A HISTORY OF EARLY CHRISTIAN DOCTRINE
BEFORE THE COUNCIL OF NICAEA

VOLUME THREE

A HISTORY OF EARLY CHRISTIAN DOCTRINE

BEFORE THE COUNCIL OF NICAEA

VOLUME THREE

THE ORIGINS
OF
LATIN CHRISTIANITY

JEAN DANIÉLOU

Translated by
DAVID SMITH and JOHN AUSTIN BAKER

Edited and with a Postscript by
JOHN AUSTIN BAKER

LONDON   PHILADELPHIA
DARTON, LONGMAN & TODD   THE WESTMINSTER PRESS

Darton, Longman & Todd Ltd
85 Gloucester Road London SW7 4SU

The Westminster Press
Witherspoon Building Philadelphia Pennyslvania 19107

First published 1977
2nd impression 1980

© 1977, Darton, Longman & Todd Ltd

ISBN (Great Britain) 0 232 48197 0

Library of Congress Cataloging in Publication Data
Daniélou, Jean.
　The origins of Latin Christianity.
　(A History of early Christian doctrine before the Council of
Nicaea, v. 3)
　Translation of Les origines du christianisme latin.
　Includes bibliographical references and index.
　1. Theology, Doctrinal – History – Early church,
ca.30–600.　　I. Title.　　II. Series.

BT25.D2713.　　230′.1′2　　76–44380

ISBN (U.S.A.) 0–664–21064–3

Text set in 12/13 pt Photon Bembo
Printed in Great Britain by The Anchor Press Ltd and bound by
Wm Brendon & Son Ltd, both of Tiptree, Essex

CONTENTS

List of Abbreviations   ix

Acknowledgments   xi

General Introduction   xiii

PART 1 LATIN JUDAEO-CHRISTIANITY

Introduction   3
1. THE TRANSLATIONS   5
   The Latin Bible   5
   Translations of Judaeo-Christian Writings   8
   The Muratorian Fragment   13

2. LATIN JUDAEO-CHRISTIANITY: ANTI-JEWISH POLEMICS   17
   V Esdras   17
   The *Adversus Judaeos*   31
   The *De Montibus Sina et Sion*   39

3. LATIN JUDAEO-CHRISTIANITY: THE CONFRONTATION
   WITH PAGANISM   59
   The *Passio Perpetuae*   59
   The *De centesima, sexagesima, tricesima*   63
   The Sermon *De aleatoribus*   93

4. THE SURVIVAL OF JUDAEO-CHRISTIANITY IN THE
   THIRD CENTURY   99
   Commodian's Theology   99
   The *De Pascha computus*   126
   The *De Fabrica mundi*   130

PART II CHRISTIANITY AND LATIN CULTURE

Introduction   137

5. TERTULLIAN AND JUDAEO-CHRISTIANITY   139

Tertullian's Reaction against Judaeo-Christianity   140
Tertullian and the Jewish Apocrypha   161
   1. *I Enoch*   162
   2. The *Book of Adam*   167
   3. The *Sibylline Oracles III*   173
Tertullian and Tradition   176

6. MINUCIUS FELIX AND HIS SOURCES   189
   The Theology of the *Octavius*   189
   The World and Man   198

7. TERTULLIAN AND STOICISM   209
   Tertullian and Philosophy   209
   Tertullian's Stoicism   214
   Tertullian's Criticism of Platonism   223

8. NOVATIAN AND THE COSMIC RELIGION   233
   The Beauty of the World   233
   The Harmony of Opposites   238
   The Cosmic Chariot   240
   Freedom   245

9. CYPRIAN AND THE AGE OF THE WORLD   251

PART III   THE LATIN FATHERS AND THE BIBLE

Introduction   261
10. THE TESTIMONIA   263
   Tertullian's *Adversus Judaeos*   263
   Commodian's *Testimonia*   273
   Cyprian's *Ad Quirinum*   288

11. TYPOLOGY   297
   The Types of Christ   298
   Types of the Church   306
   Types of the Sacraments   312

12. THE EXEMPLA   321
   Daniel and the Three Young Men   321
   Job   324
   Tobit   327

13. NOVATIAN AND THE THEOPHANIES   329

PART IV   LATIN THEOLOGY

Introduction   341
14. TERTULLIAN AND HIS METHOD   343
    Substantia   345
    Census   348
    Status   352
    Gradus   356

15. TERTULLIAN'S SYSTEM   361
    The Trinity   361
    The Creation of the World   366
    The Soul of Man   371
    The Flesh of Christ   383
    The Intermediate State   390
    The Resurrection of the Dead   395

16. THE TWO CITIES   405
    Idolatry and Demonology   405
    Pompa diaboli   412
    The Empire as the Persecutor of Christians   419

17. CYPRIAN'S ECCLESIOLOGY   429
    The Essence of Christianity   429
    The Christian Society   432
    Vigor Ecclesiae   440
    Militia Christi   448
    Unanimitas concordiae   453

Conclusion   464

Postscript by John Austin Baker   469
Bibliography   478
Textual Indexes
    a. Old Testament   487
    b. Apocrypha (Biblical)   489
    c. New Testament   489

d. Jewish Writings   490
e. Jewish Christian Writings   491
f. Gnostic Writings   494
g. Fathers of the Church   494
h. Miscellaneous Writings   503

General Index   505

LIST OF ABBREVIATIONS

BIFAO	Bulletin de l'Institut Français d'Archéologie Orientale, Cairo
CA	Cahiers Archéologiques
CCL	Corpus Christianorum, series Latina, Turnhout-Paris
CLCP	Graecitas et Latinatis Christianorum primaeva, Nijmegen
EVV	English Versions
GNO	Gregorii Nyssae Opera
JAC	Jahrbuch für Antike und Christentum, Münster
JTS	Journal of Theological Studies, London
NKZ	Neue Kirchliche Zeitschrift, Leipzig
NRT	Nouvelle Revue Théologique, Tournai
NTS	New Testament Studies, London
PG	Patrologiae Graecae cursus completus, ed. Migne
PL	Patrologiae Latinae cursus completus, ed. Migne
PO	Patrologiae Orientalis, ed. Graffin-Nau, Paris
RAC	Reallexikon für Antike und Christentum, Stuttgart
RB	Revue Biblique, Paris
RHPR	Revue d'Histoire et de Philosophie Religieuses, Paris
RSLR	Rivista di Storia e Letteratura Religiosa, Florence
RSR	Recherches de Science Religieuse, Paris
SP	Studia Patristica
SPL	Supplementum, Patrologiae cursus completus, series Latina (Migne), ed. Hamman, Paris
SVF	Stoicorum veterum fragmenta, Leipzig
Th. Rv.	Theologische Revue
TU	Text und Untersuchungen zur Geschichte der altchristlichen Literatur, ed. Gebhardt-Harnack-Schmidt, Leipzig-Berlin
VC	Vigiliae Christianae, Amsterdam
ZNW	Zeitschrift für die neutestamentlichen Wissenschaft und die Kunde der älteren Kirche, Berlin
ZTK	Zeitschrift für Theologie und Kirche, Tübingen

PUBLISHERS' NOTE

The Publishers regret that, because of the Author's death before a full revision of his work could be completed for the English language edition, it has in some cases proved quite impossible to trace and include the appropriate detailed references to the work of scholars whose opinions are mentioned. With a view to a subsequent edition, the Publishers would welcome information whereby such deficiencies can be remedied.

ACKNOWLEDGMENTS

Extracts from the following copyright English translations of ancient texts are used by permission of the copyright holders named after them, to whom grateful acknowledgement is made:

Early Latin Theology by S. R. Greenslade: S.C.M. Press Ltd, London, and The Westminster Press, Philadelphia.

The Loeb Classical Library: *Minucius Felix and Tertullian*: Harvard University Press and William Heinemann Ltd.

The Early Christian Fathers ed. and trans. H. Bettenson: © Oxford University Press 1969.

Cyprian: De Lapsis and De Ecclesiae Catholicae Unitate ed. M. Bévenot: © Oxford University Press 1971.

GENERAL INTRODUCTION

THIS is the third and last volume of my history of the cultural forms in which early Christianity found expression. In the first volume, *The Theology of Jewish Christianity,* I dealt with its expression within the framework of Jewish apocalyptic ideas. In the second volume, *Gospel Message and Hellenistic Culture,* I considered the encounter between Christianity and Hellenism. In the present volume, I am concerned with the meeting between the Christian message and the Latin world. As in the case of the first two books, I confine myself here too to the first three centuries.

The undertaking was, of course, fraught with difficulties and I would not wish to disguise the hypothetical nature of some of my findings. On the contrary, I would prefer to state this a little more clearly. Most histories of Latin Christianity begin with Tertullian, but Tertullian's work seems to have been strongly marked by what had gone before. Certainly it was Greek Christian thought, both orthodox and heterodox, which was Tertullian's primary antecedent. He knew Greek perfectly; he was deeply influenced by Justin and Irenaeus, was familiar with the writings of Melito and reacted against those of Valentinus and Hermogenes, Marcion and Praxeas.

One question that has preoccupied me, however, was whether Tertullian's thought was not also connected with Christianity originating in a Latin environment, especially since, in my research, I came across several anonymous works – *spuria* – which prompted me to ask three basic questions. First, were these *spuria* originally Latin works or had they been translated from Greek originals? Secondly, what was the precise environment with which they were connected? Thirdly, were they written before the time of Tertullian?

These are clearly controversial questions, but I think that it is possible to answer them positively and this is what I hope to do in the first part of this volume. First, were these works originally Latin? It is well known that certain Judaeo-Christian works were translated at the end of the second century from Greek into Latin. These include, for example, the *Epistle of Clement* and the *Shepherd of Hermas.* I believe, however, that we are justified in claiming that the works that are to be discussed in this book were originally written in Latin. There is now general agreement that the *Passio Perpetuae,* for example, was originally a Latin text and, according to van Damme, this would seem also to have been so in the case of the *Adversus Judaeos.* Everything points in the direction of Latin too in the case of *V Esdras.* The *De montibus Sina et Sion* and the sermon *De centesima* were also clearly Latin.

Secondly, did these works come from a Latin Judaeo-Christian environment? This is a perfectly reasonable question, since it is well known that there were many Jews both in Rome and in Carthage, and the gospel was first proclaimed everywhere among Jews. Judaeo-Christian communities therefore certainly existed in a Latin environment. The question is, then, whether these communities left any literary records. My study of a number of texts has convinced me that they did. This is undoubtedly so in the case of the *Passio Perpetuae, V Esdras,* the *Adversus Judaeos,* the *De montibus Sina et Sion* and the *De centesima, sexagesima et tricesima.* My reasons for claiming this will emerge from the detailed examination of these texts in the first part of this book.

To have established this, however, does not of itself resolve the problem of chronology. The two questions must be kept distinct. What I think I have shown is that we can identify the particular Judaeo-Christian works against which Tertullian reacted so strongly; but this does not mean that the whole of this literature antedates him. It is well known that Tertullian was an isolated figure in the early Church, and that Latin Judaeo-Christianity persisted after his time. There are still problems, therefore, in dating some of these Judaeo-Christian works. My own view is that the *Passio Perpetuae,* the *Adversus Judaeos,* the *De aleatoribus* and *V Esdras* were written before Tertullian and that the *De centesima* and the *De montibus* were of the same period as Tertullian. Commodian can, as Thraede has shown, be placed between Tertullian and Cyprian, and the *De Pascha computus* can be dated at A.D. 340/341.

The other aspect of our study in this volume, that of the encounter between Christianity and Latin culture, presents us with no less serious difficulties. Tertullian knew both Latin and Greek perfectly and, whereas it is easy to demonstrate the Latin character of his secular sources from the literary point of view, matters are more complicated as regards their philosophical aspect. Both the early and the contemporary authors quoted in his works are, for the most part, Greek — for example, Plato, Chrysippus, Albinus and Soranus. Is it possible to find, in the philosophical influences in Tertullian's writing, that distinctively Latin character which is, after all, what we are looking for? This may, however, be the wrong question to ask. The problem with regard to Tertullian is basically similar to that in the case of Cicero, namely that these Latin authors were concerned to leave their own mark on material which was mainly Greek.

This does not, however, mean that the first Latin authors were not acquainted with the Latin philosophical works that had been written before their time. Tertullian, for example, frequently quotes Cicero and Seneca. The dependence of less original writers, such as Minucius Felix and Novatian, is even more marked, the former being influenced by Cicero and the latter by Apuleius. This brings us to the thorny question of the relationship between Minucius Felix and Tertullian. Taking into account the work of Quispel and the fact that everything that specifically characterises Tertullian's writings is absent from those of Minucius, I am inclined to conclude that it was Tertullian who depended on the *Octavius* of Minucius.

Having placed these early Latin authors in their different contexts, it is necessary to show what is specifically Latin in their work. This is to be found first of all in their biblical theology. On the one hand, the Greek authors of the School of Alexandria were preoccupied with an allegorical form of exegesis, while those of the School of Antioch followed a literal approach to the Bible. On the other hand, however, the Latin Christians preserved and elaborated the typology of primitive Christianity which had been kept alive by Justin and Irenaeus, and the theology of history which formed its context. In this, their achievement was beyond price.

At the level of systematic theology, we are faced with an untypical situation. Tertullian, using distinctively Latin methods, created a remarkably coherent theological synthesis. He was above all at pains to emphasise the difference between the various orders of reality, the *census,* and to classify each of these orders in all of its aspects, the *suggestus.* Tertullian was more sensitive to distinctions than to connections, being in intellectual type akin to Pascal, to whom he displays some astonishing similarities. In this extraordinary enterprise he had no successors. But his work remained as a model, and was to prove sufficient on its own to establish the greatness of early Latin theology.

Finally, the Latin authors were more concerned than the Greeks with institutions of society, and closer to the heart of the Empire and the Church. They were therefore led to tackle the problems of ecclesiology, both in the concrete issues raised by the actualities of Church life and in the Church's historical confrontation with the ideology of the Empire. In this area the work of Cyprian displayed an originality and relevance of permanent value He succeeded in disentangling both the true structure and the fundamental mystery of the Church from the controversies within it which divided the Christian West and from the confrontations between the Church and pagan society.

These first expressions of Latin theology set the pattern for the future. The great theologians of the period that followed in the fourth century were less typical. As Latin authors, they were conscious of the need to remain constantly in dialogue with Greek culture and were strongly influenced, even fascinated by neo-Platonism. Despite the fascination that Greek Platonism has from time to time exercised over Western Christianity, however, there have been equally regular demonstrations of certain reservations in this respect, especially in the thought of Luther, Pascal, Kierkegaard, Newman and Barth. In tracing how the three great cultural expressions of early Christianity came to be juxtaposed, we have thus at the same time brought out the inter-relation of three permanent components of Western thought.

PART ONE

LATIN JUDAEO-CHRISTIANITY

INTRODUCTION TO PART ONE

THERE can be no doubt that the gospel was first preached in the Latin world in Greek by Greek-speaking missionaries. Paul wrote to the Romans in Greek, Clement used Greek in his letter to the Corinthians, and the author of the *Shepherd of Hermas* expressed himself in Greek in his exhortation to his brethren in Rome. The official language of the Church in Rome continued to be Greek until the middle of the second century, although Latin was to be used earlier in the liturgy at Carthage. These are indisputable facts, but they should not blind us to the further fact that, at a very early stage, there were Christians both in Rome and in Carthage who spoke nothing but Latin. Alongside the official language, Greek, which persisted for a long time, there was also a popular form of Christianity using Latin.

Traces of this popular Latin form of Christianity are to be found in a Greek work like the *Shepherd of Hermas*. Christine Mohrmann has pointed out that there are several Graecised Latin Christian terms in this text such as λέντιον, συμψέλιον and στατιῶν. There is therefore a hint in the *Shepherd* that a Christian spoken Latin was in existence from the beginning of the second century. No doubt it took time for this to emerge in written works, but it is not improbable that this could have taken place from the second century onwards, both in Rome and in Carthage. What is certain is that work so developed from the literary point of view as that written by Tertullian presupposes an advanced state of Latin used among Christians.

CHAPTER ONE

THE TRANSLATIONS

BEFORE any original works were produced in the Latin language, there was a preliminary period, which may have begun very early indeed, in which Christian works written originally in Greek were translated into Latin. The very earliest examples of Christian writings in Latin, then, were translations. The first of these that we have to consider are the oldest Latin translations of the Old and New Testaments. The question raised by these translations of the Bible is extremely complex and cannot be dealt with as a whole, since it is still in process of investigation, but it will be necessary to make some brief comments upon it. An area in which there are more generally accepted conclusions is that of Jewish Christian writings, some of which were translated at a very early stage into Latin, although in the case of others no agreed view has yet emerged.

1. THE LATIN BIBLE

In considering the Latin translations of the Old and New Testaments, we have first of all to bear in mind that the biblical Latin which was to become such an important element in Latin Christianity was formed in these translations. Quotations in the works of Tertullian and Cyprian point clearly to the existence of Latin translations of the Old Testament at the end of the second century. Cyprian's *Testimonia* are particularly valuable in this respect because they form a unique collection of Old Testament quotations. There is considerable divergence between these and the quotations found in Tertullian's writings. This can be explained partly by the freedom with which the latter sometimes makes his own translations, but they too point to the possible existence of earlier versions. The first Latin Christian author in Rome, Novatian, used a translation which was quite different from the one employed by the African Christians and which was also made before his time, probably during the second century.

These translations were made from the Greek version of the Old Testament, the Septuagint, which itself formed the basis of biblical Greek, so that, in this sense at least, it is true to say that biblical Latin was derived from biblical Greek. There is, however, another parallel possibility. Early Christianity in Rome and Africa first developed in a Jewish environment and it is very likely that these Latin-speaking Jews were able to make use of Latin translations of the Old Testament that had been in existence for a long time. It is well known that the Bible was read in the synagogues first in Hebrew and then in the language of the people, that is, Aramaic, Greek and Latin. These translations were, of course, at the same time interpretations and often quite free interpretations. We are therefore justified in asking whether Jewish Latin did not exist before Christian Latin.[1]

Whatever the answer to this question may be, it is clear that these early Latin translations of the Old Testament had a decisive influence on the formation of Christian Latin. The language of these translations was certainly quite distinctive and different from that of classical Latin. In the first place, they are strictly literal translations, duplicating the Hebrew even to the point of following the same word order. This resulted, on the one hand, in the formation of a distinctive vocabulary, containing numerous neologisms. These were either lexicological, in other words, completely new words were created, or else semantic, that is to say, existing Latin words were given a new meaning. On the other hand, Semitic forms were used in the syntax of the Latin translations. These biblical translations furthermore used a form of Latin which completely disregarded the classical models and had its basis in the popular language of the period. It was this

---

1. These Jewish translations were, after all, based not on Greek, but on Hebrew originals. Several authors such as Baumstark, Blondheim and Sparks have, moreover, pointed to various points of contact between certain Latin translations used by Christian authors and the original Hebrew.

which gave the Christian Bible that barbaric character which offended the taste of many educated readers. These translations were, however, primarily intended for popular use. At Rome, in particular, Greek continued to be the official language of the liturgy until as late as the fourth century.

We must now consider the early Latin translations of the New Testament. There is evidence in the *Acts of the Scillitan Martyrs* that such translations existed in Africa from 180 onwards. When they were asked by the proconsul what they had in their wallets, they replied that it was the Epistles of Paul and, since these were ordinary Christians, the texts must have been in Latin. There is also evidence in the Muratorian Canon of about the same period that a Latin translation of the whole of the New Testament probably existed in Rome. Here too, we can learn something about the African text from Tertullian's and Cyprian's quotations and about the 'European' text from Novatian's. There are, of course, many variants, but we can, by means of these quotations, reconstruct two major families of Latin translations.

Several versions of the New Testament in a Latin translation which clearly precedes that of Jerome's Vulgate have also been preserved in a number of codices. These versions vary quite widely in several respects from the ordinary version and have moreover several points of contact with the Syriac. The most striking example of these versions is the *Codex Bezae,* which has many affinities with Tatian's *Diatessaron.*

What was the environment in which these versions originated? In view of the fact that there were few Christians and that these spoke only Latin, it is obvious that there must have been a Latin translation of the New Testament at a very early stage. In the case of Jn 1:13, for example, Tertullian has *natus est,* using it as a basis for his argument in favour of the virgin birth of Jesus. The problem is more complicated, however, in the case of the European and in particular the Roman texts. Latin translations here could have emanated from several different sources. One theory is that various fringe groups may have used them as a means of proselytising among the people. This, it has been suggested, may have applied particularly to Marcionite groups, since there is evidence of the existence of Marcionite Latin prologues to the gospels at the end of the second century. In recent years, however, it has been argued that these prologues should not be dated so early. There must, on the other hand, undoubtedly have been Marcionite translations into Latin; and there was very probably a Latin translation of Tatian's *Diatessaron*, providing a kind of popular 'Life of Jesus'. This would certainly explain why readings or interpretations closely related to the *Diatessaron* and to the Syriac tradition persisted in some of the Latin codices.

If the Latin translations of the Old Testament played an important part in fashioning biblical Latin, those of the New Testament helped to form Christian Latin as such. The translators of these early versions of the New Testament were as literally faithful to the original Greek as the translators of the Old Testament were to the Hebrew. One result was that certain Greek words were simply transliterated: for example, *anastasis, apostolus, baptismus, diabolus, eremus, episcopus* and *martyr*. These words had, from the very beginning, been associated with important features of Christianity in a community of Christians who spoke nothing but Greek. When Christians began to speak Latin, these same words clearly continued to be used as technical terms. They were not understood by non-Christians and were often avoided by later Christian authors who were conscious of the classical Latin models. Alongside this specialised vocabulary of Latinised Greek words, there were also many neologisms, such as *revelatio, resurrectio, salvator* and *salutare*. These were, like the Latin neologisms in the Old Testament, either lexicological or semantic.

2. TRANSLATIONS OF JUDAEO-CHRISTIAN WRITINGS

The Latin translations of the New Testament are not the only translations into Latin of texts which were originally written in Greek. The first case of a non-biblical Greek text translated into Latin that we have to consider is that of the *Didache*. The brief treatise, *De duabus viis*, which was edited by Schecht, corresponds to the parallel texts in the *Didache* and the *Epistle of Barnabas*, but is not strictly a translation of either of them. It has certain features in common with *Barnabas*, in particular the reference to the two angels at the beginning of the treatise. Elsewhere, the text of the *De duabus viis* coincides with that of the *Didache*. What is particularly interesting, however, is that all the strictly Christian part of the *Didache* is absent from the Latin version. According to Audet, what we have is a purely Jewish text in a Latin translation, which probably goes back to the second century. There is no good reason for rejecting this opinion, since a later date is hardly acceptable in view of the very ancient character of the teaching contained in the translation. A further factor, namely the omission of the original condemnation of augury (3, 4), points to a possible origin in Rome, where the status of the augurs would have made it dangerous for Christians to condemn them.

Otherwise, however, there are fragments of a Latin tradition of the *Didache* as we know it in various other Latin texts which will be discussed later in this work. A good example of this is to be found in the sermon *De centesima, sexagesima et tricesima,* which contains the double commandment to love God and one's fellow-man in a form which is not scriptural, but rather a variant of the text of the *Didache* (1, 2) and the *De duabus viis*: 'To love the Lord from your whole heart and the one who resembles you as yourself' (58, 12–13). The golden rule also occurs in the same form as in the *Didache* and the *De duabus viis* (1, 2): 'What you do not want to be done to you, do not do to another' (65, 6–7).

These elements are found in both the *De duabus viis* and the *Didache,* but there are others which are distinctively Christian and can be derived only from an early Latin translation of the *Didache.* An example of this is the sentence: 'If you can carry out all the Lord's precepts, my son, you will be perfect' (58, 9–10), which is a simple translation of *Didache* 6, 1, but 'carrying the yoke' in the *Didache* is replaced here by 'carrying out the precepts'. It is therefore probable that the author of *De centesima* was acquainted not with the *De duabus viis* but with a Latin translation of the *Didache.*

We also have an ancient Latin version of *I Clement,*[2] which apparently goes back to the beginning of the second century, that is, to a period little later than the original text itself. The reason

---

2. Edited by DOM MORIN, *Anecdota Maredsolana*, 2 (1894), 1–60.

usually given for the existence of this translation is that the text had considerable authority in Rome. The fact that the MS does not also contain *II Clement*, a text with which the Epistle was associated at a very early stage, shows that our Latin version goes back to a very ancient document.[3] The translation is literal, often juxtalinear, and is in popular Latin. The translator also employs certain Latinisms which were not preserved in later usage and which are clearly archaisms. For example, he translates λαϊκός by *plebeius*, σχίσμα by *scissura*, as in the Latin version of the *Shepherd of Hermas*, and διάκονος by *minister*.[4] Sometimes the translator places the original Greek word and its Latin equivalent side by side, as in the case of *testimonium martyrii*. There are also archaic renderings such as *contrarius* for ἀντικείμενος applied to the demon, as in the Latin translation of *Barnabas*. There are also specific Christian words such as *ambulare* for πορεύεσθαι, which is biblical Latin. The translator was, moreover, concerned with artistic effects.[5]

The *Shepherd of Hermas* is a similar case. Its popularity in the West is well known, mainly because Tertullian protested against the abuse that was made of it, and the existence of a Latin translation is probable.[6] Do we in fact still possess this version? We know that two Latin translations of the *Shepherd* exist. Of these, one, the Palatine, is a later revised version, in correct Latin, of the earlier translation, the Vulgate, which is marked by the same crudity as the early translations of the Bible or the Latin version of the *Epistle of Clement*, namely, incorrect words and constructions resulting from a desire to translate literally.

More definite evidence of the antiquity of this Vulgate version

---

3. CHRISTINE MOHRMANN, who has studied the text in great detail, has emphasised this particularly: *Etudes*, 3, 78–106.

4. It is interesting to note that, in Pliny's letter to Trajan, which was written at about the same time, the word *ministrae* was used for 'deaconesses'. The word is also found in Commodian, where it is clearly an archaism (*Instr.* I, 26).

5. CHRISTINE MOHRMANN, *art. cit.*, has drawn attention to his use of alliteration.

6. The *Shepherd* is, of course, mentioned in the Muratorian Canon; but this raises the question whether works existing in Latin were or were not listed in the Canon.

of the *Shepherd* is provided by the fact that it is quoted in an early sermon, the *De aleatoribus*.[7] The *Shepherd* is here quoted as Scripture in the very words of our early version: 'Holy Scripture says: Woe to the shepherds! But if the same shepherds are found to be neglectful (*negligentes;* V: *dissipati,* scattered), what will they reply to the Lord about (*Domino pro:* om. V) the flocks (add. V: *huius*)? What will they say (*quid dicent;* V: *numquid dicunt*)? Will they say that they have been harried (om. V) by the flock? No one will believe them. It is impossible to believe that a shepherd can be made to suffer anything (om.V) by the flock. And there will be greater unity because of their falsehood' (*De aleatoribus* 2).

There is no doubt that the two texts are identical. The text of the *De aleatoribus* is in fact better than that of V. In particular, it allows us to restore the words *Domino pro,* which are necessary for the sense and which are absent from V, from which there are moreover other omissions. This quotation is important evidence of the authority of the *Shepherd* in the Church in Rome as well as of the antiquity of our translation. It also provides us with clear testimony that the Latin translation of the *Shepherd* included in the Vulgate was made probably at the end of the second century and certainly before the *De aleatoribus,* in which it was quoted as Scripture.

Other early Christian documents may also have been translated at a very early period into Latin. The *Apocalypse of Peter* is mentioned after the *Apocalypse of John* in the Muratorian Canon, which, however, adds the comment, 'although some among us refuse to have it read publicly in the Church'. This, of course, means that the text must have been read publicly in some churches and this in turn means that there was probably a Latin translation of this Apocalypse. The text was used in the middle of the second century in the *De laude martyrii,* which is evidence of its having been known at that time in Latin-speaking Christian circles.

---

7. This was apparently written by a bishop of Rome, because the author declares that he has received from God 'apostolic leadership' (*ducatum apostolicum*) and the 'representative throne of the Lord' (*vicariam Domini sedem*).

We also have an early Latin version of the *Epistle of Barnabas.* [8] This version includes only the exegetical section of the *Epistle,* which is a sign of early date. It has many characteristics in common with the Latin translation of *I Clement.* There are archaic renderings, such as *nationes* for ἔΘνη, *honestus* for πλούσιος and *contrarius* for ἀντικείμενος. [9] There are also several rare words, such as *propalavit* for ἐγνώρισεν (1, 7).

It is particularly instructive to study biblical quotations in this connection. One can see the author hesitating between a direct translation of the quotations as given in the *Epistle* and the use of an already accepted translation close to that which Cyprian was to employ in his *Testimonia.* An example of this is the author's quotation of Is. 6:7. He was first prompted to use a version which went back to the common Roman Bible, namely *omnem consignationem iniustam dissipa,* for which *Barnabas* has *omnem consignationem iniquam dele.* Then the same quotation is repeated in a different form, *omnem cautionem malignam dissipa,* which is his own rendering. As a second example of this phenomenon, we may mention Ex. 3:8, referring to the 'land flowing with milk and honey'. The usual translation is found in 6, 10: *Terram bonam, fluentem lac et mel,* but a different translation is found in 6, 13: *Terram quae trahit lac et mel* (see also 6, 8). [10]

Whenever he uses his own personal translation, the author of the Latin *Epistle of Barnabas* evinces a certain clumsiness. For example, in the case of Is. 49:6 ('I will make you the light of the nations so that my salvation may reach to the ends of the earth'), he translates the Greek as *Posui te in lucem nationum, ut sit sanitas tua usque in novissimum terrae* (14, 8). There is no equivalent elsewhere in any other translation into Latin for the two words *natio* and *novissimus* here, yet this passage was often quoted by the Latin

8. Edited by J.-M. Heer, *Die versio latina des Barnabasbriefes.*
9. Cf. p. 10 above.
10. This second text is of particular interest. The Latin translator of Barnabas clearly favoured the words *trahere* and *tractus.* Whereas Tertullian has *exitus* for διεξόδους, for example, in Ps 1:3, he used *iuxta tractus aquarum* (11, 6). The word *trahere* for *fluere* is also found in the *Passio Perpetuae* (8, 3), and occurs again in the *De montibus Sina et Sion,* a Christian work dating back to the second century. It would certainly seem as though this was a feature of the early Latin Christian tradition.

fathers. It is difficult to imagine that such a translation could have existed at a time when the African or Roman Vulgate had become widespread, as was the case in the age of Cyprian. We are at a stage when such a translation from the Greek did exist alongside the normal versions.

3. THE MURATORIAN FRAGMENT

The Muratorian Canon provides us with invaluable evidence of the situation at the end of the second century with regard to Latin translations of Greek texts. The Canon itself is one of the most securely dated late second century Latin texts that we possess, mainly because of the reference made in it to 'the Shepherd . . . written very recently in our time by Hermas, in the city of Rome'. The purpose of the document is to provide a canon of the New Testament writings, but at the same time it also refers to a number of apocryphal writings. We cannot be sure, of course, that all the writings mentioned by the author had been translated into Latin at the time at which he was writing, but, as the texts he lists are ones that were read in the churches, it is very likely that popular Latin translations of them were in existence.

In the case of the gospels, what is most striking is the emphasis laid on the Fourth Gospel. The author of the Canon records a tradition that the evangelist John summoned 'his fellow-disciples and bishops', in other words, the apostles, and suggested that they should fast with him for three days, and 'then let us relate to each other whatever may be revealed to each of us'. The author of the Canon continues: 'On the same night it was revealed to Andrew, one of the Apostles, that John should narrate all things'. The *Gospel of John* is therefore seen as a summary of and a conclusion to the Christian revelation.

This story directs our attention first of all to the circle of Roman Christians in which the Muratorian Canon originated. It is known that one group of Romans headed by Gaius rejected both the *Gospel* and the *Apocalypse of John*. One of their opponents was Hippolytus. They were akin in their beliefs to the monarchians, who denied the theology of the Word and were content with a Jewish monotheism, and who were very strong in Rome at the end of the second century. The Muratorian Canon bears witness to a movement in the opposite direction, developing the theology of the Logos. This theology had already been taught in Rome by Justin, but the emphasis here placed on the person and *Gospel of John* is undoubtedly due to Asiatic influence. The tradition reported in the Muratorian Canon is very reminiscent of those coming from Papias, and both Melito and Irenaeus place a similar stress on the *Gospel of John*.

The passage we have been considering is of great importance for the history of the canon of the gospels. First, it is evidence that the collection of four gospels was officially recognised. It also testifies to the fact that this collection was closed by the *Gospel of John,* which formed an explicit conclusion to it. What is more, it had a very special significance in that it synthesised the teaching of the Twelve, whereas the other gospels bore witness to particular traditions.[11]

The use of the Johannine tradition to determine the contents of the canon applies not only to the gospels but also to the Pauline epistles. In writing seven major epistles, addressed to seven churches, Paul is held to be following John, who also addressed seven churches in the *Apocalypse*.[12] Here again we have a formal criterion of canonicity, fixing the epistles at seven in number alongside the four gospels.

The Muratorian fragment, however, recognises other documents as canonical. These include the epistles to Titus and Timothy, which were written 'for the regulation of Church discipline'. In this connection, it is interesting to note that the *De aleatoribus,* which was written at about the same time as the Muratorian Canon, contains a synthesis of passages from 1 and 2 Tm relating to Church discipline (*De aleat.* 4). All these passages

11. See ISIDOR FRANK. *Der Sinn der Kanonbildung,* 1971. It will be remembered that Irenaeus regarded the four beasts of the *Apocalypse* as symbolising the four gospels, and that therefore he too must have regarded the *Gospel of John* as closing the collection.
12. The epistles to the *Thessalonians* and *Corinthians* were counted as single letters in two parts. The apocryphal epistles to the *Athenians* and *Laodiceans* were excluded.

in the *De aleatoribus* are, of course, in Latin, which means that there was probably a Latin translation of these epistles at the end of the second century and that it was to this translation that the Muratorian Canon refers.

The Muratorian Canon calls the *Acts of the Apostles* 'the Acts of all the Apostles', and this phrase also carries important implications. At the time when the Muratorian Canon appeared, various apocryphal Acts of individual apostles were in circulation. The Canon excludes these, and in the case of the canonical book of *Acts* emphasises the notion of completeness just as it had done in the case of the four gospels and the epistles. It should also be noted that the author mentions Peter and Paul, alluding to Peter's martyrdom,[13] and Paul's journey to Spain, neither of which are included in the *Acts of the Apostles*. For him, then, Peter and Paul sum up the whole of the apostolate.

The Fragment is not only important in connection with the canon of the New Testament at the end of the second century. It is also a valuable source of information with regard to the apocryphal writings. The reference to the *Apocalypse of Peter* has already been mentioned. The author of the Canon was clearly not certain as to whether the *Apocalypse of Peter* was canonical and he seems to have lacked any precise criterion for solving the problem.

Of particular interest is the attitude of the Muratorian Canon to the *Shepherd of Hermas*. First, it provides direct evidence of the fact that the *Shepherd* was given its final editing in Rome during the pontificate of Pius I. It also stresses its importance, saying 'it ought to be read'. As we have already indicated, this is clearly an argument in favour of the existence of an early Latin translation. On the other hand it did not form part of the canon of the New Testament, the criterion here being that it was non-apostolic. It will be remembered, however, that the *Shepherd* was treated by the author of the *De aleatoribus* as Scripture, which suggests that the *De aleatoribus* itself is earlier than the Muratorian Canon. The fact, therefore, that the *De aleatoribus* quotes the *Shepherd* in Latin is further proof of the antiquity of the Latin version.

13. The earliest witness to this is, of course, Clement of Rome.

CHAPTER TWO

LATIN JUDAEO-CHRISTIANITY
ANTI-JEWISH POLEMICS

IN THIS chapter we shall consider first a number of texts concerned with the conflict between Judaism and Christianity. It is well known that this conflict was a common theme in many of the Greek Judaeo-Christian texts written during the second century, from the *Epistle of Barnabas* onwards. Certain features are found in all these documents. To begin with, they testify to the vigour of Judaism. There were flourishing communities of Jews at Rome and Carthage and it was from these that the first Christian communities to emerge in the West were formed, which accounts for their strongly Judaeo-Christian character. At the same time, however, it was Judaism which was Christianity's most serious competitor, and this gave rise to intense Judaeo-Christian polemic against Judaism. This is especially striking in the *Adversus Judaeos* and the *De montibus*, and the writings of Commodian.

1. *V ESDRAS*

The name *V Esdras* is given to the two chapters which precede *IV Esdras* in the appendix to the Latin translations of the Bible. [1] Several well-known verses contained in the Roman liturgy are quotations or adaptations from *V Esdras*; in particular *Lux perpetua luceat eis*, 'Let perpetual light shine on them' (cf. 2:35); *Requiem aeternam dona eis, Domine*, 'Eternal rest grant to them, Lord' (cf. 2:34); *Modo coronantur et accipiunt palmas*, 'Now they are crowned and receive palms' (2:45); *Accipite iucunditatem gloriae vestrae*, 'Receive the joyfulness of your glory' (2:36) and *Gratias*

1. EVV: *II Esdras* 1–2.

agite ei qui vos ad caelestia regna vocavit, 'Give thanks to the one who has called you to heavenly kingdoms' (cf. 2:37).

The text of *V Esdras* has been handed down to us in two different families of manuscripts, one known as the French and the other as the Spanish.[2] At the beginning of the present century, Labourt favoured the Spanish manuscript tradition, but more recently Duensing has argued for the French. The substance of the text is not, however, affected by the variants, though in the view of the present writer the Spanish tradition is the earlier.

V Esdras is undoubtedly a Christian document, but there is no general agreement about the language in which it was originally written or about its date. Labourt believed that it was a late Latin work, from the fifth or sixth century.[3] Nowadays, however, the majority of critics agree on a date around the end of the second or the beginning of the third century. The general view now, moreover, is that *V Esdras* is a Latin translation of a Greek text.[4] The arguments put forward in favour of an early date seem decisive; the work does come from the end of the second century. On the other hand, Labourt was probably right in claiming that it was originally written in Latin, principally because the work is not quoted by any writer in Greek or in any Oriental language, all of whom seem to have been completely ignorant of its existence. What is more, there are certain similarities between our text and other Latin works written at the end of the second century, such as the *Passio Perpetuae* and Pseudo-Cyprian's *Adversus Judaeos.* It belongs to the same world as the *Shepherd of Hermas,* which was written in Greek but at Rome. I believe therefore that *V Esdras* is an example of Latin Christian literature written before the time of Tertullian.

The structure of the treatise is quite clear. The first part announces to Israel that she has been rejected because of her unfaithfulness; the second part proclaims to the nations that it is they who are to receive the inheritance. *V Esdras* shares this

---

2. Cf. DUENSING in HENNECKE & SCHNEEMELCHER. *Neutestamentliche Apocryphen,* II, pp. 488–489 (*E. T. New Testament Apocrypha,* II, ed. Wilson).
3. 'Le cinquième livre d'Esdras', *RB,* 17 (1909), pp. 412–434.
4. See DUENSING. op. cit., p. 489; SCHNEEMELCHER, art. 'Esra', *RAC* 604–605.

pattern with other works of the same period, such as Melito's *Homily on the Passion* and the *Adversus Judaeos*. There is no need to discuss in detail the first part of *V Esdras*, which is basically a *cento* of quotations from the Old Testament prophets, many of which are also to be found in the *Adversus Judaeos*.[5]

The concluding verses (1:38–40) of this first part, which are of a somewhat enigmatic character, do, however, call for comment. The text reads: 'And now, father, look with glory and see a people coming from the east, to whom I will give as a guide (*ducatum*) . . .' – here follow the names of Abraham, Isaac and Jacob, and of the twelve minor prophets. The last name is that of Malachi, 'who is also called the angel of the Lord'. What we have here is clearly a Jewish tradition concerning a group of Jews exiled in the East and manifested at the end of time. There is evidence of the existence of this tradition in Commodian (*Inst.* II, 42; *Carm. Ap.* 337–338).[6]

Not only is the theme the same in both writers, there are also certain verbal parallels. In *Carm. Ap.* 969–970, for instance, we read: *Praemittetur enim ante illos Angelus alti qui ducatum eis pacificum praestet eundo,* 'An angel will therefore be sent out before them who will act as their leader making peace', while in *Carm. Ap.* 345, the prophet Malachi is also called an angel. These passages may be compared with *V Esdras:* 'to whom I will give as a guide (*ducatum*) . . . and Malachi, who is called the angel of the Lord'. In *Inst.* II, 42, 11, reference is also made to the resurrection of the 'choir of holy prophets' in order that they should be with the people.

The principal point of interest in the second part of *V Esdras* is the doctrine of the Church. The Church is presented as the true Zion: 'Receive your number, Zion' (2: 40–41), and, in the next verse: 'I saw on Mount Zion a huge multitude, which I could not count'.[7] Early in this second part, the 'kingdom of Jerusalem' is

5. This literary genre is known to us from other Jewish or Judaeo-Christian works of the period, such as the *Apocryphon of Ezekiel*, edited by CAMPBELL BONNER.

6. SCHMIDT has suggested that this may be an Essene tradition: 'Une source essénienne chez Commodien', *Pseudépigraphes de l'Ancien Testament et manuscrits de la Mer Morte*, I, pp. 11–27.

mentioned (2: 10). The text is based on a contrast between the abandoned and deserted Zion of the Jews and the new Jerusalem, but there is less emphasis placed on a fundamental opposition between the two than on a continuity. Zion is always the same, the Church which has existed 'from the beginning' (2: 41). It has, however, been abandoned by its first children and has received others in their place.

The teaching contained in this part of *V Esdras* is clearly an extension of the New Testament theme of the replacement of the synagogue, which had rejected Christ, by the Church of the gentiles.[8] Especially striking are the resemblance between our text and that of Ga. 4:24–27, in which Mount Sinai is contrasted with Zion and Is. 54:1 is quoted (*Laetare, steriles*, 'Shout for joy, you barren women . . .'), and the clear parallel with the new Jerusalem of the *Apocalypse of John*. The emphasis, however, is not on criticism of Judaism, but rather on Israel's faithlessness. In this respect *V Esdras* differs from other Latin treatises of the same period, such as the *Adversus Judaeos*.

The most striking aspect of the ecclesiology of this apocalypse, however, is the way in which the Church is presented as a mother.[9] An entire section of the second part of *V Esdras* is taken up with the theme of the Church as mother: *Mater, amplectere filios tuos, educa illos cum laetitia*, 'Mother, embrace your children; bring them forth with joy' (2:15); *Noli timere, mater filiorum*, 'Do not be afraid, mother of children' (2:17); *Nutrix bona, nutri filios tuos*, 'Good nurse, nourish your children' (2:25); *Jucundare, mater, cum filiis tuis*, 'Rejoice, mother, with your children' (2:30) and finally *Amplectere filios tuos usquedum venio*, 'Embrace your children until I come' (2:32).[10]

---

7. This is, of course, a quotation from Rv. 7:9, with the addition of *in monte Sion*.

8. Cf., e.g., Mt. 21:43, which has 'kingdom of God', *regnum Dei*, whereas *V Esdras* has *regnum Jerusalem*.

9. This forms another parallel with Commodian: cf. *Inst.* 42:36, 44. -

10. J. C. PLUMPE, *Mater Ecclesia*, Washington, 1943, pp. 33–34, referred more than thirty years ago to the important position occupied by *V Esdras* in the whole matter of the origins of the theme of the Church as mother in early Christianity. As he was unable to date the work with any degree of certainty, however, he made little use of it.

The same theme appears in Ga. 4:26: 'Jerusalem above is free, which is our mother', and is common in Judaeo-Christian literature. Thus, the image of the Church as fertile after having been barren occurs in *II Clem.* 2:1, where again reference is made, as in Ga. 4:26, to Is. 54:1: 'Shout for joy, you barren women who bore no children . . .'. The theme was also to be elaborated by Irenaeus, Clement of Alexandria and Tertullian. Our text, however, is one of the earliest and most important examples. According to *V Esdras,* the Church carries out her task as mother by nourishing her children (2:25), guiding their steps (2:15, 25) and bringing them up (2:15) and fulfils her mission during the period before the Lord's coming (2:32), when she will see her children gathered together in glory. The Church is thus presented as both the Church of history and the eschatological Church.

One particularly interesting feature is the comparison of the Church to a dove. This image was clearly current in apocalyptic of the first and second centuries A.D., for example, in *II (4) Esdras* 5:26, where it denotes Israel. The symbol of the dove also occurs frequently in Jewish iconography, where it has the same significance.[11] It has even been suggested that, in the light of this symbolism, the dove in the baptism of Jesus represented the Church.[12] This symbol was, moreover, one especially dear to Cyprian, and was generally speaking widely used in Latin Christian circles. In *V Esdras,* the dove guides and supports her little ones as they walk (2:15, 25), which is a remarkable use of this image.

This theme of the dove seems to have originated in the Old Testament, where, in the *Song of Songs,* the bride is called a dove (Cant. 6:8). It was undoubtedly this text which influenced the author of *IV Esdras;* and the same no doubt applies to *V Esdras.*

---

11. Cf. GOODENOUGH, *Jewish Symbols,* VIII, 43–44.
12. H. SAHLIN, *Studien zum dritten Kapitel des Lukasevangeliums,* pp. 101–105. This theory was taken up again later by A. Feuillet, 'Le symbolisme de la colombe', *RSR,* 46 (1958), pp. 536–542. F. J. DÖLGER, *Antike und Christentum,* 2 (1930), pp. 46–49, has pointed out that the symbol of the Church as a dove lies behind Tertullian's phrase *Nostrae columbae domus,* 'the house of our dove' (*Adv. Valent.* II, 3).

The theme of the dove is combined with the idea of election: 'I have chosen you' (2:15), a combination also found in the *Song of Songs*, where the dove is presented as the beloved (Cant. 6:10). In the *Song of Songs* too, the dove is 'unique': *Una est columba mea* (Cant. 6:8). We may therefore conclude from this evidence that *V Esdras* is, in this respect at least, an extension of the rabbinical and apocalyptic exegesis of the *Song of Songs*. The theme of perfume (2:12) in *V Esdras* can also be understood in the same sense.

A second aspect of the text we are considering is that it presents the *parousia* as imminent: 'the end of the world is near' (2:34). Christians are invited to pray for 'their days to be shortened' (2:13), which is, of course, a well-known element in Christian apocalyptic writing (cf., e.g., Mt. 24:22). The last days will be a time of testing for the Church: 'Days of trouble and anguish will come' (2:27). 'The nations will envy the Church (2:28), but will not be able to do anything against her, because God will protect her, especially by sending Elijah and Jeremiah to help her (2:18).[13]

It is clearly too the task of the Church, in the words of the author of *V Esdras*, to 'embrace your children until I come' (2:32), but hope is kept alive in the Church during this short period of waiting by a vision of eschatological blessings, the description of which forms a major element in this second part of *V Esdras*.

These passages display some of the classic features of Jewish and Judaeo-Christian apocalyptic, and are closely akin to the eschatological discourse in the *Gospel of Matthew*. They also indicate an early date for the text, which portrays the Church in a time of persecution. It is 'those who have confessed the Son of God in the world' to whom the rewards are promised (2:47). What we have here is a spirituality of martyrdom, continuing the teaching of the *Apocalypse of John* and heralding the *Passio Perpetuae*, in which the presentation of the world to come is very much the same.[14]

13. The reference to Jeremiah is an archaic feature. Victorinus of Pettau explains the 'second witness' of Rv. 11:3 as Jeremiah, and ascribes this interpretation to an ancient tradition (*Comm. Apoc.* 11, 3; *SPL*, 1, 146).
14. All these data are important in any attempt to date the text. Labourt has nothing to offer in reply to his insistence that *V Esdras* was a late document.

The eschatology of our text has to be seen in this light. Attention is concentrated exclusively on the blessings promised to faithful Christians, since the purpose of the message is to sustain them in a time of testing. This makes the eschatology of V Esdras very close to that of the Jews. There is no question of a general resurrection. God's coming is imminent, but nothing is said about an intermediate state or about the condition of the dead while they wait for the parousia. They are simply called the 'children who are asleep' (2:31), and it is quite definitely the resurrection of the body which is envisaged. There is also no hint of millenarianism. The hope expressed in V Esdras is concerned entirely with 'eternal rest' (2:34) and the 'heavenly kingdoms' (2:37).

This absence of any reference to millenarianism is an interesting feature of the eschatology of V Esdras, and seems to be characteristic of the early Roman tradition. Millenarianism is, for example, also absent from the writings of Clement of Rome and from the Shepherd of Hermas. It appears to have been introduced into the West from Asia Minor in the works of Justin, Irenaeus, Tertullian and Commodian, and is known to have encountered considerable reservations in traditional Roman circles. This is clear from Callixtus' opposition to Montanism and Gaius' rejection in the third century of the Apocalypse of John. It is this aspect of the document more perhaps than any other which lends support to the opinion that V Esdras was fundamentally an expression of Judaeo-Christian believers in Rome during the second century.

It will be noticed that this type of eschatology is that of the Petrine catechesis. In I Peter we read of 'an inheritance . . . being kept in the heavens' (1 P. 1:4), which is about to be made manifest, and it is the expectation of this joy which is to sustain the patience of Christians, even though they may 'for a short time have to bear being plagued by all sorts of trials' (1:6). The Church is furthermore presented as the true Zion (2:6) and Christians are called the real people of God (2:9). The contrast between the world and eternity is depicted as a contrast between darkness and 'wonderful light' (2:9), and the theme of light is, it will be recalled, also to be found in V Esdras (2:35). In 1 P. 5:4, we also read of the shepherd who gives 'the crown of unfading glory' (cf. *V Esdr.* 2:45f.), and finally, both *I Peter* and *V Esdras* stress the importance of constant vigilance (cf. *V Esdr.* 2:13).

These various elements in the eschatological teaching of *V Esdras* must now be discussed in more detail. The first is the resurrection of the just. In 2:16, we read: *Resuscitabo mortuos de locis suis et de monumentis educam illos, quoniam cognovi nomen meum in eis,* 'I will raise up the dead from their places and I will bring them out of their tombs, because I have known my name in them'.[15] The opening words are also to be found in a text quoted by Clement of Rome as Scripture: 'It is written: I will raise you up (ἀναστήσω) from your coffins (Θηκῶν)'(L, 4). In the text that we are studying, the word *locus* is used as a technical term for 'coffin' or 'ossuary'. *Locus* and *loculus* are frequently to be found in descriptions of tombs or burials at this period.

The next phrase, *de monumentis educam illos,* is clearly a quotation from Ezk. 37:12: 'I will raise you from your graves', which is a passage that was used at a very early stage in the *testimonia* of the resurrection. It was quoted, for example, by Irenaeus (*Adv. Haer.* V, 4, 1) and, what is even more interesting, in our context at least, is that it appears in Cyprian's *Testimonia ad Quirinum* (III, 58) in the same form exactly as it is found in *V Esdras*. Clearly, then, *V Esdras* can in this case be regarded as evidence of the antiquity of this *testimonium*. Its merging with the apocryphal fragment quoted by Clement of Rome is an example of the composite quotations typical of Judaeo-Christianity.

The same theme of the resurrection of the body occurs later in *V Esdras:* 'When I find your dead, I will raise them up again; I will look at the signs and I will give them the first seats at the time of the resurrection' (2:23). In *V Esdras* 2:31, however, there is a new element: 'I will remember your dead children; I will bring them out of the depths of the earth (cf. *I En.* LXI:5) and I will establish the sea in the greatness of its glory'. The second part of this text has undoubtedly been falsified, in order to provide an explanation of the question of the dead recovered both from 'the

---

15. It is clear from the end of this text that what we have here are dead marked with the *sphragis*.

depths of the earth' and from 'the depths of the sea'. [16]

This theme was obviously well known in the Latin tradition, since Tertullian wrote: 'So that the resurrection of bodies does not seem to be only for those who are called from their tombs, you have said in Scripture: I will command the fish of the sea to restore the bones that they have eaten' (De reso, **XXXI**, 1). Tertullian's text here recalls that of *I En.* LXI:5 and would appear to be an allusion to it.[17]

Another apocalyptic theme in *V Esdras* is that of the number of the elect. There are three references to this theme in the second part of the text: 'Of those whom I have given you, not one will perish. I will look for them from among your number' (2:26); 'Receive your number, Zion' (2:40); and finally 'See the number of those who are marked by the seal' (2:38). The last statement also occurs in Rv. 7:4: 'the number of those who were sealed'. This theme of the predetermined number of the elect also appears in *IV Esdras* 4:36 and in *I Clem.* 2, 4 and 59, 1.[18] It is interesting to find this theme in the Roman tradition. It is specifically apocalyptic, and related to the imagery of the heavenly books, according to which everything has been determined from the beginning.[19]

The place of blessedness inhabited by the elect is described in *V Esdras* and the language, which is rich and varied, is derived from many different images. It has been suggested that this wealth of terminology is a sign of early date, and that Tertullian was reacting against it.[20] First of all, there is the term 'the kingdom', which is described in various ways. It is first called 'the kingdom of Jerusalem' (2:10), which shows to what extent the theme was

16. Cf. M. R. JAMES, on *I Enoch* LXI:5 and the *Sibylline Oracles* (II, 233).
17. It should not be forgotten that *I Enoch* 37–71, 'the Similitudes', to which these quotations belong, was a Christian apocalypse, written in Greek and closely related to the *Sibylline Oracles*, as J. T. Milik has shown.
18. On the latter passages cf. W. C. VAN UNNIK, 'Le nombre des élus dans la Première Epître de Clément', *RHPR*, 1962, pp. 237–236; see also 'Die Zahl der Vollkommenen Seelen in der Pistis Sophia', *Abraham unser Vater (Festschrift Michel)*, 1963, pp. 467–477.
19. This conception should be distinguished from the Platonist idea that the total number of souls is predetermined, which is linked with the Greek notion that everything perfect is determinate.
20. FINE, *Die Terminologie der Jenseitsvorstellungen bei Tertullian*, 1958, p. 187.

still connected with the Promised Land, a type of the eschatological Jerusalem. Later, the text refers to *praemia regni*, the
'rewards of the kingdom' (2:35); and finally to the 'heavenly
kingdoms' (2:37), indicating that the expected reward is heavenly not earthly in nature.

Secondly, there is the theme of 'rest'. The word *requies* occurs
at least twice in *V Esdras: Veniet requies tua*, 'Your rest shall come'
(2:24), and, *Requiem aeternitatis dabit vobis*, 'He shall give you eternal rest' (2:34).[21] The sense attached to *requies* in *V Esdras* is
typical of its use in the earliest Latin patristic writing.[22] It has
nothing to do with the repose of the soul after death, which is its
meaning in the pagan inscriptions of the period. On the contrary,
it refers to the rest of the seventh day, the sabbath rest, and is
therefore synonymous not with quiet repose but with festivity. In
Jewish apocalyptic writing and in early Judaeo-Christian texts
(*Barn.* XV, 8), it denotes eternal life.[23] It is, in other words,
synonymous with blessedness, as in *V Esdras*.

This use of *requies* in the sense of 'eternal life' is very early. In
Irenaeus and sometimes in Tertullian, the term was to be used to
denote the seventh millennium, preceding the eighth day, which
is eternal life.[24] This was not the primitive meaning.[25] *V Esdras* is
still in the Jewish tradition, according to which the seventh day
was eternal life. In Latin Christianity from the time of Tertullian
onwards, a rather different usage developed in which the term
requies came to mean the blessed state of the souls of the righteous
after death, a meaning which was not unknown in Jewish
apocalyptic and which in fact predominated from the time of
Cyprian onwards. In *V Esdras*, however, *requies* clearly means the
eternal rest of those who have been raised up from death.

Another image, that of the *convivium Domini*, the 'feast of the
Lord' (2:38), is closely connected with the theme of rest.[26] There
are many examples of this classical apocalyptic theme in the

---

21. The phrase, *requies aeterna*, occurs in Irenaeus, *Adv. haer.* IV, 66, 3.
22. Cf. FINE, *op. cit.*, pp. 142–147.
23. Cf. O. HOFIUS, *Katapausis*, 1970, pp. 113–114.
24. Cf. FINE, *op. cit.*, pp. 142, 147.
25. Cf. HOFIUS, *loc. cit.*
26. As FINE has observed, *op. cit.*, p. 166.

gospels. It can also be found in the Similitudes of Enoch (*I Enoch* 62, 14) and in *II (4) Esdras* 8:52, while in Latin Judaeo-Christian literature it occurs in the *Adversus Judaeos*: 'Freely may you take your place at the banquet (*in convivio*) and feast at the marriage supper of the bridegroom (*epulari nuptias sponsi*)' (47, 173, van Damme). There is also a reference in *V Esdras* to 'glorious garments' (2:39), which gives emphasis to the fact that it is a wedding feast (cf. the 'garments of glory' associated with the feast in *I Enoch* LXII:15).

Another important image used in *V Esdras* to describe the blessedness of the elect is that of the radiant glory that surrounds them. God 'admits the blind man to the sight of his glory (*claritatis*)' (2:21), *claritas* being an archaism for *gloria*. The most striking phrase, however, is *Lux perpetua lucebit vobis per aeternitatem temporis,* 'Perpetual light will shine on you for eternity' (2:35). The words *Lux perpetua* were, of course, chosen by F. Cumont as the title of his work on the ways in which the life hereafter was presented in early Christian thought. The same words have also become very well known because of their inclusion in the Mass of the Dead according to the Roman rite. In our text, this 'perpetual light' is contrasted with the 'shadow of this world', the *umbra saeculi* of 2:36, 39 and linked (v. 36) with the 'joyfulness of glory'.

This idea of 'everlasting light' is undoubtedly derived from the apocalyptic writings. It occurs in Is. 60:19f. to express the unfailing radiance of God's glory in the Jerusalem of the future; and this image is taken up in the *Apocalypse of John* (Rv. 21:23), though without the adjective αἰώνιος qualifying Φῶς. The same theme of the light of God's glory recurs in Latin Christianity in the *Passio Perpetuae* (11, 4) in the form, *lucem immensam,* 'boundless light', and in 1 P. 2:9 we find the phrase 'wonderful light'.

The description of the state of blessedness also draws on the imagery of Paradise. In *V Esdras* 2:12, for instance, we read: 'They shall have the Tree of Life for perfumed ointment (*in odorem unguenti*)'; and again, a little later on in the same chapter: 'I have prepared for you twelve trees laden with fruits, and as many fountains flowing with milk and honey, and seven immense mountains on which roses and lilies grow' (2:18f.). It is interesting to note the works which offer parallels to these images. In the NT *Revelation of John* twelve specimens of the Tree of Life line the banks of the crystal river, flowing from God's throne, and bear twelve different kinds of fruit in turn, month by month (Rv. 22:21 cf. Ezk. 47:12). In *Revelation* the Tree of Life is not scented. But in *I Enoch* 24f. its fragrance is a strongly emphasized feature: '. . . fragrant trees encircled the Throne. And amongst them was a tree such as I had never yet smelt . . . it had a fragrance beyond all fragrance' (24:4). After the final Judgement the elect feed on the fruit of this tree, and 'its fragrance shall be in their bones' (25:5, 6). The standard apocalyptic theme of God's 'preparing' these things for his elect also appears in this passage of *I Enoch* (25:7), as it has already done just before in *V Esdras* (2:11). That the trees are twelve in number is a detail found in the work of the gnostic Justin (Hippolytus, *Elench.* VII, 26), where they symbolise twelve angels.[27] Finally, the 'seven immense mountains' of *V Esdras* 2:19 echo the 'seven magnificent mountains' of the same passage in *I Enoch* (24:2f.).

The flowers mentioned in *V Esdras* as growing on the seven mountains are roses and lilies. Roses figure in the *Passio Perpetuae* (2, 5; 13, 4), in which Perpetua meets another person in a rose garden; while in the *Apostolic Tradition* of Hippolytus (32) the only flowers that can be offered are lilies and roses.[28] Lastly, 'milk and honey', which are, of course, part of the biblical imagery of the Promised Land, are also mentioned in the *Apostolic Tradition* (21), where they are used in the Roman Eucharistic liturgy.

One final group of images in *V Esdras* is connected with the Feast of Tabernacles, which is well known to have played an important role in Judaism during the earliest years of Christianity as prefiguring the Messianic Age:

I, Esdras, saw on Mount Zion a huge crowd of people . . . In

---

27. Cf. R. M. GRANT, *Gnosticism and Early Christianity,* New York, 1959, pp. 39–70. The debt of gnostic writers to apocalyptic imagery is well-known.
28. See later CYPRIAN, *Epist.* X, 5.

the midst of them was a young man of high stature (*celsus statura*), taller than the others. He placed crowns on each of their heads and grew greater and greater. So I asked the angel and said to him: Lord, who are these? He answered me: They are those who have taken off the mortal garment and have put on the immortal one. They have confessed the name of God. They have just been crowned and are receiving the palms (*modo coronantur et accipiunt palmas*). I said to the angel: Who is the young man who is crowning them and putting palms in their hands? He answered me: It is the Son of God (2:42–47).

All these images are, as we have said, connected with the Jewish Feast of Tabernacles interpreted eschatologically. As we noted above, God's people have 'everlasting tabernacles' prepared for them (2:11; cf. Lk. 16:9; Rv. 7:15; 21:3). The palms refer to the procession on the eighth day of the Feast (Rv. 7:9), but the theme of the crowns is less commonly encountered. Crowns certainly formed part of the rites of the Feast of Tabernacles – this is clear from *Jub.* XVI, 30 and from Tacitus, *Hist.* V, 5. Christians too seem to have made some liturgical use of crowns (cf. *Odes of Solomon,* XXI, 7), but this practice ceased very early in the West because of the danger of confusion with pagan rites. The custom was attacked, for example, by Tertullian in his *De corona.* In spite of what Goodenough has said about this practice,[29] it certainly originated among the Jews. Lastly, the representation of the Son of God as a man of 'high stature' is, of course, a classic feature of Christian apocalyptic (cf., e.g., *Gospel of Peter* 40).

There are several points of contact between *V Esdras* here and the vision of Perpetua, according to which Christ was of great stature (*Pass. Perp.* 10, 6) and carried a green branch (10, 9) and the martyrs were clothed in white robes (4, 8; 21, 1). The most interesting comparison, however, is with the Eighth Similitude of the *Shepherd of Hermas:* 'Under the willow stood the glorious angel of the Lord, of immense size' (*Sim.* VIII, 1:2). This angel is

29. Cf. E. GOODENOUGH. *Jewish Symbols in the Graeco-Roman Period,* IV. New York, p. 157; also J. DANIELOU. *Primitive Christian Symbols,* pp. 14–23.

the Son of God.[30] This passage continues: 'The angel commanded that crowns be brought . . . and crowned the men who had handed over the branches (= the palms). He marked them with a sign. All those who went into the tower wore garments as white as snow' (*Sim.* VIII, 2:1–4). The same themes are clearly grouped together here, in the *Shepherd,* as in *V Esdras* 2:42–47. It is difficult not to conclude that the two documents belong to the same period and in the same circle.

In conclusion, we may mention two features in the above passage from the *Shepherd* which are also to be found in *V Esdras.* The first of these is the 'sign' or 'seal'. The word *signati* occurs in 2:38 and earlier in the text we find the phrase 'I have known my name in them' (2:16). The seal is the mark of the name, the *taw,* which comes from Ezk. 9:4 and reappears in the *Revelation of John* (7:3–8). Those who were chosen were marked with this seal and it was by this seal that they were known to God. The second feature is that of the white garments. In *V Esdras* 2:40 occur the words *candidati tui,* 'those of yours who are clothed in white', and in 2:39, 'they received glorious garments from God' (*splendidas tunicas a Deo acceperunt*). The theme of the chosen ones being dressed in white is well known in the *Revelation of John* (3:4–5). The word *candidatus* also occurs with the same meaning of 'dressed in white' in the *Passio Perpetuae* (4, 8) and, in 12, 1, the four angels dress Perpetua and her companions in white robes before they enter the light-filled dwelling place in the hereafter, Paradise. The same theme is also found in the *Odes of Solomon* (XI, 9, 10: XXV, 8), where it contains an echo of the baptismal rite.

All that has been said in this section about *V Esdras* points clearly to the fact that it is a Latin Judaeo-Christian apocalypse dating back to the second century. The dominant message is a vision of the messianic kingdom which Christ will set up when he comes again in a transformed Jerusalem. The imagery of *V Esdras* is, moreover, very close to that of the *Shepherd of Hermas* and the *Passio Perpetuae.* It is, however, different in spirit from the *Adversus Judaeos,* which lays more stress on the break with the Old

---

30. Cf. DANIELOU. *The Theology of Jewish Christianity,* pp. 123f. It is interesting to note that he is also called the 'shepherd' in *V Esdras* (2:34), as in the *Passio Perpetuae* (4, 6).

Testament. In contrast to Tertullian there is still no point of contact with secular culture. *V Esdras*, together with the *Shepherd of Hermas*, with which it may be contemporary, may have influenced the imagery of the *Passio Perpetuae*.

2. THE *ADVERSUS JUDAEOS*

The authorship of the *Adversus Judaeos*, which is to be found among the *spuria* of Cyprian, has been variously attributed, mostly without foundation. Some time ago, however, the attention of scholars was recalled to the work by Eric Peterson,[31] who demonstrated that there were definite links between the text of the *Adversus Judaeos* and that of Melito's *Homily on the Passion*. This was followed by a study of the *Adversus Judaeos* in depth by D. van Damme,[32] who concluded that it was a Latin homily written at the end of the second century. Despite recent objections[33] this point now seems firmly established, though van Damme's argument that the author of the *Adversus Judaeos* had not Jews, but Jewish Christians in mind as the target of his polemic is more disputable.

The sermon opens by recalling both the blessings lavished by God on the Jews and their unfaithfulness, resulting in God's breaking of his covenant with them and his making of a new covenant with the pagans. It is, however, the author points out, always possible for the unfaithful Jews to turn back to God.

The structure of this part of the *Adversus Judaeos* is very similar to that of *V Esdras*, and some of the ideas resemble each other quite closely. Thus, in the *Adversus Judaeos*, we read that the Jews are stripped both of their temporal and of their spiritual inheritance: *Plebs autem derelicta, nuda deserta viduata regno caelesti et terrestri*, 'the people are abandoned, naked, forsaken and widowed, deprived of their kingdom in heaven and on earth' (*Adv. Jud.*

31. ERIC PETERSON, 'Pseudo-Cyprians Adversus Judaeos und Melito von Sardes', *VC*, 6 (1952), pp. 34–43, revised and enlarged in *Frühkirche, Judentum und Gnosis*, Rome, 1959, pp. 137–146.
32. D. VAN DAMME, *Pseudo-Cyprians Adversus Judaeos. Gegen die Judenchristen die älteste lateinische Predigt* – *Text, Uebersetzung, Kommentar*. Paradosis 22, Freiburg (Switzerland), 1969.
33. K. THRAEDE. *Th. Rv.*, 67 (1971), pp. 45–48.

64). This is very similar to what is said by Jerusalem in *V Esdras* 2:2: *Ego sum vidua et derelicta,* 'I am a widow and abandoned'. This double inheritance, temporal and spiritual, is transferred to the Gentiles – a further point of contact between the two texts, illustrated, for example, in *Adv. Jud.* 59: *Non est iam regnum Hierusalem, sed in nobis,* 'No longer is there a kingdom of Jerusalem – it is now in us', and in the parallel text in *V Esdras* 2:10: *Dabo eis regnum Hierusalem quod daturus eram Israel,*[34] 'I will give them the kingdom of Jerusalem which I would have given to Israel'.[35]

What is clearly stressed in the *Adversus Judaeos* is that the new covenant is addressed to all men: *Nulla hic exceptio est,* 'there is no exception here' (45). Certain items in the list of those included are of interest: *licet senes, licet iuvenes,* 'both the old and the young are admitted' (46), *etsi oculis viduatos,* 'even those deprived of sight' (47) and *valetudine fractos,* 'broken in health' (51). He has restored sight to the eyes of the blind, has made the lame walk and has raised the dead to life (49). All may freely take their places at the banquet (*libere licet discumbere in convivio,* 47).

These points are, of course, paralleled in *V Esdras: Confractum et debilem cura,* 'heal the broken and the weak', *claudum irridere noli,* 'do not mock at the lame', and *caecum ad visionem claritatis meae admitte,* 'let the blind man enter the vision of my glory' (2:21). Again, *senem et iuvenem intra muros tuos serva,* 'keep both the old and the young safely within your walls' (2:22). There is also the statement: *Dabo tibi primam sessionem in resurrectione mea,* 'I will give you the first place in my resurrection' (2:23). Finally, *V Esdras* also speaks of admission to the *convivium,* the banquet (2:38).

The cure of the blind and the lame is clearly a theme which is

34. It should be noted that van Damme's correction of the text by the addition of *in Hierusalem* is without foundation.

35. Other similarities are: *Haec omnia auxilia, munitiones, propugnacula transtulit gentres,* 'He has transferred all these troops, fortifications and defences to the nations' (*Adv. Jud.* 58), which may be compared with *Transferam me ad alias gentes,* 'I will turn to the other nations' (*V Esdras* 1:24). The *munitiones,* 'fortifications', correspond to the *plateas munitas,* the 'fortified streets' of *V Esdras* (1:13).

derived from Isaiah and Matthew, but what is of special interest in our text is that the idea of cure is less stressed than that of admission to the kingdom. What lies behind *Adv. Jud.* 47, then, is the parable of the guests who were invited to the banquet, and this impression is reinforced by the allusion in *Adv. Jud.* 47 to the 'wedding feast' (*epulari nuptias sponsi*). This theme, first introduced in *V Esdras*, was elaborated in the *Adversus Judaeos*.

There is, however, an important difference between the two texts. In *V Esdras*, the continuity of the two covenants is emphasised. The Church, which has existed *ab initio*, 'from the beginning' (2:41), is the same Jerusalem which first existed for the children of the Jews and which, after the Jews had rejected Christ, received the Gentiles. In the *Adversus Judaeos*, on the other hand, this idea of continuity is replaced by that of the breaking of the covenant with the Jews and the establishment of a *novum testamentum*, a 'new testament' with the nations.[36] Whereas Jerusalem is regarded as a mother in *V Esdras*, it is called *impia*, 'ungodly' in *Adv. Jud.* 68. There is a distinct element of Roman anti-Semitism in the *Adversus Judaeos*, which is not found in *V Esdras*.[37]

The biblical quotations in the *Adversus Judaeos* have been carefully studied.[38] As far as the Old Testament is concerned, some of the *testimonia* exhibit abbreviations, additions or modifications typical of this type of work. Thus, Is. 2:3 is quoted in the form: 'From Zion the word of God will go out from Jerusalem' (*De Sion Dei exiet verbum de Hierusalem*). Van Damme suggests that the text is corrupt, but this is always a risky suggestion. In any case, it would be more normal for this to be a shortened form of the verse in Isaiah, with the word *lex*, 'law', suppressed. The quotation of Is. 8:6–7 displays a Targumic type of addition: 'which will level out your mountains and enter your

---

36. Cf. VAN DAMME, *op. cit.*, pp. 21–24 and 27–30.
37. This would be reinforced if the words *possederunt lychnum septem luminum*, 'they possessed a lamp of seven lights', are an allusion to the bas relief on the Arch of Titus, as VAN DAMME, *op. cit.*, p. 166, has suggested. In this respect the *Adversus Judaeos* is, in spirit, close to the *De montibus Sina et Sion*.
38. Cf. VAN DAMME, *op. cit.*, pp. 39ff.

lands' (qui montes vestros in planum dabit et introibit terras vestras). The most interesting example, however, is the version of Is. 1:15, 'when you stretch out your hands I turn my eyes away', in which ἐκτείνητε in the plural is replaced by extenderis in the singular, thus changing the verse into a prophecy of the Passion. This is a well-known type of Judaeo-Christian modification.

Apart from quotations properly so-called, certain allusions to Scripture are worthy of note. The creation of man, for example, is described as follows: Dominus et Pater in principio fecit hominem sua manu, 'The Lord and Father made man with his hand in the beginning' (Adv. Jud. 9), where the singular, 'hand', is exceptional. It occurs in Tertullian (Adv. Marc. II, 4, 4), and the word pugnus, 'fist', is similarly found in the singular in the De montibus Sina et Sion: Pugno comprehendi terram et confinxi hominem, 'With my fist I seized hold of the earth and fashioned man' (De mont. 4). There is also confusion in Adv. Jud. 17 (even more marked in 77) between Sinai (Horeb) and Zion; and again it is interesting that the two are also identified in the De montibus Sina et Sion and the Epistle of Barnabas.[39]

There are also in the Adversus Judaeos several quotations from the New Testament in a translation which is different from that of the known Latin translations of Scripture. A good example of this is Mt. 11:28–30: 'Come to me, all you who labour . . .'. The version in Adv. Jud. 62 reads: Venite ad me omnes qui sub onera laboratis. Est enim iugum meum placidum et onus lenissimum, 'Come to me all you who labour under burdens, . . . for my yoke is gentle and my burden most mild'. Two further variants of the usual Latin translation of Matthaean texts are found in Adv. Jud. 62. These are Immunis et innocens sum ab huius sanguine, 'I am free from and innocent of the blood of this man' (Mt. 27:24) and Ideoque nos gentes humeris nostris crucem Domini gestamus, 'And so we Gentiles carry the Lord's cross on our shoulders' (Mt. 10:38). Equivalents of these translations are found in Ephraem Syrus, which would seem to indicate that the author of the Adversus Judaeos made use

---

39. VAN DAMME wrongly attributes this to the fact that an earlier document has been shortened, op. cit., pp. 46, 148.

of the *Diatessaron* in its Latin translation.[40] This is unquestionably an archaic feature.

Certain elements in the work are clearly derived from Judaeo-Christian traditions. A typical example is the reference to the angel abandoning the Temple of Jerusalem at the moment of Christ's Passion (*Adv. Jud.* 28 and 34). The same reference is also found in Melito's *Homily on the Passion*, and it is in fact a taking over of the Jewish tradition concerning the abandonment of the Temple by the Angel of the Presence when the Temple was destroyed by the Emperor Titus in A.D. 70. (Josephus, *Bell. Jud.* VI, 5:3).[41] In later tradition, this angel was to be replaced by the Holy Spirit. In the same paragraph of the *Adversus Judaeos*, there is also an interesting reference to the Father seized with indignation (*indignatione*) because of the crime committed by the Jews, just as, in the same context, the *De montibus* speaks of the Father made angry, *exacerbatus*, by this crime, before going on to mention the 'veil of the Temple torn' (*De mont.* 8).

In the *Adversus Judaeos* the signs that accompanied Christ's death are called by God as witnesses to the writing of the New Covenant: *Adhibitis testibus caelo et terra et angelo de templo, adsistentibus Moyse et Helia. Hos enim testes adhibuit cum pateretur in Israel,* 'Heaven and earth and the angel of the Temple were called as witnesses; Moses and Elijah also stood by. For he brought the latter as witnesses when he was manifested in Israel' (*Adv. Jud.* 28). A little further on in the text, the author says again: *Testis est caelum et terra et quae in eis sunt elementa in mortem Christi,* 'Heaven, earth and all the elements that are in them are witness to the death of Christ' (*Adv. Jud.* 33).[42] It is also worth noting in this context that Moses and Elijah take the place here of the saints who are raised from the dead.[43]

40. Cf. VAN DAMME, *op. cit.,* pp. 31–39. The same applies to the *De centesima:* cf. p. 77, below.
41. Cf. J. DANIELOU. *The Theology of Jewish Christianity,* pp. 145f.
42. Mt. 21:38 too is interpreted in the light of Is. 1:2: *Audi, caelum, et praebe aurem, terra,* 'Hear, O heaven, and give ear, O earth' (*Adv. Jud.* 29). It should also be noted that the quotation from Is. 1:2 is also found in the *Epistle of Barnabas* IX, 3 and in *V Esdras* 2:14.
43. See EPHRAEM, *Diatessaron,* 21, 6.

The author also makes use of the story of the transfiguration in the following passage: *Coactus est Dominus facere novum testamentum consignantibus septem spiritibus, teste Moyse et Helia in montem, ubi praecepit ne patefient scripturae sacramentum, nisi filius hominis resurrexisset a mortuis,* 'The Lord was compelled to make a new covenant with the certification of the seven spirits and the witness of Moses and Elijah, on the mountain, where he commanded them not to reveal the mystery of the scripture until the Son of Man had risen from the dead' (*Adv. Jud.* 43). This last passage is different from the first in that, apart from Moses and Elijah, seven spirits appear as witnesses. The need for seven witnesses to be present when an official document of God was promulgated was a Judaeo-Christian concept. It is found in Elkesai (Hippolytus, *Elench.* V, 9, 15). The seven witnesses in this case are 'heaven and water, the holy spirits, the angels of prayer, oil, salt and earth'. What is interesting about this list in the *Elenchos* is that some of the elements found in the *Adversus Judaeos* occur here too, though in a different order – heaven and earth, the elements, the angel and the spirits. The theme of the seven witnesses is also distinct from that of the three, in that it is both Jewish and archaic.

We must now consider the more fully developed themes in the *Adversus Judaeos*. These fall into three main groups, the first being that of the series of covenants with Adam, Noah, Abraham and Moses. The same series is also to be found in the *Demonstratio* of Irenaeus (11–29), and it has been suggested that the *Demonstratio* and the *Adversus Judaeos* are both here based on an earlier text which has been shortened in the *Adversus Judaeos.*[44] It may, however, be unnecessary to look in this direction for an explanation. The same series of covenants is found in Clement of Alexandria, whose phraseology is even closer to that of the *Adversus Judaeos,* since he speaks of 'testaments' (διαθῆκαι). It occurs also in an exegesis by Origen, which may with good reason be regarded as traditional. Origen connects this series of covenants, moreover, with workers engaged at the eleventh hour in the parable of the Labourers in the Vineyard, which is also com-

44. Cf. VAN DAMME, *op. cit.,* p. 49.

mented in the *Adversus Judaeos*. This theme, which is found in any case in the Old Testament itself, is therefore completely traditional and is in no way derived from Irenaeus.

The second theme is that of the persecution of the just as a figure of Christ's persecution (*Adv. Jud.* 24–25). Certain aspects of this theme should be noted. In the first place, the author of the *Adversus Judaeos* uses Jewish traditions concerning the martyrdom of the prophets: *Hieremiam lapidabant. Esaiam secabant,* 'they stoned Jeremiah and sawed Isaiah in two' (25). The reference to Zechariah's martyrdom, the last in the list, is particularly interesting. Mt. 23:34–35 refers to Zechariah as the last of the prophets put to death. This is a Jewish tradition, taken over by the author of the *Adversus Judaeos,* which implies that the priest Zechariah mentioned in 2 Ch. 24:20 was the same as the prophet Zechariah. These two Zechariahs are, moreover, identified with the Zechariah who was the father of John the Baptist. In addition there is a legend of the martyrdom of Zechariah, to which Origen is the first extant witness, but which has been proved to go back to the second century.[45] Our present passage in the *Adversus Judaeos* is undoubtedly the earliest attestation of this legend.

Lists of the just who were persecuted are found also in *I Clem.* XIV, 6–33, the *Homily on the Passion* of Melito of Sardis (**XXVI**), Tertullian's *Scorpiace* (**VIII–IX**) and Cyprian's *De Pat.* X and XIX and *Ad Fort.* Broadly similar lists are a feature of Jewish *haggada.*[46] In Christian writing the additional point is made that in persecuting the prophets the Jews were already persecuting Christ. This element, which occurs in the *Adversus Judaeos,* is already found in Melito's *Homily,* and, earlier still, in *I Clem.* XVI and XVII, 1. The list in the *Adversus Judaeos* is not, however, derived from either. In particular, it should be noted that the list begins with Moses and not with Abel, and that the emphasis throughout is on the prophets.

One final feature that calls for mention here is the linking of each righteous man who is persecuted with an evil man who is

45. H. VON CAMPENHAUSEN, 'Das Martyrium des Zacharias', *Historisches Jahrbuch,* 77 (1958), pp. 383–386.
46. K. BEYSCHLAG. *Clemens Romanus und der Frühkatholizismus,* pp. 48–135.

admired. The fact that the righteous are persecuted by the wicked is a commonplace; but the device of pairing them off, one to one, is a distinctive feature found, for example, in the *Damascus Document* and in the true and false prophets of Ebionism and the *Pseudo-Clementines*. Lists closely parallel to these in the *Adversus Judaeos* are in fact found in the pseudo-Clementine *Homilies* II, 16ff and *Recognitions* III, 61. This points clearly to the existence in our treatise of a specifically Judaeo-Christian tradition. There are, however, certain interesting variants in the treatment given to these pairs in the *Adversus Judaeos*. Aaron, who in *I Clem.* is presented as an example of jealousy, in our document is a type of Christ, an unusual evaluation which may have been influenced by Qumran. Other pairs include: Elijah and Ahab, Jeremiah and Hananiah, Isaiah and Manasseh, and Zechariah and Judas.

Turning now to the question of date, it has been pointed out that there is a passage in the *Scorpiace* of Tertullian which has certain phrases in common with the *Adversus Judaeos*, in particular, *Helias fugatur*, 'Elijah is put to flight', *Hieremias lapidatur*, 'Jeremiah is stoned', *Esaias secatur*, 'Isaiah is sawn asunder', and *Zacharias trucidatur*, 'Zechariah is slaughtered' (VIII–IX). [47] The listing of the prophets in this particular order, with Jeremiah preceding Isaiah, and Zechariah mentioned last suggests that there is a relationship between the *Scorpiace* and the *Adversus Judaeos* at this point, and it must be Tertullian's treatise which is secondary. Since the *Scorpiace* has been dated at A.D. 212, this gives us a *terminus ante quem* for the date of the *Adversus Judaeos*.

There is also convincing evidence that the author of the *Adversus Judaeos* was acquainted with Melito's *Homily on the Passion*. [48] Melito's *Homily* has been dated at around A.D. 180, which gives us our *terminus post quem*. We may therefore assert with some confidence that the *Adversus Judaeos* comes from the closing years

---

47. Cf. VAN DAMME, *op. cit.*, pp. 81–84. Like the author of the *Adversus Judaeos*, Commodian also places the martyrdom of Zechariah after that of John (see *Carm. Ap.* 227–229). It is worth noting that Tertullian cut out certain legendary elements from the story of Zechariah, whom he did not identify with the father of John the Baptist. Cyprian was to do the same (*Ad. Fort.* 11).
48. This suggestion was originally made by Peterson. VAN DAMME, *op. cit.*, pp. 62f., gives a long list of parallels.

of the second century. This date is supported by the archaic nature of some of the terms used, such as *machina* for *arca*, and *testificatio* for *testamentum*. It is almost certain that it was first delivered or written in Rome, in circles permeated with Jewish traditions, but in which there was intense antagonism between Christians and Jews. The use of the *Diatessaron,* and certain linguistic characteristics such as *genui* for *generavi,* reinforce this impression.

Further confirmation that the *Adversus Judaeos* dates back to this period is provided by one last allusion. The following quotation from Celsus, given by Origen, is well known: 'Listen to which men these Christians call – anyone who is a sinner, anyone who is weak-minded, anyone who is a little child, in a word, anyone who is lacking in gifts. Will he be received into the Kingdom of God? By sinners do you not mean the criminal, the thief, the poisoner?' (*Contra Celsum* III, 59). Now, it is certain that the *Adversus Judaeos* is vulnerable to similar criticism: 'Do not be afraid, you who are sinners. Be the first to enter life. Let not the man who has been a murderer be afraid, nor the man who has stolen be in despair. Those whom the Lord desires are those who have been humiliated, who are without beauty and who are sick' (*Adv. Jud.* 49). We know what the writer is trying to say, but it is clear that his words could be misunderstood. Without denying that the invitation to faith in Christ was unconditional, Clement of Alexandria, Tertullian and Origen all stress demands involved in conversion to Christianity. The *Adversus Judaeos* reflects an earlier state of affairs, the one which Celsus was caricaturing.

3. THE *DE MONTIBUS SINA ET SION*

The last treatise that we must consider in this chapter is the Pseudo-Cyprianist *De montibus Sina et Sion*. Various dates have been suggested. Hugo Koch was of the opinion that it was later than Cyprian, but Corssen argued strongly in favour of the end of the second century, and this view has recently been revived by Vogels.[49] The vocabulary of the *De montibus* is certainly archaic.

49. Cf. H. KOCH, *Cyprianische Untersuchungen*, 1926, pp. 421–425; CORSSEN, 'Eine Theologie aus der Werdezeit der kirchlichen Literatur des

An example of this is the word *contrarius* (*De mont.* 7) as a translation of ἀντικείμενος for the 'adversary' or devil. This word was used neither by Tertullian nor by Cyprian, but is found in the Latin translations of the *Epistle of Clement*, the *Epistle of Barnabas*, the *Adversus Judaeos* and the *De centesima*. Another word which occurs in the *De montibus*, but which was avoided at a later period because of its pejorative meaning is *credulus*. In *De mont.* 3, it simply means 'believing'; it was also used in this sense in the *De centesima*. Another archaism is the word *puer*, as a translation of παῖς in the sense of 'servant', applied to Christ. *Depalare* (*De mont.* 11), meaning to divide by a wall, is also to be found in the Latin translation of the *Shepherd of Hermas*. The adjective *dominicus*, used instead of the genitive *Domini*, is another early feature. The author of the *De montibus* also uses a rare expression, *dicto audientia*, which is elsewhere found only in Cyprian's biblical *Testimonia* (II, 27) and the Latin translation of Irenaeus (IV, 41, 2). It is clear that the author of the *De montibus* did not know Latin very well, since he often uses words in their purely etymological sense and not in accordance with their contemporary meaning. Examples of this are his use of *execrare* for 'put to another use' (*De mont.* 3) and *probatio* for 'proof'. He also confuses *speculum*, 'mirror', with *specula*, 'watch-tower'.

The translations of biblical texts in the *De montibus* display some unusual features. Some of the renderings are peculiar to this work. Thus, Jn. 2:19 is translated, *Destringite fanum istud et ego in tribus diebus excitabo illud,* 'Destroy this sanctuary, and in three days I will raise it up', where the pagan word *fanum* may be a deliberately anti-Jewish polemical feature.[50] The translation is also in certain cases closer to the Hebrew than that of Cyprian. In Ps. 2:7, for instance, where Cyprian, following the Septuagint, has *praedicans praeceptum Domini*, 'proclaiming the commandment of the Lord', the author of the *De montibus* prefers *adnuntians im-*

Abendlandes', *ZNW*, 12 (1911), pp. 1–36; VOGELS, 'Die Tempelreinigung und Golgotha', *Biblische Zeitschrift*, 6 (1962), pp. 109–110. Bardenhewer, Harnack and Schwarte argue for the beginning of the third century.

50. In early Christian literature, *fanum* is elsewhere used exclusively to describe pagan temples; see, for example, COMMODIAN, *Inst.* XXXV, 19; Pseudo-Cyprian, *Dupl. Mart.* 29.

perium eius, 'making known his dominion'. Sometimes, too we find a variant version created by conflating two separate biblical passages. Thus Sg. 1:6, *Posuerunt me custodiam in vineam,* 'They made me keeper of the vineyard', is given correctly in *De mont.* 14, but in *De mont.* 7 appears as, *Posuerunt me velut custodiam pomarii,* 'They set me as a keeper of the orchard', by contamination from Is. 1:8.

Again, in *De mont.* 9 we have the well-known Christian addition to Ps. 96:10: *Dominus regnavit a ligno,* 'The Lord has reigned *from the Tree.*' Another quotation, this time from the Fourth Gospel, is unusual in that the second part is an addition: 'The world hates me and I hate the world' (Jn. 7:7). This text may, of course, be an agraphon. This is also possible in the case of the statement: 'You see me in yourselves as a man sees himself in the water or in a mirror' (*De mont.* 13), which is ascribed to an apocryphal *Epistle of John.*

There are also several composite quotations, one of the most notable being the inclusion of Mt. 27:40–43 in the middle of a quotation from Ws. 2:19–22. Even more remarkable, however, is the passage: *Palmo mensus sum caelum et pugno comprehendi terram et confinxi hominem ex omni limo terrae,* 'With my hand I measured the heaven and with my fist I grasped hold of the earth and fashioned man from all the slime of the earth'. The first part of this text is a quotation in abbreviated form from Is. 40:12, which occurs also in the Latin version of the *Epistle of Barnabas* and in Novatian (*Trin.* 3), though there the word *comprehendi* is lacking. Tertullian, on the other hand, shortens the quotation in a different way: *Qui totum orbem comprehendit manu,* 'Who grasped the whole earth with his hand' (*Adv. Marc.* III, 25, 2). The second part of the quotation is, of course, from Gn. 2:7, but *confinxit,* 'he fashioned', is found only here for ἔπλασε and the addition of *ex omni limo* 'from *all* the slime', is an allusion to the tradition that Adam's body was formed from elements derived from all the earth. All these features come from the Judaeo-Christian use of the Bible, and are developments in the style of the Targums or the midrashim.

One of the most striking aspects of our text is the author's interpretation of the etymology of Jewish names. Adam, for example, is translated as *terra caro facta,* 'the earth made flesh', a rare etymology found elsewhere in some Greek *Onomastica* as γῆ σαρκουμένη (*Vatic.* 14, 56). Abel 'received a Hebrew name describing his parents' grief' (*nomen accepit hebraicum designans parentorum luctum: De mont.* 5). This etymology, which goes back to the *Book of Jubilees* (IV, 7) also reappears in the *Onomastica.*[51] Enoch is translated, *innovatus,* 'the one renewed', which reproduces ἐγκαινισμός, an interpretation found in the *Onomastica* in the form, *dedicatio* (Jerome) or *renovatio.* Two interpretations of the name Moses are even more extraordinary, namely *temptatio Dei* and *inventio.* The second of these etymologies is found in the *Onomastica;*[52] the first is based on the analogy of the accusative σήν (Latin *sen*) and the Hebrew *sin.* Sinai is translated as *tentatio aeterna* and *odium,* the 'everlasting temptation' and 'hatred'. The first of these etymologies is found in Jerome and in the *Onomastica,* where it is related to the Hebrew root *sin.*[53] The second etymology comes from a play on words well known in the midrashic tradition.[54] Finally, there is the name Zion, which is translated as *temptatio exacerbationis,* 'temptation to anger', and *speculatio,* 'vision'. The second meaning is, of course, standard; the first is found in the *Onomastica* in the form *tentatio callida,* 'skilful trial' (*PL* XXIII, 1245), and this too is linked with a certain confusion over the root *sin.*

Various questions are raised by these etymologies in the *De montibus.* In the first place, they are in no way connected with the Alexandrine tradition of Philo or Origen. On the other hand, they exhibit certain affinities with the etymologies found in Hilary,[55] though they are not identical with them. They also presuppose an author who knew Hebrew, thus confirming what we have already noted with regard to the biblical translations. They are, moreover, to be found, at least partly, in the Greek

51. See H. J. SCHOEPS, *Aus frühchristlicher Zeit,* p. 9.
52. In what WUST, *op. cit.,* p. 89, has called the Lactantius group.
53. The Lactantius group again (WUST, pp. 78 and 81). *Sin* is translated as *tentatio* in *PL* XXII, 1247; so too is Sennacherib; *ibid.,* 1247.
54. Cf. STRACK and BILLERBECK, III, p. 571.
55. Cf. DANIELOU, 'Hilaire et ses sources juives', *Hilaire et son temps,* Paris, 1969, pp. 143–147.

Onomastica, though never used in a literal way. It would seem, then, that the author of the *De montibus* was himself responsible for them, translating them directly from Hebrew into Latin. From this, we may conclude that he was a Latin Jew, probably a Roman, who spoke Hebrew. Finally, we should note that these etymologies are at the same time plays on words, with a deliberately polemical sense, and it is in this sense that the author uses them. This therefore suggests an anti-Jewish polemical intention on the part of a Jewish convert to the Christian faith, something which is, of course, characteristic of Judaeo-Christianity as found, for example, in the *Epistle of Barnabas* or the *Adversus Judaeos.*

The Hebrew names were, however, the subject of other speculations, not simply etymological ones. This applies especially to the author's commentary on the name Adam:

> The Hebrew word Adam translated into Latin is 'the earth made flesh' (*terra caro facta*), because God held Adam in his fist from the four points of the compass, with the result that the one who was made of the four points of the compass had to be called Adam. For we find in Scripture that four stars were established, one for each of the points of the compass. The first was the eastern star, *anatole,* the second the western star, *dysis,* the third the northern star, *arctos,* and the fourth the southern star, *mesembrion.* From the names of these four stars, numbering four (*de singulis stellarum nominibus*), take each of the initial letters – from the star *anatole* A, from the star *dysis* D, from the star *arctos* A and from the star *mesembrion* M. In these four letters you have the name Adam and this name denotes Adam in Greek letters (*De mont.* 4).

It will be noted that the author claims that this interpretation comes from Scripture. The etymology of the name Adam occurs in the *Sibylline Oracles* (III, 24), which may have been the author's source. (It is known that the third book of these oracles was familiar to Tertullian, for example.) The interpretation of the spelling, however, is found in a Judaeo-Christian apocalypse, *II Enoch,* which is extant in an Old Slavonic version: 'I establish his name (Adam) from the four elements, the Rising, the Setting, the

North and the South and I establish on it four special stars'.[56] The combination of these two themes, the spelling and the stars, means that there can be no doubt that the *De montibus* was derived from *II Enoch*. The original language of the latter work was Greek, and it dates from the beginning of the second century, so that it may well have been known in Christian circles by the end of that century. Clearly, this adds to our information regarding the date of our treatise and its connections with apocalyptic writings.[57]

This is, however, not the only explanation of the name Adam provided by the *De montibus*; it is followed by another, which is an example of gematria. The four Hebrew letters forming the name Adam have the numerical value of $1 + 4 + 1 + 40 = 46$. According to the *De montibus*, 'the number 46 denotes the passion of the flesh of Adam, the flesh which was in itself figurative and which Christ carried when he hung from the wood. The number 46 expresses the passion, because, having suffered the sixth millennium at the sixth hour, after his resurrection he went up to heaven on the fortieth day, or else because Solomon built in forty-six years a temple to God, and Christ likened his flesh to this temple' (*De mont.* 6); and the author goes on to quote Jn. 2:19: 'It has taken forty-six years to build this sanctuary (*fanum*); are you going to raise it up in three days?' Gematria of this kind was frequent in Judaeo-Christian circles. It occurs especially, for example, in the *Sibylline Oracles* (I, 326, 330).

We have noted above that reference is made in the *De montibus* to Jn. 2:19. We may go further and say that it is quite possible that the number 46 may have had a symbolic meaning even in the text of the Fourth Gospel and have referred to Adam. It is, after

---

56. Cf. edition by A. VAILLANT, p. 101, 11.25f.
57. Augustine also alludes to this symbolism surrounding the name Adam in his *Tract. in Joh.* IX, 14. An even more certain allusion is made in the *De Pascha computus,* the date of which is known to be A.D. 243. Finally, further references occur in the strange *Commentary on Mark* contained in Jerome's *spuria*, and in the *Expositio quattuor Evangeliorum* (PL 30, 638A). The source of all these would appear to be the *De montibus*.

all, nowhere stated that the building of the second Temple took forty-six years. This would mean, then, that the relationship between Jesus and the Temple was to do with Jesus and Adam. What is more, the theme of the rock of the Temple as the place where Adam was buried formed part of the Jewish tradition. It should be noted that, in his *Tract. Joh.* X, Augustine discussed this interpretation at the same time as the interpretation based on the four points of the compass, which makes it even more obvious that his source was the *De montibus*. Finally, by speaking of the Temple as built *in mysterio Adae* (12), and giving the same explanation (16), the author of the *De Pascha computus* also apparently refers to our text. [58]

In his alternative interpretation of the number 46 in the passage quoted above, the author of the *De montibus* associates it on the one hand with the sixth millennium and the sixth hour and on the other hand with the forty days from the resurrection to the ascension of Christ. These again are ideas typical of apocalytic, this time in its millenarian form. Christ is held to have died in the year 6000, at the end of the sixth millennium. Apart from Adamantius in the fourth century, our author is alone in maintaining that the death and resurrection of Christ took place at the beginning of the seventh millennium. It has been argued from this that he was a representative of the primitive eschatology according to which the *parousia* was bound to follow immediately upon the resurrection, [59] which would make the *De montibus* a very early text; but this theory has been disputed. [60] We can, however, safely conclude that we have here an example of the early apocalyptic imagery of the cosmic week, antedating the chronological calculations of the kind found in Hippolytus' *Commentary on Daniel* IV, 21. [61]

Turning now to the central theme of the treatise, the contrast

---

58. See VOGELS. 'Die Tempelreinigung und Golgotha', *Biblische Zeitschrift*, 6 (1962), pp. 102–107.
59. Cf. M. WERNER, 1955, p. 85.
60. Cf. K. H. SCHWARTE, *Die Vorgeschichte der augustinischen Weltalterlehre*, Bonn, 1966, pp. 123–128.
61. Hippolytus may perhaps have been critising our author in referring, in the same context, to the sixth hour.

between Sinai and Zion, it will be remembered that in Ga. 4:24f. Sinai is linked with the Old Testament and with the earthly Jerusalem, while the new Covenant is symbolised by 'Jerusalem which is above'.[62] Similarly in Heb. 12:18ff. Sinai, as the scene of the giving of the old Law, is contrasted with 'mount Zion, . . . the heavenly Jerusalem', of which Christians are citizens. In the *De montibus* both Sinai and Zion are presented as the mountain on which Jerusalem is built, but one represents its terrestrial (and Jewish) reality and the other its eschatological (and Christian) reality.[63]

From this starting point a striking parallelism was developed with perfect logic. Sinai, the Jerusalem on earth, became the Old Testament on which the Temple was built. Zion, the mountain of the new covenant, became the cross on which Christ died: *In montem sanctum ascendit lignum regni sui,* 'the wood of his kingdom went up to the holy mountain', and, *montem Sion sanctum esse crucem sanctam,* 'the holy mountain of Zion was his holy cross' (*De mont.* 9). The body of Christ was placed on this cross, just as the temple was placed on Mount Zion (*De mont.* 4). This striking interpretation of the mountain as the cross was based on an etymology of Zion as a *speculatio* or 'observation post' – hence the necessity for these etymologies.[64] What is more, from the very outset, the theme of the two mountains is associated with that of Jacob's two wives according to Gn. 29:15–30 (*De mont.* 3). This is also a prominent theme in Tertullian's *Adversus Judaeos*; and the relationship between the two authors is a question to which we shall have to return.

The point of departure for this interpretation was provided by

---

62. In Ga. 4:24 ff, Sinai is associated with Abraham's two wives, Hagar and Sarah, whereas, in the *De mont.* 3, it is associated with Rebekah's two sons, Esau and Jacob.

63. In this context, it is interesting to note that a similar confusion between Zion and Sinai occurs in the *Epistle of Barnabas* (XI, 2), which reads Sinai in a quotation from Is 16:1, where the Septuagint has Zion.

64. In this context, it should be noted that in the *Gospel of Philip* (125) the cross, regarded as an ark, replaces the Holy of Holies as the place where God was present when the veil of the temple was torn.

the text of Is. 2:3 applied to Christ coming from Zion. This particular verse was one of the early *testimonia*, cited in Justin's *Dialogue with Trypho*, Cyprian's *Testimonia* (I, 10) and in the *Adversus Judaeos*, 307–308. A special feature of its use in the *De montibus*, however, is that it is quoted in the context of the passion of Christ. The only other text where this occurs, to my knowledge at least, is Tertullian's *De anima*, in a passage in which Tertullian is criticising the gnostic Menander, who was of the opinion that baptism conveyed resurrection life directly and preserved one from death. To this, Tertullian replied: 'According to him, even dying for God is not a law, whereas, on the contrary, from henceforward all nations are to go up to the mountain of the Lord and to the house (*aedes*) of the God of Jacob, the house of this God who requires of them by martyrdom that death which he demanded even of his own Son. No one will allow even to magic the power of exempting from death or of transplanting (*repastinet*) life like a vine (*vitis modo*) in order to renew it' (*De anima* L, 4).

The biblical passage alluded to here is obviously from Is. 2:2–3:[65] *Omnes nationes ascendunt in montem Domini et in aedem Dei Jacob*, 'All nations go up to the mountain of the Lord and to the house (*aedes*) of the God of Jacob'. The same quotation can be found in exactly the same form in Tertullian's *Adv. Marc.* IV, 21, 3, this time followed by the rest of the sentence: *quia ex Sion exibit lex et sermo Domini ex Hierusalem*, 'for the law will go forth from Zion and the word of the Lord from Jerusalem'. The same text is also found in *Adv. Marc.* V, 4, 3 and in the *Adversus Judaeos* III, 8, in this case with a variant: *Ascendamus in montem Domini et in domum (= aedem) Dei Jacob*, 'Let us go up to the mountain of the Lord and to the house of the God of Jacob'. This quotation from Is. 2:2–3 was clearly taken by Tertullian from the earlier tradition of the *Testimonia*. He is known to have drawn on Justin in the *Adversus Marcionem* and, in the Latin world before him, the second half of the quotation is found in the *Adversus Judaeos* in

65. It is strange that Waszink did not, in his excellent commentary, recognise this quotation. Waszink believed that the allusion was to Jacob's ladder (pp. 524–525), but that clearly has nothing at all to do with what Tertullian is saying here.

the form *De Sion Dei exiet verbum de Hierusalem,* 'From Zion the word of God shall go forth from Jerusalem'.

A number of similarities exist in the way in which this quotation was interpreted on the one hand in the *De montibus* and on the other by Tertullian. A characteristic feature of the *De montibus* is that God's abode, which is situated on Mount Zion and which is both Jerusalem and the Temple, is a figure of Christ, the new Temple. This feature is also present in Tertullian's *Adversus Marcionem: Aedes Dei super summos montes* (Is. 2:2) *utique Christus, catholicum Dei templum, in quo Deus colitur,* 'The house of God towering above the mountains (Is. 2:2) is certainly Christ, the universal temple of God, in which God is worshipped' (*Adv. Marc.* III, 21, 3).[66] In the *De montibus,* we read that 'Jesus compared his flesh to the temple' (*De mont.* 4). The curious comparison of Mount Zion to the cross, which, as we saw, is found in the *De montibus,* does not occur in Tertullian's writings. He does, on the other hand, quote (*Adv. Marc.* III, 21, 2) the *testimonium, Dominus regnavit de ligno,* 'The Lord has reigned from the tree', which is also cited in the *De montibus* (9), and clearly inspired two other phrases in the same section: *lignum regale,* 'the royal tree', and *lignum regni,* 'the tree of the kingdom'. The same text is also quoted in other instances in connection with the conversion of the nations.

More striking, however, than these detailed similarities is the way in which it is applied by both writers to Christ's death on the hill of Zion. It is quite clearly used in this sense in the passage that we have quoted above from the *De anima.* To 'go up to the mountain' means to undergo death for God, and this is what Christ did and what Christians have to do in imitation of Christ. This is the meaning of martyrdom, which is the theme running through the whole of the *De montibus.* Not only is the mountain of Is. 2:2–3 linked to the death of Christ – it also becomes the symbol of the cross from which Christ hung, just as the Temple was situated on Mount Zion. The difference between Tertullian and the *De montibus* here is that the former alludes to this theme in

---

66. In *Adv. Jud.* III, 8, Christ is presented both as the dwelling place and as the mountain, following Dn. 2:34–35.

passing, whereas in the *De montibus* it is elaborated into a long allegory. It seems certain that Tertullian was making use of a theme which was well known in his time, and to which the *De montibus* bears witness. In the *De montibus*, however, this theme is presented in a more archaic, Judaeo-Christian form which Tertullian strips away.

There is an affinity between the *De anima* and the *De montibus* on another point, and that is the theme of the birth of the Church, prefigured by the water and the blood pouring from the pierced side of the crucified Christ.[67] The relevant passages here are: *De latere sanguis aqua mixtus profusus affluebat, unde sibi ecclesiam fabricavit*, 'Blood mingled with water poured abundantly from his side, from which he fashioned the Church for himself' (*De mont.* 9) and *De iniuria perinde lateris eius vera mater viventium figuraretur ecclesia*, 'In the same way, the true mother of the living, the Church, was formed from the wound in his side' (*De anima* XLI, 10). What very clearly lies behind both these passages is a parallel between the birth of Eve from Adam's side and the birth of the Church from the side of Christ.[68] This theme, which was to undergo considerable development, makes its first appearance in these two works. As Waszink points out, the *De montibus* and the *De anima* were contemporary writings. Since the theme of the birth of Eve and that of the Church is not to be found in the writings of Justin or Irenaeus, both of whom made considerable use of Adamic typology, this must mean at the very least that Tertullian found this theme in the Latin Judaeo-Christian world.

In the *De montibus*, however, the theme of the birth of Eve is merged with that of the living water flowing from the temple. The author continues by saying: '*In quam (ecclesiam) legem passionis suae consecrabat, dicente ipso: qui sitit veniat et bibat, qui credit in me flumina de ventre eius fluent aquae vivae*, 'He consecrated the law of his passion for the Church, as he said: whoever is thirsty, let him come and drink, and whoever believes in me, from his belly shall flow rivers of living water' (*De mont.* 9). This passage, of course, contains a well-known quotation from Jn. 7:37–38. What is of

---

67. As WASZINK, *op. cit.*, *ad loc.*, has rightly pointed out.
68. See J. DANIELOU. *Sacramentum Futuri*, pp. 37–38.

particular interest, however, is that the author of the *De montibus* identifies the water and blood flowing from the side of the crucified Christ with the living water flowing from the rock of the Temple. This shows that he thought that Jn. 7:37–38 was an allusion to Ezk. 47:1–11. This becomes even clearer when we read on and find a quotation in the text of the *De montibus* from Ps. 1:3: *Et erit velut lignum quod plantatum est secus decursus aquarum,* 'He will be like a tree planted beside streams of water', which, of course, is reminiscent of Ezk. 47:8–9. What we have here, therefore is clear evidence that the author of the *De montibus* interpreted Jn. 7:38 as referring to the rock of the Temple.[69]

We can, however, go further, and establish a relationship in the *De montibus* between the hollow of the rock and the wound in the side of the crucified Christ. The author of the *De montibus* achieves this in three stages. The first is a quotation from Is. 2:3: *Et declaravit montem Sion sanctam Dei esse crucem dicens: De Sion exiet lex,* 'And he declared that the mountain of Zion was the holy cross of God when he said: from Zion the law will go out'. The second stage is a quotation from Ps. 40:8: *Lex christianorum crux est sancta Christi filii Dei vivi, dicente aeque propheta: Lex tua in medio ventris mei. Percussus in lateris ventre,* 'The law of Christians is the holy cross of Christ, the Son of the living God, as the prophet said: your law is in the midst of my belly. He was struck in the hollow of the side'. The most important part of this text is the quotation *in medio ventris mei* (Ps. 40:8). *Ventris* is a translation of κοιλίας, 'belly', which is the reading that appears in the Codex Sinaiticus, although the received text has *cordis* (= καρδίας). The third stage is the quotation from Jn. 7:38: *Flumina de ventre eius fluent aquae vivae,* 'from his belly shall flow rivers of living water'.

What is especially interesting about the use of the word κοιλίας is that it can be applied both to the hollow of the rock of Zion and to the hollow in the side of the crucified Christ. The proof of this is to be found in a text of Justin (*Dial.* CXXXV, 39), which refers to Is. 51:1, in which the Jewish peo-

---

69. See J. DANIELOU. 'Joh. 7.38 et Ezech. 47, 1–11', *Stud. Evang.*, II, 1964, pp. 158–163.

ple in their descent from Abraham are compared to stones hewn
from the rock (ἐκ πέτρας). Justin applies this Isaian text to
the birth of the Church, sprung from Christ, replacing the word
πέτρας by κοιλίας. This would certainly seem to be an
allusion to the comparison between the hollow of the rock and
the hollow wound in the side of Christ. It is therefore evidence
that this theme was known in the second century.

The same theme is also found in the *Epistle of Barnabas* (XI,
1–11), where the whole chapter is devoted to an elaboration of
the parallel between Christ and the rock of the Temple. In connection with the water from the rock, for example, the same
quotation from Ps. 1:3 that appears in our text, *Erit velut lignum
. . .* is used in the *Epistle of Barnabas* (XI, 6), which also contains a
testimonium based on Ezk. 47:1–11, in which the water from the
rock and the trees of life are compared (XI, 10). Now, in the *De
montibus* there is a composite quotation (Jn. 7:38 and Ps. 1:3)
which brings together another pair of the texts we are discussing:
*Flumina de ventris eius fluent et erit lignum plantatum iuxta tractus
aquarum*, 'Rivers will flow from his belly and he will be a tree
planted next to streams of water'. This may be compared with
the following from the Latin version of the *Epistle of Barnabas* (X,
1): *Flumen trahens a dextra et ascendebant inde arbores speciosae*, 'The
river was flowing on the right hand and the beautiful trees went
up from it'. There are two interesting points here: first, the
choice of identical themes in the two works, which suggests an
early date; and secondly, the very close similarity of wording in
the various quotations, which indicates that there was also a common collection of *testimonia* connected with the water and the
rock, and the water and the cross. All this points to the
dependence of the *De montibus* on the *Epistle of Barnabas*. [70] We
have already noted that *Barnabas* replaces Zion by Sinai in the
quotation from Is. 16:1 (XI, 3), which is reminiscent of the identification of Sinai and Zion in the *De montibus*. It is, however,
possible to go even further and point to the translation *iuxta tractus aquarum* of the quotation from Ps. 1:3, which is in fact unique.
Both Tertullian and Cyprian have *exitus* here, and the only other

70. Cf. J. DANIELOU, *Etudes d'exégèse judéo-chrétienne*, pp. 122–141.

instance known to me of a rendering using the *traho*-root is in fact in the Latin version of the *Epistle of Barnabas,* which, of course, raises the question as to whether this Latin version was used by the author of our text. This is, after all, not the only point of contact between the two texts. Attention has already been drawn to the quotation from Is. 40:12: *Palmo mensus sum caelum et pugno comprehendi (apprehendi, Barn.) terram (De mont.* 18, 2), 'With my hand I measured the heaven and with my fist I seized hold of the earth'. In both cases, the quotation from the Septuagint is shortened in the same way, namely by the suppression of *manu aquam et.*

Finally, we must consider the apocalpytic character of a popular parable, of the same kind as those used in the *Shepherd of Hermas,* which appears in *De mont.* 14: 'When the time has come and the vintage is near, the servant responsible for guarding the vineyard is placed in the middle of the vineyard on a tall tree set in the middle of the vineyard. On this tree a square watch-tower *(speculum)*[71] with broken reeds is built and on each side of the square three holes *(caverna)* are made, making twelve holes in all. Through this square of holes the watchman, overlooking the whole vineyard, guards it by singing'. When the thieves *(fures)* come, the servant shouts to make them run away.[72]

The interpretation of this parable is given as follows: 'This practice *(conversus)* of the world is similar to spiritual grace. The situation of God's *(deifico)* people is like that in the earthly vineyard. The Lord's vineyard, the spiritual one, is the Christian people, guarded at the command of God the Father by Christ the servant, raised up on the wooden watch-tower. If the devil, travelling about, crosses the vineyard and dares to harass, or to carry off from the vineyard a man belonging to the Lord's people *(dominicam),* he is at once challenged by the heavenly servant and corrected by spiritual punishments and, pursued, he runs away to barren and deserted places' *(De mont.* 15). The theme of the

71. *Speculum* is confused in this passage with the word *specula* (watch-tower), which is evidence of the author's barbarous Latin.
72. STUIBER has pointed out that there is pictorial evidence for this practice in Africa and elsewhere: 'Die Wachhütte im Weingarten', *JAC,* 1959, pp. 86–89.

watchman and watch-tower in the vineyard can be found in Sg. 1:6 and Is. 5:2, but our author has developed it in a clearly allegorical direction. It is interesting in this context to note that Tertullian compared God, seeing Adam the sinner, to the *speculator* or guard: *Speculatorem vineae vel horti tui lepus aut furunculus non latet*, 'the hare or the petty thief is not concealed from the guard in the vineyard or your garden' (*Adv. Marc.* II, 25, 3).

As already suggested above, this is a popular parable of the kind found in the *Shepherd of Hermas* (cf. *Sim.* V, 1–7). It is apocalyptic in style. The watch-tower or look-out post is square (*quadratus*) and there are three holes (*caverna*) in each of the sides of the square (*quadraturas*). The *speculum*, meaning *speculatio*, 'observation post', is, of course, Jerusalem. Previously in his treatise, the author had spoken of Jerusalem as 'coming down from heaven' like a new city 'four-square on the four gospels' (*De mont.* 10). This is quite clearly an allusion to the New Jerusalem of Rv. 21:2, which was 'square' (Rv. 21:16) and had three gates in each of its four walls (Rv. 21:12). The *speculum* of the *De montibus* is therefore the new Jerusalem of the *Apocalypse of John*.

The *De montibus* seems to have been written by a Jew who knew Hebrew, but whose Latin was not good. He writes literally and his vocabulary is poor. On the other hand, he draws liberally on Scripture and uses composite quotations and *agrapha*, a clear indication that the work is archaic. The author's knowledge of the rabbinical traditions is good, especially those concerning Zion as Adam's birthplace. He makes use of very much the same symbolism based on numbers as that found in the *Apocalypse of John* and the *Epistle of Barnabas*. His parable of the vineyard, discussed above, is very reminiscent of the *Shepherd of Hermas*. Both are, as it were, a midrash on Is. 5:1–7, but, in the *De montibus*, the emphasis is placed on the watch-tower, whereas, in the *Shepherd*, it is placed on the surrounding fence.

This emphasis on the watch-tower once more raises the question of the relationship between the *De montibus* and Tertullian. The latter quotes Is. 1:8 several times in his writings, translating it on four occasions as *Derelicta filia Sion tamquam specula in vinea*, 'The daughter of Zion is left like a watch-tower in a vineyard'

(*Adv. Jud.* XIII, 26; *Adv. Marc.* IV, 25, 11; 31, 6; 42, 6). The verse is rendered differently by Cyprian, who has *Derelinquetur filia Sion sicut casa in vinea,* 'The daughter of Zion will be left as a hut in a vineyard' (*Test.* I, 6). Now, Tertullian himself uses this version with *casa* in an earlier chapter of his *Adversus Judaeos* (III, 4) than the one just mentioned, in which he adopts the rendering *specula* (XIII, 26). The translation employing the word *casa,* that is, a hut where men sheltered or where tools were stored, was clearly the standard African translation in Tertullian's time. It is, in any case, the normal rendering, being the sense of the Hebrew text. The Septuagint has σκηνή, which can also mean 'hut'.

Why, then, did Tertullian use the word *specula,* 'watch-tower', and thus introduce a new theme, that of the look-out post in the vineyard, which was foreign to the biblical text? Certainly there is a reference to an African practice with which he was acquainted, but in all probability there is also a much more specific allusion, namely to the parable in the *De montibus.* Both in the *De montibus* and in Tertullian's work, the parable is applied in the same way. For Tertullian, the *specula* was also the Temple of Jerusalem, in which the angel of the Lord dwelt and which he abandoned: *Scissum est et Templi velum, angeli eruptione derelinquentis filia Sion, tamquam in vinea speculum,* 'the veil of the Temple was torn, and by the bursting forth of the angel leaving (the Temple), the daughter of Zion became like a watch-tower in a vineyard' (*Adv. Marc.* IV, 48, 5). The angel was therefore the power of God dwelling in the *specula* or watch-tower, and the *speculator* or guard of Israel.

We may go even further in our comparison of the *De montibus* and Tertullian in this instance. In the *De montibus,* the task of the *speculator* is said to be that of watching out for thieves (*fures*). This idea is found almost word for word in another passage in Tertullian's work, part of which we have already quoted: *Speculator vineae vel horti tui lepus aut furunculus non latet,* 'The hare or the petty thief is not concealed from the guard in the vineyard or your garden', *et Deum puta de sublimioribus oculatiorem aliquid subiecti praeterire non posse,* 'And reflect that God, who is more watchful from heaven, cannot overlook anything that is under his eye' (*Adv. Marc.* IV, 23, 2). Tertullian was not, of course, referring here to the temple on earth, but to the heavenly temple, but the theme is no different. This is clear evidence that he was acquainted with the theme of the *specula* or watch-tower and its purpose, namely the idea of keeping watch over the vineyard. It is therefore even more likely that is was this which led Tertullian to change the word *casa,* 'hut', in his translation of Is. 1:8, into *specula.* This in turn seems to confirm that Tertullian was dependent on the *De montibus* for his precise application of the parable of the Temple.

The point can, moreover, be established from the opposite direction. It is remarkable that the author of the *De montibus* does not in fact quote Is. 1:8, but Sg. 1:6, because of his use of the word *custodem* (*De mont.* 17). The same text is also quoted in another translation in *De mont.* 7: *Speculum vero altitudinem ligni declarat dicente Salomone: Posuerunt me sicut custodiam pomarii,* 'Solomon declared that the watch-tower was in fact at the top of the tree when he said: They placed me as a guard in the orchard'. This rendering has clearly been influenced by Is. 1:8, since the words, *custodiam pomarii,* instead of *custodem in vineam,* 'guard over the vineyard', would seem to come from Is. 1:8, at least according to the Latin translation in general use at the time, as attested by Cyprian's use of the word *custodia.* Nonetheless, it is strange that the author of the *De montibus* does not quote Is. 1:8 directly. The fact that he does not tends to prove that he knew the text in its usual form, that is, the text containing the word *casa,* 'hut', but did not know it in the form which included the word *specula* or watch-tower, as used by Tertullian. Otherwise, he would have quoted it. This is a further proof that the *De montibus* was not derived from the work of Tertullian, but that, if there was any question of one text being derived from the other, it was Tertullian who relied on the *De montibus.*

Finally, there is one aspect of the theology contained in the *De montibus* which calls for consideration, namely the presentation of the Holy Spirit as the power of God which, by uniting itself to the flesh, constitutes the Son of God. There is no ambiguity in the text with regard to this question: *Spiritus Sanctus filius Dei rex constitutus est,* 'The Holy Spirit is made into the royal son of God' (*De mont.* 3) and later in the same text: *Spiritus Sanctus qui de caelo descendit Christus, id est unctus Dei vino, Deo vocatus est. Spiritus Sanctus carni mixtus Jesus Christus,* 'The Holy Spirit, who came down from heaven was called by God Christ, that is, the One anointed with the wine of God. The Holy Spirit mingled with flesh is Jesus Christ' (*De mont.* 4).

This concept, according to which the Son had no pre-existence, but was the result of a union between the power of God and the flesh, is also found in the *Shepherd of Hermas*: 'The Son, he is the Holy Spirit, and the Servant, he is the Son of God' (V, 5:2; cf. also V, 6:1; VIII, 10:1). The author of the *Shepherd* draws his inspiration from the figure of the servant in Is. 42. Christ is flesh perfectly submissive to the Spirit, which is not a person, but the power of God. The Son, according to this theology, is not pre-existent — he is constituted eschatologically by the union of the Spirit and the flesh.[73]

This conception is that of Praxeas.[74] It consisted in allowing a certain distinction between the Father and the Son but a distinction 'of nature, not of person' between the Father and the Son, the Father being, according to Praxeas and his followers, the Spirit, that is to say, the divine nature signified by the name of Christ. Cantalamessa quotes Tertullian's description of Praxeas' teaching: 'In one person, they distinguish between the Father and the Son, saying that the Son is the flesh (*carnem*), that is, the man, that is, Jesus, and that the Father is the Spirit, that is, God, that is, Christ' (*Adv. Prax.* 27, 1).

The statement made in the *De montibus* is curiously similar: *Spiritus Sanctus, qui de caelo descendit Christus . . . Deo vocatus est. Spiritus Sanctus carni mixtus Jesus Christus,* 'The Holy Spirit, who came down from heaven, was called by God Christ. The Holy Spirit mingled with flesh is Jesus Christ'. The formula, *Spiritus Sanctus filius Dei rex constitutus est,* 'The Holy Spirit is made into the royal Son of God', which we quoted above, has to be interpreted in the same way, as the union of the Spirit, that is, the divine nature, with the flesh which is the Son of God. On the one

---

73. Cf. PERNVEDEN, *The Concept of Church in the Shepherd of Hermas,* p. 48.
74. It has been well analysed by RANIERO CANTALAMESSA. 'Il Cristo Padre negli scritti del II–III sec.', *RSLR,* 3 (1967), p. 24.

hand, the Holy Spirit, God and Christ are equated with each other and, on the other, the Son of God, the flesh and Jesus. Jesus Christ (Jesus = the flesh, and Christ = the Spirit) is constituted by the union of the flesh and the Spirit.

In the same context another text in the *De montibus* is of interest: 'We see Solomon call the Saviour himself a spotless mirror of the Father, by virtue of the fact that the Holy Spirit as the Son of God sees himself divided, the Father into the Son and the Son into the Father, each one seeing himself in the other. That is why it is a mirror without blemish (*De mont.* 13). According to this formula, the Saviour is a mirror of the Father insofar as the Holy Spirit, which is the divine nature, exists simultaneously in the Father, of whom it is the substance, and in the Saviour, to the extent that it is present in him by virtue of the incarnation and so makes him the Son of God. The divine nature is therefore, as it were, divided into two. This is not really a trinitarian but rather a christological formula.

Because of this, it is tempting to regard the *De montibus*, as Corssen does, as a Monarchian work. In that case it would represent the teaching of the African Monarchians, which was refuted by Tertullian, but would not be by Praxeas himself, though deriving from his circle.[75] Two related conclusions may safely be drawn from our discussion of this aspect of the *De montibus*. The first is that it is further evidence that the work was written before the *Adversus Praxean* and the appearance of Tertullian's doctrine of the Trinity. The second conclusion is that there is a clear link between this Monarchianism, which has its equivalent in the *Shepherd of Hermas,* and one trend in Judaeo-Christianity.

75. J. Moingt has observed that it is not entirely certain whether Praxeas ever went to Africa.

CHAPTER THREE

LATIN JUDAEO-CHRISTIANITY
THE CONFRONTATION WITH PAGANISM

CONFRONTED with competition on the part of the Jews, Latin Judaeo-Christians were simultaneously exposed to persecution by the pagan world. Later, at the time of Minucius Felix and Tertullian, we shall see the Christian message facing the encounter with Greek culture. Before this took place, however, the clash was simply between Christianity, which was still basically Jewish in culture, and pagan society; and this found expression particularly in various Judaeo-Christian writings dealing with martyrdom or with the conflict with pagan morality. Of the texts which we shall be considering in this chapter two can be dated with certainty. The *Passio Perpetuae*, which is an expression of popular Christianity, dates back to the very beginning of the third century. The *De aleatoribus* goes back to a period when the canon of the New Testament was at a less developed stage than it had attained in the Muratorian Canon. The sermon *De centesima sexagesima tricesima* provides evidence of theological and moral ideas in the very earliest period.

1. THE *PASSIO PERPETUAE*

The first work that we have to study, the *Passio Perpetuae*, describes the Visions of Perpetua and Saturus. These visions are genuinely apocalyptic in character because they reveal sacred time and space. The ascent of Paul into the third heaven, the *Apocalypse of John* and the *Visions of Hermas* all belong to this category. Even if the *Passio Perpetuae* in its present state was edited either by Tertullian or by another member of the Christian community in Carthage, it still retains many elements coming from the martyrs themselves. This applies particularly to the three visions of Perpetua and to the vision of Saturus. There is, moreover, no doubt that the language is archaic. This is borne out by the number of Greek words that occur in this part of the work — *machaera, draco, tecnon, catasta, horoma, diastema, philela, agon, afa* and *fiala* — which are not to be found anywhere in the writings of Tertullian and are clearly evidence of a popular Christian idiom which has not yet created Latin equivalents for the original Greek words.[1] The visions are also described with many repetitions in a clearly oral style of narration, and this is further evidence of the preservation by the editor of an original testimony. What we have in this part of the *Passio Perpetuae* therefore is a spiritual experience interpreted in terms of the culture of those who received the visions; and this culture is clearly Judaeo-Christian.

There are very many apocalyptic elements in the three visions of Perpetua. The first theme to note is that of 'the bronze ladder of amazing size which reaches heaven and whose narrowness (*angustia*) allows only one person to go up at a time'. This image of the ladder which passes through successive heavens and leads up to the highest heaven is very similar to the ascent through the seven heavens described in the *Ascension of Isaiah*. The dragon's attempt to bar the way corresponds to the abode of the demon in one of the lower heavens in the *Testament of Levi*. In the *Passio Perpetuae* (4, 7), however, the dragon is in fact below the first rung of the ladder. The reference to the 'narrowness' of the ladder is, of course, reminiscent of the 'narrow way', and is also to be found, combined with the theme of the ladder, in the *Paschal Homily* of the Pseudo-Hippolytus (51). The visions of paradise as a 'boundless space of garden' (*spatium immensum horti*) and of Christ as a 'man with white hair and of great stature' come from Judaeo-Christian apocalyptic. In the *Gospel of Peter*, Christ is said to be taller than the angels and, in the third vision of Perpetua, he is described as being of great stature (10, 8). The angels are said to be beautiful young men (10, 6) and Christ holds 'a green branch from which golden apples hang' (10, 9). This description is clearly reminiscent of the *'ethrôgh*, the 'choice

1. J. FONTAINE, *Aspects et problèmes de la prose d'art latine au IIIe siècle*, pp. 85–97.

fruits', and the *lûlābh*, the 'palm tree branches, boughs of leafy trees and willows' of the Feast of Tabernacles (see Lv. 23:40). Christ is also described, as in *V Esdras*, as surrounded by a huge crowd.

The vision of Saturus is more elaborate in character. There is, as in the visions of Perpetua, a series of ascensions, but the stages are more clearly defined. The ascent is, moreover, not made by ladder, but by a gentle slope (*mollem clivum*). After they have left their bodies, the martyrs are supported by four angels, who carry them towards the East (11, 3). After they have crossed the first world, they emerge into a great light. (This is reminiscent of *V Esdras*.) They then come to a great space, like an orchard (*viridarium*), which recalls the garden (*hortus*) in the vision of Perpetua. Here there are rose-trees and other flowering plants. The trees are as tall as cypresses and their leaves never cease to sing (reading *canebant* with Robinson rather than *cadebant*). The first four angels are then replaced by four other, more dazzling angels, with whom they converse. All then cross the meadow (*stadium violatum*) and come to a building with walls of light (12, 1). At the door stand another four angels, who clothe the martyrs in white robes. Entering the building, they hear singing: *agios, agios, agios*. In this place stands an aged man (*canum*) with hair like snow but a youthful face. His feet are invisible. On his right and on his left four old men are standing and there are others behind him. The angels conduct the martyrs to the aged man, who kisses them. They leave the building and meet other martyrs in the garden with whom they converse in Greek, the language of paradise. All those in paradise are fed by an indescribable fragrance, and never become weary.

The vision of Saturus is slightly more erudite than that of Perpetua, which is evidence of the fidelity with which the tradition has been transmitted. Once again we find apocalyptic imagery: there are the angels who accompany the soul in its ascent; paradise is situated in the East; Christ is presented as having both a young face and the white hair of old age; the higher angels are old men; and the martyrs are clothed in white robes (cf. Rv. 7:9 – the *candidatus exercitus* of the *Te Deum* already makes its appearance here).

The most striking apocalyptic theme in the vision of Saturus, however, is the succession of abodes. First of all, the martyrs leave the world and enter a sphere of light. The second stage is the garden of paradise, and the third is the heavenly city. This idea of the three abodes is also to be found in Irenaeus (*Adv. Haer.* V, 35, 2), but, as Peterson has pointed out,[2] it comes ultimately from Jewish apocalyptic. Two further themes that should not be overlooked are the dialogue between the angels, which is also found in the *Ascension of Isaiah,* and the theme of the perfumes of paradise, which occurs in *I Enoch.*

The *Passio Perpetuae,* however, does not simply contain general apocalyptic themes such as those outlined above. There are also precise details which parallel features occurring in the *Shepherd of Hermas.* In *Vis.* I, 4:3 of the *Shepherd,* two angels carry towards the East the throne in which the Woman, representing the Church, is seated, and in *Vis.* IV, 2:1, the Church appears clearly as a woman with white hair but with a young face. Both in the *Passio Perpetuae* and in the *Shepherd* (*Vis.* V, 1: σχήματι ποιμενικῷ), the figure of the shepherd plays an important part. In *Vis.* I, 1:3, Hermas passes through 'an impassable place' (δι' ἀνοδίας τινος) and reaches level ground (ὅμαλα) Peterson has pointed out that Perpetua passes *per aspera loca et flexuosa,* 'through uneven and tortuous places' (10, 3). The field (ἀγρός) mentioned in the *Shepherd of Hermas* (*Vis.* II, 1:1; IV, 1:2) clearly corresponds to the orchard in Perpetua's vision. Finally, Hermas encounters the young woman with white hair who is the Church (IV, 2:1), after having passed an enormous monster which rose up on his way (IV, 1:6). Both the *Shepherd* and the *Passio Perpetuae* contain the theme of playing (*ludere*; παίζειν) as the occupation of the blessed in paradise (*Perp.* 8, 4; *Sim.* IX, 10). Similarly, both contain the distribution of palms. In conclusion, it should be noted that, apart from the first vision in the *Passio Perpetuae,* there is no question of a heavenly ascension – on the contrary, it is an ascent by ladder that is described.

2. ERIK PETERSON. *Frühkirche, Judentum, Gnosis,* p. 291.

2. THE *DE CENTESIMA, SEXAGESIMA, TRICESIMA*

The *De centesima, sexagesima, tricesima* comes to us from the sphere of Latin Judaeo-Christian apocalyptic writing of the second century. It was first edited by Reitzenstein,[3] who believed that it was a second century document which had, in view of the doctrine contained in it, originated in a gnostic environment. H. Koch, on literary grounds, thought that it originated at the end of the third century, mainly because of certain terms which occur both in the *De centesima* and in the writings of Cyprian,[4] but his reasons are not entirely convincing. It is well known that Cyprian reproduced almost word for word the language of the authors whose work he used. The most famous example of this is his quotation from the *Octavius* of Minucius Felix XVIII in the *Quod idola non sint* (9), but other examples can also be found in his *De habitu virginum* 14 and the *Ad Demetrianum* 16. It should therefore not surprise us to discover in the *De habitu virginum* two passages which are present in the *De centesima*. It is clear that Cyprian drew his inspiration from the *De centesima* at the beginning and at the end of the *De habitu virginum,* but in the rest of his treatise he relied on Tertullian's *De cultu feminarum.* We shall discuss the question of his use of biblical quotations later on in this work. The term *lavacrum vitale,* for example, is found both in Cyprian's work and in the *De centesima* and is an archaic Latin Judaeo-Christian expression of the same kind as *lignum vitale* (Commodian, *Carm. Ap.* 130). There is nothing, therefore, to prevent our text from being earlier than the writings of Cyprian.

Nor are the comparisons that have been made between the *De centesima* and Cyprian convincing evidence for the reverse chronology. At the beginning of the *De habitu virginum* (2), Cyprian says that discipline appears in Scripture as the *fundamentum,* the 'foundation' of religion; therefore, *domiciliis nostris super petram robusta mole solidatis inconcussi ad procellas et turbines saeculi stemus,* 'with our houses made firm upon the rock and strongly

---

3. R. REITZENSTEIN. 'Eine frühchristliche Schrift', *ZNW*, 15 (1914), p. 64; reproduced in *SPL*, I, pp. 53–67.
4. H. KOCH. *ZNW*, 31 (1932), pp. 248–272.

constructed, let us stand unshaken against the storms and whirlwinds of the age'. In *De centesima* 55,[5] there is also a commentary on the parable of the house founded on the rock: *Fundamentum autem Christi saxea mole spiritaliter solidatum petram robustam conversationis maximae maiestate voluntatis intelligere debemus*, 'We must understand the foundation of Christ, spiritually made firm on the rocky mass, as the strong rock of the most disciplined behaviour, achieved by the sovereign power of the will'.

We see therefore that the application of the parable is spelled out in the *De cent.*, whereas Cyprian treats it as already well known and simply makes an allusion to it. What is more, the phrase *petram robustam* represents the image of the στέρεα πετρά, 'firm rock', used by Pseudo-Barnabas and apparently not understood by Cyprian, who speaks of *robusta mole*, 'with a strong structure'. Finally, both synoptic accounts, Mt. 7:24 and Lk. 6:48, are merged together in the *De centesima*, which is evidence of its early composition. Cyprian later used the parable, in the form in which it appears in Mt. 7:24–28, in his *Test*, III, 96 and *De unit.* 2, following his use of it in *De habit.* 2.

Later in the *De habitu virginum*, Cyprian makes use of the theme of the human body as God's temple, stressing that it is wrong to let it become defiled (*violari*): 'We must take care that nothing impure or profane is introduced into the temple of God, for fear that, offended (*offensus*), he may leave the seat (*sedem*) which he occupies' (*De habit.* 3). Similarly, three columns further on in the *De centesima*, we read: 'We begin to be the temples (*templa*) and the sanctuaries (*delubra*) if we are in the one who dwells in us and we in him, as it is written: You are the temples of God and the Holy Spirit lives in you. If anyone defiles (*violaverit*) the temple of God, God will scatter him. Let us pray, then, beloved brothers, that the Lord, offended (*offensus*), will not leave (*derelinquat*) his spiritual seat (*sedem*).'

The last sentence would seem to suggest that Cyprian's text was derived from the *De centesima*. Once again Cyprian is con-

5. References are to the *Supplement to the Patrologia Latina*, I, with column and line.

tent to allude to Scripture instead of quoting it verbatim as the *De centesima* does. On the other hand, he adds an explicit mention of the body as the 'temple of the Holy Spirit' (cf. 1 Co. 3:16; 2 Co. 6:16). The quotation forms part of a group of quotations taken from 1 *Corinthians*, which, as we shall see later, come from an early collection. What is more, the connection between the theme of the foundation and that of the temple can be explained only by referring to 1 Co. 3:10, where it occurs explicitly. It would therefore seem that, here too, Cyprian simply summarises what is contained in a more developed form in the *De centesima*, adding the allusion to the body, however, because he is discussing virginity. Finally, the theme of the Spirit leaving the temple that has been defiled is characteristically Judaeo-Christian and reminiscent of the *Epistle of Barnabas* and the *Shepherd of Hermas*. It should not surprise us that Cyprian makes use of a quotation from the *De centesima* in view of the fact that he gathers together passages from Tertullian throughout the *De habitu virginum*, as well as others from Minucius Felix further on in the treatise (*De habit.* 14). As in the case of the *Quod idola non sint*, he has made a *cento* or collection of quotations here.

Towards the end of the *De habitu virginum* (22), the author's view becomes wider and more general. He summarises the doctrine of the three rewards, alluding to it three times: *Martyres pergunt, eunt virgines, iusti quoque gradiuntur*, in other words, the martyrs, the virgins and the righteous go to their rewards. He then speaks about the 'hundred for the martyrs' and the 'sixty for the virgins', but does not refer to the *iusti*. In *De habit.* 23, however, there is reference to 'many abodes' and it is explicitly stated that the abode of the ascetics is above that of ordinary baptised Christians. All this gives the impression that Cyprian is dealing here with a well-known doctrine and that he does not regard it as worth while to explain it in great detail.

It is, moreover, of interest to note that, although the main part of the treatise is concerned with virgins, the opening sections are not. Similarly, in one of the concluding sections (*De habit.* 23), which is in many ways closely parallel to the *De centesima*, there is reference to those who 'are able to preserve continence (*continentiam*), and in order to live like eunuchs (*spadonum*) castrate

themselves (*castrantur*) for the sake of the kingdom' (see Mt.
19:11–12). *Spadones* are also mentioned in *De cent.* 60, 54; 62, 3,
but not virgins. It would seem, then, that Cyprian applied to
virgins a teaching which was applied, in the *De centesima*, to
ascetics. In the same way, when commenting on Mt. 19:11–12,
Cyprian feels the need to explain why he had taken it on himself
to apply to virgins what was said in the gospel of Matthew about
those who were continent (*De habit.* 4). Again, Cyprian has, as
we have seen above, *eunt virgines*, where the *De centesima* has *eunt
agonistae*.

Finally, all that Cyprian says about the righteous in the *De
habitu virginum* is that they should not fall back into sin (23). He
also applies to virginity the antithesis between the time of fertility
and the time of continence (*De habit.* 23) and the quotation from
Lk. 20:34–35 about the contrast between the sons of this age and
those 'who are judged worthy of a place in the resurrection' (*De
habit.* 24). In the *De centesima*, on the other hand, these ideas are
applied to husbands who remain continent within marriage (*De
cent.* 63, 27; 64, 45). They are certainly more in keeping with the
idea of encratism reflected in the *De centesima* than with the standpoint of Cyprian's *De habitu virginum*. It would seem that Cyprian
applied exclusively to virgins what the author of the *De centesima*
taught with regard both to ascetics and to husbands.

It should finally be noted that the *De habitu virginum* contains
terms and ideas which occur nowhere else in Cyprian's works.
The phrase *iterata nativitas* for 'new birth' is unusual in Cyprian –
iterare baptismum means in fact 'to repeat baptism', a practice
which Cyprian condemned (*Epist.* 63, 8). The antithesis between
the time of fertility and the time of chastity was one that was
alien to his way of thinking as was the idea that there was a
group of *continentes*. The word is in fact found only in this context.

Turning to the vocabulary of the *De centesima*, we find that it
contains certain archaisms. *Celebrare* is used in the simple sense of
'to do'; with *peccata*, for example, it means to commit sins (59, 3),
with *messis*, to gather in the harvest (61, 45), and with *martyrium*,
to suffer martyrdom (58, 44). *Credulus* is used in our text in the
sense of 'believing' (54, 29), a usage which was soon to be aban-

doned. Other examples of archaic words in the *De centesima* are the Hellenism *agonista* (61, 41), which is also found in Irenaeus' *Adv. Haer.* IV, 37, 7; *sufferentia corporis* (63, 21), which occurs in the *Passio Perpetuae* (3); and *fornicaria* (65, 7), which is used in the Latin version of *I Clement* (XII, 1).[5] *Consummatio*, in the sense of 'perfection', is also archaic, and occurs in the Latin versions of *I Clement* (L, 3)[6] and of *Barnabas* (XIII, 7). *Conversatio*, meaning not 'mode of being' but 'abode', is also rare and early. The same applies to certain quotations from the Bible found in the *De centesima*. Two examples of words used in such quotations are *gloria* in 1 P. 1:24, where Cyprian (*De habit.* 7) has *claritas*, and *felix* for *beatus* in Si. 31:8.[8]

Great freedom in the citation of scriptural texts is a typical feature of the Christian *testimonia*, and it frequently points to an early date of composition. There are several examples of free adaptation of the Old Testament in the *De centesima*. Gn. 2:1, for instance, appears in our text (61, 12–16) as *Et consummatum est caelum et terra die quinto; et sexto die requievit ab operibus suis; et benedixit Deus diem septimum, quem et sanctificavit et custodire constituit*, 'And heaven and earth were completed *on the fifth day* and *on the sixth day* he rested from his works and God blessed *the seventh day*, which he made holy and ordered them to keep'. We shall be returning later to discuss this strange theme of resting on the sixth day, but in the meantime would point to another quotation from *Genesis* which is worth noting: ' "Eat of the tree of the knowledge of good and evil and your eyes will be opened" (Gn. 3:5), says the demon to Adam' (*De cent.* 64, 29–30). The translation of Ps. 119:1 in *De cent.* 66, 24–25: *Beati immaculati, qui in via ambulant et lege Domini*, 'Blessed are the spotless, who walk in the way and the law of the Lord', may be connected with the Judaeo-Christian and, before this, the Jewish teaching of the Two Ways.

The author also quotes Is. 10:23 in a shortened form which is

6. See 1 Co. 5:13 in *De aleat.* 4.
7. See also *De cent.* 58, 49; 51, 45.
8. See E. HOPPENBROUWERS, *Conversatio, CLCP*, Supplement, I, pp. 76–77.
9. See R. BRAUN, 'La notion du bonheur dans le latin des chrétiens', *SP*, 13 (1970), pp. 177–182.

characteristic of the *testimonia: Sermonem breviatum et consummatum faciet Dominus super terram*, 'The Lord will carry out his word, shortened and perfected, over the earth' (*De cent.* 57, 7–8). The same quotation is found in a complete form in Cyprian's collection (*Test.* II, 3; *De Dom. orat.* 28). The shorter form is, as we have noted, typical of the early *testimonia* and was usually connected with catechetics.[9] Another curious quotation is from Pr. 7:3–5: *Describe legem in latitudinem (V: tabulas) cordis tui. Dic sapientiam sororem tuam esse ut te liberet a muliere compta et ornata (V: extranea)*, 'Write the law on the breadth (= the tablets) of your heart. Say that wisdom is your sister so that she may set you free from the woman who is ornamented and adorned (= foreign)' (*De cent.* 65, 15, 17). *Latitudo* is used here to translate the word πλάτος (breadth) which is found in the Septuagint and which replaces πλάκος (Hebrew *lûah*, tablet). Clement of Rome quotes the same text, using πλάτος (Latin *latitudinem*) (III, 3). The same also applies to *mulier compta* (Si. 9:8). A long quotation from Ws. 6:12–21 in the *De centesima* changes the order of the verses as these are found in the received text.

The same phenomenon occurs in the case of quotations from the New Testament. In the *De centesima* Ga. 1:15–16 is given in the following form: *Postquam complacuit ei qui me contulit donum spirituale, continuo non consensi carni et sanguini*, 'After it had pleased him to bring me as a spiritual gift, I did not at once confer with flesh and blood'. The words *donum spirituale* are not in the biblical text, though they are found in the *Epistle of Barnabas* 1, 2. They may come from Acts 2:3, where the expression *donum Spiritus Sancti* means baptism. The author of the *De centesima* uses the translation *Felices qui habent uxores tanquam non habentes*, 'Happy are those who have wives as if they had none' for 1 Co. 7:29, where there is no reference in Paul's text to *felices*. Instead of 'those who are judged worthy of a place in the other world' (Lk. 20:35), the *De centesima* has *filii illius aevi*, 'sons of that age'. (These changes in the biblical texts will be discussed more fully later in this chapter — all that need be done here is to draw attention to

10. Tertullian's version is different again: *Sermonem decisum faciet Dominus super terram (Adv. Marc.* IV, 1, 5; see also IV, 16, 17, with *recisum*).

them.) One last example of this kind of change is found in *De cent.* 59, 53: *Benedicentur in eo decem civitates Dei*, 'Ten cities of God will be blessed in him', which is a modification of the text of Lk. 19:17 (the parable of the pounds). The usual significance of the quotation is found in Cyprian's *Epist.* 8, 3.

In addition to these biblical quotations, some of which go back to the literature of the *testimonia*, there are also non-scriptural quotations or *agrapha*. Three such quotations are attributed to Paul. The first of these is *Omnia ista in saeculo nata et hic cum saeculo remansura*, 'All these things were born in the world and will remain behind here with the world' (*De cent.* 55, 5–6),[10] which is also found in Cyprian, although not as Scripture.[11] Two *agrapha* in the *De Centesima* attributed to Paul are: *Si corpore castus et mente corruptus es, nihil prodest*, 'It is useless if your body is spotless and your mind is debased' (*De cent.* 60, 5–6), and *Qui continens est in omnibus, continens permaneat, non tantum corpore, sed spiritu*, 'Let the man who is continent in all things continue continent, not only in his body but in his spirit' (*De cent.* 60, 6–8).

The *De centesima* also contains elements of traditional Judaeo-Christian catechesis. This catechesis, the best known illustration of which is perhaps contained in the *Didache*, began with the golden rule and the two commandments. Both these elements are found in our treatise in their Judaeo-Christian forms. The golden rule is given as follows: *Si furantem tibi prohibes, cur alienum furaris? Si iniuriam corporis pati vetas, cur eadem alii imputas? Quod tibi fieri non vis, alio ne feceris*, 'If you forbid others to steal from you, why do you steal what belongs to others? If you refuse to endure an injury done to your body, why do you criticise others for doing the same? What you do not want to be done to you, do not do to another' (*De cent.* 65, 4–7). The negative form of this golden rule is, of course, the Jewish form which continued in Judaeo-Christian circles.[12] The text in the *De centesima* is,

11. This led SEEBERG to argue that Cyprian's work was derived from the *De centesima*: 'Eine neugefundene lateinische Predigt aus dem 3. Jahrhundert', *NKZ*, 25 (1914), p. 525.
12. Cf. ALBRECHT DIHLE. *Die Goldene Regel*, pp. 106–107. This form is found in Scripture only as an addition to the text of Acts 15:29, in D and a few minuscule texts and in some ancient versions.

moreover, exactly the same as that of the *De duabus viis* 1, 2, a Latin Judaeo-Christian document of the second century. In *Adv. Marc.* IV, 16, 17–18, Tertullian gives both forms one after the other and Cyprian uses the positive form in *De Dom. orat.* 28.

The first two sentences preceding the golden rule in the text quoted above are also of interest. Similar formulas about theft and violence are also found in Judaeo-Christian texts. In the *Clementine Recognitions* VIII, 66, for example, we read: *Quod ipsi fieri nolumus, ne hoc aliis inferamus. Sicut enim ipse occidi non vis, caveas oportet ne alium occidas . . .; furtum pati non vis, nec ipse facias* (*Rec.* VIII, 66). Similarly, in the *Didascalia* I, 9, 10: 'As you do not want a man to take your clothes, do not take another's clothes. As you do not want to be injured, humiliated or struck, do not do that to your neighbour'. All this is clear evidence of an early Judaeo-Christian catechetical tradition.

We must now consider the two great commandments. They occur in the *De centesima* in this form: *Si potes quidem, fili, omnia praecepta Domini facere, eris consummatus: sin autem vel duo praecepta amare Dominum ex omnibus praecordiis tuis et similem tibi quasi teipsum,* 'If you can carry out all the Lord's precepts, my son, you will be perfect. But if you cannot perform them all, keep the two commandments: to love the Lord from your whole heart and your fellow-man as yourself' (*De cent.* 58, 10–13). The second part of this text is a non-scriptural version of the biblical theme of the two commandments. The word *praecordia* for καρδία is an archaism which is also found in the Latin version of the *Epistle of Barnabas* and in Tertullian's version of the same quotation in *Adv. Marc.* V, 8, 10. The first half is found with a variant in the *Didache* (VI, 1): instead of 'carrying out the precepts', the *Didache* has 'carrying the yoke'.[13] In the sermon *De centesima*, it is clearly an allusion to the ideal of perfection represented by continence.[14]

---

13. There has been a certain amount of discussion about this interpretation of the formula in the *Didache*. Cf. J. LIEBAERT, *Les enseignements moraux des Pères apostoliques*, p. 115; A. STUIBER.'Das ganze Joch des Herrn', *SP*, 4 (1961), pp. 323–329. See also F. RORDORF, 'Les deux voies', *Judéo-Christianisme* (*Mélanges Daniélou*).

14. Is. 10:23 is also applied to the two commandments as a summary of the law in Irenaeus' *Demonstratio* (87), Tertullian's *Adv. Marc.* IV, 15, 1–7 and

Another Judaeo-Christian theme is the contrast between *dubius* and *sincerus*, which corresponds to the characteristic contrast in Judaeo-Christianity between δίψυχος, 'double-minded', and ἀπλοῦς, 'single-minded'.[15] As an example of the first, we read in *De cent.* 60, 41: *Corde ac mente libatus et dubius*, 'weak and wavering in heart and mind', *libatus* being used here in the archaic sense of 'weak' (see also *De cent.* 60, 47). The contrast comes out very clearly in, 'After the baptism of life, let there be no more wavering (*dubia*) faith, but only a prayer that is single-minded (*sincera*) and continuous (*iugis*)' (*De cent.* 65, 45). *Sincerus* is also contrasted with *dubius* in *De cent.* 59, 6, 60, and another typical passage illustrating the use of this term is 59, 47–49: 'In his concern to please the Lord, let him strive to prove himself to be single-minded (*sincerum*)'.[16] There is also a connection between this single-mindedness and the *voluntas Dei* which is the central theme of *De cent.* 55. Finally, the phrase *simplici corde placeat*, 'let him please God in singleness of heart', occurs in *De cent.* 60, 19.

Certain symbolic elements in the *De centesima* also point to the early date of the document. Tobias' fish is used to symbolise Christ – its flesh is eaten for food as Christ's is. This is clearly an example of the theme of the eucharistic fish, of which there is evidence in the inscription of Abercius, the *Sibylline Oracles* and the frescoes of the early catacombs.[17] The reference to the theme of the fish occurs in *De cent.* 65, 35–39. F.-J. Dölger[18] has drawn attention to the importance of this theme in the *De centesima*. The gall of the fish represents the Christian law, which is bitter at first, but becomes sweet. This gives rise to a play on words between *fel*, 'gall', and *mel*, 'honey', which is, of course, evidence of the Latin origin of the document. A similar theme of bitterness becoming sweetness is also found in Hippolytus' *Apostolic Tradi-*

Cyprian's *De Dom. orat.* 28.

15. Cf. DANIELOU, *The Theology of Jewish Christianity*, pp. 362–365.

16. See J. AMSTUTZ, *Haplotes*, pp. 42–43.

17. The theme of Tobias offering the fish to the angel is shown in the catacomb of Thrason (third century). The theme of the 'great fish' is also found in the *Gospel of Thomas*.

18. ʼΙΧΘΥΣ. *Der Heilige Fisch in der antiken Religionen und im Christentum*, pp. 33–34; 451–453; 463.

tion (21) in a similar text and in connection with milk and honey. There is also a comparison between *fel* and *mel* in the Muratorian fragment. The three letters of *fel* and of *mel* are also given a Trinitarian significance in the *De centesima*, the words being linked with baptism as a profession of faith in the Trinity and as 'illumination' (*De cent.* 65, 41).

Some of the terms used in the sermon are without doubt Judaeo-Christian. The first is *zeli et livoris stimulum*, the 'goad of jealousy and envy' (*De cent.* 5, 9, 32). This phrase may perhaps come from 1 Co. 3:3, which speaks of 'jealousy and wrangling', especially since the author quotes 1 Co. 3:16 immediately previously. On the other hand, however, it is related in a general way to the Judaeo-Christian theme of ζῆλος – Φθονός, that is, 'jealousy and envy', as an expression of the evil spirit which has inspired God's enemies from Cain down to those who persecuted the apostles, an idea developed particularly in *I Clem.* III, 1.[19] Cyprian wrote a treatise, *De zelo et livore*, on this subject, which shows that the theme was known in African Christian circles in the third century. Finally, the word *stimulus*, 'goad', suggests the action of the demon (cf. 2 Co. 12:7).

Another term is also worth noting. We must, the author of our sermon writes (*De cent.* 58, 33–35), keep free from the promptings of jealousy and envy if we are to be united with the Holy Spirit and allow him to be 'in us not only as our guest, but also as our ruler (*rectorem*)'. The term *spiritus rector* would seem to be a reference to the πνεῦμα ἡγεμονικόν of Ps. 51:10. This text is quoted in *I Clement* XVIII, 12, and the application of the text to the Holy Spirit is an early exegesis which is also found in the *Apostolic Tradition* of Hippolytus (3, 3) and the *Muratorian Canon* 19, which was written, in Latin, at about the same time as the *De centesima*.[20]

19. Cf. esp. BEYSCHLAG, *Clemens Romanus und der Frühkatholizismus*, p. 132. The concept of ζῆλος–Φθονός occurs also in the *Testaments of the XII Patriarchs* (*Sim.* IV, 5; *Benj.* IV, 4).

20. In Western Christian circles, and under the influence of Origen, the same verse was later applied to the Father: Cf. H. C. PUECH, 'Origène et l'exégèse du Ps 50, 12, 14', *Aux sources de la tradition chrétienne (Mélanges Goguel)*, pp. 180–195.

Turning now to theology in the strict sense, we find the concept of the Word as the seventh day. This is without question Judaeo-Christian, and occurs here in a form demonstrably related to the *Shepherd of Hermas*. 'When the Lord created (*creavit*) the angels from fire to the number of seven, he determined to make one of them his Son. He it is whom Isaiah was to proclaim as the Lord Sabaoth. We see that there remained then six angels created with the Son . . . Let us therefore consider the origin of past time, at the end of which day the Lord ceased to work – he who set out the ordinance of the creation of all things, saying, Heaven and earth were completed on the fifth day and God rested from his works on the sixth and he blessed the seventh. It is this day that the ascetic (*agonista*) imitates without knowing it, by resting from works of wickedness.' There follows a quotation from Rv. 4:6: *Et vidi quatuor animalia habentia alas senas*, 'And I saw four living creatures each having six wings'. The text of the sermon then continues: *Non ignorandum est igitur de hoc titulo quod Christiani animalibus insistunt, propter quod et alas senas possident quibus in medio filius Dei graditur*, 'You ought not therefore to be ignorant concerning this passage, that Christians lay great stress on these living creatures, because they also each have six wings, and in the midst of them moves the Son of God' (*De cent.* 60, 50–61, 37).

This text has been examined at length by Barbel.[21] Three themes can be distinguished in it. Firstly, there is that of the creation of the angels from fire, an idea found elsewhere principally in *II Enoch*. More important is the image of the six angels with a seventh angel in their midst who is the Son of God. There is only one other patristic text in which this idea occurs and that is the *Shepherd of Hermas*, which describes the six angels who were created first (πρῶτοι κτισθέντες), in the midst of whom stands the Son of God (*Sim.* IX, 12, 8). The word *principum* in the *De centesima* seems to fit very well with the idea of the protoctists. It is true that Clement of Alexandria also speaks of the πρωτόκτιστοι, but there were, according to him, seven protoctist angels and the Son was not counted among them. The third theme is that of the identification of the six angels with the

---

21. J. BARBEL, *Christos Angelos*, Bonn, 1941, pp. 192–224.

six days of creation and of the Son with the seventh day.[22] In the *De centesima*, then, the angels are explicitly called 'days' and the Son is called the seventh day, 'the one which God blesses'. This calling of the Son a 'day' is a Judaeo-Christian theme found in the *Preaching of Peter*, and is related to certain Judaeo-Christian speculations on the first chapter of *Genesis*.[23] The angels are not explicitly identified with the days of creation in the *Shepherd of Hermas*, but the idea would seem to be assumed in the text.

Another interesting feature is the use of the name Sabaoth to refer to the Son. This, of course, derives from Is. 6:3ff. In apocalyptic writing (*Or. Sib.* I, 304, 316) Sabaoth is the name of an angel, and was taken up by the gnostics. One passage of especial interest occurs in the *Hypostasis of the Archons*. Here the chief of the seven archangels, Ialdabaoth, is said to have a son called Sabaoth. Although Ialdabaoth is a fallen angel, Sabaoth is converted and raised up on the heavenly chariot (141, 413–431). Similarly, in the *De centesima* Sabaoth – here the Son of God – goes forward in the chariot borne by the four animals with six wings (*De cent.* 61, 25–37). The imagery as it appears in the *Hypostasis of the Archons* derives from Jewish apocalyptic,[24] and the same undoubtedly applies in the case of the *De centesima*.

Another interesting feature of the passage is its teaching that the work of creation was completed at the end of the fifth day, which is in accordance with the Septuagint version of Gn. 2:2. Seen in this light, the sixth day was essentially a day of rest in the sense of ceasing from material works and not a day of rest in the sense of reward for work done. (The seventh day was a day of rest as reward.) It is applied in our text to the practice of the Christian ascetic in refraining from works of the flesh and thus imitating the angels. It is not impossible that the text also contains an allusion here to Friday as a fast day. There is a similar reference to the sixth day in Victorinus of Pettau: *Sexto die ob passionem Domini Jesu Christi aut stationem Deo aut ieiunium facimus*, 'On the sixth day, because of the Passion of the Lord Jesus Christ, either we meet to worship God or else we fast'. In this context, it

22. See M. T. D'ALVERNY, 'Les anges et les jours', *CA*, 1957, pp. 274–300.
23. See J. DANIELOU, *The Theology of Jewish Christianity*, pp. 168–172.
24. Cf. BULLARD. *Hypostasis of the Archons*, Berlin, 1970, pp. 110–112.

is worth while noting the phrase νηστεύειν τὸν κόσμον, 'fasting from the world',[25] which indicates quite clearly that fasting had a symbolic meaning and referred to a renunciation of the world.

Another feature deriving from an archaic, semitic anthropology is the idea of 'blood' as a principle in opposition to the spirit, and contesting with it for the body. The starting-point of this concept is Ga. 5:17: ἡ γὰρ σὰρξ ἐπιθυμεῖ κατὰ τοῦ πνεύματος, τὸ δὲ πνεῦμα κατὰ τῆς σαρκός, which sees the desires of the flesh and of the Spirit as in mutual conflict. Starting from this text, the *De centesima* continues: 'The Spirit possesses the power and the flesh possesses the blood. The one over whom the angels in heaven testify to their joy (Lk. 15:7) is the man who, triumphing over the sinful flesh by the witness of blood (*cruoris*) or by his care (*cogitatione*) to weaken the life (of the flesh), does not cease to multiply martyrdom. The sheep held by the devil in the desert (Lk. 15:4) is the body possessed by the blood. The one who wishes to free himself from it (sc. the blood) must press toward martyrdom. The martyr can only be crowned if he sheds his blood and if his body is made holy by the virtue of suffering. So long as he is possessed by much blood, he is exposed to (spiritual) death (*leto*). He views everything with ill-will, and jealousy (*zelus*) abounds, sins increase in number (*celebrantur*), and killings continue. All evils come through the flesh and also through the blood' (*De cent.* 58, 38). Elsewhere in the *De centesima* the words occur: *Sanguis est omnium (malorum) radix,* 'blood is the root of all (evils)' (*De cent.* 60, 16).

The fundamental idea developed in this passage is that the principle of the flesh is blood, which is the source of all human faults and their 'goad' (*stimulum: De cent.* 38, 32). The blood keeps the body a prisoner and drives away the Spirit. This is why it is essential to 'free oneself from the blood', something which the martyr supremely achieves by pouring out his blood. Blood, therefore, is an evil power by which man is possessed and from which he is set free by martyrdom.

25. See A. GUILLAUMONT. ' Νηστεύειν τὸν κόσμον', *BIFAO,* 61 (1962), pp. 15–23.

From two points of view, this idea is Semitic. In the first place, the soul is identified with the blood and, in the second, this blood is an evil principle which is opposed to the Spirit. This dualism is found in Essenism, in the Qumran documents, and in the *Clementines*. It is usually known as the doctrine of the two *yetserim* or tendencies. The words, 'Deliver me from blood' (Ps. 51:14) are quoted by Clement of Rome (*I Clem.* 18, 14). In connection with this passage, Reitzenstein has pointed out that the theme of martyrdom as blood-shedding is an archaic feature.[26] Both Tertullian and Clement of Alexandria react against this materialistic concept of martyrdom, the former also objecting to a crudely realistic interpretation of Ga. 5:17: 'Flesh and blood do not signify substances, but the operations of the substance' (*Adv. Marc.* V, 10, 12).

To the author of the *De centesima* the same materialistic conception held good for the blood of Christ, although he stressed that, because Christ's blood had been made holy, it became sanctifying: 'When he fulfilled his passion in order to do the good pleasure of the Father, Christ himself shed his blood, but made holy, and offered himself in witness of this. And we think that the blood (*cruorem*) which comes to us from him protects us against the arrows of the devil in that we, who have triumphed over the sinful flesh by the body and the spirit of Christ, weaken the blood (*sanguis*) (of sin) by the blood (*cruorem*) of the passion' (*De cent.* 59, 5, 13). A point to note here is the use of the word *sanguis* for blood in the ordinary sense and *cruor* for Christ's blood made holy and sanctifying.

A very early tradition would appear to underlie this teaching, especially as regards the blood of Christ 'made holy' or 'consecrated'. Clement of Alexandria quotes *I Clement* (21, 6) in the form: οὗ τὸ αἷμα πρὸ ἡμῶν ἡγιάσθη (*Strom.* IV, 17; 107, 8), whereas the word ἐδόθη occurs in the original text. This curious variant, which probably did not orginate with Clement, testifies to an early tradition. There is also the question of the contrast between the sinful blood, which according to the

26. REITZENSTEIN, *op. cit.*, p. 66. With reference to the same point, Dölger compares this passage with the *Passio Perpetuae* (21, 2–3).

De centesima is the evil principle in man, and the blood of Christ, which enables man to triumph over the blood of sin.

Finally, it should be noted that the passage is not simply referring to martyrdom. Alongside the reference to the 'witness of blood', there is also an allusion to the 'will to weaken (*diminutionis*) the life (of the flesh)', which is reiterated later in the second quotation discussed above: 'we ... weaken (*minuamus*) the blood (*sanguis*) (of sin) by the blood (*cruorem*) of the Passion'. What we have here is apparently an allusion to blood as the principle of desire, ἐπιθυμία, in man. Man has therefore to weaken the excess of blood and dry out his body.[27] This is a familiar theme in Syrian asceticism, and is found especially in the *Spiritual Homilies*, traditionally ascribed to Macarius. As we shall see later on, the *De centesima* is marked by encratite influence coming from the Syrian, Tatian.

The central theme in the *De centesima*, however, is that of the parables. The first point to note is that their presentation is different from that in the New Testament and may come from another tradition. This is clear in the case of the parable of the pounds (Lk. 19:11–27). In *De cent.* 57, 32–35, we read: 'A father of a family had two servants. Going away on a journey, he called them and gave each of them ten pounds, commanding them to make a profit on them. One of the servants acquired a hundred pounds for the ten pounds he had received, by which he showed that the ten words are multiplied by ten'. In the Lucan text, on the other hand, the parable speaks of a king and not of a father of a family and of ten, not two servants. Each servant, moreover, receives one pound, not ten, and the first brings back ten pounds, the second five and the last nothing. The Matthaean parable of the talents is, of course, a special version of the same theme, and other differences occur in the *Gospel of Thomas*. This clearly points to the possible existence of a non-canonical tradition.

The author of the *De centesima* also provides us with an original version of the parable of the sower. The most obvious difference is that, in his version, the seed falls first among thorns and then on

27. See ERIK PETERSON, *Frühkirche, Judentum, Gnosis*, pp. 302–303.

rocky ground (*petra*).[28] The second difference is that in the *De centesima* there are two separate lists, one mentioning only the places where the seed falls, and a second describing what happens to the seed. Again, whereas in the gospels the seed is said to fall 'beside' (*secus*) the path, here it falls *in via*, 'on the path', as in the *Diatessaron*.[29] Similarly, where Matthew, for instance, says 'the birds came and ate it up' (Mt. 13:4), our author says that this seed 'was crushed underfoot by the passers-by before it yielded fruit' (*conculcatum est a transeuntibus priusquam fructificaret*). In Lk. 8:5, both themes are present: the seed 'was trampled on and the birds ate it up', pointing to a possible merging by Luke of two traditions, one preserved in the Matthaean account and the other by our text.

Of the seed which fell among thorns the *De centesima* remarks, *suffocatum est a cogitationibus iniustis*. The second part of this statement corresponds to, but is not exactly the same as the interpretation of the parable given in the synoptics. The *cogitatio iniusta* of our sermon is temptation and this term corresponds to the λογισμός, which is a translation of the Jewish *yeṣer hā-rā'*, a concept which plays an important part in Judaeo-Christianity. Even more interesting is the version of the seed that fell on rocky ground: *Per tempus adolescebat viridis et viso radio solis aruit, quia non habuit lentorem salutis*, 'In time it grew green, but the plant withered in the sun's rays, because it did not have the sap of salvation'. According to the synoptics, the seed sprang up, but the plant withered almost at once because of lack of water and earth. These elements are not mentioned in our text, which speaks of the *lentor salutis*, which is not paralleled in the gospel accounts.[30]

The common theme of all these parables is introduced immediately after the parable of the sower. The author's aim is to show how the Lord helps a hundred seeds to be harvested from

---

28. The same order is also found in the *Shepherd of Hermas, Sim.* IX, 19–21, and, as HEER, *op. cit.*, p. 170, has pointed out, in Justin, *Dial* CXXV, 1.

29. See G. QUISPEL, 'Das Heiland und das Thomasevangelium', *VC*, 16, 1962, pp. 146–147.

30. The word *lentor* is found in secular Latin in the first century B.C. in the work of Columella.

one. The first example of this is the case of the lost sheep. Perfection consists of a hundred sheep. The ten commandments, in other words, are multiplied by practice, which makes them bear fruit. The same principle is also illustrated by the parable of the pounds. It is, however, only the effectiveness of Christ's passion which makes it possible for the ninety-nine just men to become a hundred. The one sheep, then, is Christ. (In the *Gospel of Thomas*, Christ is the one sheep loved more than all the others.) Similarly, in the parable of the lost drachma, Christ is, according to the *De centesima*, the one *drachma* that is lost and has to be found, so that the other nine can become ten. In the same way, it is Christ who sums up in himself alone the ten commandments.

Martyrdom, according to our text, is the outstanding expression of this principle, as the author shows in his exegesis of the parable in Lk. 14:31. The king who goes to war with ten thousand men against the other king who has twenty thousand is the martyr who, relying on Christ, who is 'one', *unus*, fights against flesh and blood. The hundred just men, who still represent the ninety-nine completed by the one Christ, are multiplied for him by ten times ten (*decem per denos*) and thus become ten thousand. This is the supremely perfect fruit, which nevertheless is still the product of the one seed.

There is no doubt that the author of the *De centesima* has made use here of a biblical collection dealing with the number ten and relating to Is. 5:10; Ps. 33:2; Ps. 92:3, etc. Similar collections are found in the work of Victorinus of Pettau in connection with the number seven. Another aspect of our text is that the lost drachma or the lost sheep have a very special character in contrast with the just men because they represent Christ. This may be compared with the *Gospel of Thomas* (107), in which the parable of the lost sheep is identified with the parables of the kingdom, and the sheep found by the shepherd is interpreted as the gnosis found by the gnostic and loved infinitely more than the other ninety-nine.[31]

The author of the *De centesima* also applied the idea of the lost sheep to Adam. This goes back to a typically Judaeo-Christian

31. See P. SINISCALCO, *Mito e Storia della Salvezza*, pp. 62–63.

form of exegesis which is concerned with the history of salvation. It was used by Irenaeus, but is earlier than he, reminding us, for example, of the interpretation given to the Good Samaritan by Papias. The author of our text also applies this interpretation to the righteous of the Old Testament, which would seem to be an allusion to the descent into hell in its Judaeo-Christian sense. He then applies it to the righteous of his own time and in the future. It is clear that the parable of the lost sheep is interpreted as referring to the liberation of the Christian with regard to death, not to the conversion of the sinner. Even more remarkable is the fact that the lost sheep is interpreted as Christ's liberation from his own body and the Christian's liberation from his body in martyrdom.

It should also be remembered in this context that the drachma found by the woman is also Christ, an identification which may be influenced by the parable of the pearl or that of the treasure. As for the parable which forms the object of the sermon, the hundredfold, the sixtyfold and the thirtyfold are the martyrs, the continents and the husbands who live in continence. [32] Cyprian speaks of the first two of these interpretations as though they were already well-known, and may well have been referring to our sermon (De habitu virginum, 21; Epist. 76, 6; 69, 14). The gnostic interpretation of the hundredfold, the sixtyfold and the thirtyfold was that they were the pneumatics, the psychics and the hylics (cf. Hippolytus, Elench. V, 8, 29). Irenaeus (Adv. haer. V, 36, 1) and Clement of Alexandria (Strom. IV, 6; 36, 3; VI, 11; 86, 2; VI, 14; 114, 3; VII, 7; 40, 4) both thought that it illustrated the diversity of merits. [33] Origen's is the only interpretation which corresponds exactly to that of our treatise (Hom. Josh. II, 1). It is clearly very old, since the De centesima is the earliest extant text on the subject. Later, in the fourth century, the three categories were to be interpreted as the virgins, the widows and the husbands.

32. See B. GERHARDSSON. 'The Seven Parables in Matthew 13', NTS, 19 (1972), p. 31.
33. See A. ORBE, 'Las tres moradas de la casa paterna de san Ireneo a Gregorio de Elvira', Diakonia Pisteos (Mel. de Aldama), pp. 69–97.

The question has been posed as to whether the interpretation given in the *De centesima* may not have been directed against the gnostics. The interpretation of the parable of the wise and the foolish virgins in the *Epistle of the Apostles* at the end of the second century was certainly a reaction against the interpretation given, according to Tertullian (*De anim.* XVIII, 4), by the Valentinians.[34] In the same way the categories proposed in the *De centesima* for the hundredfold, sixtyfold and thirtyfold are in direct opposition to those of the Valentinians. The same applies also to the parable of the lost sheep, which had also been given a gnostic interpretation as early as the Simonians. It should, moreover, be added in this context that the treatise as a whole is anti-gnostic in tendency by virtue of the emphasis which it places on martyrdom. The *De centesima* was written within a framework of anti-gnostic Judaeo-Christian gnosis. Corssen was mistaken here, because he confused gnosis and gnosticism; the speculations of gnosis were parallel to those of gnosticism, but the two were sharply opposed in content.

The importance accorded to the symbolism of numbers in the interpretation of the parables will have been noted. This applies particularly to the four closely associated parables that we have been considering. There are a hundred sheep in Lk. 15:4, ten drachmas in Lk. 15:9, the hundred, sixty and thirty in Mt. 13:23 and the ten thousand and the twenty thousand in Lk. 14:31. This symbolism of numbers was very common in both orthodox and heterodox Judaeo-Christian gnosis. This type of exegesis was, moreover, prevalent among the gnostics and can also be found in the work of Irenaeus.

It is, however, worth noting that it was opposed by Tertullian, who wrote, in his *De pudicitia* IX (*CSEL,* 235–236): 'Because we do not interpret realities according to parables, but parables according to realities, we do not go to great lengths to make everything complicated in exegesis. Why a hundred sheep? Why ten drachmas? And what are these brooms?' It is clear that Tertullian was here criticising exegesis of the type found in the *De*

34. Cf. STAATS, 'Die törichten Jungfrauen von Mt 25 in gnostischer und anti-gnostischer Literatur', in W. ELTESTER, *Christentum und Gnosis,* pp. 98–115.

centesima. There may, however, be something else in what he says with reference to the *scopae* or 'brooms'. In the first place, this is an allusion to the parable of the drachma, in which the word σαροῖ in Lk. 15:8 was translated in some early Latin versions by *scopis mundet.* The treatise *Ad Novatianum,* attributed to Pseudo-Cyprian, has simply *mundare.* The *scopae* are mentioned in the *De centesima* (57, 24).[35] What is more, although Tertullian mentions the parable of the lost drachma several times, he does not once refer to the *scopae.* It would seem therefore as though he was, in the passage quoted above, alluding to the *De centesima.*[36]

Reitzenstein has observed that Tertullian referred to the application of the parables of the lost sheep and the lost drachma to the martyrs and commented that, although he did not reject this interpretation of the parables, he preferred to confine himself to the purely scriptural meaning (*De pud.* IX, 21). In contrast to Tertullian, both parables are applied to martyrdom in the *De centesima.*

We must now turn to another example of the same symbolism of numbers in the second part of the *De centesima,* where it occurs in connection with the *agonistae.* As we have already seen, these are likened in our text to the angels, which was no doubt the result of the influence exerted by the Lucan text: 'They are as the angels' (Lk. 20:36). This verse, which is quoted in the *De centesima* was a major theme in encratism, to which we shall be returning. At the end of the second century, Luke's term ἰσάγγελοι was applied by Clement of Alexandria to the true gnostics (*Strom.* VII, 12; 78, 6; VII, 14; 84, 2). For our author the number which corresponds to the state of the angels is six, since there were six protoctists, one for each of the six days of creation, and since the sixth day was the last day of creation and therefore the day of rest from material works.

To obtain the sixty, which is the reward of the *agonistae,* however, another element is necessary in order to multiply the six by ten, and this is the ten words, *decem verba,* or the decalogue

---

35. DE BRUYNE prefers the reading *scopus,* but this correction cannot be justified.

36. It should however, be pointed out that, in his *De praescr.* X, 4, Tertullian has *didragmis* as the text quoted in *De centesima.*

(*De cent.* 61, 21–22). Is it, however, nothing but the ten commandments of the law that are involved here? These, after all, are the concern of all Christians, not simply of the *agonistae*. The answer to this question may be found in a passage in the *Stromateis* where Clement of Alexandria is talking about the symbolism of numbers, and allegorises the decalogue, applying it to the true gnostics (*Strom.* VI, 16; 133–148). His ten parables signify the practice of those virtues by means of which the *agonista*, who is represented by the number six, merits the reward, which is the number sixty. It is noteworthy that, in this passage in the *Stromateis*, Clement's symbolism has several elements in common with that in the parallel passage in the *De centesima*. The number six, for example, is in both the number of creation. Both texts, moreover, quote Lk. 20:35, which speaks of those who neither marry nor are given in marriage. This suggests that both Clement and the *De centesima* are here dependent on the same encratite source.

It would seem therefore that the essential elements in the sermon *De centesima* were derived from Judaeo-Christian sources. We must now try to define this origin a little more precisely. On several occasions in this chapter, we have pointed to the encratite tendencies in the text. The central theme of the sermon, the universal call to perfection or *consummatio*, is clearly influenced by encratism. We drew attention to this in particular in connection with the text borrowed from the *Didache*. We can, however, go even further, since it is apparent that the final reward includes, according to the interpretation given in the *De centesima*, an appeal to husbands to be continent in marriage. The author contrasts the commandment to increase and multiply given in the Old Testament with the revelation of *sanctimonia* in the New Testament (*De cent.* 63, 30–32; cf. also 14–16). *Sanctimonia* means here, as elsewhere, consecrated celibacy and the author of the *De centesima* calls husbands to this *sanctimonia* (*De cent.* 63, 6). [37]

One passage in particular is typical. Discussing those who are afraid that they may be deprived of inheriting the kingdom

---

37. See the Greek equivalent ἀγιωσύνη in the *Acts of Thomas*, (Klijn, p. 85). See also A. VOOBUS, *History of Asceticism in the Christian Orient*, I.

because they have not suffered martyrdom, the author says: 'If you have not been able to follow *sanctimonia* because you have been previously bound by marriage, at least, after the washing of life (*lavacrum vitale*) which has redeemed you, imitate the ascetic' (*De cent.* 66, 3–6). It is in this connection that the author uses the quotation, which we have already mentioned, of Ga. 1:15–16 in a modified form and says: 'It is necessary to act like St Paul who, after having received the spiritual gift (= baptism), no longer obeyed flesh and blood'. The Pauline text is clearly interpreted here as a renunciation of sexual activity after baptism. It is also worth noting in this context that Tertullian distinguished three *gradus* or 'steps' in *sanctificatio,* the last of which was the same renunciation by husbands and wives of sexual life after baptism (*De exhort. cast.* I, 4; *Ad uxorem* VI, 2). This theme no longer appears in the works of Cyprian.

If the quotations used in the sermon are studied with care, it becomes clear that they form a whole which is based on a collection with a marked encratite tendency. We have already pointed to one such quotation from a *testimonium*: 'Happy are those who have wives as if they had none', a verse which is obviously reminiscent of 1 Co. 7:29, but which is found, in precisely this form, in the *Acts of Paul* (5) and in Ephraem. [38] The similarity is so great that we are bound to conclude that our author was familiar with the *Acts of Paul* or with the source of that text. Both came from the same encratite environment; and since we have already seen that Tertullian criticised these *Acts of Paul,* which date back to the end of the second century, this was probably within the Latin world and before Tertullian's time. [39]

Another quotation, this time inspired by Lk. 20:35, is used by our author but with an important variant: *Filii aevi huius nubunt et nubuntur; filii autem illius aevi, qui digni habentur esse resurrectione a mortuis, neque nubent neque nubentur,* 'The sons of this age marry and are given in marriage, but the sons of that age, who are thought to be worthy of the resurrection from the dead, will

38. Assemani, I, 16 B; see also A. RESCH, *Agrapha,* Leipzig, 1906, p. 274.
39. This Pauline formula was also used by the encratite Cassian, at least according to Clement of Alexandria (*Strom.* II, 14, 95, 7), and possibly in the same form as it was used in the *Acts of Paul.*

neither marry nor be given in marriage'. It should be noted that, unlike our author, Luke did not speak about 'the sons of that age', but about 'those who are *judged worthy* of a place in the other world', which is what is found in Cyprian's *De habitu virginum* (22). In his desire to contrast the 'sons of this age' with the 'sons of that age', the author of the *De centesima* has introduced a dualism which is quite absent from Luke and which, moreover, makes it clear that our author was deeply concerned with the antithesis between the two worlds. Quispel has pointed out that this particular text is a primary one in encratism. The encratites believed, not merely that there would be no marriage in the other world, but that it had to be rejected in this life. [40]

This is further evidence of the fact that the *De centesima* originally formed part of an encratite collection. Clement of Alexandria wrote: 'In the same way, these men support their argument by quoting, "the sons of the other age neither marry nor take wives" ' (*Strom.* III, 12; 87, 1), which is, of course, what is said in the *De centesima*. Clement goes on: 'The question about the dead and those who ask about their fate in the future does not show that the Lord condemned marriage. What is more, the words "the sons of this age" were not said by him in contrast to the sons of some other age, since all who are born into this world, being sons by birth, are born and begotten' (III, 12; 87, 3). It is clear, then, that this quotation was at the very heart of the debate with the encratites and, in the form in which it appears in the *De centesima*, formed part of their collection of texts.

Finally, it should be pointed out that, in Lk. 20:35, Jesus is replying to a question asked by the Jews. In the *De centesima*, we read: *Cum Thomas a Judaeis lege Moysi urgeretur,* 'When Thomas was pressed by the Jews regarding the law of Moses' (*De cent.* 64, 37). This reference to Thomas, which certainly does not occur in the gospel, can be explained by the pre-eminent place occupied by this disciple in encratite circles. The *Gospel of Thomas* itself, of course, came from such circles. This is, in fact, a logion similar to those found in the *Gospel of Thomas* and one which must have come from the same tradition. [41]

---

40. G. QUISPEL, *Makarius, das Thomasevangelium und das Lied von der Perle*, p. 83.

The situation is very similar in the case of a quotation attributed to Paul. We have already mentioned this hitherto unidentified text: *Qui continens est in omnibus continens permaneat, non tantum corpore, sed spiritu,* 'Let the man who is continent in all things continue to be continent, not only in his body but in his spirit' (*De cent.* 60, 7–9). This seems to be a quotation with certain modifications, of 1 Co. 9:25: πᾶς δὲ ὁ ἀγωνιζόμενος πάντα ἐγκρατεύεται, meaning 'every man who strives (in the contest) exercises self-restraint in all things', the word ἀγωνιζόμενος corresponding to the word *agonista,* which occurs frequently in the *De centesima,* where it is equivalent to *continens.* The end of the text in *De centesima* is an addition, and is echoed in an *agraphon* in the same collection: *Si corpore castus et mente corruptus, nihil prodest,* 'It is useless if your body is spotless, but your mind is debased' (*De cent.* 60, 5–6).

Clement also quotes the received text of 1 Co. 9:25, commenting, 'Instead of εἰς πάντα ἐγκρατεύεται, not abstaining from everything, but using ἐγκρατῶς what he judged good' (*Strom.* III, 16; 101, 4). Clement must therefore have known a version of the quotation in which πάντα was replaced by εἰς πάντα. This is also the version which Cassian used. Clement was critical of this version, which speaks of total continence, whereas Paul spoke simply of self-restraint in dealing with things. It would, moreover, seem that the words *in omnibus* used in the *De centesima* correspond to Cassian's εἰς πάντα. Here again, it would appear, Clement was familiar with a modified Pauline text, similar to the one found in the *De centesima.* This practice of modifying the Pauline texts to give a tendentious meaning, which was something that Marcion had already done, would seem to have recurred in Cassian.

The appeal in the *De centesima* to total renunciation is also based on another text put forward as scriptural: *Si quis non dimiserit patrem aut matrem aut omnia quae possidet et secutus me fuerit, non est me dignus,* 'If a man has not sent away his father or mother or

---

41. See F. BOLGIANI, 'La tradizione ereseologica sull'encratismo', II, p. 47. The Marcionites used the same text against marriage, but changed it in a different way; see Tertullian, *Adv. Marc.,* II, 35, 7. See also VOOBUS, *op. cit.*

everything that he possesses and followed me, he is not worthy of me' (*De cent.* 54, 10–12). Once again, what we have here is a text which has certain similarities with the New Testament – in this case, with Mt. 10:37–38 – but which is nonetheless independent of the New Testament. It is remarkable in the case of this particular text that it is also found in the *Spiritual Homilies* (XLV, 1) and in the Persian *Diatessaron* (III, 10; Messina 209). We know that there was a Latin *Diatessaron* in the West at the end of the second century, and this must therefore be the source of our text; but this *Diatessaron* was Tatian's, and he was an encratite. As Quispel has pointed out, the tendentious character of the present version is most apparent in the term *dimiserit*.[42]

Several other points need to be made in connection with this quotation. It appears in a similar form in the *Gospel of Thomas* (55), which, of course, leads us back to encratism. Furthermore, in his collection of texts on encratism, Clement of Alexandria quotes this particular text among those used by Cassian's disciples (*Strom.* III, 14; 96, 2).[43] It is therefore possible to say that what we have in the *De centesima* is a typically encratite quotation and, what is more, in the very form which that movement had given it. This is in itself a strong argument for the fact that this treatise came from a circle which was close to that of Tatian and the encratites against whom Clement of Alexandria fought. We may add here another quotation which also points in the direction of total renunciation, but which appears in the *De centesima* in its ordinary biblical form (*De cent.* 56, 8–11). This is the text of Mt. 16:24: *Qui voluerit sequi vestigia mea abneget semetipsum sibi et tollet crucem suam et sequatur me*, 'Any man who wants to follow in my footsteps, let him deny himself and take up his cross and follow me'.

There is another interesting case in the *De centesima* of a biblical text being misused to emphasise the author's argument. It is based on Rm. 7:23: *Alia est lex mentis devotae, alia corporis, sicut scriptura divina dicit: Video aliam legem, inquit, in membris meis expugnantem*

42. G. QUISPEL, *Makarius, das Thomasevangelium und das Lied von der Perle*, pp. 82–83.
43. See F. BOLGIANI, 'La tradizione ereseologica sull'encratismo', II, Turin, 1962, p. 53.

legem mentis meae et captivitantem, 'The law of the faithful mind and that of the body are different, as holy scripture says: "I see a different law," he says, in my members, overcoming the law of my mind and making (it) captive' (*De cent.* 63, 41). A little later on, our author adds: *Sed quod nolo hoc facio, non consentio legi* (*De cent.* 63, 48–49). The first quotation from Paul is abbreviated, since the text in Romans in fact continues *captivitantem me in lege peccati,* 'Making me captive in the law of sin', while the second is clearly changed. Our author's version reads: 'But I do what I do not want to do; I do not consent to the law' (*non consentio legi*). The Pauline text, on the other hand, reads: 'But *if* I do what I do not want to do, I consent to the law, that it is good' (*consentio legi quod bonum est:* Rm. 7:16). In the first quotation, then, the author of the *De centesima* suppresses the reference to sin and only speaks of the 'members'. The second quotation is interpreted on the basis of the preference given to the law of the body over the law of the rational mind. This is made explicit in the introductory sentence.

Both these texts are, moreover, quoted by Clement of Alexandria in his controversy with the encratites. His version of Rm. 7:23 is: 'Sin, battling against the law of God and my mind, he says, makes me captive in the law of sin' (*Strom.* III, 11; 77, 1). Clement stresses that man is a prisoner of sin acting through the body, and his criticism of the encratites is that they do not quote the part of the text concerned with sin. This is, of course, precisely what our author also omits to do.

The second text is quoted by Clement not in the form which it has in Rm. 7:16, but from Rm. 7:20: *Si quod nolo hoc facio, iam non ego operor illud, sed quod habitat in me peccatum,* 'If I do what I do not want to do, it is not I acting, but sin that lives in me', which shows clearly that, for Clement, it was sin that was the essential element. It is also evident that our author's position, as far as this passage is concerned, was the same as that of the encratites whom Clement was criticising.

The encratites, whom Clement calls ἀντιτασσόμενοι here (*Strom.* III, 11; 61, 2), made use of the Epistle to the Romans, but interpreted it in the sense of a dualism of body and mind and of a condemnation of the body as the source of sin. Clement, on the other hand, taught that the body was good and that it was only sin that made it an instrument of evil. The author of the *De centesima* made use of the Pauline texts only to draw attention to the antithesis between the body and the mind. The whole of the last part of his work is aimed at married people and the author's main object is to show that, after his conversion, Paul renounced flesh and blood, in other words, marriage, and that he is consequently a model for all married Christians to renounce intercourse.[44]

In the same context, another passage in the *De centesima* is noteworthy: *Spiritum cotidie adversus carnem conluctari . . . Spiritus concupiscit spiritaliter; caro autem quae carnis sunt quaerit,* 'The Spirit struggles every day against the flesh . . . The Spirit desires spiritually, but the flesh seeks the things of the flesh' (*De cent.* 58, 39–42). The first part of this text is an allusion to Ep. 6:12. Paul's text, however, reads: ὅτι οὐκ ἔστιν ἡμῖν ἡ πάλη (= *conluctatio*) πρὸς αἷμα καὶ σάρκα, 'For us it is not a struggle against blood and flesh', which is, of course, quite the opposite. The second part of the text in the *De centesima* is derived from Ga. 5:17, which, as we have seen, reads: 'The desires of the flesh are (ἐπιθυμεῖ = *concupiscit*) against the Spirit and those of the Spirit against the flesh'. What matters is the alteration of the text. Clement of Alexandria quoted the same verse with the comment that 'these things are not opposed to each other like good and evil', (*Strom.* IV, 8; 60, 4) which implies that the text was also used by the encratites as evidence of the evil of the flesh.

There are, moreover, other texts, quotations or allusions found both in the *De centesima* and in the collection used by Clement in his polemics against the encratites. There are references to 1 Co. 7:29 (*Strom.* III, 14; 95, 3) and to Mt. 10:17 (III, 15; 97, 2), and to the formula 'Be holy as I am holy' from 1 P. 1:16 (*De cent.* 62, 43–44), which our author interprets as *sanctimonia*, that is, continence in marriage. Clement interprets it, as he does others, in a non-encratite manner. It is clear that, in all these cases as well as in the case of his quotation of 1 P. 1:24 (*Strom.* III, 16; 103, 2),[45] he

---

44. The author similarly corrects the phrase *opera tenebrarum* ('works of darkness', Rm. 13: 12) into *opera carnis* ('works of the flesh', Ga. 5: 19) (*De cent.* 58; 34).

was discussing texts which had been used by the encratites, and restoring their true meaning.

More significant, however, is the interpretation given in the *De centesima* of Gn. 2:16. For the author of our sermon, the 'tree of the knowledge of good and evil' was sexual intercourse, and God's commandment to Adam and Eve not to eat the fruit of the tree was interpreted by him as an appeal to continence. He insists that Adam and Eve were urged by the devil to violate this commandment (*De cent.* 64, 13-31). The same argument occurs in Cassian, whose thesis Clement expounds and discusses (*Strom.* III, 17; 103, 1–104, 5). Clement agrees that the tree of knowledge signifies marriage, but argues that, according to the text, marriage could be used well or badly. Finally, it should be pointed out that the symbolism of the tree of the knowledge of good and evil as representing concupiscence (66, 2) is found in the *Odes of Solomon* III, 9. It would seem as though it was in the same sense that the author of the *De centesima* interpreted it.

The theme of the second part of the sermon is, of course, concerned with the ascetic or *agonista* and this has a number of characteristic features. The ascetic leads a life that is similar to that of the angels, which refers, of course, to Lk. 20:34–36. The author clearly has in mind the man who renounces sexual life entirely, but this does not mean simply a physical renunciation. It also implies interior perfection. He insists that it is not simply the members (*membra*), but above all actions which make the true eunuch (*spado*) (61, 54–55). This teaching is, of course, based on Mt. 19:11–13, a text quoted by the disciples of Basilides when they condemned marriage (see Clement, *Strom.* I, 2). Clement took this as his starting-point in his discussion of encratism.

Clement also refers to the fact that Cassian had written a treatise (*Strom.* III, 13; 91, 13; 91, 1) on self-restraint or castration (περὶ ἐγκρατείας ἤ περὶ εὐνουχίας), in which he had insisted on the Lord's condemnation of the use of the sexual organs (μόρια) . This, of course, is also what is discussed in the *De centesima,* which stresses, as we pointed out in the

---

45. Tertullian also quoted 1 P. 1: 24 as an argument in favour of celibacy *(De monog.* III, 7), together with 1 Co. 3: 2.

previous paragraph, that it was not the organs (*membra*, μόρια) which made the true eunuch, but the inner dispositions. If this were not so, our author argues, 'the man who had been made a eunuch by men might seem to be an ascetic by virtue of this accident' (*De cent.* 51, 55–62, 2). Clement affirms almost exactly the same doctrine: 'The eunuch is not the man who has undergone the deprivation in his members, but the man who refrains from sin' (*Strom.* III, 14; 91, 1).

Clement also emphasises that what makes the ascetic (ἀγωνιζόμενος) is 'to be victorious in the struggle, not to be crowned without an effort' (*Strom.* III, 16; 101, 4). This is the final theme of the section of the *De centesima* under discussion, namely that 'where there is no enemy, there is no struggle (*pugna*)', and that 'those whose bodies are weak are not crowned (*coronantur*) in the manner of fighters (*agonistico more*)' (*De cent.* 92, 12–16). The fact that Clement quotes a Pauline text changed by Cassian precisely at this point makes it all the more certain that he and the author of the *De centesima* have the same context here. The text in question is 1 Co. 9:25, which appears in the *De centesima* as *Qui continens est in omnibus continens permaneat*, which corresponds to Cassian's text: πᾶς ὁ ἀγωνιζόμενος εἰς πάντα ἐγκρατεύεται. It should finally be noticed that Clement uses the verb ἀγωνίζεσθαι when he speaks of the encratites (*Strom.* II, 20; 110, 2; 110, 3).

The fact that the author of the *De centesima* clearly made use of an encratite collection enables us to reply to those scholars who insist that the *De centesima* was dependent on Cyprian because about fifteen or so quotations from scripture are found both in the *De centesima* and in Cyprian's *De habitu virginum* and *Testimonia ad Quirinum*. A careful examination of these quotations, however, will show that this argument is unconvincing. Several of these biblical texts are found in a modified form in the *De centesima* and this form is moreover often archaic, whereas the form that is found in Cyprian's work is usually correct. This is certainly the case with Mt. 7:21, which is found in Justin, *I Apol.* XVI, 9–10 with the same modification; 1 Co. 7:30, which comes from the *Acts of Paul*; Lk. 20:35; Ps. 119:1; Mt. 22:40; Jn. 3:6; 1 Co. 6:15; 1 Co. 10:23; Rv. 14:4. It is therefore very unlikely that these quotations were borrowed from Cyprian.

The solution to this problem would seem to be that both the author of the *De centesima* and Cyprian made use of a collection of unpublished *testimonia*.[46] At least five of the quotations that appear both in the *De centesima* and in Cyprian's work have been shown by Reveillaud to have been borrowed by Cyprian from this collection. These are Jn. 6:38; 1 Jn. 2:17; Is. 10:23; Mt. 22:40 and Jn. 5:14. This collection was ascetic in character and was used first by the author of the *De centesima* in an encratite manner and then, Reveillaud believes, by Cyprian, who corrected the texts that he took from it and eliminated the tendentious aspects in them. The *agraphon* which is found both in the *De centesima* and in Cyprian's *De habitu virginum, Omnia ista in saeculo nata et cum saeculo remansura,* 'All those things were born in this world and will remain behind with this world', also comes from this collection.

Certain conclusions may be drawn from our discussion of the *De centesima*. The treatise, which was undoubtedly known to Cyprian, in whose circle the rather primitive Latin of the text was probably corrected and improved, is a Latin Judaeo-Christian sermon from the end of the second century. It exhibits characteristically Judaeo-Christian features: freedom in the use of biblical quotations, an allegorical exegesis of the New Testament parables and an angelomorphic Christology. Tertullian, as we know, reacted strongly against all these characteristics.[47]

The author of our sermon also made use of a collection of Pauline texts which would seem to have been in large measure the same as that which, according to the information provided by Clement of Alexandria, was used by Tatian and by Cassian. In addition he may have used Tatian's *Diatessaron* in its Latin translation. Finally, his work is decidedly encratite in character and he bears witness to the existence of a Judaeo-Christian encratite tendency in Africa at the time of Tertullian.

46. As M. REVEILLAUD has demonstrated: *Saint Cyprien, L'Oraison dominicale,* pp. 8, 198.
47. For other traces of Judaeo-Christianity in North Africa before the time of Tertullian the reader is referred to G. QUISPEL, 'The Discussion of Judaic

3. THE SERMON *DE ALEATORIBUS*

The sermon, 'On the Dice-players' also derives from the confrontation between Christianity and the pagan world. The title of the sermon is prompted by the fact that the game of dice was accompanied by idolatrous practices which made it unacceptable to Christians. Harnack, in his study of the sermon, demonstrated its archaic character.[48] It may, he believed, have been given by a bishop of Rome, for it was certainly addressed to other bishops, and gives clear evidence of the special status of the author. At the beginning of the sermon, he speaks of his responsibility towards the whole group of his brothers (*universam fraternitatem*): 'In his goodness, the Father has entrusted me with the leadership of the apostolate (*apostolatus ducatum*) and has placed me as his representative in the seat of the Lord. It is from the one who went before us (*superiore*) that we derive the source of our apostolic authenticity' (*De aleat.* 1). Harnack was of the opinion that the author was Victor, who was originally from Africa and occupied the see of Rome at the end of the second century.

Many reasons can be suggested in support of this early date. Many of the terms used in the text are clearly archaic. A good example of this is the use of *rector* for bishop, which would seem to correspond to the Greek ἡγούμενος ;[49] another instance is the term *procurator* (*De aleat.* 3). The word *oraculum* (*De aleat.* 5) would seem to mean a place of prayer. The expression that occurs in the passage quoted above, *in superiore nostro*, meant, according to Harnack, 'in our predecessor' (*De aleat.* 1), but it is unusual. Two other terms are worth noting. The first is the rather clumsy phrase *inductio corrumpens* for the 'cunning of the Devil' and the other is the word *extollentia*.

The author seems to have used an existing Latin translation for his quotations from the Bible, which are textually close to Cyprian's. They are, however, used with a freedom typical of the earliest period, a characteristic that we have observed in the case of other texts. The author of the *De aleatoribus* too does not

---

Christianity', *VC,* 22 (1968), p. 93.
48. A. VON HARNACK. 'Der pseudocyprianische Tractat De aleatoribus', TU, 5 (1888), pp. 1–135.
49. See COMMODIAN, *Inst.* XXIII, 3.

hesitate to abbreviate and modify the biblical texts. Some of his quotations merit closer attention. Thus, in *De aleat.* 4, several passages from *I* and *II Timothy* are quoted in succession and this sequence may come from an earlier tradition. It will be remembered that, according to the Muratorian Canon, the *Epistles to Titus* and to *Timothy* were written 'for the regulation of church discipline', and extracts may have been made from the letters with this in mind. It is worthy of note that the same catena occurs in Hippolytus' *Apostolic Tradition*.

It is, however, the non-biblical quotations which establish the early date of the *De aleatoribus*. In this respect, the *De aleatoribus* is a prime witness to the earliest phase of Roman Christian culture, of which it provides us with evidence from early Latin translations or original texts. Some of the non-biblical texts found in the *De aleatoribus* can be identified. One quotation comes from the old Latin version of the *Shepherd of Hermas* (*Sim.* IX, 21, 5).[50] It is important to note in this context that the *Shepherd* is regarded by the author of the *De aleatoribus* as Scripture (*scriptura sacra*). This would not have been possible after the publication of the Muratorian Canon and even less possible after Tertullian. This means that our text must date back to a time when the canon of scripture was still uncertain.

Harnack was of the opinion that the statement: *Quicumque frater more alienigenarum vivit et admittet res similes factis eorum, desine in convivium eius esse; quod nisi feceris, et tu particeps eius eris,* 'If any brother lives like a pagan and accepts things that are similar to what the pagans do, cease to live in his company. If you do not do this, you will be sharing his (sin)' (*De aleat.* 4), was a quotation from the *Shepherd* (*Mand.* IV, 1, 9). It cannot be denied that the text is very close to the following passage in the Latin translation of the *Shepherd: Qui simulacrum facit . . . quod si in his factis perseveret . . . nisi convivere cum illo; sin autem, et tu particeps eris peccati eius,* 'Whoever makes an image . . . if he continues to do these things . . . do not live any more with him or you will be sharing in his sin', but there is really no very close relationship between

---

50. This is prime evidence of the influence of the *Shepherd* and of the existence of a Latin translation of the text in the last quarter of the second century.

the two passages. Both are stereotyped formulae of the kind found in collections of canons. Harnack has in any case listed other allusions to the *Shepherd*[51] in the *De aleatoribus* which show that there was a connection between the two documents as far as vocabulary and thought were concerned.

Another quotation (*De aleat.* 3) has certain features in common with the *Didache,* but is not taken from that work. It is apparently a quotation from a more developed form of the *Didache* which was perhaps the law of the Church in Rome at the end of the second century, in which case this would be a development parallel to that of the Syriac *Didascalia.* The quotation mentioned above, which Harnack ascribed to the *Shepherd of Hermas,* may have come from the same collection. It may be recalled that the *De centesima,* like the *Didache,* had developed the theme of the Two Ways. It is, in this context, interesting to note that a Church law perhaps existed in Latin at the end of the second century, before the appearance of Hippolytus' *Apostolic Tradition,* which in any case would seem to be the product of a specifically Greek emigré environment.

In the same text as the quotation from the *Shepherd* (*De aleat.* 2), there is another, also presented as scriptural, which in fact comes from an apocryphon: 'Regard the priest as a worshipper (*cultorem*) and think of all the delights of full granaries being near him, so that my people will eat as much as they want'. This is a very strange text. It will be remembered that the bishops are compared in *I Clement* with the Jewish high priests. This may be due to Zadokite influence, and would suggest a Jewish apocryphon originating in Essene circles. The text, moreover, is presented as scriptural. It must therefore have come from a document which was regarded as authoritative in the Church of Rome. This would only have been possible at a very early date.

Another group of quotations all have as their main aim the condemnation of idolatry. None of these quotations are scriptural. In *De aleat.* 8, for example, we read: *Omnis immundus non tanget sacrificium sancti,* 'Let no unclean person touch the sacrifice of the holy thing' and this quotation is followed by another: *Om-*

51. A. VON HARNACK, *op. cit.,* pp. 126–128.

nis manducans carnem sacrificii, et immunda eius super ipsum, peribit anima illa de populo, 'Any one eating the flesh of the sacrifice and having uncleanness on him, will be cut off from the people'. The second quotation is from Lv. 7:20, but the first is not found in Scripture, although the words *sacrificium sancti* would appear to be a semitism. Two other quotations, aimed at those who do evil (*De aleat.* 9), have a markedly Semitic turn of phrase, so that we may conclude that they too come from a Jewish apocryphon.

Two other quotations come from a Christian apocryphon. They are closely related in form and content: 'Do not grieve the Holy Spirit who is in you' and 'Do not put out the light that has been lighted in you'. Although the first of these quotations is close to Ep. 4:30 ('Do not grieve the Holy Spirit of God') the second, though reminiscent in general sense of Lk. 11:35, is certainly not scriptural. They would in fact both seem to be non-canonical *logia*, similar to those found in the *Gospel of Thomas*, and are precisely the kind of text used in the Roman Church during the second century, and forming part of the tradition of that Church.

The *De aleatoribus* is therefore a valuable source for the Roman Judaeo-Christian literature of the second century. What is more, the fact that these quotations are presented as scriptural is clear evidence of the fact that it is a very early document. This claim to scriptural authenticity is especially important in the case of the quotations from the *Shepherd of Hermas* – such a claim could not have been made in the third century, when the *Shepherd* was still respected, but had been excluded from the Canon. There is an interesting confirmation of this in the eighth letter in the collection of Cyprian's *Epistles,* which comes from the Roman clergy. This contains an allusion to the passage from the *Shepherd* quoted in the *De aleatoribus,* but it is not attributed to the *Shepherd.* In the same way Cyprian himself takes up from the *De centesima* a quotation from the *Acts of Paul,* without, however, attributing it to Paul.

The teaching contained in the *De aleatoribus* is above all moral and there are few noteworthy theological developments. There are, however, certain points of contact with the *De centesima.* The first is the theme of the indwelling of the Holy Spirit. In *De aleat.*

3, we read, for example, 'We have received the Holy Spirit as a guest (*hospitium*) in our hearts. Do not grieve the one who dwells with you'. Harnack has drawn attention to the similarity between this statement and what is said in the *Shepherd*, but the same idea is also to be found in the *De centesima* (56), in which the Holy Spirit is called 'our guest' (*hospitem*) and which declares: 'Let us pray ... that the Lord, offended, will not leave his spiritual seat'. It should be noted that both the *De aleatoribus* and the *De centesima* quote 1 Co. 3:16: 'You are the temple of God, and the Spirit of God dwells in you'.

Another theme occupies an important place in both documents, that of the scandal when a baptised Christian returns to a life of sin. In the *De aleatoribus*, we read: 'How can it come about that, having once escaped from the demon's nets, you allow yourself to be caught again?' (5). The author of the *De centesima* returns several times to this theme, especially in paragraph 62: 'If you have renounced the devil and his works, why do you return to him by living in a lewd way?' Elsewhere, sin is contrasted in both documents not only with baptism, but also with the Eucharist: 'Do your hands, which have been purified (by baptism) of human sins and have been admitted to the sacrifice of the Lord ... allow themselves to be caught again in the demon's nets?' (*De aleat.* 5), and, 'Having been born again of the Holy Spirit and receiving every day the holy body of Christ, how can you return to such defilement?' (*De cent.* 63).

One of the most remarkable of the modified quotations found in the *De aleatoribus* is: 'Do not conform to the world, *to its pomps, to its delights* or *to its pleasures*, but preserve yourself (*coninete*) from all the world's iniquity (*iniustitia*)'. This is, of course, clearly based on Rm. 12:2: 'Do not be conformed to this world', with certain additions (here indicated by italics) by the author of the *De aleatoribus*. These would appear to have come from the baptismal formula in which the devil and all his works are renounced. This is paralleled in *De cent.* 62, which refers, in the context of renouncing the demon, to *deliciis* and *libidinibus*, in other words, to 'delights' and '(sexual) desires'. Both works are dominated by the theme of the baptised Christian's conflict with the demon, though the imagery tends to differ – the author of the *De aleatoribus* prefers the image of 'nets', whereas the author of the *De centesima* speaks of 'arrows'.

The characteristic feature of the treatise is its rigorism. It lays down as a matter of principle that the Christian cannot be allowed, after baptism, to lapse into such sins as idolatry or fornication, and pastors are warned against the danger of offering such sinners too easy a reconciliation. This tendency is, of course, very much in accordance with the whole practice of the Church at the end of the second century. The author of the *Shepherd* had exactly the same attitude, so that it is hardly surprising that our author should have quoted from the *Shepherd*. Koch, who was inclined to favour a later date for the *De aleatoribus*, had to admit that the rigorism that characterised both documents raised a considerable difficulty as far as his suggested dating was concerned. He was therefore led to conclude that a rigoristic tendency must have persisted underground throughout the whole of the second half of the third century.[52] It is, however, more usual to regard this rigorism as a characteristic of Christianity at the beginning of the third century. This is undoubtedly a further argument in favour of an early date for the *De aleatoribus*.

---

52. H. KOCH, 'Zur Schrift Adversus aleatores', *Festgabe Karl Müller*, 1922, p. 67.

CHAPTER FOUR

THE SURVIVAL OF JUDAEO-CHRISTIANITY
IN THE THIRD CENTURY

THE texts that we have discussed so far in this book may be
dated back to the second or the beginning of the third
century. The movement of which they are represen-
tative, however, persisted into the first half of the third century,
when it existed alongside the earliest developments in Latin
pagan Christianity. Commodian bears striking witness to this
continuation of Judaeo-Christianity in the first half of the third
century, and Thraede has demonstrated clearly that his writing
reflects the intense rivalry between Jews and Christians in the
attempt to convert the pagans. This is, of course, in accordance
with the historical situation obtaining at the end of the second
and at the beginning of the third century. In this chapter, we
shall leave aside the question of Commodian's use of *testimonia*,
which will be discussed later in connection with Latin biblical
theology; but we shall compare Commodian's work with the *De
Pascha computus*, the date of which has been fixed at A.D. 243.

1. COMMODIAN'S THEOLOGY

Several attempts have been made to date Commodian's work
and results have differed widely. Brewer and Courcelle favour
the fifth century, but the majority view now is that the texts are
archaic in character. This is, at any rate, the view of the most recent study of Commodian, that of Thraede,[1] who has pointed
out that the arguments against an early date are unconvincing,
and that there can be no certainty that Commodian was dependent on Cyprian. An examination of this question must wait for

1. Cf. K. THRAEDE, 'Beiträge zur Datierung Commodians', *JAC*, 2 (1959),
pp. 90–114.

the third section of the present work, when we shall be considering Commodian's *testimonia*. Even at this stage, however, it can be pointed out that Commodian's language preserves certain early characteristics.

Thraede concludes that the evidence as a whole pointed to the end of the second century or the beginning of the third as the most probable date. He draws attention, for example, to the monarchian aspects of Commodian's theology, and to the presence of millenarianism and of Jewish influences in his writing. There is also the non-technical manner in which Commodian uses such words as *senior, propheta* and *doctor*. His use of the word *timere* in the sense of the Greek Φοβεῖσθαι, to refer to the 'God-fearer', points to a period when Jewish proselytism was still intense. Commodian was reacting against this and, in Thraede's opinion, such reaction was a characteristic of the second century. Similarly, the word *iudaizare*, which was later to be used of the Judaising Christians, is employed by Commodian in the sense of the adoption of Judaism by pagans.

There are further interesting examples of Commodian's use of words. The word *lex*, for example, is used in the Jewish sense of 'covenant' and certainly not in the Pauline sense, in which it is contrasted with grace, a sense which was later to be developed by Augustine. Commodian also uses both *lavacrum* and *baptismus* interchangeably. He does not, on the other hand, seem to have known the word *baptizare* and instead uses the word *mergere* as the verb corresponding to the noun *baptismus*, which is evidence of the fact that the actual image evoked by the word was still alive at his time. All this evidence points not merely to the end of the second century, but to a Judaeo-Christian environment, and to a situation of conflict with Jewish proselytism.

Thraede was also of the opinion that the author's reference to the Goths (*Cdrm. Ap.* 810) makes it impossible for us to date the work before A.D. 240, when the Goths were first mentioned by Latin writers. What is more, as it is hoped to show when we come to the discussion of Commodian's *testimonia*, Commodian's works preceded those of Cyprian, but followed those of Tertullian. It would seem therefore that they must be dated between A.D. 220 and 240. As Thraede has observed, however, the at-

titude and the situation reflected in Commodian's writing correspond closely to those of the second century, so that it is
reasonable to regard it as the continuation after Tertullian of an
earlier situation.

To turn to Commodian's theology as such, this is of particular
interest in that it reflects the Roman theology written in Latin at
the beginning of the third century, that is, the theology of
Zephyrinus, Callistus and Praxeas, against which the new
theology of Tertullian and Hippolytus, written under the influence of the learned Greek theology of Justin and Irenaeus, was
a reaction. It is presented as the articulation of three main
elements: the order of Adam, created in the beginning by God;
the order of Christ, restoring what was lost in Adam; and the
parousia which is the fulfilment of the promise made to Adam and
is moreover imminent. Two notable gaps indicate the peculiar
character of this Latin theology when compared with the more
learned Greek theology. The first is the absence of speculation
concerning the Word, either in the creation or in the Old Testament. The second is that, in keeping with Commodian's an-
ti-Judaism, little importance is attached to the history of Israel.

Commodian begins his theological teaching by stressing the
unity and transcendence of God:

Est Deus omnipotens, unus, a seipso creatus (*Carm. Ap.* 51)
('God is almighty and one, created by himself')
This transcendence means that God is totally inaccessible:
In primitiva sua qualis sit a nullo videtur (109)
('What he is like in his primal state is not seen by anybody')
He is surrounded by his glory, which encircles him like fire:
Quod Dei maiestas quid sit sibi conscia sola est (102).
Relucet immensa super caelos et sine fine
Aureum est totum, quod est quasi flammea iustus (104–105).
('Because what the majesty of God is is known only to himself
. . .
It blazes infinite above the heavens and all is endlessly golden,
for he is righteous like a fire')
His secret plans are hidden in this glory:
Illa sunt secreta solo Deo nota caelorum (106)

('These are the secrets of the heavens, known only to God') This idea of God's secret designs is quite common in the work of Commodian (see, for example, 502; I, 27, 18; I, 29, 11). Although God transcends everything, however, he sees and hears everything.

Quidquid tenet caelum prospicit ubique de caelo
Et penetrat totum oculis et auribus audit
('Whatever heaven contains he sees everywhere from heaven and looks through everything with his eyes and hears with his ears')

Because of his sovereign freedom, God is able to manifest himself as he wishes:

At tamen cum voluit sciri de seipso qui esset
Numine de tanto fecit se videri capacem (117–118)
('But, whenever he wished it to be known who he was in himself, from such great godhead he made himself capable of being seen')

Detransfiguratur sicut vult ostendere sese (110)
('He is changed in form as he wishes to show himself')

Cum sit invisibilis facit se videri quibusdam (112)
('Since he is invisible, he makes himself appear to certain people')

When he reveals himself to the angels, he takes the form of an angel, but when he reveals himself to men, he takes on a human form. It is in this sense that the word *detransfiguratur* above is used, being the Latin equivalent of μεταμορφοῦται. It is thus that God revealed himself in the Old Testament:

Sunt quibus in ignem apparuit voce locutus (119)
('These are some to whom he appeared in a fire, having spoken with his voice')

but this was a form which was dissolved immediately afterwards:

Qui formatus modo (modo) se diffundit in auras (127)
('Now he takes shape, now disperses himself into the air')

This theology calls for comment, since it contains certain features which go back to Judaeo-Hellenistic theology, such as the reference to God who sees and hears everything. Other features, however, are of a different character. Such are the idea of glory as a divine radiance making God invisible, and the theme of God taking the form of the angels, the latter being a Judaeo-Christian conception developed especially in the *Ascension of Isaiah*. Another such feature is the ascription of the theophanies of the Old Testament to God himself rather than to the Word. This is not the case in the theology of Justin or Tertullian.

According to Commodian, God first created (*factos*) the angels as beings inferior to himself, with the task of ruling the heavens, the earth and what is beneath the earth (96–97). What Commodian stresses particularly is that the angels are lower than God and that God is inaccessible to them too:

Hunc ergo nec ipsi nuntii dinoscere possunt (109)
('Not even the messengers themselves can discern him')
Est honor absconsus nobis et angelis ipsis (101)
('It is an honour hidden from us and from the angels themselves')

What Commodian retained from the Judaeo-Christian teaching about the angels, then, was the part that they played in the government of the cosmos, which was, of course, one of their essential characteristics. What he eliminated, on the other hand, was any assimilation of the Word to an angel, such as we find for instance, in the *De centesima*. This is linked with the fact that in his theology the Word plays no part in the creation.

Of the angels some fell. Commodian here (I, 3) takes up the Enochian tradition, retaining the following elements: it was God's will that the earth should be visited by the angels, who were then seduced by the beauty of women (I En. 6, 1–2) and because of this condemned by God and excluded from heaven (16, 1); from the unions of the angels and the women the giants were born (7, 3); these giants taught men the various trades, but especially the dyeing of wool; after God slew them, their souls became evil spirits and, wandering abroad, caused great distress to men (15, 11); and it was these giants whom the pagans worshipped as gods. In one respect, however, Commodian differs from the author of *Enoch*. The latter taught that it was the fallen angels, not the giants, who communicated hidden secrets to men. Commodian may have been influenced here by the *Sibylline Oracles*.

Commodian's work also bears witness to another Judaeo-Christian tradition, namely that God entrusted the earth to a guardian angel, who, out of jealousy, caused Adam to fall:

> *Rectorem dederat in terra Deus angelum istum*
> *Qui, dum invidetur homini, perit ipse priorque* (153–154) [2]
> ('God had given that angel as a ruler on earth who, while he envies man, himself dies first')

This tradition appeared first in the work of Athenagoras. It was later elaborated by Irenaeus and then taken up again by Methodius of Olympus. It is particularly interesting to compare Commodian's treatment of it with that of Irenaeus, and not only of this tradition, but also of many themes. There is a close parallel between the *Demonstration of the Apostolic Preaching* of Irenaeus and the whole of Commodian's *Carmen*. Both authors teach the transcendence of God, the creation of the angels, the fall of man, the history of the people of the Old Testament, and the coming of Christ, and both include a collection of *testimonia*. Commodian also describes the last days and his teaching is clearly derived from the *Adversus haereses* of Irenaeus.

Commodian's account of the first stage of human history is set within this general framework. Man was created, he taught, by God to be eternal, but he fell and became mortal because he neglected God's commandments (149–150). Man's primal state is of crucial importance because it dictated the precise character of his redemption. The first law was given to Adam in paradise; it is in fact this law which is signified by the tree of the knowledge of good and evil:

---

2. See also I, 35, 1–2, where this angel is called Belial.

Lex a ligno data est homini primitivo timenda (I, 35, 11)

('It was from a tree that the law was given to the first man that
he should fear it')

Adam was, however, able to choose between good and evil,
obedience and disobedience. Because of what Belial did, he
himself violated God's commandment and this led to his fall into
death. The tree thus became for him a source of death:

Gustato pomo ligni mors intravit in orbem (I, 35, 7)
('When the fruit of the tree had been eaten, death entered the
world')

Life was to be restored to man only at the end of time.

A number of interesting features may be detected here. First of
all, the word *lex* is used to denote God's will, which man must
obey if he is to live. The word thus has a positive sense. The law
of Christ will do no more than reinstate this original law:

Est Dei lex prima fundamentum posterae legis (I, 35, 10)
('God's first law is the foundation of the later law')

This is the meaning of the word in Judaeo-Christianity, in particular in the *Shepherd of Hermas*.[3] As Thraede has pointed out,[4]
there is no question here of any Pauline opposition between law
and grace. For Commodian, moreover, the law is not the Mosaic
law, but the commandment given to Adam. This is a conception
which was developed by Tertullian (*Adv. Jud.* II).

Secondly, there is Commodian's interpretation of the tree of
the knowledge of good and evil as signifying the law. In the first
place, *lex* is connected etymologically by Commodian with
lignum, an idea found elsewhere only in the *De montibus Sina et
Sion* (9). (There are other similarities between Commodian's
work and the *De montibus*, to which we shall return later.) This is

---

3. See PERNVEDEN, *op. cit.*, pp. 84–86.
4. K. THRAEDE, *op. cit.*, pp. 100–103.

therefore clearly a Judaeo-Christian theme, the Jewish origins of which have been pointed out by Lyonnet.[5] In the *Shepherd of Hermas,* the tree mentioned in *Sim.* VIII is the law, which is in turn the same as the Son of God. As Pernveden has shown, this is connected with Gn. 2:9 and with a long tradition in which the tree of the knowledge of good and evil is identified with the tree of life. The same tradition is also found in Theophilus of Antioch (II, 15) and the *Gospel of Philip.*[6]

The tree is also connected by Commodian with the choice between the two ways:

Contulisset nobis seu boni seu mali quod egit
Dux nativitatis . . . (I, 35, 3–4)
('The fount of our birth had bestowed upon us whatever he did of good or evil')

This theme of the two ways occurs quite frequently in Commodian's work:

Sunt tibi praepositae duae viae: elige quam vis (699; cf. I, 12, 5)
('Two ways are put before you – choose which you wish')

This is, of course, a quotation from Dt. 30:15, which was a favourite text in later Judaism and in Judaeo-Christianity. There is a close relationship between this theme and that of the tree of the knowledge of good and evil, indeed the very concept of good and evil lent itself to such a relationship.

There are furthermore several early texts which show that Commodian was using an already existing theme here. An example of this is found in Justin: 'The prophetic Spirit makes God say through Moses to the first man coming from his hands: "You have before you good and evil. Choose the good"' (*I Apol.* XLIV, 1). Commodian also compares Gn. 2:9 with Dt. 30:15, 19, which he quotes in the form given above, merging together verses 15 and 19. Clement of Alexandria also juxtaposes Gn. 2:9

5. S. LYONNET, 'Tu ne convoiteras pas', *Neotestamentica et Patristica* (Mélanges O. Cullmann), pp. 158–163.
6. See also Hippolytus, *Com. Dan.* I, 17; Asterius, *Hom. Psalm* I, 112.

and Dt. 30:15 (*Strom.* V, 11; 72, 2–5), and Tertullian does the same in his *Exhortation to Chastity: Ecce posui ante te bonum et malum*; *gustastis enim de agnitionis arbore,* 'Behold, I have put before you good and evil; for you have tasted of the tree of knowledge' (*De exhort. cast.* II, 3). The word *gustastis* here is an Africanism, which is also found in Commodian (I, 35, 7), but the rest of the quotation is different. As is so often the case, Tertullian's text is entirely his own.[7]

Adam, as progenitor of the human race (*dux nativitatis*), chooses evil and this choice leads to death for all his descendants:

Morimur idemque per illum (I, 35, 4; see also 324)
('We likewise die through him')

What is more, from the time that Adam sinned, the effects of evil were spread abroad:

In scelere coepit versari gens omnis humanus (157)
('The whole of the human race began to be engaged in crime')

God, however, continues to intervene in an attempt to thwart Satan's plans:

Propter quae storias tantas Deus esse paravit
Ut inventiones diaboli detegeret omnes (151–152)
('Because of this, God prepared stories such as would expose all the devil's ruses')

After the flood, God tries, with Abraham, to create a people for himself, but this people, Israel, is unfaithful to him, like the rest of mankind.

In this context, a theme of special interest emerges, namely that of the persecution of the prophets by the Jews. This is, of course, a classical theme in the Judaeo-Christian tradition and one which we have already encountered in *V Esdras* and the *Adversus Judaeos*.

---

7. See his *Adv. Jud.* II, *arbor; De anim.* XXXVIII, 1, *agnitio boni et mali; De ieiun.* III, 2, *arbor agnitionis boni et mali; De virg. vel.* XI, 2, *arbor agnitionis.*

The form which it takes in Commodian's *Carmen* is obviously inspired by the Jewish *Vitae Prophetarum:*

Esaiam serrant, lapidant Hieremiam erecti,
Ioannem decollant, iugulant Zachariam ad aras (221–222)
('They saw Isaiah in two, they stone Jeremiah, they cut off John's head, and they cut Zechariah's throat at the altars').

The martyrdom of Isaiah and Jeremiah goes back to the Jewish tradition and was taken up again by Judaeo-Christianity. The martyrdom of John the Baptist and Zechariah, on the other hand, comes from the New Testament. The formation of lists of this kind clearly comes, however, from a Jewish *haggada* which was revived by the Judaeo-Christians (see, for example, Heb. 11:37: 'stoned, sawn in two or beheaded'). It should, in this context, be noted that Commodian mentions Zechariah after John the Baptist, an order which cannot be due simply to metrical reasons. It is, however, the same order as that found in the *Adversus Judaeos*. Later in the *Carmen*, however, Commodian gives a similar list of martyrs and the fate that they suffered in a different order:

. . . *Esaias de serra secatur,*
Alter lapidatur, alter mactatur ad arus,
Alterum Herodes iussit decollari seclusum (512–516)
('Isaiah is cut up with a saw; one is stoned, another is sacrificed at the altars, while Herod ordered another to be beheaded in secret')

The order of the martyrs given in this passage is the normal one and therefore does not require an explanation. The only satisfactory explanation that can be given for the order in the previously quoted passage (221–222) is that it was composed under an influence, and the only possible influence that could have existed was that of the *Adversus Judaeos*. There are in fact other such lists in the works of the early Fathers, but none of them are presented in the same way as Commodian's.[8] Tertullian, who according to

8. See K. BEYSCHLAG, *Clemens Romanus und der Frühkatholizismus*, pp. 75–103; 215–225.

van Damme was also dependent on the *Adversus Judaeos,* does not mention John:

Hieremias lapidatur, Esaias secatur, Zacharias trucidatur,
('Jeremiah is stoned, Isaiah cut up and Zechariah slaughtered'
— *Scorp.* VIII)

The second part of Commodian's presentation of the history of man's salvation deals with the coming of the Son of God, who gives man the new law and restores to him the life that he lost in Adam. It is possible to distinguish three important theological themes in this part of Commodian's work. The first is that it is only from the incarnation onwards that he speaks of the Son at all — before mentioning the incarnation, he speaks, as we have seen, only of the one God, the single reference to the Son being in ll. 91–94:

Est Deus omnipotens, unus, a seipso creatus
Quem infra reperies magnum et humilem ipsum
Is erat in verbo positus, sibi solo notatus
Qui pater et filius dicitur et spiritus sanctus
('God, the almighty and one, was created by himself.
You will find him below, great and humble.
He was placed in the Word, known only to himself.
He is called Father and Son and Holy Spirit.)

According to this passage, it will be noted, it is God as such who becomes lowly. The reference to the three persons of the Trinity at the end of the passage is clearly liturgical, and signifies no more than three 'names' for the one God. There is, moreover, no mention of the pre-existence of the Word, a theme which Justin, Irenaeus and Tertullian all elaborate, nor does the Word play any part, according to Commodian, in the creation. Finally, the Old Testament theophanies are also ascribed to the one God and not, as in the case of Justin, Irenaeus and Tertullian, to the Word. In other respects, the Son is presented in rather ambiguous terms:

Hic Pater in Filio venit, Deus unus ubique,

Nec Pater ipse dictus est, nisi factus Filius esset (277–278)
('This Father came in the Son, one God everywhere.
Nor was he himself called "Father" unless he had become the
Son'.)

It is the one sole God who by assuming flesh becomes the Son.

Idcirco nec voluit se manifestari quid esset,
Sed Filium dixit se missum fuisse a Patre.
Sic ipse tradiderat semetipsum dici prophetis
Ut Deus in terris Altissimi filius esset (162–166)
('Therefore he did not wish what he was to be revealed, but
said that he was the Son who had been sent by the Father. He
had handed himself over to be spoken of by the prophets, so
that he might be God, the Son of the Most High, on earth'.)

In this passage, 'Son of God' would seem to denote God in his
self-manifestation. We may quote another passage, unfortunately
mutilated, which clearly has very much the same meaning:

De virtute sua carna(liter na)sci (se fecit)
. . . .
. . . . *licet facere fimbriam unam*
Iam caro (Deu)s erat, in qua Dei virtus agebat (281–284)
('By his power he caused himself to be born in the flesh.
. . . .
. . . . He allowed one fibre to be made.
Now God was flesh, in which the power of God was active'.)

The word *fimbria* in this passage is reminiscent of Novatian's *con-
tribularet* (*De Trin.* 23), pointing to the union between God and
man. Finally, Commodian never speaks, in his treatment of the
redemption, of the Word or the Son, but only of Almighty God.

Commodian's theology is neither profound nor fully
elaborated, but from this brief survey of his ideas it is possible to
come to a fairly clear conclusion with regard to the date of his
work.[9] He obviously bears witness in his theology to the

9. In this, I would agree with Thraede, *op. cit.*, pp. 91–93.

monarchian tendency which was prominent at the end of the second century in Latin Christian circles. This is clear from the fact
that he has nothing to say about the theology of the Word,
which was very much in favour in the East, and which Tertullian
and Hippolytus were disseminating in the West during his time.
Commodian stands in the tradition of Judaeo-Christian
monotheism which acknowledged the Son of God only during
the incarnation. As Pernveden has pointed out, the author of the
Shepherd of Hermas similarly speaks about the Son of God only in
connection with the redemption.

The second point of importance is the parallel that he draws
between the fall and the redemption. He elaborates this
parallelism on several different levels. The fall began with
Belial's ruse, which deceived man and brought about his death.
In the redemption, it is the demon who is deceived by God and
man is delivered from death:

> *Sic Dei lex clamat fieret cum humilis Altus*
> *Cederet infernus, ut Adam levaretur a morte,*
> *Descendit in tumulum Dominus suae plasmae misertus*
> *Et sic per occulta inanivit fortia mortis*
> *Obrepsit Dominus veteri latroni celatus*
> *Et pati se voluit, quo magis prosterneret ipsum.*
> *Ille quidem audax et semper saevus ut hostis*
> *Dum sperat in hominem saevire victus a summo est* (313–320)

('So the law of God declared it should be, when the humble
High One yielded as one who is low, so that Adam might be
raised from death. Pitying his own creature, the Lord descended into the tomb and so through *hidden things* emptied the
strength of death. In concealment the Lord *took by surprise* the
old *thief*, and willed to suffer, so that he might cast him down
even lower. He is bold and always savage, like an enemy.
While he hoped to vent his rage on man, he was conquered by
the Most High'.)

This passage contains several elements which can be traced
back to a very early form of theology. There is, first of all, the
way in which God is hidden. The words *occulta* ('hidden'), *celatus*

('in concealment'), and *obrepsit* ('he took by surprise') are connected with the Judaeo-Christian theme of the hidden descent of the Son (see also 176). There is also the idea of the demon who is deceived and who is conquered when he believes himself to be triumphant, thus exchanging situations with Adam. Finally, there is the word *latro* used for the demon. This is connected with the interpretation of the parable of the Good Samaritan in terms of Adam's fall.

The author also makes use of the theme of the descent into hell to bring about Adam's deliverance from death. The idea that the purpose of the descent was to deliver the righteous is Judaeo-Christian.[10] It plays a particularly prominent part in the *Shepherd of Hermas*. In Commodian's theology, however, Christ's descent into hell illustrates God's mercy on his *plasma,* man whom he fashioned in the beginning. Irenaeus dealt with it in this way in opposition to Tatian (*Adv. haer.* III, 23, 1–9), and it is quite likely that Commodian is here dependent upon Irenaeus – the word *plasma* (πλάσμα) , 'fashioned' or 'created' thing, hence creature, would seem to point to this. It is also worth noting that the same theme occurs at least twice in the *De centesima.*[11]

Finally, Commodian stresses that it was the tree that brought about man's fall and his salvation: 'That by which the evil one long ago brought men down in death is that by which he was conquered. It is also thence that life comes to us' (321–322). He also states even more precisely that Adam died and that we died after him because of 'having eaten the fruit' (*degustato pomo*). Now, he goes on, 'the man who eats of the tree of life (*ligno vitali*) will live for ever in glory' (326) and concludes:

Mors in ligno fuit et ligno vita latebat (327)
('Death was in a tree and life also was concealed in a tree')

In the same passage, Commodian also says: 'The man who believes in Christ eats of the tree of life' (333), and, 'Eating of the

---

10. See J. DANIELOU, *The Theology of Jewish Christianity,* pp. 233–248.
11. *SPL* I, pp. 60, 64.

fruit of the tree of life is being nourished by the commandments of Almighty God' (330), which results in man's escaping death (331).

This is not simply a question of imagery, but of an entire theology, as the parallel passages in Commodian's *Instructions* make plain. For example, just as the tree of the knowledge of good and evil signified the primal law, so too the tree of the cross, which is the tree of life, is the new law. Furthermore, just as disobedience to the original law was the source of death for Adam, so too adherence to the new law is the source of life (I, 35, 11–14):

Lex a ligno data est homini primitivo timenda
Mors unde provenit neglecta lege primordi.
Nunc extende manum et sume de ligno vitali.
Optima lex Domini sequens de ligno processit
('It was from a tree that the law was given to the first man that he should fear it, whence death arose by the neglect of the original law. Now stretch out your hand and take from the life-giving tree. The Lord's best law came next from a tree.')

And a little further on in the Instructions (I, 36, 11), we read:

Lex in ligno fuit prima et inde secunda
('The first law was in a tree and thence came also the second')

The theme of the law as obedience to God and the condition of life for man is the predominant theme of the redemption in Commodian's theology.

One final aspect of Commodian's teaching on the subject of man's salvation is his use of the archaic theme of the replacement of the synagogue by the Church, which accords with his emphasis on the provisional nature of God's choice of Israel. From the beginning, Commodian points out, Israel had been warned that its role was no more than preparatory and that it would have to make way for the gentiles. This was the meaning of a number of episodes in the Old Testament, the most important of which was the story of Esau and Jacob:

> *Duos enim populos distinxerat in se Rebecca.*
> *Hic prior est factus, alter ut succederet illi* (189–190)
> ('Rebecca had distinguished two nations in herself; the one was made first so that the second might supplant him')

The Jews therefore had no more reason, Commodian insists, to be surprised at their being set aside than Esau had when Jacob deprived him of his birthright (252–253). [12]

Here again we are dealing with a theme frequent in early Christianity (cf. Rm. 9:10–13). It is found in Irenaeus (*Adv. haer.* IV, 21, 3), Tertullian (*Adv. Jud.* I; *Adv. Marc.* III, 24, 8–9) and Cyprian (*Test.* I, 19, 20). It occupies an important place also in the *De montibus* – one might even say that it is the dominant theme of the whole treatise. Commodian quotes other examples – the two sons of Tamar, Perez and Zerah, and of Joseph, Ephraim and Manasseh; Cain and Abel; and Jacob's second wife, Rachel, who replaced Leah (I, 38, 1–10). Cyprian too mentions Esau and Jacob and Ephraim and Manasseh (*Test.* I, 21). Commodian concludes:

> *Sic ergo percipite iuniores Christo probati* (I, 38, 11)
> ('In this way, therefore, perceive that it is the younger who are approved by Christ')

The last-mentioned of Commodian's examples is also found in Cyprian's *Testimonia* in very similar terms, since in both cases Rachel is presented as a type of the Church, *typus Ecclesiae* (I, 38, 4; cf. *Test.* I, 20). The same terms, however, had been used, before both Commodian and Cyprian, by Irenaeus and Justin (*Dial.* CXXXIV, 3–5).

The third period in the history of the world, according to Commodian, is the millennium. His view of the world of the present time since the fall is radically pessimistic:

12. Cf. also I, 38, 5.

Tormentum est totum quod vivimus isto sub aevo (309)
('The whole of our life in this age is torment')

Man's only hope, Commodian teaches, is to return to life after
the resurrection in a new world:

Hinc adeo nobis est spes in futuro quaerenda . . .
Ut resurrecturos nos credamus in novo saeclo (310–312)
('Hence, indeed, our hope must be sought in the future,
. . . that we may believe that we shall rise in a new age')

Commodian announces this theme at the beginning of the
Carmen by introducing the image of the phoenix (132–140).[13]
This pessimistic view of the present age is part of the
Judaeo-Christian tradition, and underlies the imagery of the two
aeons, to be found especially in the Clementine texts. This hope
of resurrection, however, has a distinctively Judaeo-Christian
form in Commodian, according to whom it is an expectation that
will be fulfilled during the seventh millennium and will basically
be a restoration of the paradisal state of man which was lost by
Adam when he fell:

Finitis sex millibus annis immortales erimus (I, 35, 6)
('We shall be immortal when six thousand years have come to
an end')

Commodian was one of the most thoroughgoing exponents of
the millenarianism inherited from Judaeo-Christian apocalyptic
writing. This is clear from his theory of the seven millennia and
the emphasis that he places on the seventh millennium and its imminence. In his teaching, the cultural trappings of millenarianism
express an existential situation in that they help to keep alive the
expectation of an imminent resurrection which will deliver men
from an evil world and from death which lies at the end of it. In
this respect, Commodian's work is a direct extension of the

13. Cf. Tertullian, *De res.* XIII, 2–4.

Apocalypse of John, so far as the doctrine of the first resurrection and of the reign of a thousand years is concerned, and of the thought of Israel with regard to the first six millennia. It also contains, however, other elements.

Before we discuss Commodian's treatment of the reign of a thousand years, it is worth while examining his description of the events directly preceding that reign:

> *Sed quidem hoc aiunt: Quando haec ventura putamus?*
> *Accipite paucis quibus actis illa sequantur*
> ('But they say this: "When do we think that these things will happen?" Know that, when a short time is over, these things will follow'.)

The first of these events was, according to Commodian, the seventh persecution, which was imminent and would coincide with the invasion of the Goths, who would take Rome and treat the Christians well. But then would come a Syrian emperor, *Nero redivivus,* whose coming would be directly preceded by the return of Elijah to Judah. The Jews would denounce Elijah to the new Nero, who would make him come to Rome, where he would be killed together with many Christians. Four days later, these martyrs would be raised from the dead and taken up to heaven (804–864). The persecution of the Christians would continue, however, and they would be driven out of Rome and pursued throughout the universe.

After this, a king is to arise in the East and gather all the nations together in an attack against Rome. His coming is accompanied by such signs as the sound of trumpets from heaven and the arrival of a chariot of fire and torches heralding the imminent cosmic conflagration. In the battle, Nero is killed and Rome destroyed. On returning to Judah, however, the king leads the Jews astray. He is, in fact, their Antichrist, just as Nero was the Antichrist of the nations. 'These are the two false prophets of the end of time.' The Jews, however, tire of him and turn back to God, who raises up a group of Jews who have remained hidden for a long time. These are the two and a half tribes of Israel which had remained in Babylon at the time of the exile, leading an extremely austere life there, abstaining from meat and waiting for the resurrection. Their return to Judah is accompanied by many marvels:

> *Omnia virescunt ante illos, omnia gaudent,*
> *Umbraculum illis facient nubes ne vexentur a sole*
> *Praemittitur enim ante illos Angelus Alti*
> *Qui ducatum eis pacificum praestet eundo* (967–970)

('Everything becomes green before them. There is universal rejoicing. The clouds will give them shade so that the sun will not trouble them. For an angel of God is sent before them, who is to act as their leader making peace'.)

The Antichrist and his allies resist them, but are crushed by the angels. He and the false prophet are thrown into the lake of fire; and after the fire has laid waste half the earth the saints enter the millennial kingdom. (It should, in conclusion, be noted that the same data are to be found in *Inst.* I, 41–43.)

This passage is a typical example of the influence on Commodian of Judaeo-Christian apocalyptic writing. It contains elements not only from the *Apocalypse of John* but also from other apocalyptic sources. In connection with the doctrine of the two Antichrists, Commodian himself writes:

> *De quo pauca tamen suggero quae legi secreta* (936)

('About this matter, however, I suggest a few secret things which I have read')

Other texts must clearly have influenced Commodian in his reference to *secreta* here. The Antichrist is certainly identified with *Nero redivivus* in the *Ascension of Isaiah* (IV, 2), but this theme was very common and is also found, for example, in the *Sibylline Oracles*. These were undoubtedly the most immediate source for Commodian, who borrowed frequently from them. They contain, for instance, the idea of the Antichrist making men worship him like a god (VIII, 135). The theme of the angels fighting the enemies of the people of God is also found in the *War of the Sons of Light and the Sons of Darkness,* and it must have occurred in other apocalyptic texts. The description of the flood of fire was undoubtedly inspired by the *Apocalypse of Peter.* [14]

The most unusual theme is certainly that of the hidden people. It is, moreover, clearly one to which Commodian attached some importance, because he deals with it at length in his *Instructions* (I, 42) and in *Carm. Ap.* 941–990. Some of his sources can, however, be identified. The theme of the two and a half tribes, for instance, is found in *IV Esdras* 13, 40–50 and above all in *II Baruch,* LXXVIII. Commodian's description of the holy way of life of these tribes is reminiscent of *II Baruch* LXXIII, 2–5; LXXIV, 1; LXXVII, 19–22. The *Apocalypse of Baruch,* a Christianised Jewish apocalypse, was undoubtedly also one of Commodian's sources. There is also a very striking parallel, which has hitherto passed unnoticed, between Commodian's description of the triumphant march of the people of God towards the holy land and a text in *V Esdras,* where we read about 'a people coming from the East' and led (*ducatum*) by an angel, who in this case is the prophet Zechariah. *V Esdras* is, of course, also a Latin apocalyptic work. [15]

Another remarkable feature of this theme in Commodian's text is that the Antichrist of the Jews is introduced alongside the Antichrist of the Romans. After having crushed the power of Rome, this Antichrist insists on the Jews of Jerusalem worshipping him as a god and, just as Nero is the ruin of the city, the Antichrist of the Jews is the ruin of the earth (934). Now it is, as we have seen, just at this point that Commodian alludes to the *secreta* (936). It is obvious that his source must have been an unknown apocryphon, which alluded to the Jews' expectation that an Eastern ruler would deliver them from their subjugation to the Romans, an expectation which may have stimulated a messianic movement of a worldly kind. The author of this apocalypse denounced this expectation, and presented in opposition to it his view of an ideal Jewish people inspired by a purely religious messianic hope. Commodian then gave a Christian content to the theme.

14. See M. R. JAMES, 'Notes on Apocrypha', *JTS,* 16 (1915), pp. 405–406.
15. F. SCHMIDT, 'Une source essénienne chez Commodien', *Pseudépigraphes de l'Ancien Testament et manuscrits de la Mer Morte,* I, 1967, pp. 11–27, believes that this theme goes back to an Essene source, but his arguments are not very convincing.

The question still remains, however, as to what kind of situation might have given rise to this particular genre of writing. A possible answer to this question may be found in the campaigns of the Parthians coming from Iran during the second century. These seem to have inspired the Jews with the hope of shaking off the Roman yoke. Apparent evidence in favour of the existence of a messianic tendency of this kind may be found in the frescoes of Dura-Europos at the beginning of the third century. What is more, the apocalypse which Commodian used as his source says that the prince who would deliver the Jews would come from Persia. This apocalypse may therefore have reflected the mood brought about in the Jewish world by this situation and have been written by a Jew who was anxious to put an end to false hopes. Commodian may well have come to know this apocalypse which dated back to the end of the second century through the Jews with whom he was in contact, have summarised its teaching in the *Carmen*, and taken from it his doctrine of the two Antichrists. If this theory is correct, then Commodian will have summarised the content of this apocalypse for his readers, to whom it was unknown, because it was a very recent work. It should be noted that Commodian did not make use of this apocalypse in his *Instructions*, according to which it was *Nero redivivus* who insisted on being worshipped at Jerusalem.

This brings us to the theme of the reign of a thousand years at the end of time before the last judgement and the conflagration of the world. In itself, this does not depend on speculation about the seven millennia, but goes back to the biblical idea of a thousand years as the length of life in paradise. This is, of course, what is found in the *Apocalypse of John*, in which the reign of a thousand years is inaugurated by the first resurrection, that of the just. Both these ideas, that of the first resurrection and that of the thousand years, are found in Commodian's theology. His use of the expression *anastase prima*, with the Greek word (ἀνάστασις) for resurrection, which is a direct reference to Rv. 20:5, is an archaic feature (I, 43, 1; see also 992). [16]

16. See J. DANIELOU, *The Theology of Jewish Christianity*, pp. 377–404; *Etudes*, pp. 135–137.

A distinctive feature of Commodian's millenarianism is his emphasis on the material nature of life during the thousand years. In this, he was clearly not following the *Apocalypse of John*, but Jewish apocalyptic teaching and especially that of *I Enoch* 10, 17–19. Great fertility, both in the natural world and among men, was to be a feature of the millennium:

> *Recipiunt bona, quoniam mala passi fuere*
> *Et generant ipsi per annos mille nubentes*
> *Comparantur ibi tota vectigalia terrae*
> *Terra quia nimium fundit sine fine novata*
> *Inibi non pluviam, non frigus in aurea castra*
> *Obsidiae nullae, sicut nunc neque rapinae* (I, 43, 8, 13)

('They receive good things, because they have suffered evil, and marrying they have children for a thousand years. There all the produce of the earth is furnished in tribute, because the earth pours forth (her fruits) exceedingly, being endlessly renewed, but neither rain nor cold there on the golden camp. There are no sieges there, nor is there any plundering'.)

This very materialistic conception is also found in Judaeo-Christianity in the teaching of Papias and of Cerinthus, at least according to Irenaeus (see *Adv. haer.* V, 33, 3 for Papias and III, 3, 4 for Cerinthus). According to Irenaeus himself, however, and to Justin, there might be fertility in nature in the millennium, but there is no reference to marriage.

Another characteristic of Commodian's treatment of this theme is that he establishes a relationship between the Johannine doctrine of the millennium and the idea of the cosmic week of seven millennia, which seems to have been the result of speculation about the seven days of creation.[17] It can be found in (17), and again derives from Jewish apocalyptic. The first author who explicitly merged together these two themes was Irenaeus (*Adv. haer.* V, 28, 3). Bearing all this in mind, we can see how Commodian came to identify the reign of a thousand years with the seventh day, following the six thousand years:

17. Cf. SCHWARTE, *Die Vorgeschichte der augustinischen Weltalterlehre*, pp. 70–105.

Finitis sex millibus annis immortales erimus (I, 35, 6)
('We shall be immortal when six thousand years have come to
an end')

an idea which is also found in his *Carmen* (791):

Sex millibus annis provenient ista repleta
('In six thousand years, those things will come forth in
fullness')

This teaching, which might otherwise have preserved a general
character, was, however, to be used to create a chronography
with claims to scientific objectivity. This is certainly what
Theophilus of Antioch did with it, and at the beginning of the
third century Julius Africanus also distinguished between the first
three millennia from the creation up to Abraham and the last
three from Abraham until the end of time. Richard has shown
that chronological calculators consistently tried to make their
calculations fit into this framework and it is interesting to note
that the same idea that is found in Julius Africanus is also found in
Commodian's *Carmen* (45–49):

Iam paene medietas annorum sex milibus ibat
Et nemo scibat Dominum passimque viventes.
Sed Deus, ut vidit hominum nimis pectora clausa
Adloquitur Abraham, quem Moyses enuntiat ipsum
('Now almost half of the six thousand years went by and no
one knew the Lord, though men were living everywhere. But
when God saw the hearts of men exceedingly closed, he spoke
to Abraham, of whom Moses spoke'.)

This calculation, however, is much earlier than Julius Africanus,
whom Commodian did not necessarily use as his source.

On the basis of this estimate, of course, the question was bound
to arise of the date of the end of time and of the beginning of the
seventh millennium. Several authors, including Theophilus of
Antioch (*Ad Autol.* III, 28), Hippolytus of Rome (*Com. Dan.* IV,
23–24) and Julius Africanus himself, calculated the coming of

Christ in the middle of the sixth millennium and dated it more precisely at 5500. This meant that, at the time at which they were writing, the end of the world was not imminent. Commodian, on the other hand, regarded it as imminent (809), but he did not make use of any calculation to determine its precise date. As we have already seen, the author of the *De montibus* believed Christ's Passion took place at the end of the sixth millennium and Commodian comes very close to this, which is also another indication of the archaic nature of his work.

The end of the world was to follow the seventh millennium. Commodian believed that it would take place by means of a cosmic conflagration which would destroy the structure of the world (*fabrica mundi*):

In una flamma convertit tota natura (II, 45, 6)
('The whole universe is changed in one great fire')

The wicked would be thrown into gehenna:

Nam vide post annos mille gehennae tradentur (II, 43, 8)
('For behold, after a thousand years they will be given up to gehenna')

whereas the just would be sent to their abodes (*habitacula*) (I, 45, 12), which seem to be the same as the abodes of the saints in Irenaeus. As for the wicked during the millennium, some of those who were living on earth would be destroyed in a first flood of fire (I, 43, 9) and would therefore join the souls of the wicked in death, whereas others would be preserved from death so that they could serve the saints:

Flamma tamen gentis media partiturque servans
In annis mille ut ferant corpora sanctis (II, 43, 16–17).[18]
('But the flame in the midst of the people divides them, preserving some to bear burdens for the saints for a thousand years')

18. See also *Inst.* II, 42, 43; I, 35, 12–19; *Carm Ap.* 987–988; 998.

This idea is also found in Irenaeus (*Adv. haer.* V, 33, 3).

Two observations have to be made concerning this doctrine as it is found in Commodian. The author to whom he is closest here is certainly Irenaeus, and there are many similarities between their teachings about the millennium. Commodian would also seem to have been writing before the emergence of the chronographical speculations about the date of Christ's return. He was in fact living and writing in an atmosphere of intense eschatological expectation. As in the case of Irenaeus, moreover, the importance given to the millennium in Commodian's theological thought would seem to be linked to the importance which he attached to Adam's resurrection and to the restoration of paradise (I, 35, 7). What is more, nothing comparable to this doctrine can be found in Eastern Christianity. Commodian's millenarianism is distinctively Western and Latin.

Another author who continued to concern himself with the question of millenarianism (at the end of the third century) was Victorinus of Pettau. His interest in allegorical interpretation and in the symbolism of numbers will be discussed in the third section of this chapter but it is worth while drawing attention here to his millenarianism, which he sets out in his short treatise *De fabrica mundi*.

In the first place, it should be noted that it is very much in line with the millenarianism of Irenaeus and Commodian. Secondly, it is interesting how clearly he relates this theme to the symbolism of the seven days of Genesis, which was certainly the origin of the symbolism of the seven millennia. He writes: 'The true and just sabbath is the one observed in the seventh millennium (*miliario*). The Lord has in fact pointed, in these seven days, to as many millennia. In your eyes, Lord, a thousand years are as a day (Ps. 90:4). That is why, as I have said, the true sabbath is the seventh millennium in which Christ will rule with his saints' (*De fabrica mundi* 6).

The Johannine *Apocalypse* is interpreted in Victorinus' *Commentary on the Apocalypse* according to millenarian concepts. He draws attention first of all to the signs preceding the seventh millennium. Familiar Judaeo-Christian traditions are also included – the tradition of *Nero redivivus* (XIII, 3) and that of the adoration of Satan in the temple (XIII, 3). The naming of Jeremiah and Elijah as the two witnesses comes from *V Esdras*, but it is presented in the *Commentary* as a tradition derived from the Elders (XI, 3). Finally, he also makes use of the Jewish tradition that the leader of the fallen demons was kept in the (second) heaven until he was thrown down into the world (XII, 6). [19]

Victorinus also makes a clear distinction between the two resurrections, the first being, in his view, the resurrection of the just who were to enter into glory and the second the resurrection of the wicked who were to be punished. He also connects these two resurrections with the trumpet mentioned in 1 Th. 4:15 and 1 Co. 15:52, which he calls *novissima* (XX, 2), while the Jerusalem coming down from heaven (Rv. 21:2) corresponds to the millennial reign (XXI, 1). Unlike Commodian, however, and following the tradition of Justin, Victorinus teaches that the kingdom of a thousand years is situated in the East and is in fact the land that was promised to Abraham (XXI, 1). In that kingdom, Victorinus claims, all the saints will be gathered: *Ubi illi primi steterunt et ecclesiam confirmaverunt, id est in Iudea, ibi omnes sancti conventuri sunt et Deum suum adorabunt*, 'Where those first men abode and established the Church, that is, in Judea, was where all the saints are in the future to meet together and to worship their God' (I, 6). [20]

Victorinus' description of the way of life in the age of a thousand years is, like Commodian's, materialistic. The whole of creation would, he taught, be preserved in the kingdom of a thousand years and would cause all the good things that it contained to be poured out at God's command. God would bring to the kingdom all the treasures of the sea and the wealth of nations mentioned in Is. 61:6. The inhabitants of this kingdom would drink wine and be anointed with perfume and there would be great rejoicing (see Am. 6:6; Is. 67:4). There would, however, be no question of marriage. Victorinus, we may conclude, was continuing here in the realistic tradition of Irenaeus which persisted until the time of Lactantius. Its main emphasis was a description

19. DANIELOU, *The Theology of Jewish Christianity*, pp. 190–191.
20. See H. BIETENHARD, *Das tausendjährige Reich*, p. 90.

of a materialistic fulfilment of the Messianic prophecies.

One particularly interesting characteristic is Victorinus' allusion to the fertility of the vine in the reign of a thousand years: *De hoc regno meminit Dominus, priusquam pateretur, ad apostolos dicens: Non bibam de fructu vitis huius iam nisi cum bibam vobiscum novum in regno futuro, quod est centum partibus multiplicatum, decies millies ad maiora et meliora,* 'Before his Passion, the Lord recalls this kingdom and says to the apostles: I will not drink of this fruit of the vine now until I drink it new with you in the kingdom which is to be and which has been increased a hundred times, ten thousand times for greater, better things'.

The first part of this text is, of course, from Mt. 26:29, while the second refers to those who will receive a hundredfold in the kingdom (Mt. 19:29). At the same time, however, the second part of Victorinus' statement comes from Papias, who presented it as a doctrine taught by the Lord: 'The day will come when vines will grow each with ten thousand branches and ten thousand grapes on each cluster' (see Irenaeus, *Adv. haer.* V, 33, 3). Victorinus was clearly making use here of a Judaeo-Christian tradition going back at least to Papias. The allusion to Mt. 26:29 may, moreover, point to the original reason for attributing this logion, which comes from Jewish apocalyptic (*II Baruch*, XXIX, 3), to Jesus.

Finally, the idea reappears in Victorinus that during the reign of a thousand years the nations which have not been destroyed when Christ came will be set aside to serve the saints: *Ceterae autem, quae fuerunt nobiliores servabuntur in servitutem sanctorum,* 'The rest of the nations, those which were more noble, will be kept for the service of the saints' (XIX, 1). Even these, however, are to be destroyed at the end of the millennium when the Devil is released: *Quas et ipsas quidem oportet in novissimo tempore consummato regno sanctorum . . . dimisso diabolo interfici,* 'These must also be slain at the last time, when the kingdom of the saints has been completed and the devil dismissed'.

This is a commentary on Rv. 20:4–10 and is similar to that first made by Irenaeus.

2. THE *DE PASCHA COMPUTUS*

We can be quite certain about the date of the *De Pascha computus*, because the author's explicit aim was to establish the date of the Passover in the year 243. It is not proposed, however, to study the text as a calculation of the date of the Passover, since its main interest in our present context is that it is directly in the tradition of Judaeo-Christian symbolism. The author himself states that his investigations have a direct bearing on the *alta mysteria* and the *obscura sacramenta* of faith (*De Pascha comp.* 1). This, of course, points to an esoteric tradition. Some of the elements in this tradition can be traced back to gematria and others to chronology, but the author's point of departure is the biblical calendar. In his attempts to establish dates, however, he also points out the various mysteries concealed in the calendar and, in this process, draws freely on a previously existing tradition.

The theme that first strikes the reader's attention is that of Abraham's three hundred and eighteen servants. The author's interpretation of this theme is basically that of *Barnabas*, but is rather more complicated. Like *Barnabas*, he believes that 300 corresponds to the letter T, which symbolises the cross, and 18 to the first two letters of the name Je(sus). In addition, he interprets the fact that Abraham was a hundred years old when he became the father of Isaac and that Isaac carried the wood for his sacrifice as both allusions to the cross (10). This again is a well-known theme, of which there is evidence not only in the *Epistle of Barnabas*, but also in Tertullian. The author must clearly have used the early Latin translation of the *Epistle*.

The author, however, adds further complications, by his references to the symbolism of the Temple built in the image of Adam, a theme which we have already encountered in the *De montibus*. The temple was destroyed, according to our author, by Nebuchadnezzar 1006 years after the exodus. The restoration of the Temple after seventy years is symbolised by the faith of Abraham who, at seventy, belongs figuratively to the Pentateuch, which is 5, and Jesus, who is 1. The total of Abraham, the Pentateuch and Jesus (70 + 5 + 1) is therefore 76. All we have to do is to take 76 from 1006, which leaves 930, the age of Adam when he died and therefore the symbol of his fault.

It may be because of the Latin influence that Jesus is represented by the figure 1, since the letter I and the numeral have the same form in Latin, but the reason given by the author of the *De Pascha computus* is different. It is that, as Christ is the paschal lamb and that lamb must be one year old, *anniculus,* Christ must be one. It will be remembered that Hippolytus used the word 'year' as a name for Christ in relation to the twelve apostles (*Ben. Mos.; PO* XXVII, 171). The same imagery is connected by Clement of Alexandria with an early tradition according to which Christ's ministry lasted only one year (*Strom.* V, 6; 37, 4), [21] an idea which also appears later in the *De Pascha computus.* These are examples of traditional Judaeo-Christian elements used by our author as keys to his system.

We shall return to the theme of Adam and the Temple later, but what interests us here is that the author of the *De Pascha computus* also uses the symbolism of numbers that is found in the *De montibus* with regard to the letters of the name Adam. The total of these numbers is, it will be remembered, 46 and this is the number of years which, according to the Jews in the Fourth Gospel, the second Temple had taken to build, when Christ spoke of its destruction and restoration in three days, thus alluding symbolically to the restoration of Adam himself (*De Pascha comp.* 16). This is directly derived from the *De montibus.* [22] The author of the *De Pascha computus,* however, also draws attention to the theological implications behind these symbols. One of the most striking aspects of the Latin theology of this period is the parallelism between the two Adams.

In the *De Pascha computus* 17, the author discusses the number 49, in other words, the number of the seven weeks of seven days 'in which God willed, not without reason, that so magnificent a work should be carried out'. This number symbolises the six millennia and eternal life: 'This world, in which the just and the unjust have lived together since the beginning of the world, is

21. See *Symboles,* pp. 132–133 and 137–138. This tradition persisted in the West in Gregory of Nyssa and Gaudentius of Brescia.
22. Cf. p. 44 above.

fulfilled in six days, at the end of which the seventh day will come, the blessed day of the eternal sabbath'. Our author is no more concerned with millenarianism than the author of the *De montibus,* but he is convinced that the number 49 symbolises not only the six millennia, but also Christ himself, who has led everyone, through himself, to perfection and who is himself the true Temple. What is more, 49 consists of 18, which, as we have already seen, corresponds to the first two letters of Je(sus), and 31, which is the length of Jesus' life, on the assumption that his ministry lasted only one year.

In chapter 10, the author points out that Christ was born on a Wednesday, that is, on the fourth day of the week, the day when the sun was created. The *De Pascha computus* thus provides the earliest evidence that we have of the relationship between the birth of Christ, the *nativitas Christi,* and that of the sun, the *natale solis.* For the author, however, the date was the fifth day before the calends of April, which reveals the Roman character of the text very strikingly. The author explains first of all that the solar year is a symbol of Christ in that it has 365 days and a quarter. The quarter consists of three hours: 'The three hours bear the image of the three days which were without sun and moon at the beginning of the world. And as these three hours were multiplied by four, they made the day of twelve hours'. In the same way, the three months multiplied by four make the year of twelve months. This interpretation sees the three days as a sign of the Trinity, the twelve hours as a symbol of the twelve apostles, and in the four seasons the one gospel written by the four evangelists.

The author of the *De Pascha computus* thus assembles a number of traditional data. That the three days before the creation of light represent the Trinity is an idea which appears in the work of Theophilus of Antioch (*Ad Autol.* II, 15). The relationship between the twelve months of the year and the twelve apostles goes back to a tradition in which the twelve patriarchs and the twelve signs of the zodiac were connected.[23] The parallel between the four seasons and the four evangelists also goes back to an earlier tradition. It is clear, then, that the exegesis contained

23. See *Symboles,* pp. 131–142.

in the *De Pascha computus* is closely connected with a whole symbolism in art, in which these themes already occur frequently in the Jewish synagogues.

The 365 days can be shown, by a simple process of calculation, to point to Christ himself. Jesus died in the sixteenth year of the reign of Tiberius Caesar at the age of 31. To 16 and 31, add Jesus' name – 18 – making 65. To this add 300, which is the sign of the Hebrew letter tau. We thus have 365, which is the completion of the sun's cycle, in other words, the day when the sun was born. Christ, then, was born on the day that the sun was born, but, since the solar cycle began, for our author, not in January, but in April, Christ was born in April.

Having established the Saviour's birthday by means of the solar cycle, our author then proceeds to establish the date of his resurrection by means of the lunar cycle. Adam, he argues, was born on the third day after the moon was created on the fourth day, in other words, on the sixth day of creation. In the same way, Christ was raised from the dead on the third day of the moon: *Et sic Adam ipsi et omnibus credentibus in se restituit vitam aeternam,* 'And so he restored eternal life in himself to Adam and to all believers' (*De Pascha comp.* 21). Our author therefore concludes: 'Just as both the sign of tau and the time of the Passion have been indicated by the course of the sun, so too has the third day of the resurrection been established beyond all doubt by the course of the moon'.

It is important to draw attention to two points in this context. The first is that the *De Pascha computus* is firmly based on a parallelism between Christ and Adam, on the Jewish traditions connected with the symbolism of the name Adam and on the link between Adam and Golgotha. The second is that the treatise contains several themes which formed part of the Judaeo-Christian symbolism of numbers. The author makes use of these themes to carry out his chronological aims. It is also interesting in that it bears witness to the persistence after the time of Tertullian of that Judaeo-Christian tradition which he rejected.

3. THE *DE FABRICA MUNDI*

At the end of the third century, Victorinus of Pettau, the author of the *De fabrica mundi*, continued to use the Judaeo-Christian symbolism, but incorporated into it elements from secular culture. In his little treatise, he omits the first three days and begins with the fourth. He first lists some secular examples of 'tetrads', such as the four elements and the four seasons (*De fabr. mundi* 3), then goes on to the Bible, where he finds the four animals before God's throne, the four gospels, the four rivers of paradise and the four generations from Adam to Christ. He then mentions the fast on the fourth day as the day on which Christ was arrested by the soldiers. This is an interesting piece of evidence in favour of the existence of an early tradition in which the Last Supper took place on the Wednesday, as Annie Jaubert has pointed out.

The sixth day is important for Victorinus, since, in his opinion, it was on this day that God created not only man, but also the angels. On that day, the angels were, he taught, created before man, *spiritalia terrenis anteponens,* 'giving precedence to spiritual over earthly beings' (4).[24] Victorinus' reason for placing the creation of the angels on the sixth day is that it would in this way be possible to avoid the angels claiming that they helped God in the work of creation. This is a Jewish tradition, similar to one en- countered in the *De centesima.* In addition, Victorinus teaches that the sixth day was the day of preparation for the kingdom, the *regnum* in his system being the reign of a thousand years. The sixth day is thus the sixth and last millennium.

The symbolism of the number seven is the most elaborate of all in the *De fabrica mundi.* Victorinus emphasises in the first chapter of his treatise that the seven days symbolise the structure of heaven and earth. Since his perspective is millenarian, he first gives the seven millennia, the seventh millennium being, in his own words, the one 'in which Christ will reign with his elect'. The eighth day symbolises the judgement that will follow the millennium (*De fabrica mundi* 6). Next come the seven heavens,

24. See Tertullian, *Adv. Marc.* II, 10, 4.

each of which has its cosmic function; thunder and lightning, for example, come from the seventh heaven. The heavens correspond to the seven spirits of Is. 11:1–4, and these spirits in their turn signify the various aspects of the creative Word expressed in the seven days: 'Wisdom when he makes light; understanding when he makes the heaven; . . . piety when he makes man; fear when he blesses him'. Irenaeus also made this connection between the seven days and the seven spirits of Isaiah and it is possible that Victorinus derived the idea from him.

Victorinus then lists examples of the number seven found in Scripture: the seven horns of the lamb (Rv. 5:6), the seven eyes of God (Zc. 4:10), the seven spirits and the seven women in Isaiah (Is. 11:2; 4:1), the seven churches to which Paul's letters were addressed, the seven angels, the seven deacons, the seven weeks of Pentecost, the candlestick with seven branches, the seven pillars of Wisdom, and so on. Almost exactly the same selection can be found in Cyprian's *Testimonia* (I, 20). Such lists bear witness to the same concern as the collections of *testimonia,* with the difference that they are on the symbolic level.

The next chapter of the *De fabrica mundi* is even more interesting since it contains further evidence of the link that Victorinus makes between biblical and profane symbolism. He points out that the number seven is also found in the life of Christ and gives two examples of this. The first example points to a parallel between the days of creation and the days in which the body of Christ was formed: 'The Holy Spirit made the Virgin Mary conceive on the day when light was created. He was changed into flesh on the day that he made the earth and the water. He was changed into milk on the day that he made the stars. He was changed into blood on the day that the earth and the sea produced their fruit. He was changed into flesh on the day that he fashioned man from the earth'.

This parallelism between the stages in the formation of the world and those in the fashioning of Christ's body testifies to an interest in biological questions. There are, moreover, in Victorinus' work new ways of expressing the parallel between Christ and Adam, a theme which, we have observed, plays a leading part in the Latin theology of this period. Victorinus gives yet another slant to this in what he has to say about the mysteries of Christ: 'The Angel Gabriel announced the birth of Jesus to the Virgin Mary on the day that Eve was seduced by the serpent. Christ suffered on the day that Adam sinned. He rose from the dead on the day that the light was created'. Obviously Victorinus is not concerned here with any fixed order of events – he is, for example, not troubled by the fact that Christ rose on the first day. His parallel between Adam's sin and Christ's Passion is clearly reminiscent of Irenaeus, who insisted that Adam died on the sixth day (*Adv. haer.* V, 13), and he was probably using a Jewish tradition concerning Eve's relationship with the serpent in his reference to her seduction by the Devil. It is not hard to see why he identified the day on which this latter event took place with the day of the Annunication, when it was reversed by the obedience of Mary, but the source from which he took this symbolism, if any, is not known.

Victorinus also applies the seven ages of life found in secular Greek thought to Christ. These are *nativitas, infantia, pueritia, adolescentia, iuventus, perfecta aetas* and *occasus* (birth, infancy, childhood, adolescence, youth, maturity and declining years). Augustine also applied the same seven ages of life to the seven ages of the world. The aims of the two authors were different, but they followed the same procedure, using a secular conception to throw light on a biblical one. It would, moreover, seem that Victorinus was the first to do this.

One last theme to which we must draw attention in the *De fabrica mundi* is that of the number twelve. Victorinus believed, in fact, that two groups of twelve hours each were formed by the separation of the day from the night in the creation. This led to his teaching that 'Twelve angels of the day and twelve angels of the night were certainly appointed in accordance with the number of hours. These are the twenty-four witnesses seated before God's throne. They are called *seniores* because they are older than the other angels and than men' (*De fabrica mundi* 30). In this, Victorinus is apparently acknowledging that some angels were created on the first day of creation. He also uses this theme again in his treatise on the *Apocalypse*. Victorinus' interpretation of the twelve hours is different from that given by the author of the *De Pascha computus,* and clearly has nothing to do with Judaeo-Christianity. In passing, we may finally note that he provides another interpretation in his *Commentary on the Apocalypse* (3), according to which the twenty-four elders are the twelve patriarchs and the twelve apostles.

PART TWO

CHRISTIANITY
AND
LATIN CULTURE

INTRODUCTION TO PART TWO

THE texts studied so far testify to the existence of a popular, Latin-speaking Christianity which emerged in the second century and was to continue until the end of the third. It was basically Judaeo-Christian in character. There was, however, also a reaction against this Judaeo-Christianity, a movement with the aim of freeing Latin Christianity from its Jewish ancestry and giving it a respectable pedigree within the Latin tradition. Tertullian is a witness to this reaction, and his work can in fact be fully understood only in these terms, as various examples will indicate.

A form of Christianity which was fundamentally Jewish in its mode of expression, then, was followed by various attempts to express the Christian faith in a Latin way, attempts which we shall study in the works of the third century authors Minucius Felix, Tertullian, Cyprian and Novatian. Up to their time, Latin Christianity had remained popular; and even in the West its literary forms were Greek. In the works of Minucius Felix and Novatian, the derivation is from classical Latin tradition. It was, as we shall see towards the end of this work, in Tertullian that Latin Christianity found its own genuinely original voice.

CHAPTER FIVE

TERTULLIAN AND JUDAEO-CHRISTIANITY

ERTULLIAN lived in an African Christian environment which was saturated with Judaeo-Christian culture and was to remain fundamentally Judaeo-Christian at least in its popular forms for a very long time. It was precisely against this Judaeo-Christianity that Tertullian reacted so strongly and for several reasons. In the first place, he wanted to dissociate the Christian message from its Jewish trappings in order to give it a truly Latin expression. Secondly, he was anxious to overcome the criticism common among pagans that Christian faith was unacceptable because of the mythical elements contained in the Judaeo-Christian expression of Christianity. Celsus, for example, had only recently attacked the Christian faith for this reason. Tertullian's response was to attack Judaeo-Christianity in its heterodox forms, not only Valentinian gnosticism, but also in certain aspects of the Church itself as it was in his day. His rejection of Judaeo-Christianity became progressively more pronounced as one treatise succeeded another.

Tertullian's attitude emerges clearly from a passage in his *De resurrectione*. He is asking what sources the heretics he is attacking can find to lend colour to their teachings. He refers first to their corruption of the biblical text (*stilo*) and then to the results of their false interpretations (*interpretationes*). Finally, he declares: 'They also introduce secrets of the apocrypha (*arcana apocryphorum*), the inventions of blasphemy'. The apocrypha to which he is referring here are the Judaeo-Christian writings, and he even uses the same word in connection with the *Shepherd of Hermas*. These apocrypha are concerned with hidden things (*arcana*), such being the specific material of apocalyptic writing. Finally, he speaks of the interpretations to which the parables lend themselves (LXV, 6 and 9). We shall encounter these questions elsewhere in Tertullian's work.

1. TERTULLIAN'S REACTION AGAINST JUDAEO-CHRISTIANITY

As we have already seen, one of the outstanding characteristics of the Judaeo-Christian authors, at least in the texts that we have examined, was their freedom in using Old Testament quotations. This is a practice that is closely related to the Jewish tradition of the Targums, according to which the Bible is a living reality within a tradition. It is particularly noticeable in the *testimonia*, in which quotations from the Bible appear in a shortened or in a lengthened form or merged into each other. Of these *testimonia*, Tertullian preserved those which formed part of the tradition, such as Dt. 28:66 with the addition of *in ligno*, and Ps. 96:10 with *a ligno*. Apart from a few such traditional *testimonia*, however, he is characterised by a marked concern to quote the authentic scriptural text.

Tertullian recognised only two authorities: Scripture and the official tradition of the Church. This led him to break with the unofficial tradition of Old Testament exposition, represented in the *testimonia*, and to refer directly to Scripture itself. Furthermore, it seems that the Scripture to which he thus appealed was the Greek Bible, the Septuagint, though with certain interesting variants. He must have known of the existence of a contemporary Latin Bible, but he did not make use of it and this accounts for the freedom of his translations from Scripture. His attitude was entirely different from that of Cyprian, whose work bears witness to the Old Latin version.

It is informative to examine some of the better known *testimonia* used by Tertullian. In the case of Dt. 28:66, for example, Tertullian keeps to the traditional form of the *testimonium* as it appeared, for example, in the work of Irenaeus, that is, with the addition of *in ligno*, 'on the tree', and excising the words 'day and night'. On the other hand, however, he quotes this *testimonium* in its biblical context by beginning the quotation at verse 63 (*Adv. Jud.* XI, 9).

Another well-known testimonium is *Venite mittamus lignum in panem eius,* 'Come, let us put wood in his bread' (Jr. 11:19). Tertullian uses this quotation, but takes it to the end of the verse. By contrast, Commodian, who relied on the Judaeo-Christian tradition, uses the shortened form. Tertullian also continues Is. 65:2: *Expandi manus meas tota die,* 'I stretched out my hands all the day', another common *testimonium,* to the end of the verse (*Adv. Jud.* XIII, 10). Clearly, then, he made use of traditional *testimonia,* but preferred to place them within their original biblical context.

A further example is Jr. 2:13, which Tertullian gives in the form in which it appears in the Latin *Epistle of Barnabas* and in Cyprian. This suggests that he was in this instance following the Old Latin: *Me dereliquerunt fontem aquae vitae,* 'They have abandoned me, the fountain of the water of life'. The Septuagint and the Greek *Epistle of Barnabas* both have *aquae vivae,* 'of living water'. Tertullian does, however, place the quotation back into context by quoting the whole passage, Jr. 2:10–13 (*Adv. Jud.* XIII, 13–14).

A final example is Is. 2:3: *De Sion exiit lex et verbum Domini ex Ierusalem,* 'From Zion the law went out and the Word of the Lord from Jerusalem', a *testimonium* very dear to Judaeo-Christian circles in Africa. Tertullian puts this *testimonium* too back into its context, by quoting Is. 2:2–4.

Certain conclusions can be drawn from these examples of Tertullian's use of *testimonia.* It is in the first place characteristic of him that he preserves those *testimonia* which form part of the common tradition, but not specifically as *testimonia.* That is to say, he no longer regards the *testimonium* as such as a living form, and when he quotes Scripture, he does so with great respect for the text itself. He almost always takes pains to place the *testimonium* that he uses back into its biblical context, although he usually leaves the actual wording of the *testimonium* itself unchanged. His position is therefore a central, intermediate one between that of the Judaeo-Christians, who regarded the *testimonium* as an isolated, independent datum derived more from tradition than from Scripture, and that of Cyprian, who not only restored the *testimonium* to its original context, but also corrected it to the form given in the Old Latin.

We drew attention, in our examination of *V Esdras* and the

Passio Perpetuae, to the abundance of material referring to the life after death. This characteristic feature of Jewish apocalyptic reappears in Christian apocalyptic and especially in the *Apocalypse of Peter,* with its description of the torments of the damned and the joys experienced by the elect. Latin apocalyptic takes up the theme. The *Apocalypse of Peter* is in fact mentioned in the Muratorian Canon ('the Apocalypse of Peter, which some of us refuse to have read publicly in the Church'), so that it must have been translated at quite an early date into Latin. A later document, the *De laude martyrii,* continues the tradition: 'In the cruel place known as Gehenna can be heard the great groaning of the imploring souls of the damned and, in the horrible night of thick darkness, the deadly chimneys belch forth unceasing fires with gushing flames' (20). The place where the blessed dwell, on the other hand, is described as 'an abundant land covered with grass in verdant fields and fed by scented flowers' (21).

There is nothing of this sort in Tertullian. As Finé observed, all this descriptive aspect has been eliminated, and the apocalyptic imagery has totally disappeared. Even the geography of the next world is simplified in the extreme. Tertullian in fact reduces it to three basic elements. The first is that the *inferi,* where the dead live, are found below the earth and consist of different places for the guilty and the righteous. The part where the righteous live is called 'Abraham's bosom'. Secondly, there is Gehenna or hell, into which the wicked are to be cast at the end of time. Finally, there is the place of blessedness, into which the righteous are to enter after the resurrection, and which is called either paradise or heaven. Only the martyrs go there as soon as they die. [1]

Tertullian was similarly hostile to Judaeo-Christian angelology. He condemns as Jewish the teaching that the angels played a part in the creation of man (*Adv. Prax.* XII, 2). He passes over in silence the Judaeo-Christian doctrine regarding the activity of the angels in the cosmos and in the history of Israel. He rejects the theory of the *potestates ianitrices* who were supposed to judge the souls of men (*Scorp.* X. 6–7). There are in fact only two doctrines which he retains, the first being that of the guardian

1. FINE. *Die Terminologie der Jenseitsvorstellungen bei Tertullian,* p. 187.

angel, who watches over the child from the time that it is at its mother's breast (*De anim.* XXXVII, 1) and accompanies the soul on its journey after death (*De anim.* LIII, 6). The angel of birth belongs, of course, to Judaeo-Christian teaching, which Clement of Alexandria presents as a doctrine that he had received from an elder (πρεσβύτης) (*Ecl. proph.* 50, 1).[2] The doctrine of the angel of death also belongs to Judaeo-Christian angelology (cf. Lk. 16:22).[3]

The second aspect of the Judaeo-Christian tradition concerning angels which Tertullian preserves in his teaching is the connection between the angels and the life of the Church; and he does so within the context of the liturgical tradition which was so dear to him. His teaching on this point is found principally in the *De baptismo*. An angel, for example, 'is present to set out the waters for the salvation of man' (V, 6). Tertullian also mentions the angel at the pool of Bethesda as a figure of baptism (V, 5). 'Purified by the water', he teaches, 'we are led to the Holy Spirit' by this angel. 'The judicial angel of baptism prepares the way for the coming of the Holy Spirit by wiping out the sins of man on the supplication of faith by the seal of the Father, the Son and the Spirit' (VI,.1). The doctrine of baptism that is implied by these statements cannot be discussed here, since we are principally concerned with the part played by the angel in making the catechumen ready for baptism. Finally, Tertullian speaks of an angel of prayer (XVI, 6), the presence of angels in the Christian community at prayer (III, 3) and an angel of the Church (14–27).

All these are, of course, Judaeo-Christian doctrines. The 'angel of the Church' appears in the *Ascension of Isaiah* (III, 15) and the presence of angels when the community was praying is a favourite theme in the Qumran texts. There can be little doubt that it was prompted by Paul (1 Co. 11:10). Tertullian gave particular emphasis to the part played by the angel in baptism. There are parallels to all these features in the literature of the period, especially in the writings of Origen (*Hom. 1 Cor.* II, 8; *PG* 6, 403). But these were doctrines which had already entered the common tradition of the Church, which Tertullian respected. If his work

2. See J. H. WASZINK, *Tertullianus: De anima*, p. 424.
3. *Ibid.*, p. 546.

is compared, however, with that of Clement of Alexandria, who was his contemporary, the difference is enormous. In Tertullian's teaching, everything that is derived from Judaeo-Christian gnosis and speculations about the angels is systematically eliminated.

Another aspect to consider is Tertullian's attitude towards millenarianism. He stated his millenarian views clearly, for example, in his treatise against Marcion: 'For we do profess that even on earth a kingdom is promised us, but this is before we come to heaven and in a different polity – in fact, after the resurrection, for a thousand years, in that city of God's building, Jerusalem, brought down from heaven, which the Apostle declares is our mother on high' (*Adv. Marc.* III, 24, 3). Other similar passages are to be found in the *De anima* (LVIII, 8) and the *De resurrectione* (XXV, 2), but these passages mention only the second resurrection and the kingdom and do not refer to the thousand years. It is also likely that the lost treatise *De spe fidelium*, to which Tertullian refers in *Adv. Marc.* III, 24, 2, dealt with this question.

Certain aspects of this millenarianism of Tertullian's, however, call for comment. In the first place, Tertullian bases what he has to say exclusively on Ezk. 48:30–35 and Rv. 21:12–13 (*Adv. Marc.* III, 24, 3–4). First and foremost, therefore, this is, for Tertullian, a scriptural doctrine, and his defence of it is linked with the controversy at the time over the canonicity of the *Apocalypse of John.* Secondly, it should be noted that it is in the treatises that Tertullian wrote when he was moving towards Montanism that he discusses this doctrine. Millenarianism was, of course, an element in Montanist teaching, especially so far as the expectation of the coming of the new Jerusalem was concerned (cf. for example, *De anim.* LVIII, 8). Finally, Tertullian's realistic interpretation of John's text goes back to his criticism of allegorical interpretations (*De res.* XXVI, 1) and is also connected with his own realistic understanding of the resurrection (*Adv. Marc.* III, 24, 3).

On the other hand, however, Tertullian does not mention at all the specifically Judaeo-Christian aspects of millenarianism. In the first place, he carefully avoids any attempt to locate the new Jerusalem in Palestine (*De res.* XXVI, 11), thus going contrary not only to the Jews, but also to Judaeo-Christians such as Commodian. In this, his attitude towards millenarianism was characteristic of the Montanists, for whom the heavenly Jerusalem had nothing at all to do with Judaea. He also insisted that the kingdom of a thousand years did not consist of the enjoyment of material blessings (*De res.* XXVI, 9). Nor did it, in his opinion, include any of the miraculous aspects on which Judaeo-Christians from Papias to Victorinus of Pettau had placed such stress – especially that of extraordinary fertility in man and in nature. He regarded it as essentially a sharing in spiritual blessings: 'This city, we affirm, has been provided by God for the reception of the saints by resurrection and for their refreshment with abundance of all blessings – spiritual ones – for it is just . . . that God's servants should be filled with joy' (*Adv. Marc.* III, 24, 5).

Finally – and this is very typical of Tertullian – there is no allusion at all in his work to the doctrine of the seven millennia. This, of course, is not a scriptural teaching and, as we have seen, is based on speculations about the seven days of creation. It is a doctrine that is found in the writings of Irenaeus, in the Latin Judaeo-Christian texts such as the *De montibus* and the *De Pascha computus,* and in such authors as Commodian and Victorinus of Pettau. It is also to be found in Cyprian's *Ad Fortunatum:* 'Already almost six thousand years have gone by since the Devil fought against man' (*Ad Fort.* 1; see also 11). This theme is, however, completely absent from Tertullian's work; and this is in keeping with the similar absence of all numerical symbolism, despite the fact that this symbolism plays an extremely important part in Latin Judaeo-Christian apocalyptic, in the *De centesima* and the *De montibus,* not to mention the *De Pascha computus.* We may therefore conclude that Tertullian's rejection of these themes was the result of a conscious attitude on his part of opposition to Judaeo-Christianity.

Another area in which we see Tertullian reacting in the same way is that of the exegesis of the parables. It is well known that this exegesis occupied an important position in early Christianity, in gnosticism and in Judaeo-Christian thought. In his *Commentary on Matthew,* for example, Origen gives as many as five possible interpretations of certain parables in the gospel. We have already come across this question in our discussion of the *De centesima*. The common characteristic of all these interpretations is their allegorical nature. There may be differences in the interpretations themselves, notably as between gnostics and the orthodox, but the principle determining the interpretation is in each case the same. It is this principle to which Tertullian is opposed, whether it is applied to Judaeo-Christian or to gnostic exegesis.

In his treatise on the flesh of Christ (*De carne Christi*), Tertullian alludes to an exegesis of the parable of the labourers in the vineyard (Mt. 20:1–16), according to which the labourers who came last were the Old Testament prophets, each of whom had been led by an angel, and Christ, who followed them and was inspired by an even more glorious angel. Tertullian regarded this exegesis as Ebionite. In fact it is completely in accordance with a certain Judaeo-Christian tradition in interpreting the parables. In his exegesis of this very parable, Origen, for instance, gives very similar examples. Tertullian rejects this interpretation and, in his *De resurrectione*, stresses the fact that the parables are ambiguous and the need for an authentic interpretation.

In the *Adversus Marcionem* (IV, 29–31), Tertullian discusses Marcion's exegesis of the parables contained in the gospel of Luke, referring to those of the servants waiting for their master's return (Lk. 12:35–40), the mustard seed (Lk. 13:18–19), the yeast (Lk. 13:20–21) and the guests who made excuses (Lk. 14:16–24). In the parable of the servants, Marcion interprets the thief who broke into the house as the Demiurge and teaches that the Son of Man will come to judge those who allow themselves to be deceived by him (*Adv. Marc.* IV, 29, 7). Tertullian points to certain contradictions contained in Marcion's exegesis of this parable and of that of the guests. He does not, on the other hand, believe that there can be only one interpretation of each parable. In the parable of the mustard seed, for example, he thinks that the sower could be Christ sowing the word in the world or man sowing the word in his heart (*Adv. Marc.* IV, 30, 2). In the parable of the guests, the evangelist might have been referring to the Church or to eternal life. The most important aspect in any interpretation of a parable, Tertullian believed, was coherence (*Adv. Marc.* IV, 31, 7).

It is in the *De pudicitia,* however, that Tertullian directly takes issue with the Judaeo-Christian allegorical interpretation of the parables, in this particular case, of the parables dealing with mercy and forgiveness in Lk. 15. What is particularly interesting in this context is that it is clear that Tertullian was acquainted with a variety of allegorical interpretations. In the case of the parable of the lost sheep, for instance, he refers to Simon Magus' interpretation, according to which the lost sheep was the soul who had become subject to the demonic powers of the cosmos and whom the Saviour had come to set free. He was, however, also familiar with Marcion's exegesis of the same parable and of the parable of the lost drachma (*Adv. Marc.* IV, 32, 1). In the *De paenitentia* (XII, 6), he interprets the parables of the lost sheep and the prodigal son as examples of forbearance. His interpretation was therefore moral, but already in the *De paenitentia* he criticizes those who used these three parables to argue that discipline in the Church should be relaxed. He agreed that there was a place for repentance after baptism, but this should be the fruit of an arduous conversion (*De paen.* IX, 1).

Tertullian's treatise on chastity, *De pudicitia,* is a late work and much more radical, in that it excludes post-baptismal repentance. What concerns us here, however, is Tertullian's attitude in this late work towards the exegesis of parables. He does not exclude the possibility that they can be correctly interpreted symbolically and in other ways, but he warns his readers against an allegorical interpretation which replaces their real meaning with personal conjecture: 'There is a danger in interpreting parables, and this is that facility in comparisons (*facilitas comparationum*) may lead to our interpreting them differently from the way the material of the parable calls for. It is the same as in the stories – we admire the talent, but it has nothing to do with the theme discussed. The heretics therefore lead the parables the way they want them to go, not where the parables themselves ought to go. The parables simply give these heretics the opportunity to express their own views. We, on the other hand, do not start from the parables to elaborate on their detailed content – we use the content to interpret the parables' (*De pud.* VIII, 10–12).

Up to this point, Tertullian is clearly concerned with interpretation which is not in accordance with the truth. He goes further than this, however, and criticises allegorical interpretation as such: 'We do not exhaust ourselves in an attempt to explain everything. Why a hundred sheep? And why ten drachmas? And what are all these brooms? If the intention was to say that the salvation of one sinner was very precious to God, then it was necessary to name a certain number, one of which was ready to perish. It was necessary to say that the search for the lost drachma in the house required a number of brooms and a lamp. But curious elements of this kind make certain aspects of the interpretation suspect and our attention is turned away from the truth by them because the explanations are so subtle' (De pud. IX, 2). It is clear from this passage that Tertullian questions the whole process of allegorical interpretation of the parables among Judaeo-Christians. What is more, he may also have been alluding, as we pointed out earlier in this book, to the De centesima here. It should be noted, in this context, that Tertullian does not condemn these allegorical exegeses of the parables, as he does the heretical ones, but he does warn his readers against the dangers inherent in such interpretation. The principal fault of allegorical exegesis was, in his opinion, the attempt to give meaning to details which were there only because they were required by the story: 'We would prefer to understand less of Scripture if that were necessary, than to understand it badly' (De pud. IX, 22).

In an earlier work, the Scorpiace, Tertullian criticised the allegorical interpretation of the parables in connection with the interpretation of the parable of the sower (Mt. 13:4–9) given by those exegetes who changed the evidence given by Christians before courts of justice on earth into evidence given before the heavenly courts. In the relevant passage, he says: 'If things are not interpreted as they are said, they are inevitably understood in a manner contrary to what they say. There will then be one thing in the words and something else in the meanings, as in allegories (allegoriae), parables (parabolae) and riddles (aenigmata)' (Scorp. XI, 4). Tertullian stresses that the concrete imagery used to convey the parables' message proves that they ought to be taken literally. What he has in mind here is, of course, the gnostic exegesis of the parables, but beyond this lies a criticism of all allegorical interpretation. This close parallel between the teaching found in the *De pudicitia* and that in the *Scorpiace* is an argument in favour of a late date for the composition of the latter text.[4]

It is clear, then, that Tertullian reacted against a good deal of the presentation of Judaeo-Christianity, and in particular of Latin Judaeo-Christianity. In addition to this immediate object of his reaction, however, there was a more ultimate one, namely the theology which this presentation expressed and which derived from Semitic tradition. Several times throughout this book, we have had occasion to note various theological elements, for example, in the *De montibus* or the *De centesima*, which are specifically Judaeo-Christian and there can be no doubt at all that Tertullian was explicitly opposed to this type of theology. Indeed, we may go as far as to say that, even behind the heresies he attacks, it is frequently the Judaeo-Christian attitude which he is really criticising. He often in fact makes a distinction between what is the result of heresy properly so-called, and what springs from archaic and often clumsy elaboration. Three examples will serve to illustrate this distinction.

In the first place, Tertullian rejects all angelomorphic christology. One feature of this teaching was the application of the term, 'angel', meaning 'one who is sent', to Christ. This occurs frequently in the works of the Apologists, and, among Latin writers, Novatian was to give it particular prominence. This idea of Christ as an envoy or angel does not appear at all in Tertullian's work. This is clearly evidence of the fact that he was anxious to avoid all cause of confusion between the Son and the angels. It is obvious from his *De carne Christi* (XIV, 3) that he knew of this doctrine and that he did not condemn it: 'I would rather say, if I have to, that Christ is an angel (*angelum*), in other words, an envoy (*nuntium*) from the Father, than speak of an angel in the Son' (*De carn.* XIV, 4). He preferred to avoid the teaching because it was equivocal. In his *Adversus Praxean*, he makes a radical distinction between the ministry of the angels, at the disposal of the divine 'monarch', and the relationship between the Father and the other two persons of the Trinity

4. Barnes (*Tertullian*, pp. 171–172), however, prefers an early date.

(*Adv. Prax.* III, 4). This was undoubtedly a reaction against the development of an angelomorphic Christology in Judaeo-Christianity. It may, in conclusion, be noted that this form of Christology plays an important part in the *Shepherd of Hermas* and in the Latin *De centesima*.

Tertullian also devotes a chapter of the *De carne Christi* (XIV) to this theme. He does not mention the heretics, but gathers together a number of data connected with the theme of Christ the angel. It is difficult to avoid the conclusion that this was in particular an attack against the *Shepherd of Hermas*. Tertullian's fundamental statement here is 'They say that Christ took the form of (*gestavit*) an angel'. This teaching, that the Son took on the form of angels when he came down to the world, before he assumed the form of men, was widespread in Judaeo-Christianity and can also be found, for example, in the *Ascension of Isaiah* (XVII, 12) and the *Epistle of the Apostles* (24).

Tertullian also examines the reasons for this doctrine that Christ assumed the form of an angel. The first is that the Son may have taken on the nature of the angels in order to save the angels, just as he took on human nature, in order to save men. To this Tertullian replies that: 'he received no commission from the Father to save the angels' (*De carn.* XIV, 2). He then goes on to discuss the other possible reasons: did he perhaps assume angelic form as that of an 'assistant (*satelles*), with whom he would bring about man's salvation? Was he not able, then, to save man by himself? Or did he want the angel's help to save man? Why, then, did he come himself?' (*De carn.* XIV, 3). The reasons advanced are, of course, not the real reasons for this theme of Christ in the form of an angel in Judaeo-Christianity, but they enabled Tertullian to reject the idea emphatically. It should, however, be noted that he also rejected the real reason, namely, to conceal the descent of the Word from the angels (*Adv. Marc.* V, 6, 6).[5]

Other possible reasons are also discussed by Tertullian, who says: 'He is called *Angelus magni cogitatus* (Angel of mighty counsel)' (*De carn.* XV, 9, 5). Tertullian's reply to this is that the word means 'envoy' (*nuntius*) and that it describes his function,

5. J. DANIELOU, *The Theology of Jewish Christianity*, pp. 206ff.

not his nature.[6] He also says that this word is not used here in the same sense as it is used for Michael or Gabriel. Here too, however, it is difficult not to see an allusion to the practice of referring to the Son as Michael or Gabriel, in the same way that the Word is identified with Michael in the *Shepherd of Hermas* (*Sim.* VIII, 1–3) and with Gabriel in the *Sibylline Oracles* (VIII, 456–461).[7] As we have seen, Tertullian was familiar with both of these texts. Finally, he alludes to an interpretation of the parable of the labourers in the vineyard according to which the labourers were identified with the angels and the Son was similarly regarded. We shall be returning to this question later.

We must now turn to a doctrine which Tertullian explicitly affirmed to have been Judaeo-Christian in origin, since he attributed it to 'Hebion': *Poterat haec opinio Hebioni convenire qui nudum hominem et tantum ex semine David, id est non et Dei Filium, constituit Jesum, plane prophetis aliquot gloriosiorem, ita ut in nonnullis angelum fuisse dicatur, quemadmodum et in aliquo Zacharia,* 'This view was in accordance with that of Hebion, who regarded Jesus as a mere man and simply a descendant of David, that is, not as the Son of God, although certainly somewhat more glorious than the prophets, so that by some he is said to have been an angel, as, for example, somewhere in Zechariah' (*De carn.* XIV, 5). This text is in fact a fair summary of Ebionite teaching, as reported by Epiphanius (*Pan.* XXX, 14), in other words, that Christ was not the Son of God, but an archangel who was greater than the other angels. This archangel helped Adam, Moses and the other prophets (*Pan.* XXX, 3). He was revealed in a more perfect way in Jesus, who was otherwise a man like other men. It will be noted that the heresy of which the Ebionites are accused by Tertullian is in fact that of denying the virginal conception of Christ. The Ebionite theology of the Son as a glorious angel is, however, one which they shared with other, orthodox Christians, such as the authors of the *Shepherd of Hermas* and of the *De centesima*.

Tertullian thus provides us with a summary of various aspects of the Judaeo-Christian theology of Christ as angel, both that

6. As Novatian explains at great length in the *De Trinitate* 18–20.
7. See BARBEL, *Christos Angelos,* Bonn, 1941, pp. 224–269.

which identified the Son with an angel and that according to which he assumed the form of an angel. It is clear from Tertullian's text that he had a very precise knowledge of these forms of Judaeo-Christian theology. Some of his sources are known to us – for example, the *Sibylline Oracles* and the *Shepherd of Hermas* – but it is quite possible that others were from Latin Judaeo-Christian literature, since the *De centesima* and Commodian's texts also contain similar doctrines. This explains why Tertullian was so reluctant to call the Son an angel, even in the sense of an envoy (*nuntius*), while Novatian, for example, had a very different attitude.

It may be helpful at this point to consider Tertullian's attitude towards the *Shepherd of Hermas*. In the first place, it should be borne in mind that the *Shepherd*, a work originally written in Greek at Rome, was translated at an early date into Latin, apparently at the end of the second century. It is mentioned at some length in the Muratorian Canon, and was regarded in some churches as scriptural, as Tertullian himself confirms (*De orat.* XVI, 1). This points to the existence of a Latin translation of the text, at least in Africa, where it had a considerable influence on African Judaeo-Christianity. There are also, as we have seen, traces of its influence in *V Esdras*, the *Passio Perpetuae* and the *De centesima*, while Commodian refers to the parable of the vine and the young elm tree and makes use of the *Shepherd* on several occasions. Tertullian also testifies to the important position occupied by the *Shepherd* in Christian thought in his own day, which makes his evidence all the more interesting.

His first reference to the *Shepherd* occurs in the *De oratione*, where he speaks about attitudes towards prayer: *Si Hermas ille, cuius Scriptura fere Pastor imponitur, transacta oratione non super lectum assedisset, verum aliud quid fecisset, id quoque ad observationem vindicaremus? Utique non,* 'If the famous Hermas, whose "Shepherd" is very nearly set up as Scripture, had not sat on a couch after praying, but had done something different, would we justify that too as a rule to be observed? Not at all!' (*De orat.* XVI, 1). The allusion is to *Vis.* V, 1. What first strikes one's attention is Tertullian's reservations as to whether the *Shepherd* really belongs to the canon. Secondly, Tertullian's attitude is distinctly negative, and is aimed at those who accept the slightest details of the text as binding upon them. 'It is a story, not a law', Tertullian states later (*De orat.* XVI, 2), and earlier in the same work he treats such practices as superstition (XV, 1). The very tone in which he expresses himself reveals the freedom which he felt with regard to this Judaeo-Christian heritage, and shows that in no way did he put them on a par with the official tradition of the Church.

In his second reference to the *Shepherd*, Tertullian displays definite hostility. The subject is Hermas's teaching about post-baptismal repentance. 'I would agree that you are right', Tertullian writes (*De pud.* X, 12), 'if the Scripture of the *Shepherd*, which loves only adulterers, had merited inclusion in the body of Scripture itself, if it had not been condemned by the unanimous consent of the churches (*consilia Ecclesiarum*), even yours, as false and apocryphal, itself adulterous and therefore supported by companions of the same sort.' His hostility was originally aroused by the fact that the *Shepherd* was adduced in support of their case by those Christians who allowed repentance after baptism, especially at Rome. He called it an adulterous book because it justified adultery. Tertullian, however, takes advantage of the opportunity to stress the fact that the *Shepherd* was not regarded as scriptural in the churches,[8] although he overstates his case by using the word 'false', since the book was respected, even if it was not included in the canon of Scripture.

Tertullian does not, however, confine his criticism simply to the author's attitude towards repentance. 'It is by this Scripture that you can be initiated into other things. The Shepherd will, if need be, give them his blessing. After all, the Shepherd appears on your chalice. He corrupts the Christian sacrament, and is rightly called an idol of drunkenness, and a refuge of that adultery will follow the chalice of which you yourself would in no way drink more easily than the sheep of the second penance' (*De pud.* X, 12). To admit Christians to post-baptismal repentance was therefore, in Tertullian's view, to encourage drunkenness and adultery, since those who were admitted to it and who shared once more in the Eucharist would inevitably fall into sin again.

8. See T. P. O'MALLEY, *Tertullian and the Bible*, pp. 20–21.

It will be noticed in this passage that Tertullian calls adultery *moechia*, which is a transliteration of the Greek word μοίχεια. This is an archaism similar to those that occur in the *Passio Perpetuae*, in which several Greek words are used. Since Tertullian himself said that he preferred the Latin word *adulterium*, this suggests that he was here quoting an existing Latin translation of the *Shepherd* in which the Greek word *moechia* was bound to have been used. This is further evidence of the fact that the *Shepherd* was widely known in the African church. The reference to the 'Shepherd' engraved on the chalice is also a clear indication of liturgical practice in Africa which aroused Tertullian's hostility. (See also *De pud.* VII, 1.) There can be no doubt he is deliberately confusing this image with that of the *Shepherd of Hermas*; but his reason for rejecting even the imagery of the *Shepherd*, such a familiar feature of early Christian art, is that it expresses an early Judaeo-Christian theology.

This does not, of course, mean that Tertullian was not sometimes influenced by the *Shepherd*, especially in his earliest works. One example of this is his description of the activity of the Holy Spirit in his *De spectaculis*: 'God has instructed (*praecepit*) us to treat the Holy Spirit, since from the goodness of his nature he is tender and sensitive (*tenerum et delicatum*), with tranquillity and gentleness, in quietness and peace, and not to distress him by madness, bile, anger and trouble' (*De spect.* XV, 2). In this passage, the word *praecepit* is reminiscent of the Mandates (or *Praecepta*) of the *Shepherd*, in which we read: 'The Holy Spirit, who is delicate (τρυΦερόν) ... seeks to live in gentleness (πραότητος) and peace (ἠσυχίας) ' . This is, moreover, precisely the passage which contains a praise of patience, and Frédouille has pointed to this influence of this passage on Tertullian's *De patientia* XV, 3.

One of the most striking aspects of Latin Judaeo-Christian writings is the tendency to quote apocryphal texts as scriptural. Let us recall some examples. The author of the *De montibus*, for instance, quotes: 'You see me in yourselves as a man sees himself in the water or in a mirror' (*De mont.* 13), a passage which was attributed to Christ and quoted as coming from 'the *Epistle of John* to the people'. Several examples of this practice can, as we have seen, be found in the *De centesima*. The first of these is a text which is quoted as if it were Scripture (*cum scriptum sit*): *Omnia ista in saeculo nata et hic cum saeculo remansura,* 'All these things were born in the world and will remain here with the world' (*De cent.* 55, 5–6). The second is another text attributed to Christ 'teaching us by the Holy Spirit and by his vessel of election', in other words, Paul: *Si corpore castus et mente corruptus es, nihil prodest,* 'It is useless if your body is spotless, but your mind is debased' (*De cent.* 60, 6–7).

The author of the *De centesima* also includes in his treatise two passages which are apparently Pauline, but which are in fact *agrapha,* quoted as Scripture. The first of these is, as we have already seen, *Felices qui habent uxores tanquam non habentes,* 'Happy are those who have wives (and behave) as if they have none', which is a quotation from the *Acts of Paul*. This text is preceded by the words: 'Remember Scripture and doctrine, when it says:' (*De cent.* 62, 41–44). Then, there is the quotation *Qui continens est in omnibus continens permaneat, non tantum corpore, sed spiritu,* 'Let the man who is continent in all things continue to be continent, not only in his body but in his spirit' (*De cent.* 60, 7–8). This is also presented by the author as scriptural, but, although it does reflect Paul's thought in 1 Co. 9:25, it is certainly not an original logion.

There is another quotation in the *De centesima* which is also found in the Syriac *Didascalia:* 'If you do not want others to steal from you, why do you steal from others?' (*De cent.* 65, 4–5). This is, of course, a development of the golden rule, which is quoted earlier in the same passage. This particular text is not, however, quoted as Scripture. Earlier on, however, the author quotes a text from the *Didache* (VI, 1): 'If you can carry out all the Lord's precepts, my son, you will be perfect' and this is indeed quoted as though it were scriptural (*De cent.* 58, 10–11). The first passage must also come from a more elaborate version of the *Didache,* which may have been the rule of the Roman community. It is possible that there are allusions to this rule in Tertullian (*De orat.* XI, 1; XI, 2; XVIII, 6), but they are not presented as scriptural.

The *De aleatoribus* also provides valuable evidence of this practice. As we have seen, the author of this treatise quotes the

Shepherd of Hermas as Scripture. He does the same with the *Didascalia apostolorum* (4), where the passage in question contained a developed form of a passage in the *Didache*. This particular text is quoted among several Pauline texts and is placed on the same level as the latter. The text from the *Didascalia* is presented in another passage which apparently also forms part of an 'apostolic' regulation: *Quicumque frater more alienigenarum vivit et admittet res similes factis eorum, desine in convivium eius esse; quod nisi feceris, et tu particeps eius eris,* 'If any brother lives like a pagan and accepts things that are similar to what the pagans do, cease to live in his company. If you do not do this, you will be sharing his sin' (*De aleat.* 4).

This treatise also contains, in parallel with a quotation from Si. 32:1, a strange passage which we have already discussed: 'Regard the priest as a worshipper (*cultorem*) and think of all the delights of full granaries being near him, so that my people will eat as much as they want' (*De aleat.* 2). Later in the treatise, there are two other texts which are not scriptural, but which are quoted as words of the Lord (*De aleat.* 11). They would seem to go back to Christian Targums. *V Esdras* contains an example of this practice, which is basically that of quoting an amplification of Old Testament texts. Finally, there is the case of the quotation: 'Do not put out the light that has shone in you' (*De aleat.* 3), which is presented as a word of the Lord, but would appear to be a logion.

We may therefore conclude that various texts were regarded by the second century Roman and African communities of believers as scriptural. Apart from a Latin translation of the *Shepherd of Hermas,* these texts included an amplified Latin version of the *Didache,* an apocryphal *Epistle of John* which was unknown elsewhere in the Christian world, a Latin version of the *Acts of Paul,* a Latin commentary of Paul's Epistles which was encratite in tendency, Latin Targums of the Old Testament and logia of Christ. This, of course, represents the earliest stage in Latin Christian literature, and the very fact that they were quoted as Scripture shows that the texts in which they were quoted are of a very early date.

Tertullian, on the other hand, reacted strongly against this quoting of apocryphal texts as scriptural. We observed this in the case of the *Shepherd* and it is clear that in the case of one of the texts from which we quoted above, namely the *Acts of Paul*, Tertullian's attitude was one of rejection, since he regarded it as a forgery. The only authority that he recognised was in fact that of Scripture. He did not merely dispute the authority of the Christian apocrypha, he rejected them completely. The only agraphon that can be found in his work is the formula: 'No one, without having been put to the test, will reach the heavenly kingdom' (*De bapt.* XX, 2). This formula is moreover simply put forward by Tertullian as a dictum, not as a word of God. Even the possible allusions in the same treatise to the *Didache* are very doubtful. Here again Tertullian's attitude marks a complete break with the Judaeo-Christian tradition.

We must now turn to another aspect of Judaeo-Christian theology against which Tertullian reacted strongly, in this case in his treatise against Praxeas. Here the point at issue is not the use of apocalyptic images in expressing the doctrine of the Trinity, but rather the persistence of a Jewish-type monotheism which refused to make any distinction between the three persons of the Trinity. It would seem to be quite certain that this particular doctrine originated in Judaeo-Christian circles. For one thing, this is asserted by Tertullian himself: 'This goes back to the Jewish faith, namely, belief in one sole God in the sense of refusing to associate with him the Son and, after him, the Spirit' (*Adv. Prax.* XXXI, 1). This was in fact a popular idea, held by the *simplices* (III, 1), who in their adherence to monotheism were afraid of any further development resulting from speculation.

In this, Tertullian had not only Praxeas, but also an entire theological tendency in mind, a movement which seems to have originated in Asia Minor. Cantalamessa has located its real beginning in the *Paschal Homily* of Pseudo-Hippolytus, which, he believes, was written at the end of the second century in Asia Minor. Judaeo-Christian *testimonia* were freely used in this movement: 'They say that Genesis begins in Hebrew in the following way: "In the beginning, God made a Son for himself"' (*Adv. Prax.* 5, 1). This is an instance of a rendering of *beresîth* found also in Irenaeus' *Demonstratio* (43). It is clearly Judaeo-Christian in origin, because it was, according to Jerome at

least (*Quaest. hebr.* I, 1), in the *Dialogue of Jason and Papiscus,*
written by Ariston of Pella.[9]

Another quotation is interesting in this context, this time from
Lamentations: 'The breath of our face is Christ the Lord' (Lm.
4:20). In *Adv. Prax.* 15, 10, Tertullian uses the form: *Spiritus per-
sonae eius Christus Dominus,* but, quoting it on his own account in
Adv. Marc. III, 6, 7 and V, 11, 12, he uses the form *Persona spiritus
nostri Christus Dominus,* 'the person of our spirit, Christ the Lord'.
This is clearly Tertullian's own free translation of the text from
the Greek, whereas, in the first case, that occurring in the *Adversus Praxean,* it is a traditional *testimonium,* which is, moreover, also
found in Irenaeus' *Demonstratio.* It must therefore have been part
of an Asiatic Judaeo-Christian collection, used by Praxeas or at
least by the Judaeo-Christians living in the same environment as
Praxeas and borrowed from them by Tertullian.[10] The
monarchians made use of it in an attempt to justify their claim
that Christ was the same as the Spirit of the Father (*Adv. Prax.* 27,
1).

All this is clear evidence of Tertullian's reaction against
Judaeo-Christianity. It is, however, possible to go even further
and say that he was reacting against Judaeo-Christianity above all
in Africa, associating this form of Christianity with the name of
Praxeas, because the latter was opposed to Montanism. He
wanted to discredit Praxeas and to this end treated him as a
heretic. It cannot be denied, however, that he came across the
doctrine in Africa and attributed it to the *simplices,* in other
words, to the African Judaeo-Christians who spoke Latin. Once
again, it is not a question of a heresy promulgated by educated
people, but of a popular movement.

There is, moreover, evidence of the existence of
monarchianism in African Judaeo-Christianity and, what is
more, precisely in the form in which it was criticised by Tertullian, in a document which we have already considered in this

9. See DANIELOU, *The Theology of Jewish Christianity,* pp. 167–168; P. NAUTIN,
'Gen. 1, 2 de Justin à Origène', *In Principio. Interprétations des premiers versets de
la Genèse,* 1973.
10. See J. DANIELOU, *Etudes d'exégèse judéo-chrétienne,* pp. 76–99.

book, namely the *De montibus*. We have discussed the passages in this treatise containing elements of Monarchianism and have seen that these elements are certainly in accordance with the teaching attacked by Tertullian. As Thraede has shown, this same monarchianism is also to be found in Latin Judaeo-Christianity, as represented especially by the theology of Commodian.

Tertullian was also opposed to the Judaeo-Christians with regard to their teaching about man. In the *Adversus Hermogenem*, he insists that the human soul is neither a purely corporeal nor a divine reality, but a distinct entity with its origin in the breath of God. Similarly, in the *Adversus Marcionem* he attacks the dualistic teaching of Marcion, who interpreted 1 Co. 15:50 in terms of the conflict within man between flesh and blood, which are to be strangers to the kingdom of God, and the Spirit, which is the only heir to the kingdom. Tertullian's own interpretation of 1 Co. 15:47 displays the same standpoint, that is to say, not that man is of two substances, one earthly and the other heavenly, but that man had two attitudes, one closed and the other open to God.

Tertullian's primary targets in these works are, of course, Hermogenes' Platonism and Marcion's dualism. But, as we have already seen in the other cases, it is the underlying Judaeo-Christian ideas which he has in mind quite as much as the extreme forms which they take in the teachings of the heresiarchs. The identification of the human soul with blood, in other words, the idea that it is biological in nature, is highly Semitic. It is also to be found a little later in Heraclides, an Arab bishop whom Origen attacked, and in the *Book of Degrees*. Tatian too stresses the opposition between the two souls, the animal soul which he identifies with man's blood and the heavenly soul which he identifies with the *pneuma;* and Tatian was a Syrian.

The same idea is also found in the *De centesima,* which, as we have seen, was influenced by Tatian, especially in its encratism. In one text, for example, we read: 'The first flesh, taken from the mud of the earth, possesses a soul inspired by God. The Spirit (*spiritus*), however, comes from heaven. The Spirit possesses the strong things, but the flesh possesses the blood' (*De cent.* 58, 35–37). This is a clear reference to 1 Co. 15:47, which is moreover quoted earlier in the *De centesima* in the received form: *Primus homo de terrae limo, secundus de caelo. Qualis de limo quales et qui de limo, et qualis caelestis, quales et caelestes,* 'The first man was from the mud of the earth, the second was from heaven. As was the one from the mud, so too are those who are from the mud and as the heavenly one is, so too are those who are heavenly' (*De cent.* 55, 23–26). Later in the treatise, there is a quotation from Ga. 5:17: 'It is necessary to understand, dear brothers, that the desires of the Spirit are daily in conflict with the flesh'. What should be noted especially here is the exegesis of 1 Co. 15:47, according to which the soul inspired by God (Gn. 2:7) is identified with the gift of the Pneuma, that is, the Spirit, and with the heavenly principle.

Commenting on these texts, Tertullian gives them a completely different interpretation. In the case of 1 Co. 15:47, he says: 'Let us now discuss the crux of the whole question, the flesh and blood. The way in which these substances are excluded by the Apostle from the kingdom of God can be understood in the light of the preceding passage. "The first man is from the earth, earthy", that is to say, made from mud (*limacius*), refers to Adam. "The second man is from heaven" refers to the Word of God, in other words, Christ, who is still man even though he was from heaven, because he is flesh and soul, that is, what man is and what Adam was' (*De res.* LXIX, 1–21). It is not a question of substance, but of 'discipline'.

This text is of interest in the present context because it is not directed against the heretics, but against those Christians who denied the resurrection of the flesh and blood. Tertullian comments on the same Pauline text in very much the same way in the *De carne* VIII, 5–7, although here he is replying to those Christians who denied that Christ had an intellectual soul and recognised only his fleshly soul (*De carne* XIII, 5), which is precisely the Semitic view of man as a material soul united with the blood. In attacking this view, Tertullian bases his argument on the distinction in kind between man's biological life and his intellectual life, a teaching which he had previously outlined in the *De anima*.

As a final example, we may quote his commentary on Ga.

5:17: 'Although the Apostle says that nothing good lives in the flesh; although he affirms that those who are in the flesh cannot please God, because the flesh lusts against the Spirit; and though he could go further and declare, for example, that it is not the substance of the flesh that he seeks to crush but its actions; despite all this we say that the flesh should not really be blamed in any way, except that it is urged on by the soul, which subjects the flesh to itself as its instrument' (*De res.* X, 3). Here again, it is not flesh and blood which are indicted, but the freedom which is the sole source of sin. Any kind of dualism in man is ruled out.

2. TERTULLIAN AND THE JEWISH APOCRYPHA

Tertullian distrusts not only Judaeo-Christian apocalyptic writing, as we have seen, but also the Jewish apocrypha. He is a man of the Bible. In the *De anima,* for example, he attributes the apocrypha to the activity of evil angels, and regarded them as one of the sources of the errors made by the philosophers: 'What if it was there the philosophers came across those things which we have condemned because we regarded them as apocryphal, since we are certain that nothing should be received which is not in accordance with the teaching of the true prophets, who are in fact earlier even (sc. than the philosophers), and since we remember the false prophets and, long before them, the apostate spirits who shaped the whole face of this world with false inventions of this kind?' (*De anima* II, 3).

Nonetheless, Tertullian recognised certain non-canonical Jewish documents, some of which had in any case been received in the churches. Like so many others living at the time, he was convinced of the antiquity of such pseudepigrapha as *I Enoch* and the *Sibylline Oracles.* What is more, these writings were in no way regarded as containing false teaching. It is interesting to note what Tertullian retained from this inheritance. We shall be concerned essentially with the two works just mentioned, but he also probably made use of an apocryphon of Adam, a part of which is known to us as the *Life of Adam and Eve.*

1. *I. Enoch*

In the early Christian centuries, *I Enoch* enjoyed a privileged position of authority. It was quoted in the second century by both Justin and Irenaeus. Tertullian has explained his reasons for regarding this authority as well-founded (*De cultu fem.* III, 1–3). He admits that the book 'is not accepted by some, because it is not in the Jewish canon (*armarium*)', the reason for this being that it could not be by Enoch himself, since then it must have been destroyed in the Flood. Tertullian, on the other hand, accepts that it is authentic and puts forward two hypotheses to explain how this might be so. The first is that Noah may have received the revelation of Enoch, his great-grandfather, orally from his grandfather Methuselah.[11] The alternative is that the revelation may have been rediscovered by inspiration after the Flood.

More noteworthy are two reasons which he gives to justify the status of *Enoch* as Scripture. In the first place, 'this Scripture of Enoch speaks about our Lord. From that time, nothing should be rejected by us of what concerns us' (*De cultu fem.* III, 3). This is clearly an allusion to the *Book of the Weeks,* which treats of the Son of Man. This part of *Enoch* was not found at Qumran and is believed by some scholars to have been a Christian work. In the second place, Tertullian claims, correctly, that Enoch is mentioned in the *Epistle of Jude.* We may conclude that *I Enoch* was accepted by at least some churches at the time of Tertullian, and that he is conforming to this tradition.

Tertullian mentions *I Enoch* quite frequently in his writings. In *De orat.* XXII, 5 there is an apparent reference to *I Enoch* VI, 1–2, which tells of the fall of the angels who became enamoured of the daughters of men. This is, of course, a midrash on Gn. 6:1–2, and Tertullian may here be dealing either with Gn. 6:1–2 or with *I Enoch* VI, 1–2.

Another reference, also to the fall of the angels, is contained in the *De cultu feminarum* (I, 2, 1) and the same theme is elaborated at greater length in the *De virginibus velandis* (VII, 1–4), in which Gn. 6:1–2 is again quoted. It is therefore possible that Tertullian

---

11. See *I Enoch* LXXXII, 1.

was drawing here exclusively on Genesis, but, in view of the fact that he goes straight on to speak about *Enoch,* it is clear that he had both works in mind.

The theme in *I Enoch* dealt with at greatest length by Tertullian is that of the revelation of hidden secrets by the apostate angels (*I Enoch* VII, 1–VIII 3). The first reference to this theme in Tertullian's writings is to be found in *Apol.* XXXV, 12, where he discusses the arts of 'the astrologers, the soothsayers, the augurs and the magicians' and says that these are 'arts made known by the angels that forsook God'. This is without doubt an allusion to *I Enoch* VIII, 2. It will be remembered that in *De anima* II, 3 he also speaks of the possibility that the errors made by the philosophers came in part from the teachings of 'the apostate spirits'.

In the *De idololatria* IX, 11 it is astrology he has in mind, just as he had done earlier in the *Apology*: 'I suggest one thing – the angels who deserted God, in becoming enamoured of women, revealed this form of curiosity (*curiositas*)'. The word *curiositas* is interesting. Tertullian uses it to mean every kind of empty, futile and false search. This is precisely what was revealed by the fallen angels. In Tertullian's opinion, all *curiositas* was demonic in origin, and he bases his condemnation of all occult knowledge on what he found in *I Enoch.*

What, however, seems to interest Tertullian particularly in *I Enoch* VIII, 1–3 is the revelation to women of the secrets of vanity in dress and behaviour. He deals with this theme in particular in the works in which he quotes *I Enoch* most, the first being the *De cultu feminarum* II, which is really prior in date to the *De cultu* I. In the first place, Tertullian discusses the question of golden jewellery: 'Such jewels are good, not because they are by nature so, but because of their rarity. What is more, the fallen angels, who had already supplied the substances themselves, also introduced the art of working them, so that skill combined with rarity made them precious and the object of women's desires' (II, 10, 2).

After discussing the connection between the fallen angels and jewels and precious stones, Tertullian goes on, still following *I Enoch,* to talk about cosmetics: 'The same angels who revealed the substances and attractions of this kind, that is, gold and precious stones, and who taught (us) to work them, also taught (women), among other things, to paint their eyelids and to colour their cheeks, as Enoch tells us' (II, 10, 3). All these elements can be found in *I Enoch* VIII, 1–3, namely the revelation of the substances themselves, that is, gold and precious stones, and of the materials which make it possible for them to be worked, and finally of the cosmetics.

The whole of what is contained in *I Enoch* VIII, 1–3 is resumed in the *De cultu feminarum,* with certain material added by Tertullian himself: 'The fallen angels disclosed certain materials which had with good reason been hidden, and wrongly revealed most trades to a too uncultivated world, if it is true that they disclosed the work of the mines (VIII, 1), made known the properties of herbs (VII, 1), divulged the virtue of incantations (VII, 1) and manifested every futile study (*curiositas*), even the interpretation of the stars (VIII, 2)' (*De cultu fem.* I, 2, 1). The added elements are, of course, the 'work of the mines', the 'properties of herbs' and the 'incantations'. In Tertullian's block criticism of progress useful crafts and occult arts are all lumped together.

There is a further parallel between Tertullian and *I Enoch* on the subject of female coquetry: 'In particular, they gave women that instrument of feminine vanity – the brilliance of stones which give variety to their necklaces, the gold rings which they wear on their arms, the dyes which enable them to colour their fabrics and the black powder with which they lengthen the corners of their eyes (VIII, 1)' (*De cultu fem.* II, 1, 1). These are almost verbatim quotations from *I Enoch,* with the result that this passage in Tertullian's treatise is one of the earliest testimonies to the pseudepigraphical text.

Tertullian makes the greatest use of this particular passage in *I Enoch,* but he also mentions others, including, for example, that which describes the demons as the souls of giants born of the marriage between the angels and women (XV, 9): 'How certain angels corrupted themselves and how from them was produced a brood of demons yet more corrupt, condemned by God with the authors of their race and that prince whom we have named – all this is made known in the sacred books' (*Apol.* XXII, 3). This is very clearly an allusion to *I Enoch* and it will be noted in this context that Tertullian includes the work among the 'sacred books' or Scriptures.

In his *De idololatria* (IV, 1–3), Tertullian claims that, even before the time of Moses, idolatry was condemned in the book of Enoch. The first part is interesting in itself: 'Enoch foretold that the demons and the spirits of the fallen angels would turn to idolatry all the elements, all that the world contains (*census*) and all that is embraced in heaven, earth and sea, with the result that they would be revered like gods against God' (*De idol.* IV, 2). Tertullian follows this with an exact quotation from *I Enoch*: 'Enoch threatens both those who make and those who worship idols with punishment' (*De idol.* IV, 3), and then cites a passage of some lines, which corresponds to *I Enoch* XCIX, 6.

Tertullian also refers explicitly to *I Enoch* in the *De idololatria* in connection with the deities presiding over the doors in Latin paganism: 'Foreseeing things from the beginning, the Holy Spirit prophesied, through the early prophet Enoch, that even the doors (*ostia*) would become objects of superstition' (*De idol.* XV, 6). What is particularly interesting about this reference is that it both names *Enoch* explicitly as its source and is further evidence of Tertullian's conviction that the pseudepigraphical work was inspired by the Holy Spirit. We are therefore justified in concluding that Tertullian regarded *I Enoch* as scriptural in the strict sense, and that this is the reason for the value he attached to it.

The references to *I Enoch* in the *De idololatria* nonetheless raise a certain difficulty. One of these references, that which occurs in *De idol.* IV, 3, is a literal translation of the Greek text of *I Enoch* XCIX, 6: 'Then Enoch threatens both those who make and those who worship idols with punishment'. This text is, however, preceded by a passage saying that the fallen demons turned men towards idolatry, that is, towards worship of the elements, everything contained in 'heaven, earth and sea' (*De idol.* IV, 2), of which images, that is, idols, are made. Those who make these idols are, Tertullian claims, as guilty as those who worship them (*De idol.* IV, 3). Tertullian attributes all of this teaching to Enoch, but none of it is found in any version that we possess of the text. The same applies to the allusion in *De idol.* XV, 6 to the worship offered at the 'doors' of houses, a reference which Tertullian similarly claims to have found in Enoch.

The only possible parallel that exists in *I Enoch* is the following text: 'The angels who married women will be thrown (into hell) and, taking on many different forms (as demons, sons of angels, and women), their spirits will harass men and lead them astray by persuading them to offer sacrifices to the demons (δαιμονίοις)' (*I Enoch* XIX, 1). This is, however, not in any sense a close parallel, since it contains no explicit reference to the worship of the elements or of idols, but refers only to the worship of the demons. It would therefore seem as though Tertullian was familiar with a Greek text of *I Enoch* which contained a criticism of the cult of the elements. This may have come in the fifth section of the book, from which the quotation that we have identified is borrowed.

Several times in the course of the *De idololatria*, Tertullian mentions the damnation of the fallen angels, a topic treated in *I Enoch* XII–XVI. Thus, in *De idol.* IX, 1, Tertullian affirms that the apostate angels 'were condemned by God' for having revealed the mysteries of astrology. We have already mentioned the passage in his *Apology* (XXII, 3), in which he speaks of the condemnation by God of the fallen angels, their prince, and the demons, their offspring.

Before concluding this section on Tertullian's use of the Jewish apocryphon *I Enoch,* we must discuss a final quotation which raises a special problem. In connection with the resurrection of the body, Tertullian states: *Habes Scripturam: Et mandabo piscibus meis et eructabunt ossa quae sunt comesta et faciam compaginem ad compaginem et os ad os,* 'You have the Scripture: I will command my fishes, and they will belch up the bones that have been eaten and I will put joint to joint and bone to bone' (*De res.* XXXII, 1).

The first part of this text is a fairly free quotation of *Enoch* LXI, 5. The second is a quotation from Ezk. 37:7. The quotation from Ezekiel is a well-known *testimonium*, which is also found in Justin (*I Apol.* LII, 5) and in Irenaeus (*Adv. haer.* V, 15, 1).[12] Sometimes

12. See *Etudes*, pp. 111–121.

it occurs in association with other texts, as a composite quotation, as here in Tertullian's treatise on the resurrection, though this is the only example of its being associated with a text taken from *I Enoch*. The very fact, on the other hand, that this is a composite quotation leads one to suspect that Tertullian found this *testimonium* in precisely this form. If this supposition is true, it means that this particular quotation is of little value to us in our attempt to ascertain what direct knowledge Tertullian had of *I Enoch*. It is, however, a very important indication of the importance of the apocryphal text in the early Latin Christian tradition and of its authority in the Latin Church before the time of Tertullian.

We may conclude from our examination of these various passages that Tertullian was personally acquainted with the book of *Enoch* as a whole. We may go further and say that he probably read it in its Greek translation. Tertullian is therefore in this respect a valuable witness to the history of the text. Moreover, the respect which he shows for the book derives from the fact that, in the Church of his day, it was considered by many to be canonical. This is especially the case in the Western Church.

Tertullian is, moreover, by no means the only witness to the authority of the book of *Enoch* in the Western Church – it is also quoted by Commodian, Minucius Felix, Cyprian and the anonymous author of the *Ad Novatianum*. Minucius speaks briefly about the part played by the demons in the origin of idolatry (*Oct.* XXVI, 8) and Cyprian follows him in this (*Idol.* VI). Cyprian follows Tertullian in mentioning the secrets of female coquetry (*De habit.* 14), but adds certain details which seem to point to a knowledge of the text of *I Enoch* on his own part. Tertullian alone, however, displays an extensive knowledge of the text.

2. The *Book of Adam*

Tertullian seems also on several occasions to have taken another Jewish apocryphon, the *Book of Adam,* as a source. A number of texts which can be connected with an apocryphon of Adam are in existence. There is, for example, a *Life of Adam and*

Eve which has been preserved in a Greek and an Armenian version, each following a clearly different tradition. The first is usually known as the *Apocalypse of Moses* and the second as the *Life of Adam and Eve.* There is also a *Repentance of Adam,* which is mentioned in the Gelasian Decree, and which seems to be the same work under another name. Finally, there is a *Testament of Adam,* which we have in a very fragmentary form in Syriac. All these various elements seem, however, to be fragments of the same work.[13] Jewish and Judaeo-Christian writings were often in fact compilations from different works: *I Enoch* itself is a good example of this. This is the case with the *Book of Adam;* and since Tertullian seems to attest a variety of aspects of the work, his references are of considerable value in any attempt to reconstruct it.

This apocryphon of Adam is midrashic in character, and is related to the *Book of Jubilees.* It is very different in type from some apocalyptic speculations about Adam, of which we have an echo in Philo of Alexandria, and which are related to the apocalyptic exegesis of the first chapters of *Genesis.* The *Book of Adam* is, on the contrary, a very literal account, very far removed from the kind of speculation that is found, for example, in the *De montibus.* It is quite possible that some of Tertullian's themes, especially those of Adam as fashioned from the virgin soil of paradise, of the angel's jealousy with regard to Adam, and of Cain as conceived by the sexual union of the serpent and the woman, come from this tradition; though it should be noted that they occur also in Irenaeus.

Tertullian's first allusion to Adam occurs at the end of his *De paenitentia,* the last sentence of which reads: 'The one who is the origin both of the human race and of man's faithlessness to God, Adam, having been restored to his paradise by confession (*exomologesi*), is not silent' (*De paen.* XII, 9). Tertullian is speaking here of a confession made by Adam of his sins, an incident which features in the *Apocalypse of Moses* (**XXVII**, 2, 7). Adam's

13. See A. DENIS, *Introduction aux pseudépigraphes grecs d'Ancien Testament,* pp. 3–14; H. HENGEL, *Pseudepigrapha,* I (*Entretiens sur l'Ancien Antiquité classique,* XVIII), p. 272.

penitence brings about his restoration to *his* paradise, that is to say, the earthly paradise. This is different from the paradise of which Tertullian speaks in most other contexts, namely the eschatological paradise which he identifies with heaven. It would therefore seem that he is here reproducing a tradition which is not in accordance with his own thought.

This theme is developed at greater length in the *Adversus Marcionem*, in which Tertullian interprets God's word to Adam, 'Where are you?' (Gn. 3:9) as a summons rather than as a question: 'The one in hiding through consciousness of sin should be summoned to come out into God's presence by the mere calling of his name, but along with some rebuke ... and in a case which allowed either of denial or of admission, he gave him the opportunity of willingly confessing his sin and on that account making it less grievous' (*Adv. Marc.* II, 25, 1, 3). Tertullian thus presents God in this passage as a father who is ready to forgive and Adam as a model of the truly penitent believer.

The text of the *Adversus Marcionem* goes on: 'If, because of the order of the law, Adam had been handed over to death, his hope was nonetheless preserved, the Lord saying to him: "See, Adam has been made like one of us" – this referring to man's sharing in the deity in the future. And what follows is: *Et nunc, ne quando extendat manum et sumat de ligno vitae et vivat in aevum* ("And now, lest he stretch out his hand and take of the tree of life and live for ever"). By the addition of *et nunc,* which points to the present, he shows that it is only for a time and for the present that he holds back life from him. In this way, he does not curse Adam himself or Eve, both of whom are candidates for restoration and are raised up by their confession' (*Adv. Marc.* II, 25, 4).

Here, once again, we find the themes of Adam's penance, his death and the proclamation of his return to paradise. We may, however, go further and say that this passage in Tertullian's treatise contains a very striking exegesis of Gn. 3:22, in which the commandment against eating the fruit of the tree is presented as purely provisional, and the text becomes a prophecy of the restoration of Adam to paradise in the future. This same exegesis can also be found in almost exactly the same form in the *Apocalypse of Moses* (XXVIII, 3), with the same emphasis placed on the word 'now' as an indication of the provisional nature of the prohibition: 'You will not take any now; when, however, the resurrection comes, I will give you access to the tree of life'. There can be no doubt that Tertullian was drawing here on the *Apocalypse of Moses*.

The same theme also occurs in the *De resurrectione mortuorum,* in which the sentence *Terra es et in terram ibis,* 'You are earth and you will go to earth' (Gn. 3:19) is discussed. Tertullian suggests various interpretations and concludes: 'Even if someone is bold enough to interpret the word "earth" as the holy earth of paradise, and to understand it to refer to the protoplasts, Adam and Eve, then it is the restoration of paradise which would appear to be promised to the flesh which had received it to keep and cultivate it, so that man would be recalled to the place from which he had been expelled' (*De res.* XXVI, 14). What is particularly noteworthy in this interpretation is that Tertullian calls it 'someone's boldness' and does not claim it as his own. Once again, the exegesis is also found in the *Apocalypse of Moses* (XLI, 2), where the return to the earth is interpreted as the resurrection. A similar type of interpretation, in this case of the continuation in the world of the elements of which Adam's body had been composed and of their restoration at the resurrection, is also found later in the same treatise. Tertullian writes: 'It is in this flesh that Adam will again be made present to hear the Lord say: "See, Adam has been made like one of us, really capable of evil, from which he has escaped, and of good, into which he has entered" ' (*De res.* LXI, 1).

Another group of unusual texts dealing with prayer may be connected with a form of the same apocryphon. The first example is the last sentence in the *De oratione,* in which Tertullian discusses the prayer of the animals: *Orant angeli omnes, orat omnis creatura,* ('All the angels pray and every creature prays'). Tertullian continues: 'The animals and the wild beasts bend their knees and leave their byres and their lairs to raise their eyes to heaven, not without uttering sounds and making their breath heard in their own way. And the birds, now (*nunc*) as they rise, turn towards heaven and form a cross with their wings like hands, saying something that seems like a prayer' (*De orat.*

XXIX, 4). The word *nunc* seems to be an allusion to morning prayer at sunrise.

This theme of the prayer of the animals linked with that of the angels is found in several places in the apocryphal writings which deal with the Adam cycle. In the *Life of Adam and Eve,* for instance, we read: 'Then the angels came together and all the animals and they prayed for Adam' (IX, 1). The order is exactly the same as in Tertullian's text. Closely related to this is a *horarium* which has been preserved in several versions and is connected with a *Testament of Adam* and which describes the prayer of the angels, of the animals and of the birds (*Patr. Syr.* II, col. 1325). It would in fact seem as though the theme of the prayer of the animals is connected with the Adam cycle, because Adam is connected with the animals in the book of Genesis, and at the same time with the theme of paradise. Tertullian, however, does not simply reproduce this theme — his comparison between the birds' wings and men's hands stretched out in prayer and the allusion to the cross are clearly Christian.

Chadwick was of the opinion that this apocryphon was the source of the theme of the silent prayer of creation as a whole in the middle of the night, a theme which occurs in the *Didascalia of the Apostles,* 26. It is also, in his view, the origin of the midnight prayers, mentioned by Tertullian in *De oratione* XI.[14] One of the features of this apocryphon is that it lays down the hours of prayer for every category of creature. Of all these hours, midnight possessed a particular fascination, as Chadwick notes, because it was the moment of silence separating one day from the next. This theme of the religious silence of creation at midnight is also found in a passage in the *Gospel of James* (XVIII, 2) which has recently been examined by de Nola[15] in relation to the birth of Christ. This theme again takes us back to the second century.

One last passage in Tertullian's work can be linked with the *Book of Adam,* in which, as we have seen, the angels occupy a

---

14. 'Prayer at Midnight', *Epectasis* (Mélanges Daniélou), pp. 47–49.

15. ALFONSO M. DE NOLA, *Il motivo della suspensione della vita cosmica come problema di relazioni interreligiose,* Milan, 1970; see also ALLEN CABANIS, *Liturgy and Literature,* 1970, pp. 53–56.

significant place. Writing about the devil and quoting Ezk. 28:16, Tertullian says: '"In the delights of the paradise of your God you were born" – there, he means, where, in the second creation, under the figure of animals God made the angels' (*Adv. Marc.* II, 10, 3). This is obviously an allusion to Gn. 2:18: 'From the soil Yahweh God fashioned all the wild beasts and all the birds of heaven'. This is the 'second fashioning' to which Tertullian is referring, the first being that of Gn. 1:24. He believed that the second fashioning was that of the angels, something that can be explained if it is remembered that the serpent was called 'the most subtle of all the wild beasts' made in this fashioning.

This fits in with the theme of the angel's jealousy of man as the source of the angel's sin, which is elaborated by Tertullian in the same passage (*Adv. Marc.* II, 10, 4), and which occurs also in the work of Irenaeus and Athenagoras. Now, it is precisely this idea which is found in the *Life of Adam and Eve* (XIV, 1–3). This work is thus its most probable source. This is interesting as showing that this apocalypse was known to Christians in the second century, and therefore that Tertullian is not the only witness to its popularity in Christian circles. It is also a reason for believing that Tertullian borrowed the themes of the creation of the angels in paradise, and of the fall of the 'most subtle' of them, from this same apocalyptic work.

The *Apocalypse of Adam* is also mentioned by a copyist in the margin in connection with a *testimonium* quoted in the *Epistle of Barnabas* II, 10: 'A broken heart is a sacrifice for God, an odour of sweetness for the Lord is a heart which gives glory to the one who has made it (τὸν πεπλακότα)'. The first part of this *testimonium* is a quotation from Ps. 51:17. The second part, however, is not scriptural, so that this is a *testimonium* of the composite kind that was so common at this period. In his marginal note, the copyist connects this composite *testimonium* with the *Apocalypse of Adam*. James, who has studied the question in some detail, notes on the one hand that the text fits Adam very well, with its reference to the πλάσμα, and on the other that it is quite in place in the mouth of a forgiven sinner. He has therefore suggested that this quotation reflects the fact that the *Apocalypse of Adam* was the story of Adam's repentance.

This *testimonium* is also found in various forms in other second century documents, especially in the works of Clement of Alexandria (*Paedag.* III, 12. 90, 4; *Stromat.* II, 18. 79, 1; IV, 5. 19, 2) and in Irenaeus (*Adv. haer.* IV, 29). But it is also to be found in Tertullian, who uses it in a shortened form consisting of the first part only, that is, of the quotation of Ps. 51:17: *Cor contritum et humiliatum hostia Deo est,* 'A bruised and lowly heart is a sacrifice to God' (*Adv. Jud.* V, 5). This first part of the *testimonium*, however, is very similar to the text in the *Epistle of Barnabas* (although Tertullian adds *humiliatum*), in that the quotation from Ps. 51:17a, Θυσία τῷ Θεῷ is merged together with that from Ps. 51:17b, καρδία συντετριμμένη. It is therefore possible that Tertullian, in quoting the text from the *Apocalypse of Adam,* retained only the biblical element and excluded the non-biblical part, since this would have been completely in accordance with his normal practice of restoring the *testimonia* to their originally biblical form.

3. The *Sibylline Oracles III*

The *Sibylline Oracles* are similar to *I Enoch* in that Tertullian recognised them as authoritative because of their antiquity. He states this explicitly in the *Ad nationes:* 'I shall not overlook the important evidence contained in the divine letters, which are worthy of faith because of their great antiquity. For the Sibyl is older than all your literature, that Sibyl who was a prophetess of the true God' (*Ad nat.* II, 12, 35). It would seem that what Tertullian is referring to here is the Jewish tradition, according to which the first Sibyl was Noah's daughter (*Sib.* III, 827). He believed that the pagans had usurped the Sibyl's name in order to apply it to their own oracles: 'You have covered with her name the words of the prophets of the demons' (*Ad nat.* II, 12, 25).

The *Sibylline Oracles* had been quoted frequently by early Christian authors before the time of Tertullian. Quite long passages occur in the work of Theophilus of Antioch and, among the early Latin Christians, Commodian quotes them, which points to the possible existence of a Latin translation. For all these writers the Sibyl, like the book of *Enoch,* belonged to a genre of sacred literature which was both ancient and authoritative. The link between authority and antiquity is a common theme of Greek and pagan culture at this time, as Tertullian himself bears witness in his *Apology* (XIX, 1). He himself was to quote Hermes Trismegistus as an author who, he believed, expressed a very ancient pagan wisdom, and to recall that he was regarded by many as the author of Plato's ἀρχαῖα λόγια.

Tertullian quotes the *Sibylline Oracles* three times. The first reference occurs in his *Ad nationes,* in connection with his attempt to demonstrate the human origin of Saturn, his *census* (*Ad. nat.* II, 12, 2). After having brought forward a variety of evidence from pagan sources, Tertullian speaks of the testimony of the Sibyl: 'In different verses, she speaks in the same way of the cradle and of the affairs of Saturn, saying that, in the tenth generation after the flood came upon the men of old, Saturn reigned, with Titan and Japheth, the mighty sons of heaven and of earth' (*Ad nat.* II, 12, 36). This is, of course a quotation from *Sib.* III, 108–111. Tertullian believed that the testimony provided by the Sibyl was valuable because it was close to the events reported: 'If we can put any faith either in your writers or in writings earlier than theirs, and for that reason all the closer to the events themselves because they are of the same period, then we may regard it as proven that Saturn was a man' (*Ad nat.* II, 12, 37).

Tertullian's second reference to the *Sibyllines* is in the *Apologeticum.* Here, in the text transmitted by the Fulda MS, which would seem to be a first draft, he returns to the same question. The wording of the relevant passage is in fact very close to that in the *Ad nationes,* the authority of the Sibyl being presented in much the same terms: 'You too, I think, have a Sibyl, inasmuch as this name, belonging to a true prophetess, has on various occasions been improperly extended to cover others who seemed to prophesy. This is the case with the name of your Sibyl, who is deceitful concerning the truth, like your gods' (*Apol.* XIX, 10). What Tertullian is stressing here is that the true Sibyl is the Jewish Sibyl. In the second edition of the same treatise, however, he cut out the reference to the Sibyl, no doubt because the data presented in it were not in accordance with those provided by the Roman historians on whom he was relying, and perhaps also because he wanted to confine himself to the authority of Moses.

There is a third explicit reference to the *Sibylline Oracles* in the *De pallio*. Wishing to show how everything changes in the world, he cites the example that there was a time when the sea covered everything: 'Even now, it is possible to see shells and molluscs that have strayed on to the mountains, trying to testify, with Plato, that even the high places were submerged. The universe, however, on re-emerging, once again changed its form. Now its appearance changes locally – when a site is destroyed, when, among the islands, Delos is made invisible and Samos becomes sandy – the Sibyl does not lie – when a land equal to Africa or to Asia is sought in the Atlantic or when remainders are seen in Sicily of what was once a side of Italy separated from it by the waves of the Adriatic and the Tyrrhenian seas' (II, 3).

This is a quotation from *Sib.* III, 263, although the text also contains allusions to Plato. Tertullian is not trying to prove a point here, but is quoting the Sibyl simply as a sign of his erudition, and the interesting thing to note is that she forms part of his general cultural background. In the same work he shows a knowledge of Josephus (*Apol.* XVIII, 7; XIX, 6), but there is no reference to Philo. This all points to a familiarity on his part with Hellenistic Jewish literature. We may go further and note that the Sibylline book that he knows best is the Jewish Sibylline, namely Book III. He does not refer to the Christian Sibyllines, some of which undoubtedly existed at his time. This is further evidence of his interest in inter-testamental Judaism, but not in Judaeo-Christianity.

Another Latin Christian author who was acquainted with the writings of Josephus was Minucius Felix, who refers explicitly to him (*Oct.* XXXIII, 4). Minucius also knew a Jewish apology which was used in the *Clementines,* as Quispel has pointed out. He does not, however, name the *Sibylline Oracles* at any point and does not appear to have borrowed at all from them. In the debate about the relative dating of Tertullian and Minucius, this would seem to point to the fact that Tertullian is the later. With regard to Saturn, Tertullian cites the same authorities as Minucius, but adds data taken from the *Sibyllines* and discusses these at considerable length. An interest in the Sibyllines is therefore a feature specific to Tertullian's writing.

Apart from quoting from these three Jewish books, *I Enoch*, the *Book of Adam* and the *Sibylline Oracles* III, Tertullian borrowed very rarely in his writing from Jewish apocryphal literature. Delcor has pointed out that the description of Job which Tertullian gives in the *De patientia* XIII, 8 includes certain characteristics which are not in any sense biblical, but which are found in the *Testament of Job*.[16] This is a possible borrowing, but not an important one, since it is only a question of realistic details. Quotations such as *Peperit et non peperit*, which is taken from the *Apocryphon of Ezechiel* (*De carne* XXIII, 2–6), or the application of Jacob's prophecy regarding Benjamin to Paul, *lupus rapax*, 'the ravening wolf' (*Adv. Marc.* V. 1, 5), which comes from the *Testaments of the XII Patriarchs*, do not necessarily mean that Tertullian knew these works. The most that we can say is that they formed part of the tradition of widely known *testimonia* and that Tertullian was consequently acquainted with them.

3. TERTULLIAN AND TRADITION

The various doctrines against which Tertullian reacted so strongly – speculations about the angels, an esoteric interpretation of the parables and so on – can be traced back to Judaeo-Christian gnosis, which in turn was derived from Jewish apocalyptic. This gnosis had both orthodox and heterodox forms and its existence is clearly attested both by the work of a Papias or a Clement and by the various fragments that have been directly preserved. It was claimed that this gnosis had apostolic origins and that it represented the secret teaching imparted by Christ after his resurrection. It was not to be proclaimed indiscriminately to all Christians, but only to those who were capable of hearing it. There were certain differences concerning the content of this

---

16. M. DELCOR, 'Le Testament de Job, la Prière de Nabonide et les traditions talmudiques', *Bibel und Qumran (Mélanges Bardtke)*, pp. 57–74.

gnostic teaching, but the principle behind it was universally accepted.

Tertullian explicitly opposed this conception in his *De praescriptione,* arguing vehemently against the thesis that there was, in addition to the accepted Christian tradition, an esoteric tradition which was concerned with more exalted doctrines dealing with the abodes of heaven and hell, the names of the angels and the eschatological realities. This is, of course, the thesis that is contained in the heterodox gnoses such as the *Apocryphon of John* and also in works which are in no way heretical, such as the *Epistle of the Apostles* and the *Apocalypse of Paul,* discovered at Nag Hammadi.

In the *De praescriptione* Tertullian calls both the members of the Church and the heretics to account with regard to the apostolic and the gnostic traditions (*De praescr.* VIII, 1). He is questioning the attitude of both when he says: 'Sometimes they say that the apostles did not know everything. Then they change their ground and say that, while the apostles indeed knew everything, they did not hand everything on to everybody' (**XXII**, 2). Tertullian then goes on to comment: 'Both suggestions are the product of the same demented state of mind, and in both they are exposing Christ to blame for sending out apostles who were either inadequately instructed or not sufficiently straightforward'.

Clearly, then, he rejects both arguments: 'Who in his senses can believe that the men whom the Lord gave to be teachers were ignorant of anything? For he kept them in his company, taught them and lived with them inseparably. He used to explain all difficulties to them privately, saying that they were permitted to know secrets which the people were not allowed to understand, (**XXII**, 3). After his resurrection, did not Christ expound the Scriptures to his disciples, Tertullian argues, and did he not promise that the Holy Spirit would lead them into all the truth? That promise was fulfilled at Pentecost. What is, however, particularly interesting in this context is that those whose teaching Tertullian opposed did not accept the *Acts of the Apostles* as a canonical work.

A further argument put forward by those whose teaching was

rejected by Tertullian is that the apostles' knowledge was at the most imperfect, since Paul criticised Peter and the other apostles: 'That proves that something was lacking, they say. Thus they hope to build up their argument that a fuller knowledge could have supervened later on, such as came to Paul when he reproved his predecessors' (**XXIII, 2**). Tertullian, however, who takes this to be an allusion to the incident in Ga. 1, goes on: 'How can their point that Peter was reproved by Paul prove that Paul introduced a new form of gospel, different from that which Peter and the rest put out before him?' (**XXIII, 5**).

But, say the other side, 'Was not Paul caught up to the third heaven and borne to paradise, and there heard certain things?' To this, Tertullian replies, 'But they were things which could not possibly equip him to preach a different doctrine, since by their nature they must not be communicated to any human being . . . But then either Paul is guilty of betraying the secret or else they must show that someone else was caught up into paradise after Paul, someone who was permitted to utter what Paul was not allowed to utter' (**XXIV, 6**). Tertullian's opponents here are clearly using 2 Co. 12 as a justification for the Judaeo-Christian apocalyptic conception of hidden secrets of the heavenly world coming from the apostles and forming an esoteric body of teaching separate from the common tradition.

Tertullian now turns to the second hypothesis, according to which the apostles were the recipients of a secret tradition which they communicated to only a few people. According to this view, then, there were two different levels at which the Church existed, both linked to the apostles – the level of the simple believers, who were given an elementary knowledge, and that of the initiated, who received the fullness of knowledge. Tertullian is referring to this teaching when he says, in the *De praescriptione:* 'It is just as demented to allow that the apostles were in no respect ignorant and did not differ in their preaching, and yet to have it that they did not reveal everything to all alike, but entrusted some things openly to all and some things secretly to a few' (**XXV, 1**). The reference is to the deposit entrusted to Timothy. Tertullian is here criticising the attitude of the gnostic heretics, but the criticism could equally well be applied to orthodox gnostic teaching, in other words, to Judaeo-Christian apocalyptic writing, of the kind referred to by Clement of Alexandria at the same period.

Tertullian's reply to these false teachers is that the saying about the deposit entrusted to Timothy does not imply in any sense esoteric doctrine (*remotior doctrina*), but is rather a commandment to hand on intact the apostolic teaching. There is, he claims, no other doctrine handed down by the apostles other than the teaching that they proclaimed publicly. It is therefore evident that Tertullian was not here discussing simply a heretical gnosis, the content of which was different from that of the common faith, but an esoteric knowledge of a more exalted kind that was hidden from the majority and imparted only to a few. Since Tertullian was certainly not acquainted with the works of Clement of Alexandria, the esoteric teaching that he had in mind could not have been simply that of Clement. It must have been esoteric teaching in general, in other words, the kind that is largely identified with apocalyptic writing.

It is clear that the teachings that Tertullian has primarily in mind in his *De praescriptione* are those of Valentinus and Apelles, since he mentions these explicitly. He does not, however, reject these teachings simply as heretical – he repudiates them also because they allege the existence of an esoteric tradition alongside the one shared by all. It is, in other words, not only heretical but also Judaeo-Christian teaching, of the kind accepted by the Church of Alexandria, that Tertullian refuses to accept. He is therefore reacting not only against heretical gnosticism but also against Judaeo-Christian gnosis.

Tertullian was less concerned in the *De praescriptione* to refute one particular heresy than to search for a criterion which would allow him to judge between what is in accordance with faith and what is not. Scripture as such could not be used to this end, since all the heretics claimed that their teaching was based on it, the Marcionites comparing the Old and the New Testaments and using this as the basis for their teaching, and the Valentinians claiming that they possessed the key to an authentic interpretation of the Bible. What Tertullian had therefore to do was to discover if there was in fact any criterion by which these different interpretations of Scripture could be discerned. A purely intrinsic criterion was difficult to apply and Tertullian himself believed that a spiritual as well as a literal exegesis was necessary. What had to be found, then, was a previously existing principle or *praescriptio*.

The origins of the use of the word *praescriptio* by our author have been discussed frequently and at length, and J. C. Frédouille, who is the scholar who has most recently devoted his attention to this question, has summarised these origins and has examined in detail the ways in which Tertullian employs the word.[17] His main conclusion is that the origin of Tertullian's use of *praescriptio* is not to be found in legal terminology. This is very much in accordance with the conclusions drawn by Barnes, who has disputed the traditional view that Tertullian had received a sound legal training.[18] In the Latin of Tertullian's time, the word *praescriptio* had, broadly speaking, two possible meanings. In the first place, the purely etymological meaning of preface or information given in advance soon acquired a more precise technical value in juridical language, so that the word came to mean the title of a law or a previous reference. In the second place, *praescriptio* was frequently used, by Tertullian and by other authors of the same period, to mean a precept, a rule or a law.[19] Tertullian was, of course, notoriously free in his use of words, and he evolved from *praescriptio* a personal neologism by making these two meanings overlap and combining in the one word the *praescriptio* of the orators of the first century A.D., who used it in the sense of 'objection' and the *praescriptio* of the ordinary language of the period, in which it was used with the meaning of 'precept'.[20] His purpose was to find the irrefutable principle

---

17. J. C. FREDOUILLE, *Tertullian et la Conversion de la Culture Antique*, Paris, 1972, pp. 195–234.

18. Cf. T. D. BARNES, *Tertullian*, pp. 22–29. Barnes himself, however, does accept a technical legal background to Tertullian's use of the term *praescriptio*: 'Tertullian has cast a whole treatise into the form of a legal simile. To paraphrase his own words, he applies for an injunction to restrain any heretic from trespassing upon holy Scripture, which is the sole property of Christians' (*ibid.*, p. 64).

19. FREDOUILLE, *op. cit.*, p. 232.

20. *Ibid.*, p. 233.

on the basis of which a conclusion had to be drawn.[21]

Tertullian deals with this question of the need for a *praescriptio* in order to judge between different interpretations of Scripture in a series of steps. His point of departure is that a pure reference to Scripture is not enough, because everyone claims to base his argument on it. He therefore states: 'It follows that we must not appeal to Scripture . . . One point should be decided first . . . namely, who hold the faith to which the Bible belongs and from whom, through whom, when and to whom was the teaching delivered by which men became Christians? For only when the true Christian teaching and faith are evident will the true Scriptures, the true interpretations and all the true Christian traditions be found' (XIX, 1). He thus sets out in order the points that he proposes to discuss – the origin of faith, the handing on of that faith, the time that it was transmitted and those who accept it. What he does, in other words, is to use a historical rather than a logical argument to connect the faith of Christians in his own period to the principle and foundation of that faith.

In answer to the first question, Tertullian states that the origin is Christ. This is a fact which everyone accepts. 'What he was and what he had been, how he was fulfilling his Father's will . . .', Tertullian continues, he declared principally to 'the disciples, twelve of whom he had especially attached to his person and destined to be the teachers of the nations' (XX, 2). It was these apostles, Tertullian insists, who were sent officially to teach the nations. They began by 'bearing witness to their faith and founding churches' in Judaea and then went out into the whole world. The Christian faith began, then, with these early 'apostolic' churches and was handed on by them to the other churches. This work of handing on the apostolic tradition continues, the authenticity of the faith being guaranteed by this link with the apostolic churches. Tertullian bases this on the principle of the *census: Omne genus ad originem suam censeatur necesse est,* 'Things of every kind must be classified according to their origin' (XX, 7).

21. *Ibid.*, pp. 208–211.

This brings Tertullian to his first *praescriptio* (Frédouille has observed that this is the first time that the word appears in the treatise): 'On this ground we base our "prescription". If the Lord Christ Jesus sent the apostles to preach . . . I shall "prescribe" now that what they preached should be proved only through the identical churches which the apostles established by preaching to them both viva voce and afterwards by letters. If this is so, it follows that all doctrine which is in agreement with these apostolic churches . . . is to be deemed true on the ground that it preserves what the churches received from the apostles . . . It remains for me to show whether this doctrine of ours, the rule of which I have set out above, does originate in the tradition of the apostles (*de apostolorum traditione censeatur*)' (**XXI**, 6). Like Irenaeus, Tertullian defines tradition as that which derives from the teaching of the apostles.

What, then, is this apostolic tradition? This question is important, since the gnostics also claimed that their teaching was derived from the apostles. The whole question is therefore connected with the one which we mentioned earlier in this section, that of the secret doctrines. Tertullian himself speaks of the oral tradition, but this was, in his opinion, essentially part of the tradition preserved in the apostolic churches. He could not accept that the apostles had taught a doctrine that was different from that taught by the churches. The apostles may have communicated more of the one Christian teaching at one time and less at another, but there was one teaching and its content was the same throughout (**XXVI**, 9–10).

But even if it is established that the apostles taught 'the whole content of the rule to all' (**XXVII**, 1), is it equally certain that the churches preserved the apostles' teaching intact? Here Tertullian touches on the basic question of the authority of the churches in relation to that of the apostles and his answer is to refer to the Holy Spirit present in the churches: 'Suppose the Holy Spirit had no regard for any church . . . Suppose the steward (*vilicus*) of God, the vicar (*vicarius*) of Christ, neglected his office!' (**XXVIII**, 2). In this way, he stresses the presence of a divine authority in the churches which are linked to the apostolic tradition, the only authority of the heretical groups being that of their founders.

Tertullian frequently drew attention to the fact that the Church was not a purely human institution, but the instrument of the Spirit, whom he described, in his treatise against Marcion, as the 'wise master-builder' who builds the Church (*Adv. Marc.* III, 23, 21).

A further argument in favour of the apostolic tradition, in Tertullian's opinion, is that from the unanimity of the Church: *Quod apud multos unum invenitur non est erratum, sed traditum*, 'What is found among many in one form is not error, but tradition' (*De praescr.* XXVIII, 3). Indeed, unity in a common faith among all the churches is a criterion of the presence of the apostolic tradition. Whereas different doctrines are taught by each heretical body, the one faith professed by all the churches bears the mark of apostolicity. We may note, in passing, that, although he is dealing with an essential question here in plain language, Tertullian elsewhere uses biblical images when he discusses the unity of the Church. The images of the bride, of paradise and of the house, all of which express a profound theological truth, were employed by Tertullian long before they were used by Cyprian.

Finally, Tertullian emphasises above all the need for authority: 'However error arose, it reigned, I suppose, as long as there were no heresies. Truth was waiting for a Marcionite or a Valentinian to set her free! Meanwhile, everything was done wrong – the preaching of the gospel, the acceptance of the creed, the thousands upon thousands of baptisms, the works of faith, the miracles, . . . even the martyrs were wrongly crowned . . . But was heresy before true doctrine? The real thing always exists before the representation of it; the copy comes later. It would be quite absurd that heresy should be taken for true doctrine!' (XXIX, 2–4).

This *praescriptio* would certainly seem to be the one which Tertullian regarded as the most important of all, since, as Frédouille has observed, he refers to it again and again in his later works. [22] It also forms a link between his argument and the general principle of the *census*, to which we shall return later. [23]

---

22. J. C. FREDOUILLE, *op. cit.*, p. 430.
23. See Tertullian, *Apol.* LXIX, 10 and *Adv. Marc.* IV, 5, 1: *Id verius quod prius,*

The arguments which Tertullian puts forward in favour of the tradition of the Church and against the gnostic tradition are, of course, not his own. They are all to be found in the work of Irenaeus, on whom Tertullian drew freely in his attempts to refute gnosticism. Apostolicity as a criterion of faith, the tradition of the apostles continuing in the churches that they founded, the presence of the Holy Spirit in the Church, the unity of faith and the fact that orthodoxy came before heresy, all these arguments are to be found in Irenaeus. All that Tertullian in fact does is to bring them all together in the space of a few paragraphs and to present them more systematically and more rigorously. In passing, it may be noted that he makes no explicit reference to the special part played by the bishops in the authentic handing on of the apostolic tradition, at least in the *De praescriptione*. He does, however, refer explicitly to this in his treatise against Marcion: 'The succession of bishops (in Asia), when traced back (*recensus*) to its origin, will be found to rest in John as originator' (*Adv. Marc.* IV, 5, 2).

There can be no doubt that, in his defence of the apostolic tradition, Tertullian had above all the heterodox gnostic sects in mind. As we have seen, however, he deals with this gnosis in its essential aspect of a framework of speculations derived from Judaeo-Christian apocalyptic writing. This is stressed in the first part of the *De praescriptione*, in which Tertullian discusses these speculations as such and not exclusively as heretical speculations, as *curiositas* and not simply as *scrupulositas*. In the early part of his treatise, he writes: 'I come, then, to the point which members of the Church adduce to justify speculation (*curiositas*) and which heretics press in order to import scruple and hesitation (*scrupulositas*). It is written, they say: "Seek and you shall find" ' (*De praescr.* VIII, 1).

Numerous attempts were made in the second century to interpret this verse (Mt. 7:7; Lk. 11:9). It is absolutely correct that the heretics used it to introduce their teaching. Irenaeus mentions it several times (*Adv. haer.* II, 13, 30; 18, 3 and 6; 30, 2); but the

---

id prius quod est ab origine, 'What is earlier is truer and what is from the beginning is earlier'.

final proof is supplied by the *Gospel of Thomas,* the leit-motiv of which is Mt. 7:7. Logion 3 says: 'Jesus said: may he not cease, he who seeks, to seek until he has found and, when he has found, he will be deeply troubled'; and logion 92 says: 'Seek and you will find. But what you have asked me in these days it now pleases me to say and you will not seek'. It is clear, then, that a gnostic interpretation is given to the text 'seek and you shall find', since the one who must seek is interpreted as the ordinary believer, who will find when he has gnosis. The verse is, however, also found in the writings of members of the Great Church, who use it to justify their own researches. A particularly good example of this is Clement of Alexandria.[24]

Tertullian opposes both groups. The principle that he insists on is that search is meaningful for the one who has not found, but not for the one who has already found. The words 'Seek and you shall find' are addressed, Tertullian claims, to the Jews or the pagans, but not to Christians: 'You must seek until you find and, when you find, you must believe. Then you have simply to keep what you have come to believe' (IX, 4). Christ's teaching is the end of our search, beyond which there is nothing: 'There is, then, nothing more to seek. Otherwise, what end will there be to seeking?' (X, 6). Not to cease seeking when one has found is a sign that one lacks discipline.

What one must do, therefore, is to hold fast to the *regula fidei,* or 'rule of faith', which Tertullian expounds. According to this, 'we believe that there is but one God, ... who produced everything from nothing through his word ...; that this Word is called his Son and ... was seen in different ways by the patriarchs, was always being heard in the prophets and was finally brought down by the Spirit and the power of God the Father into the virgin Mary, was made flesh in her womb, was born of her and lived as Jesus Christ; who thereafter proclaimed a new law and a new promise of the kingdom, worked miracles, was crucified, on the third day rose again, was caught up into heaven and sat at the right hand of the Father; that he sent in his place the

24. J. DANIELOU, 'Recherche et Tradition chez les Pères du II et III᷾ siècles'. *NRT,* 104 (1972), pp. 453–457.

power of the Holy Spirit to guide believers; that he will come with glory to take the saints up into the fruition of eternal life and the heavenly promises and to judge the wicked to everlasting fire, after the resurrection of both good and evil with the restoration of their flesh' (XIII, 1–6).

This is a particularly valuable text because it provides us with the full content of the 'rule of faith' at the time of Tertullian. It is in fact a summary of the Christian catechetic tradition which came from the apostles and which was handed down by the churches. All that was required of the Christian was that he should adhere to and believe in this traditional rule of faith. Tertullian does not condemn discussion around the rule of faith; he only repudiates what goes contrary to that rule. Nevertheless, he does not conceal his distrust of such speculations: 'Provided the essence of the rule is not disturbed, you may seek and discuss as much as you like. You may give full rein to your itching curiosity (*libidinem curiositatis*) . . . But these exercises come from curiosity and they glory in their virtuosity. In the last resort, it is better to remain ignorant, for fear that you come to know what you should not know. For you do know what you should know . . . Let curiosity give place to faith and vainglory to salvation' (XIV, 1–5).

Clearly, Tertullian is not speaking about heretics here, but about faithful members of the Church. He does not condemn them, but it is obvious that he is very suspicious of such speculative researches, which are the result of what he calls *curiositas*. We have already encountered this word when we were considering Tertullian's attitude towards the Jewish apocrypha and in particular towards the book of *Enoch*. Frédouille has also provided a sound analysis of Tertullian's use of the term *curiositas*, pointing out that he took it from the philosophical tradition. In employing the word, then, he was not condemning intellectual activity as such, but intellectual activity which was concerned with 'curious' and not with vital questions. In pointing out this aspect of Tertullian's use of the word *curiositas*, Frédouille has thus to a great extent resolved the apparent dilemma between Tertullian's learning and intellectual power on the one hand and his condemnation of idle *curiositas* on the other. The contradiction is not real, but only apparent, because the word does not apply to rational, intellectual enquiry about essential matters.[25]

For Tertullian, the supremely typical expression of *curiositas* is gnosis. Referring to 1 Tm. 1:4, he writes: *Hinc illae fabulae et genealogiae interminabiles et quaestiones infructuosae a quibus apostolus refrenat,* 'From this come those fables and endless genealogies and fruitless questionings, from which the apostle holds us back' (*De praescr.* VII, 7). The same allusion to 1 Tm. 1:4 occurs in *Adv. Marc.* I, 4: *Et ibitur in illas iam indeterminabiles quaestiones, quas apostolus non amat,* 'And we will run into those interminable discussions of which the apostle disapproves',[26] and in the *Adversus Valentinianos: Iam et cum genealogias indeterminatas nominet,* 'And when he lists these interminable genealogies' (*Adv. Val. 3*). It is clear from the term γενεαλογίας ἀπεράντους that Paul is referring in 1 Tm. 1:4 to Judaeo-Christian speculations especially about the world of the angels. Here too, then, it is not heresy in the strict sense of the word that is under fire.

In the context of the *De praescriptione,* however, it is Greek philosophy that is being attacked by Tertullian, who is above all concerned with the use that his fellow-Christians were making of Greek thought. This is fundamentally what is meant by *curiositas.* As Waszink has pointed out, however, Tertullian is emphasising here 'the relations existing between heresy and philosophy'.[27] What is in the background here is Tertullian's theory that gnosis originated in Greek philosophy, a view which he elaborates in *De anima* 3.

This is, however, just a polemical theory, not a historical fact. Historically, gnosis undoubtedly originated in Judaeo-Christianity, both in its orthodox and in its heterodox forms, so that the *curiositas* which Tertullian is criticising in his treatise is in fact Judaeo-Christian gnosis. In attacking this *curiositas,* therefore, in the teaching of orthodox Christians – he speaks of *scrupulositas* in the case of the heretics – he is in the last resort questioning Judaeo-Christian gnosis.

25. J. C. FREDOUILLE, *op. cit.,* pp. 412–426.
26. For the meaning of the term *indeterminatae quaestiones,* see WASZINK, *op. cit.,* pp. 113–114.
27. See WASZINK, *op. cit.,* p. 113.

This is in itself important, since it shows how different Tertullian was in this respect from his contemporaries in the Church of Alexandria, especially Clement and Origen, who were to condemn gnosticism, but to some extent to assimilate Judaeo-Christian gnosis. This involved certain risks, but it gave their thinking a contemplative dimension which was to persist in Greek Christianity. By contrast, Tertullian's radical rejection of gnosis was to orient Latin Christianity towards a stricter but less fruitful orthodoxy. This does not mean, of course, that Tertullian did not make serious attempts to understand and explain Scripture and the 'rule of faith', but he did so by excluding all *curiositas* and kept very close to the common faith of the Church. He means to speak *simpliciter,* as we shall see when we come to consider his theology.

CHAPTER SIX

MINUCIUS FELIX AND HIS SOURCES

Minucius Felix' *Octavius* is the earliest work in Latin Christian literature testifying to the encounter between the Christian revelation and the classical, literary and philosophical culture of the Latin world. It is indisputable that the *Octavius* has many points of contact with Tertullian's *Apologeticum*, but, as Quispel has argued, it is almost certain that the *Octavius* was the earlier work, dating from the end of the second century.[1] It clearly emanates from Rome and bears witness to the use of the Latin language by Christians living in Rome under the later Antonines. The author goes to great pains to use classical Latin and to avoid 'christianisms'. We cannot, however, consider the *Octavius* from the literary point of view here, despite the obvious interest of this aspect of the work, because our main preoccupation is the author's appeal to Latin philosophy, to Cicero and Seneca, in his presentation of Christian faith.

1. THE THEOLOGY OF THE *OCTAVIUS*

The *Octavius* is first and foremost a theological treatise, beginning, in the section defending the Christian faith, with proof of the existence of God. Just as a 'neat, orderly and well-kept' house points to a master, Minucius says, so too do the 'providence, order and law' prevailing in the world presuppose a Lord who is 'fairer than the stars themselves or than any portions of the entire world' (XVIII, 4). The source which is closest to this theme of the house is the *De nat. deor.* II, 5, 15 of Cicero, who links it with Cleanthes; but it is equally common in Seneca (*Nat. Quaest.* VII,

1. Cf. QUISPEL, 'Anima naturaliter christiana', *Latomus*, 10, 1951, pp. 163–169.

30, 3; *Benef.* VII, 1, 7; *Epist.* XC, 42), to mention only Latin authors. It was to be taken up by Novatian, who went back to the same sources, but was not dependent on Minucius.

Minucius goes on to argue in favour of monotheism, showing by examples from human society – Eteocles and Polynices, the Theban brothers, Romulus and Remus, Caesar and Pompey – that it is impossible for more than one ruler to govern (XVIII, 5–6). He also takes examples from the world of nature: *Rex unus apibus, dux unus in gregibus, in armentis rector unus,* 'Bees have but one king, flocks one leader, cattle one monarch of the herd' (XVIII, 7). This theme has its origin, as Erik Peterson has pointed out, in a tradition which goes back to Aristotle and is found not only in the Περί κοσμοῦ of Pseudo-Aristotle, but also in the Stoic and especially the Posidonian tradition. It comes from the standard polemic against polytheism, which is romanised by Minucius.

Some of the characteristics of this one God are now outlined. He is described as *summa maiestas* and *divini imperii potestas* and as *parens omnium,* as 'having neither beginning nor end'. As the one 'who brings all to birth' (*qui nativitatem omnibus praestet*) he is himself the principle of his own eternity. He is sufficient to himself: *ante mundum fuerit sibi ipse pro mundo,* 'Before the world, he was a world unto himself' and he governs all things: *Verbo iubet, ratione dispensat, virtute consummat,* 'By his word he orders (all things that are), by his reason he arranges (them) and by his goodness he perfects (them)' (*Oct.* XVIII, 7).[2] These are all major themes in the writings of the Christian apologists living during the second century. They reflect the preoccupation at that period with Platonism and Stoicism, but the distinctive marks of Latin language and thought also come through.

Some of the terms mentioned in the quotations from the *Oc-tavius* given in the preceding paragraph were very quickly adopted by Christians writing in Latin. The phrase *summa maiestas,* which means transcendence, and the word *potestas,* meaning sovereign authority, are examples of this. *Maiestas* is found in *I Clement,* the author of which preceded Minucius in his

2. The words *verbum, ratio* and *virtus* also occur in Tertullian's *Apol.* XVII, 1 and the phrase *ipse sibi mundus* occurs in his *Adv. Prax.* V, 1.

translation of δόξα and μεγαλωσύνγ in the Septuagint as *maiestas*.[3] In the same way, *potestas* is a translation of the εξουσία, the authority of God in the Bible. *Parens* (in the phrase quoted above, meaning 'the parent of all') and *imperium*, 'authority', are, on the other hand, classical rather than Christian words. The former is especially dear to Minucius (apart from XVIII, 7 above, see also XVIII, 4; XIX, 1 and 15; XXXV, 4), and seems, from XIX, 14, to be a rendering of Plato, *Tim.* 28 c. As for the phrase mentioned above, *qui nativitatem omnibus praestet* (XVIII, 7), *nativitas*, 'birth', is equivalent to the Greek γένεσις and is a Christian word which was frequently used in early Latin Christianity, where it is often contrasted with the word *perpetuitas* (cf. Tertullian *Adv. Val.* XI, 4).[4] The three words *verbum, ratio* and *virtus*, pointing to the action of God in his creation, also go back to early Christian usage, where the emphasis is above all on the creative word of God (*verbum*) and on his *virtus*.[5] The word *ratio*, however, introduces a Stoic note.

Minucius says that 'God cannot be seen (*non videri potest*), . . . nor grasped (*nec comprehendi*), . . . nor measured (*nec aestimari*)' (XVIII, 8) and many other passages parallel to this text have been found by Pellegrino. We shall be returning to the subject of the invisible nature of God, but in the meantime it is important to draw attention to the Stoic emphasis of the phrase *nec comprehendi*. The fact that God is incomprehensible (ἀκατάληπτος) is expressed in the *Octavius* by the two words *infinitus* (ἄπειρος), 'infinite', and *immensus* (ἀμέτρητος) 'measureless'. The consequence of this is that God alone knows himself as he is and 'our breast (*pectus*) is too narrow to take him in (*ad intellectum*)' (XVIII, 8). The human breast or heart as the seat of understanding is another common Stoic theme, and the word *pectus* in this sense is used in classical Latin. Later, in Christian circles, it was replaced by the biblical term *cor*.

The word *inaestimabilis*, which occurs in the same context, was coined by Cicero as a translation of the Stoic phrase

---

3. See R. BRAUN, *Deus Christianorum: Recherches sur le vocabulaire doctrinal de Tertullien*, Publications de la Faculté des Lettres et Sciences Humaines d'Alger, 41, Paris, 1962.　　4. See BRAUN, *op. cit.*, pp. 318–319.
5. See BRAUN *op. cit.*, pp.106–109.

τὴν ἀναξίαν ἔχων (Fin. III, 6, 20), but whereas this has a depreciatory meaning, in the second century, the term acquired a more positive sense, that of being beyond man's capacity to value. It is in this sense that it is used, for example, in the *Asclepius* 31. What is even more interesting is that, in his *Idol.* 6, Cyprian gives it as a Hermetic quotation: *Hermes quoque Trismegistus unum Deum confitetur eumque incomprehensibilem et inaestimabilem confitetur*, 'Hermes Trismetistus also confesses that there is one God and that he is incomprehensible and inestimable'. It should incidentally be noted that the only place in which Tertullian uses the words *incomprehensibilis* and *inaestimabilis* is in *Apol.* XVII, 2, and here he is clearly drawing on Minucius. This shows that Tertullian bears witness here to a previous tradition, which he does not continue. It should also be noted that the word *inaestimabilis* applies firstly to a knowledge based on the senses and only secondly to knowledge based on the intellect.

The divine transcendence to which this vocabulary points means that the one who thinks that he knows the greatness of God in fact reduces God, and that, if he is not to reduce God, he must recognise that he does not know God. This recurrent theme of the ἄγνωστος θεός, the *docta ignorantia*, was, for Philo, an important element in Jewish apologetic. Minucius goes beyond Stoicism in his emphasis on the negative theology, and it is difficult not to detect here the influence of second century Judaeo-Christian thought and especially of gnostic thinking. In the third century, there was to be a reaction against this negative theology, both in the case of Tertullian and in that of Origen. Minucius, on the other hand, remained a Stoic insofar as he believed that God could not be known either by the senses or by the intellect. There is therefore no trace of dualism in Minucius' thinking in this respect.

The question of names also plays a part in Minucius' presentation of the transcendence of God. Names, Minucius insists, are only required when it is necessary to distinguish individuals from a great diversity, whereas, in the case of God, only the word *deus* names him. 'Father', 'king' or 'Lord' (*dominus*) are all names which reduce God. 'Away with names', Minucius concludes, 'and you will see him in his splendour (*claritatem*)' (XVIII, 10).

This is clearly a very radical passage in the *Octavius*, since in it Minucius appears to do away entirely with analogy in connection with God. In this too, he is following the Stoics, who regarded names as natural (Φύσει), not as conventional (Θέσει). Because of this, *deus* is the name which points to God in his absolutely unique and incommunicable character. Tertullian follows Minucius here, although he does not, like Minucius, reject all the titles usually given to God. Minucius regarded God above all as characterised by *claritas*, in other words, by absolute transcendence.

As evidence, Minucius calls on universal custom (*consensus*) and popular usage (*vulgus*) – in both cases, the word *deus* points to a unique and transcendent reality. He also gives various formulas as examples – *deus magnus est,* 'God is great', *deus verus est,* 'God is true', and *si deus dederit,* 'if God grants it' – which prove that this is the *naturalis sermo*, the 'natural language' of the people, and that the word *deus* is what naturally names God. Quispel was right when he pointed out that this is the Stoic view that words have a natural affinity with what they denote.[6] According to Stoic thinkers, words are used to indicate the essence of each reality. Minucius is not concerned here to prove the existence of God by universal consent, nor is he offering a philosophical theory about the innate character of the idea of God. On the contrary, his aim is to emphasise the specific, unique and transcendent character of God. To do so, he has recourse to the evidence of nature, which, he believes, refutes false ideas of God.

The same theme and indeed almost the same terms recur in Tertullian's *Apol.* XVII, 4–6 and *De test. an.* II. Here, as in Minucius, Tertullian's purpose is to establish that God is one, in opposition to the pagan beliefs. To prove this, it is essential to use even the language of the pagans against paganism and to show that it is in accordance with Christianity. This is precisely what Minucius means when he says: *Vulgi iste naturalis sermo est an christiani confitentis oratio?,* 'Is that the natural language of the people or the prayer of some confessing Christian?' (*Oct.* XVIII, 11). Tertullian says exactly the same thing in his famous formula: O

6. G. QUISPEL, 'Anima naturaliter christiana', *Eranos Jahrbuch*, 18, 1950, pp. 176–178.

testimonium animae naturaliter christianae, 'O witness of the soul, in its very nature Christian!' (*Apol.* XVII, 6), which concludes the passage in his *Apologeticum* which is parallel to that in Minucius' *Octavius*. Both authors are making the same affirmation and, underlying their statements, there is the Stoic argument that there is a natural relationship between the word and the reality itself, the word expressing the natural essence of the reality.

The whole of this passage in the *Octavius*, what is more, is repeated, sometimes word for word, by Cyprian in his *Quod idola non sint*. In the first place, Cyprian sets out to demonstrate that God is one by means of examples taken from human society – the same examples as those found in the *Octavius* (Eteocles and Polynices of Thebes, Romulus and Remus, and Caesar and Pompey, of Rome) – and from the society of animals: *Rex unus est apibus et dux unus in gregibus et in armentis rector unus, qui universa quaecumque sunt verbo iubet, ratione dispensat, virtute consummat,* 'Bees have but one king and flocks one leader and cattle one monarch of the herd, (God) who by his word orders all things that are, by his reason arranges them and by his goodness perfects them' (*Idol.* 91). Cyprian has here taken a fragment of Minucius and inserted it without acknowledgment straight into his own text. This brings out once again the feature noted earlier in connection with the *De centesima*, namely that Cyprian apparently does reproduce word for word the works of which he makes use.

In the passage that follows, Cyprian again repeats almost verbatim the text of Minucius' *Octavius* (XVIII, 8–10): *Hic nec videri potest: visu clarior est; nec comprehendi: tactu purior est; nec aestimari: sensu maior est. Et ideo sic Deum digne aestimamus, dum inaestimabilem dicimus. Nec nomen Deo quaeras: Deus nomen est. Illic vocabulis opus est, ubi propriis appellationem insignibus multitudo dirimenda est: Deo qui solus est Dei vocabulum totum est,* 'God cannot be seen – he is too bright for sight; nor grasped – he is too pure for touch; nor valued – he is beyond all sense. Therefore we can only value God aright by calling him "inestimable". Seek not a name for God: God is his name. Terms are needed when individuals have to be distinguished from the mass, by proper marks and designations; for God, who is unique, the term "God" sums up all'. This passage is such a literal quotation from the *Octavius* that it actually enables us to improve the text of Minucius. And when Cyprian concludes the passage, it is Minucius' thought which he expresses: *Nam vulgus in multis Deum naturaliter confitetur. Dici frequenter audimus: O Deus, et: Deus videt, et: Deo commendo, et: Deus mihi reddet, et: Si Deus dederit,* 'For the people naturally confess God in many cases . . . We often hear it said: "O God; God sees it; I commend it to God; God give it back to me; if God grants it" '.

All that Cyprian has done here is to replace Minucius' Roman phrases by Tertullian's African ones (as found in the *De testimonio animae*), with the exception of the final phrase *Si Deus dederit.*[7]

Later in the *Octavius*, Minucius returns to the question of God, not in the context of debate with the philosophers, but within the framework of a critical discussion of the popular pagan religion and especially of the statues, the temples and the sacrifices of the pagans. This is, of course, a longstanding theme both of the Bible and of Greek philosophy, but, as Philo testifies, it had acquired a place of special importance in Jewish missionary writing, in imitation of which it was frequently taken up by apologists of the second century. The Jewish and Christian authors are characterised by three arguments in particular, which are different from those of the Greek philosophers. Against the temples, they argued that God could not be contained; he is ἀχώρητος. Against the sacrifices, they prove that he is ἀνενδεής, in need of nothing. Against the statues, that he is invisible, ἀόρατος.[8]

Minucius unites all three of these arguments in the *Octavius* (XXXII), developing them with the help of quotations from Cicero and Seneca. The first theme, that of the God who is ἀχώρητος, emerges clearly: *Templum quod ei extruam, cum totus hic mundus eius opere fabricatus eum capere non possit?,* 'What temple can I build for him, when the whole universe, fashioned by his handiwork, cannot contain him?' (XXXII, 1). This theme is found in Cicero (*De nat. deor.* XXXVII, 103): God's true dwelling-place is the heart of man. The central theme of this whole passage, however, is that of worship – cultic acts are above all performed to show that we observe God's will.

7. For Minucius and Cyprian, see H. KOCH, *Cyprianische Untersuchungen,* pp. 56–65.
8. See *Message,* pp. 297–302.

Minucius condemns the making of statues, because 'man himself is the image (*simulacrum*) of God'. Man's soul is broader (*latius*) than the material spaces, Minucius insists, and he asks whether it ought not to be in the mind (*mente*) that we should dedicate a sanctuary to God and in our heart (*pectore*) that we should offer sacrifices to him (XXXII, 2). (This passage appears almost verbatim in Cyprian's *Idol.* 9.) Underlying these arguments is certainly the Pauline tradition, but the same idea of God dwelling in the human soul is also to be found in Stoicism in general and in Seneca in particular (*Epist.* XLI, 2). [9]

God, who does not require statues and sanctuaries, similarly has no need of man's sacrifices of material gifts. On the contrary, it is he who has provided these for our use. This is the theme of the God who is ἀνενδεής. Minucius is at pains to point out that 'the acceptable sacrifice (*litabilis hostia*) is a good spirit (*bonus animus*) and a pure mind (*mens pura*) and a conscience without guile (*sincera sententia*)' (XXXII, 2).

This theme of external sacrifices is so common and so widespread in both Greek and Jewish writings that it is not possible to trace Minucius' use of it to one single source. [10] It can be found both in Cicero (*De nat. deor.* II, 28, 71) and in Seneca (*Epist.* XC, 50, with *bonus*). The vocabulary used by Minucius suggests that he was influenced here by the latter author, who also has the phrase *pura mente*. In the phrase *litabilis hostia*, however, the word *litabilis* is a *hapax legomenon*, so that it cannot have been taken from secular literature. The phrase as a whole is, in fact, a rendering of the Greek Φυσία δεκτή, which is found in the work of Clement of Alexandria (*Stromat.* II, 18. 79, 1) in a targum of Ps. 50:17 (EVV 51): 'A broken heart is an acceptable sacrifice (θυσία δεκτή) for God'. It would therefore appear that Minucius' text is a rendering into classical Latin of this biblical passage, the words *mens* and *animus* replacing the biblical terms *cor* and *spiritus*. [11]

Minucius then goes on to discuss the fact that God cannot be

9. See W. THEILER, *Die Vorbereitung des Neuplatonismus*, pp. 102–109.
10. See the references in M. PELLEGRINO, *Studi sull' antica Apologetica*, pp. 235–237.
11. Cf. DANIELOU, *Etudes d'Exégèse judéo-chrétienne*, pp. 163–169.

seen, but is nonetheless immanent and can be known by the activity of his *virtus* in the world. It is, Minucius insists, precisely because we cannot see him, but because we can know him (*sentire possumus*) that we believe that he is God. The very fact that he is invisible shows that he is the true God. To illustrate that a reality is not necessarily visible to man, Minucius gives three examples. In the first place, there are many natural phenomena, such as the wind, which cannot be seen, but which are nonetheless real. Secondly, 'we cannot look upon the sun', Minucius says, for 'its rays dazzle our eyesight (*acies*) . . . How, then, could you bear the sight of the author of the sun himself?' (XXXII, 5). Thirdly, Minucius gives an example which is also found in Cicero, *Tusc.* I, 25: 'Do you expect to see God with the eyes of flesh, when you can neither see nor lay hold of your own soul?' (XXXII, 6).

Despite the fact that he is invisible, however, the God worshipped by Christians is extremely near to us – 'all things . . . are full (*plena*) of him' and *ubique non tantum nobis proximus, sed infusus est,* 'He is not only everywhere close to us – he is also poured out into us'. The sun, Minucius says, is 'equally present everywhere, mingles and has part in all. Nowhere is his brightness dimmed. How much more is God, the author of all things and the spier-out of all, from whom nothing can be hidden, present in darkness and present in that other darkness of our thoughts! Not only do we act under him, but with him, I may almost say, we have our life' (XXXII, 7–9). This passage is entirely in the Posidonian tradition.[12] The phrase 'all things are full of God' can be found in Cicero (*Leg.* II, 11, 26), and the idea that God is close to all things, in Seneca (*Epist.* XCV, 47). In Seneca too can be found the image of the light of the sun being mingled with everything without being defiled (*Epist.* XLI, 5), the phrase *interest cogitationibus* (*Epist.* LXXXIII, 1), and finally the idea of God's nearness to the soul, expressed in similar terms: *Prope est a te Deus, tecum est, intus est,* 'God is near to you, with you and within you' (*Epist.* XLI, 1).[13]

Minucius' theology is to a great extent derived from the Chris-

12. See W. THEILER, *op. cit.*, p. 102.
13. See P. COURCELLE, 'Virgile et l'immanence divine', *Mullus* (Mélanges Klauser), pp. 34–42.

tian apologists of the second century and, beyond these authors, from the Platonists. It also contains a number of biblical allusions, such as the 'light present in the darkness', which would seem to have been inspired by the Prologue to the Fourth Gospel. We have seen, however, that he is also indebted to the Latin classical tradition, especially with regard to his vocabulary, and to the Latin Stoics, through the writings of Cicero and Seneca. This is particularly clear in the case of the theme of God's nearness to the soul, as indicated above. Minucius' tendency to emphasise man's inner, subjective being is in accordance with a closely related tendency in Latin thought. This preoccupation with the subjective element emerges for the first time in Minucius, is expressed more systematically by Tertullian and reaches its fulfilment in the work of Augustine. The *Octavius* is, therefore, valuable as evidence of the first beginnings of this movement in Christian thought.

2. THE WORLD AND MAN

Minucius Felix also deals with the world and with man. He begins with the general principle that, in the universe, 'things are coherent, closely combined and interconnected' (*cohaerentia, conexa, concatenata*). These terms come from the Latin Stoic vocabulary and are translations of the Greek concepts of συνέχεια, σύνδεσμος and ἀκολουθία. They are also used by Novatian. This order of the universe has its origin in the *divinitatis ratio* or 'divine wisdom' (*Oct.* XVII, 2; cf. also XVII, 6, 7), and is proof of God's providence (XVII, 8). Minucius' main aim in this section is to show the reality of divine providence in reply to the sceptical argument put forward by the pagan Caecilius, that things may be the result either of a combination of the elements, as the Stoics suggested, or of a collision of atoms, as the Epicureans believed, but that it is not possible to prove from them the existence of God (V, 7).

It should be noted that Caecilius makes frequent references to Stoic physics, while rejecting the theology associated with it: 'If in the beginning the seeds (*semina*) of all things come together (*in se coeunt*) and solidify by nature (*natura*), why is God the author?'

(V, 7). The *semina* are the elements, whose combination produces all beings by the action of Φύσις (*natura*). Caecilius continues: 'If we grant that fire (*ignis*) has kindled the stars, and hung (*suspenderit*) the heaven (*caelum*) overhead by its own substance (sc. air), and established the earth (*terram*) firmly by its weight, and if the sea (*mare*) has flowed from water (*liquore*), whence comes this religion?' (V, 7). Novatian was to adopt all these examples listed by Caecilius, but in order to attribute the diversity of creation to the Creator God not to the action of the immanent fire on the four basic elements: 'The Creator (*conditor*), who has hung (*suspenderit*) the heaven (*caelum*) in the topmost height, and has made the earth (*terram*) solid by laying down its mass, and has poured out the flowing seas (*maria*) from water (*liquore*)' (*Trin.* 1).

We seem also to have here in the *Octavius* the Stoic view that living beings are merely animal combinations of elements which dissolve: *Homo et omne quod nascitur, inspiratur, attollitur, elementorum ut voluntaria concretio est, in quae rursum homo et animal omne dividitur, solvitur, dissipatur: ita in fontem refluunt et in semet omnia revolvuntur, nullo artifice nec iudice nec auctore,* 'Man and each living thing is born, lives and grows up and consists of a spontaneous combination of elements into which once again man and every living thing is separated, dissolved and dispersed. So all things flow back to their source and return to themselves without an artificer, a judge or an author of their being' (V, 8). This is a clear statement of the Stoic conception of the cyclical movement of nature (*revolvuntur*) in which the elements return to their original state and, according to the pagan Caecilius, it points to nothing more than a natural law – there is no need for divine intervention.

The same law applies also, according to Caecilius, to other things in the universe. He says that the sun is simply a 'gathering together of seeds of fire' (*congregatis ignium seminibus*) which dissolve and re-form, so that it is necessary to speak of 'suns' (*soles*). It is the same with the phenomena of the atmosphere – the vapours rise from the earth, condense, form clouds and then fall again as rain on the earth (V, 9). Here too there is a constant flux and reflux and nothing which could be interpreted as providential intervention, especially since these atmospheric phenomena affect all men alike, both the good and the bad, without apparently taking any account of their welfare. Minucius therefore clearly puts into the mouth of Caecilius, his representative of paganism, a summary of Stoic teaching devoid of all idea of providence.

Caecilius' attitude is therefore deliberately sceptical, not Epicurean, even though it is Stoicism which he wishes chiefly to criticise. He takes the Stoic cosmology as his starting-point in order to demonstrate that this system does not allow us to infer the existence of Providence, only that the laws of nature are somehow determined. The context of the debate between the pagan Caecilius and the Christian Octavius, then, is Stoicism. It is this which defines the problematic area for discussion, and incidentally gives us an interesting indication of the terms of philosophical debate in Rome at the end of the second century.

To the position adopted by Caecilius, Minucius opposes an account of God's activity in the universe, presented in Stoic terms. This is very clear from the following passage: 'There exists some sacred power (numen) . . . by which all nature is inspired (inspiretur), moved, nourished (alatur) and directed' (XVII, 4). The word numen is indisputably a pagan term which was, as Braun has pointed out,[14] generally avoided by Christian authors. The word inspiretur also points to the Stoic concept of pneuma or breath as the principle of all movement, life and order. Minucius also insists that heaven is proof of 'the wonderful and divine balance maintained by the supreme controller' (summi moderatoris mira et divina libratio, XVII, 5). This phrase is significant, since Tertullian speaks later of God as the librator universitatis, the 'one who holds the balance of the universe' (Adv. Herm. II) and Novatian associates moderante and librata (De trin. 3). [15] Cicero also uses the word moderator (Tusc. I, 28, 68, 70).

Minucius' description of the universe is characteristic. He follows the order heaven – sea – earth.[16] His description of heaven clearly reflects the astral religion of his period and is expressed in refined rhetorical language. Heaven, according to

14. See BRAUN, op. cit., p. 38.
15. For librare, see Augustine, De civ. Dei XXII, 11.
16. Cf. Tertullian, Pall. II, 2.

Minucius is 'at night decorated (*distinguitur*) with stars, by day il-
luminated by the sun' (XVII, 5). As Pellegrino has observed, the
phrase *caelum distinctum astris,* 'heaven decorated with stars', is also
to be found in Cicero's *De nat. deor.* II, 37, 95. The year, Minucius
states, is 'made by the circling of the sun' and the month is 'determined, by waxing, waning and action of the moon' (*luna auctu
senior, labore*) and again the same is to be found in Cicero (*De. nat.
deor.* II, 37, 95).[17] Day and night mark the 'alternate renewal'
(*reparatio*) of work and rest (XVII, 6). The word *reparatio* here
would seem to be a neologism, of which Minucius was fond (XI,
7; XXXIV, 9), and in time became part of the theological
vocabulary.

Minucius then turns to discuss the stars and the part they play
in navigation at sea and in the timing of ploughing and
harvesting (XVII, 6). He emphasises the second particularly:
'Does the ordered succession (*ordo*) of the seasons and crops,
adorned (*distinguitur*) according to a regular diversity, not bear
witness to its author and parent, when spring with its flowers,
summer with its harvests, autumn with its ripe fruit and winter
with its olives (*olivatas*) all appear in their proper sequence
(*necessaria*)?' (XVII, 7). There are consequently certain forms of
providence 'so that the transitions (*transitus*) in the recurrent cycle
of the year may take place imperceptibly and harmlessly' (XVII,
7).

Minucius undoubtedly went back to Stoic sources for these
passages. He probably drew on Cicero's *De nat. deor.* II, 39, 98 for
the idea of the 'crops adorned (*distinguitur*) according to their
diversity (*varietate*)'. Whereas Minucius speaks of *transitus* for the
changes of the seasons, Cicero has *commutationes* (*Tusc.* I, 28, 68).
Beutler,[18] however, has pointed out that the idea of 'impercepti-
ble' movement is not to be found in Cicero and is a clearly
Posidonian theme.[19] This would seem to point to a Stoic source
other than the writings of Cicero for this idea, which is also

17. See also Seneca, *Quaest. nat.,* IV, 1, 2: *distinguitur astris* and *labore,* in connection with the moon.
18. BEUTLER, *op. cit.,* p. 27.
19. See also *medium temperamentum,* which recalls the μεϑόρ ιο ς of Gregory
of Nyssa (*Cant.* 5; GNO, LV, 5).

found in the work of Novatian. A Roman Stoic tradition undoubtedly existed from the time of Clement of Rome onwards
(*Epist.* XX). The theme of the 'dance of the seasons' was,
moreover, not only literary, but also artistic, figuring prominently in Roman painting at the time of Marcus Aurelius.

After discussing the heavenly bodies and the cycle of the
seasons, Minucius turns his attention to the sea, saying that it may
not go beyond the limit imposed on it. This idea is found in
Cicero's *De nat. deor.* II, 45, 116. It is also, it should be noted,
found in Jb. 38:8, 11. Minucius also mentions the trees, 'each
drawing its life from the bowels of the earth' (XVII, 9), which is
reminiscent of Gn. 1:10–11, and also refers to the waters beneath
the earth. In the same paragraph, Minucius speaks of the ocean,
the ebb and flow of the tides, the springs flowing ceaselessly, and
the rivers moving on and on. Many of these aspects are, as
Pellegrino has shown, borrowed from Cicero's *De nat. deor.* II,
39, 100; II, 39, 98 (*perennitates fontium*); II, 53, 138 (*aestus*).

Finally, Minucius discusses the earth. He first describes the
mountains, hills and plains and then the inhabitants of the earth,
drawing attention particularly to the means by which they defend themselves against each other. In this context, he lists their
horns, teeth, claws, stings, feet and wings (XVII, 10). Both of
these themes can be found in Cicero's *De nat. deor.* – the earth
itself in III, 39, 98 and the means of defence of the animals in II,
50, 127 (cf. also II, 47, 21). Cicero in fact specifies bulls' horns
and wild bears' teeth, so that, although he is probably the main
source, he is not the only one. Gregory of Nyssa also lists horns,
claws, teeth, stings, feet and wings (*De Op. if* 7; 140C). Minucius takes up the same themes, but handles them in accordance
with literary taste of his own period, and with greater erudition.

Minucius's Stoicism is very much a literary affair. In particular,
he never brings in the theory of the elements, which was essential
to Stoic physics (cf. however, XXXIV, 9). He rejects this theory
all the more because he believes that the world was *a Deo factus*,
'made by God', rather than *elementis concretus*, 'compounded of
elements' (XVII, 1). Novatian, it should be noted, was much
more of a philosopher in his use of Stoicism. In the *De Trinitate*,
the first chapter is closely parallel to the present chapter in the

Octavius, but in a second chapter he elaborates the theory of the elements and of their *conspiratio.* It would certainly seem as though Minucius was as fearful of the determinism of the Stoics as of the concept of chance in Epicureanism (see V, 7).

What then of man? After describing the activity of providence in the cosmos, Minucius demonstrates it in mankind. 'The beauty of our form declares that God was its author', he writes and goes on to describe that form in Ciceronian terms: *Status rigidus, vultus erectus, oculi in summo velut in specula constituti et omnes ceteri sensus velut in arce compositi* (XVII, 11). All these different aspects of man's form – 'the upright stature, the head erect, the eyes placed at the top as in a watch-tower and the other senses brought together as in a citadel' – can be found in Cicero's *De nat. deor.* II, 56, 140 and Pellegrino has added several other texts which include the *erectus,* the *arx* and the *speculatores.*

The same theme appears earlier in the same section of the *Octavius: A feris beluis hoc differimus quod illa prona in terramque vergentia nihil nata sint prospicere nisi pabulum, nos, quibus vultus erectus quibus suspectus in caelum datus est, sermo et ratio per quae deum agnoscimus, sentimus, imitamur, ignorare nec fas nec licet ingerentem sese oculis et sensibus nostris caelestem claritatem,* 'We are different from the wild animals in that, going on all fours and directed towards the ground, they are born to search for nothing more than food, whereas we, whose heads are erect and who have been made to gaze on heaven, endowed with speech and reason by which we may recognise, perceive and imitate God, neither may nor can ignore the heavenly brightness which imposes itself on our eyes and senses' (XVII, 2).

In this text, Minucius adds to his contrast between the physical posture of the animals and that of man the fact that man possesses 'speech and reason', by which he is able above all to 'imitate' (*imitamur*) God, that is, be his image.[20] It should, in this context, be noted also that it is the vision (*oculis*) of heaven (the result of the *vultus erectus*) which leads to man's knowledge of God, and that the same idea appears in Cicero's *De nat. deor.* II, 56, 140.

The same theme is used by Cyprian in his *Ad Dem.* 16: *Rectum*

20. See M. PELLEGRINO, 'Il topos sullo status rectus', *Mullus,* pp. 277–278.

te Deus fecit et cum cetera animantia prona et ad terram situ vergentia depressa sint. Tibi sublimis status et ad caelum atque ad Dominum sursum vultus erectus est, 'God made you erect, while the other animals go on all fours and are bent downwards, directed towards the ground. You have an exalted stature and your countenance is erect, turned towards heaven and the Lord above'. It is very likely that Cyprian has, in this passage, drawn on the same sources as Minucius Felix, namely Cicero, Ovid[21] and Seneca, but, as H. Koch has pointed out, the literary contacts with Minucius are especially close – this is above all noticeable in the phrase *ad terram vergentia.* It is clear, then, that Cyprian is continuing in the same tradition as Minucius. He is contributing nothing original, all the more because this is an aspect of Stoicism in which he is not interested.

Minucius continues with his description of man in *Oct.* XVIII, drawing attention here to certain special characteristics. The first is the wonder of the human body, nothing of which is 'not made for use or adornment' (*non necessitatis causa et decoris*), and the second is that 'while all men share a similar general shape, each individual shows personal difference of feature (*liniamenta deflexa*)'. The third aspect which Minucius discusses is generation and childbirth, the fourth the diversity of climates in the world. Three of these four elements are also to be found in Cicero's *De natura deorum* – the necessity and order of the parts of the human body (II, 47), human reproduction and birth (II, 48) and the different climates of the world (II, 52, 130). The theme of the different features present in the same fundamental body is not, however, found in Cicero, although it does occur in the *Asclepius* 36. Once again, then, we have evidence that Minucius' source was not exclusively Ciceronian. It is apparent that he drew on a wider, common Stoic tradition.

We must now consider another, related aspect of Minucius' teaching, that of eschatology. This, of course, is concerned both with the world and with man. With regard to the former, Minucius adheres to the doctrine of the ἐκπύρωσις or con-

---

21. Ovid also has *prona, sublime, caelum, erectos, vultus;* see Lactantius, *Inst.,* II, 1, 15.

flagration, which assumes, first of all, that the world is bound to come to an end. Minucius justifies this assumption by the general principle that 'all things which have come into being die, all things created perish' (*omnia quae orta sunt occidere, quae facta sunt interire*), and consequently that 'heaven and all the things that are contained in heaven cease as they began' (*caelum quoque cum omnibus quae caelo continentur, ita ut coepisse, desinere*) (*Oct.* XXXIV, 2).

Minucius then goes on to say that this end will be brought about by a conflagration in the world, an *incendium mundi*, but he does not specify the precise form that this conflagration will take: 'Either an earthly fire will fall unexpectedly down on the world or else heaven itself will begin to melt' (XXXIV, 3). The last word in this text is uncertain. *Difficile*, which is the reading in the manuscripts, is out of the question and *diffundi*, which might be confused with *difficile* in small letters, has been conjectured. Pellegrino has also suggested *desinere*. Despite this particular difficulty, however, there can be no doubt about the meaning of the passage as a whole.

Minucius himself is quite clear about the origin of this idea – it comes from the Bible. (We have already seen how important it is in the thought of Commodian.) Minucius recognises that the same idea is also to be found in the works of the philosophers, but he insists that they borrowed it from the Bible (XXXIV, 5). Although the common people are ignorant of it, the philosophers accept it. 'The Stoics', Minucius states, 'firmly maintain that when the moisture dries out, the world must all take fire' (XXXIV, 2), and the Epicureans also hold that there will be a 'conflagration of the elements' (XXXIV, 3). Finally, Minucius says, 'Plato speaks of parts of the world as subject alternately to floods and to fire ... and adds that only God himself, who created it, can make it dissoluble and mortal' (XXXIV, 4). Minucius' sources here are Lucretius for Epicurus (V, 407–410), for Plato, Cicero's Latin translation of the *Timaeus* (*Tim.* 41 a), and Cicero's *De nat. deor.* II, 46, 118 for the Stoics. The Stoic philosopher referred to in this case must be Posidonius, since Panetius held a different opinion regarding the conflagration of the world.

It is fairly obvious, however, that Minucius' main source was Stoicism, just as his own position is basically Stoic. In a mutilated passage (XXXIV, 2), he expresses what appears to be his own view of the ἐκπύρωσις: ... *fontium dulcis aqua ... marina nutrire, in vim ignis abiturum*, 'the fresh water of the springs ... to nourish marine life, will disappear into the force of the fire'. The same words are also found in Cicero's outline of Posidonius' thought: *Ad extremum omnis mundus ignesceret cum umore consumpto, neque terra ali posset*, 'At the end, the whole universe may burn when its moisture has been dried up and the earth will not be able to be nourished'. (*De nat. deor.* II, 46, 118 and later in the same work: *Ali autem solem, terram, reliqua astra aquis, alia dulcibus, alia marinis*, 'Nevertheless, the sun, the earth and the rest of the planets are nourished by the waters, some by fresh, some by sea waters', *De nat. deor.* IV, 14, 37). This is clearly the Posidonian theory of the universe fed by water, so that we may conclude that Minucius was, in this case and in others, influenced by Posidonius.

Minucius then goes on to discuss man's eschatological destiny, which is resurrection. Here too, he points out that the idea of resurrection was not entirely foreign to the pagan philosophers. Both Pythagoras and Plato preserve, in their teaching, at least half of the primitive tradition, in that they believe that, whereas the body dissolves, the souls of men remain eternal. They also believe, however, Minucius adds, that 'the souls of men pass into sheep, birds and wild animals' (XXXIV, 7). The reference to 'birds' here points clearly to Empedocles. Minucius' comment is that this theory of transmigration comes from comedy rather than from philosophy and it was in fact, as is obvious in the case of Lucian, exploited as a pretext for irony. Minucius is going back to the common tradition here – Tertullian, for example, mentions that a mime on precisely this theme was composed by a comic author, Laberius, who was writing at the time of Caesar (*Apol.* XLVIII, 1).

Minucius next sets out the arguments in favour of resurrection. God was able to fashion man in the beginning, Minucius says, and so he will be able to fashion him again: *sicut de nihilo nasci licuit, ita de nihilo licet reparari*, 'Just as he could be born out of nothing, so he can be renewed out of nothing' (**XXXIV**, 9). It is true that the body may dissolve and return to the four elements, 'but the elements remain in the keeping of God' (*sed deo elementorum custodia reservatur*) (**XXXIV**, 10). This theme is not to be found in Tertullian, but it is present in the work of Gregory of Nyssa. It is quite obviously in accordance with Stoicism, and Minucius is the first Latin Christian author to make use of it, whereas the other associated ideas had already been used by the second century Apologists. On the other hand, Minucius does not deal at all with the argument put forward by Celsus, that bodies are devoured by other bodies.

Finally, Minucius points out that the resurrection is prefigured (*meditetur*) in nature itself: 'The sun dips down and is born again; the stars sink and return; the flowers fall and renew their life; shrubs age and then break into leaf; seeds must decay in order to renew their life. The body in the grave is like trees in winter – they conceal their greeness under a show of dryness . . . We too must wait for the springtime of the body' (**XXXIV**, 11–12). This is another theme which was used by the second century Apologists. It can also be found in the work of Seneca, who employed it to demonstrate that, despite all its changes, nature was perpetual. It is therefore yet another Stoic theme, and Minucius, who calls on the Platonists to testify to immortality, also appeals to the Stoics to bear witness to man's resurrection.

Seneca's most interesting text in this connection is his *Epist.* **XXXVI**, 11: 'Death, of which we are so afraid, interrupts our existence, but does not tear it from us; the day which will replace us in the world will certainly come. Consider the recurrent cycle of things returning to themselves. In our universe, phenomena alternate between going away and returning. Summer passes, but another year brings it back; night swallows the sun, but is itself driven out by the day. The stars do nothing but return along the way on which they appeared. One half of the heaven rises while the other half dives beneath the horizon'. This is a further theme that is found in the work of the Apologists, but Minucius is closest to Seneca in his treatment of it. Tertullian also makes use of it, but deals with it at a deeper level (*Apol.* **XLVIII**, 8). This is a clear case of Minucius preceding Tertullian, who employs

Minucius' data but transforms them by his genius.

Minucius also contrasts the hope of the just in the resurrection with the punishment of the impious and at this point reintroduces the theme of fire. His teaching is based on Scripture, but he points out that it is prefigured in pagan mythology. The river of fire and the heat which comes from the Styx and from the dark chasm mentioned by Virgil (*Aen.* IX, 105) are examples of this. Like the fires of Etna and Vesuvius, which set fire to the land without consuming it, the punishing fire similarly destroys and replenishes its fuel at the same time. Hence the doom of sinners thrown into the *incendium* (**XXXV**, 3–4) will be eternal. Minucius, then, uses these themes taken from the Latin tradition to illustrate the Gospel message. Finally, we may note the phrase, *sapiens ignis*, 'wise fire', used by Minucius, a Stoic term also found in Cicero, *De nat. deor.* **XV**, 41.

CHAPTER SEVEN

TERTULLIAN AND STOICISM

1. TERTULLIAN AND PHILOSOPHY

IN THEORY, Tertullian had a very negative attitude towards pagan philosophy. He does not deny that it may contain elements of truth, and says so both in the *Ad nationes* and in the *De testimonio animae*. In the first of these treatises, he writes: 'Although, in their curiosity to examine all kinds of documents, the philosophers may appear to have come across the Scriptures as well, from the fact that these are earlier and that they have borrowed certain elements from them and from the fact that they have also rejected other elements, they show that they have either not examir ed everything or they have not believed everything. Add to ι!.s their desire for glory and it is clear that they have changed the Scriptures in order to express their own ideas. Moreover, what they have discovered has been lost in uncertainty, and from one or another kind of truth has emerged a flood of quibbles' (*Ad. nat.* II, 2, 5–6; cf. also *Test.* II, 4).

Tertullian is alluding in this passage to the theory of borrowings, which is also found in Justin. Holy Scripture is the earliest of all philosophies and it is possible that the philosophers, in their desire to know everything, may have borrowed certain truths from the Scriptures. These borrowings, however, are drowned in a flood of errors. Like Justin, Tertullian also stresses that, in striving after originality, the philosophers have built up their own personal systems of thought, instead of remaining faithful to the truth they received from Scripture. It is therefore possible to find, if it is strictly necessary, arguments in favour of the true religion in the works of the philosophers (*Ad. nat.* II, 1, 6), but this is a precarious proceeding.

It is also clear from at least one passage in Tertullian's writing that some of his predecessors had done the same: 'It is necessary to have a good deal of curiosity and an even better memory if one wants to take, from the best known works of the philosophers, poets and other masters of pagan thought and wisdom, any evidence in favour of the Christian truth in order to convince our opponents and persecutors that they are guilty of errors in what they teach and of injustice towards us. Some of our own people, in whom the effort of curiosity and liveliness of memory with regard to the literature of the past have persisted, have written little books of this kind, recalling and bearing detailed witness to the content, origin, tradition and argumentation of the ideas, by which it can be recognised that we have accepted nothing new or monstrous which would render it impossible to have recourse to the common and official works in our favour, rejecting what is false and retaining what is true' (De test. an. I, 1–2).

In this text, Tertullian is clearly stating his position with regard to those who preceded him, and one is reminded particularly, in this case, of Justin. In his *Apology,* Justin is anxious to draw attention to the seeds of truth contained in the pagan philosophies and mysteries and at the same time to avoid all error. He also argues that Christianity did not introduce any innovations which were alien to the pagan tradition, but that Christian teaching is in accordance with all that is best in that tradition. In this connection, however, it is worth noting that Tertullian may not have been alluding exclusively to Justin here, since Minucius Felix is also clearly preoccupied with seeking for aspects of the truth in the works of the pagan philosophers. This is particularly striking in *Oct.* XIX, where he presents a great deal of evidence in the writings of the philosophers and poets of the pagan world in support of the unity of God.

Tertullian, however, does not employ this method. The only authority that he accepts is that of revelation, although he adds, while stressing the novelty of this argument, the witness borne by religious experience. He also emphasises that the pagan philosophers were wrong in their manner of interpreting the relationship between God and the world. If his early works are studied chronologically with this question in mind, three aspects of it emerge in turn. In his *Ad nationes,* the earliest work, Tertullian defines his position with regard to pagan philosophy. In the *Apologeticum,* he goes further and outlines his own view of God. Finally, in his *De testimonio animae,* he puts forward his own argument. In all this, however, it is important to note that he is always dependent on pagan philosophy and refers constantly to it.

In his attempt to define his position with regard to paganism, Tertullian takes the treatise *De rebus divinis,* by Varro, as his point of departure (*Ad nat.* II, 1, 8). This is a valuable indication of his sources, showing, moreover, that, in this case at least, Tertullian is opposing Latin paganism, since Varro wrote in Latin during the first century B.C. His aim was to compile a compendium of the Roman religion, in which the three aspects – the philosophical, the mythical and the civil – were distinguished. Augustine believed that this threefold division went back to the Pontifex Maximus Scaevola, who belonged to the same period. In fact, it originated with the Stoics and possibly with Posidonius.[2]

What interests us above all here is Tertullian's discussion of physical theology. What he does is to analyse that interpretation of mythology according to which myths are symbols of the realities contained in the cosmos. The question that concerns him is therefore the deification of the cosmos, in other words, the cosmic religion. Following Varro, Tertullian considers the various interpretations of this religion. 'It is from this world that we have learnt to know the gods and it is from it that the physical form of theology is derived by those who have taught that the elements are gods and who, like Dionysius the Stoic, divide the gods into three categories. Varro insists that fire is the soul of the world (*anima mundi*), to such an extent that fire governs everything in the world, just as the soul governs everything in us' (*Ad nat.* II, 14–19).

This conception is refuted by Tertullian in all its aspects. If the

---

1. See R. BRAUN, 'Tertullien et la philosophie païenne'. *BIFAO* 4th Series, 2 (1971), pp. 231–251.
2. See JEAN PEPIN, *Mythe et Allégorie,* pp. 276–306.

world had a beginning, he argues, than the world cannot be God, since God is eternal (5). If it was begotten, how, then, could the gods have been begotten by the elements? (7). If the world is a living being, how could it be God, since mortality forms part of the nature of living beings (*animalia*)? All living beings move, and whatever is moved cannot be divine. It is therefore necessary to look for that which moves (*mutatorem*), but which, unlike these, is not itself moved. This rules out all living beings. Can they then be gods, except to Egyptians? The very word for God, however, in Greek Θεός, surely comes from Θέειν, which means to move? This etymology, suggested by the Stoics, is disputed by Tertullian. Even Zeno distinguished God from the nature of the world (10). Tertullian therefore concludes that God and nature are two different words and two different things (11).

Tertullian now goes further, and discusses an idea 'which seems to come from a universal common sense and a single opinion', namely the idea of providence. Varro presents it in the following way. The basis of faith in the deity of the elements is that 'without them, nothing can be begotten or nourished or advanced (*gigni, ali, provehi*) of what contributes towards the preservation of human life' (II, 5, 2). The argument is developed as follows: 'It would not be possible for bodies and souls to exist without the balance (*temperamentum*) of the elements by which it is made possible to inhabit this world, thanks to the sanction of the conditions dictated by the spheres (*circulorum*). Were it not for this, man would be refused a home on account of the excess of cold or heat' (II, 5, 3).

As a result, it is necessary to regard as gods 'the sun which, by itself, fulfils the day, brings harvests because of its heat and ensures the sequence of the year by the stages on its course (*stationibus*); the moon which adorns the night and controls the months; the stars which act as signs of those times that are suitable for cultivation; the heaven which covers everything; the earth on which everything is found; and all that in between them conspires (*conspirat*) for the good of mankind. A divine activity also has to be recognised in the anger (*ira*) manifested in lightning, hail, droughts, pestilential winds, floods and earthquakes. It is correct to regard as gods those whose nature must be honoured in what is favourable and feared in what is unfavourable, that is, to help and to harm' (II, 5, 3–6). According to Cicero, this argument is derived from Cerinthus (*De nat. deor.* II, 5, 13–15).

Tertullian does not in any way question the reality of this harmony in nature, so that, in this respect at least, his view coincides with that of the Stoics, but he does dispute the suggestion that nature itself is the source of that harmony. In music and in medical science, for example, the prize is not given to the instrument, but to the one who uses it. 'Everything that is done must be attributed, not to that by means of which (*per quod*) it is done, but to the one by whom (*a quo*) it is done. (In all things, there are these three categories: *quod est, per quod est* and *a quo est.*) In physics, your rule is contrary to nature in that it refuses to give the highest recognition to the author and looks not for the one by whom these things are done (but for that by means of which they are done). In this way, we are led to believe in the decisions and powers of the elements, when it is really a question of services and ministries' (II, 5, 8–14).

Tertullian's positive argument follows at once: 'They should therefore know that, in the absence of passivity, freedom is recognised, in freedom governance, and in governance the deity. They should remember that, all these things, which are above us, have been established as a law in fixed cycles (*certis curriculis*), in regular paths and in proper spaces, following equal alternations. They should also recognise by simple observation that these things come following the course of time and the controlling forces (*ducatibus*) which are exercised in the times . . . These things should therefore convince you that they have been accorded a power which would seem to belong to the invisible administration (*negotiatio*) of the world in the service of mankind' (II, 5, 15–17).

Further evidence of Tertullian's use of the Stoic argument in this case can be found in his *Apologeticum* XVII, 4, where he sets out very concisely the basic proofs of the existence of God 'from his own works, in their multitude and character, those works that contain us, that sustain us, that delight us, yes – and affright us' (*Vultis ex operibus ipsius tot ac talibus, quibus continemur, quibus sustinemur, quibus oblectamur, quibus etiam exterremur*). These are precisely the arguments which Tertullian describes as Stoic in the *Ad nationes.* According to the Stoics, the divine nature of the elements is borne out by the fact that they provide habitation, services, delights and terrors. Tertullian makes use of these Stoic arguments in support of his thesis that God exists.

He is clearly not simply criticising the Stoic view of the world. Above all he accepts the providential conception of the world, which is, of course, characteristic of Stoicism, and all that is implied by this, so that his attitude is very similar to that of Minucius Felix before him and Novatian after him. On the other hand, he is critical of the interpretation of providence given by Varro and the Latin Stoics. Varro believed that the elements themselves were divine principles conditioning the world for the good of mankind. Tertullian rejected this view and regarded God as transcending the cosmos, and the elements as his instruments for the good of mankind. Indirectly, then, Tertullian's view is derived from Stoicism.

If Tertullian's attitude is compared with that of Minucius Felix, it is clear that Minucius' work is earlier. His attitude is the same as Justin's, and in his investigation of the ideas of the pagan philosophers he is clearly looking for what traces of truth can be found in them. He also latinises the pagan tradition, and in this task draws on Cicero and Seneca. He is far more dependent than Tertullian on secular Latin sources, and this dependence is obvious even in his choice of words – for example, he uses *meatibus* rather than *circulis*. Finally, he elaborates at length material of which Tertullian retains only certain elements. For example, Tertullian makes no attempt to develop the ideas of the harmony of the cosmos, or of the conspiration of the elements. He merely refers to them in passing. We may therefore conclude that, although the Stoic context – that of the cosmic religion – is the same in the case of both authors, the approach of each to the subject is different.

2. TERTULLIAN'S STOICISM

Tertullian's knowledge of philosophy was enormous and he was in particular influenced by Stoicism. In his moral teaching, he was greatly indebted, as Frédouille has pointed out, to Seneca. This is particularly noticeable in his treatment of the theme of patience. In the *De anima* (**XX**, 1), he even goes so far as to speak of *Seneca noster*. As Waszink has shown, he also adopted a number of Stoic arguments, a good example of this being his thesis on the unity of the soul. On the other hand, however, Tertullian is not, like Minucius and Novatian, dependent, from the literary point of view, on Cicero's *De natura deorum* and on the *Letters to Lucilius*. We may therefore say without hesitation that the Stoic influence in his case was less a matter of detail and more of the spirit. He kept certain basic aspects of Stoic teaching, and these were to provide both the background of his own thought and one of the ways in which he was to leave his mark on Latin Christianity.

The first question that we have to consider is Tertullian's teaching about universal corporeity. He uses the word *corpus,* in the ordinary sense of 'human body', synonymously with *caro,* 'flesh', to refer to the material aspect of man as opposed to his soul. This is, as we shall see, a constrast that is strongly emphasised by Tertullian. In this sense, too, he speaks of the 'body of Christ' and of the resurrection of the body. He also, however, uses the word in a technical sense borrowed from Stoic philosophy and one which has frequently been misunderstood both in his own writings and in Stoicism itself. Because this use of the word corresponds to one of the most important aspects of his thought, we must try to discover its real meaning.

Let us begin by examining a number of ways in which Tertullian uses the word.[3] He uses it to designate matter, writing, for example, in his treatise against Hermogenes: 'We believe that matter is corporeal, since the very substance of whatever exists is body' (*Adv. Herm.* XV). This text is very typical of Tertullian's attitude. It is not a question of a contrast between matter and substance, the former being corporeal, the latter not; on the contrary, matter is corporeal precisely because all substances are corporeal. This is even true of the soul, as Tertullian says again and again in the *De anima:* 'The soul is a body of its own peculiar

---

3. See BARNES, *op. cit.,* pp. 304–306; MOINGT, *op. cit.,* pp. 62–63.

quality' (*De anim.* IX). He also opposes Plato, who stressed the existence of 'incorporeal substances' (*De anim.* XVIII). This was a contradiction for Tertullian, who insisted that even the angels were corporeal: 'The angels are by nature of a spiritual substance, though corporeal, of a special kind' (*De carne Christi* V). Finally, the same is also true of God: 'Who will deny that God is a body, although he is spirit? For spirit is a body of a special kind'.

The most general statement that Tertullian makes concerning this universal corporeity is as follows: 'Everything that exists is a body of a special kind. There is nothing incorporeal but what does not exist. If a being has something by which it exists, it is a body' (*De carne Christi* XI). There are, however, different species of body: 'Over against spirit and soul I am not aware in man of any other substance except flesh to which this term, "body", can be applied' (*Adv. Marc.* V, 15, 8). On the basis of these quotations, then, it is possible to set out Tertullian's view of the reality of body in the following schematic way:

$$
\text{body} \begin{cases} \text{spirit} \quad = \quad \text{God} \\ \text{soul} \quad \begin{cases} \text{angel} \\ \text{man} \\ \text{animal} \end{cases} \\ \text{flesh} \end{cases}
$$

If, however, Tertullian believes that everything is body, what, in his opinion, is the opposite of corporeity? It is that which is without concrete effectiveness: 'From where does the force (*vis*) come to an incorporeal soul? How could an empty thing (*vacua*) move solid things (*solida*)?' (*De anim.* VI, 3). The contrast here is between what is firm and solid and what is not. In connection with the Word, Tertullian says: 'What could it mean to say that he is nothing without whom nothing has been done, so that what is without firmness and solidity (*inanis*) makes firm and solid things work, what is empty (*vacuus*) makes full things (*plena*) function and what is incorporeal makes corporeal things operate' (*Adv. Prax.* VII, 7). The essential opposition, then, is between what has concrete reality, firmness and solidity and can resist and act and what is without concrete reality and effectiveness.

This does not mean, however, that there is not something which is the opposite of body, but that this something does not derive from the very substance of reality, but rather from those abstractions by which reality is analysed in the mind. That is so in the case of movement: 'Movement is not a substantial thing, because it is not corporeal, but an accident of substance, that is, of substance and body' (*Adv. Herm.* XXXVI). The same applies to good and evil: 'By giving location to good and evil, you make them into corporeal things. But incorporeal things have no location, unless it be in the body when they qualify (*accidunt*) a body. By giving something a location, you transform it into a substance' (*Adv. Herm.* XLI).

Tertullian's profound vision, then, is that the name of body has to be given to what is real, and what is real is not that which is dependent on the mind, but that which imposes itself on the mind, comes into conflict with it and resists it.

What Tertullian is saying, however, is that this resistance is precisely not the work of matter, which, in a certain sense, resists the least. The soul itself resists more and God offers most resistance of all. In him existential density is at its strongest. This is not in any sense a form of materialism, as has often been suggested, but rather a striking realism. Tertullian is here affirming the objective reality of all being at all levels, and contrasting this with everything that is derived from the categories of the mind.

This conception comes from Stoicism, and Tertullian himself states that he was directly influenced by Soranus (*De anim.* VI, 6). Both the Stoics and Tertullian have frequently been accused of materialism, but, as Eric Weil has correctly observed, the charge is as false in the one case as in the other. A more correct term, Weil suggests, would be 'corporealism'.[4] The body in this case is what exists, what is solid and offers resistance (στέρεον καί ἀντίτυπον).[5] The incorporeal things are the accidents (συμβεβηκός), the non-existing things ex-

---

4. For WEIL's comments on the materialism of the Stoics, see *L'Aventure de l'esprit* (*Mélanges Loyré*), II, pp. 556–572.
5. *Op cit.*, p. 362.

isting in the existing things.[6] The spirit is therefore a body and the reality that it knows is also a body, but knowledge itself is an incorporeal thing.[7] In one sense, body is, according to what Plotinus says about Stoicism, the essence of the οὐσία, in other words, that by which a being exists. It is on the side of existence.

Although, however, Tertullian was certainly inspired by the Stoic concept of corporeity, this does not, however, mean that he accepted it just as it stood. There are certain aspects of the concept which he rejects. The first is that of the homogeneity of body. As we have already seen, he regards corporeity as concretely determined. There are, also, in his view, certain irreducible levels of corporeity, in the first place the three principal degrees of spirit, soul and matter, and secondly the different levels of souls – the angelic, the human and the animal levels. There is, therefore, according to Tertullian, a hierarchy corresponding to the intensity of corporeity or of existence itself, matter, for example, being the least corporeal and God being the most corporeal.

The second aspect of the Stoic teaching about the body that Tertullian rejects is that of τροπή or *mutatio*. Although he accepts this great Stoic principle of change, it is for him clearly something that characterises the created being, in contrast to God who is immovable. All that we have said about Tertullian in the preceding paragraph, moreover, points to the fact that, for him there can be no transformation of one being into another and especially into the being of God. 'The condition of nature must be defined as containing two determinations – what is created and what is uncreated', Tertullian writes in the De anima, 'and what is created includes, by its very nature, change (*demutatio*), whereas what is uncreated is unchangeable. God alone therefore has unchangeable being (*inconvertibilis* = ἄτρεπτος). All created beings are by nature changeable (*convertibilis* = τρεπτός) and mutable (*demutabilis* =ἀλλοίωτος)' (*De anim.* XXI, 7).

This principle was also accepted by Novatian, which in fact confirms its Stoic origin: 'Everything that changes (*vertitur* =

6. *Op. cit.*, p. 568.
7. *Op. cit.*, p. 659.

τρέπτεται) is seen to be mortal by the fact that it changes (*convertitur*). It thus ceases to be what it was, and as a consequence (*consequenter*) begins to be what it was not. The only things which come to change (*conversionem*) are those which are becoming (*fiunt*) or which are born (*gignuntur*). Insofar as there was a time when they did not exist, they learn to be in being born, and in this way their birth is a change (*converti*)' (*De Trin.* 4). The principle of change as the distinguishing mark of the created being is clearly revealed in this text, which points to the transition from non-being to being in the very origin of the creature. This is radically opposed to God, who is above all unchangeable or ἄτρεπτος. This principle in all its ramifications was elaborated at a later period by Gregory of Nyssa.

But if this *conversio* is a fact about all created being, nevertheless it has various aspects. It can be found at the level of existence, substance, or qualities. In his *Adversus Hermogenem*, he shows that matter cannot be both eternal and at the same time transformed from evil into good: 'Nature must be regarded as determined and fixed. If nature is changed (*demutabitur*) from evil into good in matter (according to Hermogenes), then it can be changed from good into evil in God' (*Adv. Herm.* XII, 1). Tertullian then introduces this principle, which occurs so often in his writing: 'If nature must lose what it was by becoming, through a change (*demutatione*), what it was not, then it is not eternal' (*Adv. Herm.* XII, 4; cf. XXXIX, 1).

The same question recurs in the *De anima* in connection with the soul. What is natural in the soul, Tertullian argues, cannot change. It cannot, in its substance, become either matter by sin or spirit by conversion. It is the error of Valentinus, that he conceives of three kinds of soul, but does not admit any possibility of transition from one to the other (XXI, 4). Only 'free will, because it is both natural and changeable (*naturalis et mutabilis*), is transformed by nature into that towards which it turns' (XXI, 6). Free will, however, is precisely not the substance of the soul.

It is also on the basis of the permanence of natures that Tertullian does not accept the possibility of the metempsychosis of the human soul into that of an animal. 'If the soul is in any way capable of being transferred (*translationis* = μεταβολῆς) into animals, will it be changed (*demutabilis*) according to the qualities of the species (*animales*) and their lives, which are contrary to human life, itself made contrary to human life by change (*demutationem*)? If its change consists in losing what it was, it will not be what it was. And if it is no longer what it was, the metensomatosis disappears, because it can no longer be attributed to a soul, which, if it is changed, will no longer exist. For there is no metensomatosis except of that which is changed while remaining in its own nature. If, then, it cannot be changed, for fear that it may no longer be what it was, nor remain in its state because it cannot accept contraries, what valid reason can there be for this change (*translationis*)?' (*De anim.* XXXII, 4).

In the *De carne Christi*, Tertullian replies to the objection based on the belief that 'God was really able to change (*conversum*) into a man', since 'to change (*convertere*) into a thing is the end of what was before' (III, 4–5). This, however, does not apply to God, 'who can change into anything and remain as he is' (III, 5). This is because the change is not a change of substance. At the same time, however, it is not a purely apparent change, but 'the assumption of a strange substance'. Tertullian also extends this principle of change to the angels, who, he claims, assume a real substance whenever they manifest themselves visibly (III, 6). This, then, is clearly a new type of change which does not always affect the substance, but is the assumption by one substance of another substance.

Tertullian returns to this question in his *Adversus Praxean,* in which he asks 'how the Word was made flesh, as transformed (*transfiguratus*) into flesh or assuming flesh' (XXVII, 6). He eliminates the first possibility, giving the same reason that he gave in the *De carne Christi*: 'Transformation (*transfiguratio* = μεταμόρΦωσις) is a destruction of what was before. Everything that is transformed into something else ceases in fact to be what it was and begins to be what it was not. God, however, does not cease to be and cannot be different from what he is' (XXVII, 8). Tertullian then goes further with the argument: 'If the Word was made flesh by transformation or change of substance, Jesus would then be one substance made of two, of flesh and spirit, a kind of mixture, as electrum is an amalgam of gold and silver. He would therefore begin to be neither gold, that is, spirit, nor silver, that is, flesh, since the one is changed into the other and becomes a third thing' (*Adv. Prax.* XXVII, 8).

Another related theme, that of the *mutatio* by which a being of flesh may become spiritual without ceasing to be flesh, is introduced by Tertullian in the *De resurrectione*. His starting-point is in 1 Co. 15:51: *non omnes demutabimur*, 'not all of us will be changed'. Tertullian says, in this context: 'the flesh, by the change that will come, will clothe an angelic mode of being' (*De res.* XLII, 3), and goes on to state more precisely: 'To change does not here mean to cease completely to be what one was; . . . change (*demutationem*) must be distinguished from all forms of destruction'. His conclusion is that 'change (*mutatio*) is destruction if the flesh is changed in such a way that it perishes' (XLII, 3). One of the examples of this type of *demutatio* which Tertullian gives is the transfiguration of Christ (LV, 8–12). Following Scripture, he uses the word *transfiguratio* in a positive sense here.

It should also be noted that Tertullian rejects in this context all change which is in effect a deterioration of substances, although he accepts a type of change which is a development from the seed of the substance itself. This is another important principle, which also originated with the Stoics. Substances themselves are unchangeable. They can, as we have already seen, be the objects of accidental changes, but they can also develop, and Tertullian applies this principle to every sphere of reality, not only at the biological level, but also at that of the soul. According to Tertullian, the soul was a unique substance which developed in the intelligence, in freedom and in various inventions, for which Tertullian uses a word that is very typical of him, namely *suggestus*.[8]

This principle of development is also to be found in the history of salvation. It is what accounts for the transition from the natural law to the Mosaic law. Tertullian sees this as a growth from a seed: 'In the law given to Adam, we recognise the hidden precepts which were given abundantly by Moses. The primitive

8. See the index of the *CCL*.

law was given to Adam and Eve in paradise as the mother of all God's precepts. In this law of God, universal and primordial, we recognise all the precepts of the later law, specifically contained, which in their time germinated outside' (*Adv. Jud.* II, 3–5).

Tertullian thus describes the primitive law as containing in nucleus everything which was to develop later in the law of God. It is very characteristic of him to give such importance to the law. It is also highly characteristic of him on the one hand to connect things with their origins – this is the *census* which we shall be discussing later – and, on the other, to emphasise their development. In Tertullian, the Mosaic law is in no sense regarded as a retrograde step in comparison with the natural law of paradise, as it was by the Pseudo-Barnabas and Justin and even by Commodian. On the contrary, he regards it as a normal development and indeed as a homogeneous growth. Nothing, in his opinion, is contained in it that is substantially new and this is undoubtedly why, as Frédouille has pointed out, Tertullian is reluctant to apply the same principle of development and growth to the transition from the Mosaic law to the law of the gospel. There was a danger of minimising what was new in the gospel.

By contrast, however, in the *Adversus Marcionem,* since this time he was dealing with the Marcionites, who taught that there was a radical cleavage between the Old and the New Testaments, Tertullian set out to show that there was a growth, an advance and an element of novelty, in other words, a *suggestus,* while at the same time continuity was preserved with the Old Testament: 'So he (Christ) made it plain that the things he was separating had once been in unity . . . In that sense we admit this separation, by way of reformation, of enlargement, of progress (*profectus* = προκοτή), as fruit is separated from seed, since fruit comes out of seed. So also the gospel is separated from the law, because it is an advance from out of the law, another thing than the law, though not an alien thing, different though not opposed' (*Adv. Marc.* IV, 11, 11).

This thesis culminated, in the *De virginibus velandis,* in a version of the four ages of mankind, seen both as progression and as continuity. These four ages are compared by Tertullian to the four periods of man's life and it is clear that the theme of growth is once again predominant. Tertullian begins by developing this theme of the transition from the seed to the tree by way of the first sprouting of the seed, then the bush and continues: 'It is the same with righteousness, since both this and creation have the same God. Righteousness was based in its beginnings (*rudimenta*) on man's natural fear of God. Then, through the law and the prophets, it advanced towards childhood (*infantia*). Afterwards, through the gospel, it entered the ardour of youth (*iuventus*). Now, by the Paraclete, it is in its maturity (*maturitas*)' (*De virg. vel.* I, 6).

Tertullian completes the image of the growth of the tree by that of the growth of man. He was certainly the first of the Fathers to make use of the latter theme, which later was to play an important part in the theology of Augustine. Schenke has noted that Augustine's theology of history takes two great frameworks as its starting-points – the traditional Judaeo-Christian exegesis of the theme of the seven days of creation, and the Stoic theme of the ages of mankind. This second theme is not found in the Greek Fathers. It is one of the points at which, under the influence of Stoic thought, Tertullian introduced a category which was to have a great influence. The whole theology of development is here in embryo.

3. TERTULLIAN'S CRITICISM OF PLATONISM

Tertullian belonged to an age when Platonism was a vital philosophical force. He was a contemporary of Ammonius Saccas, who marks the transition from the Middle Platonism of Albinus and Numenius to the neo-Platonism of Plotinus and Porphyry. Christian Platonism was represented at this period by Clement of Alexandria. As Tertullian himself points out (*De praescr.* XXX, 1), the gnostics were disciples of Plato. In Carthage itself, Apuleius was a Middle Platonist who wrote a treatise on the *Daemon of Socrates* and another on the *Teaching of Plato*. This, then, was the environment in which Tertullian lived, and it is important to ascertain his own position with regard to Platonism.

He makes frequent references in his writing to Plato himself, almost always in lists in which he gives Plato's opinion together with those of other philosophers. These references go back to the style of writing known as δοξαί and are not in any sense peculiar to Tertullian. There is, however, one question in connection with which Tertullian discusses Platonism at a very deep level. This is in the context of his teaching about the pre-existence of souls in the *De anima*. In this passage, he refers not only to Plato himself, but also to Middle Platonist thinkers such as Albinus, whom he mentions explicitly twice, and, as Waszink has pointed out, makes many allusions to Platonic thought generally at this period. Tertullian, then, is one of our witnesses for the debate about Platonism in the Latin world.

The subject is introduced by Tertullian in *De anim.* XXIII, 5: 'I am sorry that Plato should, in good faith, have been responsible for spreading all kinds of heresies. In the *Phaedo,* for example, he says that souls come from various places at various times (*Phaed.* 60 c) and, in the *Timaeus,* that the descendants (*genimina*) of God, having been given the task of begetting (*genitura*) mortals, received the immortal principle of the soul and made a mortal body freeze around it (*circumgelaverint*) [9] (*Tim.* 69 c). He also teaches that this world is simply the image of another world'. As Waszink has correctly pointed out, Tertullian mentions these three points precisely because they had been developed by the gnostics into doctrines which Tertullian had just criticized. He wanted therefore to point to the Platonic origins of these gnostic themes. What should also be noted in this context is the accuracy of Tertullian's translation from the Greek of Plato. In the contrasting terms *genimina/genitura,* the original contrast between γεννήμασιν and γένεσιν is preserved.

In *De anim.* XXVI, 1, Tertullian returns to the first of these three points, giving an account of Albinus' interpretation of the passage in the *Phaedo.* This has led many scholars to believe that Tertullian did not look out the three quotations for himself in Plato's work, but found them in Albinus. It is on these grounds that Waszink bases his view that Tertullian borrowed his account

9. Cf. IX, 5, with *gelata.*

of the fall of the souls and of metempsychosis from Albinus, not from the *Didaskalikos,* which is extant and in which the question is not treated, but from a more fully elaborated work.

Tertullian criticises the various arguments on which these theses are based in Platonic thinking. His first criticism is directed against the place occupied by memory: 'In order to obtain consent regarding all these things and the fact that the soul previously lived in higher places with God in the interchange of ideas and that the soul is here thinking again about those things that it previously learnt in the models, he (Plato) developed a new argument, that of knowledge through remembering' (*De anim.* XXI, 6). Plato's argument is subjected to a number of criticisms by Tertullian, who, on the one hand, insists that the soul cannot be regarded as divine, as Plato believed, and at the same time possess the defect of forgetfulness and, on the other, maintains that, if it is natural for the soul to have knowledge of ideas, it cannot forget a knowledge that forms part of its very nature. With this argument, 'all the rest collapses, namely that souls are unbegotten (*innatae*), that they dwell in the heavenly world and have knowledge of divine things there and that, having fallen from there, they recall that knowledge here' (**XXIV**, 12).

Another theory which Tertullian criticises is that of the animation of the infant at the moment of birth, when, according to the philosophers and others, the child breathes in the soul. Both philosophers and others were of the opinion that the soul was not conceived in the womb and was not present when the body was formed, but was imparted after birth from outside to the child who was, until then, not alive (**XXV**, 2). Two questions arise in this context. The first is whether animation takes place at conception or only at birth and, as is clear from Porphyry's treatise on *The Animation of the Embryo,* Platonist thought was very divided about this. Tertullian attacks the idea of animation at birth, which undoubtedly was the position adopted by his Platonist source. (This must have been Albinus, who holds what is effectively this view in the *Didaskalikos* (25).) The second question is whether the soul is imparted from outside or whether it is transmitted in the act of procreation. It is known that the latter was Tertullian's view, since it is the one which he expounds in

De anim. XXVII. This view had its origin in Stoic thought. [10]

Tertullian follows this by a consideration of the problem of metempsychosis, which he describes as the *animarum reciproce discursu* (*De anim.* XXXVIII, 1) or *animarum recidivatu revolubili semper ex alterna mortuorum atque viventium suffectione,* which can be freely translated as 'the movement by which souls pass unceasingly from the dead into the living and conversely'. This teaching is usually attributed to Pythagoras, though, according to Albinus (XXIII, 1), it came from a divine oracle. Tertullian bases his criticism of it in the first place on the classical contrast between the ἕξις and the στέρησις, the 'state' and the 'deprivation'. According to Stoic logic, it was possible for death to follow life, but not for life to follow death, just as blindness can follow sight, but not the reverse. According to Tertullian, Albinus had tried to reply to this objection, which suggests that it was from Albinus that he himself derived it.

Tertullian's second objection is that, in that case, 'there would always have been the same number of souls, that is, the number of those which first entered life' (XXX, 1). The 'commentaries on human antiquities', however, show that the human race has gradually developed, the proof of which is to be found in the gradual population of the earth by the migration of peoples and in demographic growth. None of this, Tertullian argues, would have taken place if the number of souls had remained constant. He also points out that the Platonic theory of a return after a thousand years would risk bringing about the end of life on earth before the coming of a new wave of souls (XXX, 2, 5). Waszink has shown that the 'antiquities' referred to are those of Varro, and that they had been used by Tertullian on this very subject in *De pallio* II, 6, and before him by Seneca (*Cons.* VII, 1–2). What we have here, then, is a Latin Stoic criticism of Platonic thought.

These two basic objections are followed by a number of detailed criticisms. If a woman has several children, for example, is the number of souls not therefore increased? Does this not imply an acceptance of traducianism? If souls leave bodies of various ages, how can they return to bodies with the age of a child? Will they

10. See WASZINK, pp. 344–345.

return with the character which they had before? If they do not, they will not be the same. These and other objections were, in Waszink's opinion, invented by Tertullian, but, since the second is also found in Gregory of Nyssa, it must clearly have been traditional. A Stoic thesis is, moreover, the starting-point for the first. This seems to point to a collection of Stoic objections to the principle of metempsychosis as the basis of Tertullian's arguments.

Tertullian then goes on to discuss the type of metempsychosis which extended to animals and plants, a theory which originated with Empedocles, to whom Tertullian refers explicitly, quoting Empedocles' statement: 'I have been a shrub and a fish'.[11] In the first place, Tertullian says, each animal has a special affinity with one of the elements, whereas the human soul cannot be reduced to any of these elements (*De anim.* XXXII, 3). What is more, in none of the animals is the seat of the soul the same as it is in Man. Man's soul has its own dimension; it cannot fill an elephant or be confined within a fly. It cannot change its nature without ceasing to exist. This assimilation with animals has a purely moral significance and is used to point to a trait of character (XXXII, 1–9). Here again, Waszink believes that these are Tertullian's own objections. It is true that his argument that the soul occupies a certain space implies corporeity, but this idea may have originated with a Stoic thinker who shared the same view.

The problem of Tertullian's sources in this whole discussion is raised both by his account of Platonist theory and by his refutation of it on the basis of Stoicism. For what we have is a highly characteristic block of ideas: criticism of the theory of the fall of souls; coming and going between heaven and earth; criticism of the theory of metempsychosis; and the simultaneous origin of the body and the soul. This group as a whole occurs, so far as the present writer is aware, only in one other patristic author, namely Gregory of Nyssa[12] (*De anima et resurrectione* 188B–225B).

It is interesting therefore to examine the points of contact

---

11. See Diels, B 117.
12. Waszink refers to Gregory several times, especially in connection with the theory of the simultaneous origin of the body and the soul.

between Gregory and Tertullian. In the first place, Gregory distinguishes between metempsychosis from men into men and from men into animals or plants. He ascribes the second type to Empedocles, and quotes the same fragment as Tertullian (108 B–C). He accuses this theory of confusing two different natures (110 B–C), and points out that it is absurd to think of the human soul as flying with birds, swimming with fishes, or feeding like animals (110 C; see De Anim. XXXII, 6D). This assimilation with animals, he stresses, has a purely moral significance. He then goes on to discuss the question of the fall of souls, and points out that there is a cyclical movement (κυκλικός = revolubile) of the soul, which leads to a coming and going between the heavenly region (οὐράνιον χῶρον) and earth (112C–113C). He also discusses the two theories of the soul's introduction into the body at the time of conception in the womb or at the time of birth (116C–117B). Next, he considers the doctrine of the simultaneous appearance of the body and the soul (123B–C). After this, he states that, on the basis of the principle of ἕξις and στέρησις, life cannot come from death (128A). Finally, he deals with the determination of the number of souls, but sees this as something which occurs at the end of a process of growth (128C).

It goes without saying that Tertullian could not have influenced Gregory of Nyssa here, but it is at the same time difficult not to conclude that each author made use, in his own special way, of already existing material. If this is so, then the treatise in question undoubtedly came from a Middle Platonist source. As we have already seen, Tertullian referred to Albinus, and Gregory's treatise is basically a continuation of Porphyry's teaching. It would seem, moreover, that Porphyry himself made use of Albinus, and it is certainly in keeping with the practice of the latter to have systematised Plato's teaching by comparing the various passages in his work which relate to the same themes. Apuleius did the same in his De dogmate Platonis. If this theory is sound, then Tertullian would be the earliest witness to a lost treatise by Albinus which was used by Porphyry and also indirectly by Gregory of Nyssa.

We must now consider the questions raised by the refutation of the Platonist argument, the first being the question of rebirth in another human life. In the *Apologeticum* Tertullian recognises the possibility of metempsychosis (*Apol.* XLVIII, 3), but insists that the same soul must return to the same body. This, he says, is in accordance with the Christian belief in the resurrection and in God's judgement. Gregory of Nyssa also recognises the validity of this type of metempsychosis and he too says that the same soul enters the same body (109 A–B). Both authors adopt a standard approach of Christian apologetic which sees the Platonist teaching about metempsychosis as one of the cases where truth and error are mixed together.

In the *De anima,* however, the position is different. Here Tertullian is striving to collect all the available arguments against metempsychosis. Waszink has pointed out that some of them seem to be Tertullian's own invention – those from quintuplets, for example, or from acquired characteristics. But, in the case of the questions regarding the age at which men are reborn and the dispositions with which the soul will be endowed at rebirth, the arguments are also to be found in the *De mortuis* of Gregory of Nyssa (533 B–C), in the form of objections to the resurrection to which Gregory replies. They must therefore have formed part of a collection, no doubt sceptic in origin, of objections to metempsychosis of the Platonist type.

As regards metempsychosis of the Empedoclean type, that is, of souls being transferred to animals and plants, there is much more material. One can see all the jokes to which the subject might lend itself, and Tertullian refers to these in the *Apologeticum* (XLVIII, 3), quoting a line from the Latin comic author, Laberius, 'The man comes from the mule, and the viper from the woman' (*Apol.* XLVIII, 1). There is also the risk, he points out, of eating one's ancestors: 'A man must be careful not to eat a bit of his own grandfather in his beef' (XLVIII, 1). The same objection is also raised by Gregory of Nyssa (112 A–C). It clearly formed part of a scholarly criticism of the Pythagorean and Empedoclean theory.

A much more important subject, however, is that of the permanence of natures. For Tertullian, first of all there is the permanence of the nature of the soul, for a human soul differs by nature from that of an animal (*Apol.* XLVIII, 2, Vulg.). Gregory makes precisely the same point (109 B). Both authors are here following a Platonist tradition which can be found in the work of Iamblichus and Hieracles, the latter being, as Theiler has pointed out, closely connected with Ammonius Saccas. Ammonius being a contemporary of Tertullian's, it would seem that we have here an echo of controversies within Platonism at the time when Tertullian was writing.

In the *De anima*, however, Tertullian, goes even further, postulating not only that there are different natures of souls, but also that there are different natures of bodies. He develops this thesis in *De anim.* XXXII, 1–10, thus correcting the F manuscript of the *Apologeticum,* which reads: 'The same soul must come back into the same body, that is, the human body' (XLVIII, 2). This is not to be found either in Gregory of Nyssa or in the Platonist tradition. The way in which Tertullian elaborates this argument points to the possibility that he may himself have invented it, as Waszink suggests. On the other hand, however, he also uses data taken from biology and this is something that he did not invent, but borrowed from Pliny.[13] The idea that, although always made from the four elements, the body has uses which are different from those of the elements is probably derived, in Tertullian's case, from an Aristotelian tradition.

There are two quite different problems involved here. In the first place, there is the question of the reincarnation of human souls in human bodies. Here Tertullian borrows his arguments, so far as the soul is concerned, from the Platonists and, for the body, from the Aristotelian and Stoic tradition. In the second place, there is the question whether it is the same souls that are reincarnate in the same bodies. This is, of course, a theological argument which is bound up with the question of judgement. Tertullian makes a clear distinction between the two problems in *Apol.* XLVIII, 3 and 4, but in the *De anima,* he tries to apply philosophical arguments as well. Finally, there is the question of the transmission of the body and the soul by means of procreation and the closely related question of man's development since the

13. See WASZINK, *De anima,* pp. 385–387.

time of the primal pair, which are, of course, both Stoic themes.

Before concluding this chapter, it should be noted that there are other points of comparison between Tertullian's *De anima* and Gregory of Nyssa. A good example of this is the reference in *De anim.* XIV, 4 and in Gregory (38 A–B) to the hydraulic organ. Tertullian mentions Posidonius explicitly in this context and Gregory is clearly also dependent on Posidonius, so that this author of the Middle Stoa may well be their common source.

In the case of Tertullian, however, this influence was mediated through the Latin Stoa. Thus, Waszink has drawn attention, in the passage that we have been considering here, to borrowings from Pliny the Elder, whose Natural History follows the tradition of the scientific work of Posidonius, and from Varro, whose writings are in the same tradition. What is more, Posidonius' followers were mainly Latin authors, the most important being Cicero and Seneca. Tertullian is undoubtedly within this tradition, and witnesses to it, and even though his interpretation of Stoic teaching was original, he was one of its great representatives. As Barnes has justly remarked, Tertullian was the greatest intellect of his time.

CHAPTER EIGHT

NOVATIAN AND THE COSMIC RELIGION

THE Stoic influence on Novatian has been studied above all from the point of view of his moral teaching,[1] but there are in his writings also cosmological and anthropological doctrines which are worthy of attention. The main source of their inspiration is the opening chapters of Genesis, but their vocabulary and certain of the concepts are philosophical. It is therefore interesting to investigate whether here too there is any question of Stoic influence. The examination of this question which follows is a modest contribution to this study, offered in homage to the scholar who has with such skill defined the philosophical sources of Tertullian and Calcidius.

1. THE BEAUTY OF THE WORLD

In his *De Trinitate*, Novatian provides us with a description of nature which includes three sections – the visible world, man and the angels – and it is the first with which we shall be principally concerned. It displays certain points of contact with other descriptions of the same type, among Latin works notably with Cicero, *De nat. deor.* II, 39, Apuleius, *De mundo* 2–3,[2] and Seneca, *Quaest. nat.* II, 4. We shall also be referring to the *De Opificio* of Gregory of Nyssa, since this work derives, as von

---

1. Cf. Most recently H.-J. VOGT, *Coetus Sanctorum*, Bonn, 1968.
2. We are referring here to the Latin translation of the Περὶ κόσμου. As FRANZ REGEN has pointed out in his *Apuleius philosophus platonicus*, Berlin, 1971, this translation seems to have been due to Apuleius. It is in any case a Latin translation that was apparently used by Novatian. See also JEAN BEAUJEU, *Apulée. Ouvrages philosophiques*, pp. 111–119.

Ivanka has shown, from the same source as Cicero. It is quite plain that Novatian draws inspiration from biblical sources, but he has secular ones as well. Is it possible to ascertain which these were?

One preliminary question is the order in which Novatian describes the different parts of the cosmos. He mentions heaven with the stars first, then the earth with the plants and the animals, and finally the sea with the fish. In *Spect.* 9, he then adds the air. This is not the same order as that of the hierarchy of elements as we find this in the section dealing with the harmony of opposites. Water ought to be placed, strictly speaking, before the earth, but Novatian is here working from a more descriptive standpoint which contrasts heaven on the one hand with the earth and the sea on the other. Nor is this, of course, the perspective of Gn. 1, where the earth is mentioned last.

This is an important factor in the attempt to determine Novatian's sources, since the same sequence, earth-sea, is also found in parallel texts, notably Cicero's *De nat. deor.* II, 39, the *De mundo* 4, and Gregory of Nyssa's *De opif.* I, 132 B–C. What we have here, then, is undoubtedly a current conception which was originally Stoic and, in particular, Posidonian, as the agreement of Cicero and Gregory of Nyssa would seem to indicate. Taking all four parts of the cosmos into account, however, the order in the *De natura deorum* is not the same as that followed by Novatian, for the pair earth-sea comes first, followed by the air and the heaven. Novatian's order, however, is the same as that of the *De mundo,* which is an indication of his relation to that work.

Turning to the detailed description of the different parts of the world, we find that Novatian's account of heaven is based on that given in Genesis, in which the sun and the moon are mentioned first and then the stars. The reference to the regular cycles (*meatus*) of the stars is found in all the texts. More interesting is Novatian's description of the earth: *In terris quoque altissimos montes in verticem sustulit, valles in ima deiecit, campos aequaliter statuit, animalium greges instituit, fruges in cibum elicuit, silvarum quoque robora solidavit . . ., fontium ora reseravit et lapsus fluminibus infudit. Post quae varies florum coloribus ad voluptatem spectantium cuncta vestivit,* 'On the earth, he also raised the highest mountains to

their peaks, cast the valleys down to their depths, likewise evened
out the fields, ordered the animals into herds, brought out crops
into food and set firm the trees of the forests . . . He marked off
the edges of the fresh water springs and filled the courses of the
rivers. Next he clothed everything with flowers of various
colours for the pleasure of all who see them' (*De Trin.* 1). A brief
summary of this is also given in the *De spect.* A comparison with
Cicero reveals various common elements: *altissimos montes, campos, fruges, fontium, vestita floribus,* and the references to the rivers
and the animals. Gregory of Nyssa also speaks of flowers
(ἄνθεσιν) , vegetables (βοσκήματα) and the summits of
the mountains (ἀκρώρειαι) and adds the valleys
(κοίλοις) and the flocks (κατ' ἀγέλας) . These points
of comparison, however, are only concerned with fairly commonplace expressions. There are much more striking comparisons to be made between Cicero and Gregory, among the
most interesting being the reference in both to rocks
(ῥαχεῖαι = *rupes*) and to metals hidden in the earth (*De opif.*
134 A; *De nat. deor.* II, 39).

There are also many points of comparison between Novatian's
detailed description of the earth and that given in the *De mundo,*
both as far as content and vocabulary are concerned. Apuleius'
list of the beauties of the earth includes, for instance, the high
mountains (*altitudines montium = altissimos montes, De Trin.*), the
evenness of the plains (*camporum aequore = campos aequaliter*), the
animals (*animantibus = animalibus*), the forests (*silvae = silvarum*)
which are a 'clothing' (*vestituta = vestivit*) and which the other
authors do not mention at all, the springs (*fontes = fontium*), the
courses of the rivers (*fluminum lapsus = fluminibus lapsuis*) and the
varied colours of the flowers (*infinitis coloribus florum = variis
florum coloribus*).[3] It is therefore probable, on the basis of these
similarities, that Novatian drew on the *De mundo.*

Novatian points to two features of the sea – the great variety
of animals inhabiting it and the fact that the coastline acts as a
frontier against invasion by the sea. The former comes from

3. Cf. also *Florides* 10: *Montium vertices arduos extulit* (= *in verticem sustulit, De
Trin.*).

Cicero; as to the latter, Cicero does mention the coastline, but merely remarks that the earth and the sea seem to form a unity. The same idea is found in Gregory of Nyssa in a more developed form; and the coastline is also mentioned in *De mundo* 4. Here Novatian starts from a hint which he found in his sources – the *De natura deorum* and the *De mundo* – but his use of the theme is personal and was inspired by the Book of Job.

As we have already noted in the *De Trinitate*, Novatian does not mention the air, but deals with it in the *De spectaculis*, after the other elements. This points to a desire on his part to complete the description given in the first treatise and is at the same time a further proof of the authenticity of the second. The text given in the manuscripts is: *Interim constantem pariter summa conspiratione nexibusque concordiae extensum aerem medium tenuitate sua cuncta vegetantem, nunc imbres contractis nubibus profundentem, nunc serenitatem refecta raritate revocantem.* The beginning of this passage is incomprehensible as it stands. *Inter haec* has been suggested by Latinius and *pariter ac* appears in Z, but, in my opinion, a much simpler correction is preferable. My reading is: *Inter ima constantem pariter et summa.* The word *ima* appears in the parallel text of *De Trin.* 1 in contrast with *altissimos* and *pariter et* is frequently used by Novatian.[4] The passage may now be translated as follows: 'Situated between the things below and the things above, in harmony and connection, the air, spread out in the midst, impregnates everything by virtue of its rarefied substance, now pouring forth showers when the clouds have condensed, now calling back fine weather when the rarefaction of the air has been restored'. This emendation is supported by a parallel passage in Seneca (*Quaest. nat.* II, 4, 1): *Aer caelum terramque conectit qui ima ac summa sic separat ut tamen iungat. Separat, quia medius intervenit, iungat, quia utrique per hunc inter se consensus est,* 'The air joins the sky to the earth, separating the depths from the heights in such a way that nevertheless it unites them. It separates them because it comes in between, and joins them because through it there is harmony between them both'.

What is particularly striking here is that air is the sole in-

---

4. Cf. H. KOCH, *Cyprianische Untersuchungen*, p. 6, note 1.

termediary between heaven and earth and that, as we have already seen, the water is regarded as forming part of the earth. This is not a Stoic idea. According to Gregory of Nyssa, both the air and the water formed 'the intermediate creation between the extremes — that is, heaven and earth, partly sharing in their neighbours and bringing about a mediation (μεσιτεύει) between the extremes (ἄκρα), so that they may reveal the concord (συναφεία) of opposites by the mediation of what is in between (διὰ τοῦ μέσου) ' (De opif. 7; 139A). This is also the conception implied in the De nat. deor, so that it would seem to point to a Stoic view and, in particular, to that of Posidonius.

On the other hand, the more descriptive conception, which is more in accordance with the various levels of the cosmos than with the theory of the elements, is the one that is found in the Latin De mundo. This is all the more interesting in that, as Regen has pointed out, this concerns one of the points at which Apuleius modified the Περὶ κόσμου, by introducing a reference to the air into several passages (1, 29; 33), apparently under Platonist influence.[5] In the Timaeus, Plato develops this tripartite conception: 'It is not possible for only two terms to form a good composition without a third, since there must be a link between them (in the middle = μέσον) which connects them' (Tim. 31c — 32a). The same idea is also found in Albinus: 'After the ether, there is the sphere of the air and at the centre the earth with its moisture' (Didask. XV, 4).

Two other characteristics of the air are also mentioned in the text of the De spectaculis. The first is that it gives life because of its subtlety, tenuitate sua cuncta vegetantem. This phrase is found almost word for word in Cicero: 'By its subtlety (tenuitate), it provides for the living (animantibus) a life-giving and beneficial breath' (De nat. deor. II, 35). The second characteristic is alternating rains, connected with the condensation of the air (contractis), and fine weather (serenitatem), connected with the rarefaction of the air (raritate). Here too, the text that is closest to this is Cicero's Tum autem concretus in nubes cogitur, tum fusus et extenuatus sublime fertur, 'Then, however, hardened together, it is forced into the clouds,

5. Cf. JAEGER, Nemesios von Emesa, p. 101, note 1.

then diffused and made less dense it is borne on high'. The word
serenitas is also found in the Latin *De mundo* 8.

We may therefore conclude that Novatian seems to have
drawn on Apuleius' *De mundo* for his account of the cosmos,
which is more descriptive than methodical. He has also borrowed
certain elements in his description of the world from Cicero's *De
natura deorum*, but he is independent of him in his arrangement of
the material as a whole. Finally, in the matter of the air as an intermediary between heaven and earth, he displays a literary
affinity with Seneca.

2. THE HARMONY OF OPPOSITES

After this descriptive section in the *De Trin.* 1, Novatian goes on,
in chapter 2, to demonstrate the coherence of the universe: 'God,
holding all things together (*continens omnia*), leaves nothing empty of himself . . . He is always present in his work, penetrating
(*vadens*) all things, moving all things, connecting (*conectens*) in
order to achieve concord (*concordiam*) between the discordant
(*discordantes*) matter⁶ of all the elements, so that, from the
different (*disparibus*) elements, one world, both single (*unus*) and
firm (*solidatus*), would be formed by the harmony (*conspiratione*)
of the elements brought together (*coagmentata*)'.⁷

This passage clearly contains two different aspects – that of the
harmony of opposites and that of the activity of providence. The
theme of the harmony of opposites is found, with certain
differences in each case, in the Platonist, Aristotelian and Stoic
traditions. In the case of the latter, Cicero speaks, in the *De nat.
deor.* II, 7, of the *rerum consentiens*, 'agreement of things', *con-
spirans*, 'harmony', and *continuata cognatio*, 'perpetual kinship'; and
later in the same treatise says: *Illa mihi placebat oratio de convenientia
consensuque naturae quam quasi cognatione continuatam conspirare
dicebas*, 'I was pleased by the discourse on the agreement and har-

---

6. Cf. also *De Trin.* 5: *materiarum . . . diversitas consuevit excitare discordiam*,
'diversity of matter has usually provoked discord'.
7. Cf. also *De Trin.* 18: *ex coagmentis corporalibus*, 'from the combination of
corporeal things'.

mony of nature which you said continued to harmonise as though through kinship' (III, 11). The word *coagmentatio* is also found in *De nat. deor.* II, 46: *Quae copulatio rerum, et quasi consentiens ad mundi incolumitatem coagmentatio naturae,* 'This union of things and, so to speak, this combination of nature agreeing together for the safety of the world'. Otherwise, however, neither the thought nor the language of Cicero coincides with those of Novatian here.

This is not the case with the *De mundo.* In paragraphs 19–21, the author follows his description of the world with his general conception of it, which is, as we have just seen, what Novatian does. According to his view, the world is fundamentally a concord (*concordia*) between the various elements (*elementorum*) of air, water and earth: 'The nature of the world is made of different elements, warring among themselves' (*De mundo* 19). By the unity 'of these disparate (*impares*) principles', however, 'nature has composed (the universe) like a piece of music, by an agreement (*consensu*) that is harmonious and without discord (*discordante*)', so that 'the distinct (*inconfusa*) substance' of the elements has been led to this 'concord (*concordia*)', in which a harmony is achieved between 'the disparate (*disparibus*) qualities of nature' (*De mundo* 21).

Despite apparent resemblances, there are in fact two quite different views of nature here. The first view is that of the Stoics, who insist on the unity of nature, of which all the elements come from the primal fire, are transformed into each other, and will return to the fire. The second view is Aristotle's. He taught that there were different natures, which could not be reduced to each other and which had opposite qualities, but between which a harmony had been established. The ideas and the language of our two authors obscure these differences. The Stoic view of Cicero is ultimately a biological one – he speaks of *conspiratio* (σύμπνοια) and says himself that *consensus* is his own translation of συμπαθεία (*De nat. deor.* III, 11).

How does Novatian deal with this question? He emphasises in fact both the difference between the elements and their concord and, generally speaking, his vocabulary overlaps with that of the *De mundo.* The difference between the elements is stressed by the use of the word *dispares,* but by far the most important term in the passage is *concordia,* which appears altogether five times in the passage from the *De mundo.* Now this word is a favourite with Novatian also, who uses it again in the *De spectaculis,* with reference to the harmony existing between the elements. He also employs it to express the harmony or union of both natures in Christ. Very frequently, too, it is paired with *discordantes,* as in the *De mundo.* Finally, the term *elementa* should also be noted.

Novatian also makes use of a number of Stoic themes, especially that of the *conspiratio.* This is a translation of the Greek word σύμπνοια and was originally a medical term, used in the first place by Hippocrates.[8] It was later employed by Chrysippus in the sense of 'the living unification of the parts by the *pneuma'.*[9] Cicero too uses the word *conspiratio* in his *De nat. deor.* II, 7; III, 11, as we have already pointed out. The Greek word σύμπνοια is also found in Gregory of Nyssa, *De opif.* 138C, with whom it is in general a favourite theme.[10] In the same chapter, Gregory speaks about the σύνδεσμος (138 C) or 'binding together', which is associated with the βεβαιότης or 'firmness' that corresponds to Novatian's *soliditas.* Here, therefore, it is Gregory to whom Novatian is closest.[11] It should, in conclusion, be noted that the word *conspiratio* is found not only in Novatian's *De Trinitate,* but also in his *De spectaculis,* where it appears in the text that we have quoted above: *conspiratione nexibusque concordiae.* Here the σύμπνοια is concerned above all with the harmony of the elements, and the use of the word is closely related to Gregory's in the *De opificio.*

3. THE COSMIC CHARIOT

We must now consider more closely the first part of Novatian's statement in the *De Trin.* 2, in which he speaks of the source of cosmic harmony as 'God, holding all things together

8. Cf. JEAN DANIELOU, *L'être et le temps chez Grégoire de Nysse,* pp. 51–58.
9. Cf. BEINHARDT, *Cosmos und Sympathie,* p. 55.
10. *Op. cit.,* pp. 51–69.
11. Tertullian also uses the word, in descriptions of Stoic philosophy (*Ad nat.* V, 5; *Adv. Marc.* I, 13, 3).

(*continens omnia*)' and 'leaving nothing empty (*vacuum*) of himself
. . . always present in his work, penetrating (*vadens*) all things,
moving all things (and) connecting (*conectens*) all things'. This
passage can be compared with another of Novatian's in which he
defines God as 'an intelligence begetting and completing all
things and governing the causes of things according to a natural
connection (*naturaliter nexas*) and according to superior and
perfect reason (*ratione perfecta*)' (*De Trin.* 2, 12).

It is quite obvious that Novatian's thought and language here
are both Stoic − clear examples of this are the parallels with the
πνεῦμα διῆκον, the σύνδεσμος, the λόγος and the
Φυσικὸς εἱρμος of the Stoics (SVF 948; II, 274). Cicero is,
moreover, Novatian's immediate source here: *Natura est igitur
quae contineat mundum omnem. Quo circa necesse est naturam eam, quae
res omnes complexas teneat, perfectione rationis excellere*, 'Nature,
therefore, is that which contains the whole universe. Consequently, it is necessary for nature, which embraces all complex
things, to excel by the perfection of reason' (*De nat. deor.* II, 11).
The word *conexa* appears in the context[12] and the idea that
'everything is full of God' is also to be found in Cicero (*Leg.* II,
11, 26), as well as the theme of God penetrating all things.

It is a striking fact, moreover, that the author of the *De mundo*
writes polemically against the idea of God's immanence, using
language which is very similar to that employed by Novatian.
He criticises, for instance, those poets who claim that everything
is 'full of Jupiter' (*De mundo* 24) and that nothing is 'empty'
(*viduata*) of his help. It is possible to say that 'God penetrates
everything (*per omnia permeare*)' and that 'his power extends to us'
(*De mundo* 25), but only on condition that he remains in heaven
and that his activity in the world takes place through intermediaries. This is, of course, an example of teaching based on
the esoteric writings of Aristotle and their denial of the exercise
of providence in special cases.

It would therefore seem as though Novatian drew more on
Cicero than on the *De mundo* here, but the question is in fact not
quite so simple as it first appears. For though Novatian uses

12. Cf. Seneca, *Quaest. nat.* II, 4: *conecti.*

language closely related to that of Cicero, he also criticises Cicero's argument, according to which God is identified with the immanence of nature: 'As for the regular alternation of night and day, we do not think that the maker (*artificem*) of this is some nature (*naturam*) or other, but would more readily acknowledge that it is God the creator' (*De Trin.* 3). This is a direct criticism of the teaching of Zeno as outlined by Cicero: 'Nature is not merely skilful (*artificiosa*) but is called "craftsman" (*artifex*) outright by Zeno' (*De nat. deor.* II, 22).[13]

It is clear, then, that Novatian makes use of Cicero's idea that providence penetrates everything, but it is equally evident that providence is not, in his opinion, the same as nature. It is, on the contrary, the transcendent God. Conversely, he retains from the *De mundo* the idea of God's transcendence over the universe, but rejects the idea of a divine activity that can affect the world only through intermediaries. We can see from this both the complexity of Novatian's sources and the freedom with which he uses them, retaining only what was in accordance with Christian faith.

A good illustration of this can be found in a text in which Novatian interprets the vision of the chariot (Ezk. 1) as an expression of the universal providence of God who is otherwise transcendent (*De Trin.* 3). In his view, the chariot is the world and all that it contains, including the stars and their regular movement. God governs the world with the help of the angels, represented in the vision of Ezekiel by the winged animals. The wheels of the chariot are interpreted by Novatian as the cyclical rhythm of the days and the seasons, and the feet as the movement of time. The eyes on the rims of the wheels signify the providence of God, from whom nothing can be hidden. The fire symbolises either the final conflagration, or the vital force which animates the world or the heat without which a world made of earth would become numb. Finally, Novatian interprets the reins which restrain or release the animals as the natural law (*naturalis lex*).

This text contains a number of data derived from Stoicism —

---

13. Cf. WEYER, *Novatianus De Trinitate*, p. 50, note 23.

the idea of universal providence extending to individual realities, time conceived as progressive, the doctrine of the ultimate conflagration, fiery breath seen as a vital universal principle, heat and cold as primordial qualities and finally the idea of the natural law (Φυσικὸς νόμος). At the same time, however, Novatian christianises this Stoic view by emphasising that God is transcendent and that he surveys everything. In this task, God is, according to Novatian, helped by the angels and the stars; these play an important part in governing the world,[14] but they are in no sense intermediaries, necessary to God's activity in the world.

This theme of the word represented as a chariot, with God as the charioteer, derives ultimately from the *Phaedrus* of Plato.[15] The same theme is also found in the work of Philo (*Quis rer.* 301; *Quaest. Gen.* IV, 51; *Migr.* 131) and in that of Dio Chrysostom. The allusion in Novatian's text to the reins, stretched or loose, is, moreover, a reference to another passage in the *Phaedrus,* in which Plato speaks of the harnessing of the horses and of the charioteer being the spirit. The theme is transferred here to the concept of the world-soul. Finally, in this connnection, it is interesting to note the presence of this theme of God the charioteer (ἡνιοχοῦσα) in the chapter of the *De opificio* which we have already quoted.

Even before Novatian, however, other patristic authors had identified Plato's chariot of Zeus with the chariot in Ezekiel's vision. The theme is found in the *Cohortatio* of Pseudo-Justin (31) and in the *Adversus haereses* of Irenaeus (III, 11, 8). Later, it was considerably developed by Methodius (*De res.* II, 10) and then by Ambrose (*Abr.* II, 8, 54). Novatian's interpretation, however, cannot be compared in its details with any of these texts. His exegesis is quite original. The basic question that arises is how the theme came to appear in his treatise and it would certainly seem as though it was originally suggested by the *De mundo.*

The whole of the last part of the *De mundo* is in fact dominated by the theme of Zeus as the chief driver and charioteer (*in cursus rector*) of the universe: 'The whole of the world is governed; it

14. Cf. JEAN DANIELOU, *Les anges et leur mission*, pp. 25–27.
15. Cf. esp. P. BOYANCE,'Sur l'exégèse hellénistique du Phèdre, 246c', *Miscellanea Rostagni,* 1963, pp. 45–53.

has a driver (*rector*) who watches over (*speculatur*) everything'. This driver is identified with the law, which maintains the balance. He dwells on high and from there controls the whole of the universe. This, in the first place, means heaven, which moves along a course without deviating and the stars, each of which follows its own path. We may finally note that the concluding sentence of the *De mundo* is an extra quotation from Plato in addition to that from *Leg.* 715 c. which appears in the Περὶ κόσμου, and that in this additional quotation Regen believes that it is possible to detect the passage relating to the chariot of Zeus.

Several elements in this imagery are also to be found in Novatian's treatise. Above all, he includes the same image of the cosmic chariot with God as its driver. He also speaks of the *lex naturalis*, the natural law, acting as a yoke balancing the horses. Another element that appears in both the *De mundo* and the *De Trinitate* is that of the stars, their regular course and the part that they play in the government of the world. Both texts also speak of God as dwelling high above the heavens. As a whole, the theme is elaborated in Novatian's treatise with the help of Stoic ideas and biblical images, but it would certainly seem to have originated with the idea of the winged chariot in Plato's *Phaedrus* as taken up by the Platonist Apuleius in the *De mundo.* [16]

The theme, then, is basically Platonic and Aristotelian, but Novatian adds to it the Stoic idea of the presence and the activity of God in the world. He does not therefore accept either the Stoic idea of God's complete immanence in the world, nor does he accept the Aristotelian idea of divine transcendence. He does, in other words, emphasise that providence is able to reach even the most lowly of the realities found in the cosmos.

All this goes to confirm what has so far been said in this section, namely that Novatian does not take all his ideas from one source. His basic inspiration is the book of *Genesis,* but the main framework for his ideas is clearly the *De mundo* of Apuleius and he also introduces many Stoic elements, implying that he had a knowledge of Cicero's *De natura deorum* and of Seneca's letters.

16. It should be noted that Tertullian quotes the *Phaedrus* (246 e) in his *Apol.* XXIV, 3.

4. FREEDOM

Novatian's teaching about man too is impregnated with Stoicism. He says, for example, that the world was created before the creation of man in order to be his dwelling place and that man appeared afterwards (*De Trin.* 1; 3, 10f.; cf. also 21; 7–15). He was placed in charge of the world (*ibid.*) and everything was put at his service (1; 3, 14). All these aspects are found, in exactly the same order, in Cicero's *De natura deorum,* but the parallel with Gregory of Nyssa is even more striking: 'Man was introduced last after creation, not thrown back to the end as contemptible, but called to control what was made subject to him from the moment of his creation' (2; 134 A). Even before Gregory, moreover, the same theme had occurred in Methodius (*De res.* I, 34). Novatian also teaches that man's body was formed from the elements (*primordia*) of the earth, but that his substance was breathed into him by a breath (*halitus*) which was heavenly and divine (1; 3, 12-14). In the same way, we find Gregory writing: 'God places in him the principles of a double creation, having mingled the divine with the earthly' (134 B).

The place in which the first man and woman were put was paradise. This is, according to Novatian, in the world: 'God established for the first human beings, as a private world designed for a life that was to be eternal, a garden in the East' (8; 24, 9-11). The tree of the knowledge of good and evil and the tree of life were planted in this garden (24, 11-12). Novatian emphasises that the tree of the knowledge of good and evil is not in itself evil, and that all that is evil in it is the use to which man puts it, that is, his use of it despite God's prohibition. Novatian takes up this idea again in his *De cibis iudaicis,* in which he states that all foods are good in themselves and that they are made harmful only by being used wrongly. The tree of life confers immortality, which is man's destiny and God forbids Adam to touch its fruit after he has sinned, so that he will not be a sinner for ever (1; 5, 1-4). This latter feature undoubtedly comes from Irenaeus (*Adv. haer.* III, 23, 6). It is noteworthy that, as in his description of the cosmos, Novatian is very literal in his interpretation of the biblical account and that his view of the material world is extremely optimistic.

The exclusive cause of evil is man's will. God created man free (1; 3, 15) — if he had not been created free, he would not have been the image of God (4; 1-2). On the other hand, however, God gave him a law (*lex*), 'so that an unbridled freedom could not lead him to despise the giver' (1; 2, 3). Man, however, incited by the jealous angel (4, 5), rejected this law, and was deprived of his immunity from death (4, 6; see also 10; 35, 1-2). In accordance with the Stoic tradition, then, Novatian clearly stresses man's freedom. The same emphasis is found in Gregory's *De opificio*. Novatian's definition of freedom also corresponds to the Stoic 'choice' or προαίρεσις :'Having it in his power for his will to tend, according to the movement of the spirit, in one direction or the other' (4; 4-5).

Will, however, cannot be separated from law. Just as God rules the world by the natural law, Novatian argues, so too he governs man's freedom by the moral law (1; 3, 7-9). Left to itself and not restrained (*soluta*) by anything (1; 3, 15) freedom is at risk. It becomes what Novatian calls 'unbridled' (*effrenata*) freedom — if 'the reins are loosened' (*Cib.* 4; 959 B), the passions run wild. This is, of course Plato's image in the *Phaedrus* — the body as the chariot, the charioteer as the spirit and the reins restraining the passions (*Pud.* 14). This is why, Novatian insists, the law was given to the sons of Israel — they had to be led back to the good morals that they had received from the patriarchs, but had lost in Egypt (*Cib.* 3; 956 C). The law of the gospel brings this law of the old covenant to perfection (6; 962 A).

Because Adam broke this law, he was as a necessary consequence (*consequenter*) punished, just as, had he been faithful to the law, he would have been rewarded. He was, however, not changed for the worse in his essential being (10; 9-10), but simply made subject to the penalty of work: 'God has kindly ordained (*indulgenter temperavit*) man's punishment insofar as he does not curse man himself so much as his work on earth' (1; 4, 8-10). In his reference here to God's goodness, Novatian is very close to Irenaeus.[17]

In a curious passage in the *De cibis iudaicis*, Novatian explains

---

17. Cf. H. VOGT, *Coetus sanctorum. Die Kirchenbegriff des Novatians*, pp. 57–61.

the meaning of this punishment in the form of work: 'To consider things from the beginning, the first man's only food was the produce and fruit of the trees. It was in fact sin which made him turn from eating the fruit of trees to cereals, the posture of his body corresponding to the state of his conscience. For innocence made men upright, to reach up and gather their food from the trees. They had at that time a good conscience. Once they had, however, committed their fault, they bent down towards the ground and the earth to look for their food' (*De cib.* 2, 955 B).

This passage is again very close to the account in Genesis, according to which the first human beings were nourished by the fruit of trees (Gn. 1:29) and were later punished for their sin by having to work the earth (Gn. 3:17–19). Novatian, however, introduces another idea – that of man's upright posture in paradise and of his bending downwards towards the earth after having sinned.[18] This theme of man's upright stature as an expression of his dignity is a very old one (cf. for example, Plato, *Tim.* 90 a-b). It is found in the Stoics (Cicero, *De nat. deor.* II, 56, 140) and in Minucius Felix (*Oct.* XVII, 2) and Gregory of Nyssa devotes a whole chapter of his *De opificio* to it (8). It is, however, always dealt with in the form of a contrast between the upright posture of man and the lowly posture of the animals.

In the text that we have just quoted from Novatian the treatment is different. The contrast is between man before he has sinned and man after having sinned, between man during the golden age, living by gathering fruit (cf. Ovid, *Met.* I, 201-208) and, in classical literature, man working the earth as an expression of his will to power (Seneca, *Epist.* XC, 37). This theme forms part of the Cynic's criticism of human culture,[19] and is directly anti-Posidonian. Nevertheless, a Stoic like Seneca could take it up, bringing the contrast between man's upright posture and his bent posture into line with this idea: 'This invention (sc. of the hammer and tongs) is the result of a prudent, but not of a great and elevated (*elati*) spirit'. The same, Seneca

---

18. Cf. Tertullian, *Adv. Marc.* II, 2, 6.
19. Cf. F. LAMMLI, *Homo Faber: Triumph, Schuld, Verhängnis,* pp. 34–43.

continues, applies to 'everything that man has to look for with his body bent (*corpore incurvato*) and with his spirit turned towards the earth' (*Epist.* XC, 110; see also *Quaest. nat.* V, 15, 3).

It would therefore seem as though Novatian took this theme from a Stoic source. But this is a Stoicism which exalts nature and celebrates the golden age, not the philosophy of culture characteristic of Posidonius. On the other hand, it is not concerned to criticise that philosophy as Seneca does, referring explicitly to Posidonius. Novatian is concerned with the contrast between fruit and cereals or vegetables as man's food, not with that between spontaneous fertility and the need to work the earth. From this, all that Novatian retains is the contrast between man's upright stature and his bent posture, the two positions which correspond to the two types of food. Finally, he interprets this contrast liturgically: man is upright when he is praising God in prayer and prostrate when he is praying to God in repentance.

Novatian goes on from discussing man's use of cereals to speak of his use of meat: 'Then the use of meat (*carnis*) was added, God's grace providing suitable foods for man's needs according to his circumstances. A lighter kind of food should have been sufficient to feed weak and uncivilised men, even if it had not been produced without work, with a view to correcting their fault and because they might want to sin if the work imposed on them did not encourage them to innocence. But since they no longer had simply to care for paradise, but had to cultivate the whole earth, meat, as a more substantial food, was given to them so that something might be added to the strength of their bodies to enable them to cultivate the earth' (*De cib.* 2. 955 B).

Here too, Novatian draws initially on the Genesis account (Gn 9:3), but at the same time he also interprets this idea in the light of Stoic teaching. The use of meat as a food is not seen as the result of sin, in the sense of signifying the end of the peace that prevailed between men and animals during the golden age. Meat is, on the contrary, seen as related to the providence of God who gives man the food that he needs with regard to the circumstances in which he finds himself (*opportunis temporibus*). Novatian's source here is clearly the medical tradition as expressed by Hippocrates, who states that the first men were vegetarians, but that they later became aware of the insufficiency of purely vegetable food (*Vet. med.* 7). Meat as food therefore marks a step forward.

Novatian adds to his statement: 'All this takes place by a disposition of the grace of God, who feared that, if men were nourished by elements which were not substantial enough, they would be weakened by their work and, if they were nourished by foods which were too heavy, they would be overcome and would not be able to endure them' (*De cib.* 2; 955 B).[20] This again clearly comes from the same medical tradition, which stresses the balance which has to be kept between the different foods and which is ultimately based on the balance of the humours. It is worth noting that Gregory of Nyssa has a very similar passage: 'It is necessary to guard against an absence of moderation in one direction or the other by taking care, on the one hand, that an excessive cosseting of the flesh does not weaken the mind and, on the other, that extreme emaciation does not make it feeble' (*Virg.* XXI, 1; Aubineau, p. 512, with notes).

What once again is clear from this teaching in Novatian's *De cibis iudaicis,* then, is firstly that all God's creatures are fundamentally good. These introductory passages in Novatian's treatise point to the theme of the treatise as a whole – that there are no naturally pure or impure foods, the distinction between the two being simply allegorical. In the second place, Novatian stresses that all things are disposed according to their time and order. This is an idea which he expresses in almost the same words in his *De Trinitate:* 'The Holy Spirit is always the same, but he distributes his blessings according to the times (*tempora*), circumstances (*occasiones rerum*) and moments' (*De Trin.* 29, 17–18).[21] This is all the work of providence, God governing everything by his *dispositio.*

It is possible to draw a number of conclusions from what we have said in this chapter. Stoic elements and biblical ideas are present in Novatian's cosmological teaching. These can be

---

20. In this passage, *minus* governs the two comparisons, whereas *amplius* simply amplifies the *et.*
21. Cf. also De Trin. 5, 20, 1: the *tempus fidei* referring to the age of faith.

summarised as the harmony of the elements in the cosmos, the law of the connection between natural phenomena, the anthropological view of the universe and the absence of any dualism in the cosmos. The language which Novatian uses to express these ideas is typical, but it should be noted that he extends it to include what is strictly theological. The same applies to his teaching about man, in which he stresses man's upright posture, the importance of human freedom and the parallel between the natural law and the moral law.

It is quite certain that, for this teaching, Novatian is dependent upon the Latin Stoic authors, especially Cicero (*De natura deorum*) and Seneca (*Letters*). Both his thought and his language point to this dependence. On the other hand, however, this explanation is not entirely sufficient, since the comparison that we have made between the passages in the work of Gregory of Nyssa which go back to Posidonius and Novatian's texts undoubtedly point to a common Stoic source. Finally, to judge from the close literary affinities, it would certainly seem as though Novatian borrowed from Apuleius' *De mundo*. Our conclusion that Novatian was dependent on Stoic Christianity which originated in Asia is, moreover, confirmed by his theology of the Word.

CHAPTER NINE

CYPRIAN AND THE AGE OF THE WORLD

As WE have seen, Tertullian uses the Stoic theme of the ages of man's life to illustrate the stages in the history of salvation, which rules out old age. Cyprian, on the other hand, retains this idea in its cosmological application, and derives from it his doctrine of the ageing of the world. This is, in fact, one of the few points at which Stoicism has affected his theology. It is, as Koch has pointed out, chiefly in the sphere of Cyprian's moral teaching that the influence of Seneca shows itself. Cyprian's deeply pessimistic view of the imminent end of all things is not without its Judaeo-Christian elements – he believed, for instance, that the world was close to the end of the sixth millennium (*Ad Fort.* 1) – and the tragic events that took place between A.D. 251 and 253, wars, famine and plague, undoubtedly helped to shape this conviction. The form in which he expressed this vision was, however, philosophical.

The theme appears in his treaty on idols (*Idol.* 11), in the phrase *vergente saeculo,* and in general terms in his treatise on the Unity of the Catholic Church (*De unit.* 16), in which he speaks of the *occasus mundi* and of the approaching end of the world. The signs of this approaching end, however, seem to be the growth of evil in the Church. All this, of course, derives from Scripture. Similar phrases can be found in Cyprian's letters written at this time. In *Epist.* LVIII, he writes of the 'fall (*occasum*) of the world and the approaching time of the Antichrist' (1) and of the 'world already dying' (2). In *Epist.* LXVII, 7, he laments the evils in the Church and reminds his readers that these evils had been predicted for the time when 'the world was about to pass away'.

Cyprian expresses himself more precisely in the *De mortalitate,* written a year later in 252: 'What the servants of God have to do at all times they ought to do even more when the world is collapsing (*corruente*) and is beleaguered by the storms of evils that attack it, so that, as we begin to see these serious things and know that even more serious things are on the way, we shall regard it as a great advantage to withdraw from here' (*De mort.* 27).

In the same treatise, Cyprian describes the situation as he sees it: 'In your house, if the walls begin to lean over with age (*senectute*) and the roof begins to shake above your head, and if you see that the house is already tired, exhausted and threatened with the ruin which lies in wait for buildings falling with age (*senectute*), would you not leave it as quickly as possible? Now the world is also leaning over and collapsing. By its ruin, it is bearing witness to the fact that it is dying less from old age (*senectute*) than from the end of all things' (*De mort.* 25). Two images can be distinguished here. The first is that of the world presented as a house. We have already come across this image and it is worth noting Seneca's text (*Benef.* VII, 1, 7) in this context: *Mundus est una omnium domus.* The second theme is that of the ageing of things.

This theme of the age of the world, however, figures most prominently in the *Ad Demetrianum,* a treatise which Cyprian addressed to a pagan, and in which the philosophical allusions become more precise as the theme takes on its full importance. Koch has pointed out that Stoic themes are present in this treatise, for example, that of the equal state of man, the *sors nascendi* and the *condicio moriendi* in the case of both master and slave (*Ad Dem.* 8; cf. also Seneca, *Epist.* XLVII, 10; *De ira,* II, 22, 1).[1] Another is that of man's upright posture (*Ad. Dem.* 17). Both are also found in Minucius Felix (*Oct.* XXXVII, 10 and XVII, 2).

The theme of the ageing of the world is presented in terms that leave no doubt as to its secular origins. The pagan Demetrianus, to whom Cyprian replies in his treatise, blames the Christians for having caused the evils that are afflicting the world, an argument which Augustine also had to refute at a later period. Cyprian's reply is that these evils are simply an expression of the natural course of events: 'You are ignorant of the knowledge of God and

1. Cf. KOCH, *op. cit.,* p. 62.

are a stranger to truth. You should, however, know in the first place that the world is already old (*senuisse*), that it is no longer established in the powers in which it has hitherto been established and that it no longer enjoys the health (*vigore*) and strength (*robore*) which it previously enjoyed. We have no need to speak of Holy Scriptures and divine doctrines or to produce any of these documents – the world itself says so and bears witness by its fall (*occasum*) to the decadence of things' (*Ad Dem.* 3).

What is interesting in this case is that Cyprian, who is here addressing a pagan, does not use scriptural arguments, but confines himself to natural reasoning. On the other hand, when he is addressing Christian readers, he always relies mainly on Scripture, although he does at the same time make use of originally pagan ideas. It is therefore easy to distinguish the two eschatological tendencies in his writing: the Judaeo-Christian eschatological strain, containing allusions to the Apocalypse and to the catastrophes preceding the end of time, and the secular element, stressing the decadence of the world whose vital forces (*vigore et robore*) are exhausted.

Cyprian provides a number of examples of the growing exhaustion of nature, and does so in a style which owes nothing to the Bible and everything to Latin rhetoric. The *Ad Demetrianum* and the *Ad Donatum* are the works in which Cyprian provides the clearest evidence of the fact that he was a teacher of rhetoric in Africa before his conversion. Take, for example, the passage: 'There is no longer the great abundance of rains in winter, necessary to nourish the seed, nor in summer the usual heat to warm the crops (*frugibus*). The springs (*verna*) no longer rejoice (*laeta*) in their climate (*temperies*), and the autumns are no longer so fertile in the products of the trees' (*Ad Dem.* 3).[2] The literary theme of the seasons also occurs in his *Epist.* XXXVII, where it is applied to the martyrs. Terms that are common to both texts are *verna, temperies, laeta* applied to the spring, and *frugibus* applied to the summer.[3]

2. See FONTAINE, *Aspects et problèmes de la prose d'art latin au IIIe siècle*, pp. 172–176.
3. See Minucius Felix, *Oct.* XVII, 7.

Even more striking in this exhaustion of nature is the failure of subterranean resources: 'Fewer blocks (*crustae*) of marble are removed from the hollowed out and tired mountains. The mines (*metalla*) are exhausted and produce less wealth of gold and silver. The impoverished seams become reduced from day to day.' Civilisation too is affected by the phenomenon of decadence: 'Everything diminishes and fails — the labourer in the fields, the sailor at sea, the soldier in the camp, innocence in the forum, justice in the tribunal, concord in friendships, skill in trades and discipline in morals' (*Ad Dem.* 3). It is not only nature but human civilisation itself which is in decline.

Cyprian goes beyond statements of fact, however, and maintains that this is the result of a law which decrees that all things are to pass from youth to old age: 'Do you think that there can be as much substance in something which is growing old as there is vitality to be revealed in a youth still fresh and full of sap (*vegeta*)? Everything that tends to decline and cease at the approach of the end must diminish. When it sets, the sun sheds its rays with a less brilliant and burning ardour. At the end of its course, the moon wanes and its horns become thinner. The tree which was previously green and fertile becomes barren and its branches become dry; it is made ugly by decay. The spring which flowed abundantly from its sources, which were previously gushing, dries up with old age and only pours forth a few weak drops. Such is the law of the world and the law of God — that everything that is born dies, everything that has grown up becomes old, everything that was strong becomes weak and everything that was big becomes small and dies' (*Ad Dem.* 3).

Cyprian's argument is here based on common sense. It is as absurd 'to blame Christians for the diminishment of things and for the ageing of the world (*senescente mundo*)', as it would be to attribute to them the weakening of powers that takes place in old men (*Ad Dem.* 4). If today, Cyprian argues, this ageing process begins at an earlier stage, 'if this age is old from the start', it is because it shares in the general ageing: 'Thus birth hastens at its very beginning towards its end and everything that is born now degenerates with the ageing of the world (*ipsius mundi senectute*). Thus no one should be surprised that each thing in particular begins to weaken in the world, when the whole world is failing and at an end' (*Ad Dem.* 4).

This idea of the old age of the world and of the exhaustion of the world's energies can also be found in the *De laude martyrii*, which Koch dates after Cyprian.[4] Three texts from this treatise will demonstrate the parallel: 'The world itself is collapsing and the universe partly shaken and nature (*natura*) becoming exhausted (*deficiens*) bears witness to its ultimate end' (*De laude* 13); 'At the end of time, there will be the exteme old age of all things' (27); and, 'If, situated in these uncertain misfortunes of nature, you were given the promise of life, would you not rejoice with all your heart? If, shaken by the storms of this world, you had a meal within your reach, would you not regard death as a remedy?' (14).

Only the author of the *De laude* and Cyprian, among Christian writers, teach this doctrine;[5] and Cyprian, of all the writers of the ancient world, is the one who developed the idea most fully. It owes nothing to Christianity, but is ultimately a purely biological conception. It was a current notion that everything in the world had youth, growth and old age. The following is a typical example from the work of Seneca: 'Everything comes in its time. Things must be born, grow up and become adult. There is nothing which does not have its old age' (*Epist.* XXI, 13; cf. *Dial.* XI, 10). For a closer parallel, Cyprian is, in fact, quoting Sallust almost word for word here: *Omnia orta occidunt et aucta senescunt,* 'All things that come into being die and things that have grown become old' (*Jugurtha* 2, 3).[6] This theme is clearly connected with that which links together birth and death and was also common in the ancient world, being especially favoured by the Cynics: 'to be born is to be already moving towards death'.

What is of special interest in the passage from the *Ad Demetrianum* is that this biological theme is in fact applied to the whole universe, which is seen as a living being experiencing youth, maturity and old age. This is clearly a specific

4. See *Cyprianische Untersuchungen*, pp. 341–343.
5. See SPANNEUT, *Le Stoicisme des Pères de l'Eglise*, pp. 413–414.
6. This text is quoted by Jerome as a proverb; cf. *In Ezech.* III, *praef.*

philosophical doctrine, but it is not immediately obvious where it originated. Minucius Felix, however, has an interesting comment in his *Octavius* which has so far not been utilised: *Quis enim sapientium dubitat, quis ignorat, omnia quae orta sunt occidere, quae facta sunt interire, caelum quoque cum omnibus quae caelo continentur, ita ut coepisse, desinere,* 'What philosopher doubts, who does not know, that all things which have come into being die, that all things created perish, that heaven and all the things that are contained in heaven cease as they began' (*Oct.* XXXIV, 2). This is obviously the same theme as Cyprian's, and Minucius regards it explicitly as a common doctrine, giving examples in Stoic and Epicurean thought: *Stoicis constans opinio est, quod consumpto umore mundus hic omnis ignescet. Et Epicureis de elementorum conflagratione et mundi ruina eadem sententia est,* 'The Stoics firmly maintain that when the moisture is dried out, the universe must take fire. And Epicureans hold the same about the conflagration of the elements and the destruction of the universe' (*Oct.* XXXIV, 2–3).

This, then, is obviously a doctrine which was quite widespread at the time when Cyprian was writing. It is also found, for example, in the Latin *Asclepius* (26) and in Aulus Gellius (III. 10. 11). The Stoic – or more precisely the Posidonian – form of this doctrine of the drying up of the water in the world and of the final conflagration was used by many Christian authors, including Justin (I *Apo.* XX, 1–4). In the case of Cyprian, however, the ἐκπύρωσις or 'conflagration' is not mentioned. In fact, the opposite takes place – summer becomes less warm and the sun's rays are weaker as the world becomes older. This is obviously a different idea and it has been frequently suggested that it is fundamentally Epicurean, all the commentators referring here to Lucretius' *De nat. rerum*, II, 1104 ff. It cannot be denied that this text is very close to Cyprian's, but it has been pointed out by Hagendahl that there is no literary dependence.[7] In fact, this biological idea of the world can be traced back to a very early period in Greek thought,[8] even, as Marrou has shown,[9] as far back as Hesiod.

7. *Latin Fathers and the Classics*, p. 76.
8. 'La fin du monde n'est pas pour demain', *Lumiére et Vie*, 11 (1953), pp. 56–87.

It is interesting to note in this context that the same doctrine of
the ages of man is used by Tertullian as the basis of his theology
of history, although he retained no more of it than the sequence
infancy, youth and adulthood, thus at a stroke depriving it of its
cyclical character. What is more, in Tertullian's case, this doctrine applies only to the religious history of mankind and not to
the history of the cosmos. With Cyprian, however, we are faced
not with a transposition of the idea of the ages of man but with
its rigorous application. He regards it as the law of everything
that is in the world, and indeed of the world itself. It characterises
creation in its aspect as material life, and this creation is moving
towards its end.

Over against this, however, stands deified humanity, whose
life is not biological but spiritual. It is this humanity which is established in the Church, and which exists in an ageing world
without being touched by that ageing. This humanity is
dominated by a vitality (vigcr) which knows nothing of discon-
tinuity. (We shall be returning to consider this idea more fully
later.) What matter if even now the world is collapsing like an
old building? Christians already belong to a different world –
hence their scorn of the present life. Why should one want to remain in a house with its walls collapsing and its roof falling in?
What Cyprian is doing here in fact is to place side by side a
cyclical conception of cosmic history, derived from pagan
sources, and a Christian conception of sacred history, which is
not cyclical but genuinely historical. These two views of history
cannot be merged together. The end of the world is not a reality
of sacred history, in accordance with God's plan. Cyprian, as has
been pointed out, does not refer to the expectation of the parousia
and, even though he does in fact mention the seven millennia (Ad
Fort. 11), this doctrine plays no part in his view of history. [10]

It is interesting to note, however, that Cyprian does come to
make a connection between the old age of the universe and the
decadence of the Church. He stresses, however, that this happens

9. See FRANZ LAMMLI, Homo Faber, pp. 132–133.
10. K. H. SCHWARTE, Die Vorgeschichte des augustinischen Weltalterlehre, pp.
159–162.

precisely to the extent that the Church compromises with the world and so shares in its decay. This emerges clearly from his *Epist*. LXVII, 8: 'Do not be troubled if, in these last days, in the case of certain believers, a failing faith bends, fear without respect for God vacillates and peaceful agreement does not last. These things were proclaimed as having to take place at the end of the world (*in fine saeculi*) and it has been predicted by the way of the Lord and the witness of the apostles that, when the world begins to fail (*deficiente*) and the Antichrist comes near, good things will cease to appear (*deficere*) and evils will increase'.

This text is obviously addressed to Christians and the references contained in it are biblical, but the underlying teaching is philosophical. This is clear above all from the non-biblical vocabulary, which is concerned especially with the failure or decline (*deficiente*) of the universe. But even if part of the Church, Cyprian argues, is involved in this universal decline, the spiritual power of the Church will resist its being entirely carried away. Even if, 'in these last days', the evangelical power (*vigor*) falls in the Church of God or the strength (*robur*) of faith becomes weak, a number of priests will nonetheless not allow themselves to be involved in this ruin (*ruinas*) of things and this shipwreck of faith (*Epist*. LXVII, 8). This is, of course, the theme of the declining *vigor* which we met at the beginning of the *Ad Demetrianum*. In both cases, the idea is basically the same – that of the forces of the world becoming exhausted. This exhaustion is found in the Church to the extent that it is dependent on the world, but it is not found there insofar as some believers are sustained by the unfailing strength of God.

PART THREE

THE LATIN FATHERS
AND
THE BIBLE

INTRODUCTION TO PART III

HAVING placed the earliest Latin theology within its dual environment of Judaism and paganism, we must now proceed to discuss the theology itself under three main heads – biblical theology, systematic theology and ecclesiology. In all three spheres, the period we have been studying was one of striking originality. In the field of biblical theology, it was the Latin Fathers, Tertullian and Cyprian who were the heirs of the typological tradition of primitive Christianity, and developed it, whereas the Greeks were to be tempted away, at Antioch by the scientific study of the Bible, at Alexandria by allegorism. In the sphere of systematic theology, Tertullian evolved a remarkably original synthesis throughout which the characteristic features of Latin thought find expression. Finally Cyprian was to inaugurate a tradition of thought about the Church and its structure which has no equivalent in the Greek world, and was to remain characteristic of the Latin West.

CHAPTER TEN

THE TESTIMONIA

BEFORE discussing early Latin biblical theology as such, it is important to consider the question of sources. The authors whose work we shall be studying did not write continuous commentaries on any of the biblical books. The first to do anything of this nature in Latin was Victorinus of Pettau. What Tertullian, Cyprian and Novatian did was above all to make use of the early Christian *testimonia* that they had inherited. Cyprian was the first Latin author to undertake a systematic regrouping of these *testimonia* and to standardise their form in accordance with the accepted translation of the Bible. Tertullian and Commodian mark the transition from the Judaeo-Christian use of *testimonia* to their standardisation by Cyprian.

1. TERTULLIAN'S *ADVERSUS JUDAEOS*

The authenticity of the first text that we shall study, Tertullian's *Adversus Judaeos*, has been discussed by Tränkle.[1] Few scholars doubt that the first part of the treatise at least is the work of Tertullian. From chapter IX onwards, however, the continuity of the treatise breaks down. The second part is, moreover, at least partly to be found, almost word for word, in the *Adversus Marcionem*. Certain scholars, notably Neander, Corssen, Akermann and Quispel, are of the opinion that this second part of the *Adversus Judaeos* was added as a supplement by an editor who drew on Tertullian. On the other hand, Nöldeke, Harnack and Monceaux have insisted on the authenticity of the

1. Q.S.F. *Tertulliani Adversus Judaeos. Mit Einleitung und kritischem Kommentar,* Wiesbaden, 1964.

second part, although they have not been able to support their claim with convincing proofs. On the basis of strict philological criteria, Säflund, a pupil of G. Thörnell, established this authenticity in a study published in Uppsala in 1955.

The problem of the strange literary structure of the work and of its obvious relationship with the *Adversus Marcionem*, however, still remains. Tränkle is of the opinion that the *Adversus Judaeos* is no more than an outline which Tertullian did not develop into a complete treatise. This is possibly true of the first part, insofar as the differences which so many scholars have claimed to detect between the first and the second parts of the treatise do not exist. It does not, however, take account of the differences that there are, especially in Tertullian's use of biblical quotations. In my view, the first part is a work, complete in itself, which Tertullian wrote in his youth, and to which he added a supplement at the time that he was writing the *Adversus Marcionem* IV, with which indeed there are striking similarities.

On first reading the *Adversus Judaeos,* one is struck by the apparent disorder in the author's presentation of quotations from the Old Testament, some of which occur several times, while others are grouped in a rather disconcerting way. The same apparent disorder is found, however, in Justin's *Dialogue,* on which Tertullian drew to some extent in writing his treatise. In both cases, the authors were not primarily concerned with an orderly presentation of scriptural texts. Such an order can certainly be found in the collections of *testimonia,* in which the texts are grouped around particular themes – the criticism of legal observances, or the messianic prophecies. Both Tertullian and Justin, on the other hand, draw on these collections according to the demands made by the progress of their arguments.

The *Adversus Judaeos* is just such an argument, and very characteristic of Tertullian. It sets out to show why the people of Israel was replaced by the Church of the gentiles. Tertullian bases his answer on a theology of salvation-history which he defines in *Adv. Jud.* II, 8: *Omnibus gentibus eamdem legem dedit quam certis statutis temporibus observari praecepit,* 'He gave the same law to all nations and ordered that it should be observed at certain stated times'. There is, in other words, only one divine law, Tertullian argues, but it is unfolded according to the *statuta tempora*. There is the period from Adam to Abraham, the period of the people of Israel, and the period inaugurated by Christ in his hidden parousia; and there will be the period of his glorious second coming. The essential point in the argument is to prove that a new period was inaugurated with Christ: *Probare debeamus tam illam veterem legem cessasse quam novam promissionis nunc operari*, 'Let us be as pleased that the old law has ceased as we are that the new law of the promise is in operation now'.

It is to this that the heart of the work is devoted. The fact of this new period in the history of salvation is stated in *Adv. Jud.* VI, and in the following chapter (VII) established chronologically in accordance with Dn. 7. In the succeeding chapters, the special prophecies begin (*incipiamus*): IX, on the birth of Christ; X, on his passion, in accordance with the scriptural sequence of Isaac, Joseph, Moses and Isaiah. This is the same as the order used by Melito of Sardis in his *Homily on the Passion*. In *Adv. Jud.* XIII, Tertullian stresses a vital point, namely that it is the Jewish Scriptures themselves which show that the Christians are right: *Praescribamus eis de ipsis Scripturis*, 'Let us give them a precept from these very scriptures'. The material in this chapter of the *Adversus Judaeos* is otherwise very similar to that of the preceding chapter. We may note, however, that Tertullian does not refer here to the texts that he has already used (Dt. 28:66; Ps. 96:10; Dn. 9 etc.), but draws on another type of collection concerned with the passion of Christ, namely texts on the *lignum* or wood of the cross. The novelty of the chapter, however, lies in the type of argument used, which is that of the *praescriptio*. It only remains to show how the actual contemporary situation, which includes the Jewish diaspora, confirms the argument that the present order will be followed by the second coming. The excellent construction of the argument can be followed by certain key words and phrases, which mark out the stages of the treatise; for example: *gradum conseramus*, 'let us plant our step' (*Adv. Jud.* II, 1), *ostendimus*, 'we show' (III, 5, 1), *in isto gradum conseramus*, 'let us plant our step on this' (VII, 1), *incipiamus probare*, 'we shall begin to prove' (IX, 1), *probabimus*, 'we shall prove' (X, 14), *praescribamus* 'let us give a precept' (XIII, 1).

One question remains, that namely of Tertullian's sources in the *Adversus Judaeos*. Two factors contribute to the difficulty of tracing these. The first is simply that most of the literature of the second century A.D. has been lost, the second that the use of the same biblical quotations does not necessarily indicate dependence. Two of his sources, however, are beyond dispute. The first is the *Epistle of Barnabas*. Tertullian is closer to this *Epistle* than to Justin (*Dial.* XL, 4) in his use of the symbolism of the two goats (*Barn.* VII, 4). A second instance is Ps. 51:17. Tertullian quotes *Cor contribulatum et humiliatum hostia Deo est*, 'A troubled and humbled heart is a sacrifice to God', which combines elements from both parts of the verse of the psalm. The quotation is found in this form in *Barn.* II, 9 (cf. also Clement, *Stromat.* II, 18; 69, 1 and Irenaeus, *Adv. haer.*, IV, 17, 1). What is more, the association of Ps. 1:3 with Jr. 2:13 in the same context (*Adv. Jud.* XIII, 11 and 14) is also based on the *Epistle of Barnabas* (XI), in which the *testimonia* about the rock and the water are compared with those relating to the wood and the water.

In the view of the present writer, Tertullian was undoubtedly also influenced by Melito.[2] Attention has already been drawn to this influence in connection with Tertullian's way of listing the prophecies in their historical order. Furthermore, in the case of the *Adversus Judaeos*, the series of figures of the passion, beginning with Isaac, then Joseph, and so on, is also to be found in Melito's *Homily on the Passion*. The typology of the sacrifice of Isaac does not occur in Justin's work, but is dear to Melito. In the same way, the etymology of πάσχα, Passover, through πάσχειν, to suffer, which underlies *Adv. Jud.* X, 18 is not found in Justin, but is used by Melito (*Hom. Pasch.* 46), as is the symbolism of the bitter herbs in the same passage. Other examples are, moreover, not difficult to find. It is also known that Melito published a collection of *testimonia*. Above all, however, Tertullian's dependence on Melito is clear from the fact that his central theme in the *Adversus Judaeos*, that of the *statuta tempora* or the three ages

---

2. See J. DANIELOU, 'Bulletin d'histoire des origines chrétiennes', *RSR*, 49 (1961), pp. 583, 593–594.

of salvation, is already spelled out in Melito's *Homily on the Passion.*[3]

The most important influence, however, was exerted by Justin. We have already mentioned that a collection of *testimonia* on the criticism of Jewish legal observances is to be found in the *Adversus Judaeos*. This part of the treatise is, moreover, dominated by the theme of the two peoples of God. The theme is presented at the very beginning of the treatise (*Adv. Jud.* I, 4) and Tertullian then takes it up again in the form of a contrast between the Jewish observances which were given as a sign, and the Christian law which was given as salvation. In this, he is making use of a traditional element in anti-Jewish polemical writing, for this criticism of Jewish observances is to be found both in the *Epistle of Barnabas* and in Justin's *Dialogue*. The first book of Cyprian's *Testimonia* was also to be devoted to it. What is of particular interest to us in the present context, however, is Tertullian's use of scriptural material.

A first group of quotations is concerned with circumcision (*Adv. Jud.* III). Tertullian supports a quotation from Jr. 4:3–4 – *Innovate vobis novitatem et ne seminaveritis in spinis: circumcidimini deo et circumcidite praeputium cordis vestri,* 'Renew newness for yourselves and do not sow among thorns; be circumcised to God and circumcise the foreskin of your heart' – with a number of quotations which point, in a more general way, to the temporary nature of the Jewish law and to the coming of the new law. These supporting quotations include Jr. 31:31–32, which speaks of a *testamentum novum* or 'new covenant', Is. 2:2–3, which mentions Mount Zion raised above the other mountains, with a reference to Dn. 2:34 (the stone growing into a mountain), Is. 2:3, *Ex Sion exibit lex,* 'The law will go out from Zion', and Ps. 18:43, which is taken to refer to the new people of God. To this list must be added Is. 1:7–8, the 'desolate land'.

It is fairly clear that Tertullian drew on Justin for this rather

3. See H. WIDMANN, 'Irenäus und seine theologischen Väter', *ZTK*, 54 (1957), p. 16; J. DANIELOU, 'Figure et événement chez Méliton', *Neotestamentica et Patristica, Freundesgabe Oscar Cullmann*, Leiden, 1962, pp. 282–292. Incidentally, we know from Jerome the store which Tertullian set by Melito (*Vir. ill.* 24).

loosely connected group of biblical quotations. In his *Dial.* XXVIII, Justin combines Jr. 4:3–4, in the same form in which Tertullian uses it, with Ps. 8:3, although there is no real reason for these two texts to be associated, and with Ml. 1:10, which Tertullian uses later in his treatise. In *Dial.* XXIV, moreover, Justin criticises circumcision on the basis of Jr. 31:31–32 and Is. 2:3. These texts are not, however, found grouped together in Cyprian's *Testimonia*. There is no obvious similarity between them, and if both Tertullian and Justin bring them both together, we may safely conclude that the later of the two was following the earlier. To this we must add the theme of circumcision as a sign (*signum* = σημεῖον) which makes it possible for the Jews to be distinguished at the time of punishment. This theme is also taken from Justin, and the verbal affinities in this case make Tertullian's dependence on Justin assured.

There are, however, other collections of quotations in the same chapter of the *Adversus Judaeos* which are of a different character. In the case of the theme of circumcision, for example, Tertullian makes use of a number of quotations, all of which are taken from Is. 1, and which therefore derive from a different type of grouping from those just examined. These quotations are Is. 1:2, *filios genui,* 'I have begotten sons'; 1:15, *si extenderitis manus,* 'If you stretch out your hands'; 1:4, *vae gens peccatrix,* 'ah, sinful people!'. All these texts bear on the faithlessness of Israel and the nation's rejection by God. Although one of them is used by Justin, the collection as a whole is not derived from him.

Tertullian follows this collection with another on the sabbath which has no equivalent in Justin. The quotations in this collection include Is. 1:14; Ezk. 22:8; Is. 54:15; Jos. 6:20, 21; 1 M. 2:38–44. None of these texts are, in fact, quoted anywhere by Justin, so that we are bound to conclude that this collection of quotations against the Jewish sabbath has a different origin. It is possible, of course, that it was built up by Tertullian himself, but is much more likely that it comes from another source, a collection, in other words, of *testimonia* on the true sabbath.

The same applies to Tertullian's polemic against sacrifices. Tertullian here lists Ml. 1:10–11; Ps. 96:7–8; Ps. 51:19; Ps. 50:14; Is. 1:11–13. The only one of these texts used by Justin is Ml.

1:10–11, which is in any case so frequently quoted that there is no reason to use it as a basis for regarding Justin as Tertullian's source in this instance. Ml. 1:10, Is. 1:11 and Ps. 50:14 are, on the other hand, grouped together in Cyprian's *Testimonia* (II, 16), which suggests that Cyprian drew in this case on Tertullian, and that here we have a collection of *testimonia* which existed in the Church of Carthage before Tertullian's time. The same probably applies to the sections dealing with circumcision and the sabbath.

We must now turn to the second part of the *Adversus Judaeos*, which begins at chapter IX and is concerned with the messianic prophecies. Tertullian here follows the same plan as Justin in his *Dialogue*, but once again it is certain that Tertullian's source, in the case of some quotations at least, is Justin. One example of this is the linking of Is. 7:13–15 and Is. 8:4 (*Adv. Jud.* IX, 1), which are similarly associated in Justin's *Dial.* LXVI, 2–3. The fact that Tertullian is dependent on Justin in this case is further strengthened by Tertullian's interpretation of these quotations, which is very similar to Justin's.

The same applies to chapters X and XI, which bring together the prophecies of the passion. Here, the collection of quotations includes Dt. 33:17, the horns of the unicorn; Gn. 49:6, *taurus*, the 'bull'; Ps. 96:10, *Dominus regnavit a ligno*, 'The Lord reigned from the tree'; Is. 9:6, *imperium super humeros*, 'the government on his shoulders'; Jr. 11:19, *lignum in pane*, 'wood in your bread'; Ps. 22:16, *foderunt pedes*, 'they pierced my feet'; Ps. 22:21, the horns of the unicorn; Is. 53:8–10, *nec dolus in ore*, 'no deceit in his mouth'; Is. 57:2, *sepultura sabbata*, 'burying the sabbath'; Am. 8:9, *occidet sol*, 'the sun will go down'; Ezk. 9:1–6, the sign of *tau*; and Dt. 28:66, *pendens in ligno*, 'hanging on the wood'.

Of the above quotations, Jr. 11:19, Is. 53:8–10 and Ps. 96:10 are found in Justin's *Dialogue* (LXXIII, 2; LXXVI, 1 and LXXIII, 1 respectively). The gap which follows *Dial.* LXXIV seems, moreover, to have contained Dt. 28:66. Later in the same work we find Ps. 22:16 and 21:21, Is. 57:2 and Dt. 33:17 (CIV, 1; CV, 1; XCVII, 2 and XCI, respectively). Some of these quotations, of course, undoubtedly formed part of a common catechesis and were known well before Tertullian's time. This is in particular the case with Ps. 96:10, with the addition of *a ligno*. Nevertheless, the grouping of the quotations on the one hand and the exegesis of Dt. 33:17 are two powerful reasons for believing that Tertullian drew on Justin here.

In the case of a third group of quotations, this time in the *Adv. Jud.* XIV, it seems to be almost certain that Tertullian's source was the *Dialogue* of Justin. The subject of this group is the two parousias. On the one hand, there is no doubt that the quotations in both treatises are strikingly parallel. The first example is Is. 53:2, *non erat species*, 'he had no beauty', which is contrasted with Dn. 7:13–14. The same comparison is also made by Justin (*Dial.* XIV, 8). This is followed by Ps. 45:2–5, which is also quoted by Justin (*Dial.* XXXVIII, 3). There is also a quotation from Zc. 12:10, *cognoscent quem pupugerunt*, 'they will know the one whom they have pierced', in both the *Adv. Jud.* XIV, 6 and *Dial.* XIV, 8. This quotation follows directly after the first two texts. Is. 53:8 occurs both in Tertullian (*Adv. Jud.* XIV, 6) and in Justin (*Dial.* XLIII, 3). Finally, in the case of the incident of the high priest Joshua (Zc. 3:1–2), not only does this quotation occur both in the *Adv. Jud.* (XIV, 7–10) and in the *Dialogue* of Justin (CVI, 3), but Tertullian's exegesis is also clearly derived from the interpretation given by Justin. We may therefore conclude that this is another case of convergence established by a similar grouping of biblical texts and similar interpretations.

These three groups of quotations which show the influence of Justin, are not, however, the only ones. In chapter IX, for example, several texts are grouped together – Ps. 38:17, *homo in plaga positus*, 'a man set in the plague'; Is. 53:7, *tanquam ovis*, 'like a sheep'; Is. 42:2, *neque contendit*, 'he did not strive'; Is. 42:3, *arundinem contusam*, 'the bruised reed'; Is. 58:1, *exacta voce*, 'with raised voice'; Is. 35:4, *ecce deus noster*, 'behold our God'. None of the texts found in this collection are found in Justin, nor does the collection seem to go back to one on a special theme. We seem to be faced here with a collection of different origin.

The same applies to chapter X, where there is another collection, this time on the passion, in which all the quotations are taken from the Psalms: Ps. 63:5; 22:17; 69:21 and 22:19. The quotations from Ps. 22 certainly occur in the *Dialogue*, but they can also be found in many other treatises, and none of the others are found in Justin's work. It is, of course, possible that Tertullian made his own collection, but in this case he seems to have made use of an existing one, which can be found in Irenaeus' *Adv. haer.* IV, 33, 12. We know, from his use of Irenaeus' treatise in the *Adversus Valentinianos,* that he had read Irenaeus. We may therefore conclude that the *Adversus haereses* was probably his source for this collection and the one last mentioned.

Chapter XIII presents a collection of prophecies concerning Israel's rejection, a subject already treated in chapter III. The first quotation in this collection is Is. 1:7, which was known to Justin (*Dial.* LII, 4). This is followed by Is. 33:17, which also appears in Justin (*Dial.* CX, 2), and Is. 65:2, *expandi manus,* 'I stretched out my hands', which occurs in *Dial.* XCV, 2. The next quotations are from two psalms, Ps. 22:17 and Ps. 69:22, both of which we have met in *Adv. Jud.* X. Finally, there are two quotations from the prophets — Jr. 9:10–13, *dereliquerunt me,* 'They have forsaken me', which occurs in *Dial.* XIV, 1, and Is. 65:13–15, which does not appear in the *Dialogue,* but which is in a chapter of the book of Isaiah from which Justin often quotes. This first group certainly seems to have been taken from Justin.

After *Adv. Jud.* XIII, 24, however, there is no equivalent in Justin's *Dialogue* for the collection of quotations that occurs in Tertullian's treatise at this point. This consists of Is. 2:20, which Tertullian presents as a prophecy of the conversion of the gentiles; Is. 3:3, *sapientem architectum,* 'wise master-builder'; Is. 5:6, *imbrem super vineam Sorech,* 'rain over the vineyard of Sorech'; Is. 52:5, *nomen meum blasphematur,* 'my name is blasphemed'; Is. 1:7–8, in a different version from the one which we have encountered earlier in this book, when discussing the *De montibus,* in that the word *specula,* 'watch-tower', is used for *casa,* 'hut', and *casula,* 'little hut', for *custodiarium,* 'watch-tower'; Is. 1:3, *Israel non cognovit,* 'Israel does not know'; Is. 1:20, *gladius nos comedet,* 'the sword will eat us'; Ps. 59:11, *disperge eos,* 'scatter them'; and finally Is. 50:11, *in anxietate dormietis,* 'you will sleep in uneasiness'. This group is entirely missing from Justin, nor does it occur in the *Testimonia* of Cyprian.

This situation is similar to that which we encountered in the first part of the *Adversus Judaeos,* where Tertullian was criticising the Jewish observances, in that, in both cases, almost all the quotations are taken from Is. 1, and most of them were not to be found in Justin's collection, namely: 1:2; 1:4; 1:7–8; 1:15; 1:14; 1:11–13. At that point the evidence seemed to suggest a traditional African collection of anti-Jewish polemical quotations. These same quotations are, at least to some extent, found in the *Adversus Judaeos* of the author known as Pseudo-Cyprian, which we discussed at some length earlier in the present volume (Is. 1:2; 1:13; 1:15; 2:3–5; 8:1; 8:6).

We are now in a position to draw a number of conclusions concerning the collections of *testimonia* that occur in Tertullian's *Adversus Judaeos.* First, it is clear that Tertullian made use of the Greek authors who preceded him. He was acquainted with the writings of Melito and Pseudo-Barnabas and drew on a collection compiled by Irenaeus. Above all, however, he depended extensively on Justin's *Dialogue* as his source for *testimonia* and their exegesis. It should, however, be stressed that all these authors on whom Tertullian drew were simply handing down *testimonia* which they had themselves received from the Judaeo-Christian tradition, and that it was this tradition, therefore, which Tertullian inherited through them.

It is, however, important to point out that, although Tertullian received from these earlier authors the *testimonia* that they had themselves used, he did not preserve them in their original Judaeo-Christian form. We know, for example, that one of the features of *testimonia* is the modification of scriptural texts, either by abbreviation, addition, or the fusion of originally separate elements. Some of these *testimonia,* such as Dt. 28:66 and Ps. 96:10, which Tertullian undoubtedly found in Justin's writings, are preserved by him. Generally speaking, however, he tended to refashion them so that they were more closely in accordance with the Bible that he used. This version of the Bible was without any doubt the Septuagint, which Tertullian translated directly from the Greek. As we shall see, Commodian did the same.

We have already noted that Tertullian makes use, in the *Adversus Judaeos,* of many anti-Jewish texts which are not in any sense traditional *testimonia.* These are in the main taken from the Book of Isaiah. They are not to be found in any of the Greek sources on which Tertullian normally drew, and it is therefore quite reasonable to suppose that he took them from a Latin source. This assumption points to the existence in Africa of collections of anti-Jewish *testimonia* before the time of Tertullian. Confirmation of this supposition is to be found in the presence of these *testimonia* in Judaeo-Christian texts written before Tertullian, such as *V Esdras* and the *Adversus Judaeos* of Pseudo-Cyprian. The existence of such *testimonia* further implies that African Christians had to combat Jewish proselytism among the pagans.

All this is quite clear from the great amount of anti-Jewish Christian literature that existed in Africa in the second and third centuries. This literature was directed against the Jewish proselytes. Tertullian himself was opposing a proselyte in his *Adversus Judaeos* (I, 1), and it is quite likely that the anonymous treatise of Pseudo-Cyprian had the same audience in mind. It is certainly Jewish proselytism that Commodian was attacking in his *Instructions*. All these factors confirm what Marcel Simon and Frend have said about the importance of Judaism in Africa in the first Christian centuries.

2. COMMODIAN'S *TESTIMONIA*

The second part of Commodian's *Carmen apologeticum,* that is, verses 265–494, consists mainly of a collection of *testimonia* referring to Christ. There are in fact sixty of these texts, all in one way or another messianic. The author's aim is to show that the Jews were mistaken in their failure to recognise that Christ was the one who had been announced by the prophets. Many of Commodian's biblical quotations can be found in the work of Justin, Irenaeus and Tertullian, so that we can be quite sure that he did not himself build up this collection. Our task therefore is to ascertain whether it is possible to trace his source or sources and whether these can be located in the history of collections of *testimonia* in the early Church.

One particularly striking factor is that there is a clear connection between Commodian's quotations and Cyprian's *Testimonia ad Quirinum,* since fifty-four of Commodian's sixty *testimonia* appear in Cyprian's collection. This whole question has been studied at length by B. Dombart.[4] Generally speaking, too, Commodian's Latin text is the same as Cyprian's. From this, Dombart's conclusion was that Commodian made use of Cyprian's work, with the result that he must have been writing at a later period. K. Thraede, however, has more recently questioned Dombart's conclusion,[5] pointing out that in a very similar case (that of the relationship between the *Altercatio Simonis Judaei et Theophili Christiani* and the *Ad Quirinum,*) Harnack, writing at about the same time as Dombart, had demonstrated that there might have been a common source here.[6] Thraede did not, however, develop this thesis. It is proposed, therefore, to undertake that task now, and to show that there are good reasons for believing that Commodian's source was not Cyprian's *Ad Quirinum*, but a collection of Latin *testimonia* which was of a much earlier date.

It will be noted that the quotations which occur in both Cyprian's *Testimonia* and Commodian's *Carmen* form only a small proportion of Cyprian's treatise. Almost the only ones in common are in fact Book II, 6–26, and not even the beginning of that, and Book I, 17–21. As Dombart noted, none of the third Book is used at all. This may, of course, be because Commodian was interested only in the quotations concerned with prophecies of the Messiah. It is, however, equally possible that the whole group of quotations used by Commodian formed a distinct collection which Cyprian incorporated into a series aimed, in Book I, at criticising Jewish legal practices, in Book II, 1–6, at stressing the divinity of Christ, and in Book III, at the precepts.

There are also several cases of *testimonia* quoted by Commodian in the *Carmen* which can be found in Cyprian's *Testimonia* in the context of a longer quotation. A few examples will illustrate the point. In *Carm.* 270, Commodian quotes Ps. 22:16: *Effoderunt, inquit, manus meas et pedes ipsi*, 'They have pierced, he says, my hands and feet', whereas, in *Test.* II, 20, the whole passage Ps.

4. 'Ueber die Bedeutung Commodians für die Textkritik der Testimonia Cyprians', *Zur Hist. Theol.*, 1879, pp. 275ff.
5. 'Beiträge zur Datierung Commodians', *JAC*, 2 (1959), p. 94.
6. *TU*, I, 3 (1883).

22:16–23 is quoted. Tertullian, on the other hand, in *Adv. Jud.* X, 13, as we have already seen, quotes the verse in isolation. Again, *Carm.* 274 quotes Jr. 11:19, *Venite, mittamus lignum in panem*, 'Come, let us put wood in his bread'. It is in this form that the text occurs in the collections of *testimonia* and is quoted by Justin, *Dial.* LXXII, 2. Cyprian, however, continues the quotation to the end of the verse (*Test.* II, 15) and Tertullian does the same (*Adv. Jud.* X, 12). A third example is *Tanquam ovis ductus ad aram, nec voce clamavi, patienter omnia gessi*, 'Like a sheep led to the altar, I did not call with my mouth; I bore everything patiently'. This text from Is. 53:7 is quoted in this form by Commodian, whereas, in *Test.* II, 13, Cyprian quotes the longer passage, Is. 53:7–9, 12.

It would not be difficult to give more examples of this phenomenon. What it is important to remember, however, is that the peculiar characteristic of a *testimonium* is that only the significant part of a text or sentence in the Bible is quoted. This is true both of the collections in the New Testament itself and of those from the second century. It is therefore unthinkable that Commodian extracted *testimonia* from longer quotations used by Cyprian, especially since there were independent collections of *testimonia* in existence before Cyprian's time. This applies in the case of several of the examples that we have given. What is most likely, then, is that Cyprian placed the *testimonia* which he found in his source or sources back into their original context.

The fundamental problem, however, is not solved by this suggestion. One of the characteristics of the early *testimonia* is their freedom with regard to the biblical text. Additions and excisions were made and texts were quite frequently merged together. Now, in Commodian we find a number of these modified texts, of well attested early date, whereas in Cyprian the standard text is established. As with Origen at Alexandria, Cyprian was writing at a time when attention was being paid to precision in biblical quotations. It is therefore possible that these were corrections made by copyists at a later date. There is, however, nothing in the manuscript tradition to allow us to assume this. The whole thesis, moreover, is made improbable because of the great number of cases.

Let us consider, as a first example, Ps. 119:120, which is clearly a case of suppression. In *Carm.* 269, we find: *David illum dixit clavis configi silentem* and further on, in *Carm.* 417: *Suffigitur clavis quod David praedixit olim* ('David said that he was silent when pierced by nails'; 'He was pierced with nails, as David once foretold'). In both cases, the context is that of the crucifixion. The first of these two quotations is placed immediately before Ps. 22:16: *Effoderunt manus meas et pedem ipsi* and the reference to David shows clearly that the quotation is from Ps. 119. This form of the quotation is very early indeed; it is found both in the *Epistle of Barnabas* V, 13, where it is compared with Ps. 22:16, and in Irenaeus, *Dem.* 79. The original text, however, reads: 'Pierce (καΘήλωσον) my soul with your fear' and is used in a moral sense. In order to turn it into a prediction of the crucifixion, the authors of the *testimonium* suppressed, 'with your fear'. It is only in this form that the text could have been included in the anthology on the crucifixion. Finally, in Cyprian's *Testimonia* II, 20, the same text appears in the form: *Confige clavis de metu tuo carnes meas,* 'Pierce my flesh with the nails of your fear'. The original form of this *testimonium* is undoubtedly that used by Commodian, and Cyprian corrects it to make it conform to the biblical text.

A second example is that of Dt. 28:66,[7] where an addition is made to the original text, which contains no reference at all to the passion: 'Your life will hang before your eyes and you will fear day and night and you will not believe in your life'. There is, however, little doubt that because of the word 'hanged' (κρεμαμένη), which also occurs in Dt. 21:23 – 'the one who is hanged (κρεμάμενος) on the wood is accursed' – this text was very early seen as a *testimonium* of the crucifixion. It is found with this meaning in Melito's *Homily on the Passion:* 'It is by the voice of the prophets that the mystery of Christ is proclaimed. Moses said to the people:"And you will see (ὄψεσΘε) your life hang before your eyes day and night and you will not believe in your life"' (*Hom.* X, 13–19). It will be noted that Melito modifies the original text of Deuteronomy by adding 'you will see'.

---

7. See *Etudes d'exégèse judéo-chrétienne,* pp. 53, 75.

This is one of the commonest *testimonia* of the second century. It occurs three times in the work of Irenaeus (*Dem.* 79; *Adv. haer.* IV, 10, 2; V, 18, 2, Harvey) and once in Clement of Alexandria (*Stromat.* V, 11; 72, 2). It is also found in Tertullian, who makes a notable addition: *Et erit vita tua pendens in ligno ante oculos tuos et non credes vitae tuae,* 'And your life will hang on the wood before your eyes and you will not believe in your life' (*Adv. Jud.* XI, 9; cf. also XIII, 11). The addition of *in ligno* is, of course, a clear allusion to the cross. This is a very typical early *testimonium* and Tertullian's text is the first evidence of this particular addition, although, as Pierre Prigent has pointed out,[8] it seems also to have been used by Justin.

It is also clear that Commodian found this text (Dt. 28:66) essential in connection with one of his favourite themes, that of the cross as the tree of life, since he quotes it at least six times. All that we can do here is to discuss those aspects of the quotation which are immediately relevant and especially the forms in which the quotation appears.[9]

The first time that Commodian quotes Dt. 28:66 is in verse 276 of his *Carmen,* where it is given together with Ps. 119:120; Ps. 22:16 and Jr. 11:19: *Ante tuos oculos pendebit vita necata* ('Before your eyes your life will hang murdered'). This is, of course, the short form that is found in Irenaeus and Tertullian, with the addition, it will be observed, of *necata.*

The second quotation contains a clearer allusion to the cross:

Qui credit in Christo de ligno vitae degustat
quo fuit suspensus Dominus Moysi praedicto (333–334)
('He who believes in Christ tastes of the tree of life, on which the Lord hung according to the prophecy of Moses')

This reference to the tree of life indicates that Commodian was acquainted with the text containing the words *in ligno.*

This supposition is further borne out by two further uses of the

8. *Justin et l'Ancien Testament,* pp. 189–194.
9. For a detailed study of these quotations the reader is referred to DANIELOU, *Etudes,* pp. 56–58.

text in his *Instructions*. The first of these is found in *Inst.* I, 35, 7–10:

> *In ligno pendet vita ferens poma praecepta.*
> *Capite nunc vitalia poma credentes*
> ('On the tree hangs life, bearing fruit taught beforehand. Believing, now receive the life-giving fruit'.)

The beginning of the first verse is a quotation from Dt. 28:66, with the addition of *in ligno,* while *ferens poma* may be a quotation from Ps. 1:3, which Tertullian linked with Dt. 28:66 (*Adv. Jud.* XII, 12). The reference is even more precise in the following passage:

> *Pars alia legis clamat: Videbitis inde*
> *suspensam in ligno vitam nec illi credetis* (I, 40, 8–9)
> ('Another part of the law exclaims: You will see life hung on a tree and you will not believe in it')

This quotation is particularly interesting in that it on the one hand contains the addition *in ligno* and, on the other, includes the *videbitis,* 'you will see', that occurs, as we have already seen, in Melito (ὄψεσθε). It is the earliest example of a text containing these two additions together, although both can be found at a later period in Novatian's *De Trin.* 9.

It is quite obvious that Commodian could not have derived this *testimonium* from Cyprian either in this form or indeed in any of the other forms to which we have drawn attention, all of which contain certain modifications, because Cyprian quotes the text in its accepted biblical form: *Et erit pendens vita tua ante oculos tuos et timebis die et nocte et non credes vitae tuae,* 'And your life will hang before your eyes and you will fear day and night and you will not believe in your life' (I, 20).

A case of some interest occurs in *Carm.* 291–292:

> *Exsurget in Israel homo de radice Jesse:*
> *in illo sperabunt gentes cuius signo tuentur*
> ('A man will arise in Israel from the root of Jesse; the nations

will hope in him by whose sign they are protected')

This is a different class of *testimonium,* that of the composite quotation. The first part of the first line — *exurget in Israel homo* — is an echo of Nb. 24:17,[10] and the second part — *de radice Jesse* — comes from Is. 11:1. The second line is based on Is. 11:10.[11] This is a very ancient *testimonium.*[12] In Rm. 15:12 we already have Is. 11:10 apparently modified by the wording of both Is. 11:1 and Nb. 24:17. Justin has the same group of three quotations merged together, although he uses Is. 11:1a instead of Is. 11:1b: 'Another prophet, Isaiah, proclaims the same thing in different terms. A star will rise from Jacob and a flower will grow on the stem of Jesse and the nations will hope in his arm' (*Dial.* XXII, 12–13).

Nb. 24:17 and Is. 11:1 were in fact two essential messianic prophecies. They had already been combined at Qumran (I Q Ben V, 27; Qumran Caves I, 128–129), the *Apocalypse of John* (Rv. 22:16) and Justin's *Dialogue* (XXVI, 1).[13] It is therefore hardly surprising that they should have been fused into a single composite quotation. The fact that Justin ascribes it to Isaiah shows that its origin had been forgotten. The same attribution is made in Commodian's *Carmen* (290).

There is, however, no trace of this composite quotation in Cyprian's work, although the quotations from Nb. 24:27 and Is. 11:1 are found in the extant text in two different places. The first is *Test.* II, 10: *Orietur stella ex Jacob et exurget homo ex Israel,* 'A star will rise out of Jacob and a man will arise out of Israel' and the second is found in *Test.* II, 11: *Et exiet virga de radice Jesse et flos de radice ascendet et requiescet super eum spiritus Dei,* 'And a rod will come out of the root of Jesse and a flower will rise up from the root and the Spirit of God will rest upon him'. Cyprian has clearly expanded the second quotation.[14] Finally, in a third passage (I, 21), Is. 11:10 is also quoted, again in the fully elaborated form, as indeed it is in Novatian's *De Trinitate* 9. All this serves to

10. This is also found verbatim in l.369.
11. This is also found in ll.264, 298.
12. Cf. J. DANIELOU, *The Theology of Jewish Christianity,* pp. 218–219.
13. Cf. J. DANIELOU, *Primitive Christian Symbols,* pp. 90–105.
14. It is also found in Tertullian (*Adv. Jud.* IX, 26).

demonstrate that Commodian's use of these texts was early and
not in any way dependent on Cyprian.

The sixth example that can be given is found in Commodian's
Carm. 295–296, where the author combines Ps. 96:10 and 97:1.
This case may be compared with that of Dt. 28:66:

> *In psalmis canitur: Dominus regnavit a ligno;*
> *exultet terra, iocundentur insulae multae.*
> ('It is sung in the psalms: the Lord has reigned from the tree;
> let the earth rejoice, let the many islands be glad')

This is a very early *testimonium*, which is found also in Justin, who
treats it as traditional and accuses the Jews of mutilating the text
(*Dial.* LXXIII, 1), and in Tertullian (*Adv. Marc.* III, 19, 1; 21, 1).
The biblical text does not, of course, contain the words *a ligno*,
but simply *Dominus regnavit*, *a ligno* having been added at a very
early date.[15] In Cyprian, the same text occurs in more or less the
same form as it is found in Commodian, but without the words *a
ligno* (*Test.* II, 29). In this case too the early form is that found in
Commodian, who could therefore not have taken the *testimonium*
from Cyprian.

Another quotation in the *Carmen*, this time of Is. 7:14, is in
several respects interesting:

> *Ecce dabit Deus ipse nobis signum ab alto:*
> *Concipiet virgo et pariet terra caelestem* (405–409)
> ('Behold, God himself, will give us a sign from the height
> above: a virgin will conceive and the earth will bear what is
> heavenly')

Two aspects of this quotation are worthy of comment. The first
is that the words *ab alto* are clearly taken from Is. 7:11 and the second is that *pariet filium*, 'She will bear a son' are replaced by
pariet terra caelestem, which would seem to be an allusion to
another biblical text. In the *Adversus Judaeos*, Tertullian writes:
Nam et alibi propheta praedicat, dicens: Terra dedit benedictiones suas

---

15. Cf. J. DANIELOU, *The Theology of Jewish Christianity*, pp. 96–97.

(Ps. 67:7). *Utique illa terra virgo ex qua nunc Christus secundum carnem ex virgine natus est,* 'For elsewhere the prophet foretells, saying: the earth gave its blessings (Ps. 67:7). This earth is certainly the virgin from whom Christ has now been born, of a virgin so far as physical birth is concerned' (*Adv. Jud.* XIII). What we have here is the theme of the virgin earth of paradise compared with the virgin's womb, which was a favourite theme of Irenaeus and Tertullian and which also underlies Commodian's text. In this case, it is clear that Commodian was inspired by Tertullian, since he uses the text in the same chapter. Cyprian, on the other hand, merely quotes the received text of Is. 7:10–11.

There is, however, a further aspect of this text which shows that it comes from a very early *testimonium*. This is that it is immediately followed by a quotation from Is. 8:4:

Et verbum: Samaria cap(ietur) priusquam loqueretur.
Sed haec est historia clausa, de qua docti revoluunt,
Ut parvulus lactans sine pugna praedas iniret
('And the word: Samaria will be taken before he speaks. But this is a closed book, about which learned men reflect, how an infant at the breast may enter on the booty without a battle'.)

This quotation is not found in Cyprian, but in many of the very early *testimonia* the preceding text Is. 7:14–16 is merged together with this passage from Is. 8:4. An example of this is the insertion of Is. 8:4 between Is. 7:16a and 7:16b twice in Justin's *Dialogue* (XLIII, 6 and LXVI, 3). Furthermore, both in his treatise against the Jews (*Adv. Jud.* IX) and in that against Marcion (*Adv. Marc.* III, 13, 1), Tertullian treats Is. 7:14 and Is. 8:4 as a single quotation. There can therefore be no doubt that, in this case, Commodian is quoting this particular *testimonium,* and this in turn enables us to explain the strange statement *historia clausa de qua docti revoluunt.* Justin, Tertullian and Origen all interpret Is. 8:4 as the victory of a child over the powers of the devil.[16] What Commodian means,

---

16. Cf. J. DANIELOU, *The Theology of Jewish Christianity,* p. 109.

therefore, is that the text has a hidden sense; and his mention of the *docti* seems to be a definite allusion to Tertullian and proof that he has read him.

In some cases, it is possible to discern that a similar procedure has taken place, although there is no evidence earlier than Commodian that the text already existed in its modified form. The modification may, of course, be Commodian's own, but it is also possible that he is simply making use of an earlier tradition of which no other examples are extant. By contrast, in all these cases the parallels in Cyprian use the received text. A good example occurs in *Carm.* 383–384:

> *Dictum est Christo meo, teneo cuius dexteram, illud:*
> *Exaudiant gentes et imperet gentibus ipse*
> ('This is said to my Christ, whose right hand I hold: let the nations hear and let him rule the nations')

The first part of this quotation, as far as *imperet,* is a very ancient testimonium, found in the *Epistle of Barnabas* (**XII**, 11) and known to Tertullian (*Adv. Jud.* VII, 2). It is taken from Is. 45:1. The second part of l. 384 is from Ps. 22:28. Both parts are found, separately, in Cyprian's *Testimonia* (I, 21 and II, 29), in the case of the second, as part of a longer quotation comprising Ps. 22:27–28. Clearly, the process that has taken place here is similar to the one found in the early *testimonia,* so that this quotation too must have existed before Commodian's time.

There are also cases of modifications to biblical texts which were made for metrical reasons. A good example of this adaptation to conform to the metre of the verse is Commodian's version of Is. 6:10:

> *Ipse Deus illos descripsit: Pectore clauso*
> *Nec videant oculis nec intelligent corde durato.*
> *Incrassavit enim cor populi huius iniqui,*
> *Ut nihil agnoscant donec verbo meo sanescant* (*Carm.* 399–402)
> ('God himself described these people: their heart is closed and let them not see with their eyes nor understand with hardened hearts. For the heart of this wicked people has become dull

so that they understand nothing until they are healed by my word'.)

This is a very early *testimonium*, which is found in the New Testament (Mt. 13:15; Jn. 12:40; Ac. 28:26–27). Commodian's text is closest of all to that of John, especially in its inclusion of the same abbreviations. Clearly the words *corde durato* come from John's *induravit cor eorum*, 'he has hardened their heart'. It is, however, worth noting that Commodian also uses the common version *incrassavit*. On the other hand, *pectore clauso* for *oculos claude*, and *ne nihil agnoscant* for *ne convertantur*, 'lest they be converted', are Commodian's own modifications of the Johannine text. *Verbo meo*, 'by my word', is an addition, taken from Ps. 107:20; *Misit verbum suum et sanavit eos*, 'He sent his word and cured them'. Finally, Commodian inverts the first two parts of the verse. Cyprian, on the other hand, quotes the complete text in the received version.

Commodian has modified in the same way another text (Ps. 3:5) which is also part of an early *testimonium*, in this case on the resurrection, and which is found in Clement of Rome (*I Clem.* XXVI, 2), Justin (*I Apol.* XXXVIII, 5) and Irenaeus (*Dem.* 71), also with modifications. Commodian has the following form:

> *Ego dormivi, ait et somnum cepi securus,*
> *Auxilio Domini surrexi, nihil mali passus* (*Carm.* 445–446)
> ('I slept, he said, and I took my sleep free from care;
> I rose with the help of the Lord, having suffered nothing evil')

Cyprian, on the other hand, has the following form of this *testimonium: Ego dormivi et quievi et resurrexi, quoniam Dominus suscipiet me*, 'I slept and rested and I rose, since the Lord will uphold me' (*Test.* II, 24). Several comments have to be made about Commodian's version. *Securus*, 'free from care', is a commentary; *nihil mali passus*, 'having suffered no evil', seems to be a kind of summary of verse 6, which is not quoted in Cyprian's version. It must clearly have formed part of the *testimonium* which Commodian used. The text which Commodian employs is not, however, the same as that used by Cyprian. He has *somnum cepi*, which is the received version, whereas Cyprian has the unusual rendering *quievi*. On the other hand Commodian uses the phrase *auxilio Domini*, where Cyprian has *quoniam Dominus suscipiet me*. This is further proof that Commodian could not have taken this passage from the *Testimonia* of Cyprian.

It is, therefore, certain that Commodian was not dependent on the *Testimonia ad Quirinum*. We must, however, go a stage further and ascertain the source or sources from which he derived a collection of *testimonia* which he had not himself assembled. The first possible source is undoubtedly Tertullian. We have already drawn attention to this possibility in connection with the *testimonium* combining Is. 7:13–15 and Is. 8:4 and containing the two themes of the virgin earth and the victory of the child over the powers of the devil. Other examples suggest the same possibility. In *Carm.* 171, for instance, we read:

> *Esaias autem: Tu es Deus et nesciebamus*
> *Et Deus in te est et praeter te non alter habetur*
> ('Isaiah, however, declared: You are our God and we did not know and God is in you and beside you there is no other')

This is, of course, a quotation from Is. 45:14–15. Cyprian quotes this text (*Test.* II, 6), but places it back in its context. Tertullian also uses it in his treatise against Praxeas: *In te Deus est. Tu enim es Deus noster et nesciebamus,* 'God is in you. For you are our God and we did not know' (*Adv. Prax.* XIII) and it is quite certain that Commodian knew this passage. For he writes in *Carm.* 381:

> *Certe iam apparet, qui sit Deus et quis in ipso*
> ('Certainly it now appears who is God and who is in him')

Tertullian had written: *Hic enim dicendo: Deus in te, et: Tu Deus, duos proponit qui erat et in quo erat* (*Adv. Prax.* XIII), 'For he, by saying: God is in you, and: You are God, sets forth two separate beings, he who was, and the one in whom he was'.

We should not, however, conclude too readily that Commodian inherited Tertullian's text, since the text that he quotes includes the words *et praeter non alter habetur* (LXV, 15), which are not found in Tertullian, but are included by Cyprian. Tertullian, moreover, has abbreviated the text, which must have formed part of a collection of *testimonia* which was used by all three authors, Tertullian, Commodian and Cyprian. Commodian appears to provide the most authentic version of the *testimonium*, Tertullian seems to have shortened it and Cyprian has clearly expanded it. It should also be noted that this text is combined with Jr. 17:9 in *Carm.* 370:

> *Et homo est, inquit, et quis eum novit in ipsis?*
> ('And he is man, he said, and who knew him in these things?')

This text is found in Cyprian (*Test.* II, 10), and Tertullian (*Adv. Jud.* XIV, 6; *Adv. Marc.* III, 7, 6). The continuation of the text (*Carm.* 371–372) contains a quotation from Ba. 3:36–38 combined with that from Jeremiah:

> *Hieremias ait: Hic Deus est noster aequalis*
> *Post haec et in terra visus est conversatus humanis*
> ('Jeremiah says: This God is our fellow; after this he was also seen on earth, living as man')

Here again, the passage is found in Cyprian (*Test.* II, 6) but in its complete form. It had already been used by Irenaeus (*Dem.* 37; *Adv. haer.* IV, 32, 4) and the *Testaments of the XII Patriarchs*.

Another quotation in which Commodian was probably influenced by Tertullian is Dn. 9:25–26, which is found in *Carm.* 267–268:

> *Hunc sanctum sanctorum Daniel perungui designat*
> *Et exterminari post illum chrisma regale*
> ('This Holy of Holies Daniel names as anointed and that the royal chrism is destroyed after this')

This quotation is not to be found in Cyprian, and dependence on him is therefore ruled out. On the other hand, it plays a vital part in Tertullian's *Adversus Judaeos,* where the prophecy of the Seventy Weeks is quoted *in extenso* (Dn. 9:1–27) in chapter VIII. Dn. 9:24 is expounded as follows: *Et unctus est Sanctus Sanctorum id est Christus,* 'And the Holy of Holies has been anointed, that is, Christ', so that it is difficult not to believe that this was Commodian's source, since Tertullian interprets the Holy of Holies as Christ, and says that the anointing (*unctio*) came to an end (*exterminata est*) after (*post*) the passion of Christ.

Another commentary, specifically on Dn. 9:24–26, is found in Tertullian's *Adv. Jud.* XIII: *Lex praecepit in captivitate non licere unctionem chrismatis regalis confici. Si autem iam nec unctio est illis, ut Daniel prophetavit; Dicit enim: Exterminabitur unctio. Ergo iam non est illis unctio,* 'The law taught that in captivity it was not lawful to carry out the anointing of royal chrism. But if they now have no anointing (as Daniel prophesied, for he said: The anointing will be destroyed), then there is now no anointing for them'. One of the most striking aspects of the use of this text by Commodian and Tertullian is the exact parallel between *chrisma regale* and *chrismatis regalis.* What is more, the *testimonium* is no more than one element in Tertullian's long quotation, whereas Commodian provides us with the *testimonium* in its pure state as a prophecy of the messianic High Priest. This *testimonium* is moreover combined with another particularly famous one, the prophecy of Is. 28:16 on the Messiah as the corner-stone. These two *testimonia* must clearly have been linked in the collection that Commodian used.

These three examples show quite decisively that Commodian was influenced by Tertullian and point to a *terminus post quem* of which Thraede was apparently not conscious. They do not, however, prove decisively that Commodian in fact took these *testimonia* from Tertullian. A long tradition, after all, lay behind these *testimonia,* as we have already observed in the case of the first two. In the case of the third, the *testimonium* from Daniel's prophecy of the Seventy Weeks, this too is quoted by Justin in his *Dialogue* and Irenaeus in the *Adversus haereses* V. [17] The form of these *testimonia* in Commodian is not the same as that in Tertullian's work. We may therefore conclude that Commodian was

17. See also the *De Pascha computus* 13, in which the text cited is different from that given by Tertullian and Commodian.

indebted to Tertullian, not for the *testimonia* themselves but for their exegesis.

Finally, we turn to the case of a quotation of a passage from the *Book of Wisdom* (Ws. 2:12–22) used by Commodian and Cyprian. The relationship between the way in which each of these authors uses this quotation presents us with a special problem. For here, in contrast to all the other cases that we have considered, it is Commodian who quotes the passage at length (*Carm.* 483–502) and, as it also occurs in Cyprian's *Test.* II, 14, it might seem as though Commodian took it from Cyprian.[18]

It is clear, however, that Commodian did not take this text from Cyprian's *Testimonia*. In *Carm.* 495–496, a quotation from Mt. 27:39–43 is inserted into the long quotation from the *Book of Wisdom*, but Cyprian does not refer to this text from *Matthew* in *Test.* II, 14, although he does in fact quote Mt. 27:3. In the *De montibus*, on the other hand, a quotation from Mt. 17:55 is inserted into the same place in the same quotation from the *Book of Wisdom*.[19] Again, in Cyprian's *Testimonia*, the quotation from Ws. 2:12–22 is accompanied by one from Is. 57:2; but these two texts are not associated either in Commodian or in the *De montibus*.[20] In this context it should not be forgotten that the *De montibus* was written before Cyprian compiled his *Testimonia*.

This leads us to conclude that Ws. 2:12–22 belonged to a tradition of *testimonia* that existed before the time of Cyprian, and that it had a special status within this tradition, which would explain why it plays such an important part in Commodian's *Carmen*. It would seem that the *Book of Wisdom* was regarded as especially

18. ANNE-MARIE LA BONNARDIERE has studied the problem raised by this text in early Latin literature and has drawn attention to the many different references to it. 'Le Juste défié par les impies (Sap. 2, 12–22) dans la tradition patristique africaine', *La Bible et les Pères* (*Colloque de Strasbourg*. 1–3, Oct. 1969), pp. 161–167. It is, for example, found in the *De montibus* 7, although in a shortened form. It also occurs in the *Altercatio Simonis et Theophili*, which draws on the same tradition of *testimonia* as Cyprian and Commodian.
19. LA BONNARDIERE has drawn attention to this variation.
20. In passing, it should be noted that this is not the only connection between Commodian's *Carmen* and the *De montibus* – in both treatises, as we have seen, *lex* and *lignum* are associated.

significant in the Latin Church in general and in the African Church in particular. A good example of its importance is found in the sermon *De centesima*, in which the quotation Ws. 6:12–21 occurs. Once again, the quotation is unusually long (Supp. *PL* I, 66), and the sequence of the verses is modified. We know too that *Wisdom* played an important part in the early Christian liturgy because the 'Wisdom of Solomon' is quoted in the Muratorian Canon among the books 'read publicly in the Church'. All this supports the general conclusion that Ws. 2:12–22 was a *testimonium* of special importance, introduced into Africa for liturgical purposes in a special form, and persisting in that form in the Latin Christian tradition.[21]

It would therefore seem that Commodian was not here dependant on Cyprian. The earliest form of the quotation is the composite version, including the text from Matthew (Mt. 27:39–43, 55). This is the form that occurs in the *Carmen* and in the *De montibus*, although neither author was dependant on the other. We are therefore bound to conclude that the text had a place in the tradition of the Latin Church dating from the end of the second century or the beginning of the third. In this case, as in all others, Cyprian simply reconstituted the text to make it conform to the received version, by eliminating the changes that had been made in the *testimonia*.

3. CYPRIAN'S *AD QUIRINUM*

Cyprian's work forms a most important element in the history of *testimonia*. He is the earliest author of whom we possess writings consisting exclusively of *testimonia*. (The three books of the *Ad Quirinum*, and the *Ad Fortunatum* are examples of this.) In this way, his work marks the culmination of a process which began with the first generation of Christians. Cyprian inherited a long tradition and most of the quotations that had been handed down either by Christian authors or in various catechetical collections can be found in his work. At the same time, however,

---

21. See A. LAMBERT, 'Echos du Livre de la Sagesse dans Barn. 7, 9', *Judéo-christianisme (Mélanges Daniélou)*, p. 198.

he leaves his own imprint on these texts, arranging them in his own way, adding new passages, suppressing the anomalies in the archaic versions of the *testimonia*, and quoting them in the rendering of the Latin Bible that he used. He also adds quotations from the New Testament to those taken from the Old Testament.

Cyprian's work in the field of *testimonia* comprises four undoubtedly authentic works, all of which contain previously existing collections of *testimonia*. The first volume of the *Ad Quirinum* is basically an anti-Jewish polemical work, related to chapters III and XIII of the *Adversus Judaeos* of Tertullian. The second volume consists of messianic prophecies and is similar in this respect to books IV and XII of Tertullian's treatise, which in its turn drew on Justin for several groups of *testimonia*. Volume III of the *Ad Quirinum* is more personal and deals with the problems of Christian life and morals connected with the works that Cyprian was editing at the time. Finally, the *Ad Fortunatum* is an anthology on the subject of martyrdom, and equally personal in character.

Cyprian's work in this sphere therefore stands in sharp contrast to that of Commodian. The latter is concerned only with *testimonia* on the messianic prophecies, and confines himself exclusively to quotations taken from the established tradition, never adding any *testimonia* of his own. He also preserves each *testimonium* in its archaic form, with all the suppressions, additions and combinations that characterise the *testimonia* as a Judaeo-Christian genre. In Cyprian, however, the *testimonia* no longer represent a distinctive literary genre. Everything which gave them their distinctive character is eliminated. They are simply a collection of quotations. The only feature to survive is that these are still, in the main, the traditional passages to be found in Tertullian or in the various Latin collections compiled before his time.

The first collection in the *Ad Quirinum* (volume I) consists of anti-Jewish *testimonia*, grouped according to a precise plan which makes this section of the *Ad Quirinum* a genuine treatise rather than a mere collection. The first four chapters deal with the faithlessness of the Jews, chapters 5–18 with the disappearance of Israel's privileges, and chapters 19–24 with the Church of the gentiles, who have replaced the ancient people of God. There are three obvious differences here from Tertullian's anti-Jewish polemics. The first is that Tertullian announces the theme of the two peoples, the Jews and the gentiles, at the beginning of his treatise. The second is that Cyprian stresses in the last two chapters that salvation is more difficult for the Jews to achieve than for the gentiles. Thirdly, unlike Tertullian, Cyprian insists that the Jews are bound to accept baptism and to renounce their practice of the law. [22]

Turning now to the question of the quotations themselves in *Ad Quirinum* I, two different groups can be distinguished. The first group of quotations is concentrated mainly in chapters 1–4 and 19–24. Most of these quotations can also be found in Tertullian, *Adv. Jud.* III and XIII and *Adv. Marc.* III. Cyprian is, however, distinctive in that he adds quotations taken from books of the Old Testament which were seldom used before his time, in particular the books of Kings and Samuel (1 K. 19:10; 1 S. 2:5). As we have already pointed out above, the chapters in which this first group of quotations occurs are those dealing, on the one hand, with the faithlessness of the Jews and, on the other, with the new, gentile people of God. Cyprian arranges these quotations in his own way, but the same texts are also to be found in Tertullian, who in turn derived most of them from Justin.

The second series of quotations, which can be found in chapters 5–18, is the most original. Here Cyprian lists the privileges which have been taken from Israel and replaced by those bestowed on the gentiles. This theme is not absent from Tertullian who concentrates on three aspects of it – circumcision, the sabbath and the Jewish sacrifices. Two of these are discussed by Cyprian – circumcision (8) and sacrifices (16) – and his quotations overlap with those used by Tertullian. He adds, however, a series of other privileges: the land (6), light (7), the law (9–10), the testament (11), baptism (12), the yoke (13), the shepherds (14), the temple (15), the priesthood (17) and the prophet (18). In these chapters, Cyprian often uses quotations

22. This is reminiscent of the *Adversus Judaeos* of Pseudo-Cyprian.

which are also to be found in Tertullian, but in a different context. More often, however, and especially in chapters 7, 9, 14 and 15, he uses quotations of his own.

As we have already seen, Tertullian did not use Justin as his source for quotations concerned with the Jewish practices of circumcision, the sabbath and sacrifice. We suggested that he in fact made use of an anti-Jewish, African source. It is quite possible that Cyprian may have thought of the same source, but it is certain that his main concern here was with moral and sacramental teaching. This is so because, unlike the *Adversus Judaeos*, the *Ad Quirinum* is not first and foremost a polemical writing directed against the Jews, but an account of Christian faith. This means that the meaning attached to the *testimonia* in the *Ad Quirinum* is different.

The second collection in the *Ad Quirinum* contains the prophecies of the Messiah and corresponds to what we have already found in Justin and in Tertullian's *Adversus Judaeos*. This is an even more traditional type of collection than the one that we have just discussed, and contains groupings which clearly go back to the Judaeo-Christian community. Examples of these are the theme of Christ as the stone (16) and as a mountain (17 and 18), the wood of the cross (20), the sign of the cross (21) and the sign of tau (22). In addition all the classic passages quoted in the New Testament on the virgin birth (Is. 7:14), Bethlehem (Mi. 5:1) and the Passion (Is. 53; Ps. 22) are included.

Cyprian, however, adds two other elements to this classic collection of messianic prophecies. The first six chapters are concerned with the pre-existence of the Word. Here Christ is presented in turn as Wisdom (1 and 2), as the Word (3), as God's hand and arm (4), as the one who is sent, the *angelus* (5) and as God, distinct from the Father (6). Justin also includes this collection concerning the pre-existence of the Word in his work, and Tertullian also uses it, not in the *Adversus Judaeos*, but in the *Adversus Praxean*. It would seem that the latter treatise was Cyprian's inspiration, since many quotations are common to both, though he has also enriched the collection with several passages of his own.

Furthermore, the final chapters of this part of the treatise are concerned, not with the messianic prophecies, but with the second coming of Christ at the end of time. Several important collections of *testimonia* in these chapters seem to have been compiled by Cyprian himself. For example, that in chapter 28, entitled *quod ipse index venturus est*, 'That the sign himself will come', comprising Ml. 4:1; Ps. 50:3; Is. 42:13; Ps. 68:2; Ps. 82:8, seems to be peculiar to Cyprian. Similarly, in chapter 29: *Quod ipse sit rex in aeternum regnaturus*, 'That he will reign forever as king', the first quotations are also found in Tertullian, but the eight which follow, from the Psalms, have been collected by Cyprian. The same applies to the last chapter (30).

Turning now to the strictly messianic chapters in this part of the *Ad Quirinum* (6–27), we are conscious of Cyprian's intention to arrange these prophecies according to the sequence of the mysteries of Christ. To do this, he makes use of two kinds of collection of *testimonia*. The first kind consists of *testimonia* which follow the order of the life of Christ, as in the case of certain collections found in the work of Irenaeus and Tertullian. The second type follows the order of the books of the Old Testament, as in the work of Melito. There are also groups of *testimonia* concerned with certain signs, such as the collections on the stone, the lamb and the wood of the cross, to be found in the work of Pseudo-Barnabas and Justin.

Within each chapter Cyprian follows the order of the biblical books. As we have already pointed out, he also adds quotations from the New Testament which show that the prophecies have been fulfilled. He also inserts, between the mysteries, collections on the signs. In chapter 16 he has, for instance, the sign of the stone, in chapter 18 that of the bridegroom, and in chapter 20 that of the wood of the cross. We are therefore bound to conclude that, although Cyprian uses material which is traditional, his arrangement of it is original. What he in fact does is to divide groups which contain *testimonia* traditionally associated with each other and distribute them differently.

What, however, was Cyprian's intention in grouping the *testimonia* in this way? Bearing in mind what has been said so far, it is clear that Cyprian's scheme was that of the 'rule of faith'. That is why he begins with the pre-existence of the Word and then goes on to speak about the mission of the Word in revelation and salvation, the virgin birth, Christ's two natures, his descent from David, his birth in Bethlehem, the lowliness of his manifestation of himself, the passion, the crucifixion, the descent into hell, the resurrection and exaltation, and finally his return at the end of time to judge the living and the dead, and his eternal reign. Clearly, what we have here is, in broad outline, the early Roman creed of the third century.

At least one important conclusion can be drawn from this. Until the time of Cyprian, the *testimonia* on the messianic prophecies had all appeared within the framework of anti-Jewish or anti-Marcionite polemic. This is certainly true of Commodian and Tertullian on the one hand and of Justin and the *Adversus haereses* on the other. With Cyprian, however, we find these *testimonia* used with a catechetical intention to confirm and illustrate the faith, a purpose which had already inspired Irenaeus in writing his *Demonstration of the Apostolic Preaching.*

Finally, what were Cyprian's sources? To a great extent, he seems to have derived his material from the *Adversus Judaeos* and the *Adversus Marcionem* of Tertullian, and, in the case of the first few chapters of his treatise, from the *Adversus Praxean.* For the rest, he appears to have searched out his quotations for himself. On the one hand, he widens the range of biblical books from which the passages are taken. Where Tertullian borrowed above all from the prophetic books and the *Psalms,* Cyprian makes more use of the Pentateuch and the historical books. [23] He also emphasises the sacramental aspect (*Ad Quir.* I, 2, citing Pr. 9:1) and that of the Church (I, 19, the texts on the bride).

Book III of the *Ad Quirinum,* which we must now briefly consider, is a work of moral catechesis. Its authenticity has been established by Hugo Koch, who has made a careful comparison between it and Cyprian's other works. In the first two collections, it is clear that Cyprian is handing on traditional data. In this book, however, in which his aim is more explicitly moral and practical, there are constant echoes of his own preoccupations in this field. He has clearly prepared his own collections of biblical texts in connection with his other writings and their preparation.

23. This will come out more clearly in Chapter 11, *Typology.*

The point is easily illustrated. The first chapter, entitled *De bono operis et misericordiae*, 'That work and pity are a good', may be compared with his treatise *De opere et eleemosynis*, 'On work and almsgiving'; and the same applies to chapter 2, *In opere et eleemosynis voluntatem satis esse*. Chapter 16, *De bono martyrii*, 'That martyrdom is a good', deals with a theme which was to be taken up in the *Ad Fortunatum*, while the subject matter of chapter 32, *De bono virginitatis*, 'That virginity is a good', is clearly related to the *De habitu virginum*. Chapter 58, *De idolis*, 'On idols', is reminiscent of the treatise *Quod idola non sint*; chapter 106 is concerned with patience, as is the *De bono patientiae;* and finally chapter 120, *Orationibus consistendum*, 'That there must be perseverance in prayer', is related to Cyprian's treatise on prayer, the *De oratione*. We may therefore conclude that the themes dealt with in these chapters are those which feature again and again in Cyprian's teaching.

It is quite evident that Cyprian is concerned here with an aspect of traditional Christian catechesis. From the very first extant examples, we find moral and dogmatic instruction going hand in hand, as in the *Epistle of Barnabas*, the moral teaching consisting of a treatise on Christian ethics both in its general principles and in its particular practical application. Clear echoes of this are found in the *Ad Quirinum* III, one example being the situation of the commandment to love at the beginning of the book, and the working out of this in the first three chapters. Another example is the allusion at the end of the book to eschatology, with a chapter on the Antichrist, which is reminiscent of the moral catechesis in the *Epistle of Barnabas*.

Having said this, however, it is important to add that Cyprian's work in this section is completely original. Before his time there is no methodical collection of scriptural texts drawn from the Old and the New Testaments with the purpose of establishing the basis of various aspects of Christian life. Tertullian's moral treatises are certainly of this type, but he deals in them with particular cases and makes no attempt to organise the biblical texts. All this points to the fact that Cyprian did the work of collecting the texts himself. He certainly indicates this in his preface: *Petisti ut ad instruendum te excerperem de scripturis sanctis quaedam capitula ad religiosam sectae nostrae disciplinam pertinentia,* 'You have asked that in order to instruct you I should cull from the Holy Scriptures some short passages relating to the religious discipline of our sect'.

The motivation of this section of the treatise is also original. Cyprian is concerned more with behaviour, with the ordinary practice of Christian life, than with moral theory. This is a clear reflection of his thinking generally, since he has a moralising turn of mind. He displays little originality in the first two books of the *Ad Quirinum*, in which he is concerned with dogmatic teaching, but in Book III he is on his own ground. At the same time, however, his interest in the practical aspect of Christian life is also a very typical feature of Latin Christianity. If we wish to find a model for his work, we must look for it in the collections of *sententiae* that abound in the literature of the imperial period.

CHAPTER ELEVEN

TYPOLOGY

FOR the study of typology in Latin christianity of the third century the crucial materials are the writings of Tertullian. Devoted to the literal meaning of the text, distrustful of any allegorical interpretation, he acknowledges only one spiritual sense, namely the typological, relying here on the example of St. Paul (*Adv. Marc.* III, 5, 4) and on the common tradition. His contribution is original only by virtue of the quality of his intellectual grasp. In an absolutely general way, he uses the word *figura,* which corresponds exactly to Justin's τύπος for 'figures' in the typological sense. When, in the *Adversus Marcionem,* he does use *allegoria* in the same sense, it is simply in deference to Pauline usage. In the *De resurrectione mortuorum,* however, the term has the pejorative meaning of allegorism. The word *aenigma* is used only to qualify other expressions.

Tertullian's typological exegesis is to be found principally in the *Adversus Judaeos* and *Adversus Marcionem* III. As we have already seen, the first of these two works is a draft outline going back to the earliest period of Tertullian's literary activity. His aim in this early treatise is to show how the Church of the gentiles took the place of the people of Israel, a standard theme of Christian literature in the second century. He argues, as we pointed out in an earlier chapter, that there was never more than one law, given by God in the beginning, but that this same law was developed *statutis temporibus,* 'at certain fixed times' and that Israel represents only one stage in this process. A new and indeed final period was inaugurated with the coming of Christect. [1] This is

1. Cf. T. P. O'MALLEY, *Tertullian and the Bible,* pp. 138–171; J. VAN DER GEEST, *Le Christ et l'Ancien Testament chez Tertullien,* pp. 151–191.

in fact the central message of the treatise and to convey it Tertullian has recourse to figures derived from authors writing at a previous period. Tränkle, for example, has demonstrated his dependance on Pseudo-Barnabas and Justin,[2] and to these we must add the influence of Melito. There were also, however, other collections upon which Tertullian drew, either using the material as it stood or developing elements which interested him.

1. TYPES OF CHRIST

Tertullian and Cyprian both make use of an already existing typology developed in the New Testament and by Justin and Irenaeus. Both Latin authors employ the same figures of Christ, but in their own personal way. Tertullian is more concerned with Adam as man than with Adam as a type, although the typology of Adam is certainly not absent from his work. It underlies, for example, many of the passages in which he quotes 1 Co. 15:45ff (the *novissimus* Adam). As we shall see later on, Tertullian is also interested in the typology of the Church and refers to Ep. 5:31 in connection with the birth of Eve as a figure of the Church.

Tertullian's most important treatise in this context is the *De carne Christi*, which shows clear traces of the influence of Irenaeus, especially in the following passage: 'All this new birth, prefigured (*figurata*) as it is in everything by the old birth, is so also by the spiritual economy of the Virgin at the time of the birth of the man who is Lord.[3] The earth was still virgin, not yet compressed by work or subjected to the sowing of seed. It was from her, as we know, that man was made a living being of God. This is why, if this has been handed on to us by the first Adam, it is right that the second and last Adam was produced by God as a life-giving spirit from virgin earth, that is, from flesh which had not yet been subjected to the reproductive process' (*De carne*, XVII, 4; see also *Adv. Jud.* XIII, 11).

---

2. Cf. H. TRANKLE, *Q.S.F. Tertulliani, Adversus Judaeos.*
3. This may be an answer to Marcion, who contrasted the 'first Adam' and the 'last Lord'; cf. *Adv. Marc.* V, 10.

This theme is derived, through Irenaeus, from the Jewish idea based on the etymology of Adam as 'red clay'. To this theme, Tertullian adds another, which is similarly derived from Judaism and which is a modification of the idea that Eve was fertilised by the serpent: 'God recovered his image and likeness, which the devil had seized, by a similar operation. The serpent's word, which introduced death into the world, penetrated into the virgin Eve and it was also into a Virgin that the word of God, which created life, had to be introduced, so that what had been lost by the sex of the one was restored by the same sex. Eve had believed in the serpent, but Mary believed in Gabriel. What had been lost by the credulity of the one was found again by the faith of the other. It will be said, however, that Eve conceived nothing by the word of the devil. On the contrary, she did. For the fact of her giving birth to wretched offspring and of her giving birth in pain shows that the seed in her was the word of the devil. She brought to life a devil who killed his brother.' (*De carn.* XVII, 5–6).

There is no need to examine the haggadah to which Tertullian is referring here.[4] The theme of Eve's adultery with the serpent is apparently known to Jn. 8:44; it is also found in the *Gospel of James* (131) and the *Epistle of Polycarp* (VII, 1), and figures prominently both in the *Pseudo-Clementines,* and in the gnostic writings. The *Gospel of Philip* (42) is of particular interest in this connection. The theme allows Tertullian to develop the Eve-Mary parallelism, already familiar to Irenaeus, and to give it a new dimension. The same parallel between Eve and Mary continued to be used in the typology of paradise.

Closely linked with this typology is the parallel between the tree of the knowledge of good and evil and the tree of the cross, which existed before Tertullian's time and had been exploited by Irenaeus. Tertullian refers to this in *Adv. Jud.* XIII, 11: 'The tree gave its fruit, not the tree of paradise, which gave death to the first parents, but the tree of Christ's passion, though you did not believe the life that hung thereon (Dt. 28:66)'. Since

4. Cf. N. A. DAHL, 'Der erstgeborene Satans', *Apophoreta (Festschrift Haenchen)*, pp. 70–84; A. ORBE, 'El pecado original y el matrimonio en la teologia del sec. II', *Gregor.*, 45 (1964), pp. 501–536.

the authors writing at this time used the theme of the trees of
paradise in many different symbolic ways, it needs to be pointed
out that here the parallelism is between the tree of the knowledge
of good and evil as the source of sin and the tree of the cross as
the source of salvation. The typology is of the same antithetic
type as in the case of Eve and Mary (cf. also *De pud.* VI, 16: *arbor
concupiscentiae*, the 'tree of desire' and *arbor patientiae*, the 'tree of
patience').

Cyprian portrays Abel as a figure of Christ: 'Inaugurating and
hallowing the origin of martyrdom and the passion of the
righteous man, Abel neither resists nor repels his murderous
brother, but, humble and gentle, patiently allows himself to be
killed' (*De bono pat.* 10). In this text, the author shows that 'all the
patriarchs, prophets and just men, who had previously borne in
an image (*imagine*) the figure (*figura*) of Christ, bore witness to
patience' (*De bono pat.* 10).[5] This list includes Abel, Isaac, Jacob,
Joseph, Moses, David and the prophets. In this passage, Cyprian
is clearly developing what is found in Melito's *Homily on the Passion* 59, particularly stressing Abel.[6]

Cyprian also has a typology of Noah as a figure of the passion.
This, however, is connected not with the theme of the persecution of the patriarchs, but with the symbolism of wine. This form
of typology is more archaic and allegorical, the theme being
taken from Irenaeus. The passage in Cyprian's letter reads: 'We
find in *Genesis,* in connection with the mystery (*sacramentum*) of
Noah, a prefiguration of the passion of the Lord (*praecucurisse et
figuram dominicae passionis extitisse*) in the fact that he drank the
wine that made him drunk and that he uncovered himself in his
house, that he lay down with his legs naked and visible, that this
nakedness of the father was noticed by the second son and
proclaimed by him outside, but was hidden by the eldest and the
youngest, and all the rest which there is no need to elaborate'

5. Cf. also Cyprian, *Ad Fort.* 11 (Abel, Jacob, Joseph, David, Elijah,
Zechariah); *Epist.* VI, 2 (Abel, the just, the prophets) and Pseudo-Cyprian. *De
laude martyrii,* 29 (Abel, Isaac, Joseph, with Isaiah before them).
6. In the *De zelo,* Abel is also placed at the head of a list of victims of jealousy.
This, however, is not a question of typology, but of morality and Cyprian
derives his ideas from *1 Clem.* IV, in which the same theme is discussed.

(*Epist.* LXIII, 3). The whole of this episode is therefore a figure of the passion. Cyprian does not explain how, though the explanation was obviously known to him. It should be noted that here and in the preceding example Cyprian is developing types which are not found in Tertullian.

In the *Adversus Judaeos*, Tertullian deals with the theme of the passion in a group of figures of Christ crucified: *Sacramentum passionis ipsius figurari in praedicationibus oportuerat*, 'It was necessary that the mystery of his passion should be foreshadowed in preaching' (*Adv. Jud.* X, 5). The first type is Isaac: 'When he was led by his father as a victim and carried the wood himself, he was already proclaiming the death of Christ, offered as victim by the Father and carrying the wood of his own passion himself' (*Adv. Jud.* X, 6; see also XIII, 20–21; *Adv. Marc.* III, 18, 2). This figure is also found in the *Epistle to the Hebrews*, 11:17–19 and was developed by Melito (*Frag.* 9 and 11). It is mentioned in the *Capella graeca*, does not appear at all in Justin's works, but is alluded to by Irenaeus. Cyprian refers to Isaac: *Isaac est in passionis dominicae similitudinem praefiguratus*, 'Isaac is prefigured as a type of the Lord's passion' (*De bono pat.* 12). The typology is further developed by Tertullian, who lays emphasis on the replacement of Isaac by the ram, and interprets the ram caught in the bush as a figure of Christ hanging from the wood of the cross (*Adv. Jud.* X, 7–8). Tertullian is also the first Christian author to compare the wood that Isaac carried with the cross.

Tertullian does not mention Jacob, though Cyprian speaks of 'Jacob driven into exile (*fugatus*) bearing the figure of Christ in a prophetic image' (*De bono pat.* 10). Tertullian briefly refers to Joseph as a 'figure of Christ inasmuch as he was persecuted by his brothers' (*Adv. Jud.* X, 6), but does not develop this typology in detail, *ne demorer cursum*, 'that I delay not my course' (see also *Adv. Marc.* III, 18, 3), which implies that he could have done so. It is found in Melito (*Hom. Pasch.* 59), Cyprian (*De bono pat.* 10),[7] and earlier in the *Testaments of the Twelve Patriarchs* (*Zeb.* IV, 4). This typological theme was not elaborated in the East, but became quite important in the West, Tertullian's use of it being significant in this connection.

7. Cf. *Message*, pp. 249–251.

Tertullian also provided a typological interpretation of the Blessings of Jacob and Moses in the cycle of the patriarchs. His comment in the case of Joseph, whose 'beauty is that of the bull' and whose 'horns are the horns of the unicorn' (Dt. 33:17), is 'Christ was figured in him, the bull, because of the two economies, one hard as a judge, the other gentle as a saviour. The horns are the arms of the cross, the unicorn the upright post in the centre' (*Adv. Jud.* X, 7; cf. also *Adv. Marc.* III, 18, 3, which reproduces the passage in *Adv. Jud.*). The blessings of Simeon and Levi (Gn. 49:5–6) similarly prefigure Christ because of the reference to the 'bull' (*Adv. Jud.* X, 8; see also *Adv. Marc.* III, 18, 5). Here, Tertullian is dependent on Justin.[8]

The most important of these blessings, however, is that of Judah (Gn. 49:9–10), of which Tertullian writes that it 'was Christ himself' (*Adv. Marc.* IV, 35, 10). Certain aspects of Tertullian's typology form part of very ancient *testimonia*. He mentions, for example, the expectation of the gentiles (*Adv. Marc.* IV, 11, 1), but stresses above all the importance of the text of Gn. 49:10: 'He will wash his garment in wine and his vesture in the blood of the grape', which he regards as a prophecy of the incarnation, the coat being the flesh of Christ and the wine his blood (*Adv. Marc.* IV, 40, 6).

Cyprian, on the other hand, elaborates this typology of Judah in the same way that he developed the typology of Noah: 'In the blessing of Judah, the figure (*figura*) of Christ is expressed in the fact that he had to be praised and adored by his brothers, that he had to rest on the backs of his conquered and fleeing enemies the hands with which he carried the cross and overcame death, that he would himself be the lion of the tribe of Judah, that he would rest, sleeping in his passion, that he would rise again and that he would be the hope of the people' (*Epist.* LXIII, 6).

Tertullian and Cyprian both draw on a wide variety of sources for this typology. In the first place, they make use of certain traditional figures which are especially closely related to the passion. The obvious example of this is the sacrifice of Isaac, which goes back to a common tradition. In the second place, both

8. Cf. DANIELOU, *The Theology of Jewish Christianity*, p. 293.

authors draw on Justin and Irenaeus in the main for certain
typologies which were first used at the beginning of the second
century in polemics against the Jews on the one hand and the
gnostics on the other. Finally, there is a further source of
typology concerned principally with the prefiguration of Christ's
passion in the patriarchs, the prophets and the just men who were
persecuted. This particular class of types, which comes from
Melito, is found principally in Cyprian.

The last-mentioned typology is found, for example, in the
Moses cycle. For both Tertullian and Cyprian (*De pat.* 10) the
persecuted Moses is a figure of the persecuted Christ. The Moses
cycle, moreover, contains a whole group of traditional figures
which are found in the work of both writers. It was this that
made Tertullian say that 'the whole history (*ordinem*) of Moses
was a figure of Christ' (*Adv. Marc.* V, 11, 8). Moses is a figure of
Christ's crucifixion, Tertullian claims, when he prayed with his
arms in the form of a cross on the mountain (*Adv. Jud.* X, 10).
This type had already been used in the *Epistle of Barnabas* (XII, 2)
and it occurs again in Cyprian's *Testimonia* II, 20 and in *Ad Fortunatum* 8. In Tertullian's *Adv. Jud.* X, 10 and Cyprian's work, it
is associated with the figure of the bronze serpent, which is as old
as the Fourth Gospel (Jn. 3:14). Tertullian and Cyprian also connected another figure, that of the paschal lamb, with the Moses
cycle. This traditional figure is mentioned by Tertullian in his
treatise against Marcion: 'The Passover is the figure of Christ'
(*Adv. Marc.* V, 7, 3) and by Cyprian, who speaks of 'the blood of
the lamb forming a cross on the houses of the Jews' (*Ad Dem.*
XXII) and the 'lamb offered in the evening' (*Epist.* LXI, 16).

Tertullian continues his list of types in the *Adversus Judaeos* with
Joshua. Following Justin, he writes: 'When Hoshea, the son of
Nun, was named as Moses' successor, he changed his name and
took that of Jesus. We maintain therefore that this was a figure of
the one who was to come (*futuri figura*). Jesus Christ was to introduce into the promised land, flowing with milk and honey, in
other words, into possession of that eternal life which is sweeter
than all things, the second people, that is, ourselves, the gentiles,
who had until then been living in the desert of the world. He had
to bring this about not by Moses. that is, by the discipline of the

law, but by Jesus, that is, by the grace of the new law. For these reasons, the man who had been prepared in order to portray this mystery in symbols (*imagines*) also inaugurated it by the figure (*figura*) of the name of the Lord, with the result that he was called Jesus' (*Adv. Jud.* IX, 21–22).

The above passage is very characteristic of Tertullian in many respects. He makes use here of a theme originally discussed by Justin, but deals with it with a rigour which brings out its basic meaning very clearly. (This is also true of his treatment of the typology of the sacrifice of Isaac and the exodus.) He has the gift of making interesting what might otherwise have been no more than a rather banal allusion. He makes everything that he touches new – in manner, not matter. This is a characteristic of Tertullian's genius which is particularly noticeable in this field. The words that he uses in connection with his typology are also worth noting – *figura, imagines, sacramentum*. Later in the same chapter of the *Adversus Judaeos*, still referring to Joshua, he speaks of *nominis futuri sacramentum* (*Adv. Jud.* IX, 25; see also *De monogamia* VI, 4), 'the mystery of the name that is to come'.

In the same passage, he also alludes to the stone knife with which the Jews were, at Joshua's command, circumcised: *Petra enim Christus multis modis et figuris praedicatus est,* 'For the rock which is Christ was preached in many ways and figures' (*Adv. Jud.* IX, 22). This is a very ancient theme – in the New Testament, for example, Is. 28:16 (the corner-stone), Is. 8:14 (the stumbling stone) and Ps. 118:22 (the stone rejected by the builders which became the keystone) are grouped together. In addition to these passages, Tertullian also mentions the stone which broke the statue and became a mountain (Dn. 2:34; see *Adv. Jud.* XIV, 3). The same comparisons are made by Justin, who has a collection on the theme of Christ as 'the stone' (λίθος), Is. 28:16 recurs again and again, not only in Justin, but also, for example, in Commodian (*Carm.* 265). Tertullian also adds the theme of the stone knives (Jos. 5:2), which is also found in Justin's *Dialogue* (CXIII, 6) and which is introduced into a typology of Joshua taken over by Tertullian.

The same collection is given in a more complete form by Cyprian. Although he mentions Is. 28:16; Ps. 118:22 and Dn.

2:34, he does not mention Jos. 5:2 or Is. 8:14. He does, however, quote Zc. 3:8–9, 'the stone with seven eyes'; Dt. 27:8, the stone tablets; Jos. 24:26, the 'stone of witness'; Gn. 28:11, 'the stone where Jacob's head rested', *quam lapidem consecravit et unxit sacramento unctionis Christum significans,* 'He consecrated and anointed this stone by a mystery of unction, thus pointing to Christ'; Ex. 17:12, 'the stone on which Moses sat with his arms outstretched on the mountain'; 1 S. 6:18, 'the stone on which the tabernacle is placed'; 1 S. 17:49, 'the stone by which David slew Goliath' and finally 1 S. 7:12, 'the stone erected by Samuel after his victory'.

It is instructive to compare Cyprian's collection of quotations with Tertullian's. Cyprian's is more complete. It is also earlier in origin, since it contains elements which are not found in Tertullian, but which do occur in the second century. An example of this is the quotation from Ex. 17:12, the stone on which Moses sat on the mountain. Justin uses this as a figure of Christ in *Dialogue* XC, 4. Cyprian, then, makes use of a common scholarly tradition and uses all of it, whereas Tertullian takes what suits him from this tradition and leaves the rest out. He also develops those data which he retains. A new element which is apparently introduced by Cyprian is the figures borrowed from the Books of Kings, which are not found in the Greek typological tradition of the second century.

There is one final problem which remains to be discussed. It is unlikely that Cyprian would have introduced elements of his own invention into a collection of this kind and a solution to this problem may be found in the fact that there is an author, who lived at a time between that of Tertullian and Cyprian, who developed the typology of the *Books of Kings*. This is Hippolytus, whose most important treatise in this particular context is on David and Goliath.[9] On the one hand, Cyprian may have made use of Hippolytus' work. On the other, however, the latter is an echo of the interest taken in the typology of David in the Western tradition. It is worth noting that Cyprian not only develops the typology of David (*De bono pat.* 10), which was

9. Cf. *Message,* pp. 242–243; article 'David', *RAC,* VI, pp. 594–603.

merely mentioned by Melito, but also was the first author to
regard Elijah as a figure of Christ (*Oper.* 17).

2. TYPES OF THE CHURCH

So far as the typology of Christ is concerned, Tertullian and
Cyprian are the heirs of the typological tradition of the New
Testament, Justin and Irenaeus. Tertullian expressed this
typology with especial clarity and without any concession to
allegorism, while Cyprian sought to extend it to new areas of
Scripture. In other spheres of typology, however, their contribution is more original and more closely in accordance with their
preoccupations. This applies particularly to their typology of the
Church, which, although it existed from New Testament times,
played a very limited part in the work of the second century
authors. It was much more fully developed by Tertullian and
above all by Cyprian.

First, we shall examine the various themes of the typology of
the Church in Tertullian's writings; and then turn to Cyprian,
who is here at the centre of the picture, since it was by him that
the doctrine of the Church was first fully developed.

In considering Tertullian's typology of the Church we may
begin with the theme of paradise. In *Adv. Marc.* II, 4, 4, he says
that 'man was translated to paradise – translated early as that, even
out of the world into the Church'. Tertullian is in fact the first
Christian author to use the theme of paradise as a figure of the
Church. Hippolytus was to give great prominence to it later and
it was also to feature in Cyprian's writing. It should, however, be
pointed out that there is an echo of the theme in the Roman
catacombs, where paradise is frequently portrayed in connection
with Christian baptism. This would seem to indicate, therefore,
that Tertullian was bearing witness to a western tradition.

A second theme is that of the dove. F. J. Dölger has rightly
pointed to the symbol of the dove in Tertullian's treatise *Adversus
Valentinianos* (III, 1) as a figure of the Church: *Nostrae columbae
etiam domus simplex,* 'Even the simple house of our dove'. It is
clear that, in this text, the dove indicates the Christian community. The theme is unknown in the East, where the dove represents

the Holy Spirit. In *V Esdras*, it represents the Church, the author basing his teaching on the exegesis of the *Song of Songs* and, as we shall see later, Cyprian also interprets the dove in the same way.

Finally, there is a third theme which was especially favoured by Tertullian, namely that of Eve as a type of the Church. In the earlier tradition, which was certainly known to Tertullian (see *De carn.* XVII, 5), there was, as we have seen, a typology of Eve and Mary. To this typology, however, Tertullian adds a typology of Eve and the Church. In *Adv. Marc.* III, 5, 4, for example, we read: *Apostolus suggerens Ephesiis quod in primordio de homine praedicatum est, relicturo patrem et matrem et futuris duobus in unam carnem, id se in Christum et Ecclesiam agnoscere,* 'The apostle advises the Ephesians that that which was foretold in the beginning that a man would leave his father and mother and that he and his wife would become one flesh, is seen by him to refer to Christ and the Church'. The same theme is also found in *De anima* XI, 4: *Adam statim prophetavit magnum illum sacramentum in Christum et Ecclesiam: Hoc nunc os ex ossibus meis . . .,* 'Adam at once prophesied the great mystery of Christ and the Church saying: This is now bone of my bones'. It should also be noted that Tertullian calls the Church the 'mother of the living' (see also *De anim.* XXI, 2; *De jejun.* 32; *Adv. Marc.* V, 18, 8–14).

The origin of this typology is clearly indicated in the texts that we have just quoted – Paul's interpretation (Ep. 5:31–32) of Adam's words (Gn. 2:23–24) as a prophecy of Christ and the Church. Tertullian regards this prophecy as very important and refers again and again in his works to the idea of Adam as a prophet. The theme is also closely related to the importance attached to prophecy in Montanism. In a treatise entitled *De extasi,* which has been lost, Tertullian gave great prominence to the theme of Adam's ecstasy. It should be noted that all the texts that we have quoted in this connection date from Tertullian's Montanist period.

Tertullian draws several conclusions from this analogy between the union of Christ and his Church and that of Adam and Eve, the most important being that there could only be one Church: *Apostolus in Ecclesiam et Christum interpretatur 'erunt duo in unum carnem' secundum spiritales nuptias ecclesiae et Christi – unus enim Christus et una eius Ecclesia* ... *De uno matrimonio censemus utrobique et carnaliter in Adam et spiritaliter in Christo,* 'The apostle interprets of the Church and Christ the words, "the two shall be one flesh", in accordance with the spiritual marriage of the Church and Christ, for Christ is one and his Church is one ... We think of one marriage in both cases, but carnally in Adam and spiritually in Christ' (*De exhort. cast.* V, 3–4). Very much the same thing is said in the *De monogamia* V, 7: *Christus unam habens Ecclesiam sponsam secundum Adae et Evae figuram, quam Apostolus in illud magnum sacramentum interpretatus in Christum et Ecclesiam, competentes carnali monogamiae per spiritalem,* 'Christ having one Church as his bride, according to the figure of Adam and Eve which the apostle interpreted of that great mystery, namely Christ and the Church, matching monogamy in the flesh with spiritual monogamy'. In both cases, Tertullian stresses the unity of the Church.

One feature of this typology which is worth noting is that the birth of Eve from the side of Adam is a type of the birth of the Church from the side of Christ. Tertullian draws attention to this in the *De anim.* XLIII, 10: *Si enim Adam de Christo figuram dabat, somnus Adae mors erat Christi dormituri in mortem ut de iniuria perinde lateris eius vera mater viventium figuraretur Ecclesia,* 'For, if Adam affords a type of Christ, the sleep of Adam was the death of Christ, who would sleep in death so that, from the wound in his side, the Church, the true mother of the living, might be prefigured'. As Waszink has shown, Tertullian is the first Christian author to have seen in the birth of Eve a figure of the birth of the Church.

Cyprian's use of these themes to demonstrate the unity of the Church was to make them of prime importance in the history of Western theology. The theme of the Church as a type of paradise is developed by Cyprian in *Epist.* LXXIII, 10, where he says that 'like paradise, the Church has fruit-trees within her walls, [10] and if any of them does not bear good fruit, it is cut down and cast into the fire. These trees she waters with four rivers – the four

10. Tertullian also refers to the wall (*maceria*) of fire which surrounds the heavenly paradise (see *Apol.* XLVII, 13).

gospels – by which, a saving and heavenly flood, she bestows the grace of baptism. Can one who is not in the Church water from the springs of the Church?' Cyprian also attaches to this theme the idea of the 'enclosed garden', *hortus conclusus*, that is found in the *De centesima* IV, 12 (see *Epist.* LXIX, 2; LXXIV, 11).

Cyprian also makes use of the theme of the ark as a figure of the Church in his treatise on the Unity of the Church: *Si potuit evadere quisque extra arcam Noe, et qui extra Ecclesiam foris fuerit evadit*, 'If there was anyone who could escape outside Noah's ark, then there would be someone who could escape outside the Church' (*De unit.* 6). He takes up the theme again in his letters. In *Epist.* LXIX, 2, he writes: 'There was only one Noah's ark and this was the type of the one Church'. Again, in *Epist.* LXXIV, 11, we read: 'Whoever was not in the ark was not saved by the water. Similarly, a person cannot be saved by baptism if he is not in the Church which was founded as one by the Lord, according to the figure (*sacramentum*) of the one ark'.

A third theme is that of the dove, of which Cyprian says: 'The Church is also intended in the *Song of Songs*, when the Holy Spirit says, in the person of the Lord: "My dove, my perfect one, is but one" ' (*De unit.* 4). Cyprian's conclusion to this passage confirms Dölger's interpretation of Tertullian's teaching: 'The bride of Christ cannot be made an adulteress. She is undefiled and chaste. She knows but one home, she guards with virtuous chastity the sanctity of one bed-chamber' (*De unit.* 6). The same theme is repeated in *Epist.* LXXIV, 2 and in the *Ad Novatianum* (2–6), in which the symbolism of the dove as the Church is based on Zp. 3:1–2.

Finally, the theme of Eve as a figure of the Church is found in *Epist.* LI: *Cum Paulus apostolus dicat: Erunt duo in carne una, ego dico in Christum et Ecclesiam, quomodo potest esse cum Christo qui cum sponsa Christi non est*, 'When the apostle says, They two shall be in one flesh, I say it refers to Christ and the Church; how can anyone be with Christ if he is not with the bride of Christ?' (*Epist.* LI, 1). There is, however, a difference between Tertullian and Cyprian, in that the former connnects the theme of the Church as the bride of Christ exclusively with the figure of Eve, whereas the latter draws constantly on the *Song of Songs*, not

only for the image of the dove, but also for the themes of
paradise and of marriage.

So far, in the examples that we have considered, Cyprian's
themes have been developments of those already found in Tertullian's work. We must now turn, however, to other images
which are not present in the writings of Tertullian, namely those
of the house of Rahab and of the house of the Passover meal.
Both themes are brought together by Cyprian in the *De unit.* 8:
'It was said of Rahab, the type of the Church: ". . . Whoever
shall go out of the doors of your house into the street, his blood
shall be on his head" (Jos 2:18–19). Similarly, the law in Exodus
relating to the mystery of the Passover contains only one
prescription, namely that the lamb, which is slaughtered as a type
of Christ, must be eaten in a single house (Ex. 12:46)' (*De unit.*
8). The same is found in *Epist.* LXIX, 4.

Both these figures were unknown in second century typology,
the first Christian writer to use them being Origen, [11] who speaks
about the house of the Passover in a fragment dealing with *Exodus*: 'The law says: you will eat in one house. By this is meant
the one house, the Church' (*PG*, XII, 285 D – 288 A). Origen
refers to the second figure of the Church, the house of Rahab, in
his *Homilies on Joshua*: 'All those, Scripture says, who are in the
house will be saved (Jos. 2:17). No one should have any illusions
about this – outside that house, that is to say, the Church, there is
no salvation' (*Hom. Josh.* III, 5). It is interesting to see that the
creator of this celebrated formula was in fact Origen.

The same two themes are also associated in an Easter homily
inspired by Origen, which P. Nautin has dated to the end of the
fourth century, but which definitely contains Origenist elements,
especially when compared with the two treatises *De Pascha*,
found at Tura. Comparison with the two quotations we have just
given makes it quite certain that the allusion to the two houses
forms part of the Origenist material in the two homilies. The
allusion to the house of the Passover is also found in another
homily, which is closer to Hippolytus. The date of this other
homily is disputed, but the association of the two themes is distinctively Origen's.

11. Cf. JEAN DANIELOU, 'Mia Ecclesia', *Le concile et les Conciles*, pp. 129–139.

We are therefore bound to ask whether Origen also influenced Cyprian. It cannot be ruled out, but, on the other hand, it is not very probable. On the other hand, it is not the only case where there is a point of contact between Cyprian and Origen in this matter of the types of the Church. As we have already seen, Cyprian elaborates the theme of the Church as bride and the Church as paradise by using texts from the *Song of Songs,* a development unknown to the tradition before his time. Tertullian, for example, only quotes the *Song of Songs* once (in the *Adv. Marc.* IV, 11, 8) in connection with the theme of the Church as bride. It looks, then, as if Cyprian was influenced by another author.

It is in fact not difficult to trace the origin of these quotations from the *Song of Songs,* since Firmilian quotes from this book precisely in connection with the themes of the Church as bride and as paradise in a letter to Cyprian (*Epist.* LXXV, 14) written after the *De unitate.* Michel Reveillaud has shown that these quotations formed part of a group which Cyprian was already using before the date of the *De unitate,* especially in the *De oratione,* but which is not found in the collection contained in the *Ad Quirinum.* It probably orginated, he believes, in a collection of *testimonia* which Firmilian had previously sent to Cyprian, and with which the theme of the two houses may well have been connected. Now, Firmilian was a disciple of Origen.

Another theme, that of the patriarchs' wives as types of the Church and the synagogue (*Ad Quir.* I, 10) presents us with a similar problem. This theme is present in the work of Paul, who contrasted Sarah and Hagar in Ga. 4:21–31. Cyprian calls Isaac a 'type of Christ' and then goes on to speak of Jacob's two wives: 'Jacob had two wives. The elder wife, Leah, is the type (*typum*) of the synagogue, whereas the younger, Rachel, is the type of the Church. It was she who gave birth to Joseph, who is himself a type of Christ. Elkanah (1 S. 1:5) had two wives, Peninnah and Hannah. It was Hannah who gave birth to Samuel, who is also a type of Christ'. In the *De orat.* 5, too, Hannah is the *typus Ecclesiae.* Finally, in *Epist.* XLIII, 4, Susannah is presented by Cyprian as a type of the Church.

The sources from which the groups of types in the above text have been derived are of some interest. The first example is taken from the New Testament (Sarah and Hagar). The second comes from Justin: 'Leah is your people and Rachel is our Church' (*Dial.* CXXXIV, 2). This theme was also used by Irenaeus and Commodian (*Instruct.* I, 38). Tertullian also calls the wives of the patriarchs figures of the Church (*Ad uxorem,* II, 2;˙ *De exhort. cast.* VI, 1). The third theme (the wives of Elkanah) is, however, not found in any patristic text in the second century, nor does Samuel ever occur during that period as a figure of Christ. We do know, however, that Hippolytus wrote a treatise *On Hannah and Elkanah,* fragments of which have been preserved. What is more, in his commentary on Daniel, he also calls Susannah a figure of the Church. This helps to confirm the hypothesis that the work of Hippolytus exerted an influence on the tradition between Tertullian and Cyprian.

3. TYPES OF THE SACRAMENTS

The origins of the typology of the sacraments are also to be found in the primitive Christian community, in which baptism was prefigured by the flood or the crossing of the Red Sea, and the eucharist by the manna or the water from the rock in the desert. The same typology is found in the Greek writers of the second century. Tertullian and Cyprian, however, are the earliest Christian authors to have studied and expounded this typology for its own sake. In the *De baptismo* Tertullian is the first to provide a typology of baptism within the framework of a baptismal catechesis. This typology covers both the Old and the New Testaments, though we shall here be concerned only with the former. The popular character of this typology is attested by the paintings in the catacombs and the ancient prayer for the blessing of the waters.

The first figure of baptism that we have to consider is that of the primordial waters on which the Holy Spirit rested: *Prima illa quae iam tunc etiam ipso habitu praenotabatur baptismi figurandi, spiritus qui ab initio super aquas vectabatur,* 'First that which even then was marked out by its very nature as prefiguring baptism – the Spirit which, from the beginning, hovered over the waters' (*De bapt.*

IV, 1). Cyprian mentions the rivers of paradise as a figure of baptism (*Epist.* LXXIII, 16).

The second type is that of the flood (VIII, 3–5). This goes back to 1 Peter and is also found in Justin. Tertullian develops this theme in an original way by comparing the dove to the Spirit and, more important still, the ark to the Church. [12] The same theme is also found in Cyprian (*Epist.* LXIX, 2; LXXIX, 11). In the catacombs, Noah in the ark is often depicted as a figure of baptism, notably in the *capella graeca* of the catacomb of Priscilla, which dates from the beginning of the third century, and is therefore contemporary with Tertullian.

Tertullian himself was struck with admiration for the evidential value of these types. In the *De baptismo,* for example, he writes: *Quot patrocinia naturae, quot privilegia gratiae, quot solemnia disciplinae, figurae, praestructiones, praedicationes, religionem aquae ordinaverunt,* 'How many defences of our nature, how many privileges of grace, how many practices of moral discipline, types, special providences, prophecies have the waters ordained for religion', (*De bapt.* IX, 1). He continues by listing the figures that are connected with the Moses cycle. The first of these is the crossing of the Red Sea: *Quae figura manifestior in baptismi sacramento. Liberantur de saeculo nationes, per aquam scilicet; et diabolum dominatorem pristinum in aquam oppressum derelinquunt,* 'This figure is made plain in the sacrament of baptism. For it is through water that the nations are freed from the world, and leave the devil, their former tyrant, drowned in the water' (*De bapt.* IX, 2). This type goes back to St Paul, but it is not depicted in the early catacombs. Cyprian, on the other hand, develops it (*Epist.* LXXVIII, 7; see also *Ad Fort.* 7).

Tertullian also mentions the waters of Marah sweetened by the wood: 'This wood was Christ healing with himself the streams that previously were by nature poisoned and bitter and making them into healthy water, that of baptism' (*De bapt.* IX, 2). He had already presented this idea in the *Adversus Judaeos: Hoc enim lignum tunc in sacramento cum Moyses aquam amaram indulcavit sicuti*

---

12. *Sacramentum,* pp. 69–85; J. HOOYMAN, 'Die Neo-Darstellung in der früchristlichen Kunst', *VC,* 12 (1958).

*nos ligni passionis Christi per aquam baptismatis portantes fidem, quae est
in eo reviximus vitam,* 'for this wood was then present in sacramental form when Moses sweetened the bitter water, just as we, bearing our faith in the wood of the passion of Christ through the
water of baptism, entered the new life which is in him' (*Adv. Jud.*
XIII, 12). This is another very early theme, which forms part of a
collection on the water and the wood and is also found in Justin
(*Dial.* LXXXVI, 31) and later in Cyprian (*De zel.* 17).

A fourth image is that of the rock of Horeb: *Haec est aqua quae
de comite petra populo profluebat; si enim petra Christus, sine dubio aqua
in Christo baptismum videmus benedici,* 'This is the water which
poured out for the people from the rock which accompanied
them; for if the rock is Christ, then there is no doubt that we see
baptism blessed by water in Christ' (*De bapt.* IX, 3). The words
comite petra are a clear reference to 1 Co. 10:4, but the theme is
also, of course, Johannine. It is a frequent theme of paintings in
the catacombs, where it was, from the time of the *capella graeca*
onwards, the favourite figure of baptism. Eastern tradition interpreted the incident in terms of the eucharist, but in the West the
baptismal interpretation was dominant. Cyprian also made use of
this theme, comparing Christ wounded by the lance with the
rock from which baptism flows (*Epist.* LXIII, 8). He also
criticises, in the same passage, the interpretation of the rock in the
eucharistic sense.

A fifth theme is that of the iron axehead which Elisha caused to
float in the Jordan. Justin was the first author to make use of this
figure and linked it to a mystical interpretation of the Jordan
(*Dial.* LXXXVI, 5). It is also found in Irenaeus, but not in Tertullian's *De baptismo,* which would seem to indicate that it does
not go back to the common catechesis. It does, however, appear
in the *Adversus Judaeos,* in a passage very obviously derived from
Justin: *Quod manifestius huius ligno sacramento quod duritia huius
saeculi mersa est in profundo erroris et a ligno Christi, id est passionis eius
in baptismo liberatur, et quod perierat olim per lignum in Adam, id
restituetur per lignum Christi,* 'What is more clearly manifested by
the mystery of this wood is that the hardness of this age was submerged in the depth of error, and by the wood of Christ, that is,
of his passion, is freed in baptism and what had once perished

through wood in Adam is restored through the wood of Christ' (*Adv. Jud.* XIII, 9).

Another question that arises in this context is whether Tertullian's comment in the *De baptismo* that Jacob blessed Ephraim and Manasseh 'by crossing his hands in such a way that, making the form of Christ, they proclaimed even then the future blessing in Christ' (*De bapt.* VIII, 2) means that he saw in this incident a prefiguring of the sign of the cross in baptism. This theme is also found in Novatian's *De Trinitate* XIX, 19, in which there is an indisputable reference to the cross: 'Jacob points to Christ as the author of the blessing by his stretching out his crossed hands over his children. This suggests that their father was Christ, in that his hands were placed to show the future form and figure of the passion'. In the case of Tertullian, however, the symbolism of the crossed hands may refer to the first letter of χριστός.[13] If this is so, then we have here an interesting example of a transition from a Greek symbol, which was known to Tertullian, to a Latin one.[14]

If the typology of baptism is well attested from the very first, that of the eucharist, of which the beginnings are already present in the New Testament, was to find little echo in the earliest Christian literature. There is no reference at all to it in the work of Tertullian. Cyprian was in fact the first of all the early Christian writers to elaborate upon it, as he does in *Epist.* LXIII to Caecilius, concerning heretics who forbade the use of wine for the consecration and substituted water. As this text shows, Cyprian's typology is essentially concerned with the wine of the Eucharist.

There are, indeed, other references. In *Epist.* LXIX, 14, Cyprian says that the Eucharist was prefigured by the Manna in the wilderness: 'In prefiguring future things, it (the manna) showed the food of the heavenly bread and the nourishment of Christ to come'. This idea can also be found, of course, in the

13. Bernard Botte believes that the letter X should be read in Tertullian's text, not *Christum*. This may not be necessary, but there was certainly an ambiguity in the symbolism of X in the early Latin Church; cf. 'Deux passages de Tertullien', *Epectasis*, pp. 19–20.
14. Cf. *Epistle of Barnabas* XIII, 5.

Gospel of John and in *1 Corinthians,* but until the fourth century, no other Christian author apart from Cyprian makes use of it. In a sacramental context, Tertullian alludes to 'the holy land' where milk and honey flow and this is no doubt a reference to the Eucharist, in that milk and honey played a part in the Eucharistic rites (*De res.* XXVI, 11).

Epist. LXIII, however, is the most important source, and here Cyprian lists the types of the wine of the Eucharist. The first of these figures is the drunkenness of Noah. Cyprian first recalls the whole typology of Noah, then goes on to say: 'It should be sufficient simply to remember that Noah was a type of the truth to come (*typum futurae veritatis*) in drinking not water but wine and in thus expressing the image (*imaginem*) of the Lord's passion' (*Epist.* LXIII, 3). Noah's drunkenness is therefore a typology of the passion and strictly speaking Cyprian's allusion to the wine here may refer only to the passion and not to the Eucharist. The context in which this passage appears, however, is basically a justification of the use of wine in the Eucharist, so that we are bound to conclude that the text has a Eucharistic meaning.

Later in the same letter, Cyprian returns to the question of the wine that Noah drank: 'I am astonished that some believers go against the discipline of the gospel and offer water in the cup of the Lord, when this alone cannot express the blood of Christ. The mystery (*sacramentum*) contained in this is expressed by the Holy Spirit in the *Psalms* when he says: "How excellent is your intoxicating cup" (Ps. 23:5). A cup that intoxicates is mixed with wine. The Lord's cup intoxicates in the same way as Noah was intoxicated in the *Book of Genesis* by drinking wine' (*Epist.* LXIII, 11). The allusion to Ps. 23:5 is worth noting in this context, since it is the first time that this text is used in connection with the Eucharist.

Cyprian then goes on to develop the symbolism of the wine of the Eucharist by showing what kind of intoxication results from it: 'The Lord's cup intoxicates by making the spirits sober and taking them back to spiritual wisdom, by leading us back from a taste for the world to spiritual understanding. Just as the spirit is relaxed by ordinary wine, the soul is loosened and all sadness is banished, so too does drinking the Lord's blood and the cup of salvation dispel the memory of the old man, make us forget our past life in the world and spread the joy of God's forgiveness in hearts made sad by the pain of sin' (*Epist.* LXIII, 11).

The importance of this text cannot be overemphasised. Not only is it the earliest passage in which we find a development of the symbolism of the wine of the Eucharist, but it does admirable justice to the real character of this symbolism by stressing the fact that it has to do above all with festal joy and by transposing this joy from the material level to that of the spirit. For, as Lebeau has pointed out, the symbolism of wine in Jewish ritual is precisely to express the joy experienced at a feast, and this symbolism persisted into the use of the wine of the Eucharist. The application of Noah's drunkenness to the Christian Eucharist, then, which may at first sight seem strange, is by no means without foundation.

A second type of the Eucharist put forward by Cyprian is that of the sacrifice of Melchizedek: 'Prefigured (*praefiguratum*) in Melchizedek the priest we see the sacrament of the sacrifice (*sacrificii sacramentum*) of the Lord, according to the testimony of Scripture: Melchizedek, the king of Salem, offered bread and wine' (*Epist.* LXIII, 4). This use of Melchizedek as a type of Christ is, of course, found in the *Epistle to the Hebrews* and the eschatological interpretation of the bread and wine was known long before the time of Cyprian, occurring, for example, in Clement of Alexandria (*Stromat.* IV, 25; 319, 25). Cyprian, however, was the first to develop this Melchizedek typology.

Using the quotation from Ps. 110:4, 'You are a priest for ever according to the order of Melchizedek', Cyprian begins by showing that Melchizedek is a type (*typus*) of Christ: 'Who is more a priest of the Most High God than our Lord Jesus Christ, who offered to the Father the very same that Melchizedek offered, namely bread and wine, that is, his own body and blood?' (*Epist.* LXIII, 4). Just as Melchizedek is a type of Christ, so too is his offering a type of Christ's offering. It is, moreover, a type not only of Christ's sacrifice, but also, in a noteworthy phrase, of the 'sacrament of the sacrifice' of Christ. This relationship is emphasised by the fact that the bread and the wine are identical: 'Thus the figure (*imago*) of this sacrifice, consisting of bread and wine, has already been presented in the past. It is this that the Lord completed and fulfilled when he offered the bread and the cup mixed with water. He who is fullness fulfilled the reality of the prefigured image (*praefiguratae imaginis*)' (*Epist.* LXIII, 4). The typology of the Eucharist was never to be more rigorously expressed.

Cyprian sees another typology of the Eucharist in the feast given by Wisdom (Pr. 9:5): 'The Spirit also shows us the figure of the Lord's sacrifice through Solomon, by mentioning the slaughtered victim, the bread and wine and also the altar. Wisdom, he says, has built a house and has supported it with seven pillars. She has sacrificed her victims. She has mixed water and wine in the bowl and has prepared a table. Solomon speaks of wine mixed, in other words, he prophesies the Lord's cup of water mixed with wine' (*Epist.* LXIII, 5; see also *Test.* II, 2).

Finally, Cyprian speaks of the Blessing of Judah (Gn. 49:10) as a figure of the Eucharist: 'In the blessing of Judah, the same thing is meant where it is said: "He will wash his coat in wine and his cloak in the blood of the vine". Where "the blood of the vine" is mentioned, what does "the blood" denote, if not the wine of the Lord's cup?' (*Epist.* LXIII, 6). Before Cyprian wrote these words, Tertullian had already observed that this passage in the Old Testament contained an allusion to the Eucharist: 'So now also he consecrated his blood in wine, as he had of old used wine as a figure for blood' (*Adv. Marc.* IV, 40, 6).

Several conclusions can be drawn from this study of the typology of the early Latin Fathers. Tertullian clearly inherited a common tradition, known to him through the works of Melito, Justin and Irenaeus, and made use of those aspects of that tradition which suited his purpose. (In this respect Cyprian is more scholarly in his witness to this typology.) Tertullian, however, uses the traditional themes with a profundity which his predecessors rarely attained and must be regarded, from this point of view, as one of the great masters of biblical typology. In one area, indeed, he enriches the tradition, namely that of the typology of the Church as the bride of Christ. His treatment is completely free from allegorism, and he is mistrustful of the possible abuses even of a spiritual interpretation. In this matter he has his own sure criteria. Cyprian continues along the same lines, while increasing the number of types. In this he was influenced especially by Hippolytus, as regards the *Books of Samuel*, and by Origen, in the case of the *Song of Songs*.

CHAPTER TWELVE

THE EXEMPLA

IN addition to typological exegesis, the Latin Fathers also practised a special form of moral exegesis, in which they drew attention to various virtues on the basis of models derived from the Bible. This is hardly surprising, given the moralising tendency characteristic of the Latin authors. Large numbers of Old Testament characters are drawn upon, and in some cases, such as those of Abel, Noah and Joseph, it is not easy to distinguish between this moral exegesis and the typological exegesis analysed in the previous chapter. We do not intend to give a full account of this type of exegesis here. It is, however, striking that there was special interest in the West in a group of characters connected with the book of Daniel – Daniel himself and the three young men in the furnace – and in Job and Tobit. The importance of these figures both in Rome and in Carthage is borne out not only by the literary texts but also by the paintings on the monuments. In these instances we are dealing with a feature specific to Latin Christianity, and it is on these therefore that we shall concentrate.

1. DANIEL AND THE THREE YOUNG MEN

Tertullian makes special use of Daniel in his moral exegesis as a model of the just man persecuted for having refused to worship idols (*Scorp.* VIII, 7; *De idol.* XV, 10). He also mentions Daniel as a model of the fasting which wins favours from God (*De jejun.* VII, 7–8; IX, 5) and as a model of prayer (*De jejun.* X, 4; *De orat.* XXIX, 1).

Cyprian, too, frequently refers to Daniel. First, he sees him as a model of the power of faith in persecution: 'What is there more glorious than Daniel, what is stronger than the firmness of his faith to bear witness and happier by God's reckoning than he who so often both conquered when he was in conflict and survived after he had conquered?' (*De lapsis* 19). Secondly, he is a model of the righteous man who is persecuted and of his deliverance. Again, Cyprian sees him as a model of the man who, after all these experiences nevertheless still acknowledges that he is a sinner (*De lapsis* 31). Then, in the *De opere* 5, Daniel is cited as a witness to the value of good works because of his recommending them to Neduchadnezzar, and finally, in the *De opere* 11, Daniel testifies to the fact that the just man never lacks what he needs in that he himself was fed by God in the lion's den.

Above all, however, it is as a model of the martyr that Cyprian sees Daniel, that is, as the man who would rather suffer and die than renounce God. In the *Ad Fort.* II and *Epist.* LVIII, 5, Daniel is presented as a martyr, and in *Epist.* LXI, 2, Cyprian writes: 'When Daniel was urged to worship the idol of Baal, which the people and the king adored, he bore witness in full faith and freedom to the fact that he honoured God. His example thus attests that the glory of martyrdom still exists, even if God delivers man from it'. Daniel also shows that one man on his own can bear witness, even if others do not: 'Daniel was not frightened by the loneliness of a strange country or by the attacks of his unceasing persecutors and he again and again bore powerful testimony to God' (*Epist.* LXVII, 8).

Archaeologists have found a great deal of evidence of the popularity of the theme of Daniel in the lions' den. It is depicted, for example, as early as the crypt of Lucina, where it appears together with a picture of Noah. It would seem to have a sacramental meaning, and this conjecture is confirmed by Hippolytus' grouping together Daniel in the lions' den and the crossing of the Red Sea as figures of baptism. Although the theme is found simultaneously both in Rome and in Carthage, the Romans gave it a sacramental interpretation, whereas the African Christians interpreted it in the moral sense. Cyprian in particular interpreted it from the standpoint of the confessor.

Associated with Daniel are the three young men, Ananias, Azarias and Misael, whom Nebuchadnezzar threw into the furnace. Tertullian quotes them as examples of the rejection of idolatry (*De idol.* XV; *Scorp.* VIII) and of God's action in deliverance (*Adv. Marc.* IV, 41). Their abstinence is exemplary in that 'they prefer vegetables as food and water as drink, rather than the lean meats and the wine of kings' (*De jejun.* 9; *De anima* XLVIII, 3). In every case the three young men are linked with Daniel and it would seem that Tertullian has here inherited a previously existing tradition. Daniel and the three young men are, for example, associated in *1 Clem.* 45 as models of just men who are persecuted, and this haggadic tradition must go back to the preaching of the Hellenistic Jews in the synagogues.

Cyprian mentions the three young men in the *De unitate* (12) as examples of unity in prayer. He also deals with them at length in *Epist.* VI, 3, where he clearly regards them as models of confessors of God before the pagans, even though they were no more than youths: 'Ananias, Azarias and Misael, those illustrious young men, enclosed in the furnace, saw the fires go out and the flames give well-being (*refrigerium*). This is because the Lord was with them, showing that the heat of gehenna could do nothing against his confessors and martyrs, but that those who believe in God would always remain unharmed and protected in all things'. Cyprian continues by quoting Dn. 3:16–18. It should be noted that the deliverance of the young men here denotes eschatological deliverance.

Cyprian also associates the three young men with Daniel in other passages. They are, as for instance in *Ad Fort.* 11, mentioned together as models of humility and of the confession of sins in contrast with the *lapsi,* who, in their pride, ask to be reconciled without having to submit to penance. The fact that the *Letters* also link the same four figures testifies to the popular character of this particular theme. In *Epist.* LVIII, 5, for example, Cyprian lists the three young men and Daniel as models of a refusal to worship idols. In *Epist.* LXI, 2, the confessors of the Church are shown as reproducing (*repraesentatum*) what Daniel and the young men had accomplished, 'ready to struggle in the flames rather than to serve the gods or adore the idol'. The same point is made in *Epist.* LVII, 8. The *Letters* are a kind of popular preaching written in the form of writing, and in them Cyprian comes back again and again to these particular *exempla.*

2. JOB

With the figure of Job we meet a new form of Latin moral exegesis. It is especially prominent in the treatises on patience. The
theme of patience was commonplace in Latin Stoic philosophy,
and is treated at length both in Cicero and in Seneca, being illustrated by *exempla* taken from Roman history. Tertullian's own
De patientia stands within this tradition. As Frédouille has shown,
Tertullian provides a Christian interpretation of the virtue of
patience, infused with Stoic elements.[1] As an illustration of this
ideal of patience, Tertullian takes the *exemplum* of Job from the
biblical tradition. There is no other treatise which shows more
clearly how biblical *exempla* were inspired by those of classical
Latin.

After mentioning how Isaiah was sawn in two – a story which
comes from Judaeo-Christian tradition – and Stephen was stoned
to death, Tertullian deals at length with the case of Job. He lists
the blessings of which Job was deprived – both physical and
spiritual well-being and fortune.[2] Finally, with a realism which
derives from his taste for rhetoric, he describes how Job 'playful-
ly made the vermin go back into the sore from which they had
escaped' (*De pat.* XIV, 5). We have here an example of the
transposition of biblical into Latin imagery, very similar to that
which we find at the same period in Clement of Alexandria's
handling of Homeric imagery.

The place occupied by Tertullian in the history of Christian
presentations of Job is obviously an important one. The story of
the righteous man put to the test is ancient and pre-biblical; and
this was given a monotheistic perspective in the *Book of Job.*
Certain Stoic elements were introduced in the Septuagint version. Clement of Alexandria presents a Hellenistic Job, and Tertullian gives us a Latin one, to which there seems to be parallels
in the iconography of the Job story. Later, in the Middle Ages
and in the Renaissance, there were new interpretations of this
favourite theme. Tertullian has his place in the history of the

1. *Tertullien et la conversion de la culture antique,* pp. 379–389.
2. In developing this theme he makes use of military images taken from the
Latin tradition, in particular the *feretrum* and the *vexillum:* cf. H. PETRE,
L'Exemplum chez Tertullien, pp. 94–95.

iconography of Job. His interpretation is particularly vivid, for instance, when he pictures Job between God 'laughing' and the devil 'grinding his teeth'.

Tertullian returns more briefly to the *exemplum* of Job in the *De fuga* 2, in connection with his argument that there are two different ways in which man can be handed over to the devil – either to be punished or to be put to the test. Job was put to the test. What is particularly striking in this case is that Tertullian reverts here to the importance of the theme of Satan. This is, of course, completely in accordance with his dramatic vision of the conflict between God and Satan over man. It is also worth noting that Tertullian is not concerned here with the *Book of Job,* but only with Job the man.

Cyprian deals with the theme in his own way, but in the same tradition as Tertullian. He provides a portrait of Job in his *De bono patientiae,* but the resulting image is different from Tertullian's. He speaks, for instance, of 'the extent of Job's sores, which are added (to his other trials) and his consuming sufferings, caused by the worms devouring his rotting and decomposed limbs' (*De bono pat.* 18). Cyprian also shows the devil inciting Job's wife to reproach him, 'using this old ruse of his malice, as though he could deceive every one by the woman, as he did at the beginning'. In the midst of all these trials, however, Job does not cease to bless God. Behind Job's temptation we are always conscious of that of Adam, and it should be noted that Cyprian deals with this episode of Job in a passage from that in which he lists the just men who were persecuted – Abel, Isaac, Jacob, Joseph, Moses and David, those types of Christ considered in the previous chapter.

Cyprian presents the same theme with the various trials and the reproaches of Job's wife in the *De mortalitate,* 10. Here he includes four quotations from the *Book of Job* – 1:21; 2:10; 1:22; 1:8. This is a first version, more biblical and less literary, of the portrait of Job which appears in the *De bono patientiae.* The reworking of the story in the later version is seen in a more allusive treatment of the part played by the wife and of Job's blessing God, and in certain elaborations, such as the description of the sores and the comparison between Job's wife and Eve. The two works provide a good example of the way in which Cyprian developed a biblical datum.

In the *De opere et eleemosynis* (18) Cyprian makes use of Job as a model of a man who was not prevented from offering sacrifices to God by the number of his children. Job is also mentioned in the chapter of Cyprian's *Testimonia*, entitled *De bono operis et misericordiae*, though the reference here is to another passage (Job 29: 12–16), which occurs again in *Test.* III, 113 and is concerned with the help that should be given to widows and orphans. Job is also mentioned in *Test.* III, 14 as an example that we should not complain when we are put to the test, the passages quoted (Jb. 1:8; 2:10) being two of these used in *De mort.* 10 in connection with the virtue of patience. Another of the four passages cited there, Jb. 1:21, is also quoted in *Test.* III, 4, as an example of patience. Finally, Jb. 14:4 is quoted in *Test.* III, 54 to prove that no man is without sin.

It is interesting that Job is seen not just as a model of the righteous man who is persecuted, but as an ideal of the righteous man as such, someone whose virtues should be imitated. (It should, incidentally, be noted that Cyprian is clearly familiar with the *Book of Job,* whereas Tertullian is not.) This interest in the moral aspect of the Old Testament, and especially in its hagiographical elements, is characteristic of Cyprian and of the general concern of the Latins with the moral sphere. The third book of Cyprian's *Testimonia,* which is peculiar to him, and in which he created a tradition in moral teaching to which there is no equivalent in Greek Christianity, is of special significance in this respect.

Job appears for the last time in Cyprian's writings in the *De lapsis,* where he is associated with Noah and Daniel, in a reference to Ezk. 14:14.[3] Cyprian exalts Job for his many virtues: *Quid Job in opere promptius, in temptationibus fortius, in dolore patientius, in timore summissius, in fide verius?* 'What was more prompt in good works than Job, stronger in temptations, more patient in suffering, more humble in fear and more true in faith?' To good works, patience, strength and humility is now added faith. Job has indeed become the ideal of the righteous man.

3. This text, which cites all three figures, refers in fact not to Daniel the

3. TOBIT

Tertullian, as we have seen, had used the figure of Job, but Cyprian introduced an innovation by giving a place alongside him to Tobit. This, as we pointed out above, is very much in the Latin tradition, with its interest in biblical hagiography. In Cyprian's *De mortalitate* and *De bono patientiae,* Tobit is placed after Job as a model of patience. In *De mort.* 10, for instance, we read: 'After performing these magnificent good works and after many glorious acts of mercy, Tobit became blind and, fearing and blessing God in his trial, increased in glory by the misfortune of his body. What is more, his wife tried to deprave him'. The reader will note the parallel with Job in the role of the wife as tempter.

The *De bono patientiae* does no more than summarize briefly the passage in the *De mortalitate* on the subject of Tobit's patience. In the *Ad Fort.* 11, on the other hand, Cyprian synthesises several of the traditions that we have already encountered separately in connection with the theme of the just man who is put to the test. In the first place, he groups together Abel, Jacob, Joseph and David. Secondly, he speaks of Elijah and Zechariah in connection with the theme of the martyrdom of the prophets. Daniel and the three young men in the furnace form a third group and finally Cyprian adds Tobit: 'Although he was living under the oppression of a tyrannical king, Tobit remained free both in his mind and in his spirit, preserved his faith in God, and in a sublime manner bore witness to the power and greatness of God'. This text is followed by a quotation from Tb. 13:6.

Tobit also appears in the *De dominica oratione* as a model of prayer accompanied by good works. Cyprian first quotes from Tb. 12:8: 'Prayer with fasting and alms is good' (*De dom. orat.* 32). This is followed by the theme: 'Prayers rise up at once to God when the merits of our actions commend them. The angel Raphael therefore remained with Tobit, constantly praying and acting' (*De dom. orat.* 33). A long quotation from Tb. 12:11–14 follows this passage. The quotation from Tb. 12:8 also occurs in

---

prophet but to Daniel the wise man, but Cyprian, like all early writers, confused the two.

the *De opere et eleemosynis* 5, in which Raphael is mentioned. In this treatise, the reference to Tobit is preceded by a passage on Daniel's exhortation to king Nebuchadnezzar to pray and fast (Dn. 4:24).

In the same treatise, Cyprian returns yet again to Tobit as a model of the union between prayer and good works. In this case, he quotes the advice of the aged Tobit to his son Tobias. The first quotation is from Tb. 14:8 (10): 'Serve God in truth and do what is pleasing to him. And advise your sons to act with justice and to give alms' (*De opere* 20). This is followed by a long quotation from Tb. 4:5–11. This quotation is also used in *Test.* III, 1, the chapter entitled *De bono operis et misericordiae,* where it is preceded by a quotation from Tb. 2:2.

Finally, we must add that Cyprian also uses a text from the *Book of Tobit* in *Testimonia* III, 62, a section entitled 'Marriage must not be contracted with pagans'. The quotation is from Tb. 4:12: 'Choose a wife from the race of your own kindred and do not choose a foreign wife who is not of the family of your own kindred'. This verse is followed immediately by Tb. 4:5–11, which, as we saw above, also follows the quotation in the *De opere et eleemosynis* 20. It would seem, therefore, that Cyprian's attention must have been drawn to v. 12 by its proximity to the longer quotation, and that he noted it for use in connection with the subject of this section of the *Testimonia*. Although he is not really concerned here with Tobit the man, the passage is certainly situated in the perspective of that figure as a model of goodness and wisdom. In conclusion, we may also say that Cyprian's use of Tobit testifies to the important position occupied by Jewish hagiography in his moral teaching.

CHAPTER THIRTEEN

NOVATIAN AND THE THEOPHANIES

E VIDENCE for the Roman interpretation of Scripture in the middle of the third century A.D. is found in Novatian's *De Trinitate*. In this treatise, the author makes use of the translation of the Bible that was current in Rome and different from the one used in Africa. There is practically no typology at all in Novatian's treatise, but there is a collection of *testimonia*, which is fundamentally that of the Roman catechesis and, as in the case of Cyprian, does not contain the modifications that are present in the very early *testimonia*, but is close to the received text. The only exception is the text of Dt. 28:66, which is abbreviated in Novatian's treatise: *Videbitis vitam vestram pendentem nocte ac die et non credetis ei*, 'You will see your life hanging night and day and you will not believe in it'. Finally, Novatian arranges the *testimonia* in the order in which they appear in the Bible – Moses, Isaiah and David.

Almost all of these *testimonia* are the classic ones – Gn. 49:10, *non deficiet princeps de Juda*, 'the prince will not depart from Judah'; Ex. 4:13, *provide alium quem mittis*, 'provide another whom you will send'; Dt. 18:15, *prophetam nobis suscitabit deus*, 'God will raise up a prophet for us'; Dt. 28:66, *videbitis vitam vestram pendentem*, 'You will see your life hanging', and a series of texts from Isaiah, grouped together according to the mysteries of Christ, from Is. 11:1, *prodibit virga de radice Jesse*, 'A branch will come forth from the root of Jesse', to Is. 53:3 and 5. (In this context it is worth noting that Is. 11:10 is interpreted as pointing to the resurrection of Christ because of the verb *surget*, 'will arise'.) Finally, Novatian lists quotations from the psalms – Ps. 110: 1–2; 2:7; 72:1. Taken as a whole, these are the texts which had been of central significance since the time of the apostolic catechesis.

In the course of his christological analysis in the *De Trinitate,*
Novatian interprets a number of other *testimonia* theologically.
An example of this is the text of Hab. 3:3: *Deus ab Africa veniet et
sanctus de monte opaco et condenso,* 'God will come from Africa and
the Holy One from the shady and thickly wooded mountain' (*De
Trin.* 13). This text does not form part of the African *testimonia,* in
which only the second part of the verse is quoted (cf., for example, Cyprian, *Test.* II, 21). What is particularly interesting in our
context, however, is that Novatian interprets the passage as a
prophecy of the birth of the Son of God at Bethlehem, *cuius
metaturae regio ad meridianam respicit plagam caeli,* 'Bethlehem, the
boundary of which looks towards the southern zone of the sky'.
From the theological point of view, the interpretation of Gn.
49:11, *lavabit stolam suam in vino et in sanguine vinae amictum eius,*
'He shall wash his robe in wine and his cloak in the blood of the
vine' is of considerable importance, in that Novatian links this
text with Col. 2:15: *Exutus carnem potestates dehonestavit,* 'Having
stripped off his flesh, he dishonoured the powers publicly'. He
does this to show that the Word was stripped of his humanity
(*stolam, amictum*) in death and, after having washed it in his
blood, took it up again at the resurrection. In this, Novatian
makes use of the same tradition as that found in Hippolytus, *De
Antichristo* 11, and Tertullian *Adv. Marc.* IV, 40.

Novatian thus bears witness, in the matter of types and
prophecies, to a Roman tradition which is parallel to the African
tradition, but which exhibits no really original features. The
point of particular interest, however, is his interpretation of the
Old Testament and his attribution of the theophanies to the Son.
He is in no sense original in this; in their defence of the unity of
the two covenants against the Jews and the gnostics both Justin
and Irenaeus had previously developed this idea. Tertullian had
also made use of it in the *Adversus Praxean* (16), in order to establish the distinction between the Father and the Son. Novatian
employs it to the same end, but develops *in extenso* what his
predecessors had only suggested.

The first example of this in the *De Trinitate* is based on the
passage in which God pronounces judgement on Babel (Gn.
11:7): *Venite et mox descendamus ut confundamus illic ipsorum linguas,*

'Come, let us go down now in order that we may there confuse their languages'. Novatian's commentary on this text is as follows: 'Which is the God who, in their opinion, went down, here, to this tower, seeking to visit these men? Was it God the Father? He was, in that case, confined to one place. How, then, could he encompass all things? Or does he affirm that it was an angel who came down with the angels and said: "Come, let us go down"? We would then point out that, in Deuteronomy, it is God who reported these things and God who spoke, in the passage: "When he dispersed the sons of Adam, he set their boundaries according to the number of the angels of God" (Dt. 32:8). It was not the Father, then, who came down, as the reality shows, nor was it an angel who gave the command, as the truth proves. All that remains is the Son of God and it was clearly he who came down' (De Trin. 17).

Novatian's argument in the above commentary on Gn. 11:7 is clear. When Babel was destroyed, it could not have been God the Father who came down, since the Father cannot be limited to one place. (This idea is also found in Justin.) Nor could it have been an angel, since God the Father commands the angels. It could only have been the Son. The question for Novatian is thus: at what level are we to place the Son? He is above the angels because he is God, but he is distinct from the Father because he is able to adapt himself to a place. This clearly points to an element of difference between the Father and the Son, and this in turn implies a certain distinction between their natures.

Novatian also briefly develops the theme of the judgement on Sodom and Gomorrha (De Trin. 18; 66, 3–22). This occurs also in Justin (Dial. LVIII, 5), Irenaeus (Adv. haer. IV, 10, 1) and Tertullian (Adv. Prax. XIII, 4), as well as Cyprian (Test. III, 33). Novatian says nothing, however, about the flood.

This section of the De Trinitate is followed by one on the theophanies. The first that Novatian discusses is Yahweh's appearance to Abraham at the Oak of Moreh (Gn. 12:7). What interests him here is the contrast between the visible nature of the Son and the invisible nature of the Father. He contrasts the story in Genesis with the statement in Ex. 33:20: Nemo hominum Deum videat et vivat, 'No man may see God and live'. He goes on: 'If

God cannot be seen, how is it that he was seen? If he has been seen, how could he not be seen? John, after all, also says: "No one has ever seen God" (Jn. 1:18) and the apostle Paul speaks of him whom no man has seen or can see. Since Scripture cannot lie, God has therefore been seen. Hence we can understand that it is not the Father who has been seen, that is, the One who cannot be seen, but the Son who was wont to come down and who was seen by virtue of the fact that he came down. For he is the image of the invisible God' (De Trin. 18).

This is, once again, a well known theme, found both in Irenaeus and in Tertullian. Novatian clearly drew on Tertullian, since both authors make very similar use of it. Tertullian says: 'No one will see the face of God and live, that is, the man who sees will die. Yet we find that God has been seen by many men and that none of them who saw him has died. God was seen therefore according to man's capacity, not according to the fullness of the deity. In fact, the patriarchs Abraham and Isaac said that they saw God, yet they did not die'. Tertullian then goes on to point out either that they would have had to die or that Scripture lies. 'But Scripture does not lie,' he says, 'neither when it says that God is invisible nor when it says that God was seen. This therefore implies that the one who was seen was some other, since God cannot at the same time be invisible. It follows that we understand that the Father is invisible according to the fulness of the deity and that the Son is visible in proportion to his derivation from the Father' (Adv. Prax. XIV, 1–4).

Whereas Tertullian, however, speaks only in general terms about God's appearances to Abraham, Novatian discusses them in some detail. As we have seen, he first mentions the incident at the Oak of Moreh. He then goes on to the appearance of Yahweh to Hagar (Gn. 16:7–16): 'Hagar, Sarah's servant, was driven out of the house and sent into exile. She was met by the angel near the spring on the road to Shur and he questioned her. She answered him, telling him why she had run away. He then advised her to be humble, but at the same time gave her hope that she would be called a mother and promised her that a great people would be born from her womb. What is more, this angel is presented in Scripture as Lord and God. (Indeed, he would not have been able to promise that the race would be blessed if he had not been both angel and God.) If all this is true, then what the heretics have said about this passage must be examined' (*De Trin.* 18; 63, 20–64, 8).

In commenting on the text of Gn. 16:7–16, Novatian returns to his basic argument: 'Was the one who was seen by Hagar the Father or not? He is, after all, presented as God. We, on the other hand, do not venture to call God the Father an angel, because to do so would be to make him subject to another, whose angel he would be. They, however, say that it was an angel. How, then, can he be God if he is an angel – since that name has never been given to the angels – unless the truth leads us to conclude, on the basis of these two factors, that he was the Son of God? Because he was from God, he is correctly called God, as Son of God. And because he is subject to the Father and the messenger of the Father's will, he was called Angel of Mighty Counsel (Is. 9:5)' (*De Trin.* 18; 64, 9–18).

Novatian then expounds another episode from the story of Hagar (Gn. 21:17–19): *Et vocavit Angelus Domini ipsam Agar de caelo, et aperuit Deus oculos eius,* 'And the angel of the Lord called to Hagar from heaven and God opened her eyes'. He says: 'If, then, it was the God who was with the child who opened Hagar's eyes in order that she might see the well of living water; and if, on the other hand, it was God who called to her from heaven; and if he is called an angel, even though, while he was listening to the child's voice as it was crying, he was God; one can only conclude that it was another than the angel, and one who was also God. Since that could not apply to the Father, who is only God, but could apply to the Son, who is called not only God, but also an angel, we may be sure that it was not the Father who spoke to Hagar in this case, but rather Christ, because he is a God to whom the name of angel can also be applied' (*De Trin.* 18).

It is from the same viewpoint that Novatian interprets the appearance of God to Abraham at the Oak of Mamre (Gn. 18:1–33): 'Moses adds that God appeared to Abraham near the oaks at Mamre. Although the patriarch saw three men, he called only one of them Lord. If it is thought that, in this passage, it was the Father who appeared and was welcomed as a guest, with two angels, it should be remembered that it is the heretics who believed that the Father can be seen. If, on the other hand, it is thought that it was an angel, although only one of these three was called Lord, why, then, is an angel called God, when this is, after all, contrary to the usual practice? Unless, so that the invisible nature proper to him should remain peculiar to the Father and the inferior nature (*mediocritas*) proper to him should be restored to the angel, it was the Son of God, who is also God, who appeared to Abraham' (*De Trin.* 18; 65, 9–25).

This text is especially interesting, because the theophany at Mamre is one of the *loci classici* for the theology of the Logos. Before the time of Novatian, other authors interpreted this passage in a similar way. Philo of Alexandria, for instance, sees here the Logos surrounded by the first two Powers. In an anti-Jewish polemical text, Justin develops the same theme in a way that looks forward to Novatian's anti-modalist polemics, since in both cases an attempt is made to prove the existence of a 'second God'. Finally, Tertullian deals with it among the theophanies to which he has recourse in his attack on Praxeas: *Quale est ut Deus omnipotens ille invisibilis . . . apud Abraham sub robore refrigeraverit,* 'What sort of thing is it that almighty God, he, the invisible one . . . should have refreshed himself with Abraham under an oak?' (*Adv. Prax.* XVI, 6; cf. also *De carne* III, 6).

Another example discussed by Novatian is that of Jacob. The first passage discussed is Gn. 31:11–13, according to which an angel of God appears in a dream to Jacob and says: *Ego sum Deus qui visus sum tibi in loco Dei,* 'I am the God who was seen by you in the place of God'. Novatian's commentary on this text is: 'If the angel of God says these things to Jacob and this angel goes on to say: "I am the God who appeared to you in the place of God", then we see at once that the one thus presented is not shown simply as an angel, but as God, since he says that the dedication was made to him, by Jacob, in the place of God and not in "my place". There is therefore a place of God and God is there and what is said here is "in the place of God", not "in the place of God and the angel", but only "of God". Now the one who promises these things is presented as God and angel in such a way that there is clearly a distinction between the one who is simply called God and the one who is not simply called God, but is also called angel' (*De Trin.* 19; 69, 1–17).

Tertullian does not quote this text, but Cyprian does in his *Testimonia* II, 5, under the heading *Quod idem Angelus et Deus,* 'That the angel and God are the same', so that it is clear from this that Novatian is closer to Cyprian in this question than to Tertullian. What is more, Tertullian is, as we have already seen, reluctant to give the Son the title of angel, mainly because he was writing at a time when there was a need to oppose the Judaeo-Christian angelomorphic christology. When Cyprian and Novatian were writing, however, this need no longer existed. There was no longer any difficulty involved in the use of the word *angelus* as a title for Christ. Cyprian bears clear witness to this and Novatian developed the theme in a remarkable way which was to influence the Latin theology which followed him.

Novatian also speaks of the Son in another passage in the story of Jacob. He comments as follows on the patriarch's struggle with the angel (Gn. 32:24–27): 'Why does Jacob, who displays his strength in seizing the man with whom he was struggling and demands a blessing from the one he was holding, therefore have to make a request, if not because we have here a prefiguring of the conflict in which Christ was opposed to the sons of Jacob, the end (*perfecta*) of which is told to us in the gospel?' (*De Trin.* 19; 70, 24–71, 5). Jacob's victory in this struggle prefigures the triumph of the Jews over Christ. Afterwards, however, they, like Jacob, were to limp and, Novatian says, to beseech the one whom they had persecuted for mercy (*De Trin.* 19; 71, 15–22). What is more, Jacob was called, after the contest, Israel, 'the one who sees God', which shows that it was against God that he had been struggling.

It is clear that, in this passage, Novatian's teaching is different from that of Tertullian, who regards Jacob's adversary as an angel (*De carne* 3, 6). Novatian, on the other hand, follows the tradition of Justin, who believes that the angel who wrestled with Jacob was the Son (*Dial.* LVIII, 6–10; CXXV, 3–5). There is, moreover, no question of an angel in Novatian's commentary. The word does not appear in the text of Genesis under discussion,[1] and Novatian believes that Jacob's adversary was a man and, more particularly, a prefiguring of Christ in his human and his divine nature. Clearly, then, there is an element of typology here, the struggle between Jacob and the man being a figure of the conflict between the Jews and Christ.

A final example taken by Novatian is the passage in Genesis in which Jacob blesses Joseph's two sons, Ephraim and Manasseh (Gn. 48:15–16). Crossing his hands over the heads of the boys, Jacob says: *Deus qui pascit me a iuventute mea usque ad hunc diem, Angelus qui liberavit me ex omnibus malis benedicat pueros hos,* 'May God, who has nourished me from my youth until this day, may the angel, who has freed me from all evil, bless these boys'. In this case, too, it is the same person who is called both *Deus* and *Angelus,* so that it can only be the Son, Novatian concludes. He also confirms this conclusion by drawing attention to the typology: 'This means that the one who gives the blessing is Christ, placing his crossed hands on the children, as if their father were Christ, showing, by the way in which he places his hands, the type and future form of the passion' (*De Trin.* 19; 72, 19–73, 2).

The quotation is justified in this case too by the fact that the same person is called both *Deus* and *Angelus,* with the result that it must be the Son. There can be no doubt that Novatian built up a collection of Genesis texts in which these two words were linked and that, in this way, he amplified a theme of which Cyprian gives only one example. What is more, Novatian also emphasises the typological element present in this text, Jacob's crossed hands being a 'figure of the passion' (*sacramentum passionis: De Trin.* 19; 73, 4). This is particularly interesting, in that Novatian seldom makes use of typology. Finally, it is quite certain that he takes this from Tertullian, since, as we have already seen when we were discussing the typology of the sacraments, the latter refers to this particular type in *De baptismo* VIII, 2.

We may therefore conclude that Novatian was above all influenced in his treatment of the theophanies by Justin. He drew on Justin in the case of the episode at the Oak of Mamre, in that of Jacob's struggle with the angel, and in that of Jacob's ladder.

---

1. Interestingly enough, Jacob's adversary is described as an angel in Ho. 12:4, a verse which could also be one source for Novatian's point about Jacob's later supplication for mercy (Tr.).

He also derived from Justin the main themes in his argument – the distinction between the two Gods, the name of *Angelus* given to one of them, the invisible nature of the Father and the visible nature of the Son, and the fact that the Father cannot be confined to one place, whereas the Son can. His use of the theophanies against modalism may have been suggested by Tertullian's employment of them in the *Adversus Praxean*. Finally, the theme of the adaptation of the Word to men and of men to the Word clearly comes from Irenaeus, possibly via Tertullian.

Irenaeus regarded this process as one of divine education, accustoming man gradually to God's ways, and Novatian takes up this educative function in the *De Trinitate*: 'We are acquainted with the interpretation given by Scripture to the question of the arrangement of the economy (*temperamento dispositionis*). The prophet first spoke of God in parables, in accordance with the age of faith (*tempus fidei*), not according to what God was in reality, but according to what the prophet was able to grasp' (*De Trin.* 5; 19, 14–20, 4). A new stage in this educative process was brought about in the New Testament: 'Although in the Gospel Christ speaks with men, leading to increases (*incrementa*) in their grasp of God, he also speaks of God to men in terms of what they could at that time understand and grasp' (*De Trin.* 7; 22, 10–12).

Novatian expresses this idea above all in his presentation of the Word as the visible image of the Father, accustoming man gradually to a knowledge of the Father who is invisible. In a typical passage, he says: 'It is not the Father who is seen, the one who has never been seen, but the Son, accustomed to come down and to be seen insofar as he has come down. For he is the image of the invisible God, in such a way that the smallness and weakness (*fragilitas*) of the human condition may become accustomed (*assuescat*) sometimes to see the Father in the image of God, that is, in the Son of God. Gradually (*gradatim*) and increasingly (*per incrementa*), the human weakness had to be impelled by the image of God towards this glory, so that it would one day be able to see God the Father' (*De Trin.* 18; 62, 7–63, 1).

Novatian also compares this process with the effects of the sun, saying that, if it appears suddenly and shines too brightly, it blinds the eyes, but that the eyes become accustomed to it (*assuefacit*) at dawn when its strength increases slowly (*mediocribus incrementis*). In the same way, he goes on, 'Christ, that is, the image of God and the Son of God, is seen by men, to the extent that he can be seen. The smallness and weakness of the human condition is thus fed by him, extended (*producitur*) and developed (*educatur*), so that, one day, accustomed (*assueta*) to contemplate the Son, it will also be able to see God the Father as he is. And this is so that, struck by the sudden and intolerable brilliance of the divine majesty, it may not run the risk of being crushed, with the result that it will not be able to see God the Father, whom it has always longed to see' (*De Trin.* 18; 63, 9–15).

There is no need to discuss here the subordinationist doctrine of the Word presupposed by this text, and already present in the work of Justin, but simply to point out the basic theme, that of the process of becoming progressively accustomed, and the vocabulary which goes with it – *assuescere*, to become accustomed, *incrementa*, growths or increases, and *producere*, to extend, lengthen, increase. Finally, it is important to remember that this is a doctrine which is characteristic of Irenaeus.

Novatian's distinctive contribution to this theme is the elaboration of other episodes, already mentioned by Justin, such as those of Hagar and Ishmael and of the blessing of Ephraim and Manasseh. The fact that he develops all these episodes at considerable length is evidence of the importance he attaches to them for the proof of his thesis. This is, in fact, Novatian's main argument against Sabellius and we shall have more to say later about the problem that this raises with regard to the theology of the Trinity. Novatian does provide, however, a number of principles for the development of scriptural exegesis in Latin Christianity of the third century which were to exert a considerable influence on the Latin authors of the fourth.

PART FOUR

LATIN THEOLOGY

INTRODUCTION TO PART IV

So far in this book, we have been principally concerned with the background to, the influences on and the sources of the earliest Latin theology, with all that went to form it. Beyond all this, however, it was the individual genius of two great writers which gave Latin theology of this period its distinctive character, a character consisting less in its cultural or linguistic contribution than in a certain intellectual quality. Tertullian, for example, is astonishingly original and personal, appearing like a meteor, neither ascending nor descending. Yet at the same time, despite his obvious originality, he displays those characteristics which are to be found throughout Latin Christianity: a realism which knows nothing of the Platonist devaluation of matter; a subjectivity, which gives special prominence to inner experience; and a pessimism which lays more stress on the experience of sin than on transfiguration.

Cyprian is different from Tertullian, but is no less characteristic. He is above all conscious of the Church as a social reality. Whereas the Greek Fathers of the second century were equally interested in ecclesiology, but emphasised the mystery of the Church as an eternal reality outside time, Cyprian stresses the concrete reality of the Church as a community of people. The members of the Church are, in Cyprian's view, all faced with the same destiny, the same hostility of the world that surrounds them and the same threat of persecution and martyrdom. At the same time, however, the Church is also conscious of the divine power that inspires it, strongly structured in its organisation, yet always striving toward union with God. Here again, from another viewpoint, it is the Latin Church of later centuries which is sketched out, at least in its major features.

CHAPTER FOURTEEN

TERTULLIAN AND HIS METHOD

W E have already seen the background in terms of which Tertullian's thought is to be understood. First he was motivated by a desire to oppose those doctrines which were contrary to the faith, whether these were external to Christianity, like Greek philosophy or rabbinic teaching, or internal, like the gnostic, Marcionite and other heresies. But secondly – and this is even more characteristic – his attitude toward Judaeo-Christian gnosis was, as we have seen, one of rejection. For him there could never be two levels of religious knowledge, one for simple believers and the other for the perfect. Whether operating in the field of philosophy or of theology, he kept strictly to the level of the knowledge shared by all, the *testimonium animae,* the 'testimony of the soul', and the *regula fidei,* the 'rule of faith'. What, then, does his theology consist of? It is essentially an attempt to set in order the different realities known through reason and faith. It is, in other words, a kind of phenomenology, implying a direct apprehension of these realities, and concerned essentially to define them and to place them in their true hierarchical relationship.

In this respect, Tertullian's work is systematic in character. All his writings are, it is true, oriented toward the particular doctrines that he is attacking, but they are not simply occasional pieces. This aspect of his work means only that he was concerned to make clear where he stood in the context of contemporary debate. As Siniscalco has shown, however, Tertullian's works form a kind of *Summa* which deals in succession with the various aspects of his faith. In the *De testimonio animae* and the *De praescriptionibus,* for example, Tertullian considers the problem of the sources of faith. In the *Adversus Hermogenem* and the *Adversus*

Marcionem he treats of the relationship between God and the world. The *De anima* is a study of man. The *De carne Christi* is concerned with the incarnation of Christ, the *Adversus Praxean* with the Trinity and the *De resurrectione carnis* with Christian eschatology. Taking these works as a whole, we can see that Tertullian's intention was to provide an exposition of the whole of Christian faith by contrasting it with the various deformations of that faith and by taking advantage of this contrast to throw light on points which were not sufficiently clear.

Only one other Christian author of the early centuries can be said to have made a similar attempt, and that is Origen in his treatise on 'first principles', the Περὶ ἀρχῶν. In spirit, however, these two theologians are very different. Origen is above all concerned with the inner coherence of his system and to preserve this he often sacrifices factual data. In this respect, he is undoubtedly within the gnostic and Platonic tradition, as H. Jonas has shown.

Tertullian's approach is quite different, in that he makes every effort to place concrete data in relationship to one another. He is essentially realistic in his thinking. His attempt to create a theology is therefore completely original, not only by virtue of the fact that it is in any case earlier than Origen, but also in that it reflects an entirely different attitude of mind. It is characterised by two main features. First, there is its descriptive, experiential, concrete quality; it sets out to make an inventory of reality. Secondly, there is the urge to discriminate, to arrange, to put everything in its proper place. In this respect Tertullian's work, even though it does borrow elements from his Greek predecessors, Justin, Theophilus and Irenaeus, is the product of a different and typically Latin spirit.

We shall, in this part of the book, study Tertullian's cosmology, anthropology and eschatology, but, before doing this, we must examine the formal aspect of his theology, in other words, the instrument that he uses. This is perhaps the most original feature of his system, at every level of which a certain number of special categories can be found. The words used to define these categories, *census, status, gradus* and so on, are quite original and not simply a replica of Greek philosophical terms.

All attempts to reduce them to this level have so far failed, since they are not strictly a philosophical vocabulary, but rather a descriptive one, which does not refer to technical concepts. All attempts to trace them back to legal origins have also come to nothing. They are common ideas, borrowed from the vocabulary that was current at the time and preserving a certain flexibility, and it is precisely this that makes them difficult to define.

There is no need to make a complete analysis here of these words and the ways in which Tertullian uses them, since this has already been done admirably by R. Braun and J. Moingt. This preliminary work of compilation and analysis, however, provides the tools with which we can begin to explore the formal aspect of Tertullian's thought.

1. SUBSTANTIA

The word *substantia* plays a very important part in Tertullian's works, where it is found more than three hundred times. He is in fact the first Latin Christian author to give such importance to this word.[1] Braun rejects both Harnack's theory of a legal origin, and that of Evans, who sees in it a rendering of the Greek term πρωτὴ οὐσία used by Aristotle. He is of the opinion that the word derives from everyday speech, which is an interesting theory, since, if it is true, it is further proof of the fact that Tertullian's vocabulary is more indebted to ordinary language than to technical terminology. Braun has also pointed out that, in Tertullian's works, the word *substantia* has a richer range of meaning than the same word used in the purely philosophical sense, although it does, of course, correspond at least partly to the Greek words οὐσία and ὑπόστασις. In Tertullian, the word has a concrete meaning which is closely related to its etymological sense. It points to the concrete ground which permanently underlies individual realities and persists throughout

1. For the use of the word in Tertullian's writings (and in Braun's case also before Tertullian) cf. R. BRAUN, *'Deus Christianorum'*, pp. 167–199; J. MOINGT, *Théologie trinitaire de Tertullien*, II, *Substantialité et Individualité: Etude du Vocabulaire Philosophique. Théologie*, 69, Paris, 1966, pp. 297–430; and IV, *Répertoire Lexicographique et Tables. Théologie*, 75, Paris, 1969, pp. 220–234.

the variety of qualities, actions and changing elements. *Substantia,* in other words, is what determines the fundamental characteristics of things, and their level in the scale of realities. It corresponds, therefore, to that aspect of the *res,* which is concerned with its constitutive element, not with its individual properties. Tertullian uses it to distinguish between levels in what is real, not between individual realities.

It is therefore an essential term in the vocabulary that he uses to define the different orders of reality. First, it denotes material substances, beginning with the four elements, each of which has its own specific quality (cf. *Adv. Herm.* XXX). Secondly, we must distinguish between the elements from which man is formed, namely matter and spirit, as entirely different substances (cf. *Adv. Marc.* IV, 29, 1). Tertullian rejects Hermogenes' teaching, according to which the soul is produced by matter. For him, the soul is derived from the *flatus vitae,* the 'breath of life', breathed by God into the earth that he had moulded. In this respect, therefore, it is wrong to call Tertullian a materialist. Moreover, these two aspects are permanent constituents of man. The resurrection brings about a *dispositio spiritalis* in the flesh, which nonetheless preserves its substance (*De res.* LXII, 2). The substance of the soul is, in Tertullian's opinion, single, despite its various operations, such as those of the senses, intelligence and freedom. By contrast, the Spirit, which is given to man, and which makes him partake of the divine, whether by santification or in prophecy, is of a different substance. There are thus three levels of existence in man – the corporeal, the psychical and the spiritual.

These clear distinctions between substances are also found in Tertullian's christology. First, he states clearly against Hermogenes' affirmation that Christ has a material soul, the distinction between body and soul in Christ: *Quod si una caro et una anima, salvus est numerus duarum substantiarum, in suo genere distantium,* 'But if there is one flesh and one soul, then the number of the two realities, each distinct in its own kind, is preserved' (*De carne* 13). It is important to note in this context that Tertullian's teaching is very remote from the monism of the Stoics. What is more, he affirms very clearly the distinction between the divine and the human substances in Christ: *Filium Dei et filium hominis secundum utramque substantiam in sua proprietate distantem,* 'Son of God and Son of man according to both realities, each separate in its own proper nature' (*Adv. Prax.* XXVII, 10). The word *substantia,* then, may point either to the contrast between Christ's body and his soul or to that between his divine and his human natures. Finally, in his trinitarian teaching, Tertullian also makes use of the word *substantia,* affirming that the Father, the Son and the Holy Spirit are of one substance only (*Adv. Prax.* II, 4). God's substance is 'spirit', and the term points to what is truly divine in God.

A number of comments may be made as a result of this analysis. It has frequently been pointed out that Tertullian's theological formulas are extremely precise, having an almost definitional character, whereas those used by the Greek authors of the period are much more imprecise. This is undoubtedly because the latter were much more dependent on philosophical language in their theology. Tertullian does not encumber himself with philosophical idiom, but works at the level of ordinary speech, which he adapts to the realities that he wishes to express. In this, he displays a great freedom, bending the existing language to his own terms and creating neologisms. It was only later that the influence of Greek philosophical terminology was to introduce difficulties into Latin trinitarian theology. In particular, it should be noted that Tertullian does not make use of the word *essentia,* which was the usual translation of the Greek οὐσία. In this he is simply conforming to the practice of the secular writers of the period; but it may be thought that there is also a desire not to employ a word with too philosophical a connotation, loaded with all the ambiguities of the Greek οὐσία. In the same way, he chose to use the word *substantia,* we have suggested, because of its concrete meaning and its avoidance of the ambiguities inherent in the Greek ὑπόστασις.

Similarly, when equivalents to the word *substantia* are required, Tertullian derives them not from the vocabulary of philosophy, but from everyday speech. An interesting example is his use of the term *corpus.* This word can, in his writings, denote what is material, in contrast to what is not. But Tertullian also ascribes corporeity to all *res,* in the sense that they have substantiality or concrete reality: *Ipsa substantia corpus sit utriusque rei,* 'The body is the substantial reality of both things' (*Adv. Herm.* XXXV, 2). In the same way, he teaches that the soul is a body: *Anima corpus est aliquod suae qualitatis,* 'The soul too is a body of some sort, having its own attributes' (*Adv. Marc.* V. 15, 8). In this context, corporeity signifies the concrete reality as opposed to what belongs to the order of the idea: *Nihil est incorporale nisi quod non est,* 'Nothing is incorporeal except what does not exist' (*De carne* XI, 4). The same applies also to God himself: *Quis negavit corpus Deum esse etsi Deus spiritus est,* 'Who has denied that God is a body, even though God is spirit?' (*Adv. Prax.* VII, 8), with the result that, *Sermonis corpus spiritus,* 'Spirit is the body of the Word' (*Adv. Prax.* VIII, 4).

Corpus, then, does not denote a particular substance – all substance rather is body. There are, in Tertullian's view, essentially three orders of *corpus* – the flesh, the soul and the Spirit (*Adv. Marc.* V, 15, 7). It should also be noted here that Tertullian often uses the word *corpus* for flesh. This does not, however, imply a materialist view. On the contrary, it points to a certain continuum of soul and body, which both excludes a dualist account of man, and explains how, in Tertullian's thinking, the soul can carry out both sensory and intellectual functions.

2. CENSUS

The *substantia* or reality of a thing is related to its origin. This idea is expressed by Tertullian in the word *census.* Once again, the term is not taken from philosophy, but from everyday language. The fundamental meaning of *census* is a register. The *census* is the list of persons or things belonging to one category because they all go back to the same origin.[2] The word is important in Tertullian's vocabulary insofar as it is applied to different orders of reality so as to determine their nature on the

2. Cf. Tertullian's use of the verb, *censeo: Naturali praescriptione omne omnino genus censum ad originem refert,* 'By a natural law, absolutely every category that can be classified refers back to its beginning' (*Ad nat.* I, 12, 12): cf. also *De praescr.* XXI, 7. Tertullian has a unique use of the word with reference to pagan idols: *Inde a metallis censentur dii vestri,* 'That is where your gods come from – the mines' (*Apol.* XII, 5).

basis of their origin. The *census* of a substance emphasises its concrete continuity, and gives it a historical dimension in addition to its ontological situation.

In his index, Moingt has set out the main fields in which the word *census* is used by Tertullian. Its first application is to the primacy of Adam as the origin of the natural man. The importance of the term in this context will be understood if it is borne in mind that Tertullian, as a traducianist, believed that man's substance, both his body and his soul, came from Adam: *Omnis anima eousque in Adam censetur donec in Christo recenseatur,* 'So every soul takes its origin in Adam until it receives a new origin in Christ' (*De anim.* XL, 1). Man's twofold nature is therefore derived from his twofold origin. The natural man has his origin in Adam, whereas the spiritual man has his origin in Christ: *Census noster transfertur in Christo, animalis in spiritalem,* 'Our origin is transferred in Christ, that which is psychical into that which is spiritual' (*De mon.* V, 5). It is to this origin that monogamy goes back: *Ipse census generis humani: unam feminam masculo Deus finxit,* 'This is the origin of the human race; God fashioned one woman for a man' (*De mon.* IV, 2).

Secondly, Tertullian uses the word *census* in connection with a major feature of his thought, namely to express the apostolic origin of the churches, which is the source of their authority. Used in this sense, then, *census* points to the uninterrupted handing on of a reality from its origin: *Nostra doctrina de apostolorum traditione censeatur,* 'This doctrine of ours . . . originates in the tradition of the apostles' (*De praescr.* XXI, 6). The idea comes, of course, from Irenaeus, but Tertullian formulates it in his own categories. Another text in the same treatise illustrates this factor even more clearly: *Hoc enim modo ecclesiae apostolicae census suos referunt, sicut Smyrnaeorum ecclesia Polycarpum ab Johanne collocatum refert, sicut Romanorum Clementem a Petro ordinatum est,* 'This is how the apostolic churches record their origins: the church in Smyrna, for example, reports that Polycarp was placed there by John, the church in Rome that Clement was ordained by Peter' (*De praescr.* XXXII, 2). It is clear from this statement that Tertullian believes that a *census* could be made of the bishops going back to the apostolic origin of the Church. This is the apostolic succession,

Irenaeus' διαδοχή and Tertullian's *ordo episcoporum ad originem recensus*, 'the succession of the bishops, when traced back to its origin' (*Adv. Marc.* IV, 5, 2). From this, Tertullian concludes that those churches which cannot testify to their connection with the apostles are not authentic: *Ecclesias . . . adulteras, quarum si censum requiras*, 'Churches . . . spurious, if you search out their ancestry' (*Adv. Marc.* IV, 5, 3). In this case, the substance of faith is transmitted in the succession of bishops from the time of the apostles onwards, just as the substance of human nature is handed on in the succession of men from the time of Adam.

Another particularly interesting meaning of the word *census* also relates to the doctrine of man, and, what is more, gives us a very illuminating insight into the structure of Tertullian's thought. He tells us in the *De anima*, which was written against Hermogenes, that he had also written a treatise entitled *De censu animae* against the same author. In the treatise *De anima*, Tertullian is concerned with the structure of the soul, so that it is a treatise *De statu animae*, whereas the *De censu animae* dealt with its origin. In opposition to Hermogenes, who believed that man had an animal soul which was derived from matter and also an intellectual soul, which was the image of God, Tertullian believed in the unity of the human soul and that its origin was the breath of God (*flatus vitae*) mentioned in Gn. 2:7: *De solo censu animae Hermogene congressus – ex materia (an) ex Dei flatu*, 'Having fought with Hermogenes about the unique origin of the soul – whether it comes from matter or from the breath of God' (*De anim.* I, 1). The two aspects of *status* and *census* are distinguished by Tertullian: *Post definitionem census quaestionem status patitur*, 'After defining its origin, the question of its state is discussed' (*De anim.* I, 1). It is this origin which makes man the image of God: *Hominem . . . imaginem et similitudinem suam . . . per animae scilicet censum*, 'Man was the image and likeness of God . . . since from it the man's soul took its origin' (*Adv. Marc.* II, 5, 1). Everything that goes to form man's soul and everything resulting from its substance goes back to this origin: *Omnia naturalia animae ipsi substantiae inesse pertinentia ad sensum et intellectum ex ingenito animae censu*, 'All the natural qualities of the soul pertaining to sense and intellect are inherent in its substance and derive from its unborn origin' (*De anim.* XXXVIII, 1; see also **XX**, 1). This text is especially interesting in that three characteristic terms, *natura, substantia* and *census* occur together in it and, what is more, with their precise meanings: the permanent element of the soul (its *substantia*), together with the activities which are connected with it and constitute its nature (*sensus et intellectus*), is present from the very origin (*census*) of the soul, an origin which is uncreated because it is the breath of God (*flatus Dei*).

Tertullian also uses the word *census* in his theology of the incarnation and of the Trinity. In the former case, he employs it to define Christ's twofold substance on the basis of his twofold origin: *Ita utriusque substantiae census hominem et Deum exhibuit,* 'Thus the origin of both realities displayed the man and the God' (*De carne* V, 7). What Tertullian stresses above all, however, in opposition to the various forms of docetism, is the reality of Christ's humanity. For him, the most convincing proof of this reality is the *census,* in other words, the fact that Jesus was born of Mary: *Christum ex David deputatum carnali genere ob Mariae Virginis censum,* 'Christ . . . is reckoned as derived from David by carnal descent because of the lineage of Mary the Virgin' (*Adv. Marc.* III, 20, 6). In this text, Tertullian uses the word *census* in its original sense, as in the gospel, which tells us that Joseph went to Bethlehem with Mary in order to be registered as a descendant of David. Tertullian quite often employs the term in this sense (cf. *Adv. Marc.* IV, 1; IV, 49, 6), which is basically genealogical. Genealogies are, of course, of great importance in the Old and New Testaments and it is perhaps possible that the source of Tertullian's use of the term *census* is to be found in this biblical practice.

In Tertullian's trinitarian teaching, on the other hand, the term *census* occurs only once, and that is in his treatise against Praxeas (*Adv. Prax.* III, 5). The passage is interesting for other reasons, in that it describes the unfolding of the monarchy in the Trinity from its source in the Father. It cannot be said, however, that *census* forms part of Tertullian's trinitarian vocabulary.[3] This may

3. MOINGT's index lists no instance of *census* used in a trinitarian connection by Tertullian, nor does BRAUN note any such reference.

be because the word had been used in pagan Rome in connection with the genealogies of the Roman gods. Certainly Tertullian employs it in this sense: *Existat apud litteras vestras usquequaque Saturni census*, 'The origin of Saturn is everywhere clear from your books' (*Ad nat.* II, 12, 26). This use of *census* is linked in antiquity with *humana qualitas* (cf. *Ad nat.* II, 18, 24), families and nations trying to find divine origins (*census*) for themselves, which, in Tertullian's view, simply proves that their gods were no more than men. In his *Apology*, for example, he says: *Ante Saturnum deus penes vos nemo est, ab illo census totius vel potioris et notioris divinitatis*, 'Before Saturn you had no god among you; he is the origin of all your pantheon or of the more powerful and better known' (*Apol.* X, 6). This suggests that the word *census* was used in mythological texts, and Varro confirms this. It is well known that Tertullian tends to avoid any words which might run the risk of assimilating Christian teaching to pagan myths.

There is one more way in which the word *census* is used by Tertullian which should be mentioned here. This is connected with the origins of evil. In his debate with Marcion, Tertullian rejects the suggestion that evil originated in the demiurge who created the world. Nor does it derive from the angels nor from man as such, since both were created good. The *census* of evil, therefore, can only be the limitations of created freedom. It was this, as Tertullian sees it, which led to the fall of Lucifer: 'The author of sin . . . aforetime irreproachable since the day of his creation, created by God for goodness, as by a good Creator of creatures without reproach; adorned with all angelic glory; set in God's presence as in the presence of good, yet afterwards by himself transposed to evil . . . began to sin, he sowed the seed of sin and so from then onwards he was engaged in the multitude of his merchandise, his wickedness, the full measure of his transgressions (*censum delictorum*)' (*Adv. Marc.* II, 10, 4–5).

3. STATUS

The word *status* introduces a further consideration into Tertullian's attempt to define reality. It refers to the whole complex of properties which characterise a given reality (*substantia*) and enable us to define its relation to other realities. The status of a reality is therefore more abstract than its *substantia*. It corresponds in fact to what we often call the 'nature' of a thing; and indeed the word *natura* is sometimes used by Tertullian as equivalent to *status*. At the same time, however, it also corresponds to what we call an order or level of reality, as for example, when we speak of Pascal's 'three orders' or contrast the 'divine level' and the 'human level'. The term brings in an essential aspect of Tertullian's method, his concern to introduce order into *res*, and to place them in their proper mutual relationship. Things have a 'status' which is not imposed on them by the mind, but which has, on the contrary, to be discovered by it. In this context, Braun has quoted an interesting passage from the *De fuga* IV, 1: 'It is not the task of the subjective judgement to prejudge the nature of realities (*statui rerum*). It is, on the contrary, the nature (*status*) which has to determine the judgement. For each nature (*status*) is something stable and imposes a law on the judgement to judge the nature (*status*) for what it is'.[4]

As in the case of *substantia* and *census*, Tertullian does not seem to have borrowed the word *status* from the terminology of the philosophers. Curiously enough, the word is not to be found at all in the philosophy written either before or after Tertullian's time. It is clear, then, that *status* is not a technical term that could be handed down, but a word to which Tertullian gave a meaning according to his own way of thinking. Indeed, he often uses it in a very trite sense, and frequently in a variety of phrases which have remained quite familiar. Thus, Tertullian speaks of the 'whole state of the question' (*Adv. Marc.* V, 2, 3), 'state of health' (*salutis status, De pud.* IX, 8), the 'state of things' (*De fug.* IV, 1), the 'Jewish kingdom' (*Adv. Marc.* IV, 6, 3), the 'Roman state' (*De res.* XXIV, 18), the 'state of the world' (*Apol.* XXXIX, 2) and a 'change of state' (*Adv. Herm.* XXV, 3). In all these instances, the word *status* describes a factual state or situation, and this ·is the ordinary meaning of the word.

Tertullian keeps this concrete aspect; in his writings, 'state' is something different from 'nature' or 'essence'. But he modifies

4. Cf. BRAUN, *op. cit.*, p. 200.

the meaning of *status* by laying the emphasis on the permanent aspect of a reality, that connected not with its circumstances but with its nature. It is in this way that he uses it quite distinctively. It is a word which is derived neither from juridical nor from philosophical terminology, but from everyday language, and Tertullian uses it to express one aspect of his own view of things. *Status* enables him to distinguish between certain levels of reality. As we have already seen, the peculiar task of human intelligence is, for Tertullian, to discern the distinctive characteristics of an object and thereby to decide on the particular sphere to which it belongs. In this respect intelligence has to adapt itself to what is real, to conform to being, which in its turn is formed by irreducible essence. Tertullian's thought is rigorously objectivist and phenomenological. It discerns the various *status* in the mass of empirical data, and thus allows them to be placed within the hierarchy of realities.

Some examples, covering the main levels of reality, will make this clear. In the debate with Hermogenes, Tertullian discusses the *status* of matter (*Adv. Herm.* XXV, 1). Hermogenes defines the *status materiae* as *inconditus* (disordered), *confusus* (confused) *turbulens* (turbulent) and *ancipitis motus* (having a twofold motion) (*Adv. Herm.* XLV, 6). Above all, however, he insists that this *status* is *innatus*. But to be *innatus* is part of the *status* of God; the level of the divine is characterised by the fact that it is uncreated. If so, *communis ergo status amborum,* 'then there is a state common to both' (*Adv. Herm.* VI, 4). But matter cannot be uncreated: 'Like all other things that become, it is capable, as God is not, of becoming less or more. This is the status of matter' (*Adv. Herm.* VII, 2). According to this antithesis between the created and the uncreated, then, the *status* of matter is that of everything that has been created. Tertullian's concern as we see, is to determine the 'order' to which matter belongs, to place it in relation to other orders of reality.

In the *De anima* Tertullian's opponent is again Hermogenes, but now the subject is the *status* not of matter but of the soul.[5] He

5. The *status* of the soul, not its origin (*census*), which, as mentioned above (p. 350), Tertullian treated in the *De censu animae.*

defines this in *De anim.* IV, 1. He suggests various philosophical and gnostic theories about this *status* and then comes to certain conclusions himself concerning the basic characteristics which establish it in its order: *Definimus animam Dei flatu natam, immortalem, corporalem, effigiatam, substantia simplicem, de suo sapientem, varie procedentem, liberam arbitrii, accidentibus obnoxiam, per ingenia mutabilem, rationalem, dominatricem, divinatricem, ex uno redundantem:* 'We define the soul as born of the breath of God; immortal, corporeal, having shape, simple in substance, susceptible of the functions proper to it, developing in various ways, having freedom of choice, affected by external events, mutable in its faculties, rational, dominant, capable of presentiment, evolving in plurality from one archetype' (*De anim.* XXII, 2).

This is by no means a stereotyped list of the characteristics of the *status* of the soul. Each of the words used to define this *status* is also found in the context of a question discussed by Tertullian in connection with an error that he is seeking to refute in his treatise. The passage quoted above is really a description of this *status* rather than a mere definition. The words *flatus Dei* contained in it make us aware of the author's concern with the *census* or origin of the soul as determining all the other aspects and distinguishing the soul both from nature and from God. At the same time, Tertullian also stresses the unity of the soul within the diversity of its operations. Finally, the substance of the soul is immortal, although it is changeable in its freedom.

In conclusion, we must mention the *status* of God. This follows from his *census* or origin, which in the case of God, of course, is precisely that he has none. Hence the condition (*status*) of this *census* is that God has always been and must always be, having 'neither beginning nor end' (*Adv. Herm.* IV). This *status* belongs to God alone. It separates him radically from all that is not Himself. This, for Tertullian, is the basic contrast, that between what is created and what is uncreated. As for the Trinity, all three persons share this *status* and are different not *statu*, but *gradu*. They belong, then, to the same order of reality; the problem is to discern what distinguishes them within that order.

To summarise what we have said so far in this chapter, it is possible to point, at each level of reality, to an element which corresponds to the *substantia,* the *census* and the *status* of that reality. In the case of God, for example, the *substantia* is his *spiritus.* This is the concrete reality which forms God as a body and as an objective reality. This *spiritus* is different from the *anima* in the case of men, the *substantia spiritalis* in the case of the angels, the sidereal matter of the stars and the terrestrial matter of the body. God's *census,* on the other hand, is *aeternitas,* eternity without a beginning or an end. Finally, there is the *status* of God. This is his uncreated state and the fact that he was not begotten. God's *status,* Tertullian teaches, is opposed to everything which is not God and which derives its origin from him. In all this, Tertullian is far less preoccupied with penetrating into the inner reality of things than with placing them in their correct mutual relation. This is, moreover, something that he did with exceptional clear-sightedness, if we compare his attempts with those of his contemporaries.

4. GRADUS

The heart of Tertullian's logical method is his concern with the establishment of an order in the reality of existing things or *res,* so that it is easy to understand the importance of a word like *ordo* in his writings.[6] The word is, however, employed by Tertullian in so many different ways that its study yields very few useful data. This is not so in the case of another word, *gradus,* which Tertullian uses less often, but in very meaningful contexts. *Gradus* always points to a progressive series, as we shall see in the examples given below. But it also has more precise implications, indicating the organic bond between the various data in the series. This aspect of the word *gradus* in Tertullian's work will also be examined.

First, *gradus* in several passages denotes the degrees in a hierarchy. One interesting example of this use is concerned with the different states of life: 'The first kind (*species*) of holiness is virginity preserved from birth. The second is virginity preserved from baptism. This may last either through continence in

6. The entry occupies five pages in MOINGT's index.

marriage by mutual agreement between the partners or through widowhood undertaken by personal choice. The third kind is monogamy when, after a single marriage has been terminated by the death of one partner, the surviving partner renounces sexual life, that is, does not marry a second time' (*Exh. cast.* I, 4). Later in the same treatise Tertullian resumes this theme and demonstrates that there is a descending line. This same theme of the three stages of holiness played an important part in the early centuries of Christianity, above all, as we have already seen, in the context of the three rewards. It was, in fact, the subject of the sermon *De centesima,* in which the three stages were martyrdom, virginity and continence in marriage after baptism.

The word *gradus* is also used by Tertullian in connection with the theme of spiritual progress. In *Scorpiace* VI, 7, for example, he speaks of personal progress (*profectus*) and shows that this ought to be stimulated by the hope of reward. The same also applies, in Tertullian's view, to 'progress in degree' in earthly matters. There are different mansions in the Father's house and these are related to merit. In his *De pud.* X, 8, Tertullian speaks ironically of the invitation to the psychic[7] to continue to descend by degrees since they are already sure of mercy. In the *De fuga* XI, 1, he says that the Christian occupying a low rank may rise to a higher rank by climbing several degrees (*gradus*) in patience in persecution. At the same time, however, Tertullian asks how it is possible for the believer to remain at his present stage (*gradus*) if his leaders desert. In all these cases in which *gradus* is used, however, the word is not applied to God himself: *Divinitas gradum non habet,* 'Deity does not have degree' (*Adv. Herm.* VII, 4).

We must now turn to those ways in which Tertullian uses the word *gradus* to express certain structures in his own thought. The first case of this is found in Tertullian's outline of the manner in which God's ways of acting are implied in each other and, more precisely, of the manner in which his ways of acting in the New Testament are in continuity with those reported in the Old

7. For the significance of the term 'psychics' here, cf. p. 362 below.

Testament. He discusses this several times in the *Adversus Marcionem*.

Tertullian does this in the first place in order to show that goodness presupposes justice: 'Any goodness whatsoever is in the first instance made rational by its justice. Even as, in the primary degree (*gradu*), the goodness, if it is just, will be rational, when it is exercised in respect of its own belongings, so also toward the stranger it will be seen to be rational if it is not unjust' (*Adv. Marc.* I, 23, 6; see also IV, 16, 11).

Tertullian uses the same argument to demonstrate, against Marcion, that the revelation of Christ as saviour presupposes the existence of God as creator. He begins by outlining the general rule of the *gradus*: 'Everything must be suspected if it is removed from that rule of reality (*regula rerum*) which does not allow what is first in order (*gradus principalis*) to be known later – the Father after the Son, the one holding authority after the authority itself, Christ after God. Nothing exists first in man's knowledge which does not exist first in the real succession (*dispositio*)'. Similarly: 'If these are additions to the kingdom to be administered at a second step (*gradus*), then the second step belongs to him to whom the first step (*gradus*) belongs, and the food and raiment belong to him whose is the kingdom' (*Adv. Marc.* IV, 29, 5). Hence God the redeemer is always the same as God the creator.

Another aspect of Tertullian's theological teaching which is revealed in the term *gradus* is the link between the stages in one substance and their origin. This principle is stated in a general manner by Tertullian in his *Ad nationes*. He is trying to prove that, whatever transformations the pagans may believe take place in a piece of wood for it to be made into an idol, the final stages must be linked to the original substance: 'When the third stage (*gradus*) is linked to the second and the second to the first, then the third stage is linked to the first by going through the second. It is by an ordinance (*praescriptio*) of nature that every kind of thing without exception derives its classification (*census*) from its origin'.[8] Once again we have the principle that the nature of a

---

8. N.B. the juxtaposition of *praescriptio* and *census* here.

thing must be explained in terms of its origin.

Tertullian applies this principle to the genealogy of Christ from Jesse. The statement that Jesse is the root, Mary the branch and Christ the flower has no meaning, he insists, if the flower is not of the same nature as the root. This is clearly a case of the link between the third and the first stages via the second: *Omnis gradus generis ab ultimo ad principalem recensetur,* 'Every stage of a species is traced back from the last to the first' (*De carne* XXI, 6). It will be noticed that, as in previous examples, there is no suggestion of a scale of values. *Gradus* indicates simply an order of succession. This was clearly the case with the ideas of goodness and justice discussed above; the term *gradus* merely emphasized the need for an order in this succession.

It is in this sense that Tertullian uses the word in his theology of the Trinity. The *gradus* mark the order of succession of the divine persons, but do not in any way imply a difference in *status* or *substantia*. They are simply an expression of the common *census*.

The examples in Tertullian's general thesis have been classified by Moingt, the most striking being taken from Tertullian's *Apology* and his treatise against Praxeas. In *Apol.* XXI, 13, for example, he writes: *Ita et quod de Deo profectum est, Deus est Dei filius et unus ambo. Ita et de spiritu spiritus et de Deo Deus modulo alternum numerum, gradu non statu fecit,* 'Thus, what has proceeded from God is God and the Son of God and both are one. Thus, that which is spirit from spirit and God from God makes a numerical second when counted, but by order of succession (*gradu*) not in level of reality (*statu*)'. In the *Adv. Prax.* II, 4, he says similarly but more succinctly: 'They are three, not by *statu*, but by *gradu*'.

The *gradus,* then, points not only to the difference in succession, but also to its order: 'Thus the Trinity derives from the Father by continuous and connected stages (*gradus*)' (*Adv. Prax.* VIII, 7). Once again, to illustrate this succession, Tertullian uses the image of the tree: *Tertius enim est Spiritus a Deo et Filio, sicut tertius a radice fructus ex fructice,* 'The Spirit makes the third from God and the Son, as the fruit from the tree is the third from the root' (*Adv. Prax.* VIII, 7). Tertullian is therefore one of the first Christian authors to describe in this way the nature and the position of the

Holy Spirit: 'Thus Christ shows the Spirit as other than himself, as we too show the Son as other than the Father, so that the third stage (*gradus*) appears in the Paraclete, as we show the second in the Son, because of the observance of the economy' (*Adv. Prax.* IX, 3).

CHAPTER FIFTEEN

TERTULLIAN'S SYSTEM

THE various categories that we have examined in the preceding chapter made it possible for Tertullian to formulate a theological system of remarkable coherence. As Siniscalco has emphasized, moreover, it was from the time that he wrote the *Adversus Hermogenem*, and prompted by his opponent's errors, that Tertullian began to develop the major themes in his own theology. It is these themes which we shall now examine, endeavouring in particular to see how the categories of which Tertullian makes use enable him to take up a position vis-à-vis the various trends in contemporary thought with which he was in conflict.

In this chapter we shall be dealing with the Trinity in the *Adversus Praxean*, the creation of the world in the *Adversus Hermogenem*, man in the *De anima*, the incarnation in the *De carne Christi*, and the resurrection in the *De resurrectione mortuorum*. Something will also be said about Tertullian's views on the intermediate state between death and resurrection.

1. THE TRINITY

The first area in which we can study the use Tertullian makes of the categories discussed in the previous chapter is that of the doctrine of the Trinity, a task which has been made much easier since the publication of Moingt's important work.

Tertullian's main concern is to arrive at a correct formulation of the data concerning the Trinity implicit in Scripture in order to counter the incorrect formulations made by Praxeas and his disciples. Praxeas, Tertullian's opponent, was an Asiatic who came into conflict with Montanism in Asia Minor. A little before the year 200, he came to Rome in order to combat this teaching. In Moingt's opinion, Praxeas did not himself go to Africa, but sent disciples there to carry on the campaign against Montanism. To complete the picture, it is necessary to add that Tertullian was also confronted by those whom he calls the *simplices,* that is to say, Christians who had received only basic catechetical instruction and who were disturbed by theological speculations, and the *psychici,* who were largely members of the hierarchy and maintained a politic position midway between the two extreme tendencies.

Because this conflict, which spread first to Rome and then to Carthage, began in Asia, it is important to understand the theological situation in Asia during the last quarter of the second century. What seems to have been stressed by all Asiatic theologians at this time was the fact that God is one. This was because, on the one hand, the Jews were accusing Christians of abandoning monotheism and on the other, the gnostics were contrasting the God of the Old Testament and the God of Jesus Christ. This emphasis on the oneness of God characterises the teaching not only of the Montanists, but also of Irenaeus; and it is this same affirmation of monotheism which we find in Noetus and Praxeas. Why then did the conflict ever arise? What started it appears to have been the opposition to Montanism first of Noetus and then of Praxeas. The accusations made against them were to begin with a reaction on the part of the Montanists. For it should be noted that their theology did not at first seem very different from that of most of the theologians in Asia, which found supporters in the hierarchy, firstly in Asia and then at Rome and Carthage.

We are therefore bound to ask whether the charges brought against Noetus and Praxeas were really justified. To be precise, were they simply witnessing to an archaic type of theology, so that the accusations made against them would be just as valid in the case of Melito or Irenaeus? Or did they in fact make systematic statements concerning the doctrine of the one God which brought it into conflict with that affirmation of the numerical distinction between the Father, the Son and the Spirit which Irenaeus had always made?

The second thesis is strongly favoured by Moingt, who regards Tertullian as more 'orthodox' than Praxeas and is therefore critical of Lebreton, who regarded Praxeas' theology as archaic, but nonetheless orthodox. Moingt, however, puts forward all the possible reasons that might exonerate Praxeas and it has to be admitted that these reasons are quite convincing. In some respects, Praxeas' theology anticipates that of Marcellus of Ancyra, which was favoured by Athanasius, whereas Tertullian's could be twisted in an Arian direction. Raniero Cantalamessa was, in my opinion, right to call Praxeas the representative of an archaic type of theology rather than a dangerous heretic.[1] Moingt acknowledges, moreover, that the debate with Praxeas led Tertullian to correct some of his positions.

Tertullian's problem is to demonstrate that there can be number in God without jeopardising the unity of the divine substance. In order to do this, however, it is necessary to define the reality of the Word. The first and most elementary approach is to postulate that the Word is something objective, having density. Tertullian in fact does this by using the categories *substantia, materia* and *corpus*. As Moingt has shown, these should not be understood in a materialistic sense, since the substance is *spiritus*, which is divine substance. What is more, according to Tertullian, the Word is a definite reality, a *res*, as opposed to other *res*, and has an *effigies*. The problem is therefore to determine how there can be, in God, different 'things' which are not at the same time different 'substances'.

Tertullian's solution to this problem is to distinguish the Father, who is *tota substantia*, from the Son and the Spirit, who are derived from the Father's total substance. This relationship within the Trinity is expressed above all by the word *census*, which enables Tertullian to state that the three persons of the Trinity are of the same order (*status*), namely the divine order. The distinction between them therefore comes from the *gradus*, which denotes the 'inner order of communications of the sub-

---

1. Cf. his 'Prassea e l'eresia monarchiana', *La Scuola Cattolica*, 9 (1962), pp. 28–50; 'Il Cristo Padre negli scritti del II–III secolo', *RSLR*, 3 (1967), pp. 1–27.

stance', the *species,* which is the particular type of existent resulting from this order, and the *forma,* which is the 'principle of individualisation'.

A dry analysis cannot do justice to this tentative but lucid attempt on Tertullian's part to encompass his objective, but even so it must be said that the attempt is not entirely successful. Tertullian does not succeed in reconciling the specific individuality of the persons of the Trinity and the ground of their distinct existence. It was only later reflection which hit on the insight that it was precisely the specific individuality of the Persons which was the basis of their existence; and this was possible only by distinguishing more clearly between the act of being and substantiality. Tertullian divorces the distinction and the subsistence of the three persons into two elements. The first of these is a plural unity which is the inner organisation of the divine substance, but which does not in itself imply any plurality of existents. The second is a plurality of existents, which have their basis, not in their own specific individuality, but in the Father's act of will, which causes the Son and the Spirit to come forth from him. This is the doctrine of the προβολή. The Son and the Spirit are distinguished, therefore, from the Father in that they have their own subsistent being, which is not, however, based on their eternal specific individuality, but rather on their function in relation to God's creation. Tertullian does not manage to get beyond the combination of a modalism with regard to the distinctness of the individual persons and a subordinationism with regard to their existential plurality.

This emerges quite clearly in the question of the meaning of the word *persona.* In a lengthy discussion of the ideas of Braun and Andresen concerning this question, Moingt has concluded that Tertullian was the first author to use the word *persona* in connection with the Trinity. The difficulty is to determine precisely how the word is employed in the trinitarian sense by Tertullian. It certainly does not coincide with what later theologians mean by the term *persona.* Tertullian undoubtedly uses it in the context of the οἰκονομία (economy) – the *Sermo* becoming *persona* insofar as he makes the Father manifest, his distinction from the Father at the level of individual existence being related to his coming forth from the Father in order to make him manifest. This is clear from the contrast between the invisible nature of the Father and the visible nature of the Son. This contrast does not affect the specific nature of the persons of the Trinity in eternity, but only their existence as individual figures in the economy.

How should Tertullian be interpreted on this point? According to Orbe, he presents three states of divine wisdom. In the first state, this wisdom is identical with God without differentiation; in the second, it is constituted within God with a view to the *dispositio* of creation; and in the third, it is articulated by God and comes forth from him. This is, of course, the obvious meaning of the passages in question.

Certain pertinent criticisms have, however, been made by Moingt of Orbe's thesis. In the first place, he points out that the word οἰκονομία, which, it has often been observed, expresses the underlying inner organisation of the substance of God, always has the same meaning in Tertullian's writings as it had in those of Irenaeus before him and was to retain in later times, namely the unfolding of the divine plan of salvation. This point can be taken as established. Moingt then goes on to emphasise all that can be traced back, in Tertullian's outline of the begetting of the Son, to the οἰκονομία or manifestation and not to the *dispositio* or internal structure of the divine reality. This manifestation reveals the internal structure, but does not express it directly. This is, of course, in accordance with the general rule of all trinitarian theology, which starts from manifestations of the Trinity and ends with the eternal relationships between them. Moingt argues that the real data concerning the internal structure of the Trinity in Tertullian's writings have to be sought in his use of such terms as *substantia* or *forma* rather than in his employment of words like *persona* or οἰκονομία, which relate more to the manifestation.

The truth probably lies in a tension between these two positions. Certainly Orbe is more faithful than Moingt to the letter of Tertullian's text and the comparisons that he makes between Tertullian and the gnostics in this instance are more impressive than Moingt cares to admit. It cannot be disputed that Tertullian belongs to a theological world in which the begetting of the Son was linked to the creation of the universe. It was only after the Council of Nicaea that the theology of the Trinity was set free from all connection with cosmology, a development for which, it must be admitted, we are indebted to what was valid in the thought of monarchians such as Praxeas. Having said this, however, it remains true – and it is Moingt's achievement to have demonstrated this – that Tertullian's living thought, by its very freedom in the matter of schematization, marks a very real step forward in the theology of the Trinity. He saw clearly the direction that had to be followed in order to preserve both the unity of the divine substance and the distinction of the three persons. Although he lacked the intellectual tools which might have enabled him to define the reason for the individual existence of the three persons while at the same time distinguishing that existence with more metaphysical precision than he in fact did from the divine substance, he undoubtedly moved in this direction in introducing the term *persona* into the debate.

2. THE CREATION OF THE WORLD

Tertullian deals with the question of the creation of the world in his *Adversus Hermogenem*. Hermogenes was an Antiochene by origin, and Theophilus of Antioch wrote a refutation of his theories of which Tertullian made use. Influenced by the Middle Platonism of his time, Hermogenes believed particularly in the eternity of matter.[2] The first part of Tertullian's treatise in reply to him consists of a philosophical section in which he argues that, if matter is eternal and if it is the principle of evil, evil itself must therefore be placed on the same level as God. Tertullian then goes on to discuss the *originale instrumentum Moysi* (*Adv. Herm.* XIX, 1), the creation story in Genesis, of which he gives his own interpretation in opposition to the erroneous interpretations of the heretics.[3]

This theme is particularly interesting as an illustration of Ter-

2. Orbe can even say that Hermogenes is the only example of a rigorous metaphysical dualism, such as was not taught even by the gnostics.
3. Cf. G. T. ARMSTRONG, *Die Genesis in der alten Kirche: Beiträge zur Geschichte der biblischen Hermeneutik*, 4, Tübingen, 1962, pp. 102–112.

tullian's original approach. The Judaeo-Christian apocalyptic writers had been especially drawn to the first chapter of *Genesis* and had interpreted it in one of two ways: either in terms of speculation about the heavenly world, in which, for example, the seven days of creation were interpreted as the seven angels or the angels were the waters above the firmament; or prophetically, the sun and the moon, for instance, representing Christ and the Church. These speculations are also to be found in Latin Judaeo-Christian writings. In the *De centesima*, for example, the seven days are interpreted as the seven angels. In the *De Pascha computus*, the first three days are interpreted as the three persons of the Trinity. Tertullian records these ideas, but confines himself to a literal theological exegesis.

The first question to be considered is that of the first two words of *Genesis, In principio*, 'In the beginning'. Tertullian was aware that the Greek word ἀρχή could be understood not only as *ordinativum*, but also as *potestativum*. In the latter case the opening words would mean: 'It is by reason of his sovereignty (*principatu*) and his power that God made heaven and earth' (*Adv. Herm.* XIX, 5). The heretics, moreover, 'want the *principium* in which God made heaven and earth to be something substantial (*substantivum*) and concrete (*corpulentem*), which might be said of matter' (*Adv. Herm.* XIX, 1).

Tertullian does not dispute that the world may have been made from something, but insists that this something from which it was made is divine wisdom: 'When God decided to create the world; he at once established (*condit*) and begot Wisdom in himself'. In this sense, this may be called the 'material of matter' (*materia materiarum*); but if so, then we must say that God had need only of himself and not of an alien reality (*alieni*). Even as hypostasis, however, Tertullian argues, Wisdom itself had a beginning, with the result that only God himself is without a beginning.

It is interesting to note that both the equivalence of Wisdom and the Word, and the begetting (*generat*) of Wisdom with the creation of the world in mind are reflected in Tertullian's writing. What he does in fact is to introduce speculation about the Word into the Latin Christian world. In particular, as Orbe has pointed out, the idea of Wisdom as matter from which God made the world was a common theme in orthodox and gnostic learned theology during the second century.[4] Tertullian therefore acknowledges that it is possible to apply the phrase *in principio,* to Wisdom (*Adv. Herm.* XX, 1), but insists that it cannot refer to matter, for in that case it would be necessary to have *ex principio* (XX, 2). It would therefore seem as though he ultimately rejects the theme of Wisdom as matter, after having accepted it briefly as a hypothesis in the event of matter being required at any cost.

Tertullian, then, first considers various hypotheses on the subject of *in principio* in Genesis, and rejects one as heretical, while regarding others as possible. Finally, however, he himself comes down in favour of the obvious meaning of the words: *Ad ordinationem operum principii vocabulum pertinebit, non ad originem substantiarum,* 'The word "beginning" will apply to the order in which the works are performed, but not to the origin of substances' (*Adv. Herm.* XIX, 14). This provides an excellent example of Tertullian's theological method. He defines his own position in opposition to a heretical interpretation, expresses his reservations with regard to both Judaeo-Christian and Hellenistic speculations, and then makes his own choice. In passing, it is worth noting that, shortly afterwards, Origen also made a lengthy study of the term ἀρχή in his Commentary on St John's Gospel.

Tertullian then goes on to consider Gn. 1:2: *Terra autem erat invisibilis et incomposita,* 'The earth was invisible and unorganised'. It should, however, be noted that later on Tertullian translates ἀκατασκεύαστος by *rudis,* which would appear to indicate that here he is quoting from a received text. This may have been the one quoted by Hermogenes, if this author wrote in Latin or had been translated into Latin. For Hermogenes, *terra* meant matter, but Tertullian shows that the word *terra* cannot at the same time point to both that from which the earth is made and the earth which is made from that time onwards. The word therefore must mean, he concludes, the earth in the ordinary

---

4. Cf. ORBE, 'Elementos de teologia trinitaria en el Adversus Hermogenem, cc. 17–18', *Gregor.,* 39 (1958), pp. 706–747.

sense of the word. It is invisible and *rudis* because the elements were created first and then organised (*Adv. Herm.* XXIX, 1).

Taking Hermogenes' interpretation as his point of departure, Tertullian thus formulates his own position with regard to the interpretations of Gn. 1:2 then prevailing. Clement of Alexandria, following Philo Judaeus, believed that the 'invisible' earth was the intelligible earth, the archetype of the tangible earth. Tertullian does not refer to this thesis in his *Adversus Hermogenem*, but makes use of a tradition according to which the earth, still not visible or organised, is identified with the invisible and formless (ἄμορφος) species (εἶδος) , by which in the *Timaeus* Plato denotes the primal vessel (*Tim.* 51 a). This tradition is also found in Valentinus; and Justin explains in his first *Apology*, that Plato borrowed from Moses the idea of God's 'making the universe by changing formless matter' (I *Apol.* LIX, 1). It should be noted that, in this case, Plato speaks not of ὕλη ,but of εἶδος ,but that Albinus uses the term ἐξ ἀμόρφου ὕλης, 'from formless matter'. It is clear therefore that Justin derives his teaching here from Middle Platonism, and the same is true of Hermogenes.[5]

We may go further. For Albinus, matter (ὕλη) was a principle (ἀρχή) that was co-eternal with God. We have already seen that Hermogenes too regarded the word *principium*, in the sense of ἀρχή, as denoting matter, on this point therefore reproducing the Platonist argument. What is more, Theophilus of Antioch had disputed this thesis (*Ad Autol.* II, 4). It is clear, then, that Tertullian's source, or at least one of his sources, in the whole of his debate with Hermogenes was Theophilus' treatise against Hermogenes.[6] It should also be noted that Tertullian avoids the word *informis* in this context and prefers the word *rudis* (*Adv. Herm.* XXVIII, 2), which allows him to argue that the earth had been made, since it was imperfect.

Gn. 1:2b, *Et tenebras super abyssum et spiritus Dei super aquas ferebatur*, 'And darkness (was) over the deep and the Spirit of God was borne over the waters', is interpreted by Hermogenes as

---

5. Hippolytus explicitly refers to this derivation from Plato (*Ref.* VIII, 17, 2).
6. See especially *Message*, pp. 111–114.

massalis illius molis, in other words, as referring to unformed
matter in which the elements are confused (*Adv. Herm.* XXX, 1).
Tertullian retorts that the same reality cannot at the same time
both be formless and contain distinct *species.* Hermogenes also
claims that, because of the confusion of the four elements in
primal matter, these elements were not in fact created by God,
and that primal matter was also not created by him if it and the
four elements are identical. Tertullian's reply is that, in saying
that God created heaven and earth, he implies the creation of the
darkness and the deep, which are contained in the earth, and the
spirit and the water, which are contained in heaven (*Adv. Herm.*
XXXI). He insists that there is no primal matter, even matter first
created by God, but only the elements, which were created
directly by God (XXXIII). Finally, it is evident that they were
created, Tertullian argues, because they are corruptible, as Scripture says; and everything that perishes must have had a beginning
(XXXIV).

Tertullian, then, completely rejects Hermogenes' thesis that
primal matter was uncreated, but he also attempts to show that it
never existed, although he does not entirely exclude the opposite
hypothesis (XXXII). He also points to the fact that Hermogenes
gives primal matter a contradictory character, since it is, in his
opinion, neither corporeal nor incorporeal (XXXV). Or rather,
it is both at the same time: *Corporale materiae vult esse, de quo corpora edantur; incorporale vero inconditum motum eius,* 'He wants the
nature of the matter to be corporeal, so that bodies may be
produced from it, but its uncreated movement to be incorporeal'
(XXXVI). To this hypothesis, Tertullian replies that the movement is certainly incorporeal, but is not a component of substance. It is rather, he says, an accident, deriving from the *status*
(XXXVI).

Waszink has pointed out that all the aspects of Hermogenes
refuted by Tertullian are ultimately derived from Middle
Platonism.[7] A clear example of this is Hermogenes' teaching that
matter is neither corporeal nor incorporeal, which is found in

7. 'Observations on Tertullian's Treatise against Hermogenes', *VC*, 9 (1955),
pp. 128–138.

Apuleius *De Platone* (I, 5).[8] Another example is his insistence that matter is infinite (*ibid.* I, 5). Undoubtedly the most important aspect of all is the idea of 'disordered movement' (*inconditus et confusus et turbulentus*) of matter waiting to be organised by God. This is a major concept in Plutarch (*De animae procr. in Tim.* 7), who contrasts the disorder of matter and the order which comes from God. This teaching may well have been the source of the belief that matter is both good and evil, since the evil aspect of matter is expressed in its disordered movement.

All this clearly illustrates Tertullian's theological method. His interpretation of Gn. 1:1–2 is in no way dependent on the apocalyptic type of exegesis which is still to be found at the end of the second century in the work, for example, of Victorinus of Pettau. He is obviously acquainted with the platonizing interpretations of the kind quoted by his contemporary Clement of Alexandria (cf., e.g., *Strom.* V, 14; 89, 5; 93, 4; 94, 2). He eliminates those which he regards as heretical. On the other hand, he does not dwell too long on the interpretations which seem to him to be acceptable. He only mentions these in order to point out that, even if they are accepted, his thesis still remains valid. He keeps to literal exegesis, but he interprets the *Genesis* texts on the basis of the categories outlined in the preceding chapter: *census Dei aeternitas* (*Adv. Herm.* IV, 1), 'the origin of God is eternity'; *divinitas gradum non habet,* 'deity does not have degrees' (VII, 4); *status materiae,* 'the status of matter' (VII, 3).

3. THE SOUL OF MAN

Tertullian discusses the creation of man as a continuation of his commentary on the creation of the world; and indeed he does so within a very similar framework, that of a refutation of the teaching of Hermogenes. This appeared in the treatise *De censu animae,* which is no longer extant. A summary of it, however, is provided in the *De anima.*[9] Tertullian first sets out his view of the nature and the origin of man in contrast with that held by Her-

---

8. *Op. cit.,* p. 131ff.
9. Cf. WASZINK, *Tertullian, De anima,* pp.8*–14*.

mogenes. Then, in the *De anima*, he extends this discussion to include the leading theories concerning the soul of man as found in ancient philosophy, examining the views expressed by Empedocles and Pythagoras, Plato and Aristotle, and the Stoics and Epicureans. What is chiefly important for us, however, is the conception which he expounds in the *De censu* in opposition to the Platonism of Hermogenes. At the same time, we shall have to decide whether he drew on any source for his own idea of the soul.

Hermogenes' argument consists mainly of an affirmation that the soul comes *ex suggestu materiae quam ex Dei flatu*, 'from the piling up of matter rather than from the breath of God' (*De anima* I, 1). The reason why Hermogenes states this, Tertullian suggests, is because his text of Gn. 2:7 read *spiritum* (πνεῦμα) *vitae*, 'spirit of life', and not *flatum* (πνoή) *vitae*, 'breath of life'. *Spiritus*, however, can only point to a divine principle and it is impossible to believe that the spirit of God could have fallen into sin. The source of sin is therefore in the material principle of man, which includes the soul. The spirit comprises man's higher faculties and these are alien to the soul (*De anima* II, 2).

Having outlined Hermogenes' theory, Tertullian goes on to set out his own. He rejects the rendering *spiritus* for πνoή and retains *flatus* (*De anim*. III, 4), translating the whole verse: *Et flavit Deus flatum vitae in faciem hominis et factus est homo in animam vivam*, 'And God blew the breath of life into man's face and man became a living soul' (Gn. 2:7). Secondly, he states that the soul does not originate in matter, but in the breath of God; this is its *census* (*De anim*. III, 4). Man's soul unfolds in his higher faculties, which are called by Tertullian a *suggestus*, a 'piling up' (*De anim*. XII, 17). Finally, we read *Definimus animam Dei flatum natam, immortalem, corporalem, effigiatam, substantia simplicem, de suo sapientem, varie procedentem, liberam arbitrii, accidentibus obnoxiam, per ingenia mutabilem, rationalem, dominatricem, divinatricem*, 'We define the soul as born of the breath of God; immortal, corporeal, having shape, simple in substance, susceptible of the functions proper to it, developing in various ways, having freedom of choice, affected by external events, mutable in its faculties, rational, dominant, capable of presentiment' (*De anim*. XXII, 2).

Tertullian can now place the soul at its proper level (*gradus*), which is higher than that of matter, but lower than that of God himself, who is spirit (*spiritus*). In addition to this passage in the *De anima* (XXIV, 2), however, there is another text in the *Adversus Marcionem*, which is clearly aimed at Hermogenes [10] and which is therefore also interesting in this context. In this second passage, Tertullian says: *Intellige itaque afflatum minorem spiritu esse, etsi de spiritu accidit, ut aurulam eius, non tamen spiritum . . . Capit etiam imaginem spiritus dicere flatum. Nam et ideo homo imago Dei, id est spiritus. Deus enim spiritus,* 'Observe then that breath, though a function of spirit, is something less than spirit, not spirit itself . . . One may even say that breath is an image or reflection of spirit, for it is in this sense that man is the image of God, that is, of spirit, since God is spirit' (*Adv. Marc.* II, 9, 2–3). It is precisely because of this that the soul is capable of sinning, something of which the spirit is incapable.

The main point here is the idea of the *flatus Dei* which Tertullian develops in contrast to the *spiritus*. This conception is also elaborated in the *Adversus Hermogenem* (XXXII, 2–3), which confirms the view that these texts form part of the debate with Hermogenes. In the passage just cited Tertullian is discussing the *Genesis* text 'the spirit hovered over the waters' (Gn. 1:2) and says: 'This refers to the spirit (*spiritum*) which was sent over the created earth – *librator* (surveyor) and *adflator* (breath-giver) and *animator universitatis* (life-giver of the universe), not, as some believe, meaning that this spirit was God himself'. Here the question of translation is not involved; but in commenting on the word *adflator*, Tertullian likens the breath to the principle of life in the universe, which is also that which governs man. [11] From the same standpoint he sees the angels as made of the *flatus* of God, although this is of a lower quality than that of the soul of man. [12]

---

10. Cf. WASZINK, *op. cit.,* p. 10.
11. In the *De baptismo*, in which he follows the catechetical tradition, he describes the breath of Gn. 1:2 as the Holy Spirit (III, 2; V, 1); the *De baptismo* is, however, an earlier work.
12. Cf. also *Adv. Marc.* IV, 26, 4.

In this case too, Tertullian demonstrates his originality with regard to various theological positions. He is conscious of the importance of the apocalyptic exegesis according to which Adam and Eve prefigure Christ and the Church (*Adv. Marc.* III, 4, 15). It forms part of a traditional deposit of faith, which he respects even while disentangling it from mythical elements. Nevertheless it derives from an allegorical method in which he is not primarily interested. That in opposition to which he defines his own position, while criticizing Hermogenes, is a Platonist type of exegesis which was very widespread at the end of the second century. A representative of this type of interpretation is Tatian, who believed that there were two πνεύματα in man, the first being the soul and material, the other being the Spirit and divine (*Or.* 12). Like matter, the soul is simply darkness (*Or.* 13) and when the Spirit which comes from above is united with it, it is saved. Left to itself, on the other hand, it dies together with the flesh.

This same Middle Platonist tradition is also found in the work of the Valentinian gnostics, who gave their gnosis a philosophical form. One of the leading representatives of this school is Theodotus, whose ideas are described by Clement as follows: 'Taking mud of the earth (Gn. 2:7), not of the dry land (ξήρας), but of matter (ὕλης), he makes a material (ὑλικήν) and earthly (γεωδήν) soul, without logos and consubstantial with the soul of the animals' (*Excerpts.* L, 1). In this, it should be noted that, as in Hermogenes, the 'earth' in this case denotes not the element earth, but matter in general. This is one of the points on which, as we have seen, Tertullian attacks Hermogenes. It was, in fact, a common feature of Middle Platonist Christian exegesis.

For Theodotus, then, as for Hermogenes, the ψυχή is made from this ὕλη and is therefore not radically different in man and in animals. It is contrasted with the πνεῦμα, which is the breath of God, mentioned in Gn. 2:7. The exegesis is therefore the same, although the interpretation differs in that Theodotus interprets the Middle Platonist thesis in a gnostic sense. Since God the Creator is the Demiurge, he argues, it is he who breathes into man the πνεῦμα which forms man in his image. Thus Tatian, Theodotus and Hermogenes all bear witness to a certain exegesis of Gn. 2:7 and to a contrast between the material soul and the divine soul in man.[13]

It is possible to define Tertullian's position more precisely on this basis. On the one hand, from the exegetical point of view, he disputes the translation of πνοή by the Latin word *spiritus*.[14] There was, in fact, a good deal of confusion between πνοή and πνεῦμα in the exegesis of Gn. 2:7 before Tertullian's time — it occurs, for example, in the work of Philo — although this did not necessarily involve any confusion between the πνεῦμα of Gn. 2:7 and the divine πνεῦμα. It is well known that πνεῦμα could have many different meanings for Christians in the second century, for example in Theophilus of Antioch and Athenagoras. Tertullian, however, avoids the ambiguity which could arise, as Hermogenes shows, by using two different words.

More important is Tertullian's theological position. He is concerned above all to point out that the soul of man does not have its origin in matter, but in the breath of God. The *census* of the soul, in other words, is different from that of the body. What is more, this soul, which animates the body and makes it a living thing, is also what is manifested in human thought and freedom. It is therefore, Tertullian teaches, a *flatus* of a very special kind.

This is a point of some importance for our understanding of Tertullian's thought. The *flatus Dei* is, for him, the principle which animates all living beings, but it varies in quality. There is, in other words, a difference in kind between the *flatus* which animates the animals, the *flatus* which animates the angels and the *flatus* which animates men, the latter being the highest (*Adv. Marc.* II, 8, 2). It is this *flatus* which makes man into the image of God, that is of the *spiritus*. Theodotus also identified this *flatus* and the image of God in Gn. 1:27 and 2:7, but in a different sense.

Finally, there is the question of man's participation in the *spiritus*, in other words, in God himself. Tertullian's teaching here is radically different from that of Hermogenes, for whom the *spiritus* of Gn. 2:7, that is, the divine principle in man, is intellectual man, who cannot sin because he is divine. It is, in Hermogenes' opinion, the material soul which sins and, when it sins,

13. Cf. *Message*, pp. 355–365.

it separates itself from the intellectual man. Tertullian, on the other hand, teaches that intellectual man is not part of the divine order, with the result that he is able to sin. The divine principle of *spiritus* is quite different, does not form part of man's nature and can therefore be lost. The debate with Hermogenes therefore turns on the nature of the νοῦς. As a Platonist, Hermogenes sees a divine principle in this νοῦς, whereas Tertullian sees in it the highest aspect of created life.

Tertullian makes use of 1 Co. 15:45–50 as a basis for this distinction: *Primo enim anima, id est flatus, populo in terra incedenti, id est in carne carnaliter agenti, postea spiritus qui ipsi terram calcant, id est opera carnis subigunt quia et apostolus non primum quod spiritale, sed quod animale, postea spiritali,* 'Firstly the soul, that is, the breath, is given to the people who go upon the earth, that is, who act carnally in the flesh, and then the spirit, to those who tread the earth, that is, subdue the works of the flesh, because the apostle says that it is not the first which is spiritual, but that which belongs to the soul, then the spiritual' (*De anim.* XI, 3). The reference to 1 Co. here is obvious.[15] The same passage is quoted by Tertullian in *Adv. Marc.* V, 10, 7, where the creation of Adam is interpreted as a union of the *corpus* and the *flatus*, both of which form his being, the communication of the *spiritus* being given only with Christ as a gift which does not derive from man's nature.

This does not mean that the Spirit could not have been given to man before Christ's coming, but that it was only given in an accidental manner, that is, in prophecy. In this context, Tertullian refers to a doctrine which he received from tradition and which he very much favoured, namely the doctrine of Adam as a prophet. He uses it in this instance to reply to the question in the *De anima* XXI, 2: *Quid spiritale in illo? Si quia prophetaret magnum illud sacramentum in Christum et Ecclesiam,* 'What is spiritual in him? That he prophesied that great mystery of Christ and the Church'. He explains this as coming from an intervention made by God from the outside: 'This took place when God put a madness

14. He used it, however, in his first writings; see, for example *De paen.* III, 5.
15. The first part of the passage is an exegesis of Is. 42:5 (Tr.).

(*amentiam*) into him, *spiritalem vim qua constat prophetia* ('the spiritual force by which prophecy occurs') (*De anim.* XXI, 2). Adam became psychical, Tertullian also says elsewhere, after his ecstasy (*De jejun.* III, 2). It is in this way, then, that he defines the *status* of the soul.

Tertullian is therefore quite consistent in rejecting the suggestion that the Holy Spirit had been given to Adam as a participation in God, although, during the earlier part of his life, before his debate with Hermogenes, he seems to have accepted this idea. In his treatise on baptism, for example, he writes: 'Thus man is restored by God, into his likeness, for he had of old been in his image ... For he receives back the Spirit of God which at the beginning he received from God's inbreathing (*afflatu*), but which he afterwards lost through his transgression' (*De bapt.* V, 7). This, however, shows us the state of Tertullian's thinking before he made it explicit, and contains at least two ideas which he later rejected. On the one hand, the *afflatus* of Gn. 2:7 is identified with the Holy Spirit and, on the other, a contrast is made between the 'likeness' of God and the 'image', the latter corresponding to nature and the former to grace in the future. This contrast is found in only one other of Tertullian's treatises (*De exhort. cast.* I, 3).

The question arises, however, as to whether this was an original idea on Tertullian's part. We are bound to consider the influence of Irenaeus here, since Tertullian refers to him several times in this context and undoubtedly made use of his writings in the *Adversus Valentinianos*. In his exegesis, he was certainly indebted to Irenaeus who, before Tertullian, stressed the fact that the πνοή of Gn. 2:7 was not the divine πνεῦμα (*Adv. haer.* V, 12, 2). Irenaeus also clearly makes a distinction between three principles – the body, the breath as the principle of the intellectual life, and the Holy Spirit. We may therefore conclude that, insofar as these two essential questions are concerned, Tertullian continues in the tradition of Irenaeus' teaching and was unquestionably dependent on him. At the same time, there is also a considerable difference in emphasis between them.

For Irenaeus the emphasis is essentially on the body, whose value he wishes to demonstrate in opposition to the gnostics. In his view, following a Semitic tradition, it was the body which was created in God's image. What is more, this body is called to transfiguration by the Spirit and it is this which gives it a special dignity from the very beginning. The two basic principles for Irenaeus, therefore, are the body and the Holy Spirit. The latter has been mingled with the body since the beginning, and will transfigure it fully at the end of time.

On this basis, what becomes of the soul, the rational breath with which God animated the plasma? Its role is to enable the body, which is the essential feature of man, to know the difference between good and evil and to choose the good. It is a power communicated to the plasma which makes it capable of vital and moral actions, by means of which it is to pass from the original mere mixture of body and Spirit to a composite life given shape by both body and Spirit. In other words, it plays the part of a mediator between the body, which is the image of God, and the Spirit, which is the likeness. It is clear, however, that Irenaeus does not place the emphasis on the soul. [16]

In this question, Tertullian does not contradict Irenaeus, but rather supplements his teaching. Their anthropologies are similar, but they emphasise different aspects of man. As we shall see in connection with his teaching concerning the resurrection of the flesh, Tertullian acknowledges the importance of the latter. In his debate with Hermogenes, however, he recognises that this raises the question of the nature of the soul, and that it is not enough, therefore, merely to discuss its origin (*census*). In Irenaeus' conception, however, there is a gap – the place of the soul between the flesh and the Spirit is not made explicit. Now this was a major topic with the pagan philosophers, and it was therefore essential to clarify one's position in relation to their views. This is what Tertullian sets out to do in the *De anima*, as he makes clear at the start: *De solo censu animae congressus Hermogeni, nunc ad reliquas conversus quaestiones plurimum videbor cum philosophis dimicaturus*, 'Having taken issue with Hermogenes only about the origin of the soul, I shall now turn to the remaining questions and I shall seem principally to join battle with the philosophers' (*De anim.* I, 1).

16. Cf. A. ORBE, *Antropologia di S. Ireneo*, pp. 89–170.

These questions are, of course, those relating to the *status* of the soul (*status animae, De anim*. IV, 1), which occupies the first chapters of the treatise[17] and is summarised in XXII, 2, which we have already quoted. The main points from these early chapters are as follows. First, in opposition to Plato, Tertullian emphasises that the soul has a beginning in time (*De anim*. IV). Secondly, it is corporeal. The importance of the corporeity of the soul for Tertullian is indicated by the fact that he devotes three chapters to this question (V–VII). He opposes the teaching of Plato again, but also of those, such as Epicurus and Heraclitus, who 'constitute the soul out of perceptible bodies'. Tertullian adopts the Stoic position, and expounds the views of Zeno, Cleanthes and Chrysippus.[18] He also relies to a great extent on the teaching of the physician Soranus (VIII), but adds that this *corpulentia est propriae qualitatis et sui generis*, 'of its own quality and of a special kind'. It therefore implies only certain corporeal qualities (IX, 1), among these being that it has an *effigies* (IX, 2) and colour (IX, 5).

Thirdly, an important aspect of the soul for Tertullian is that it is 'simple and uniform' (X, 1). It is one of his basic arguments that there is not a material soul and an intellectual soul, but that there is only one substance of the soul and that the soul manifests itself in many different *suggestus*. He first opposes the idea that a vegetative soul should be distinguished from a sensitive soul (XI) and then goes on to show that the νοῦς is a *suggestus animae*, a 'piling up of the soul' (XII, 1). He translates the word νοῦς by *animus* and calls it *animae concretum, non ut substantia alium, sed ut substantiae officium*, 'a concretion of the soul, not as different in substance, but as a function of the substance' (XII, 5). The soul is therefore not capable of being divided and this is linked to its immortality (XIV, 1). There is also *summus in anima gradus vitalis et sapientalis quod* ἡγεμονικόν *appellant*, 'the highest level in the soul, the seat of life and wisdom, which is called "the governing principle"' (XV, 1).

---

17. Cf. G. ESSER, *Die Seelenlehre Tertullians*, 1893.
18. Cf. E. WEIL, 'Remarques sur le matérialisme des stoiciens', *L'Aventure de l'Esprit (Mélanges Loyré)*, II, pp. 556–572.

Tertullian is not in this case outlining the Platonist theory, according to which the *animus,* as a true substance, has the *principalitas* over the *anima. Animus* is merely an *instrumentum* of *anima* (XIII, 3). This does not mean, however, that Plato's contrast between the rational and the irrational soul does not to some extent have to be preserved. What it means is that this contrast should be understood not in the physical, but in the moral sense. The soul is irrational when it does not follow reason (XVI, 2) and the intelligence and the senses are not two distinct modes of knowing which go back to two different souls – the intelligence perceives through the senses (XVIII). Here Tertullian discusses the objective value of knowledge given to us by the senses. This is a question with which he is deeply concerned and in his argument he relies above all on the Epicureans, although he makes use of their teaching to suit his own purpose. As Waszink has observed, this passage is highly characteristic of Tertullian's method, in that he derives all that he needs from his sources, but only uses this material insofar as it can be adapted to his own purpose. [19]

Fourthly, in the list of attributes of the soul given in *De anim.* XXII, 2, Tertullian includes *per ingenia mutabilem,* 'changeable in its abilities'. This is in fact discussed in XX, where Tertullian refers explicitly to Seneca: *Sicut et Seneca saepe noster: insita sunt nobis omnium artium et aetatum semina magisterque ex occulto Deus producit ingenia,* 'Just as our Seneca often says, There are planted in us the seeds of all arts and ages, and God is the master who produces abilities from hidden things'. This teaching about the seeds contained in the soul and coming from it is interesting evidence for Tertullian's Stoic sources.

Fifthly, there is freedom: *Inesse autem nobis naturaliter iam Hermogeni ostendimus,* 'We have already shown Hermogenes that this is by nature within us' (XXI, 6). This allusion to Hermogenes towards the end of the discussion is clear proof that the *De anima* and the *De censu animae* form a continuous whole.

There remains one final question which Tertullian raises for consideration: *Quod si uniformis natura animae ab initio in Adam, ergo non multiformis, nec triformis, ut adhuc trinitas Valentiniana caedatur,*

19. Cf. WASZINK, *op. cit.,* p. 240.

quae nec ipsa in Adam recognoscitur. Quid enim spiritale in illo?, 'But, if the nature of the soul was uniform from the beginning in Adam, then it is not multiform nor triform, so that there is an end of the Valentinian trinity, which is not known in Adam. For what is there of the Spirit in him?' (**XXI**, 1). The Spirit does not form part of the substance of the soul, which is no more 'spiritual' than it is material. But, just as it can become material if it turns towards matter, so too can it become spiritual if it turns towards the Spirit. If necessary, then, it is possible to speak of a *trinitas animae*, a 'trinity of the soul', but only *mutatione accidentiae, non ex institutione naturae*, 'by a change of accident, not by an inborn structure of nature' (**XXI**, 7).

This text is in fact an excellent summary of Tertullian's final position and points clearly to the originality of that position. The soul constitutes a special order, distinct on the one hand from the body and, on the other, from the Holy Spirit. What is more, because of its freedom, the soul can be transformed into that towards which it turns: *quoquo vertitur natura convertitur,* 'withersoever it is turned, so its nature is changed' (**XXI**, 6). This changes, not the substance of the soul, but its quality. It is possible therefore to discern three aspects in the soul – the fleshly, the intellectual and the spiritual aspects – but this in a sense is quite different from that of the Valentinians, for example, or from that of Hermogenes. The former taught that the soul had three distinct substances. The latter, on the other hand, believed that man had a material soul and a spiritual soul, but completely overlooked the one true soul of man which is not by nature material or spiritual, but which can become, according to Tertullian, either material or spiritual by accident.

The same text also indicates the difference between Tertullian's position in this matter and that of Irenaeus. Irenaeus believed that the soul was neither body nor Spirit, but was not fundamentally interested in the question. What is of real interest to Irenaeus in this context is the body on the one hand and the Spirit on the other. He regards man essentially as body transfigured by the Spirit. The essence of man, in other words, is the body, and the soul comes in as that which introduces the freedom by which the body can open or close itself to the Spirit. Irenaeus, however, is not interested in the process by which the soul itself becomes spiritual.

It is precisely here that Tertullian demonstrates his originality. Basing his argument on the pagan philosophers against Irenaeus, he attempts to emphasise the importance of the level (*gradus*) at which the soul exists and to define the *status* of the soul on the basis of its origin or *census*. In this, he is constrained to go counter to Irenaeus in one important aspect. The latter interpreted the creation of man 'in the image and likeness of God', as we have seen, by on the one hand making a distinction between the two terms 'image' and 'likeness' and on the other by applying the first to the body on account of its upright posture, and the second to the Holy Spirit, given to man, albeit inchoately, from the beginning. Both points are rejected by Tertullian, who, on the one hand makes no distinction between the two terms and on the other applies them both to the soul. The soul is, in Tertullian's opinion, both the image and the likeness of God, above all by its freedom, which forms the highest *gradus*: 'I observe that man was created by God as a free man, with power to choose and power to act for himself. I can think of no clearer indication in him of God's image and likeness than this, the outward expression of God's dignity (*status*). Countenance and physical shape vary so widely among mankind that the man cannot in respect of these have been moulded into the shape of God, for this is one and unchanging. Rather it was the substance (*substantia*) which he derived from God, himself the substance of the soul, which corresponds to the form of God' (*Adv. Marc.* II, 5, 5).

It is interesting to turn to the *De resurrectione mortuorum* in this context. Having praised first the soul and then the flesh, Tertullian goes on to correct in one particular the statements in the *Adversus Marcionem* just quoted. He now makes an explicit connection between the 'image of God' and God's fashioning of man's body from the mud and between the 'likeness' and God's breathing the soul into man. The essential point, however, remains valid, namely that it is man's soul which is made in the likeness of God and above all reflects his freedom.

In this, Tertullian's thought was profoundly original, and was to have a great influence on Latin theological thinking after his time. For the effect of his teaching about the human soul was to give an essential place in theology to the human person, the inner life of man and his subjective experience. We shall return to this point when we come to examine the *De resurrectione mortuorum* in the last section of this chapter, but its importance ought to be stressed here.

This whole question of the soul of man throws a very interesting light on Tertullian's theological method. His thought is clearly dominated by his special categories and what he most wants to do is to bring order into the mass of Christian, gnostic and philosophical literature, of which his knowledge is so vast. He is, in fact, original, not by virtue of the content of his teaching, but of the order he introduces into it. On reading the passage from Tertullian quoted above, one is inevitably reminded of Pascal's words about the three orders. But is this just a reminder? Is it not rather a clear echo of Tertullian in the writing of the seventeenth century French author, either direct or by way of Augustine? In any case, both authors write with brilliant order and clarity, which set the seal of permanence on their works.

4. THE FLESH OF CHRIST

The principles which enabled Tertullian to analyse the various component elements of man also enabled him to define the reality of Christ. In his treatise on the flesh of Christ (*De carne Christi*), he once again establishes his own position by reference to a number of heretical attitudes. Among the heretics whose position he attacks are Marcion, who disputed the reality of the incarnation itself, and Apelles, who admitted that Christ had a body, but denied that he was born of Mary. Another group are those who believed that the flesh of Christ was his soul that had been made visible. Finally, there are Valentinus' disciples, who taught that Christ's flesh was spiritual. Tertullian goes on, after having discussed these opinions, to deal with the question of the incarnation and in particular of the virgin conception and its significance.

It is in the debate with Apelles that he defends the reality of the flesh of Christ. Apelles was a disciple of Marcion and is known to us through the writings of Rhodon (Eusebius, *Hist: eccl.* V, 3) and Hippolytus. Tertullian had in fact written a treatise *Adversus Apelleiacos* (*De carne* VIII, 11–12), but, in the *De carne,* the only point he discusses is that, for Apelles, Christ's body could not have been born of Mary because he could not be formed of fleshly substance, which is evil and which is the creation of the demiurge. Christ, Apelles taught, had a body, but that body was made of another substance and did not come from Mary (*De carne* VI, 3). Apelles based his argument on the fact that even orthodox Christians believed that the angels could assume a body without passing through the process of human birth.

Tertullian refutes Apelles' argument in the first place by emphasising that Christ's death presupposes his birth. Death and birth are correlative and a body that has never been born cannot die. But Christ came in order to die. (It is interesting to see the principle expressed here that the incarnation was the necessary condition of the redemption.) Tertullian then goes on to discuss Apelles' argument *ad hominem.* The latter is interesting because it is based on a view which was really held by Christians. It was originally Judaeo-Christian and is found in Origen, as a Jewish tradition, and in Commodian. Tertullian does not deny that the angels took bodies of flesh, but insists that they did so in an accidental way: *In carnem humanam transfigurabilis ad tempus, ut videre et congredi cum hominibus possint,* 'capable of being transfigured into human flesh on occasion, so that they can see and consort with men' (*De carne* VI, 9).[20] This also applies, he claims, to the body assumed by the Son in the Old Testament theophanies (*Adv. Marc.* III, 9, 6).

This text is also important for the light it throws on Tertullian's theological system. The angel has a spiritual nature, that is, of a substance which is analogous to the soul. It therefore has a certain corporeity, but it is not flesh. It can be transfigured into flesh, but, for the angel, this flesh is a form which clothes its sub-

---

20. Tertullian also adds here that, if the body of Christ had been made of heavenly matter, it would not have been of the same nature as ours (*De carne* IX, 2). He also believes that it is nonetheless more pure than ours, although it is of the same *substantia* and *forma* (*De res.* LI, 1).

stance. It should be noted in this context that *transfigurari* is the word which Tertullian uses for the soul which becomes Spirit; and this too is a form which clothes the original substance. In man, on the other hand, there is both *substantia carnis* and *substantia animae*. He belongs by his very nature to both orders. For Christ to be truly man, therefore, his flesh had to form part, not accidentally but substantially of the being that it clothed.

Further on in his treatise, Tertullian also deals with attacks made against the flesh of Christ by a disciple of Valentinus, one Alexander, who is known to us only through Tertullian and who made use of syllogisms in his attempt to demonstrate contradictions in the orthodox position. One of Alexander's arguments is that it is necessary to choose between two solutions – either that Christ's flesh is earthly and therefore must, like ours, be dissolved in the earth, since it must have been born of the will of man, or that it is spiritual in its nature (*De carne* XV, 1), in which case our flesh, like his, must rise again at once (XV, 3). From this, Alexander concludes that the flesh of Christ is not of the same nature as ours.

Another of Alexander's arguments consists in exposing a contradiction in orthodox doctrine. He claims, in this context, that Christians teach that Christ was clothed with flesh of a terrestrial origin (*census*) in order that he might destroy in himself the flesh of sin (XVI, 1). Tertullian uses this as a basis for distinguishing between what is traceable to the nature of flesh and what goes back to the sin of the flesh: *Defendimus non carnem peccati evacuatam esse in Christo, sed peccatum carnis, non materiam, sed naturam, nec substantiam, sed culpam,* 'We defend the position not that the flesh of sin was done away in Christ, but the sin of the flesh – not the matter, but the nature; not the substance, but the guilt' (XVI, 2). It is not impossible that Alexander may have been alluding here to the attitude of certain Christians who were encratite in tendency.

More important, however, is Tertullian's refutation, in a passage of major significance, of a heresy which enables him to emphasise the importance of Christ's soul. Unlike Irenaeus, Tertullian, as we have already seen, laid the stress on the soul of man; and, in exactly the same way, he was also the first to stress the soul of Christ.[21] The false teachers whom Tertullian attacks in this context taught that Christ took merely *carneam animam*, a 'soul made of flesh' (*De carne* **X**, 1). They seem to have believed that the Word of God came simply to teach souls and that Christ's corporeity was only the way in which he made himself visible in order to reveal their nature to them, as though they were not aware of it (**XI**, 1).

Tertullian's first criticism of this teaching is that Christ came to save not only the body, but also the soul, which is why *in semetipso suscepit animam*, 'he took a soul in himself' (**X**, 1) and why it is impossible to accept that he should have made that soul carnal. In the case of those heretics who teach that Christ came only to save the soul, the idea is even more absurd. What is more, if Christ came only to save our souls, Tertullian says, he would not have saved them since *nostra anima carnea non est*, 'our soul is not made of flesh' (**X**, 3). Tertullian's theological principle here is of the first importance: Christ did not come simply in order to save bodies – he also came to save souls and to do this he must have had a soul.

Tertullian bases this principle, however, on a firm distinction between the soul and the body, that is to say, on the anthropology of the *De anima: Si caro est anima, iam non est caro, sed anima. Si anima est caro, iam non anima est, sed caro. Certe perversissimum ut carnem nominantes animam animam intellegamus et animam significantes carnem interpretamur. Fides nominum salus est proprietatum,* 'If the flesh is soul, it is not flesh, but soul. If the soul is flesh, it is not soul, but flesh. Certainly it is extremely perverse, whenever we mention "flesh" to understand it as meaning "soul", and when we signify the soul to interpret this as referring to the flesh. Faithfulness to the right names is the guarantee of correct meanings' (**XIII**, 1). Here again we find that firm distinction between different levels of existence, that is, between *status*, which for Tertullian is always ultimately the principle on which any problem is to be resolved. Tertullian is, in this sense, radically opposed to any form of monism. It is, incidentally, worth noting that the thesis to which he is objecting here is Stoic rather than Platonist.

21. R. CANTALAMESSA, *La Cristologia di Tertulliano*, pp. 88–90.

Tertullian also challenges, however, the reason why his opponents wanted Christ to have been made visible in the flesh, namely so that man, who did not know his soul, impeded as it was by the veil of the flesh, *impedimentum carnis* (**XI**, 1), might know it. In his reply Tertullian argues as follows, once again going back to his own teaching about the soul. In order for man to need a revelation of what his soul is, he must be ignorant of it. This presupposes that he stands, as it were, outside his soul, whereas *totum quod sumus anima sit,* 'everything that we are the soul is' (**XII**, 2). This is one of Tertullian's most emphatic statements about the importance of the soul, and is the exact opposite to the view that 'the body and the man are equivalent'.[22]

That the soul does know itself is for Tertullian a vital principle, which he establishes as follows: 'The soul is endowed with sense (*sensualis*). There is in fact nothing animal without sense and no sense without a soul. To put it more strongly, sense is the soul of the soul. This soul, which enables all to feel, how can it not have perception of itself (*sensus sui*) from the beginning?' Every soul must also have a *notitia sui,* namely a knowledge of its *qualitatem.* All the more must man, being a rational animal, have a soul of the same order, namely a soul endowed with reason (*ratio*). 'But how could his soul be rational, if it did not know its own reason, because it did not know itself? The soul therefore does not need God to teach it about its author, its judge or its status'. (In this context, Tertullian is clearly referring to his earlier treatise, *De testimonio animae.*) What man needs to learn from Christ, he concludes, is not his *effigies,* but his salvation (**XII**, 6).

Here we have once more Tertullian's whole teaching about the soul, but given certain special emphases. The soul is above all *sensus,* sensory perception, and this perception plays a part at each level of human experience, but especially at the rational level, since the *flatus* or breath of which the soul is made is rational in quality. This means that it is bound to know itself in its rational quality, by virtue of an immediate perception and by virtue of the fact that it shares the same nature as itself. It is this *sensus communis* or common sense in the strict meaning of the term which

22. *Op. cit.,* p. 71.

enables it to know itself in its relationship with God, its author and its judge. Tertullian's conception in this case derives not from Plato's innate ideas, but rather from the Stoic theory of sensory perception, συναίοθησις. [23] What he stresses once again, however, is the fact that the *anima* is firmly established in its own order.

Tertullian also attributes the teaching that 'Christ took the form (*gestavit*) of an angel' to the same group of heretics. Under this head he lists a number of heterodox positions, with the objections to them. Did Christ make use of an angel to help him bring about our salvation? But he had no need of anyone to help him in that. Is he not called *angelus magni cogitatus*, 'the angel of mighty counsel' (Is. 9:5)? This simply means that he was one sent (*nuntius*) by the Father. Is he not identified with Gabriel or Michael? This is a false identification. What is more, in the parable of the Wicked Husbandmen, are not the first messengers sent angels, and does not the fact that he follows the servants in their office show that Christ was one of the servants? But, Tertullian replies, it is quite wrong to see an angel in the Son.

All these themes can be found in Judaeo-Christian teaching, especially the very common notion that Christ took on the form of an angel, either to conceal his divinity or to bring about the salvation of the angels (XIV, 2). Justin had already criticised the Judaeo-Christian practice of quoting Isaiah's phrase as signifying the angelic nature of Christ (*Dial.* LXXVI, 3). The practice of identifying Christ with Gabriel and Michael was, of course, extremely common in Judaeo-Christian apocalyptic texts. [24] He is identified with Michael, for example, in the *Shepherd of Hermas* and, in the Fifth Similitude of the same work, the messengers in the parable of the Wicked Husbandmen are also interpreted as angels (*Sim.* V), which is entirely in accordance with the kind of Judaeo-Christian interpretation of the parables to which Origen bears witness. Tertullian himself links these interpretations with Judaeo-Christianity and suggests that this view might have suited Ebion, *qui nudum hominem constituit Deum, plane prophetis aliquot*

23. Cf. TIBILETTI, *De testimonio animae*, pp. 31–46.
24. Cf. DANIELOU, *The Theology of Jewish Christianity*, pp. 119–132.

gloriosiorem ita ut in nonnullis angelum quoque dicatur, ut in aliquo Zacharia, 'who makes of God a mere man, though plainly rather more glorious than the prophets, so that in some he is also called an angel, as in the case of Zechariah' (XIV, 5).

This is proof that Tertullian was familiar with the Judaeo-Christian gnosis. It is also clear that he is alluding to the apocrypha, and we know that he was acquainted with the *Shepherd of Hermas*. The idea that Christ was an angel was still current in Judaeo-Christian teaching in the Africa of Tertullian's period, and the doctrine of the Son as the seventh angel is, as we have already seen, to be found in the *De centesima*. Commodian speaks of incarnations of angels preceding the incarnation of the Son, and of the Son taking the form of an angel. The *De carne Christi* bears witness to Tertullian's mistrust of this gnosis. Here, therefore, he is defining his own position in contrast not to heresy but to Judaeo-Christian tradition; and here again his primary concern is to place the soul of Christ at its proper level. Now, as we have already seen, the *anima* of man is of a different *qualitas* from that of an angel.

Tertullian spends little time discussing Alexander's syllogisms, but at the end of his treatise deals with an important question raised by this disciple of Valentinus. Alexander disputed the reality of Christ's flesh on the ground of the virgin birth, and Tertullian seeks to prove that it is, on the contrary, precisely the virginal conception of Christ which is the supreme evidence for the reality both of his manhood and of his divine nature. This brings him to the climax of his treatment. He has already placed the flesh of Christ at the level of the flesh and the soul of Christ at the level of the rational breath. He now confronts these two aspects of the substance of man with the third element constituting Christ's *persona*, namely the individual concrete reality of Christ, which is his divine substance.

The virginal conception is in fact the *nova nativitas*, the 'new birth by which man is born in God by the fact that God is born in man' (XVII, 3). The gesture of God's coming to man is, in other words, the necessary condition of man's becoming deified: 'The flesh born of the old seed is taken up without the old seed in order to be remade by a new, spiritual seed, free from old stains'

(XVII, 3). Christ had therefore to be brought into being in his humanity, not by the old seed, but exclusively by the power of God so that the one who was already the Son through his eternal birth from the Father should be, not only the son of man, but also the Son of God in his birth in time. This was also necessary so that a new humanity, 'free from old stains', might be initiated; and this is the meaning of the virginal conception.

He goes further, however, and claims that the flesh is remade 'by a new spiritual seed'. He expresses this idea in the categories outlined in the previous chapter, in particular, in this case, in the category of *substantia*, He is thus the first to state that there are two substances in Christ. Earlier in the treatise he had said: *Ita utriusque substantiae census hominem et Deum exhibuit*, 'Thus the origin of both realities displayed the man and the God' (V, 7). Now, in the context of his discussion of the virgin conception, he takes up the same point: 'If he had the flesh as well as the Spirit, when he speaks of the condition of the two substances (*duarum substantiarum*) which he bore within himself, he cannot seem to have been determined by the Spirit as his own, but by the flesh as not his own' (XVIII, 7). It is not, Tertullian is stressing, a case of the man and the God, but of one who at the same time has divine and human substance. This is another example of Tertullian's originality. Here by the rigour of his thinking he has achieved the earliest expression of the doctrine of the two natures 'assumed' in the one person of Christ.[25]

5. THE INTERMEDIATE STATE

The question of the intermediate state in which man finds himself between death and the resurrection takes on considerable importance in Tertullian. Unlike the gnostics, who believed that man was liberated from the body at the end of time, he is convinced that the *perfectio* is the resurrection of the body.[26] This leads him to emphasise the contrast between the intermediate

---

25. Cf. R. CANTALAMESSA, *op. cit.*, pp. 105–107.
26. Cf. PAOLO SINISCALCO, *I significati di 'restituere' in Tertulliano*, Turin, Académie des Sciences (1959).

state which follows death and the resurrection. In this, his view is more anthropological than that of Irenaeus, who stresses that the first resurrection, that of the millennium, is no more than one stage. Although all his ideas are borrowed from Scripture and his predecessors, Tertullian arranges them in a more systematic way and derives from them a philosophical anthropology. The tendency which we see emerging here was to remain that of Western eschatology.

The first question that Tertullian considers is the localisation of the abode of the souls after death.[27] He does not use such words as *mansio, receptaculum* or *locus* for this dwelling-place, but prefers *inferi*, 'lower regions', which is in accordance with his emphatic conviction that the souls lived in the underworld. The apologists in general did not define the location of this abode. Tertullian, on the other hand, stressed that the dwelling-place of departed souls was under the earth because he was reacting against gnosticism. Characteristically, too, he describes their abode in the *inferi* quite systematically, distinguishing between the dwellings of the saved and of the damned. For the latter the *inferi* are already a place of punishment, although this is not the same as gehenna, the great abyss into which they are to be thrown after the resurrection. The same view is expressed by Hippolytus, but, since it is met with so frequently in all apocalyptic writing, it is not necessary to say that Tertullian influenced Hippolytus in this case.

Of the saved, some dwell in the abode of sinners. The word *carcer*, 'prison', may in fact denote either the place of the damned or that of the sinners. It comes from Scripture, in particular from the allegorical exegesis of Jesus' words about the debtor who is thrown into prison until he has paid the last farthing (Lk. 12:58–59). The first author to give these words an eschatological meaning was apparently Carpocrates; and it is in attacking him that Irenaeus and Tertullian take them over for their own purposes. For Tertullian, paying 'to the last farthing' refers to the debt which has to be paid in the *inferi* by the souls who are ultimately destined to be saved, so that these lower regions would

27. Cf. H. FINE, *Die Terminologie der Jenseitsvorstellungen bei Tertullian*, Bonn, 1958.

seem to be equivalent to purgatory. This, however, is expressed in the form of a delay in resurrection to the millennial kingdom.

To describe the dwelling-place of the just, Tertullian makes use of the term 'Abraham's bosom', reserving it for the intermediate state, in which it points to a place in the *inferi*. Origen, on the other hand, uses it for the place of ultimate blessedness, so that, for him, it is the same as 'heaven'. The sense in which it was used by Origen was, of course, the one which prevailed. Tertullian's position in this question, however, was linked to his controversy with Marcion and the details contributed by him to eschatology are determined by polemical considerations. He makes use of traditional data, but organizes them into his own system. A point worth noting is that he connects the phrase 'Abraham's bosom' with the idea of a common meal as a symbol of consolation and well-being.

Tertullian also discusses a second question, that of the state of the souls of the just. In his early writings, notably in the *De testimonio animae,* he sees this simply as a state of waiting, on the grounds that reward or punishment presuppose sensory experience, and that this is possible only through the resurrection of the body.[28] As we have already seen, however, Tertullian's anthropology did not remain static and his theory that the soul possessed not only intellectual, but also sensory faculties led him to say, in the *De anima,* that reward or punishment could begin from the moment of death onwards (LVIII, 2). The damned are already punished in this state, whereas the sinners begin their expiation. The just, on the other hand, are in a state of happiness, for which Tertullian uses a number of terms.

The first of these is *solatium,* which denotes consolation or comfort, with the added nuances of foretaste and reward. A second term used by Tertullian is *requies,* rest. In the Septuagint, the New Testament and the earliest Christian literature, the theme of God's rest on the seventh day and that of the rest of the dead are combined in such a way that the word *requies* has an eschatological meaning. Tertullian, however, seems to have been the first Christian author to apply this word specifically to the

28. Cf. WASZINK, *op. cit.,* p. 588.

state of the souls of the just before the resurrection. The word is later used in this sense by Cyprian, in the African inscriptions, in Spain, and finally in Rome.

Tertullian also uses a third word, *refrigerium*, which was applied, in secular usage, not simply, as Parrot has suggested, to the idea of a cool drink, but also to everything covered by rest and refreshment, including bathing, meals and relaxation in games. The eschatological use of this word apparently derives from Lk. 16:24, a passage which seems to have been definitive for representations of the eschatological state in art. The gnostics used the term *locus refrigerii* to describe the state of blessedness in the *pleroma*, and Irenaeus to describe life after the resurrection. In Tertullian it may denote either the intermediate state or eternal life. In the former sense it is equivalent to 'Abraham's bosom'. It was by way of Tertullian that it passed into the *Vetus Latina*, Cyprian, the liturgy, and finally the inscriptions.[29]

A fourth term employed by Tertullian, *in caelis*, always denotes not the intermediate state, but eschatological blessedness. It seems, therefore, that his thought is absolutely consistent in the matter of locating the intermediate state in the underworld, thus systematising the line taken by Justin and Irenaeus. In the case of all three writers this position seems to be connected with the dispute with gnosticism and especially with Marcion. For the majority of Christians at that time, however, the intermediate state could just as well be in heaven as in the *inferi*. This is certainly true of the inscriptions. From the time of Cyprian onwards it came to be located in heaven, and this gradually became the generally accepted view.[30]

There is, however, one important exception to the general rule to be found in Tertullian's teaching, in that he believes that the souls of the martyrs dwelt, not in the lower regions, but in

29. In *Pass. Perp.* VIII, 1 the term clearly goes back to pagan representations, although I am not convinced that those representations in which living water appears denote the eschatological *refrigerium*, as suggested by FINE, *op. cit.*, p. 189.
30. For this reason, it is not possible to agree with STUIBER, who believes that it was generally thought until the fourth century in circles influenced by gnosticism that the intermediate state was situated in the *inferi*.

paradise. The practice of situating paradise in the third or fourth heaven goes back to the apocalyptic representations.[31] The same idea is also found in the writings of Paul, the gnostics and Origen. Irenaeus, on the other hand, believed that, before the resurrection, paradise was situated in the garden of Eden, in other words, on earth, and that it was to this place that Elijah and Enoch, for example, were translated.[32] After the second resurrection, however, paradise was, in Irenaeus' opinion, to become one of the three celestial dwelling-places, between heaven and the city.[33] This explains why for Irenaeus the martyrs are in heaven but not yet in paradise.

Like Irenaeus, Tertullian also makes a distinction between the garden of Eden on earth, the abode of Adam and Eve before the fall, and paradise, identified with the heaven which is to be the abode of the just after the resurrection. This concept was to persist in western theology. It is found in the *Passio Perpetuae* and in the writings of Cyprian, despite what Karl Rahner has said. Tertullian's distinctive teaching is that the martyrs were admitted to the eschatological paradise in heaven immediately after their death. Cyprian, on the other hand, teaches that all the saints could be admitted to this paradise when they died. Another aspect of Tertullian's teaching is that it sees equivalents in Semitic and Hellenistic imagery, a clear example of this being the assimilation of the Elysian Fields to the biblical paradise.[34] On the other hand, Tertullian reacts strongly against the excessively luxuriant descriptions favoured by the Judaeo-Christians.

Tertullian is original in taking ideas of a general kind from earlier eschatological writings and using them to express his own, much stricter views. In other words, he takes a mythical theology and changes it into a rational theology. This is, of course, clearly in accordance with his own systematic and logical way of thinking. Some of his ideas were not accepted by later Christians, a notable example being his situation of the intermediate state in

31. J. DANIELOU, *Primitive Christian Symbols*, Paris, 1961, pp. 25–27.
32. FINE, *op. cit.*, p. 221.
33. E. PETERSON, *Frühkirche, Judentum, Gnosis*, p. 291.
34. If Kroymann's emendation is accepted, then there is also a possible allusion, in the *De corona* XV, 7, to the Platonic heavenly 'field'.

the *inferi*. Others, however, were to become part of the common teaching of the Church. He also had a considerable influence on Christian vocabulary, words such as *requies* and *refrigerium* undoubtedly owing their universal adoption to him.

6. THE RESURRECTION OF THE DEAD

Both chronologically and thematically, the last of Tertullian's treatises is the *De resurrectione*. The author's thought is basically the same in this work as in those that we have previously considered, and we shall analyse it with the method rather than with the content in mind, despite the fact that, as regards the latter, it is a work of incomparable value. One is conscious, in approaching this treatise, that Tertullian is applying his method with great mastery. Although many of the terms that we have already encountered are employed again in the *De resurrectione,* he handles them with more confidence than ever. It is this which gives the treatise its exceptional character, making it, in my own view, not only his masterpiece, but that of his works which has the most astonishing relevance today.

The background to the treatise has been well described by Siniscalco.[35] It presupposes the criticisms, endlessly repeated by pagan authors as to the impossibility of the resurrection of the body. The work is, however, more than simply a reply to pagan objections; it is also a polemic against the Marcionites and the gnostics. Siniscalco has demonstrated that Tertullian's lengthy commentary on certain Pauline texts,[36] and his emphasis on the fact that the good God and the just God are one and the same, are clearly directed against the former. As regards the latter, the proof that Tertullian had the gnostics in mind has been supplied by the discovery at Nag Hammadi of the so-called *Letter to Rheginos.* The editors of this letter noticed at once that it provided the context of the *De resurrectione* and Siniscalco has observed that the same applies to the treatise on the resurrection attributed to Justin, although, as Pierre Prigent has pointed out, this treatise

35. *Ricerche sul 'De resurrectione' di Tertulliano,* pp. 15–68.
36. *Op. cit.,* pp. 58–61.

could not have been written by Justin. It dates back to the end of the second century and was without doubt used by Tertullian. Finally, there is the problem of the *De resurrectione* attributed to Athenagoras. This, however, clearly belongs to a very different intellectual sphere.[37]

Some of the characteristic features of Tertullian's treatise can be explained by the gnostic background against which it was written. One example of this is the use of the term 'resurrection of the flesh', which, as Siniscalco has pointed out, is not biblical in origin. Nor was it invented by Tertullian himself, since Pseudo-Justin employs it frequently. Siniscalco has shown that the word 'flesh' in this context does not mean man in his wretchedness nor the whole living human being, but the natural body.[38] The context in which the expression emerged was anti-gnostic,[39] and it was to find its way into the credal formulas.[40] It was, moreover, at the end of the second century that we first find the insistence on the identity of the resurrected body with the body of flesh,[41] an affirmation made in the context of criticisms of the gnostic teachers.[42] As the *Letter to Rheginos* shows, the gnostics regarded the resurrection as something that had already been brought about by conversion to gnosis. They also believed that the eschatological resurrection would take place in bodies of a different nature.[43] This affirmation of the physical identity of the resurrection body and of the body of flesh had been made by Pseudo-Justin before Tertullian's time, and was to be repeated by Methodius of Olympus and Gregory of Nyssa in answer to Origen.

---

37. R. M. Grant has suggested that this work dates back to the end of the third century. I myself have drawn attention to certain striking similarities which it has with the treatise on the ἄωροι written by Gregory of Nyssa, both in its form and in its basis: 'Le traité sur les enfants morts prématurément de Grégoire de Nysse', *VC*, 20 (1966), pp. 159–182. We may therefore conclude that it dates back to the fourth century.
38. P. SINISCALCO, *op. cit.*, p. 110.
39. *Op. cit.*, p. 106, 105.
40. *Op. cit.*, p. 107.
41. *Op. cit.*, p. 166.
42. *Op. cit.*, p. 162.
43. *Op. cit.*, pp. 45–49.

The introduction to the treatise is followed by a number of preliminary arguments, the first of which starts from the premiss that the world belongs to God. This argument, which had already been developed by Pseudo-Justin in his *De resurrectione*, implies that the world is God's creation (*De res.* XI). It is clear that God is able to 'remake what he has already made, since it is more difficult to make than to remake, to commence than to recommence. You may therefore believe that it is easier to restore the flesh than to institute it'. Underlying this is the further assumption that God the creator and God the saviour are the same – it is the same God who fashioned Adam in the beginning and who can refashion him. Siniscalco points out how deftly Tertullian links together this argument and various traditional examples drawn from nature: 'Consider the examples of God's power. The day dies with the night and is everywhere buried in darkness. The beauty of the world goes into mourning, the whole of reality becomes gloomy and everything is extinguished, falls silent and goes to sleep (*sordent, silent, stupent cuncta*). Yet the same light comes to life again throughout the whole world in its integrity and totality and with its beauty, its adornment and its sun. The whole of this cyclical order of things bears witness to the resurrection of the dead' (*De res.* XIV). Tertullian is here arguing that the revelation of God through the order of nature bears witness to the fact that God can also manifest himself through historical events.

Tertullian's second argument is concerned with the dignity of the flesh. Here, he touches on a weakness in his adversaries' argument, since all of them, both the gnostics and the Platonists, scorned the flesh. God, however, is less scornful than they, Tertullian maintains, since he created it, and those who scorn the flesh are scorning God's creation. After having created the flesh, God would surely not cast it aside? Tertullian rightly remarks, in one of those brilliant phrases typical of him: *Caro salutis est cardo,* 'The flesh is the hinge of salvation' (*De res.* VIII). And this is true. God proves the goodness of the flesh because it is his work, and the flesh also proves the goodness of God because, if man's existence were simply *caro foenum*, 'flesh that is grass', destined only to be cast into oblivion, the world could surely not be the work

of a good God. Tertullian concludes his argument by saying that
God keeps this same flesh in reserve in the store-rooms with the
intention of using it again at the resurrection, thus showing that a
good God is revealed in the resurrection of the flesh, whereas
contempt for the flesh would necessarily argue an irrational God.
Such a God would merit only rejection.

Before Tertullian, Pseudo-Justin had already written ironically
on this point: 'We must argue with those who say that, although
the flesh is entirely the work of a good God and is regarded by
him as being above everything, for all that it does not possess the
promise of resurrection. Would it not be absurd for the one who
made the flesh according to such a great plan, flesh which is
regarded as being above everything, to scorn it to the extent of
casting it back into oblivion?' (*De res.* VIII). Tertullian takes up
this argument with his own peculiar genius: 'God fashioned this
flesh with his hands in his own image. He animated it with his
breath in the likeness of his own vitality. He established it in
order to inhabit, cultivate and have mastery over all his work. He
reclothed it with his sacraments and his teachings. How can
he not raise up again something which is by so many titles his
own possession? It is impossible that God should cast away into
eternal destruction the work of his own hands, the product of his
genius, the sister of his Christ' (*De res.* IX). Here again, the
parallel between the creation of Adam and the resurrection of
the dead controls the development of the argument, in this case
to demonstrate not so much the power of God as the great
importance of the flesh.

Tertullian's third justification of the resurrection of the flesh is
a reply to the objection raised by those who claimed that, since
sin and virtue both originated exclusively in the soul, only the
soul ought to be judged. He takes this opportunity to stress the
inseparable unity of the soul and the body. The soul, he says,
carries out all its activities through the body and is able to use its
senses only through the body (*De res.* VII, 3). 'The word itself,'
Tertullian claims, 'is an organ of the flesh' (VII, 3), and further,
'Whatever goes on in the heart is the activity of the soul in the
flesh, with the flesh and through the flesh' (XV, 3). Tertullian
thus emphasises that the same applies to the Christian sacraments:
Caro abluitur, ut anima emaculetur; caro unguitur, ut anima consecretur;

. . . *caro corpore et sanguine Christi vescitur, ut anima de Deo saginetur,*
'The flesh is washed that the soul may be cleansed; the flesh is
anointed that the soul may be consecrated; . . . the flesh feeds on
the body and the blood of Christ that the soul may be nourished
on God' (VIII, 3).

Is what Tertullian means by all this that the resurrection of the
flesh is necessary in order that the soul should receive either
tormentum or *refrigerium* (XVII, 1)? The *simpliciores* might believe
this, but this is not what Tertullian himself thinks. As we have
already seen, the soul does not, in Tertullian's opinion, need the
flesh in order to be able to suffer or to find happiness: 'We
believe that the soul is corporeal and we have demonstrated this
in the book devoted to it' (XVII, 2). 'The soul has a special kind
of solidity (*soliditas*) which enables it, even before the resurrection, when it is deprived of the body, to be unhappy or happy in
the lower regions.' This is one of the points on which Tertullian
makes his position clear in the *De anima*. It does not mean,
however, that the body does not share in the punishment or the
reward experienced at the resurrection, since the flesh has been
the instrument of sin or faithfulness (XVII, 6–8; cf. XXXIII,
9–10).

Tertullian therefore presents us with three justifications of the
argument for the resurrection of the flesh – the dignity of the
flesh, God's power, and the connection between the soul and the
flesh. There remains, however, the question of fact. Is this in-
credible assertion really to be found in Scripture? Resurrection is
possible, but does it really happen? Tertullian here confronts the
fundamental argument of the gnostics as presented in the treatise
discovered at Nag Hammadi. This gnostic thesis is that the scriptural texts on the resurrection ought to be interpreted symbolically. As Tertullian himself says: 'Having adopted a very sublime
form of prophetic language, which is most of the time allegorical
and figurative, they always interpret the resurrection of the dead,
even though it is proclaimed in an obvious way, in an imaginary
sense, claiming that death itself should be understood in a
spiritual sense. In reality, this is not death in the ordinary sense of
the word, that is, the separation of the soul from the body, but
ignorance of God' (XIX, 2–3).

Tertullian gives, in this text, an extremely accurate description of the heresy he is attacking. It contains two basic statements. The first is that the resurrection ought to take place at once: it is a passing from ignorance to knowledge, in other words, conversion to gnosticism. It also implies, however, that 'the soul's leaving the tomb at death is resurrection, because the tomb is the world and the world is the abode of the dead, that is, of those who do not know God. The soul's leaving the body is also resurrection, since the body keeps the soul enclosed in the manner of a tomb in the death of the life of this world' (XIX, 7). If this text is compared with the text of the Nag Hammadi treatise, the accuracy of Tertullian's description of the gnostic teaching is seen to be remarkable.

In his reply to this question, Tertullian acknowledges that some of the prophecies have to be interpreted spiritually and criticises the literal interpretation practised by Jewish exegetes (XXVI, 1–14). Other texts, however, those bearing on essential points, have to be interpreted literally. As examples he cites Is. 7:14 (the sign of the virgin with child) and Is. 8:4 (the victory of the child over the power of Damascus). Both these texts are, as we have already seen, to be found among his *testimonia*. The first, which is a prophecy of the virginal conception, is to be interpreted in the literal sense, whereas the second should be interpreted spiritually (XX, 3). Another example of special interest is Ezekiel's prophecy of the valley full of dry bones which come back to life (Ezk. 37). Although Tertullian agrees that this prophecy can be interpreted of the resurrection of the Jewish people, he also emphasises that it implies the reality of a resurrection of the body. This interpretation (*De res.* XXIX–XXXIII) is particularly striking.

In the New Testament, on the other hand, it is true that the resurrection is presented as having already taken place. First, however, Tertullian points out that this is not the resurrection as described in gnostic teaching. According to Paul, it consists in the fact that 'Whereas we were living in evil, we have been buried with Christ in baptism and raised in him by faith in the power of the God who raised him from the dead' (XXIII, 1). For all that, however, Scripture does not deny the eschatological resurrection of the body: 'Just as it presents us as dead spiritually, while yet acknowledging that we shall one day die corporeally, so when it declares still more that we are raised spiritually, no more does it deny that we shall rise again corporeally' (**XXXIII**, 2).

Tertullian goes on to explain a number of New Testament texts concerning man. The interest of his exegesis lies in the fact that he brings in the principles of his anthropology in order to interpret them correctly (**XXXIII**, 10). His opponents interpreted the text of 2 Co. 4:16, 'Though this outward man of ours may be falling into decay, the inward man is renewed day by day', of the destruction of the body and the salvation of the soul. Tertullian, on the other hand, observes that 'the inward man does not mean *animam* so much as *mentem* and *animum,* that is, not the *substantia* itself, but the *saporem substantiae'.* In other words the text does not imply a contrast between the soul and the flesh, but rather progress in faith and virtue by the action (*suggestum*) of the Spirit. This progress does not, however, simply concern the soul, since it is in its efficacy in the *mens* and the *animus* that the Spirit is present, not in the substance. Now, these activities are carried out by the body as intermediary (**XLVI**, 13). The phrase, the 'inward man' can therefore just as well be taken as including the flesh (**XL**, 4–5), for it relates to the whole man, which is like a 'buckle' (*fibula*), hooking together two substances (**XL**, 3; cf. also XLVI, 13).

Another contrast made by Tertullian is that between the old and the new man. Here again, some understood the old man as the body and the new man as the soul. Tertullian begins by criticizing this view from a simple anthropological standpoint. If a choice had to be made, he argues, the soul would have to be given priority. In fact, however, the soul and the body, which in man are born simultaneously, appeared almost simultaneously in the beginning: *Quantulum enim temporis inter manum Dei et adflatum?* 'For how little space of time is there between the hand and the breath of God?'. Here too, there is no conflict between substances: 'We believe that the old and the new in man derive from a moral and not a substantial difference' (**XLV**, 15). He must, Tertullian insists, 'strip himself not of *corpulentia,* the body aspect, but of *vitiosa disciplina,* wrong training' (**XLV**, 16).

Paul's text, 'Flesh and blood cannot inherit the kingdom of God' (1 Co. 15:50) also provides the point of departure for a consideration of the nature of the body and the soul and of their union. Tertullian points out in this case too that 'flesh and blood' do not signify the substance of the body, but man's evil works (XLIX, 11). What is more, this is not a direct reference to the resurrection, but a question of the 'kingdom', which, for Tertullian, is the millennium. Entry into the kingdom implies the first resurrection, that of the just alone. When Paul speaks in this context of flesh and blood not entering the kingdom, he is speaking of flesh and blood *nomine culpae, non substantiae,* under the heading of guilt rather than of substance. This does not mean, however, that the flesh and blood of those who have not yet risen again will not be raised *nomine formae* at the time of the general resurrection. It is also true in another sense that 'flesh and blood, in the sense of substance, cannot enter the kingdom on their own, apart from the Spirit' (L, 4). Finally, how can our flesh and blood, still in the sense of substance, Tertullian asks, 'not inherit incorruptibility, when Christ has already introduced his flesh and blood into heaven as an earnest of ours' (LI, 4).

It will be seen that all these interpretations are controlled by the fundamental distinctions of Tertullian's anthropology. Man is, in his view, composed of two substances – the body, which is fashioned from mud, and the soul, which is made of breath. The soul is active in sensory and spiritual perception, but these activities do not take place except through the body, and they can therefore be traced to the flesh as well as to the soul. In both his substances, moreover, man is called to be transfigured by the Spirit. It is this Spirit which, in this life, gives rise in the *mens,* by an operation common to both the body and the soul, to spiritual actions, and which, in the messianic kingdom, bestows incorruptibility on the two substances of which man is composed. Everything depends on the rigour with which Tertullian makes a radical distinction between the two substances, and yet equally radically unites their activities, insisting that the soul can do nothing without the body. He concludes that, as the Spirit is present in all these activities, the body and the soul are always transfigured together by the Spirit.

We may conclude this section on Tertullian's teaching about the resurrection by examining briefly his interpretation of another of Paul's texts: 'The first Adam became a living soul; but the second Adam has become a life-giving Spirit' (1 Co. 15:45). In the opinion of his opponents, this 'living soul' was a *corpus animale* a 'living body'. In his reply Tertullian goes back to the account of the creation. Man was first made as a body, and the body was then animated by the soul, only so becoming a *corpus animale*. Similarly at the resurrection, he argues, the body will be reunited first with the soul and then with the Spirit. The term *corpus animale,* however, is not one that can be suitably applied to the soul. The soul certainly is a body – in the sense in which Tertullian uses the word – but it is not a *corpus animatum,* or 'animated body'. How, he asks, would it be animated, since it is itself soul? A better term would be *corpus animans,* an 'animating body'. If, therefore, the first man is called a 'living soul' and the second a 'life-giving Spirit', this must, in Tertullian's opinion, mean that, if both were flesh, the first is characterised by the fact that his flesh had been animated, whereas the second is characterised by the fact that his flesh was spiritualised, without prejudice to the fact that the flesh of the second was also animated (LIII, 16).

In this chapter we have seen the mastery with which Tertullian uses his ideas, and, in conclusion, it is important to try to define them. In the first place, he is writing against certain heterodox tendencies in their most up-to-date form, as revealed in the writings, for example, of Hermogenes, Apelles and Alexander, and in the *De resurrectione* of the gnostics. His fundamental criticism of these authors and tendencies is that they lack a sound anthropology and that, as a consequence, they confuse, in their teaching, what goes back to man's structure – his body and soul – and what comes from his vocation – nature and Spirit. Tertullian therefore has to adopt an attitude towards the work of the pagan philosophers, whom he judges with considerable freedom, and criticises all alike whenever he detects errors in their teaching. When the need arises, he makes free use of their doctrines, but he does not identify himself with any of the current philosophical systems. It would be quite wrong to regard him, for example, as a Stoic. Novatian was to prove much more truly stamped with the imprint of the Stoa.

So far as Christian tradition is concerned, Tertullian distinguishes between its various elements. He dissociates himself from the teachings of Judaeo-Christianity, especially its angelology; and, although he is not ignorant of the writings of the Greek Apologists, he relies very little on their theology. By contrast he is greatly indebted to the Asiatic tradition of Melito and Irenaeus, to such an extent, indeed, that he follows them very nearly in strict continuity. It is all the more interesting, therefore, to note that he sets himself to complete their teaching by defining more fully than they had done the nature of the soul. In this task, he also relies on the teaching of Plato in his attempt to avoid a devaluation of the soul, just as he relied on the Stoics in order to give proper emphasis to the body.

The essential elements in his thought can be summarised as falling under two headings. On the one hand, he depends to a very great extent on Scripture and tradition. Argument from Scripture plays a very important part in all his treatises, although his interpretation of Scripture is very free. He defends the spiritual interpretation of the prophecies, for example, against the materialist approach of the Jews. Equally, however, he defends their historical sense against the allegorism of the Valentinians. He interprets the *Genesis* accounts in a literal sense, but he does not reject the typological exegeses inherited from tradition. In the *De praescriptione* especially, he leans heavily on tradition in attacking the innovations introduced by the heretics, but he also leaves room for charismatic gifts in his Montanist period.

The second of these elements is his use of certain categories, less in order to formulate a system than to have at his disposal certain logical means which allow him to classify and organise the various data put before him. It is in his use of these categories that Tertullian's originality is most clearly revealed. They are in great measure his own creation, or at least the use he makes of them is his own. They enable him to establish quite precisely the mutual relations of the realities with which he is confronted. I have already compared him to Pascal, and in this respect he is as impossible to classify as Pascal. He cannot be included in any theological movement, but he is a source and standard to which Latin theology never ceased to have recourse.

CHAPTER SIXTEEN

THE TWO CITIES

THE religion of Rome was above all social and juridical, its essential aim being to maintain the *pax deorum* as the necessary guarantee of success in whatever was undertaken both by individuals and by the city as a whole.[1] In the Latin world, Christianity for its part also displayed more particularly its social aspect, that of an institution founded in its turn on religion, and expressed primarily in loyalty to a society. From the start, therefore, conflict between the two societies was inevitable. Christians were to interpret this conflict, in the light of Jewish apocalyptic teaching as extended by Christianity, as one between the forces of evil and the act of God in Christ. It was the demons who reigned over the pagan city, and who stirred it up against the Church, which they saw as a threat to their power.

1. IDOLATRY AND DEMONOLOGY

Demonology formed part of both Greek and Latin philosophy, especially of Platonism. The δαίμονες were spirits, lower than the gods but intermediate between them and men. Both Xenocrates in the fourth century B.C. and Plutarch in the first century A.D. had given them an important place. This demonology was taken up by the Christian apologists, who thought of the δαίμονες, however, as evil and identified them with the fallen angels, spoken of in *I Enoch*.

This pagan demonology was also to be found in the Latin world, where it had been elaborately developed by Apuleius, in whose work it formed an essential theme. The earliest Latin

1. MICHEL MESLIN, *Pour une science des religions,* p. 25.

Christian authors, Minucius Felix, Tertullian and Cyprian in particular, were to adapt Apuleius' demonology in the same way
that Athenagoras adapted that of Maximus of Tyre.

It is in the *Octavius* of Minucius Felix that this demonology is
most fully worked out. Tertullian, Cyprian and Lactantius were
content to take it over for the most part as it stood, making additions only in detail. Minucius is concerned to expose the *fontem
ipsum erroris et pravitatis,* 'the true source of error and perversity'
(*Oct.* XXVI, 7), which is idolatry. This source, Minucius'
believes, is to be found in the demons. He identifies the demons
of the pagan world with the fallen angels of *I Enoch,* beginning
by reminding his readers of the existence of demonic beings:
'There exist unclean and wandering spirits (*spiritus*) whose
heavenly vigour (*caelesti vigore*) has been overlaid by earthly soils
and lusts. These spirits, burdened and steeped in vices, have lost
the simplicity of their original substances; as some consolation for
their own calamity, these lost spirits cease not to conspire for
others' loss, to deprave them with their own depravity and, under the alienation of depraved and heathen superstitions, to
separate them from God' (XXVI, 8). The theme in *I Enoch* of the
angels who were seduced by women and, having fallen from
heaven, took their revenge by trying to persuade men to join
them in their apostasy is here reproduced in classical language by
Minucius.

He continues by pointing out that the pagans also worship
these fallen angels, although they call them demons: 'Such spirits
(*spiritus*) are recognised as "demons" (*daemonas*) by the poets, are
discussed by the philosophers and were known to Socrates, who,
at the instigation and will of his attendant demon, declined or
pursued certain courses of action' (XXVI, 9). He goes on to mention the magi who knew the demons (*daemonas*) and 'by their aid
perform their magical tricks . . . making things visible that are
not or things that are, invisible' (XXVI, 10). He names one
magician explicitly, that is, Hostanes, who 'renders due homage
to the true God; angels, he tells us – ministers and messengers of
God – attend the throne of God and stand by to render worship
. . . He has borne witness also to demons of the earth, ranging to
and fro, the enemies of mankind' (XXVI, 11).

Minucius then turns to Plato: 'Does not Plato too, who accounted it a hard matter (*negotium*) to find out God, find it no hard matter (*sine negotio*) to tell of angels and demons? In his *Symposium*, is he not at pains to define their nature? He will have it that there is a substance intermediate between mortal and immortal, that is, between body and spirit (*substantiam inter mortalem immortalemque, id est inter corpus et spiritum mediam*), compounded of an admixture of earthly weight and heavenly lightness (*terreni ponderis et caelestis levitatis*), out of which he tells us love is fashioned and glides into the hearts of men and stirs their senses, shapes affections and instils the ardour of desire' (**XXVI**, 12).

At this point, Minucius introduces a short account of pagan demonology, which is of considerable interest and provides confirmation of his dependence on secular culture. He gives the main sources of this demonology. First of all, there are the poets – and here (**XXVI**, 9) the reference is clearly to Homer and Hesiod [2] and perhaps also to Virgil – and then the philosophers, among whom Plato is the most important. Minucius here alludes to Socrates' 'attendant demon' and it is well known that Apuleius wrote a treatise on this subject. It is not certain that Minucius is dependent on Apuleius in this respect, but the subject was in the air at the time. He then refers to the *Timaeus* (28d; 40 d–e) and the distinction between the good angels and the evil demons, which is basically Plutarch's interpretation of the text.

Finally, he mentions the *Symposium* ('Banquet') and the theme of Eros, which point clearly to his use of Plato as a source. Plato says that the δαιμόνιον is 'between mortal and immortal' (*Conv.* 202 d), which is, as we have seen, the same formula that Minucius uses. It would also seem, however, that Minucius draws on Apuleius in his commentary, for the latter writes: 'The bodies of the demons have a little weight (*ponderis*), which prevents them from climbing to the heights, and a little lightness (*levitatis*), which makes it impossible for them to go down into the depths' (*Deo Socr.* 9). He also calls them *mediae* (*ibid.* 6) and *commixta* (*ibid.* 9) and these precise words are found in Minucius' text, so that it would certainly seem as though he was familiar with

2. Cf. PELLEGRINO, p. 202.

Apuleius' treatise. It is also clear that his interpretation of Plato is that of Middle Platonism. What is more, in the phrase *inter corpus et spiritum* (XXVI, 12), *spiritus* is apparently the equivalent of Plato's Θεῖον (*Conv.* 202e), and is different from the *spiritus* as applied to demons.[3] At the end of this passage, Minucius speaks of *amor* and this is inspired by the theme of Eros in the *Symposium* of Plato (195e–196a).

Finally, Minucius speaks of the magi. He first refers in general terms to their practice of magic, the activity of demons in magic being a commonplace of the Apologists (cf., e.g., Justin, I *Apol.* XIV, 1).[4] More particularly characteristic of Minucius is his allusion to Hostanes, who, Minucius claims, knew the true God, the good angels 'attending the throne of God' in the heavenly liturgy and the evil demons 'of the earth, ranging to and fro, the enemies of mankind'. Apuleius also mentions Hostanes in his *Apol.* 90 and Minucius may have drawn on him in this passage on magic. It is certain that he had a positive appreciation of him.[5]

In the *Quod idola non sint*, Cyprian reproduced Minucius' account verbatim though in an abridged form and with certain modifications. Thus, on the subject of the magi, he attributes to the demons their power to perform 'pernicious or ridiculous actions' (*Idol.* 6), thus striking a more severe note than Minucius. He also ascribes to Hostanes the teaching that 'the form of the true God cannot be seen', that is, a doctrine of the spiritual and transcendent nature of God, and observes that both Plato and Hostanes distinguish in this way between the true God and the good or evil angels, which is an exact comment on Minucius' statement in this context. Finally, he mentions Hermes Trismegistos, saying that the latter speaks of one God, whom he calls 'incomprehensible and inestimable'. This illustrates the interest in the hermetic literature in the middle of the third century. Lactantius in particular drew heavily on these writings.

Before Cyprian, Tertullian had already taken up Minucius' theme, but, as always, with great independence of mind.

---

3. Cf. R. BERGE, *Exegetische Bemerkungen zur Dämonenauffassung des M. Minucius Felix,* pp. 9–23. Apuleius contrasts *terrea* and *aetheria.*
4. Cf. PELLEGRINO, *op. cit.,* p. 203.
5. Cf. BIDEZ, *Les mages hellénisés,* I, pp. 180, 186; II, pp. 275, 285–290.

Whereas Minucius is descriptive in his approach, Tertullian treats it logically. He first posits the existence of angels: *Dicimus esse substantias quasdem spiritales*, 'We say there are certain spiritual natures' (*Apol.* XXII, 1), explaining that the pagans too acknowledged their existence. The philosophers know of the demons (*daemones*) – here, in line with his own teaching about guardian angels and demons (*De anim.* XIV), he mentions Socrates' *daemon*, which he regards as an evil influence – as do the poets (*omnes sciunt poetae*, 'All the poets know of them', *Apol.* XXII, 2). Next, in keeping with what he says in his *De testimonio animae* (III, 2), he refers to popular testimony. This is followed by a further account of Plato's witness to the angels and that of the magi to both angels and demons. Finally, he deals with the scriptural teaching about the fall of the angels.

Whereas Minucius provides as it were a collection of pagan views concerning the angels, Tertullian constructs a miniature treatise containing his own ideas such as the testimony of the soul, the presence of the demon from the time of birth and the severe sentence passed on the demons. He deals in order with 'demons' in general, giving a pejorative meaning to the word, in the case both of Socrates and of the poets, and of the demons of popular belief. He then goes on to treat of good angels and the fact that both Plato and the magi recognise their existence as well as that of evil angels or demons. He concludes by discussing the theme of the origin of the evil angels, appealing to Scripture to show that they are good angels who have fallen. It is therefore quite clear that Tertullian makes use, in a highly personal way, of Minucius' doxography.

Turning again to Minucius, we find that after establishing the nature and existence of demons he devotes a chapter to proving that they are the source of idolatry. He deals first with the oracles: 'These unclean spirits', he writes, 'find a lurking place under statues and consecrated images and by their breath exercise influence as of a present god; at one while they inspire prophets (*dum inspirant vatibus*), at another they haunt temples, at another animate the fibres of the entrails, govern the flight of birds, determine lots and are the authors of oracles mostly wrapped in falsehood' (*Oct.* XXVII, 1). These are precisely the same as the activities which Apuleius, following Plato, attributes to the demons: the examination of entrails, the flight of birds, the drawing of lots and the inspiration of soothsayers (*vatibus inspirandis*) (*De Deo Socr.* 6).

Minucius also describes another means used by the demons to persuade people to worship them – they cause troubles, such as diseases, and, having cured them, simply by withdrawing, persuade men to believe that they are the healers (*Oct.* XXVII). Minucius may have drawn here on Tatian (*Orat.* 16, 1). One is reminded in this context of the importance at this period of the cult of Aesculapius, to which Aelius Aristides bears witness. The idea that the demons become fat from the smoke of sacrifices was originally pagan and it is clear that Minucius was indebted to paganism in his teaching about the demons. He may also have taken the idea that demons were responsible for the physical convulsions of epileptics and of the priests in certain pagan cults from Apuleius (*Met.* VIII, 27). There are also certain marvels which Minucius attributes to demons: 'Jupiter by a dream claiming the renewal of his games; Castor and Pollux being seen with their horses, and the bark towed by a matron's girdle' (XXVII, 4). It should be noted here that the appearance of the Dioscuri is also mentioned by Maximus of Tyre.

Minucius argues that the proof of demonic activity in all these cases is to be found in the demons' admission of what they are when they are exorcised: 'All this . . . the demons themselves admit to be true, when they are driven out of men's bodies by words of exorcism and the fire of prayer. Saturn himself, Serapis, Jupiter or any other demon you worship, under stress of pain, confess openly what they are; and surely they would not lie to their own disgrace, particularly with some of you standing by' (XXVII, 5–6). Idolatry therefore is nothing but a mystification on a large scale undertaken by vain and greedy demons, of whom the pagans are the dupes. In this context, it is worth noting the allusion to Saturn, who was especially venerated in Africa and to whom Tertullian refers frequently in his *Ad nationes*.

What Minucius in fact does in his demonology is to take Apuleius' teaching about the demons and to attribute to evil demons the oracles and cures which Apuleius ascribes to good demons, and to confirm that the pagan gods and the evil demons are identical by their own confession made in exorcism. Ter‑ tullian too makes use of these traditional elements of demonology in his *Apologeticum* (XXII, 6, 11–12), where he mentions their cures, oracles and wonders; but he also adds the pregnant com‑ ment that, 'their work is the destruction of man' (XXII, 4). He describes this work in full, and explains the way in which the demons operate (XXII, 7).

Demons, Tertullian says, cause physical illness and 'sudden ex‑ travagant bursts of violence' in the soul. They are able to enter both the body and the soul because of 'their subtle and im‑ palpable substance' (XXII, 4). 'Undetected by sight or sense, they are recognised more in the consequences of their action than in their action itself', as is clear, for example, from their pollution of the air and the consequent destruction of fruit and crops (XXII, 5). They are omnipresent and can therefore announce events as soon as they happen or even cause them to happen (XXII, 8). They know the writings of the prophets and are thus able to compete with God by claiming that they have fulfilled the prophecies (XXII, 9). They can also forecast the weather, Tertullian claims, because 'they have their abode in the air, the stars are their neighbours and their commerce is with the clouds' (XXII, 10). In this, Tertullian is clearly following Justin. He also has a great deal to say about their magic powers (XXIII, 1).

Above all, however, Tertullian turns to account the theme of the pagan gods who confess to being demons when they are ex‑ orcised. His argument is quite simple. The pagan deities are demons, since they themselves say that they are, and, because the demons are subject to Christians, the pagan deities are also subject to them. It is therefore absurd to worship them: 'Divinity, as you understand it, is subject to Christians, but I don't think it is really to be reckoned divinity if it is subject to a man . . . So that divini‑ ty, which you maintain, is nothing of the kind' (XXIII, 8–10). Tertullian therefore clearly makes use of various sources such as Justin and Minucius Felix for his interpretation of demonology, but he at the same time transforms them with his own original genius.

2. *POMPA DIABOLI*

Moreover – and here we come to what is specifically characteristic of Tertullian – he was convinced that the whole of public life in the pagan city was impregnated with the demonic. This is in fact the theme of his *De spectaculis,* in which he states quite clearly that everything that is in the world is 'the work of God', but that everything in the world has at the same time been changed by 'the violence of that angel, perverter of God's work and God's rival' (*De spect.* II, 12). 'The streets, the market, the baths, the taverns, even our houses, are none of them altogether clear of idols. The whole world is filled with Satan and his angels' (VIII, 9). All this is what Tertullian means by the word *pompa,* 'procession' in the narrower sense of the word, but in the wider sense the whole 'outfit of the games of the circus' (VII, 2), where 'the demons sit in conclave' (VII, 3). These places are in fact consecrated to the demons and the angels by 'statues' and 'altars' (VIII, 2–3); and the horses dedicated to Castor and Pollux, for example, 'passed from being God's gift into the service of demons' (IX, 1–2).

Tertullian judges the theatre in the same way as the public shows in the arena or circus. For him, it is not a theatre, but 'a temple of Venus' or a 'house of Liber (Bacchus)' and these two deities are no more than 'demons of drunkenness and lust' (X, 6–7). Again, we note that Tertullian identifies the evil angels, who incite men to particular vices, with the pagan deities. Similarly, Apollo and the Muses, to whom the arts are dedicated, are, in Tertullian's opinion, merely names of the dead. He goes on: 'We know that the names of dead men are nothing – just as their images are nothing – but we are not unaware who are at work under those names and behind the images set up for them, what joy they take in them and how they feign deity: I mean evil spirits, demons' (X, 10).

What is more, Tertullian claims, the arts themselves were invented by the demons: 'From the very beginning, the demons took thought for themselves and, among other pollutions of idolatry, devised those of the spectacles for the purpose of turning man from his Lord and binding him to their own glorification.

and so inspired these ingenious arts' (**X**, 12). In his condemnation of the 'most popular spectacle of all' (**XII**, 1), the cruel games which originated in the *munus* or service to the dead, Tertullian says: 'For in the images of the dead, demons have their abode . . . We must give the same interpretation to the equipments which are reckoned among the ornaments of office. The purple, the rods (*fasces*), the fillets and garlands . . . do not lack the pomp of the devil (*sine pompa diaboli*) nor the invocation of demons' (**XII**, 5–6). We may therefore conclude from this that it is not simply the spectacles of pagan society, but the state itself as revealed in its public manifestations, which Tertullian regards as contaminated by demons.

The spectacles are diabolical, not only because they are idolatrous, but because they arouse man's baser passions, which also come from the devil. We have already seen how closely these two elements are linked together in Tertullian's teaching. In a passage in the *De spectaculis* which is reminiscent of the *Shepherd of Hermas,* he contrasts the two spirits: 'God has instructed us to approach the Holy Spirit – in his very nature tender and sensitive – in tranquillity, gentleness, quiet and peace, not in madness, bile, anger and pain to vex him. For what concord can the Holy Spirit have with the spectacles?' (**XV**, 2), which, as Tertullian goes on to point out, arouse violent passions, cruelty, sensuality and partiality. How could such emotions come from a good spirit? Tertullian therefore concludes that 'the world is God's but what is worldly is the devil's' (**XV**, 8). 'All these spectacles were instituted for the devil's sake', he insists, and are the *pompa diaboli,* 'the pomp of the devil' (**XXIV**, 2). Finally, he gives examples of those who 'by communion with the devil in the shows have fallen from the Lord', adding, 'No man can serve two masters' (Mt. 6:24) and 'What has light to do with darkness?' (2 Co. 6:14) (**XXVI**, 4).

The most striking characteristic of Tertullian's teaching in this treatise on the pagan spectacles is his use of the term *pompa diaboli,* for which he is the earliest extant witness. The meaning of this term, which Tertullian particularly favoured, has been widely discussed. Two authors in particular, Salomon Reinach and Hugo Rahner,[6] thought that the term indicated the demons who followed Satan, but more recent studies have shown that the explanation of this term must be sought elsewhere.[7] In Tertullian, these later scholars have argued, the *pompa diaboli* denotes the cult of idols which accompanied the various manifestations of the life of the pagan city. Consequently, the renunciation by Christians of these 'pomps of Satan' involved a break not only with the devil and with sin, but also with the pagan world itself, its spectacles and its honours. Tertullian sums the matter up thus: 'How many lines of argument have we pursued to show that nothing connected with the games pleases God? But does a thing befit a servant of God, which does not please his Master? If we have established our point that all the spectacles were instituted for the devil's sake ... why, here you have that "pomp of the devil" that we renounce when we receive the seal of faith' (XXIV, 2).

Tertullian, however, formulates this idea in a new way: 'When we enter the water and profess the Christian faith in the terms prescribed by its law, we profess with our mouths that we have renounced the devil, his pomp and his angels. What shall we call the chief and outstanding matter, in which the devil and his pomps and his angels are recognised, but idolatry? (IV, 1–2). A similar formulation of the same idea is also found in Tertullian's *De idololatria*: 'If you have foresworn the pomp of the devil, you should know that to touch it anywhere is idolatry' (*De idol.* XVIII).

In this latter treatise, Tertullian reconsiders and amplifies many of the ideas contained in his *Apologeticum*. He points out, for example, how complicity in idolatry is involved in many occupations. Among these, he includes the profession of 'schoolmasters and other teachers of letters', who are 'bound to praise the gods of the heathen, rehearse their names, genealogies, stories and all their ornaments and attributes. They must also

---

6. SALOMON REINACH, *Cultes, mythes et religions*, I, Paris, 1905, pp. 347–362; HUGO RAHNER, '*Pompa diaboli*', in *Zeitschrift für katholische Theologie*, 55 (1931), pp. 239–273.

7. PIERRE DE LABRIOLLE, '*Pompa diaboli*', *Archivum latinitatis medii aevi*, 2 (1926), pp. 170–181; J. H. WASZINK, '*Pompa diaboli*', in *Vigiliae christianae*, 1 (1947), pp. 13–41.

keep their feasts and celebrations' (X, 1–2). Schoolmasters, Tertullian points out, have to 'consecrate the very first fee (*stipem*) of
a new pupil to the honour and name of Minerva'. They must also
celebrate the *minervalia* for Minerva and the *saturnalia* for Saturn,
in which even very young devotees are involved. Tertullian continues in the same vein: 'The schools must be garlanded for Flora,
the priests' wives and the newly appointed aediles bring their
sacrifices, the school is bedecked for holidays. It is the same on an
idol's birthday – the whole pomp of the devil is celebrated' (X,
2–4). The consequence of all this is that 'a child's belief is built up
for the devil from the beginning of its education. How, then, can
the one who catechises about idols not be guilty of idolatry?' (X,
6).

There are many arts and crafts as well as trades, Tertullian insists, which may not directly involve those who practise them in
idolatry, but which certainly involve them in complicity (VIII,
1). As an example, Tertullian quotes those who sell incense, since
incense 'fattens the demons' (XI, 2). 'If a Christian in-
cense-merchant walks through a temple,' Tertullian writes, 'can
he bring himself to spit and blow on the smoking altars' – in
order to banish the spirit – 'if he has himself provided the incense?' (XI, 9). Again, 'if a purveyor of victims for public
sacrifices comes over to the faith, will you permit him to continue in that occupation? Or if an already baptised Christian takes
up such work, will you think it right to keep him in the
Church?' Tertullian therefore concludes: 'No craft or profession
or business that ministers to the making or equipping of idols can
escape the charge of idolatry' (XI, 9), and insists that 'it is wrong
to cajole ourselves with the necessity of maintaining life by saying, after sealing our faith, "I have nothing to live on" ' (XII, 1).
It is, finally, interesting to note in this context that Hippolytus
was also to list in his *Apostolic Tradition* the occupations which
catechumens had to give up on becoming Christians.

As regards social life, Tertullian does not return in the *De
idololatria* to the subject of spectacles since, as he says, 'I have
already written a whole volume on shows and pleasures of that
kind' (XIII, 1). He speaks rather of the pagan feasts: 'Is it to
honour a god, you ask, that the lamps are put before the doors

and the laurels on posts? No indeed, they are not there to honour a god, but a man, who is honoured as a god by such attentions. Or so it appears on the surface. What happens in secret reaches the demons. For we ought to be well aware (I give some details which may have escaped those not proficient in secular literature) that the Romans even have gods of doorways. There is Cardea, the goddess who gets her name from hinges, there are Forculus, Limentius and Janus, called after the door-posts, the threshold and the gate (*ianua*). Though the names are idle fiction, we may be sure that they draw to themselves demons and all manner of unclean spirits when they are used superstitiously. Consecration creates a bond' (**XV**, 4–5).

Special difficulties were involved for the Christian in the 'ceremonies at private and family festivals, such as putting on the white toga' (*toga pura,* worn on reaching manhood), 'celebrating an engagement or a marriage or giving a name'. These, Ter-tullian believed, 'are innocent in themselves, since neither the man's clothing, nor the ring, nor the marriage bond, nor the name originate in honour paid to an idol' (**XVI**, 2). These meetings, however, were often accompanied by sacrifices and in such cases the Christian could be present provided he did not contribute to or offer the sacrifice, but was there simply as an onlooker (**XVI**, 5). But what were Christian slaves or freed men to do? If they helped their masters in the sacrificial act, in any way at all, they would be regarded as 'ministers of idolatry' (**XVII**, 1). The same question was discussed at about the same period by Clement of Alexandria, who, like Tertullian, taught that Christians might take part in such feasts purely as members of the family, but recognised that they were nonetheless always placed in a difficult situation by them.

This problem became acute in the case of official functions un-dertaken by Christians, since such matters concerned the city itself: 'Can a servant of God undertake an administrative office or function if, by favour or ingenuity, he can keep himself clear from every form of idolatry . . .? Grant that a man may succeed in holding his office, whatever it may be, quite nominally, never sacrifice, never authorise a sacrifice, never contract for sacrificial victims, never delegate the supervision of a temple, never handle their taxes, never give a show at his own expense or the state's, never preside over one . . . Well, if you think that is possible, he may hold his office' (XVII, 3).

Tertullian's attitude, then, is that it is possible in principle for a Christian to undertake such public functions, but that it is extremely difficult in practice because the whole of public life is permeated with religion. This does not, however, mean that Tertullian does not acknowledge the existence of this tension – as he says in his *Apologeticum,* the Christian is bound to be present in society, but must avoid all complicity in idolatry. It is clear, however, that this rejection of pagan society by placing him in opposition to that which constituted its ideology, made such a presence very difficult and was bound to provoke a conflict.

Tertullian also considers the question of clothing. He notes that purple can be simply 'a mark of high office', but observes that 'this decoration (*suggestus*) can also be attached to priesthoods or idolatrous functions . . . The purple robe and other marks of rank and authority which were originally dedicated to the idolatry attaching to rank and authority, these keep the stain of their profanation, since idols are still dressed up with robes of state (*praetextae*), robes with borders (*trabeae*), robes with purple stripes (*laticlavi*) and still have rods and staves (*fasces, virgae*) carried in front of them. The demons are, after all, the magistrates of this world' (XVIII, 3).

Here therefore, it is obvious that Tertullian is identifying the pagan state and the demonic powers. Christ, after all, 'rejected the glory which he did not desire' – that of the 'rods of office (*fasces*)' and the 'purple' – and 'in rejecting it, condemned it and, in condemning it, set it down as the pomp of the devil (*pompa diaboli*). He would not have condemned it but for the fact that it was not his own and what does not belong to God can belong to none but the devil. If you have foresworn the pomp of the devil, you should know that to touch it anywhere is idolatry. If you would be convinced that all authorities and ranks of this world are not merely alien to God, but also hostile to him, bear in mind that it is through them that punishments have been determined against God's servants' (XVIII, 7–8).

One other example that Tertullian takes is that of service in the army. He had already discussed this in his earlier treatise *De corona militum,* where he took as his point of departure the laurel wreath given to the soldier, and proceeded from this to the more general question of military service in the case of the Christian. In this wider context, he had stressed such points as the conflict between giving an oath of fidelity to Christ and then giving it to another master (*De coron.* XI, 1), and the obligation to be present in the pagan temples, and then asked a series of further questions: 'Will he (the Christian) bear the standard which is rival to that of Christ? Will he ask to be marked with the sign of the prince when he has already been marked with the sign of God? Will he let himself be cremated, following the military custom, when cremation is forbidden to Christians? To forsake the name of the army of light and accept that of the army of darkness is a betrayal' (XI, 4).

In the *De idololatria,* Tertullian returns to the issue of military service for the believer in connection with a particular problem: 'It is being asked whether a believer can turn to military service and whether a soldier may be admitted to the faith, at least the rank and file who are not compelled to offer sacrifices or impose capital sentences' (XIX, 1). To this question, Tertullian gives a very radical answer: 'There is no compatibility between the oath (*sacramentum*) to serve God and the oath to serve man, between the standard of Christ and the standard of the devil, the camp of light and the camp of darkness. One life cannot be owed to two masters, God and Caesar' (XIX, 2).

In this final example too, therefore, we find the same opposition to the pagan city expressed by Tertullian as in the other cases that we have considered. In his view, the Christian has to turn away from the city because of its idolatry, an idolatry inspired by the demons and the idols. The idols, the demons and the emperors are united in forming an order which is opposed to Christ's rule. Because Roman society is dominated by idolatry, by the demons who are the enemies of Christ, it is the city of Satan and opposed to the city of God.

3. THE EMPIRE AS THE PERSECUTOR OF CHRISTIANS

As we have seen, Tertullian regarded the persecution of the Christians by the Roman Empire as a sign of its demonic nature. This theme had already been exploited by the Greek Apologists and especially by Justin, who taught that 'the evil demons scattered abroad many false and godless accusations against the Christians' (I *Apol.* X, 4) and 'make men who live contrary to reason . . . kill and hate the Christians' (I *Apol.* LVII, 1). These demons have in their power unjust magistrates of the Roman Empire who are their servants (δαιμονιῶντες) (II *Apol.* I, 2). Their attacks began even before the Christian era, being made against those just men who were already partly in possession of the Word (II *Apol.* VIII, 3). This, then, is the familiar patristic theme of the demons who are hostile to man and who passionately desire to destroy him and have striven to do so from the very beginning.

The same theme is used by the Latin authors, including Minucius Felix: 'Challenged at close quarters they run away from Christians, though at a distance in mixed crowds they set you on to harry them. Worming their way into the minds of the ignorant, they sow secret hate against us based on fear, for it is natural to hate one you fear, and to launch what attacks you can upon one of whom you are afraid. They seize and close the approaches of men's hearts, to insure their hating us before they know us, for fear that when they know us they may either proceed to imitate or feel unable to condemn' (*Oct.* XXVII, 8). The demons, then, reign in men's hearts by means of idolatry and rule society by means of the pagan empire. Their attitude towards the Christians, who threaten their power, can therefore only be one of hatred.

Tertullian also clearly states, in his *Apologeticum,* that the author of the persecutions, 'that spirit of demonic and angelic nature . . . battles against us with your hearts for his base – your hearts tuned and suborned to perverse judgement and savage rage' (*Apol.* XXVII, 2). In the *De fuga* too, he takes up the same theme as that of the *De idololatria:* 'If what is sinful comes not from God but from the devil, and if persecution comes from sin, what is there, then, that is more sinful than to treat as guilty those who are faithful to the true God and disciples of the truth? It is therefore clear that persecution comes from the devil, from whom sin is at work in the world, giving rise to persecution' (De fuga II, 1).

Like Justin, however, Tertullian too is concerned not to identify political power as such with the persecution of Christians carried out by the state. It was therefore necessary first of all 'to establish whether those beings to whom sacrifice is offered can give safety (salutem) to the Emperor or to anyone at all' (Apol. XXIX, 1). Christians, Tertullian teaches, defend the 'majesty of the Emperors', but 'do not subordinate them to their property' (XXIX, 4). They also 'on behalf of the safety of the Emperors, invoke the eternal God, the true God, the living God, whom the Emperors themselves prefer to have propitious to them beyond all other gods. They know who has given them the Empire' (XXX, 1). It is clear, then, that Tertullian tends to dissociate the Empire from idolatry as such.

The politico-religious situation was different at the time of Cyprian, since the bond between the state and religion had become stronger by the middle of the third century. Whereas in the second century the ideology of the Empire had had a philosophical basis and the Christian Apologists had been able to appeal to the wisdom of the princes, in the third century that ideology was inspired by the traditional religion of Rome.[8] This resulted in a sharpening of the conflict between the state, which was consciously attached to idolatry, and the Christian community, which was radically opposed to it. It was therefore no longer possible for Christian authors to dissociate the state from pagan idolatry, as Tertullian had done. The state had, in the third century, identified itself with idolatry. It had, in other words, become the instrument of the demon. This, at least, is how Cyprian viewed the situation. Moreover, persecution was now not the only aspect of the demons' activity. Another was the work of destruction within the Church, either by temptations or

8. Cf. JOACHIM MOLTHAGEN, Der römische Staat und die Christen im zweiten und dritten Jahrhundert, pp. 70–81.

by inner divisions. It is the whole range of this demonic operation against the Church that we must now consider.

From the very beginning the devil has striven to destroy man: 'Spiritual wickedness from the very beginning (*a primordio*) designed the destruction of man' (Tertullian, *Apol.* XXII, 4). Cyprian too refers to this several times in various treatises. In his *Ad Fortunatum*, for example, he says: 'The enemy against whom we are struggling is very old. Almost six thousand years have elapsed since the devil first attacked man. Experience and age have taught him all the ways and means of tempting man and all the tricks to make him fall' (*Ad Fort.* 2). This is why it is necessary 'to prepare men, by exhortation, to combat the arrows and darts of the devil' (*Ad Fort.* 1), that is, the persecutions.

This aspect of the devil's activity is also stressed in Cyprian's *De unitate.* The adversary, Cyprian states, 'has tricked and deceived us from the very beginning of the world, his lies wheedling the inexperienced (*rudem*) soul in its reckless confidence. That is how he tried to tempt the Lord himself, approaching him secretly as if to steal upon him again and trick him. But he was understood, turned back and laid low, because he was recognised and unmasked' (*De unit.* 1). Here it is the temptation of Adam which appeared at the beginning as the first manifestation of the devil's determination to make man fall; and this is contrasted with the temptation of Christ, whom the demon also tried to seduce, but by whom he was himself exposed and overcome. This theme of the struggle against Satan and his defeat, continued in the life of every Christian, is of central importance in Cyprian's writings.

In developing this conception, Cyprian draws on the Judaeo-Christian tradition of the jealousy of Satan. This idea is expounded in the *De zelo*: 'It is through jealousy that the devil, from the very beginning of the world, was both the first to perish and to cause another to perish. He who had been endowed with angelic glory and was pleasing and dear to God, after he had seen man made in the image of God, fell into jealousy brought about by a malevolent envy. Nor did he make the other fall by inspiring him with jealousy before falling himself through jealousy' (*De zelo* 4). This theme of Satan's fall through his jealousy of

Adam came originally from Judaeo-Christianity, had been used by Athenagoras and Irenaeus, and runs side by side with that of the fall of the angels in *I Enoch.*[9]

In the *De bono patientiae,* Cyprian writes in the same vein: *Impatientia malum diaboli est,* 'Discontent is an evil of the devil himself . . . Let us go back to the beginning. The devil suffered impatiently when he saw man made in the image of God. This is why he perished and caused man to perish' (*De bono pat.* 19). It will be noted that Cyprian uses the same idea in connection with the different vices that he opposes. In this, he draws on Tertullian who also traced the origin of discontent back to Satan in his *De patientia:* 'I observe the birth of discontent (*impatientia*) in the devil himself, when in the beginning he was discontented and vexed that the Lord God himself had subjected the whole creation to man, his own image' (*De pat.* V, 5; cf. also *Epist.* XLIII, 6).

One of the forms which this struggle of Satan against man takes is that the whole of man's life is a fight against the devil: 'What else is there in the world every day but a struggle against the devil, against his arrows and darts in continuous encounters? For us it is a conflict with covetousness, impurity, anger and ambition. It is a perpetual, hard struggle against the vices of the flesh and against the seductions of the world. Man's soul is surrounded and besieged on every side by the devil's invasions, and it is right for him to resist all attacks and to oppose them. If covetousness is overcome, sensuality rises up and if sensuality is conquered, ambition emerges' (*De mort.* 4).

Cyprian also describes in a similar way the different vices, such as, in this case, jealousy: 'The Lord recommends us to be prudent, for fear that the adversary, who is constantly watching and setting traps for us where he has crept into our hearts, should light fires with sparks and, by means of the storms and tempests that he arouses, cause the ruin of our faith and the shipwreck of our salvation and life. That, brothers, is why we have to watch and work with all our strength, so that, by our vigilance, we may drive back the angry enemy who shoots his darts at all the parts

9. K. BEYSCHLAG, *Clemens Romanus und der Frühkatholizismus,* pp. 48–56.

of our bodies where we may be struck and wounded' (*De zelo* 1).

A portrait of man perpetually besieged by Satan is provided in the *De zelo* 2: 'He (the devil) goes around each of us, and, like an enemy laying siege to men enclosed (in a town), he examines the walls, looking for some part which is less solid and secure, so that he can get inside through this weak spot. He appears in seductive shapes and easy pleasures in order to destroy chastity by vice. He tests the ears by music and songs so as to melt away and soften the Christian's strength as he listens to their sonorous sweetness. He stirs up the tongue to insults and stimulates the hand to commit murder by harassing the Christian with injustices. He suggests illicit gain to encourage the practice of fraud. He promises earthly honours in order to turn the Christian away from heavenly rewards'. This psychological analysis of human temptation is clearly reminiscent of the *Shepherd of Hermas,* but in this case expressed in a style and language which is derived from the Latin tradition.

Another method employed by Satan in his attack against Christians is, according to Cyprian, to try to break by violence what he has been unable to destroy by trickery. This is the way of persecution: 'When he cannot deceive by secret ways, he threatens openly, stirring up the earth by violent persecution, never relaxing his efforts, always on the attack, so as to conquer the servants of God. He is cunning in peace and violent in persecution' (*De zelo* 2). Cyprian here clearly interprets the persecution of Christians as an activity of the demons; and it should be noted that he regards persecution less as an attempt to destroy the Church by suppression than as a form of terror used against Christians in order to break their resistance and make them renounce their faith. This was indeed the aim of Decius' persecution of Christians; and it was the very resistance of the confessors which was to be the Christian victory.

There is frequent evidence in Cyprian's writings of this idea of persecution, namely as a form of temptation by the demon, who is attempting to destroy Christians. We read, for example, in the *De bono patientiae:* 'These trials, which are experienced by everyone in the world, are experienced even more by us, who are more shaken by the attacks of the devil. We are, after all, always in the fighting line – and are tired by encounters with an inveterate and experienced foe. In our case too, in addition to the varied and constant attacks of the devil's temptations, we suffer loss of our belongings, imprisonment, chains, the sword, the wild beasts, fires and the cross' (*De bono pat.* 12).

A special form used by Cyprian to express the activity of the demon incarnate in the Empire as the persecutor of Chritians is that of the Antichrist. Cyprian employs this representation of the devil in the *Epistles* written after the first of Decius' persecutions with the intention of preparing his readers for the second: 'You must know and regard as certain that the time of tribulation (*pressura*) is already beginning to hover over your heads and that the end of the world (*occasum mundi*) and the age of the Antichrist has drawn near' (*Epist.* LVIII, 1). It is true that the persecution of the just is nothing new – it began with Abel (LVIII, 1). The things which are to come, however, are in no way similar, he suggests, to the things which happened in the past: 'A greater and more savage combat is threatening' (LVIII, 1), and 'The imminent arrival of the Antichrist is in sight, but Christ is also coming' (LVIII, 7).

This activity of the Antichrist is that of the demon, the Antichrist being the visible instrument that carries it out: 'Take up your weapons and arm yourselves with spiritual and heavenly means so that you can resist the threats of the devil on that evil day' (LVIII, 9). A choice, Cyprian teaches, must be made between Satan and Christ: 'How wretched will be those who have deserted God and rebelled against him, having done the will of the devil, on the day when (Christ's) glory is revealed' (LVIII, 10). The battle consists in refusing to sacrifice to the pagan gods: 'Let us take in our hand the sword of the spirit, so that it may firmly reject the deadly sacrifices' (LVIII, 9). Cyprian therefore obviously regards idolatrous worship, the demon and the Antichrist as identical.

This conception occurs again in *Epist.* LIX, written to Cornelius on the subject of Novatian's schism. In destroying the unity of the Church, Novatian, Cyprian claims, has made himself the devil's accomplice: 'What remains, then, but that the Church should yield to the Capitol and, after the bishops have retired and have removed the altar of the Lord, statues of the idols with their pagan altars should be introduced into the sacred place of the assembly of our clergy? . . . If they must needs threaten, let them realise that the bishops of God are not afraid of them. When he begins to come, the Antichrist will not enter the Church by threats, and Christians will not give way to his weapons and his violence just because he says that he will kill those who resist him. If any condition calls for tears and lamentations, it is that of those whom the devil has so blinded that, heedless of the eternal pains of hell, they are trying to enact the coming of the Antichrist, when his approach is already so near' (LIX, 18).

The threat of the Antichrist's devilish attacks is also the occasion of *Ep.* LX, 3: 'Does he know who the servants of God whom the Antichrist attacks are, who the Christians whom the devil fights are?' Cyprian again and again identifies the Capitol, the devil and the Antichrist, and stresses the imminence of persecution. That is why anyone causing division within the Church is an accomplice of the Antichrist, who is presented as on the point of coming and is increasingly identified with the Empire as the present persecutor of the Church. In other words, the title Antichrist denotes everything that acts as an instrument of the demon in his attempt to destroy the Church by means of persecution.

The texts just quoted indicate the final method by which the demon attempts to overcome the Church, namely by weakening it from within. One trick used by the devil to this end is to encourage a too easy reconciliation of the *lapsi,* thus preventing their effective cure: 'Dear brethren, there has now appeared a new source of disaster and, as if the fierce storm of persecution had not been enough, there has come to crown it a subtle evil, an innocent-seeming pestilence, which masquerades as compassion . . . People coming back from the altars of Satan approach the Lord's sacred body (*sanctum Domini*), their hands still foul and reeking . . . This is a new sort of persecution, a new sort of temptation, by which the crafty enemy still attacks the lapsed (*lapsi*) and ranges about wreaking unsuspected devastation' (*De lapsis* 15–16).

Cyprian says very much the same in a letter written at about the same period: 'I beseech you, brothers, to be on your guard against the lying in wait of the devil and, concerned for your salvation, to be more watchful against his deadly duplicity. There is, after all, another temptation and another persecution' (Epist. XLIII, 3). The demon, Cyprian insists, retains his powerful hold over the lapsed by preventing them from being fully cured. He therefore urges them to 'avoid the wolves which separate the sheep from their shepherds. Avoid the devil's poisoned tongue. He has been a liar since the beginning of the world and continues to lie in order to deceive, to flatter in order to harm, and to promise life in order to destroy it' (Epist. XLIII, 7). This, of course, is the familiar theme of the devil who has been active since the beginning.

Satan tries to weaken the Church, however, mainly by causing inner division. It is this type of demonic activity which Cyprian discerns in Novatian's schism and which he denounces at the beginning of the De unitate ecclesiae. The opening chapters of this treatise in fact bring together all Cyprian's teaching about the demon and the way in which he operates. Here, for example, he describes the action of the serpent from the beginning of the world, the persecution of the Christians and the devil's trickery, all familiar themes: 'It is not only persecution that we have to fear and the attack which advances openly to subvert and overthrow the servants of God. Caution is not difficult where the danger is obvious. When the adversary reveals himself, our minds are prepared for the encounter. There is more to fear, more care to be taken, with an enemy who creeps upon us secretly, tricks us with a show of peace and hides his approach by serpentine deviations (serpit), true to his name of serpent (serpens) . . . That is how he has tricked us and deceived us from the very beginning of the world' (De unit. 1).

In the present situation his strategem is to divide the Church: 'We must guard against wily trickery and subtle deceit no less than open and obvious perils. And could anything more subtle and wily have been devised than this? The enemy has been exposed and laid low by the coming of Christ . . . Yet, when he saw his idols abandoned and his seats and temples deserted through the host of believers, our enemy thought of a new trick to deceive the unwary under cover of the name of Christian. He invented heresies and schisms to undermine faith, pervert truth and break unity ... He adorns his ministers as ministers of righteousness ... and calls the Antichrist Christ' (*De unit.* 3).

More details of Cyprian's picture of the demon's activities emerge from his letters. The demon used to rule by means of idolatry. When idolatry was exposed, he carried the fight to within the Church, introducing his own servants into it, and setting up cells of his followers inside its structure. The Antichrist appears, not only in the form of the imminent persecutor, the Empire as the enemy of Christians, but also in the form of instruments already used by the devil inside the Church. Previously the name Antichrist was applied to the Emperor. Now, though still the instrument of Satan, he is the heretic or the schismatic serving the demon within the Church and seeking to destroy it from within. This image of the Antichrist was to dominate Cyprian's struggle against Novatian. By his pride Novatian shows that he has 'the Antichrist in his heart' (*Epist.* LIX, 3), and is in fact 'the Antichrist who attacks Christians' (LX, 3).

Because he regarded the heretic as Antichrist, Cyprian was inevitably driven to reject the validity of heretical baptism: 'We are bound to ask whether those who are Christ's adversaries and who can be called Antichrists are able to give Christ's grace'. In this context, Cyprian also quotes 1 Jn. 2:18–19: 'You have heard that the Antichrist is coming. From now on, however, there are many Antichrists. That is why we know that it is the last hour. They went out from us, but they were not of us. That is why they did not stay with us' (LXX, 3). According to Cyprian, then, the Antichrist is both the persecutor who is coming and the false prophet who is already present – the two aspects of the Antichrist presented in the Johannine writings, the first occurring in the *Apocalypse* and the second in *I John* (cf. also *Epist.* LXIX, 1).

This theme is developed in Cyprian's *Epist.* LXXIII, 15: 'If we try to discover what the apostles thought about heretics, we shall find that in all their letters they execrated and detested their blasphemous depravities. When they say: "Their word spreads as doth a canker" (2 Tm. 2:17), how can the word which spreads like a canker in the ears of those who listen to it give them the remission of their sins? When they say that there is no fellowship between righteousness and iniquity and no communion between light and darkness, how can darkness illuminate or iniquity justify? (cf. 2 Co. 6:14). When they say that they are not of God, but of the spirit of the Antichrist, how can the enemies of God, their hearts obsessed by the spirit of the Antichrist, minister spiritual and divine things? . . . Those who scatter and attack the Church of Christ have no rights over the saving grace of the Church. For Christ calls them his adversaries and the apostles call them Antichrists'.

From all these features of Cyprian's writings emerges a deep pessimism with regard to the world. From the Stoic tradition, he inherited the conviction that it was moving inexorably towards its end and was in a condition of decay. Under the influence of the biblical tradition he saw it as ruled by the demon. Living in the world, man is on all sides besieged by the devil and beset by temptations, persecutions and divisions: 'Every day, his soul endures persecutions. What pleasure is there in remaining for a long time between the devil's swords?' (*De mort.* 5).

Cyprian's view, then, is not dualistic, like that of the gnostics, but gloomy and profoundly pessimistic as far as man's condition here on earth is concerned. This pessimism was already noticeable in the writings of Tertullian. In Cyprian it becomes deeper and more radical, a trend that was to continue in Augustine. Through these two writers it was to leave its mark on the whole of the Latin West, from Luther to Jansenius, from Kierkegaard to Karl Barth, from Péguy to Bernanos. In all deeply sensitive spirits the reality of evil wounds, and only faith can save from ultimate despair. Minucius and Novatian, on the other hand, remained closer to the Greeks and their vision of cosmic harmony.

CHAPTER SEVENTEEN

CYPRIAN'S ECCLESIOLOGY

LIVING in and confronted with this pagan society dominated by demons, Christians constituted a different people. Not that they were strangers to the civilisation in which they lived. On the contrary, Tertullian was to stress that Christians took part in every aspect of the life of the city. They were, however, alien to everything which derived from the spirit that inspired the pagan world. These men and women constituted the society of the Church; and in contrast to the apocalyptic writings of the Judaeo-Christians and the idealism of the early Greek Fathers, the work of the early Latin theologians is characterised by this extremely concrete concept of the Church. Hence, it is in their writings that questions of ecclesiology emerge; and Cyprian's work is especially important in this respect.

1. THE ESSENCE OF CHRISTIANITY

We must begin, however, by considering their awareness of the distinctive character of Christianity. This was defined by contrast with the pagan world, on three levels, the first being that of faith. Christianity was first of all a break with the cult of the false gods, with idolatry. In the *Octavius,* the *Ad nationes* and the *Apologeticum,* and the *Quod idola non sint,* Minucius, Tertullian and Cyprian on the one hand criticise idolatry, which they regard as the worship of demons, and, on the other, affirm the existence of the true God. This affirmation is expressed in the first place in monotheistic terms which are more or less the same in Minucius, Tertullian, Cyprian and Novatian, and which there is no need to recapitulate here. But Christian faith is not simply monotheism.

It is also linked with the biblical revelation; and we have examined the attitude of the early Latin Fathers to this in our discussions of exegesis. Finally, Christianity is faith in the revelation in and through Jesus Christ.

The thought of Tertullian, in the *Adversus Judaeos* in particular, reveals the coherence of two aspects of this faith. On the one hand, Christianity is the expression of true religion, as opposed to the false religion of the pagan world. On the other hand, however, this true religion has been unfolded in three successive stages. The seed has been the same from the very beginning, but by the action of the Spirit it has developed from natural revelation, through that of Moses to the revelation of Christ. Although it is certainly the expression of the fullness of the knowledge of God, the Christian faith at the same time recapitulates the previous stages. At the level of interpretation of man's natural knowledge of God, Christianity is in dialogue with the pagans. At the level of the Old Testament revelation, it is in dialogue with the Jews. Finally, at the level of the Christian revelation, it is in dialogue with the Christians. Tertullian emphasises these three stages especially in the *Apologeticum* (XVII–XXI).

The second way in which Christians are distinguished is by their manner of life, the *disciplina*. From the very beginning, God had given a law to man – this is the meaning of the tree of the knowledge of good and evil. Man, however, preferred to obey Satan rather than to obey God. Christianity is basically the restoration of the primal order, and it is in this sense that Tertullian and Cyprian contrast Christian morality with pagan immorality. At the same time, however, like faith in God, God's law has, as Tertullian explains in the *Adversus Judaeos*, been subject to a process of development. The earliest stage is that of the natural law, the second that of the Mosaic law with its various precepts. Christ in his turn brought a new law, which does not contradict the previous laws, but extends them and goes beyond them. This point has already been considered in connection with Tertullian's concept of development.

At the level which this process has now reached it is, therefore, the law of the Gospel on which stress has to be laid; and this aspect of the matter bulks large in the works of the second century Latin writers. The moral content of their writings is considerable, and it is interesting to note the points on which they concentrate. Among the virtues, patience is discussed in treatises both by Tertullian and by Cyprian. As Frédouille has pointed out, these treatises contain clear echoes of Stoic moral teaching, especially that of Seneca. On the other hand, however, the Christian emphasis is also evident. It is, moreover, predominantly the practical problems of morality that are dealt with in the writings of this period. Tertullian, for example, writes about fasting, prayer, women's dress, the virgin's veil and the soldier's crown. Cyprian deals with the behaviour of virgins and, in his letters, with many different moral problems. In Book III of his treatise *Ad Quirinum*, he provides a collection of a hundred and twenty articles concerned with Christian *disciplina*, one of them entitled, for example, 'The discipline of God must be observed in the Church's precepts' (*Ad Quir.* III, 66). Cyprian often returns to this question of *disciplina* in his letters. In connection with prayer, for instance, he writes in *Epist.* II, 5: 'Christ is *magister disciplinae*'. In the *De oratione* too, he discusses this *disciplina*, that is, the order which the Christian should observe in the sphere of prayer.

The third characteristic of the Christian community is its eschatological orientation. All three aspects of this early Latin teaching are summarised in Tertullian's dictum: *Corpus sumus de conscientia religionis et disciplinae unitate et spei foedere*, 'We are a society with a common religious feeling, unity of discipline and a common bond of hope' (*Apol.* XXXIX, 1). Among the characteristics of the Christian life, Cyprian includes eschatological hope: *Subito venire finem mundi*, 'The end of the world will come unexpectedly' (*Ad Quir.* III, 89) and this aspect is stressed also in the treatises addressed to the martyrs – Tertullian's *Ad Martyres* and *Scorpiace*, and Cyprian's *De mortalitate, Ad Fortunatum* and various letters. In these texts we have the extreme expression of a break not just with the pagan world but with the world as such. They voice both a pessimistic view of the present world, dedicated to its own destruction, and also a joyous expectation of the life to come as promised to Christians. The Christian community, in other words, is in the world, but it finds fulfilment beyond this world.

Two passages from Cyprian are particularly striking examples of this eschatological teaching. The first occurs in the *De mortalitate:* 'We must remember, dear brothers, that we have renounced the world and that we live here as temporary guests. We look forward to the day when each of us will be given his dwelling-place and we shall be taken from here and set free from the bonds of the age, in order to be restored to paradise. Who is the exile who does not long to return to his homeland? Who does not hasten to set sail on the sea and wish for a favourable wind, so that he may all the sooner be allowed to kiss his own again? Paradise is our homeland. There are the patriarchs, our fathers. There, those who are dear to us are waiting for us in great numbers. There, we shall find the glorious choir of the apostles, the exultant group of the prophets, the countless number of the martyrs' (*De mort.* 26).

The same emphasis is found in the *Ad Fortunatum*. It is interesting that here the chapter on immortality follows directly on one in which idolatry is condemned (*Ad Fort.* 5). It is, in fact, the whole world which is subject to the power of the demon, and death is the only deliverance from it: 'In our trials, we prefer the riches and delights of paradise to the poverty of the world, the sovereign power of the eternal kingdom to temporal slavery, immortality to death, God and Christ to the devil and the Antichrist' (*Ad Fort.* 6; cf. also 7). Clearly then, Cyprian regards the world as the sphere ruled by the demon and the powers which are the visible incarnation of the demon. This apocalyptic vision is reminiscent of Commodian (*Carm. Ap.* 309–310):

> *Tormentum est totum quo(d) vivimus isto sub aevo;*
> *Hinc adeo nobis est spes in futuro quaerenda.*
> ('Our whole life in this age is torment; for this very reason our hope must be sought in the future').

2. THE CHRISTIAN SOCIETY

The *corpus* or 'society' formed by Christian believers is therefore characterised by these three features – faith, discipline, hope. But it also has a hierarchical structure, for the preservation of these things is entrusted to those who preside over the assembly, who are the successors of the apostles and to whom Christ has committed the Church. In his brief summary of Christian teaching and practice, the beginning of which we quoted above, Tertullian states precisely this: *Praesident probati quique seniores,* 'Our presidents are elders of proved worth', and adds that they are 'men who have reached this honour not for a price, but by character', in other words, by the witness they have borne in their lives (*Apol.* XXXIX, 4). Tertullian does not, however, go into details concerning the part played in the life of the Church by these *seniores.* It is left to Cyprian to develop this doctrine of the episcopate to such an extent that it was to have a profound influence on the Latin West.

The bishops, Cyprian stresses, are the successors of the apostles and derive the lawfulness of their office from this succession. In *Ep.* III, 3, for instance, he writes: 'Deacons should remember that the Lord chose the apostles, that is, the bishops (*episcopos*) and presidents (*praepositos*), but that it was the apostles who, after the Lord's ascension into heaven, instituted deacons (*diaconos*) to serve as ministers (*ministros*) both to themselves and to the Church. If we dare do anything against God, who made the bishops, then the deacons also may dare to oppose the bishops, from whom they derive'. Cyprian thus affirms the divine institution of the episcopate more clearly than any of his predecessors by making a distinction between the apostolate, which comes from God and is carried out by the bishops alone, and the ministers, who are a human institution.

This episcopate is handed down from the apostles in a legitimate succession, with the result that a man who is not lawfully ordained is not a bishop. Opposing Novatian's theory, Cyprian writes in *Ep.* LXIX, 3: 'For the Church is one . . . If it is with Novatian, it was not with Cornelius. But if it was with Cornelius, who succeeded Bishop Fabian by a legitimate ordination, . . . then Novatian is not in the Church and cannot be reckoned a bishop – a man who scorned the tradition of the gospel and the apostles, succeeded to no one and originated from himself! For one who has not been ordained in the Church can by no means possess or govern the Church'. In the same letter,

Cyprian writes also: 'How can he be regarded as a shepherd who, while the true shepherd is alive and presides in the Church of God by virtue of an ordination in regular succession, succeeding nobody and beginning from himself, becomes a stranger and an alien? (*Ep.* LXIX, 5).[1]

The bishop's task is, of course, to be vigilant so that the whole community of believers will remain at all levels within the tradition of the Church. This applies first of all at the level of faith. Cyprian, however, has little to say about this, nor does he write so much against heretics as against schismatics. Tertullian emphasises the great importance of the apostolic tradition as the criterion of orthodoxy, but he too does not deal with the special part played by the episcopate in handing down that tradition, although he does, on the other hand, frequently stress the bishops' task of supervising the observance of Church discipline. One instance where he alludes to this function is in his controversy with a bishop.[2] In this controversy, he does not dispute that the bishop has the power to remit sins, but he does criticise him for his abuse of this power by remitting sins too easily (*De pud.* XXI, 5–8). Cyprian discusses this episcopal function several times, as for example here: 'You know that we do not deviate from the tradition of the gospel and the apostles. We are firmly and constantly advising our brothers and sisters. We use every means to help and support them, always vigilant so that discipline (*disciplina*) may be maintained in the Church. We who fear God are bound to uphold the divine precepts (*praecepta*) of that discipline in full observance (*observatio*)' (*Ep.* IV, 1–2). The importance in this passage of the terms given in parenthesis should be noted.

Finally, the bishop also has the task of maintaining hope, in particular in those who are being put to the test, and very specially in the martyrs. Cyprian himself carried out this task fully by

---

1. Cf. also *Ep.* LXVII, 5; LXV, 16: 'The power to remit sins has been handed to the apostles and to the churches that these, having been sent by Christ, have instituted and to the bishops who have succeeded them by ordination' (cf. also *De unit.* 10).

2. This, as Barnes has pointed out, was certainly the Bishop of Carthage rather than the Bishop of Rome.

sending a collection of quotations to Fortunatus: 'What is more in accordance with our responsibility and our care than to prepare by means of exhortations the people entrusted to us by God and the army established in the heavenly camps against the arrows and darts of the devil?' (*Ad Fort.* 2). No words could be plainer. In addition, the theme of the conflict with Satan is reintroduced, showing that the bishop's task is to prepare his people for this struggle against the devil and his agents. The dualistic view is characteristic and occurs elsewhere in the letters (cf., e.g., *Ep.* X, 1).

In *Ep.* XXXI, 6, Cyprian congratulates Bishop Moses on carrying out this duty of encouragement, among others: 'It is a further joy to us that, despite your separation from your brothers because of special circumstances, you have nonetheless not neglected your duty as a bishop. You have encouraged confessors frequently by your letters. You have provided for various expenses by your efforts. Nowhere in your office have you ever limped as a deserter'.

Whereas the bishop, on the one hand, has certain tasks which he must fulfil, the people, on the other, have a corresponding duty to respect his authority. In several of his letters, Cyprian speaks of those who oppose that authority. In *Epist.* XLIII, 2, for example, he says: 'We can now see where Felicissimus' faction came from. These people stirred up and provoked certain confessors to quarrel with the bishop and not keep the Church's *disciplina* according to the Lord's precepts, in faith and peace'. Similarly, in another letter, he insists that the deacon 'must acknowledge the priest's honour and give satisfaction to the bishop who is set over him, in all humility. Heretics and schismatics always begin by seeking to please themselves and, inflated with pride, to scorn the one who is put over them' (*Ep.* III, 3).

This emphasis placed on order in the community of believers and on the part played by the bishop derives from a Western tradition, the earliest evidence of which is to be found in the First Letter of Clement of Rome. This was translated into Latin at a very early stage. In it the traditional teaching is given a certain secular colouring by the argument from order as natural to both animals and men: 'The bees have a king and the flocks have a guide (*ducem*) and are loyal to him. Even brigands obey their leader (*manceps*) with respect full of humility. How much better and more simple than us these wild beasts, dumb animals and bloodthirsty brigands are! Among them, the one who rules them is acknowledged and respected' (*I Clem.* 66, 6).

The Church is therefore defined by its discipline, and the bishops' duty is to be watchful to safeguard this discipline. Behind it, however, is the form of this order, which is ultimately the will of God. In the last analysis, then, it is conformity with the will of God which is the form of the Church. It is in virtue of this that the Church is the kingdom of God, as opposed to the kingdom of the demons. The various precepts are no more than detailed expressions of this supreme law, and the bishops are simply its guarantors. It would therefore seem that this is another case in which Christianity has taken over a Stoic conception. According to the Stoics, Reason is conformity with nature, and as such the regulative principle of every activity. In Christianity, conformity with the will of the personal God is the supreme rule of every good action. Cyprian, in other words, conceives the Church in terms of the Stoic image of the city.

The will of God is a constantly recurrent theme in Cyprian's work. In the *Ad Quirinum* III, 9, for instance, he includes, under the heading *Voluntati non nostrae sed Dei obtemperandum*, 'It is necessary to conform not to our own will, but to the will of God', a group of quotations from the New Testament (Jn. 6:38; Mt. 26:39; 6:10; 7:21; Lk. 12:47; 1 Jn. 2:27). The quotation from Mt. 6:10 comes from the Lord's Prayer and is developed at some length in Cyprian's *De Dominica oratione*, with reference to Mt. 26:39; Jn. 6:38 and 1 Jn. 2:15, 17. God's will is what Christ did and taught, with the result that Christ is the model for the Christian to imitate. The believer must pray for God to help him to do this, as the devil will constantly hinder him. The content of this will of God is identical with that of the precepts of the Church; for example: *in operibus misericordia, in moribus disciplina, iniuriam tolerare, cum fratribus pacem tenere*, 'Mercy in works, discipline in behaviour, bearing wrongs and keeping peace with the brothers' (*De orat.* 14–15). Similarly, in the *De habitu*, Cyprian writes: 'We must follow eternal and divine things, and do everything according to the will of God, in order to follow in the footsteps of our Lord'. There follow quotations from 1 Jn. 2:25 and Jn. 6:38. Cyprian is speaking here of virginity; elsewhere we are urged to imitate Christ's patience in carrying out the will of God, again with reference to Jn. 6:38.

An important example is the Christian's acceptance of death: 'We must bear in mind that we have to do, not our own will, but the will of God, according to what our Lord has commanded us to ask every day. What depravity it is if we ask for God's will to be done (Mt. 7:21), but, when God calls us and takes us out of this world, we do not at once observe the order of his will, but resist it and rebel against it' (De mort. 18). Here it is the eschatological aspect of the order of existence of God's people, their fundamental orientation towards the future life, which is related to the will of God. This, therefore, covers the whole field of that Christian discipline which constitutes the object of the bishop's responsibility, and of which the ultimate basis is to be found in the divine will and in the example of Christ who fulfilled that will to perfection.

The Church, as the Latin Christian authors of the third century were profoundly aware, is a holy people, because it is animated by the Holy Spirit. This aspect of the Church is closely related to the contrast between the Church and pagan society; and it is precisely because this relationship was so clearly perceived that it became the source of serious ecclesiological problems for the third century Latin church, first the conflict between Cyprian and Novatian, and secondly that between Cyprian and Stephen. In the former case, what was at stake was whether the so-called 'lapsed' could be reconciled to the Church without risk of laxity and of impairing the holiness of the Church. In the latter, it was a question of knowing whether the Spirit could be given by someone who had separated himself from the Church.

In order to understand the first of these problems, we must return to Novatian. To understand his doctrine of the Church it is necessary to recall his doctrine of man. Man, Novatian teaches, is remote from God by virtue of his biological condition. In the resurrection of his own body, Christ restored human nature to a state of union with God. In baptism, all men are able to share in this restoration to the paradisal state, which will be completed by death. But baptism already and at once establishes man in a state of perfect holiness, in which neither progress nor fall is possible. This conception clearly reflects the influence of Stoicism, with its teaching that the wise man enjoys a state of perfection which is one and unchanging. Novatian's ecclesiology is derived from this doctrine of man. The Church is the community of the saved, not the instrument of salvation. It is the spotless virgin, not the merciful mother. This inevitably rules out any reconciliation of sinners. Not only can they not be readmitted to the Church, they are not to receive any pastoral care. The inevitable conclusion, though Novatian does not state this explicitly, is that there can be no eternal salvation for sinners.

Novatian's heresy is above all to be found in these last aspects of his teaching. As Vogt has shown, his teaching is characterised not only by 'rigorism' but by 'puritanism'. Cyprian was a rigorist in that he refused to allow the 'lapsed' to be reconciled. He did not, for all that, refuse them spiritual help. For him it was a matter of the educational use of penance. By contrast, Novatian was concerned with a Church of the pure, separated completely from sinners. Both were reacting to the same situation, that of the numerous Christians who, having already once been reconciled to the Church, fell away again during the Decian persecution. Their attitudes toward these Christians were determined, however, by their differing doctrines of the Church. It is Cyprian who represents the old, traditional discipline, and Novatian who is the innovator. Cornelius represents the position most radically opposed to that of Novatian. The interest of the controversy is its bearing on the permanent ecclesiological problem of the conflict between two conceptions — that of the Church, a small community of the pure, and that of a great, mixed community of both saints and sinners.

Novatian's concept of the Church is, however, not Stoic in the moral sense of being concerned simply with a moral attitude. This Church of the saints, which he champions, is so only because it is subject to the activity of the Holy Spirit, who works miracles within it. In this respect Novatian is witness to an essential aspect of any doctrine of the Church; and before his schism, he describes, in his *De Trinitate,* this activity of the Holy Spirit in the Church: 'It was the Spirit which strengthened the souls and minds of the apostles, revealed to them the mysteries of the gospel, and enlightened them concerning divine mysteries. It was in his strength that for the name of the Lord they feared neither imprisonment nor chains. Nay more, animated and strengthened by him, they trampled underfoot the powers and torments of the world, because they had within themselves the gifts that this Spirit gives to the Church, the bride of Christ, like ornaments' (*De Trin.* 29). The Spirit, then, is the inner principle by means of which the Christian's 'body' is able to encounter the evil world.

Novatian shows how this activity of the Holy Spirit is continued in the Church, instituting the prophets, inspiring the teachers, enabling men to speak with tongues, bestowing the gifts of healing, performing miracles, discerning the spirits, helping those whose task it is to govern the Church, giving counsel and distributing every kind of charism. In this way, the Spirit makes the Church everywhere and in everything perfect and fulfilled. This description of the Church is valid; it has something true to say. Its only exaggeration is to reduce the Church to a group of charismatics. It should be noted that Novatian does not mention the bishops – for him, the Church is a Church of prophets. It was important that this aspect of the Church should be kept alive, but only on condition of not becoming exclusive.

The same tendency drove Tertullian, during his Montanist period, to see the Church as a charismatic group: 'Now what of all this concerns the Church – your Church, I mean, sir Psychic? For following Peter's person, that power will belong to spiritual man, apostle or prophet. For the Church itself is properly and fundamentally spirit, in which is the Trinity of our divinity, Father, Son and Holy Spirit. It is the Spirit who gathers together the Church which the Lord made to consist in three. From that beginning, the whole number (*numerus*) of those who agree in this faith takes its being (*censetur*) as the Church from its founder and consecrator. Therefore the Church will indeed pardon sins, but the Church which is spirit, through a spiritual man, not the Church which is a collection of bishops. Law and judgement belong to the Lord, not to the servant, to God, not to the priest' (*De pud.* XXI, 16–17).

Tertullian here pushes Novatian's implied contrast to the limit. Whereas Cyprian places the emphasis on the bishop's authority and does not mention the activity of the Spirit in the Church, Tertullian stresses the latter as constitutive for the Church, without any necessary link with the bishop. In fact, however, it is not possible to separate these two aspects. Novatian was right to stress the importance of the Spirit, but Cyprian was equally right to point out that it was to the apostles and their successors that the Spirit had first been given. One cannot separate these two aspects, and Cyprian himself did not in fact do so.

3. *VIGOR ECCLESIAE*

The pagan world and the Christian Church are completely incompatible; one cannot simultaneously serve both God and the idols. This is the theme of Cyprian's *Quod idola non sint,* and it is taken up again in the introduction to the *Ad Fortunatum.* This incompatibility is, of course, asserted by all Christians; but, in the Latin Church during the middle of the third century, the issue became particularly acute. The persecutions of Decius and Valerian confronted Christians for the first time with an ultimatum: they had to sacrifice to the idols. This order may have been applied more or less severely in differing parts of the Empire, but there is no doubt that it was enforced rigorously in Africa at the time of Cyprian.

It is important to appreciate this situation, if we are to understand Cyprian's ecclesiology. At the beginning of the Church's history, this confrontation between the Church and the world only involved relatively small groups of Christians. At the time of Tertullian, for instance, martyrdom was a glorious exception, whereas, during the period when Cyprian was writing, the whole Christian community was involved in the conflict. This gave rise to a number of new situations, such as the large number of those who fell away, the *lapsi,* and the problems which this posed for an embattled Church. The demands of the struggle inevitably led to an emphasis on certain features.

In this opposition to the pagan world, Cyprian was inspired by Tertullian, but to take a very different line. He seeks to show that the Church is a genuine expression of the reality of which pagan society is a mere caricature; and in doing so he uses various forms of expression which we shall examine because they are a characteristic aspect of the Church in the Latin world. What we have here is no longer the adoption of philosophical ideas, but the transposition of certain sociological features. These are the very data which Cyprian condemns in the pagan world — its domination, its public spectacles, its wars; and he uses them to express the nature of the Church in contrast to the world.

According to Cyprian, it is when the Church is militant that it expresses its health, vitality and vigour; and this explains his fondness for the word *vigor*. The word is not characteristic of Tertullian, who uses it in a secular sense (cf., e.g., *Scorp.* VIII, 6; *De anim.* V, 5; LIII, 3), in particular as a translation of the Greek ἐνεργεία, which derives from Stoicism (cf. *De anim.* XLIII, 3 and 5; XLVIII, 1). He speaks, for instance, of Zeno's *vigor* (*De anim.* III, 2). In cases where Cyprian might have used the word *vigor*, however, Tertullian employs other terms such as *tenor* (*De pud.* XCVIII; X, 10; XX, 2); *vires* (*De jejun.* XVII, 9); *severitas* (*De pud.* XIV, 8; XVIII, 14; XXI, 5); and *valentia* (*Adv. Marc.* V, 17, 6).

Tertullian uses the word *vigor* in the sense of spiritual power in certain quotations from the Old Testament, such as *exclama in vigore* (Is. 58:1), which he quotes in *Adv. Jud.* IX, 30. A more interesting example is the phrase, *spiritus vigoris,* 'a spirit of power', in Is. 11:2, which clearly refers to spiritual force. It may be, however, that Tertullian is here making use of an already existing translation, since elsewhere he renders the same passage in Isaiah differently, as *spiritus virtutis* in *Adv. Jud.* IX, 26 and *spiritus valentiae* in *Adv. Marc.* V, 8, 4 and 8. We cannot therefore conclude that Tertullian particularly favoured the word *vigor*. It is, moreover, interesting to note that the rendering used by Cyprian for these two quotations is *fortitudo* (*Test.* II, 11; III, 1), which shows clearly that, in his case at least, the term *vigor* was not derived from biblical Latin.

The word is, however, very important in Cyprian's writings.

It occurs in its secular sense, in *Ad Donatum* 8, in the phrase, *vigor sexus,* 'sexual vigour'. In a cosmological context, it appears in *Ad Demetrianum* 3, in a description of the decadence of the universe quoted earlier: 'You must know in the first place that the world is already old, that it no longer possesses the powers which formerly marked its existence, and that it no longer enjoys the health (*vigore*) and strength (*robore*) which it previously enjoyed'. Cyprian then goes on to describe the exhaustion of nature – the diminishing rain and sun leading to lessening fertility and pointing to a general decline of all things (*labentium*).

It is, however, in the sense of spiritual force that the word was to play a major role in Cyprian's writings. Its use in contrast to the *labes* or fall will have been noted in the passage just cited. In the same way he contrasts the *vigor* of the Church with the falling away of the *lapsi*. In the by now familiar context of the Church's confrontation with the pagan world, Cyprian here stresses, not the *patientia* of Christians, but their *vigor,* in other words, an active attitude, conscious of its power. Whereas in Tertullian Christian resistance to paganism takes on the glamour of a kind of defiance, involving a small band of *desperati,* Cyprian speaks of the tranquil power of a whole people, already certain of ultimate victory. It is the pagan resistance to the Church which strikes one as the madness of despair. The final stage in this transformation is marked by Lactantius' hymn of victory in the *De mortibus persecutorum.*

Christian *vigor* is the vitality of faith and faithfulness as expressed above all in steadfastness under persecution. It is for this that Cyprian praises a Christian in Rome: 'The full power (*vigor*) of the gospel and the firm discipline of the law of the Lord are expressed in your letter' (*Epist.* XXVII, 4). He writes in the same vein to a group of confessors in Africa: 'We have observed the solidity (*tenor*) of your discipline in the firm tone (*vigore*) of your letter' (*Ep.* XXVIII, 2).

The word *vigor* is also often used by Cyprian in combination with the verb *calcare,* to trample underfoot, which describes the attitude of the victorious athlete. In *Ad Fortunatum* XI, Cyprian uses this term in connection with one of the sons of the mother in *2 Maccabees:* 'He trampled underfoot (*calcabat*) the harsh torments by the power (*vigore*) of his faith'. In *Ep*. XXXVII, 2, he speaks of the *vigor* of the Carthaginian martyrs: 'You trample underfoot, by the power of your firmness (*roboris vigore*), the horror of the condemned cell', and, in another letter, of Cornelius, 'opposing the public edicts and trampling underfoot the cruel torments by the power (*vigore*) of his faith' (*Ep*. LV, 9).

In this attitude Cyprian displays remarkable intuition. He has detected the enfeeblement of the Empire and of pagan society, and describes their decadence in terms borrowed from the pagan authors themselves. All the *vigor*, the vitality, is on the side of Christianity. His fundamental pessimism about the future of the world is balanced by a striking joy with regard to the future of the Church. In his teaching, the decadence of the Roman Empire is closely associated with that of the world, and the *saeculum* or 'age', which he sees as being in a state of decline or *occasus*, is for him the world in the sense both of the cosmos and of human society. For him, therefore, the hope of the Church is eschatological. What he does not yet envisage is that the Church's victory may be an earthly one and that the end of the Empire may not be the end of the world.

Cyprian also insists on this *vigor* not being relaxed even during periods of peace. In the *De unitate*, for instance, he complains: 'With us, the vigour of faith has withered (*emarcuit*) and the strength (*robur*) of belief has grown faint' (*De unit*. 26). Similarly, he writes in a letter: 'We are invited by God's call to be sparing in our food and sober in our drink for fear that the pleasures of the world may weaken our hearts that have already been stirred up by heavenly vigour' (*Ep*. XI, 7). The demon, on the other hand, strives 'to soften the power (*vigorem*) of Christians by the temptations of the senses' (*De zelo* 5). This is why the weakness (*labes*) of the carnal and terrestrial body has to be trampled underfoot (*calcanda*) by heavenly vigour (*vigor caelestis*) (*De zelo* 14).[3]

3. It may be noted that in *Idol*. 6 the phrase 'heavenly vigour' denotes the life of the angels (cf. also *De habit*. 14). The words were first used by Minucius Felix in this sense, where they are applied to 'unclean spirits' (*Oct*. XXVI, 8). They indicate the contrast between heavenly incorruptibility and carnal corruptibility and may have originated in Virgil's *Aeneid* VI, 730.

This *vigor* is manifested in the first place in the confrontation with persecution. It distinguishes the *integri* from the *lapsi*: 'May those who are unimpaired (*integri*) preserve the power (*tenorem*) of their health (*salutis*) and the lasting vigour (*vigorem*) of their preserved and protected wholeness' (*Ep.* LXV, 4). It also shows itself, however, in the power of thought, its persuasiveness. Cyprian tells the pagan Demetrian that it is easy to kill bodies; he should 'enter the struggle with the vigour (*vigore*) of the mind'. It is the same vitality which is seen in the strength of virgins, Cyprian stressing that there is always virginity in the Church and that the glory of continence is not diminished by the sins of others. 'The Church is flourishing', he wrotes, 'crowned by so many virgins. Chastity and continence preserve the power (*tenorem*) of their glory and the forgiveness and penance granted to the adulterer do not destroy the vigour (*vigorem*) of continence' (*Ep.* LV, 20).

This text gives us a very precise indication of the position adopted by Cyprian. He is strenuously opposed to those who are in favour of easy reconciliation either for the lapsed or for the adulterers, since this introduces an easy-going laxity into the life of the Church and destroys its *vigor*. He is, however, also opposed to the merciless attitude of such Christians as Novatian, who reject all reconciliation. This is not Christianity but Stoicism (*Ep.* LV, 16). Reconciliation, so long as it is subject to adequate conditions, does not, Cyprian teaches, weaken the 'vigour of the gospel' (LV, 3). By way of the specific problems confronting him Cyprian thus arrives at a central and permanent problem — that of the balance that has to be found between severity and leniency.

Another very important aspect of Cyprian's teaching regarding the *vigor* of the Church is that it inspires not simply individuals or groups in the Church, but the Church as a whole. This, of course, applied particularly to the Church at the time when Cyprian was writing, since it was then the Church as a whole that was attacked and resisted the attacks. 'The one who has insufficient power to overcome everyone tries to thwart each one separately, but he is thrust back by the faith and the power (*vigore*) of the whole army' (*Ep.* LX, 2).

According to Cyprian, this *vigor* is an active force which is not, however, human in origin. It is above all *vigor caelestis,* heavenly power. The strength which animates the virgins and martyrs of the Church is a divine power. It is the power of the Holy Spirit, which was already expressed long ago in the prayer of the three young men in the furnace (Dn. 3). There we see the vigour (*vigor*) and strength (*robur*) of faith which, on the one hand, believes and knows that God can deliver from present death, and yet, on the other, does not fear to die, so that faith may be more rigorously tested. As Cyprian says in one of his letters, 'The Holy Spirit is expressed through the pure and unvanquished mouth (sc. of the three young men)' (*Ep.* LVIII, 5).[4] In the *Ad Donatum* 4, Cyprian insists that 'all our power (*vigor*) for good is derived from God'.

This *vigor,* then, is not in any way tied to human qualities, but may be manifested in weakness: 'No priest of God, lying on the ground and wretched, feeble with the frailty (*imbecillitate*) of human mediocrity, is weak (*infirmus*) to such a degree that he may not be raised by God against God's enemies and adversaries, and that his lowliness (*humilitatem*) and weakness may not be animated (*animatus*) by the vigour (*vigore*) and power (*robore*) of God who protects him' (*Ep.* LVII, 18). This passage makes it quite clear that the vigour or power which Christians possess is ultimately derived from God. Because it is a divine power it is available to the weakest of believers and cannot be overcome.

One of the uses to which Cyprian puts the word *vigor* is peculiar to him. In this special sense, *vigor* expresses the firmness which the bishop applies to the keeping of the Church's discipline and is often associated in this context with words such as *disciplina* and *censura*. It expresses both the power that resides in the episcopate as a divine institution and at the same time the firmness with which the bishop himself is bound to watch over the observance of Christ's law (*Ep.* IV, 4). The word serves to characterise the bishop's power: 'In accordance with the strength (*vigore*) of the episcopate and the authority of the bishop's throne (*cathedra*), you had the power to act at once against him (sc. a

4. Tertullian also uses the word *vigor* in the case of the three young men in the furnace (*Scorp. VIII,* 6).

rebellious deacon)' (*Ep.* III, 1). It is in virtue of this authority that priests and deacons are to resist those who are imprudent in receiving the lapsed back into the Church: 'The vigour (*vigor*) of the priesthood is available to priests and deacons to prevent the action of certain members of the Church who are so forgetful of the Church's discipline and so driven by boldness and haste that they have already begun to readmit the lapsed to penance' (*Ep.* XX, 2). In this and similar cases *vigor* consists in making the Church's discipline effective.

For this *vigor* is first and foremost required by the gospel itself. The force of the gospel's demands must be maintained against those who try to weaken it. Cyprian contrasts it with laxism: 'Dear brethren, there has now appeared a new source of disaster and, as if the fierce storm of persecution had not been enough, there has come to crown it a subtle evil, an innocent-seeming pestilence, which masquerades as compassion. Contrary to the full strength of the gospel (*contra evangelii vigorem*), contrary to the law of our Lord and God, through certain people's presumption a deceptive readmission to communion is being granted' (*De lapsis,* 15). Similarly Novatian praises those confessors who 'preserve intact the dignity of the vigour (*vigor*) of the gospel' (*Ep.* XXX, 4), but he, of course, refused reconciliation with the Church altogether to the *lapsi*.

Cyprian warns Christians against any relaxation of the Gospel demands which would favour excessive indulgence: 'Do you think, brother, that these are small crimes against God, little and insignificant offences – the fact that the majesty of an angry God is not defended by these men (sc. the laxists), that the wrath, the fire, and the Day of the Lord are not feared, and that the faith of the whole people, mobilised, is disarmed, while the Antichrist is approaching, and vigour (*vigor*) and the fear of Christ are disappearing?' (*Ep.* LIX, 13). Here, 'vigour' expresses a lively sense of holiness and the Last Judgement.

This demand of the gospel and this authority of the bishop in furthering it must be effectively exercised. The bishop's *vigor* shows itself both in animating his flock and in firmly condemning false teaching: 'I have observed that some of the people are less firm in their attitude, either because their spirit is feeble or because their faith is small, or because their life in the world is easy or because their sex is weak or — what is worse — because they have erred from the truth. For this reason, I can no longer hide or remain silent about this situation. This is also why we shall try, as far as our weakness allows us, to strengthen the weakness of those whose minds are frail with full vigour (*vigore*) by letting our words be inspired by the reading of the Lord's word' (*De mort.* 1).

This vigour must also be expressed in defending the discipline of the gospel whenever the latter is violated. It is in the first place the vigour of Christ himself: 'In his precepts, Christ has impressed on us (the duty to forgive) with great firmness (*vigore*) in all its rigour (*censurae*)' (*De orat.* 28). It will also be the *vigor* of God's avenging judgement (*ultoris vigor*) (*Idol.* 14). It is the *vigor* with which the bishops are to condemn errors. Cyprian praises Cornelius, for instance, for the position that he adopted with regard to Felicissimus, who allowed the lapsed to be received back into the Church without penance. 'I have read your letter', he writes, 'which is full of Church discipline and priestly severity (*censurae*) and in which you informed me that Felicissimus had been rejected by you with the full vigour (*vigore*) that a bishop must use' (*Ep.* LIX, 11; cf. LIX, 18).

Above all, the bishop is bound to resist those who boldly try to intimidate him: 'If things have come to such a pass that we are afraid of the insolence of wicked men, and bad men achieve, by unbridled violence, what they cannot get by lawful means, then it is all up with the strength (*vigore*) of the episcopate and with the high, God-given right of government in the Church' (*Ep.* LIX, 2). This applies especially to the fallen bishops who claim the right to carry out their ministry again: 'We must struggle with the greatest vigour (*vigore*) in order as far as possible to repel them in the boldness of their crime, so that they will not try to behave like priests — the very men who, because of the greater weight of their fall, have fallen lower than the fallen lay people' (*Ep.* LXV, 3; cf. also LXV, 5).

It is interesting to note that in this particular sense the word *vigor* is also a favourite with Novatian. This would seem to indicate that the word originated in Stoicism, since Novatian derived much of his thought and vocabulary from Stoics. The word is employed several times in *Ep.* **XXX**. Novatian declares that he is 'a mind relying on the vigor of the discipline of the gospel (*Ep.* **XXX**, 3; cf. also *De spect.* I) and that he is at one with Cyprian in a 'unity of judgement (*censurae*) and discipline' (**XXX**, 1). He goes on to say that 'nothing is more suitable in peace or more necessary in the war of persecution than the maintenance of the obligatory severity of the divine vigour' (**XXX**, 2). 'May the abandonment of vigour by worldly easiness and the relaxation of the muscles of severity, which shake the majesty of faith', he insists, 'be eliminated from the Church of Rome' (**XXX**, 3).

In *Ep.* **XXXVI**, Novatian praises Cyprian for 'his vigour and the severity which he applies in conformity with the discipline of the Church' (**XXXVI**, 1). In all these texts, however, it will be noted that Novatian uses the word *vigor* only in the sense of strictness, and associates it with the word *severitas*. It is therefore linked with his own strict and rigorous attitude. In Cyprian's writing, on the other hand, the term has many more shades of meaning, illustrating the idea of the vitality and living power of the Church, both in its positive and its negative aspects, and more use is made of the possibilities offered by the word. This only serves to emphasise Cyprian's originality in this respect.

4. *MILITIA CHRISTI*

The Jews compared the people of God with an army confronting the army of the pagan nations. A good example of this is the description of the eschatological struggle in the *War of the Sons of Light and of Darkness*. The same theme is given a spiritual meaning by Paul, who deals with the symbol of the struggle between the Christians and the 'powers of the air'. In early Latin literature, however, the image has a concrete and contemporary meaning, relating to the conflict between the Church and the pagan empire. This was, it is true, not a military conflict, but the Christian community is described in terms taken from the Roman military vocabulary.

This is clear from the first work written by Tertullian, the *Ad martyres,* which is set in the context of the persecution of Septimius Severus: 'We are called to join the army (*militiam*) of the living God as soon as we respond to the words of the oath (*sacramentum*). No soldier goes to war for pleasure and none leaves his bedroom to enter the fighting line (*acies*) – he leaves tents (*papilionibus*) put up in a hurry' (*Ad mart.* III, 1–2). After making use of these few military images, however, Tertullian goes on at once to employ other images, drawn from the vocabulary of the combats in the gymnasium, which stress the individual character martyrdom always retains in his writings.

Tertullian also describes the Christian people as an army in the *De idololatria,* but this is to contrast the Church with the armies of this world, since the Christian conflict is spiritual: 'There is no compatibility between the oath (*sacramento*) to serve God and the oath to serve man, between the standard (*signo*) of Christ and the standard of the devil, the camp (*castris*) of light and the camp of darkness. One life cannot be owed to two masters, God and Caesar' (*De idol.* XIX, 2). In this text, the contrast between the two camps, that of God and that of the idols, is clearly defined. But it is in the guise of the Roman army that the world of the idols is portrayed.

An example of this occurs in the *De corona militum,* where the terminology is very similar: 'Do we believe that he is allowed to . add a human oath (*sacramentum*) to the divine oath and to respond to another Lord, after Christ? Will he set up positions (*stationes*), either for others more than for Christ or on Sunday, when there are none for Christ? Will he carry a standard (*vexillum*) which is in rivalry to Christ's standard? Will he ask the prince for a mark (*signum*), when he has already received the sign of Christ? To have one's name transferred from the camp (*castra*) of light to the camp of darkness is a sin' (*De corona* XI, 1–4).

It is clear from an examination of this passage how easy it was to describe the Christian community in military terminology. Some words obviously had a technical meaning both in the terminology of the Church and in that of the Roman army. Examples of this are *sacramentum, signum* and *statio.* The Roman *statio,* which refers to a military position consisting of a guard and soldiers, is matched by a Christian *statio* or fast (*De jejun.* X, 7).

This does not in fact mean that the Christian terms were taken from the language of the Roman army, but simply that the fact that the same words were used made the comparison of the Church to an army easier. Some of the words are, of course, explicitly military – the standard or *vexillum* denotes the cross of Christ (*Ad. nat.* I, 12, 16). This usage is already found in Justin.

Cyprian also makes use of the traditional vocabulary of the army and warfare to express incorporation into the Church. In his very first work, the *Ad Donatum,* he writes, for example, to his friend: 'You who have already been marked (*signavit*) in the spiritual camp (*castris*) by the heavenly army (*militia*)' (*Ad Don.* 14). There is, of course, no indication in this text of a confrontation between the Church and the pagan world. It simply points to the fact that Cyprian made use of military language as something that was especially well known in the Roman Empire.

This situation changed, however, during the persecution of Christians by Decius, the militant aspect of the Church becoming more important. The whole Church was mobilised like an army, and Christian confessors were engaged in combat. Refusal to sacrifice to the idols was breaking the resistance of paganism; and the Church saluted the victors, those who had borne witness in this confrontation. There was, as it were, a breath of victory in the air. Cyprian's problem was to keep up the morale of the army; and the dramatic focus of this problem was the question of the *lapsi,* those who had allowed themselves to be overcome, who had yielded in face of the enemy. The times presented what was indeed the decisive test of faith, and all the energies of the Church had to be concentrated for the fight.

All this is clearly expressed by Cyprian in his *De lapsis* 2: 'They form the bright army of the soldiers (*militum cohors candida*) of Christ, whose steadfastness broke the fierce onslaught of persecution, ready as they were for the long-suffering of prison life, steeled (*armati*) to the endurance of death. Valiantly you resisted (*repugnastis*) the world's attack, to God you offered a glorious spectacle . . . How blessed, how happy the Church is to open her gates for you to enter as, in closed ranks, you bear the trophies of the vanquished foe!' (*De lapsis* 2).

Cyprian also encourages and congratulates the Christians who are engaged in this combat against the pagan world in his letters of this period. In *Ep.* XII, 2, for instance, he speaks of those who, 'firm (*stantes*) in faith and fighting (*militantes*) firmly with us, have not deserted the camp (*castra*) of Christ', and, in *Ep.* XXXIX, 2, of Celerinus, a brave confessor, whom he calls 'the first in the battle (*proelium*) of our times, a member of the colour-party (*antesignanus*) of Christ's soldiers'. Again, the 'deeds of those of high rank and leaders in the combat of our times have set in motion the banners of the heavenly army' (*Ep.* XXVIII, 1).

It is in this context that we are to place Cyprian's behaviour with regard to the various tendencies that showed themselves in the community. His decisions do indeed imply certain rules concerning the exercise of authority, the discipline of penance, and the admission of Christians to the sacraments; but these rules are applied in terms of a specific situation, that of persecution, and this is the crucial point. For it is because of this concrete situation that Cyprian is led to describe the Church in military terms, prompted not by the Church's structure as such but by its confrontation with the world of idolatry. Nevertheless, at another level, such language does also serve to express the militant character of the Church.

In *Ep.* LV, 4, for instance, Cyprian replies to those Christians who were surprised by his easy reconciliation of the lapsed: 'For, as long as the battle (*acies*) was joined (*inter manus*) and the glorious contest (*certaminis*) was raging in a blaze of persecution, then the utmost exhortation and encouragement was called for to spur on the energies of the combatants and, for the lapsed especially, my words must ring out like a trumpet (*classico*) to revive their spirits. These needed to pursue their way of penance not only in prayer and sorrow, but also – since the opportunity lay open for renewing the struggle and repairing their fall – my words must stir them up (*increpiti*) and inspire them with zeal to witness to their faith and win the glory of martyrdom'.

Very much the same is said in *Ep.* LVII, 5: 'When the enemy was seen to be on the point of attacking us, it seemed to us to be valuable to bring the soldiers of Christ together in the camp (*castra*) and, after examining each one's case, to restore peace to those who had fallen or, even better, to give weapons to those who were on the point of fighting'. This text clearly refers to a period between two different persecutions. Cyprian recognises that it is not the time to extend the period of penance for those Christians who had fallen during the first persecution – this would have been his normal practice in dealing with the laxists – but that he should reconcile them to the Church in order to give them the opportunity to redeem themselves in the battle ahead.

Military terms are used in every paragraph of *Ep.* LVIII, which is, from beginning to end, an exhortation to Christians to prepare for the fight: *proelium*, 'battle', *pugna*, 'combat', *milites Christi*, 'soldiers of Christ' (LVIII, 1); *militiam*, 'army, military service' (2); *milites Dei*, 'God's soldiers', *nomen militiae dedimus*, 'we gave (it) the name of armed service', *recusare militiam*, 'to object to military service', *militiam* (3) and *militem*, 'soldier' (4). A characteristic sentence from this letter is 'May God's camp (*castra*) move towards the fighting line (*acies*) pointed out to us'. All Christians, both the *integri* and the *lapsi*, those who have remained faithful and those who have fallen away, are to take up arms against the enemy. Cyprian quotes from Ep. 6:13–17: the 'breastplate of righteousness', the 'shield of faith', the 'helmet of salvation' and the 'sword of the Spirit', and in his comments applies these terms to the current situation. The helmet of salvation, for instance, protects the Christian's eyes so that they cannot see idols, his forehead so that it may preserve the seal of Christ, and his mouth so that it may bear witness to the faith. In his introduction to the *Ad Fortunatum*, which is a collection of biblical quotations intended to sustain the martyrs, Cyprian says: 'God's precepts are like weapons which have to be obtained for those engaged in the combat. They are the trumpet (*tubae*) calls, the bugles to summon the fighters'.

The situation changed with the return of peace, and now we hear Cyprian protesting against the practice of reconciling the lapsed too easily. It is true that he has only one desire, namely that all Christians should return to the Church, but he is not in favour of an easy reconciliation: 'I should like everyone to return to the Church. I should like all our fellow-soldiers (*commilitones*) to be included within Christ's camp (*castra*) and in God's tents.

It is, however, an insult to those who fought bravely to see the lapsed (*lapsi*) trying to be received back without spending any time doing penance' (*Ep.* LIX, 22). This is the issue on which Cyprian was opposed to Cornelius. He warns him against the false reports that have been made to him, accusing him of rigorism. It is clear that Cyprian adapts his attitude to changing circumstances.

Another element is stressed by Cyprian in *Ep.* LX, addressed to Cornelius, namely that persecution came up against the resistance of the whole Church: 'The adversary had made a surprise attack in order to throw Christ's camp into disorder and to spread terror. But he was repelled with an assault (*impetus*) as furious as his own. He thought that he would once again be able to bring God's servants down and shake them in the usual way like young recruits (*tirones*) and beginners, believing that they were less well prepared and less on their guard. He first attacked one Christian only, like a wolf seeking to steal one sheep from the flock. But, repulsed (*retusus*) by the faithfulness and vigour of the whole army (*exercitus*), he realised that Christ's soldiers, soberly watching out and standing at arms ready for the battle, could not be conquered. They were made invincible because they did not fear death. In the combat in which they fought the enemy, they did not fight as individual soldiers. The whole camp went forward.' Finally, in another letter, Cyprian stresses that the Christian who accepts baptism by the heretics as valid is in fact the enemy's accomplice: 'If God's discipline has to be preserved in this way, then we can only lay down our arms, break our vows with God's justice and hand over the banners of the heavenly camp' (*Ep.* LXXIV, 8).

4. UNANIMITAS CONCORDIAE

If the *vigor Ecclesiae* was to assert itself in the face of persecution by the pagan world and to be able to resist its attacks, then the Church had to have a high degree of inner cohesion. This brings us to another of Cyprian's ecclesiological themes, that of the *concordia* of the Church. There is no doubt at all that this theme originated in the Latin world. We have already encountered it at the theological level, and have established that this usage is in the tradition of Latin Stoicism. Here we shall examine its use in connection with the community of the Church, where it is closely connected with the distinctively Latin concept of the unity of the city.

This theme of *concordia* occurs in Cyprian's writings at different levels, corresponding to the various stages in his doctrine of the Church. The earliest references occur in the texts written during Decius' persecution. Here *concordia* is the unity of Christians in common prayer, expressing the unity of the Church. This theme recurs in the *De unitate Ecclesiae* and in *Ep*. LV, in connection with Novatian's schism. In these texts the stress is laid on the unity of the Church as realised through the unity of the legitimate bishops. Finally, the same theme is also found in *Epp*. LXIII and LXIX with regard to the controversy over heretical baptism. Here it is the sacramental aspect of *concordia* which is stressed.

In *Ep*. XI, Cyprian is clearly concerned about a loss of religious fervour in the Christian Church, which has become lax since Decius' first persecution, and the divisions which this has brought in its train. This is, of course, the period during which Cyprian was opposing a too easy reconciliation of the lapsed. In this letter, he insists that the unity of the Church, which has to be restored in faithfulness to the Church, is above all expressed in unanimity in prayer: 'In prayer, there are discordant (*dissonas*) voices and divergent (*dispares*) wills. It has keenly displeased the One who said: "Ask and pray", that there is inequality and conflict (*discrepant*) among the people and that there is no unity (*consensus*) among the brethren nor one uniform concord (*concordia*)' (*Ep*. XI, 3).

This close bond between unanimity in prayer and the power of the Church is clearly emphasised at the conclusion of the letter: 'Everyone should pray to God, not only for himself, but also for all his brothers, as the Lord has commanded us, when he not only recommended private prayer to all, but also ordered us, praying a communal (*communi*) prayer and a unanimous (*concordi*) inter-cession, to pray for everyone. If the Lord finds us humble and peaceful, united (*copulatos*) to one another, he will protect us from the enemy's attacks' (*Ep.* XI, 7). What Cyprian is expressing here is the need for a unity of will among all members in the communion of the one Church.

The treatise *De oratione* has as one of its main themes the *concordia* of the Church and this would seem to be a good reason for dating it at the same period as *Ep.* XI, in other words, before Cyprian's return to his diocese in the spring of 251. What is particularly interesting is that Cyprian clearly draws on Tertullian's treatise on prayer, but places much greater emphasis on communal prayer, which is further evidence of the importance of the theme of the Church and its unity in his writing. It is also noteworthy that he makes no reference to the question of schism, which he would certainly have done had this treatise been later than the *De unitate.*

In the *De oratione,* then, he writes: 'Above all, the God of peace and the Lord of concord (*concordiae*), who has taught us unity (*unitatem*), wants each of us to pray for everyone, just as he has borne us all in his unity. This law of prayer was observed by the three young men in the fiery furnace; they were united (*consonantes*) in prayer and at one (*concordes*) in unity (*consensione*) of spirit' (*De orat.* 8). The same was true of the apostles: 'They persevered unanimously in prayer, demonstrating by the unity (*concordia*) and the insistence of their prayer that God allows only those whose prayer is unanimous (*unanimis*) to enter the divine and eternal dwelling-place' (*De orat.* 8). Union with the Church in brotherhood (*fraterna concordia*) is the condition of sacrifice being acceptable to God (*De orat.* 23). What lies behind these statements is, of course, the problem of reconciliation with the Church.

The theme is taken up again in the *De unitate,* in which Cyprian clearly aims to show that it is not enough for certain individuals to pray together for prayer to be effectual – they must be united to the Church as a whole: 'The Lord was urging peace and unanimity upon his disciples ... These words (Mt. 18:19–20) prove that much is given not to the mere number but to the unanimity of those who pray. "If two of you shall agree on earth," he says, putting unanimity (*unanimitatem*) and peaceful concord (*concordiam pacis*) first ... The Lord's words were spoken about his own Church and addressed to members of the Church. If they are agreed (*concordes*), if, as he commanded, but two or three are gathered together and pray with one mind (*unanimiter*), then, although they are but two or three, they can obtain from the divine majesty what they ask . . . He shows that . . . more can be obtained by the united prayer of a few (*paucorum concordi prece*) than by the discordant petition of many (*quam discordiosa oratione multorum*)' (*De unit.* 12).

It is quite clear from this text what Christian *concordia* is. It is not simply the prayer of a few Christians gathered together, but prayer made in union with the whole Church. It is at once the prayer of the whole Church and for the whole Church. The universal character of this prayer is defined by the word *unanimis*, which is often associated with it in Cyprian's writing about this theme. From the very beginning, then, Cyprian stresses that this *concordia* is an attribute of the Church and he continues to do this in all his later work. In *Ep.* LX, 1, for instance, he writes: 'For us, the Church is one, the spirit united and the concord (*concordia*) indivisible'; and in *Ep.* LXVI, 8: 'The whole people of the Church is gathered together (*collectus*), united (*adunatus*) and at one with itself by means of an indivisible agreement (*concordia*)'. The word *concordia* clearly has a strongly distinctive sense, perhaps best translated as 'universal harmony'. This places it in the tradition of Stoic philosophy, both cosmic and political, which stressed the unity and harmony of all things.

The theme of *concordia* was to acquire a fresh nuance, however, when Cyprian was confronted in 241 with Novatian's schism. At that particular time it served to express that aspect of the Church's unity which is embodied in the unity of the lawful bishops at one with each other and with the bishop of Rome. Even before the schism of Novatian, however, this aspect of the *concordia* of the Church was present in the writings of Cyprian. An example of this is his appeal to the bishops of Africa to preserve unanimity with regard to the lapsed: 'Let us be unanimous and united (*unanimes et concordes*) in preserving a healthy attitude towards the healing of the wounds of the lapsed (*lapsi*)' (*Ep.* XXXIV, 3; cf. also XLIII, 4; LV, 7).

The theme of *concordia* as present in the unity of the bishops of the Church first appears in the context of Novatian's schism in *Ep.* LV. Even the formal opening of the letter is important in this respect: 'In the first of the letters which I have received from you, dear brother (Antonianus, Bishop of Numidia), and which firmly endorsed the unity (*concordia*) of the episcopal body and your own adherence (*cohaerentes*) to the Catholic Church, you intimated that you were refusing communion to Novatian and, following our directive, were joining in the common recognition (*unum consensum*) of Cornelius, as our fellow bishop' (*Ep.* LV, 1). Here *concordia* expresses the unity of the college of bishops, which represents the universal (*catholicae*) Church voicing a single agreed opinion (*unum consensum*).

In the same letter, Cyprian goes on to state in opposition to Novatian why Cornelius is the lawful bishop. 'It is,' he writes, 'the judgement of God who made him (Cornelius) a bishop and the testimony of his fellow bishops who all, without exception, throughout the world gave him their approval (*consensit*) in unanimous agreement (*concordi unanimitati*)' (*Ep.* LV, 8). Here we have another aspect of *concordia*. It is the recognition of a bishop by all the other bishops which makes him a member of the episcopal college. This common agreement (*consensus*) is that of the universal Church as represented by the whole college of bishops, and the catholicity of the Church is the expression of this universality.

The situation is quite different with regard to Novatian, Cyprian points out: 'Whereas . . . the Church is one throughout the world, having many members in its parts, and whereas the episcopate is one, spread out in the concordant (*concordi*) fellowship of its many bishops – he (Novatian), despite God's disposition, despite the bond (*conexam*) everywhere linking together (*coniunctam*) the unity of the Catholic Church, tries to create a Church of human origin . . . He thinks he can . . . break up the structure (*compaginem*) of the body ecclesiastic by sowing his seeds of discord (*discordiae*)' (*Ep.* LV, 24).

The vocabulary used by Cyprian in the above passage displays new elements, marking a development in the doctrine of *concordia*. This *concordia* expresses the structure or organic unity (*compago*) of the body of the Church, the term *compago* which

Cyprian uses in this context meaning a connection or an assembly of parts. It is found, for instance, in *De unit.* 23: 'The one body cannot be divided by breaking up its structure (*discidio compaginis*)'.[5] Another closely related word, *compages,* with parallel meanings, is also found, used in the secular sense, in Cyprian's *De habit.* 14, where it refers to the individual pearls in a necklace, in the *De unit.* 18, to describe the whole of the earth's crust, and in *Ep.* X, 2, in which Cyprian speaks of 'the mass of the organs' of the martyrs being broken. Finally, the word is also encountered in connection with the eucharistic body, 'formed (*solidatum*) by the bringing together (*compago*) of one loaf' (*Ep.* LXIII, 13), the reference being to the coming together of the grains of wheat.

The verb *conecti* is also used by Cyprian to express the idea of different elements linked to each other and forming a single whole. It can also be applied to the image of the human body. In the Latin translation of Ep. 4:16, where Paul speaks of the body of Christ 'joined together and compacted', we find *conexum* and *compactum* and, although the actual quotation does not occur in Cyprian's writings, there may possibly be an allusion to it. More generally, the word *conecti* is used in contexts where the image of the body is in the background. We met it earlier in Novatian, *De Trin.* 2, in connection with the structure of the cosmos thought of as a great body.

In the *De unitate,* Cyprian deals more systematically and in a more general way with the theme of the Church as a single united structure and at the same time with the need for the Church to have inner cohesion. Cyprian begins by outlining the two great dangers facing the Church. The first is the danger of attack from without, from the enmity of the pagan city. We considered this in connection with the image of the Church as an army in battle. The second threat to the Church's unity comes from within: 'When he saw the idols abandoned, . . . our enemy (the demon) thought of a new trick . . . He invented heresies and schisms to . . . break unity' (*De unit.* 3). This menace is internal division. It is important to note how often the theme of *concordia*

5. Tertullian also uses the word in the secular sense in *Ad nat.* I, 16, 12 and referring to the unity of the Church in *De pud.* V, 9 and XX, 10.

is linked, in Cyprian's writings, to a concrete situation; and it is from this standpoint that we are examining it.

Cyprian begins by deepening the foundation of the Church's *concordia,* namely its *unitas.*[6] This is in the first place the unity of the college of bishops. The latter, however, derives its own unity from the fact that it is united to the successor of Peter: 'In order to make unity manifest, he (Christ) arranged by his own authority that this unity should, from the start, take its beginning from man. Certainly the rest of the apostles were exactly what Peter was; they were endowed with an equal share of office and power. But there was unity at the beginning before any development, to demonstrate that the Church of Christ is one . . . It is particularly incumbent upon those of us who preside over the Church as bishops to uphold this unity firmly' (*De unit.* 4–5).

This constitutive unity is expressed in the accord that exists between the bishops, their *concordia.* The term occurs again and again in the *De unitate:* 'To break the peace and concord (*concordiam*) of Christ is to go against Christ' (*De unit.* 6). Later in the treatise, he emphasises how important it is even for martyrs to be in *concordia:* 'Christ gave us peace and ordered us to be of one heart and mind (*concordes atque unanimes*)' (*De unit.* 14). The formation of a community is not enough; one must also belong to the universal unity: 'He (Christ) put unanimity and peaceful concord (*concordiam pacis*) first, teaching us to agree firmly and loyally' (*De unit.* 14). The same applies even in the case of a confessor: 'If a confessor abandons the Church in which he became a confessor, rends the bond of unity (*unitatis concordiam*) and exchanges his first faith for faithlessness, he cannot flatter himself on the strength of his confession that he is elect to the reward of glory' (*De unit.* 21).

In addition to *concordia,* however, Cyprian also uses another term, which emphasises the need for cohesion. This is the verb *cohaerere,* which Cyprian uses in a variety of contexts. Thus, Christ's seamless robe is 'a proof of this mystery of unity, this inseparable bond of harmony (*vinculum concordiae inseparabiliter cohaerentis*)'. Cyprian goes on: 'Since Christ's people cannot be

6. Cf. H. KOCH, *Cyprianische Untersuchungen,* p. 103.

rent, his coat, woven throughout as a single whole (*cohaerens*), was not rent by its owners. Undivided, conjoined (*copulata*) and coherent (*conexa*), it proves the unbroken harmony (*concordiam cohaerentem*) of our people who have put on Christ' (*De unit.* 7).

The same image occurs further on in the treatise: 'There will always be charity in the kingdom; it will abide for ever in the unity of harmonious brotherhood (*fraternitatis sibi cohaerentis unitate*)' (*De unit.* 14), and: 'The sons of God ought to be peacemakers, gentle in heart, united (*concordes*) in affection, loyally holding to one another (*sibi cohaerentes*) in the bonds of unanimity' (*De unit.* 24). Rhetoric does, of course, play some part in this repetition of certain favourite formulae, but rhetoric is not the whole explanation. Each word has its own particular shade of meaning and is chosen with care. The verb *cohaerere*, for instance, emphasises the fact that the Church is not composed of separate pieces of cloth sewn together, but consists of one single fabric.

Finally, the same theme of concord is expressed by another image in the *De unitate:* 'There is one God and one Christ and one Church and one faith and one people, fastened together (*copulata*) into a solid (*solidam*) corporate unity by the glue of concord (*concordiae glutine*)'. We have already encountered the verb *copulare* in this context, denoting the mutual joining together of different elements so that they form a single, solid whole. More interesting, however, in this context is the use of the image of *gluten,* the 'glue' which binds these elements together in unity and denotes Christian love.[7]

The same image is also employed in *Ep.* LXVIII, 3, where Cyprian speaks of the bishops, in their unity, as shepherds of the one flock who are bound to seek the sheep who have been abandoned by those in schism: 'That is why, brothers, the numerous body of bishops is joined together (*copulatum*) by the glue (*glutine*) of mutual concord (*concordiae*) and by the bond of unity, so that, if one of our colleagues becomes a heretic and tries to tear apart Christ's flock, the others will make up for this'.

---

7. Cf. TERTULLIAN, *De pud.* V, 9, for the unity of the members of the Church. Courcelle has studied this theme of glue as the symbol of the love which unites Christians.

Here, Cyprian stresses the active character of the unity of the Church.

This unity, which is expressed in the concord of Christians, is made visible in the college of bishops united to the Bishop of Rome and forms a single fabric which cannot be torn or divided. There is, however, another means by which Christians are united to Christ and to each other. This ultimate basis of Church unity is found in the sacraments; and here Cyprian is seen as a theologian of originality, both in his ecclesiology and in his mystical theology, opening up a line of thought which Augustine was to develop more fully at a later period. Two occasions led Cyprian to discuss this theme: the first was his critique of those who were opposed to the use of wine in the Eucharist; the second, his controversy with Stephen, the Bishop of Rome, concerning the baptism of heretics.

For the first, we must turn to Cyprian's letter to Caecilian, *Ep.* LXIII. Here, after recalling the biblical types concerning wine, Cyprian shows how the mixing of water with the wine has theological significance, expressing the union of Christ with his Church. In Scripture, he points out, the waters 'denote the people of the nations and the wine the spiritual grace' to which the nations are called, adding the comment, 'This is exactly what we see contained in the sacrament of the cup' (*Ep.* LXIII, 12).

Cyprian develops this latter idea in the following way: 'Because Christ, who bore our sins, bore us all, we see in the water the people and in the wine the blood of Christ. When, in the cup, the water is mixed (*miscetur*) with wine, the people are united (*adunatur*) to Christ and the multitude of believers is fused (*copulatur*) and joined together (*iungitur*) with the one in whom they believe. This fusion and joining together (*copulatio et coniunctio*) of the water and wine is also mixed in the Lord's chalice so that the elements of this mixture (*commixtio*) can no longer be separated from each other. In the same way, nothing can separate the Church from Christ insofar as it adheres (*haeret*) to him and abides in him, joined by indivisible charity. When (the wine and the water) are mixed with each other by a unity of fusion (*adunatione confusa*), the spiritual and heavenly mystery is fulfilled' (*Ep.* LXIII, 13).

This passage contains a number of nouns which we have so far not encountered in Cyprian's writing: *coniunctio, copulatio, commixtio,* and *adunatio.* Some, like *copulatio,* correspond to certain verbs that we have already met. What is new in this passage is the vocabulary concerned with the mixture (*commixtio*) of the water and wine. This is borrowed from the language of the eucharistic rite and it points to the mixture of divinity and humanity of which the rite itself is a symbol.[8] This reference is made ever more precise by the use of the phrase *adunatione confusa copulatur,* which shows that this mixture results in a complete fusion or merging together. It should be noted in this context that the word *confusus* was avoided by later Latin authors to designate the union of the two natures in Christ, mainly because this term (and *confusio*) indicated a mixture in which the elements lost their properties.[9] Cyprian's vocabulary, however, is still at the formative stage.

The word *adunatio* is also of some interest in that it stresses the realism of a unity which is physical and not simply moral. It is used in this sense in Cyprian's *Ep.* LXII, 1: 'Our brothers' captivity is our own captivity, because our union (*adunatio*) is a union of one body and this is not simply love, but the bond (*religio*) which must impel us to ransom those members which are our brothers'. It is clear from this text that Cyprian's thought developed between his earlier letters, in which he regarded the unity of the Church as a *concordia* or *dilectio,* and the later ones, in which the union of charity presupposes the unity of membership of one body.

So far *Ep.* LXIII has been concerned exclusively with the union of Christ and his Church. In the latter part, however, taking up the symbolism of the bread after that of the wine, Cyprian goes on to discuss the union of Christians among themselves: 'The Lord's cup is therefore not simply of wine nor simply of water, but a mixture (*misceatur*) of the two, just as the body of Christ cannot be simply of flour or simply of water – the two are united (*adunatum*), bound together (*copulatum*) and

8. Cf. JEAN PEPIN, '*Stilla aquae modicae multo infusa vino*', *Divinitas,* 11 (1967), pp. 367–368.
9. Cf. WOLFSON, *The Philosophy of the Greek Fathers,* I, pp. 387–392.

consolidated (*solidatum*) in a single structure (*compagine*) of one loaf. In this way, the unity (*adunatur*) of our body is made manifest in the sacrament itself so that, just as many grains of wheat, collected (*collecta*), ground together (*commolita*) and mixed (*commixta*), make one loaf, we know that we are one body in Christ, who is the heavenly bread in whom our mass is joined (*coniunctus*) and united (*adunatus*)' (*Ep.* LXIII, 13).

The comparison, however, is not quite on all fours. It is obvious that the water cannot point to the divinity of Christ, since the whole letter precludes this identification. Here, the body of Christ in the Eucharist, made of many grains of wheat which are united by water, is compared in this passage with the body of the Church, made of many believers united in one body. This second half of the letter is particularly interesting, because it stresses the reality of the unity of the Church as, on the one hand, a union with Christ (*in Christo*) through the Eucharist (*qui est panis caelestis*) and, on the other, a union of Christian believers among themselves. There can be little doubt that Cyprian's source here is *Didache* IX, in which the bringing together of the many grains of wheat to form one loaf is already an image of the unity of the Church.

Cyprian takes up this image again in *Ep.* LXIX, against Novatian, combining it this time, as in the *Didache,* with that of the many 'bunches and clusters' gathered from the vine to form one wine. His aim is to show that because the bread and wine of the Eucharist signify the unity of the Church, anyone who is outside the communion of this bread and wine cannot administer baptism, since only the Church can do this. In this passage, therefore, Cyprian brings out to the full the bond linking the unity of the Church to the sacraments. He insists that no one who is not in sacramental communion with the one Church is able to give a valid sacrament. Whereas Cornelius, the legitimate Bishop of Rome, recognised the validity of baptism administered by one who was not in communion with the Church and did not therefore share the same Eucharist, Cyprian goes to the ultimate point of realism in the question of the unity of the Church.

He writes: 'The sacraments of the Lord show how Christian unanimity (*unanimitatem conexam*) is preserved by the strong and indissoluble bond of charity. When the Lord calls his body bread, bread which is made (*congestum*) by the union (*adunatione*) of many grains of wheat, he is pointing to the union (*adunatum*) of our people whom he himself carried (*quem portabat*). When he calls his blood wine, wine which is pressed from many bunches and clusters of grapes and collected together (*coactum*), he is similarly describing our flock gathered together (*copulatum*) by the commingling (*commixtione*) of the multitude into unity. If Novatian is united (*adunatus*) to this bread of the Lord, if he is commingled (*commixtus*) with the cup of Christ, if, that is, it is established that he keeps the unity of the Church, then it will be possible to believe that he can possess the grace of the one and only baptism of the Church' (*Ep.* LXIX, 5).

All the words indicated in brackets in the above passage occur in the earliest texts that we have discussed here, but it is interesting to note the development in Cyprian's thought, since his earliest writings, regarding the unity of the Church. He lays increasing stress on the reality of the physical unity of the Church, of which the moral expression is *concordia*. At all stages of this evolution in his thinking, however, this emphasis on the unity of the Church is related to the actual situation in which the Church finds itself, that is, to the various forms taken by the threat of division. The fact that the Church was faced with so many dangers called, in other words, for a strong inner cohesion, and this led Cyprian to insist more and more on unity. In this respect, his work displays a manifest originality when compared with that of Tertullian in particular. One is conscious of the bishop confronted with the responsibilities of his office, where Tertullian's testimony is more that of the theologian.

CONCLUSION

THE origins of Christianity in the Latin world, looked at from the standpoint of culture, present a special problem. The earliest Christian authors in the West and in Rome in particular wrote in Greek, the most famous texts that have come down to us being the *Epistle of Clement,* the *Shepherd of Hermas* and the writings of Hippolytus. From the second century onwards, however, popular Christian writings in Latin began to appear; and in the present work we have tried to gather together the surviving traces of this early Latin Christianity, whether in the form of Latin translations of Greek texts or in that of original Latin works. In addition, of course, there are the earliest inscriptions in Latin. We have seen that this very early Latin Christianity was strongly marked by Jewish culture.

Later, however, Latin Christianity became more literary and works written in Latin tended to replace those written in Greek. The leading figure in this movement is, of course, Tertullian, whose plan was to equip Latin Christianity with a complete library of its own which would take the place of the Greek works. His *Adversus Judaeos,* for example, supersedes Justin's *Dialogue with Trypho,* and likewise his *Apology* those of Justin. He also wrote a treatise against the Valentinians (*Adversus Valentinianos*) which was inspired by Irenaeus's treatise against heresies, and a treatise against Marcion which had Justin as its source. Tertullian's theological treatises covered the whole area of faith, with the possible exception of ecclesiology, a gap which was to be filled by Cyprian.

In his attempt Tertullian was inspired by Greek models; but in imitating them he showed himself a mind of remarkable originality. His writings contain features which were to become those of Western Christianity at large. These aspects are in fact more prominent at this stage, when they come fresh from his genius, than they were to be in Western Christian authors of the fourth century, since the latter drew more on Greek models. Three features in particular seem to stand out in Tertullian's writing and at the same time point to the Latin Christian genius of the future. Firstly, unlike the Greek Fathers, who emphasise Christ's glory almost to the point of neglecting his human, earthly nature, Tertullian stresses his flesh and the mystery of his passion. Secondly, whereas the Greek authors were optimistic, contemplating man in his paradisal state and his eschatological restoration, Tertullian is conscious of man as a sinner and presents us with the pessimistic vision which was later also to characterise the work of Augustine, Luther, Pascal and Karl Barth.

In the third place, Tertullian is clearly interested in the inner life of man, the subjective aspect of the Christian way of life; and this too is new. Unlike Irenaeus, who concentrates mainly on the salvation of the body, Tertullian stresses the importance, above all in the *De anima,* of human psychology. Here again, Tertullian goes contrary to the tendency of the Greek authors to emphasise the objective aspect of salvation in Christ, and makes a vital preliminary contribution to a subject which was to find outstanding expression in Augustine, the founder of Western spirituality, and to be explored afresh in modern times by Christian existentialism.

It clearly required a powerful and original thinker to do this, but Tertullian's genius can be understood only if what went before him is borne in mind. It has been the attempt of the present work to do precisely this. This or that detail may be open to dispute, but the argument as a whole seems well-founded. Tertullian can be related to two distinct currents of thought. On the one hand, there is popular Christianity, Judaeo-Christian in type, still tied to its Jewish cultural origins, and confusing the tradition with the socio-cultural elements encrusting it. On the other hand, there is the attempt made by Minucius Felix to create a Latin Christian work by using classical models. This is closely related to that form of Latin writing which so frequently does no more than betray somewhat ponderously the Greek models which lie behind it. In the case of Tertullian, however, we are conscious of the young sap of Christian faith, springing up from Latin soil, and at the very first attempt bringing forth a corpus of writing of such originality that it can never be imitated and of such genius that it is impossible to forget.

POSTSCRIPT

JOHN AUSTIN BAKER

THERE is a particular responsibility in speaking for those who can no longer intervene in the debates of this world to speak for themselves. Had Jean, Cardinal Daniélou, so wished he could have corrected the Postscripts which it was my privilege to contribute to the previous two volumes of this great survey of Christian doctrine during the first three centuries, seen in terms of its cultural matrices. Since he did not, we may hope that they did at least not distort their subject matter in the effort to draw out its significance for the theology of our own day. In the present instance there can, sadly, be no such check, and that in respect of the branch of Christian tradition to which the great scholar himself belonged and at the conclusion of the whole enterprise.

Since, however, we are now at the end of a work with which I have been intimately associated off and on for seventeen years, I may perhaps be allowed to say something very briefly about the grand design which the author attempted to realise. The whole conception of trying to disentangle the elements in early Christian thought deriving from Jewish, Hellenistic and Latin culture has been seriously criticised both in principle and in detailed execution; and one can only agree that some of these criticisms have had weight. It has been asked, and with justice, whether the whole picture has not been distorted by excluding the New Testament from the material to be analysed, seeing that in the New Testament Jewish and Hellenistic culture are already intermingled. Indeed, in the light of modern understandings of the New Testament one may well ask whether in any future history of Christian doctrine the canonical texts will not have to be included, despite the obvious problems created by their rapid promotion to a special status as a source of truth, since it is precisely that special status which makes the varied cultural elements they contain especially influential. Again, there have been questions raised about the category of 'apocalyptic' so widely used by Daniélou – though if he errs here, he does so in good company, for no question has proved more slippery than the proper reference of that term. There have also been doubts whether there were ever any actual human beings or groups which corresponded to the concept, 'Jewish Christian' or 'Judaeo-Christian', and anxieties about the circularity of a method of analysis which seems at times to say that such and such a feature is Judaeo-Christian because it appears in an allegedly Judaeo-Christian work and then to argue that any other work in which the same feature appears thereby betrays Judaeo-Christian influence. Finally, the far-reaching syncretism of thought in the Mediterranean world at the beginning of the christian era inevitably makes some distinctions arbitrary. On what grounds, for example, is Stoicism treated in this volume as part of the Latin cultural matrix when, although popular and influential in the Latin world, it is in origin a Greek system, when its Latin exponents are not markedly original, and when it also affects Greek Christian theologians?

Nevertheless, despite these and other questionable features this massive work will, I believe, be judged in time to come to have been worthwhile, and does here and now offer the student something very important which he cannot get elsewhere. For it is a mark of the intellectual life of our century to have become aware in many spheres as never before of the cultural forms in which ideas are expressed. No one would argue today that Christianity was miraculously exempt from this universal feature of human life; and so it was highly desirable that someone should pioneer a conspectus of its early doctrinal development in a way that would take account of this fact. Daniélou, with his unrivalled knowledge of research in the field, was uniquely qualified to do this. As to his threefold pattern, it will again hardly be disputed that, however much cross-fertilisation there may have been, the world of early Christianity did have in it ingredients which were (at any rate proximately) mediated by

Semitic, Hellenistic and Latin culture. Whatever refinements may later be found necessary, this is a valid starting-point. It is true that the cultures are not co-extensive with the incidence of the languages. Both Semitic and Latin cultural elements appear in works written in Greek, and Semitic and Greek in Latin. That is why certain authors appear in more than one volume, and why the view of them in any one volume alone is misleading. But – and this can hardly be too strongly emphasised – this work is not primarily a portrayal of theologians or of doctrines, though such portrayals are part of what it has to offer, but of the interaction of cultural resources with the Christian mind seeking to articulate and structure its faith. In creating such a portrayal *de novo,* intuition born of familiarity with the literature is indispensable, whatever subjective errors it may bring with it, and this intuitive sense Daniélou magnificently possessed. I am convinced that many of his insights will find a permanent place in the history of Christian doctrine, a conviction confirmed in writing these Postscripts on the continuing relevance of the ancient material, for this relevance has emerged as strikingly different and individual in each case.

This is true even of the notoriously imitative and derivative Latin culture. The reader will have noticed throughout the present volume the extensive borrowings by Latin authors from material discussed in *The Theology of Jewish Christianity* and in *Gospel Message and Hellenistic Culture.* Nevertheless there are fresh contributions here, and Daniélou has himself drawn attention to them in a stimulating way by indicating the points at which lines of development began, leading down eventually to figures as various as Luther, Pascal, Kierkegaard and Péguy. The present assessment will, however, be as before in terms of themes and attitudes to truth rather than of personalities.

From the material under review four characteristic major themes emerge. The first, and most obvious, is the emphasis on *Christian institutions.* There is a difference of emphasis here between East and West which, for all that it is one of emphasis and therefore relative not absolute, has yet been of permanent significance. In the East, the Church and its sacraments are felt first and foremost as part of a continuum reaching into eternity, as the communion within which the true gnostic, the orthodox catholic believer, grows into fulfilment in that heavenly world which so far transcends the joys and glories of this earth. It is this faith, passing almost into sight, nourished by contemplation and study of the Scriptures, rather than any organisational framework, which creates the Church and makes it indestructible. In the West, by contrast, it is the discipline and structural cohesion of the Church which defend and perpetuate the faith. As the Christian community ceases to be a low-class minority and draws into its membership more and more individuals from the governing strata, so the ethos of the Empire begins to shape the Church's image of itself. Just as the bureaucratic and military organisation of Rome upheld the kingdom of the false gods, so the iron discipline of the Church was to create a city and a camp within which salvation would be safeguarded for ever. The individual Christian, however frail, would find the courage to endure from the corporate devotion and will to victory and from the assurance of a reward beyond this life mediated by the divinely guaranteed sacraments. His contribution, therefore, was primarily to obey; and this was the easier part. The really terrible burdens fell on those whose task it was to rule and who were ultimately responsible for the eternal destiny of those under them. It is in this perspective that we begin to understand the emotional voltage of the controversies over those who lapsed under persecution, and the logic of the bishops' various policies toward them. The overriding strategic priority was to keep the institutional Church strong and undivided, because this church as an institution was the basic means of salvation to mankind, and without her the very gospel itself would perish. Hence a man like Cyprian is perfectly consistent when, like a general on campaign, he judges at one point, when the outlook is sombre, that it is his duty to live to fight another day, and later, when victory is in the air and he has discharged his responsibility to those under his command, that he must now claim his own personal crown of triumph by martyrdom.

The Latin tradition here speaks directly to one of the major questions exercising Christian thinking today: which forms and structures are the right ones for the Church in the pluralistic and socially and politically volatile world in which we now live? One view, obviously in tune with some central New Testament insights, sees the future in terms of small, cell-like, local Christian communities, living and working almost anonymously as the salt or leaven in human society and stripped of any international or even denominational superstructures that might appear to echo the institutional power-systems of the world. This conception of the Church is in part a conscious reaction against some later developments of the very tradition we have been studying. But this tradition, and Cyprian in particular, have serious points to put in this debate. Historically it would seem to be true that the energy and vitality of the Christian people in its world mission have derived in large measure from having been more highly organised and more disciplined than any other great world religion. Do the hard facts of human psychology mean that these two things necessarily go together? Furthermore, Christianity is the most truly inter-racial and international of all the great religions, as befits a faith which early in its career broke through the barriers between Jew and Gentile. Ought there not then to be some visible personal structure to express this fact and sustain it? No doubt Christians are at fault when they succumb to triumphalism, or try to vie with the rulers of this world in outward trappings of influence and authority, whether these be the gold plate and social status of an earlier day or the buildings and bureaucracies of modern governments and multi-national corporations. But this does not mean that the Christian communities within a nation or in the world as a whole ought not to have some means of speaking with a single voice or of coming to a single mind on vital issues or of being recognised by their fellow-men as belonging to a single family. On the contrary, these are surely necessities, if the words, 'one in Christ', are to have any effective significance; and these are precisely the things for which, in the form of the unity and consensus of the episcopal college, Cyprian is arguing as necessities. They are not a substitute for the local vocation of christians, but they provide the framework without which that vocation must inevitably lose much of its driving force and sense of meaning. And if – as well may happen – Christians everywhere find themselves one day the victims of savage persecution, as so many of their brothers and sisters are today, then, as in Cyprian's time, the wider fellowship of the Church will do a very great deal to create the spiritual resources to meet it.

The second major theme that emerges from the writings of this period is that of *order and simplicity* in theology. This goes hand in hand with the concern for the institutional life of the Church. Both are primarily pastoral and soteriological in motivation – indeed, the distinction of emphasis between East and West in the institutional sphere can here be extended and more clearly defined. For the struggle against gnosticist tendencies developed rather different preoccupations in the Greek and Latin branches of the Church. In Eastern theology the emphasis is on the task of leading those who can take advantage of it to deeper spiritual understanding and holiness. The theologian sees himself essentially in the role of master speaking to disciples, and controversy tends in this early period to be a straight fight between experts, orthodox versus gnostic or pagan. In the West the theologians of the same era are more conscious of the *simplices.* Their task is to defend the salvation of those who cannot defend themselves against falsehood or guileful argument, and to rout their enemies. What emerges from the debate must be clear and comprehensible and in accord with the *regula fidei,* that fundamental pattern of the content of the faith which is the same among all Christians, educated or uneducated. The figure bridging these two theological emphases is Irenaeus, in whom pastoral concern animates both the huge, rambling mass of the *Adversus haereses* and the compact basic handbook of the *Demonstratio.* But when we compare Irenaeus's writings with those of Tertullian, a difference that strikes us at once is that even in his largest and most erudite controversial works Tertullian's aim is not only to arrive at results which will consolidate and defend the faith of the ordinary believer but to do so in a form which can be clearly understood and unambiguously used in teaching and discipline. It is a paternalist view of the theologian's vocation, and one which has always been a favourite in the West.

To fulfil such a task order and simplicity are vital. Dubious speculations, unnecessary side-issues must be ruthlessly excluded.

We must see clearly how one thing follows from another, how everything hangs together. Here are the beginnings of systematic theology; and it is interesting to note that it was in the West that systematic became one of the main tools for training the ordinary clergy, and long remained so, whereas in the East no comparable use has been made of the work of such great systematists as Maximus the Confessor and John of Damascus. Today we are in a period of great theological confusion, and theologians sometimes seem to have scant sense of any vocation to convey to the ordinary believer a clear, comprehensible and intellectually satisfying faith which will still carry the saving and sanctifying power of the gospel. The approach of men like Minucius Felix, Novatian and Tertullian has much to offer us in this respect.

Closely linked in its turn with this is a third feature that has emerged throughout the present volume, and that is the *openness to secular thought* of these theologians. This is, of course, not peculiar to the Latins. We had occasion to comment on it in the Postscript to the second volume with regard to Hellenistic culture. But interestingly enough there is a certain difference between Greeks and Latins even here; and it lies in the kind of secular thought in which each is most interested. In the East this is logical philosophy in the form of Middle Platonism, that of Albinus in particular, interpreting the nature of thought; in the West it is cosmological philosophy, especially Stoicism, interpreting the nature of the world. It would be anachronistic to call this an inclination toward science, for scientific thought in the modern sense did not exist at this period. But it would not be improper to see here at any rate intimations of that interest in the material and empirical which later characterised the West and which has made it possible for Western theology to try to come to terms honestly, however painfully and so far incompletely, with the scientific understanding of the world. The lesson which perhaps we have still to learn from these earliest centuries is that theologians need not be restricted to justifying their own language as still viable in its own sphere despite the findings of science in other spheres. Complementary to this is a bolder, more dangerous, but in the end possibly more creative course, and that is to learn how to use the terms and concepts of science to communicate the faith, and so to do this more effectively.

Finally, we must draw attention to a notable feature of this period which is far less likely to attract the modern Christian, and that is its *moralism*. It would be unfair to apply the term without qualification to the writers of our period since their faith is very far from reduced to morality and nothing more. Nevertheless it is perhaps the nearest single label to mark their overmastering tendency to see the substance of Christian living as expressed almost exclusively in moral conduct. Mysticism or meditation on Scripture to attain divine truth for its own sake – both elements of great importance in the East – are largely ignored. Everything – sacraments, prayer, grace – gets drawn into the one frame of reference of right behaviour; and one of the main duties of the bishop as pastor is to define this in considerable detail and to impose penance on those who transgress. There is no need to spell out how this has been a salient feature of Western Christianity, both Catholic and Protestant, ever since. It undoubtedly owes a great deal to both the Roman and the Stoic mental pictures of human life.

At present Western society is going through a phase of revolt against this ethos and is striving to shake free of it; and many in the Christian churches are, as always, being drawn by the spirit of the age to modify, sometimes drastically, their traditional rules and mores. Whether this phase is temporary and there will be a swing back to a more disciplined and less self-regarding set of standards in all departments of life, or whether the present trend will continue and infect larger and larger proportions of the population, it is impossible to say as yet. But unpalatable, and in some senses undesirable though this may be to a Church which has learned a good deal in this century about making morals more humane and less unthinkingly rigoristic, the time may well be drawing near when the Christian Church will have to say once again, 'If you are a Christian, there are certain things you do not do, whatever the world may say.' This was found indispensable in the early centuries of the Church, and has proved recurrently so ever since; and here too the Latin Fathers of the first three centuries have guidance for us that we neglect at our peril.

At the same time we must never lose sight, as the West has

done at certain sombre stages of its history, of the *anima naturaliter christiana,* the fact that by its very nature the human soul is designed by God for true fulfilment only in himself. The magnificent confidence that radiates from writers like Minucius Felix, Tertullian and Cyprian, from the appalling verses of Commodian, and from the artless but invincible faith of Perpetua and her Companions, was based not on some egotistical conviction of arbitrary election to bliss hereafter, but on the assurance that the Way, the Truth and the Life they had embraced were right for all men, that they were the key to the human situation. In the end what we most need to learn from these forerunners of ours is the gift of vision: a vision that reads the nature of the world and of man and the signs of the times, and sees in them the potential for which the gospel is the one true and eternal hope, and seeing is able to express that hope in words that speak to the contemporary condition.

BIBLIOGRAPHY

Acts of Thomas, ed. A. F. J. Klijn (Novum Testamentum Suppl. 5), Leiden 1962.

ALVERNY, M. T. D'., 'Les anges et les jours', *CA,* 8, 1957, pp. 274-300.

AMSTÜTZ, J., ʾΑπλότης: *eine begriffsgeschichtliche Studie zum jüdisch-christlicher Griechisch* (Theophaneia 19), Bonn 1968.

Apocryphon of Ezechiel. See under Melito.

ARMSTRONG, G. T., *Die Genesis in der alten Kirche: die drei Kirchenväter Justin der Märtyrer, Irenaeus, Tertullian* (Beiträge zur Geschichte der biblischen Hermeneutik 4), Tübingen 1962.

BARBEL, J., *Christos Angelos: die Anschauung von Christus als Bote und Engel in der gelehrten und volkstümlichen Literatur des christlichen Altertums. Zugleich ein Beitrag zur Geschichte des Ursprungs und der Fortdauer des Arianismus* (Theophaneia 3), Bonn 1964.

BARNES, T. D., *Tertullian. An Historical and Literary Study,* Oxford 1971.

BAUMSTARK, A., *Die christlichen Literaturen des Orients,* Leipzig 1911.

BAUMSTARK, A., *Geschichte der syrischen Literatur mit Ausschluss der christlich-palästinensischen Texte,* Bonn 1922.

BEAUJEU, J., *Opuscules philosophiques — Du dieu de Socrate, Platon et sa doctrine, Du monde — et fragments (d') Apulée,* Paris 1973.

BERGE, R., *Exegetische Bemerkungen zur Dämonenauffassung des Minucius Felix,* Diss., Fribourg 1928.

BEUTLER, R., *Philosophie und Apologie bei Minucius Felix,* 1936.

BEYSCHLAG, K., *Clemens Romanus und der Frühkatholizismus: Untersuchungen zu I Clemens 1-7* (Beiträge zur historischen Theologie 35), Tübingen 1966.

BIDEZ, J., *Les mages hellénisés: Zoroastre, Ostariès et Hystaspe d'après la tradition grecque,* Paris 1938.

BIETENHARD, H., *Das tausendjährige Reich: eine biblisch-theologische Studie,* Zurich 1955.

BLONDHEIM, D. S., *Les parlers judéo-romans et la Vetus Latina: étude sur les rapports entre les traductions bibliques en langue romane des juifs au moyen âge et les anciennes versions,* Paris 1925.

BOLGIANI, F., *La tradizione ereseologica sull'encratismo* (Atti della Academia delle Scienze di Torino 91), Turin 1965-7.

BOTTE, B., 'Deux passages de Tertullien', *Epektasis (Mélanges patristiques offerts au Cardinal Jean Daniélou),* Paris 1972, pp. 17-20.

BOYANCÉ, P., 'Sur l'exégèse hellénistique de Phèdre 246c', *Miscellanea di studi alessandrini in memoria A. Rostagni,* Turin 1963, pp. 45-53.

BRAUN, R., 'La notion du bonheur dans le latin des chrétiens', *SP,* 10, 1970, pp. 177-182.

BRAUN, R., *Deus Christianorum. Recherches sur le vocabulaire doctrinal de Tertullien* (Publications de la Faculté des Lettres et Sciences Humaines d'Alger 41), Paris 1962.

BRAUN, R., 'Tertullien et la philosophie païenne', *Bulletin* 4th Series, 2, 1971, pp. 231-251.

BRUYNE, D. de, *Les fragments de Freising, épîtres de S. Paul et épîtres catholiques* (Coll. biblica latina 5), Rome 1921.

CABANISS, A., *Liturgy and Literature: selected essays,* University of Alabama 1970.

CAMPENHAUSEN, H. von, 'Das Martyrium des Zacharias', *Historisches Jahrbuch,* 77, 1958, pp. 383-386.

CANTALAMESSA, R., *La cristologia di Tertulliano* (Paradosis 18), Fribourg 1962.

CANTALAMESSA, R., 'Prassea e l'eresia monarchiana', *La Scuola Cattolica,* 9, 1962, pp. 28-50.

CANTALAMESSA, R., 'Il Cristo Padre negli scritti del II-III secolo', *RSLR,* 3, 1967, pp. 1-27.

CHADWICK, H., 'Prayer at midnight', *Epektasis (Mélanges patristiques offerts au Cardinal Jean Daniélou),* Paris 1972, pp. 47-49.

I Clement, ed. G. Morin, *Anecdota Maredsolana,* 2, 1894, pp. 1-60.

COURCELLE, P., 'Virgile et l'immanence divine', *Mullus (Festschrift T. Klauser,* ed. A. Stuiber-A. Hermann) = *JAC,* Ergänzungsband 1, Münster 1964, pp. 34-42.

CORSSEN, P., 'Eine Theologie aus der Werdezeit der kirchlichen Literatur des Abendlandes', *ZNW,* 12, 1911, pp. 1-36.

CUMONT, F., *Lux perpetua,* Paris 1949.

CYPRIAN, *L'Oraison dominicale. Texte, traduction, introduction et notes,* ed. M. Réveillaud (Etudes d'histoire et de philosophie religieuses publiées sous les auspices de la Faculté de Théologie Protestante de l'Université de Strasbourg 58), Strasbourg 1964.

PS.–CYPRIAN, *Adversus Judaeos: Gegen die Judenchristen: die älteste lateinische Predigt* (Paradosis 22), ed. D. van Damme, Fribourg 1969.

DAHL, N. A., 'Der erstgeborene Satans und der Vater des Teufels (Polyk.7[1] und Joh.8[44])', *Apophoreta (Festschrift für Ernst Haenchen zu seinem 60 Geburtstag am 10 Dezember 1964*, ed. W. Eltester-F. H. Kettler), Berlin 1964, pp. 70-84.

DANIÉLOU, J., 'Le traité *Sur les enfants morts prématurément* de Grégoire de Nysse', *VC*, 20, 1966, pp. 159-182.

DANIÉLOU, J., 'Recherche et Tradition chez les Pères du IIe et IIIe siècles', *NRT*, 94, 1972, pp. 449-461.

DANIÉLOU, J., 'Joh.7.37 et Ezech. 47.1-2', *Stud. Evang.*, 11, 1964, pp. 158-163.

DANIÉLOU, J., *Études d'exégèse judéo-chrétienne, les Testimonia* (Théologie historique 5), Paris 1966.

DANIÉLOU, J., 'Mia Ekklesia chez les Pères grecs des premiers siècles', *L'Église et les Églises* (Études et travaux offerts à Dom Lambert Beauduin I), Chevetogne 1954-1955, pp. 129-139.

DANIÉLOU, J., *The Theology of Jewish Christianity*, trans. and ed. J. A. Baker (A History of Early Christian Doctrine before the Council of Nicaea I), London and (Baltimore, Md) 1964, Philadelphia 1977.

DANIÉLOU, J., *Les anges et leur mission d'après les Pères de l'Église* (Coll. Irénikon 5), Dinant 1953[2].

DANIÉLOU, J., *L'être et le temps chez Grégoire de Nysse*, Leiden 1970.

DANIÉLOU, J., *Sacramentum futuri, Études sur les origines de la typologie biblique*, Paris 1950.

DANIÉLOU, J., 'Hilaire de Poitiers, évêque et docteur', *NRT*, 90, 1968, pp. 531-541.

DANIÉLOU, J., 'Hilaire et ses sources juives', *Hilaire de Poitiers 368-1968* (Actes du Colloque de Poitiers 29 Sept.-3 Oct. 1968), Paris 1968, pp. 143-147.

DANIÉLOU, J., 'Figure et événement chez Méliton', *Neotestamentica et Patristica (Freundesgabe Oscar Cullmann zu seinem 70 Geburtstag*, ed. H. Baltensweiler-B. Reicke), Zurich 1962, pp. 282-292.

DANIÉLOU, J., 'Bulletin d'histoire des origines chrétiennes', *RSR*, 49, 1961, pp. 146-152.

DELCOR, M., 'Le Testament de Job, la Prière de Nabonide et les traditions targoumiques', *Bibel und Qumran (Beiträge zur Erforschung der Beziehung zwischen Bibel und Qumranwissenschaft, H. Bardtke zum 22.9.1966*, ed. S. Wagner), Berlin 1968, pp. 57-74.

DENIS, A. M., *Introduction aux pseudépigraphes grecs de l'Ancien Testament* (Studia in Veteris Testamenti Pseudepigrapha I), Leiden 1970.

Didaché. Instructions des apôtres, ed. J.-P. Audet, Paris 1958.

DIHLE, A., *Die goldene Regel: eine Einführung in die Geschichte der antiken und frühchristlichen Vulgärethik* (Studienheft zur Altertumswissenschaft 7), Göttingen 1962.

DÖLGER, F.-J., *Der heilige Fisch in den antiken Religionen und im Christentum* (ΙΧΘΥΣ. Das Fischsymbol in frühchristlicher Zeit IV),

Münster 1922.

DÖLGER, F.-J., *Antike und Christentum*, Münster 1930.

DOMBART, B., 'Über die Bedeutung Commodians für die Textkritik der Testimonia Cyprians', *Zur hist. Theol.*, 1879, pp. 275ff.

DUENSING, H., 'Epistula Apostolorum', *New Testament Apocrypha*, trans. and ed. R. McC. Wilson, London 1963-1965, I, pp. 189-227.

II Enoch. Le livre des secrets d'Hénoch: texte slave et traduction française, ed. A. Vaillant (Textes publis par l'Institut d'Études Slaves 4), Paris 1952.

EPHRAEM, *Opera*, ed. J. S. and S. E. Assemani, 6 vols, Rome 1732-1746.

ESSER, G., *Die Seelenlehre Tertullians*, Paderborn 1893.

FEUILLET, A., 'Le symbolisme de la colombe dans les récits évangéliques du baptême', *RSR*, 46, 1958, pp. 536-542.

FINÉ, H., *Die Terminologie der Jenseitsvorstellungen bei Tertullian*, Bonn 1958.

FONTAINE, J., *Aspects et problèmes de la prose d'art latine au IIIe siècle: la genèse des styles latins chrétiens* (Lezioni 'Augusto Rostagni', a cura dell'Istituto di Filologia classica dell'Università di Torino 4), Turin 1968.

FRANK, I., *Der Sinn der Kanonbildung. Eine historische-theologische Untersuchung der Zeit vom I Clemensbrief bis Irenäus von Lyon* (Freiburger Theologische Studien 90), Freiburg-Basle-Vienna 1971.

FRÉDOUILLE, J. C., *Tertullien et la conversion de la culture antique*, Paris 1972.

GEEST, J. van der, *Le Christ et l'Ancien Testament chez Tertullien: recherche terminologique* (Latinitas christianorum primaeva 22), Nijmegen 1972.

GERHARDSSON, B., 'The Seven Parables in Matthew 13', *NTS*, 19, 1972-1973, pp. 16-37.

GOODENOUGH, E., *Jewish Symbols in the Graeco-Roman Period*, 11 vols, New York 1953-1963.

GRANT, R. M., *Gnosticism and Early Christianity*, New York 1959.

GREGORY OF NYSSA, *De virginitate*, ed. M. Aubineau.

GUILLAUMONT, A., 'ΝΗΣΤΕΥΕΙΝ ΤΟΝ ΚΟΣΜΟΝ(P. Oxy. 1. verso, pp. 5-6)', *BIFAO*, 61, 1962, pp. 15-23.

HAGENDAHL, H., *Latin Fathers and the Classics. A study on the Apologists, Jerome and other Christian writers* (Studia graeca et latina Gothoburgensia 6), Göteborg 1958.

HARNACK, A.-GEBHARDT, O. von, *Texte und Untersuchungen zur*

Geschichte der altchristlichen Literatur, Leipzig 1883ff.

HARNACK, A., 'Der pseudocyprianische Traktat *De aleatoribus*', *TU*, V, 1888, pp. 1-135.

HEER, J.-M., *Die versio latina des Barnabasbriefes und ihr Verhältnis zur altlateinischen Bibel*, Freiburg-i.-B. 1908.

HENGEL, M., 'Anonymität, Pseudepigraphie und "literarische Fälschung" in der jüdisch-hellenistischen Literatur', *Pseudepigrapha* I (Entretiens sur l'Ancienne Antiquité classique XVIII), Geneva 1971, pp. 229-308.

HOFIUS, O., *Katapausis: die Vorstellung vom endzeitlichen Ruheort im Hebräerbrief* (Wissenschaftliche Untersuchungen zum Neuen Testament 11), Tübingen 1970.

HOOYMAN, R. P. J., 'Die Noë-Darstellung in der frühchristlichen Kunst. Eine christlich-archäologische Abhandlung zu J. Fink: Noë der Gerechte in der frühchristlichen Kunst', *VC*, 12, 1958, pp. 113-135.

HOPPENBROUWERS, H., 'Conversatio: une étude sémasiologique', *GLCP* Suppl. I, Nijmegen 1964, pp. 45-95.

Hypostasis of the Archons. The Coptic Text, Codex II from Nag-Hammadi, with translation and commentary, ed. R. A. Bullard (Patr. Texte und Stud. 10), Berlin 1970.

IRENAEUS, *Adversus haereses*, ed. W. Harvey, 2 vols, Cambridge 1857, new impression Cambridge 1949.

JAEGER, W. W., *Nemesios von Emesa. Quellenforschungen zum Neoplatonismus und seinen Anfängen bei Poseidonios*, Berlin 1914.

JAMES, M. R., 'Notes on Apocrypha', *JTS*, 16, 1915, pp. 403-413.

JONAS, H., in *Theol. Zeitschr.*, 1948, pp. 101-119.

KOCH, H., *Cyprianische Untersuchungen*, Bonn 1926.

KOCH, H., 'Zur Schrift *De aleatoribus*', *Festgabe von Fachgenossen und Freunden Karl Müller zum 60 Geburtstag dargebracht*, Tübingen 1922, pp. 58-67.

KOCH, H., 'Zu Tertullian *De pudicitia* 21.9ff', *ZNW*, 31, 1932, pp. 68-72.

KOCH, H., 'Die pseudocyprianische Schrift *De centesima, sexagesima et tricesima* in ihrer Abhängigkeit von Cyprian', *ZNW*, 31, 1932, pp. 248-272.

LA BONNARDIÈRE, A.-M., 'Le "Juste" défié par les impies (Sap. 2, 12-22) dans la tradition patristique africaine', *La Bible et les Pères* (Travaux, Université de Strasbourg. Centre d'Etudes supérieures spécialisé d'histoire des religions. Colloque 1-3 Oct. 1969), Paris 1971, pp. 161-186.

LABOURT, J., 'Le cinquième livre d'Esdras', *RB*, 17, 1909, pp. 412-434.

LABRIOLLE, P. de, 'Pompa diaboli', *Archivum latinitatis medii aevi*, 2, 1926, pp. 170-181.

LÄMMLI, F., *Homo faber: Triumph, Schuld, Verhängnis?* (Schweizerische Beiträge zur Altertumswissenschaft 11), Basle 1968).

LIÉBAERT, J., *Les enseignements moraux des Pères apostoliques* (Recherches et synthèses des sciences religieuses. Section de morale 4), Gembloux 1970.

LYONNET, S., 'Tu ne convoiteras pas', *Neotestamentica et Patristica* (*Freundesgabe Oscar Cullmann zu seinem 70 Geburtstag*, ed. H. Baltensweiler-B. Reicke), Zurich 1962, pp. 158-163.

MELITO, Bishop of Sardis, *Homily on the Passion, with some fragments of the apocryphal Ezechiel*, ed. C. Bonner (Studies and Documents 12), London 1940.

MESLIN, M., *Pour une science des religions*, Paris 1973.

MESSINA, G., *Notizia su un diatesseron persiano tradotto dal siriaco* (Biblica et Orientalia 10), Rome 1943.

MILIK, J. T., *Dix ans de découvertes dans le désert de Juda*, Paris 1957.

MINUCIUS FELIX, *Octavius*, ed. M. Pellegrino, Turin 1947, 1950.

MOHRMANN, C., *Études sur le latin des chrétiens*, Rome 1965, III, pp. 78-106.

MOINGT, J., *Théologie trinitaire de Tertullien*, 4 vols (Théologie 68-70, 75), Paris 1966-1969.

MOLTHAGEN, J., *Der römische Staat und die Christen im zweiten und dritten Jahrhundert* (Hypomnemata 28), Göttingen 1970.

NAUTIN, P., 'Gen. 1.2 de Justin à Origène', *In Principio. Interprétations des premiers versets de la Genèse* (École pratique des hautes êtudes, Paris, section des sciences religieuses. Centre d'étude des religions du livre), Paris 1973.

NOLA, A. M. de, *Il motivo della suspensione della vita cosmica come problema di relazioni interreligiose*, Milan 1970.

NOVATIAN, *De Trinitate. Über den dreifaltigen Gott. Text und Übersetzung mit Einleitung und Kommentar von H. Weyer*, Düsseldorf 1962.

O'MALLEY, T. P., *Tertullian and the Bible* (Latinitas Christianorum Primaeva 21), Nijmegen-Utrecht 1967.

ORBE, A., 'Las tres moradas de la casa paterna de san Ireneo a Gregorio di Elvira', *Diakonia Pisteos* (*Mélanges de Aldama*), pp. 69-97.

ORBE, A., 'Elementos de teologia trinitaria en el Adversus Hermogenem cc. 17-18', *Greg.*, 39, 1958, pp. 706-746.

ORBE, A., 'El pecado original y el matrimonio en la teologia del siglo

II', *Greg.*, 45, 1964, pp. 501-536.

PELLEGRINO, M., *Studi sull'antica apologetica*, Rome 1947.

PELLEGRINO, M., 'Il "Topos" sullo "Status rectus" nel contesto filosofico e biblico', *Mullus (Festschrift T. Klauser*, ed. A. Stuiber-A. Hermann) = *JAC*, Ergänzungsband 1, Münster 1964.

PÉPIN, J., 'Stilla aquae modicae multo infusa vino', *Divinitas*, 11, 1967, pp. 331-375.

PÉPIN, J., *Mythe et Allégorie: les origines grecques et les contestations judéo-chrétiennes*, Paris 1958.

PERNVEDEN, L., *The Concept of Church in the 'Shepherd of Hermas'*, trans. I. and N. Reeves and M. Went (Studia theologia lundensia 27), Lund 1966.

PETERSON, E., *Frühkirche, Judentum und Gnosis: Studien und Untersuchungen*, Fribourg 1959.

PÉTRÉ, H., *Caritas, Étude sur le vocabulaire latin de la charité chrétienne* (Spicilegium sacrum lovaniense 22), Louvain 1948.

PÉTRÉ, H., *L'exemplum chez Tertullien*, Dijon 1945.

PLUMPE, J. C., *Mater Ecclesia. An inquiry in the concept of the Church as Mother in early Christianity*, Washington 1943.

PRIGENT, P., *Justin et l'Ancien Testament: l'argumentation scripturaire du traité de Justin contre toutes les hérésies comme source principale du 'Dialogue avec Tryphon' et de la première 'Apologie'*, Paris 1964.

PUECH, H. C., 'Origène et l'exégèse du Ps. 50, 12, 14', *Aux sources de la tradition chrétienne (Mélanges offerts à M. Goguel)*, Neuchâtel 1950, pp. 180-195.

QUISPEL, G., 'The discussion of Judaic Christianity', *VC*, 22, 1968, pp. 81-93.

QUISPEL, G., 'Anima naturaliter christiana', *Eranos Jahrbuch*, 18, 1950, pp. 173-182.

QUISPEL, G., 'Anima naturaliter christiana', *Latomus*, 10, 1951, pp. 163-169.

QUISPEL, G., *Makarius, das Thomasevangelium und das Lied von der Perle (in den Thomasakten)* (Novum Testamentum, Supplementum 15), Leiden 1967.

QUISPEL, G., 'Der Heiliand und das Thomasevangelium', *VC*, 16, 1962, pp. 121-151.

RAHNER, H., 'Pompa diaboli', *ZKTh*, 55, 1931, pp. 239-273.

REGEN, F., *Apuleius philosophus platonicus: Untersuchungen zur 'Apologie' – 'De magia' – und zu 'De mundo'* (Untersuchungen zur antiken Literatur und Geschichte 10), Berlin 1971.

REINACH, S., *Cultes, mythes et religions*, I, Paris 1905.

REITZENSTEIN, R., 'Eine frühchristliche Schrift von den dreierlei

Früchten des christlichen Lebens', *ZNW*, 15, 1914, pp. 60-90.

RESCH, A., *Agrapha: Aussercanonische Schriftfragmente*, Leipzig 1906.

SAHLIN, H., *Studien zum dritten Kapitel des Lukasevangeliums*, Uppsala 1949.

SCHMIDT, F., 'Une source essénienne chez Commodien', *Pseudépigraphes de l'Ancien Testament et manuscrits de la Mer Morte*, Paris 1967, I, pp. 11-27.

SCHNEEMELCHER, W., 'Esra', *RAC*, VI, cols 595-612.

SCHOEPS, H. J., *Aus frühchristlicher Zeit: religionsgeschichtliche Untersuchungen*, Tübingen 1950.

SCHWARTE, K. H., *Die Vorgeschichte der augustinischen Weltalterlehre*, Bonn 1966.

SEEBERG, E., 'Eine neugefundene lateinische Predigt aus dem 3 Jahrhundert', *NKZ*, 25, 1914, pp. 472-494.

SINISCALCO, P., *Mito e Storia della Salvezza: ricerche sulle più antiche interpretazioni di alcune parabole evangeliche* (Università di Torino, Facoltà di lettere e filosofia. Filologia classica e glottologia 5), Turin 1971.

SINISCALCO, P., *Ricerche sul 'De resurrectione' di Tertulliano*, Rome 1966.

SINISCALCO, P., *I significati di 'restituere' in Tertulliano*, Turin 1959.

SPANNEUT, M., *Le stoïcisme des Pères de l'Eglise, de Clément de Rome à Clément d'Alexandrie* (Patristica Sorbonensia 1), Paris 1957.

SPARKS, H. F. D., *The Old Testament in the Christian Church*, London 1944.

SPARKS, H. F. D., *The formation of the New Testament*, London 1952.

STAATS, R., 'Die törichten Jungfrauen von Matthäus 25 in gnostischer und antignostischer Literatur', *Christentum und Gnosis*, ed. W. Eltester (Beiheft ZNTW 37), Berlin 1969, pp. 98-115.

STRACK, H. J.-BILLERBECK, P., *Kommentar zum Neuen Testament aus Talmud und Midrasch*, 2 vols, Munich 1922, 1924.

STUIBER, A., 'Das ganze Joch des Herrn (*Didache* 6, 2-3)', *SP*, 4, 1961, pp. 323-329.

STUIBER, A., 'Die Wachhütte im Weingarten', *JAC*, 2, 1959, pp. 86-89.

TATIAN, *Diatesseron persiano*, ed. and trans. G. Messina (Biblica et Orientalia 14), Rome 1951.

TERTULLIAN, *Opera*, ed. A. Kroymann, III (*CSEL XLVII*), Vienna 1906; V/2 (*CSEL LXX*), Vienna 1942.

TERTULLIAN, *De anima*, ed. J. H. Waszink, Amsterdam 1933, 1947.

TERTULLIAN, *Adversus Judaeos. Mit Einleitung und kritischem Kommentar von H. Tränkle*, Wiesbaden 1964.

TERTULLIAN, *De testimonio animae. Introduzione, testo e commento*, ed.

C. Tibiletti (Università di Torino, pubblicazioni della Facoltà di lettere e filosofia, II/ii), Turin 1959.

THEILER, M. W., *Die Vorbereitung des Neoplatonismus* (Problemata 1), Berlin 1930.

THRAEDE, K., 'Beiträge zur Datierung Commodians', *JAC*, 2, 1959, pp. 90-114.

TIBILETTI, C., 'Il cristiano e la Sacra Scrittura in un passo di Tertulliano (*De testimonio animae* 1, 4)', *Giornale italiano di filologia*, 15, 1962, pp. 254-256.

UNNIK, W. C. van, 'Die "Zahl der vollkommenen Seelen" in der "Pistis Sophia" ', *Abraham unser Vater* (*Festschrift für Otto Michel zum 60 Geburtstag*, ed. O. Betz-M. Hengel-P. Schmidt), Leiden-Cologne 1963, pp. 467-477.

UNNIK, W. C. van, 'Le nombre des élus dans la première épître de Clément', *RHPR*, 42, 1962, pp. 237-246.

VOGELS, H. J., 'Die Tempelreinigung und Golgotha (*Joh*. 2, 19-22)', *Biblische Zeitschrift*, 6, 1962, pp. 102-107.

VOGT, H.-J., *Coetus Sanctorum. Die Kirchenbegriff des Novatians*, Bonn 1968.

VÖÖBUS, A., *History of Asceticism in the Syrian Orient: a contribution to the history of culture in the Near East*, 2 vols, Louvain 1958, 1960.

WASZINK, J. H., 'Pompa diaboli', *VC*, 1, 1947, pp. 13-41.

WASZINK, J. H., 'Observations on Tertullian's Treatise against Hermogenes', *VC*, 9, 1955, pp. 129-147.

WEIL, E., 'Remarques sur le matérialisme des stoiciens', *L'Aventure de l'esprit* (*Mélanges Loyré*), II, pp. 556-572.

WERNER, M., *Die Entstehung des christlichen Dogmas, problemgeschichtlich dargestellt*, Berne-Tübingen 1954[2] (ET *The Formation of Christian Doctrine*, London-New York 1957).

WIDMANN, H., 'Irenäus und seine theologischen Väter', *ZKTh*, 54, 1957, pp. 156-173.

WOLFSON, H. A., *The Philosophy of the Church Fathers*, Cambridge, Mass. 1970[3].

TEXTUAL INDEXES

OLD TESTAMENT

GENESIS
1   234
  1–2   371
  2   368, 369, 373
  10–11 202
  24   172
  27   375
  29   247
2 1   67
  2   74
  7   41, 160, 350,
        372, 374, 375,
        377
  9   106
  16   90
  18   172
  23–24 307
3 5   67
  9   169
  17–19 247
  19   170
  22   169
6 1–2   162
9 3   248
11 7   330–331
12 7   331
16 7–16 332, 333
18 1–33 333
21 17–19 333
28 11   305
29 15–30 46
31 11–13 334
32 24–27 335
48 15–16 336
49 5–6   302
  6   269
  9–10   302
  10   302, 318, 329
  11   330

EXODUS
3 8   12
4 13   329
12 46   310
17 12   305
33 20   331

LEVITICUS
7 20   96
23 40   61

DEUTERONOMY
18 15   329
21 23   276
27 8   305
28 63   140
  66   140, 265, 269,
         272, 276, 277,
         278, 280, 299,
         329
30 15   106, 107
  19   106
32 8   331
33 17   269, 270, 302

NUMBERS
24 17   279

JOSHUA
2 17   310
  18–19 310
5 2   304, 305
6 20   268
  21   268
24 26   305

I SAMUEL
1 5   311
2 5   290
6 18   305
7 12   305
17 49   305

I KINGS
19 10   290

II CHRONICLES
24 20   37

II ESDRAS (NEHEMIAH)
  1–2   17

JOB
1 8   325, 326
  21   325, 326

  22   325
2 10   325, 326
14 4   326
38 8   202
  11   202

PSALMS (MT)
  (Vulg. refs. in brackets)
1 3   12n, 50, 51,
         266, 278
2 7   40, 329
3 5(3.6) 283
  6(3.7) 283
8 3(8.4) 268

18 43(17.44) 267
22(21) 291
  16(21.17) 269, 274, 276,
             277
  16–23(21.17–
  22)   275
  17(21.18) 270, 271
  19(21.20) 270
  20(21.21) 269
  21(21.22) 269
  27–28
  (21.28–
  29)   282
  28(21.29) 282
23(22) 5 316
33(32) 2 79
38 17(37.18) 270
40 8(39.9) 50
45 2–5
  (44.3–6) 270
50(49) 3 292
  14   268, 269
  19   196
51 10(50.12) 72
  14(50.16) 76
  17(50.19) 172, 173, 196,
             266
  19(50.21) 268
59 11(58.12) 271

63 5(62.6) 270
67(66) 7 281

68 2(67.3) 292
69 21   270
   22(68.23)271
72 1(71.2) 329
82(81) 8   292
90(89) 4   123
92 3(91.4) 79
96(95) 7–8 268
   10   41, 140, 265,
           269, 272, 280
97(96) 1   280
107(106) 20 283
110(109)1–2 329
   4   317
118(117) 22 304
119(118) 1 67, 91
   120   276, 277

PROVERBS
7 3–5   68
9 1   293
   5   318

SONG OF SOLOMON
(Canticles)
1 6   41, 53, 55
6 8   21
   10   22

ISAIAH
1 2   35n, 268, 272
   3   271
   4   268, 272
   7   271
   7–8   267, 271, 272
   8   41, 53, 55
   11   269
   11–13   268, 272
   13   272
   14   268, 272
   15   34, 268, 272
   20   271
2 2   48
   2–3   47, 48, 267
   2–4   141
   3   33, 47, 50,
           141, 267, 268
   3–5   272
   20   271
3 3   271
4 1   131
5 1–7   53
   2   53
   6   271

   10   79
6 3ff   74
   7   12
   10   282
7 10–11   281
   11   280
   13–15   269, 284
   14   280, 291, 400
   14–16   281
   16   281
8 1   272
   4   269, 281, 284,
           400
   6   272
   6–7   33
   14   304, 305
9 5   333, 388
   6   269
10 23   67, 70, 92
11 1   279, 329
   1–4   131
   2   131, 441
   10   279, 329
16 1   47n, 51
28 16   286, 304
33 17   271
35 4   270
40 12   41, 52
42   56
   2   270
   3   270
   5   376n
   13   292
45 1   282
   14–15   284
49 6   12
50 11   271
51 1   50
52 5   271
53   291
   2   270
   3   329
   5   271, 329
   7   270, 275
   7–9   275
   8   270
   8–10   269
   12   275
54 1   20, 21
   15   268
57 2   269, 287
58 1   270, 441
60 19f   27
61 6   124

65 2   141, 271
   13–15   271
67 4   124

JEREMIAH
2 10–13   141
   13   141, 266
4 3–4   267, 268
9 10–13   271
11 19   141, 269, 275,
           277
17 9   285
31 31–32   267, 268

LAMENTATIONS
4 20   158

EZEKIEL
1   242
9 1–6   269
   4   30
14 14   326
22 8   268
28 16   172
37   24, 400
   7   166
47 1–11   50, 51
   8–9   50
   12   28
48 30–35   144

DANIEL
2 34   267, 304
   34–35   48n
3   445
   16–18   323
4 24   328
7   265
   13–14   270
9   265
   1–27   286
   24   286
   24–26   286
   25–26   285

HOSEA
12 4   336n

AMOS
6 6   124
8 9   269

MICAH
5 1   291

HABBAKUK		ZECHARIAH		MALACHI	
3 *3*	330	**3** *1–2*	270	**1** *10*	268, 269
		8–9	305	*10–11*	268
·ZEPHANIAH		**4** *10*	131	**4** *1*	292
3 *1–2*	309	**12** *10*	270		

APOCRYPHA (Biblical)

II(4) ESDRAS		*11–14*	327	ECCLESIASTICUS (*Sirach*)	
4 *36*	25	**13** *6*	327	**9** *8*	68
5 *26*	21	**14** *8*	328	**31** *8*	67
13 *40–50*	118			**32** *1*	156

TOBIT				BARUCH	
2 *2*	328	WISDOM		**3** *36–38*	285
4 *5–11*	328	**2** *12–22*	287		
12	328	*19–22*	41	I MACCABEES	
12 *8*	327	**6** *12–21*	68, 288	**2** *38–44*	268

NEW TESTAMENT

MATTHEW		*39–43*	287, 288	JOHN	
6 *10*	436	*40–43*	41	**1** *13*	7
24	413	*55*	288	*18*	335
7 *7*	184, 185			**2** *19*	40, 44
21	91, 436, 437	LUKE		**3** *6*	91
24	64	**6** *48*	64	*14*	303
24–28	64	**8** *5*	78	**5** *14*	92
10 *17*	89	**11** *9*	184	**6** *38*	92, 436, 437
37–38	87	*35*	96	**7** *7*	41
38	34	**12** *35–40*	146	*37–38*	49, 50
11 *28–30*	34	*47*	436	*38*	50, 51
13 *4*	78	*58–59*	391	**8** *44*	299
4–9	148	**13** *18–19*	146	**12** *40*	283
15	283	*20–21*	146		
23	81	**14** *16–24*	146	ACTS OF THE APOSTLES	
16 *24*	87	*31*	79, 81	**2** *3*	68
17 *55*	287	**15**	147	**15** *29*	69
18 *19–20*	455	*4*	75, 81	**28** *26–27*	283
19 *11–12*	65, 66	*7*	75		
11–13	90	*8*	82	ROMANS	
29	125	*9*	81	**7** *16*	88
20 *1–16*	146	**16** *9*	29	*20*	88
21 *38*	35n	*22*	143	*23*	87, 88
43	20n	*24*	393	**9** *10–13*	114
22 *40*	91, 92	**19** *11–27*	77	**12** *2*	97
23 *34–35*	37	*17*	69	**13** *12*	89n
24 *22*	22	**20** *34–35*	66	**15** *12*	279
26 *29*	125	*34–36*	90		
39	436	*35*	68, 83, 84, 85,	I CORINTHIANS	
27 *3*	287		91	**3** *2*	90n
24	34	*36*	82	*3*	72

10	65	
16	65, 72, 97	
5 13	67n	
6 15	91	
7 29	68, 84, 89	
30	91	
9 25	86, 91, 155	
10 4	314	
23	91	
11 10	143	
15 45	403	
45ff	298	
45–50	376	
47	159, 160	
50	159, 401	
51	221	
52	124	

II CORINTHIANS
4 16	401
6 14	413, 428
16	65
12	178
7	72

GALATIANS
1	178
15–16	68, 84
4 21–31	311
24ff	46
24–27	20
26	21
5 17	75, 76, 89,

	160, 161
19	89n

EPHESIANS
4 16	458
30	96
5 31	298
31–32	307
6 12	89
13–17	452

COLOSSIANS
2 15	330

I THESSALONIANS
4 15	124

I TIMOTHY
1 4	187

II TIMOTHY
2 17	427

HEBREWS
11 17–19	301
37	108
12 18ff	46

I PETER
1 4	23
6	23

16	89
24	67, 89, 90n
2 6	23
9	23, 27
5 4	23

I JOHN
2 15	436
17	92, 436
18–19	427
25	437
27	436

REVELATION
3 4–5	30
4 6	73
5 6	131
7 3–8	30
4	25
9	20n, 29, 61
15	29
11 3	22n
14 4	91
20 4–10	125
5	119
21 2	53, 124
3	29
12	53
12–13	144
16	53
23	27
22 16	279
21	28

JEWISH WRITINGS

APOCALYPSE OF MOSES
XXVII	2, 7	168
XXVIII	3	169
XLI	2	170

II BARUCH
XXIX	3	125
LXXIII	2–5	118
LXXIV	1	118
LXXVII	19–22	118
LXXVIII		118

I ENOCH
VI	1–2	162
VII	1	164
	1–VIII,3	163

VIII	1	164
	1–3	164
	2	163, 164
X	17–19	120
XII–XVI		166
XV	9	164
XIX	1	166
XXIV	2f	28
	4	28
	5	28
	6	28
XXV	7	28
LXI	5	24, 166
	15	25n
LXII	14	27
	15	27

LXXXII	1	162
XCIX	6	165

JOSEPHUS
(War of the Jews)
VI	5:3	35

JUBILEES, BOOK OF
IV	7	42
XVI	30	29

LIFE OF ADAM AND EVE
IX	1	171
XIV	1–3	172

PHILO (Migr.)
	131	243

PHILO (*Quaest. in Gen.*)
IV   51   243

PHILO (*Quis rer.*)
       301   243

I Q *Ben.*
V   27   279

QUMRAN CAVES
I   *128-129* 279

SIBYLLINE ORACLES III
     24   43
     108-111 174
     263   175
     827   173

JEWISH CHRISTIAN WRITINGS

ADVERSUS JUDAEOS
3   8   48n
9   34
17   34
24–25   37
25   37
28   35
29   35n
33   35
34   35
43   36
45   32
46   32
47   27, 32, 33
49   32, 39
51   32
58   32n
59   32
62   34
64   32
68   33
77   34
148   63
173   27
307–308   47

ASCENSION OF ISAIAH

III   *15*   143
IV   *2*   117
XVII   *12*   150

I CLEMENT
II   *4*   25
III   *1*   72
       3   68
IV   300
XII   *1*   67
XIV   *6–33* 37
XVI   37
XVII   *1*   37
XVIII *12*   72
       14   76
XX   202
XXI   *6*   76

XXVI   *2*   283
XLV   323
L   *3*   67
       4   24
·LIX   *1*   25
LXVI   *6*   436

II CLEMENT
II   *1*   21

CLEMENTINE HOMILIES
II   *16ff* 38

CLEMENTINE
RECOGNITIONS
III   *61*   38
VIII   *66*   70

COMMODIAN
(*Carmen apologeticum*)
17   120
45–49   121
51   101
91–94   109
96–97   103
101   103
102   101
104–105   101
106   101
109   101, 103
110   102
112   102
117–118   102
119   102
127   102
130   63
132–140   115
149–150   104
151–152   107
153–154   104
157   107
171   284
176   112
189–190   114
221–222   108

227–229   38n
252–253   114
264   279n
265   304
265–494   273
267–268   285
269   276
270   274
274   275
276   277
277–278   110
281–284   110
290   279
291–292   278
295–296   280
298   279n
309   114
309–310   432
310–312   115
313–320   111
321–322   112
324   107
326   112
327   112
330   113
331   113
333   112
333–334   277
337–338   19
345   19
363–366   110
369   279n
370   285
371–372   285
381   284
383–384   282
384   282
399–402   282
405–409   280
417   276
445–446   283
483–502   287
495–496   287
502   102
512–516   108

699	106
791	121
804–864	116
809	122
810	100
934	118
936	117, 118
941–990	118
967–970	117
969–970	19
987–988	122
992	119
998	122

COMMODIAN (*Instructions*)

I	*2*	26	10n
	3		103
	6	1–2	103
	8	1–3	103
	12	5	106
	15	3	103
	16	1	103
	23	3	93n
	27	18	102
	29	11	102
	35	1–2	104n
		3–4	106
		4	107
		6	115, 121
		7	105, 107,123
		7–10	278
		10	105
		11	105
		11–14	113
		12–19	122n
		19	40n
	36	11	113
	38		312
		1–10	114
		4	114
		5	114n
		11	114
	40	8–9	278
	41–43		117
II	*26*		10n
	42		19,118
		11	19
		36	20n
		43	122n
		44	20n
	43	1	119
		8	120,122

	9	122
	13	120
	16–17	122
45	6	122
	12	122
65	15	285

DE ALEATORIBUS

1	93
2	11, 95, 156
3	93, 95, 97, 156
4	14, 67n, 94, 156
5	93, 97
8	95
9	96
11	156

DE CENTESIMA

4	*12*	309
5	*9*	72
	32	72
38	*32*	75
51	*45*	67n
	55–62, 2	91
54	*10–12*	87
	29	66
55		64, 71
	5–6	69, 155
	23–26	160
56		97
	8–11	87
	7–8	68
57	*24*	82
	32–35	77
	9–10	9
58	*10–11*	155
	10–13	70
	33–35	72
	34	89n
	35–37	159
	38	75
	39–42	89
	44	66
	49	67n
59	*3*	66
	5	76
	6	71
	13	76
	47–49	71
	53	68
	60	71

60	*5–6*	69, 86
	6–7	155
	6–8	69
	7–8	155
	7–9	86
	16	75
	19	71
	40	71
	41	71
	47	71
	50–61,	*37* 73
	54	65
61	*12–16*	67
	21–22	83
	25–37	74
	41	66
	45	66
	54–55	90
62		97
	3	65
	41–44	155
	43–44	89
63		97
	6	83
	14–16	83
	21	67
	27	66
	30–32	83
	41	88
	48–49	88
64	*13–31*	90
	29–30	67
	37	85
	45	66
65	*4–5*	155
	4–7	69
	6–7	9
	7	67
	15	68
	17	68
	35–39	71
	41	72
	45	71
66	*2*	90
	3–6	84
	24–25	67
92	*12–16*	91

DE DUABUS VIIS

1	*2*	70
58	*9–10*	9
	12–13	9
65	*6–7*	9

DE MONTIBUS
SINA ET SION
3		40, 46, 55
4		34, 43, 46, 48, 56
5		42
6		44
7		40, 41, 55, 287n
8		35
9		41, 48, 49, 105
10		53
11		40
13		41, 57, 154
14		41, 52
15		52
17		55
18	2	52

DE PASCHA COMPUTUS
1	126
10	126
12	45
13	286n
16	45, 127
17	127
21	129

DIDACHE
I	2	9
III	4	9
VI	1	9, 70, 155
IX		463

EPISTLE OF BARNABAS
I	2	68
	7	12
II	9	266
	10	172,173
V	13	276
VI	8	12
	10	12
	13	12
VII	4	266
IX	3	35n
X	1	51
XI		266
	1–11	51
	2	46n
	3	51
	6	12n, 51
	10	51
XII	2	303
	11	282

XIII	5	315n
	7	67
XIV	8	12
XV	8	26

EPISTLE OF POLYCARP
VII	1	299

EPISTLE OF THE APOSTLES
24	150

V ESDRAS
1	13	32n
	24	32n
	38–40	19
2	2	32
	10	20, 25, 32
	11	28, 29
	12	22, 27
	13	22, 24
	14	35n
	15	20, 21, 22
	16	30
	17	20
	18	22
	18f	28
	19	28
	21	27, 32
	22	32
	23	24
	24	26
	25	20, 21
	26	25
	27	22
	28	22
	30	20
	31	23, 24
	32	20, 21, 22
	34	17, 22, 23, 26, 30n
	35	17, 23, 26, 27
	36	17, 27
	37	18, 23, 26
	38	25, 26, 30, 32
	39	27, 30
	40	25, 30
	40–41	19
	41	20, 33
	42	19
	42–47	28–29, 30
	45	17,
	45f	14
	47	22

GOSPEL OF JAMES
18	171
131	299

GOSPEL OF PETER
40	29

HYPOSTASIS OF THE ARCHONS
141,	
413–431	74

ODES OF SOLOMON
III	9	90
XI	9	30
	10	30
XXI	7	29
XXV	8	30

PASSIO PERPETUAE
2	5	28
3		67
4	6	30n
	7	60
	8	29, 30
8	1	393n
	3	12n
	4	62
10	3	62
	6	29, 60
	8	60
	9	29, 60
11	3	61
	4	27
12	1	30, 61
13	4	28
21	1	29
	2–3	76n

PSEUDO-CYPRIAN
(Dupl. Mart.)
29	40

SHEPHERD OF HERMAS
(Mandates)
IV	1	9	94
V	1	3	154

SHEPHERD OF HERMAS
(Similitudes)
V		388
	1–7	53
	5, 2	56
	6, 1	56

VIII		106		4, 3	62		330	44
	1, 2	29	II	1, 1	62	II	233	25n
	1–3	151	IV	1, 2	62	VIII	135	117
	2, 1–4	30		1, 6	62		456–461	151
	10, 1	56		2, 1	62			
IX	10	62	V	1	62, 152	TESTAMENTS OF THE XII		
	12, 8	73				PATRIARCHS—		
	19–21	78n				TESTAMENT OF BENJAMIN		
	21, 5	94				IV	4	72n
			SIBYLLINE ORACLES			TESTAMENT OF SIMEON		
SHEPHERD OF HERMAS			I	304	74	IV	5	72n
(Visions)				316	74	TESTAMENT OF ZEBULON		
I	1, 3	62		326	44	IV	4	301

GNOSTIC WRITINGS

GOSPEL OF PHILIP		GOSPEL OF THOMAS			
42	299	3	185	92	185
125	46	55	87	107	79

FATHERS OF THE CHURCH

ACTS OF PAUL
5   84

AMBROSE (Abr.)
II   8, 54   243

ASTERIUS OF CAPPODOCIA
(Arian) (Hom. Pslam)
I   112   106

AUGUSTINE (De civ. Dei)
XXII   11   200n

AUGUSTINE (Tract. Io.)
IX   14   44n
X   45

CLEMENT OF ALEXANDRIA
(Eclogae Propheticae)
50   1   143

CLEMENT OF ALEXANDRIA
(Exc. ex Theod.)
50   1   374

CLEMENT OF ALEXANDRIA
(Paedag.)
III   12.90   4   173

CLEMENT OF ALEXANDRIA
(Stromat.)

I	2		90
II	14.95	7	84
	18.69	1	266
	79	1	173, 196
	20.110	2	91
		3	91
III	11.61	2	88
	77	1	88
	12.87	1	85
		3	85
	13.91	1	90
		13	90
	14.91	1	91
	95	3	89
	96	2	87
	15.97	2	89
	16.101	4	86, 91
	103	2	89
	17.103	1–104,	
		5	90
IV	5.19	2	173
	6.36	3	80
	8.60	4	89
	17.107	8	76
	25.319	25	317
V	6.37	4	127
	11.72	2	277

		2–5	107
	14.89	5	371
	93	4	371
	94	2	371
VI	11.86	2	80
	14.114	3	80
	16.133–		
	148		83
VII	7.40	4	80
	12.78	6	82
	14.84	2	82

CYPRIAN (Ad Dem.)
3   253, 254, 442
4   254, 255
8   252
16   63, 203
17   252
22   303

CYPRIAN (Ad Don.)
4   445
8   442
14   450

CYPRIAN (Ad Fort.)
1   145, 251, 421

2 — 322,421, 435
5 — 432
6 — 432
7 — 313, 432
8 — 303
11 — 38n,145, 257,300n, 323,327, 442

CYPRIAN (*Ad Nov.*)
2–6 — 309

CYPRIAN (*Ad Quir.*)
See below under
Testimonia

CYPRIAN (*De bono pat.*)
10 — 37, 300, 301,303, 305
12 — 301, 424
18 — 325
19 — 37, 422

CYPRIAN (*De habitu virg.*)
2 — 63, 64
3 — 64
4 — 66
7 — 67
14 — 63, 65, 167,443n, 458
21 — 80
22 — 65, 85
23 — 65, 66
24 — 66

CYPRIAN (*De lapsis*)
2 — 450
11 — 322
15 — 446
15–16 — 425
19 — 322
31 — 322

CYPRIAN (*De mort.*)
1 — 447
4 — 422
5 — 428
10 — 325,326, 327
18 — 437

25 — 252
26 — 432
27 — 252

CYPRIAN (*De op. et el.*)
5 — 322, 328
10 — 328
11 — 322
17 — 306
18 — 326
20 — 328

CYPRIAN (*De oratione*)
5 — 311
8 — 455
14–15 — 436
23 — 455
28 — 68, 70, 71n, 447
32 — 327
33 — 327

CYPRIAN (*De unit.*)
1 — 421, 426
2 — 64
3 — 427, 458
4 — 309
4–5 — 459
6 — 309, 459
7 — 460
8 — 310
10 — 434n
12 — 323, 456
14 — 459, 460
16 — 251
18 — 458
21 — 459
23 — 458
24 — 460
26 — 443

CYPRIAN (*De zel.*)
1 — 423
2 — 423
4 — 421
5 — 443
14 — 443
17 — 314

CYPRIAN (*Epist.*)
II   5 — 431
III 1 — 446
     3 — 433, 435

IV   1–2 — 434
     4 — 445
VI   2 — 300n
     3 — 323
VIII — 96
     3 — 69
X   1 — 435
     2 — 458
     5 — 28n
XI — 454, 455
     3 — 454
     7 — 443, 455
XII   2 — 451
XX   2 — 446
XXVII 4 — 442
XXVIII 1 — 451
       2 — 442
XXX see under Novatian
XXXI   6 — 435
XXXIV 3 — 456
XXXVI see under Novatian
XXXVII — 253
       2 — 443
XXXIX 2 — 451
XLIII 2 — 435
       3 — 426
       4 — 311, 456
       6 — 422
       7 — 426
LI   1 — 309
LV — 454, 457
       1 — 457
       3 — 444
       4 — 451
       5 — 444
       7 — 456
       8 — 457
       9 — 443
       16 — 444
       20 — 444
       24 — 457
LVII   5 — 451
       8 — 323
       18 — 445
LVIII — 251, 452
       1 — 251, 424, 452
       2 — 251, 452
       3 — 452
       4 — 452
       5 — 322,323, 445
       7 — 424
       9 — 424

10	424
LIX	424
2	447
3	427
11	447
13	446
18	425, 447
22	453
LX	453
1	456
2	444
3	425, 427
LXI 2	322, 323
16	303
LXII 1	462
LXIII	315, 316, 454
3	301, 316
4	317, 318
5	318
6	302, 318
8	66, 314
11	316, 317
12	461
13	458, 461, 463
LXV 3	447
4	444
5	447
16	434n
LXVI 8	456
LXVII 5	434n
7	251
8	258, 322
LXVIII 3	460
5	445
LXIX	454, 463
1	427
2	309, 313
3	433
4	310
5	434, 464
14	80, 315
LXX 3	427
LXXIII 10	308
15	427
16	313
LXXIV 2	309
8	453
11	309
LXXV see under Firmilian	
LXXVI 6	80
LXXVIII 7	313
LXXIX 11	313

CYPRIAN (Quod idola dii non sint)

6	167, 192, 408, 443n
9	63, 196
11	251
14	447
91	194

CYPRIAN (Testimonia)

I	267, 274, 289
1–4	289, 290
2	293
5–18	289, 290
6	54, 290
7	290, 291
8	290
9	291
9–10	290
10	47, 311
11	290
12	290
13	290
14	290, 291
15	290, 291
16	290
17	290
17–21	274
18	290
19	114, 293
19–24	289, 290
20	114, 131, 276, 278
21	114, 279, 282
II	289
1	291
1–6	274
2	291, 318
3	68, 291
4	291
5	291, 335
6	284, 285, 291
6–26	274
6–27	292
10	279, 285
11	279, 441
13	275
14	287
15	275
16	269, 291, 292

17	291
18	291, 292
20	274, 291, 292, 303
21	291, 330
22	291
24	283
27	40
28	292
29	280, 282, 292
30	292
III	274, 289, 293–295, 326
1	326, 328, 441
1–3	294
2	294
4	326
9	436
14	326
16	294
32	294
33	331
54	326
58	24, 294
62	328
66	431
89	431
96	64
106	294
113	326
120	294

DE LAUDE MARTYRII

13	255
14	255
20	142
21	142
27	255
29	300n

DIDASCALIA

I	9	70
	10	70
XXVI		171

EPHRAEM (Diatesseron)

21	6	35n

EPIPHANIUS (Panarion)

XXX	3	151
	14	151

EUSEBIUS (*Hist. eccl.*)
V   3   384

FIRMILIAN (*Letter to Cyprian*)
(=*Cypr., Epist.* LXXV)
14   311

GREGORY OF NYSSA (*Cant.*)
5   201

GREGORY OF NYSSA
(*De anim. et res.*)
PG 38A–B   231
    108B–C   228
    109A–B   229
    B   230
    110B–C   228
    C   228
    112A–C   229
    C–113C   228
    116C–117B   228
    123B–C   228
    128A   228
    C   228
    188B–225B   227

GREGORY OF NYSSA
(*De hom. opif.*)
1 PG 132B–C   234
2   134A   235, 245
    134B   245
7   138C   240
    139A   237
    140C   202
8   247

GREGORY OF NYSSA
(*De mort.*)
PG 533B–C   229

GREGORY OF NYSSA
(*De virg.*)
XXI   1   249

HIPPOLYTUS (*Apost. Trad.*)
3   72
21   28, 72
32   28

HIPPOLYTUS (*Comm. Dan.*)
I   17   106n
IV   21   45
    23–24   121

HIPPOLYTUS
(*De Antichristo*)
11   330

HIPPOLYTUS (*Elenchos*)
V   8, 29   80
VII   26   28
VIII   17, 2   369
IX   15   36

PS.-HIPPOLYTUS
(*Hom. pasch.*)
51   60

IRENAEUS (*Adv. haer.*)
II   13.30   184
    18. 3   184
    6   184
    30. 2   184
III   3. 4   120
    11. 8   243
    23. 1–9   112
    6   245
IV   10. 1   331
    2   277
    17. 1   266
    21. 3   114
    29   173
    32. 4   285
    33.12   271
    37. 7   67
    41. 2   40
    66. 3   26n
V   286
    4. 1   24
    12. 2   377
    13   132
    15. 1   166
    18. 2   277
    28. 3   120
    33. 3   120, 123, 125
    35. 2   62
    36. 1   80

IRENAEUS (*Demon.*)
11–29   36
37   285
43   157
71   283
79   276, 277
87   70n

JEROME (*De vir. illust.*)
24   267n

JEROME (*In Ezech.*)
III   praef.   255n

JEROME (*Quaest. hebr.*)
I   1   158

JUSTIN (*I Apol.*)
X   4   419
XIV   1   408
XVI   9–10   91
XX   1–4   256
XXXVIII   5   283
XLIV   1   106
LII   5   166
LVII   1   419
LIX   1   369

JUSTIN (*II Apol.*)
I   2   419
VIII   3   419

JUSTIN (*Dial.*)
XIV   1   271
    8   270
XXII   12–13   279
XXIV   268
XXVI   1   279
XXVIII   268
XXXVIII   3   270
XL   4   266
XLIII   3   270
    6   281
LII   4   271
LVIII   5   331
    6–10   335
LXVI   2–3   269
    3   281
LXXII   2   275
LXXIII   1   269, 280
LXXIV   269
    2   269
LXXVI   1   269
    3   388
LXXXVI   5   314
    31   314
XC   4   305
XCI   269
XCV   2   271
XCVII   2   269
CIV   1   269
CV   1   269
CVI   3   270
CX   2   271
CXIII   6   304

CXXV 1 78n
    3–5 335
CXXXIV 2 312
    3–5 114
CXXXV 39 50

PS.-JUSTIN (*Cohortatio*)
31 243

LACTANTIUS (*Inst.*)
II 1, 15 204

MACARIUS (*Hom. spirit.*)
45 1 87

MELITO (*Frag.*)
9 301
11 301

MELITO (*Hom. Pasch.*)
X 13–19 276
XXVI 37
XLVI 266
LIX 300, 301

METHODIUS (*De res.*)
I 34 245
II 10 243

MINUCIUS FELIX (*Octavius*)
V 7 198, 199, 203
  8 199
  9 199
XI 7 201
XVII 1 202
    2 198, 203, 247, 252
    4 200
    5 200, 201
    6 198, 201
    6–7 198
    7 198, 201, 253n
    8 198
    9 202
    10 202
    11 203
XVIII 63, 204
    4 189, 191
    5–6 190
    7 190, 191
    8 191

    8–10 194
    10 192
    11 193
XIX 210
    1 191
    14 191
    15 191
XXVI 7 406
    8 167, 406, 443n
    9 406
    10 406
    11 406
    12 407, 408
XXVII 410
    1 409
    4 410
    5–6 410
    8 419
XXXII 195
    1 195
    2 196
    5 197
    6 197
    7–9 197
XXXIII 4 175
XXXIV 2 205, 206, 256
    2–3 256
    3 205
    4 205
    5 205
    7 206
    9 201, 202, 207
    10 207
    11–12 207
XXXV 3–4 208
    4 191
XXXVII 10 252

MURATORIAN CANON
19 72

NOVATIAN (*De bono pud.*)
14 246

NOVATIAN (*De cib. Iud.*)
2 PG 955B 247, 248, 249
3 956C 246
4 959B 246
6 962A 246

NOVATIAN (*De spect.*)
1 448
9 234

NOVATIAN (*De Trin.*)
1 199, 202, 235, 236, 238
  3 246
2 7–9 246
3 10f 245
  12–14 245
  14 245
  15 246
  101 245
4 5 246
  6 246
  8–10 246
5 1–4 245
2 203, 238, 240, 458
  12 241
3 41, 200, 242
4 219
  1–2 246
  4–5 246
5 238n
19 14–20 4 337
20 1 249n
22 10–12 337
24 9–11 245
  11–12 245
9 278, 279
10 9–10 246
35 1–2 246
  330
13 331
17 238n, 333
18
62 7–63 1 337
63 9–15 338
  20–64 8 333
64 9–18 333
65 9–25 334
66 3–22 331
18–20 151n
19 315
69 1–17 335
70 24–71 5 335
71 15–72 335
72 19–73 2 336
73 4 336
21 7–15 245
77 245

23	110	11	212		1	265
29	439	12 2	174		3–5	222
17–18	249	25	173		8	264
		26	352	III		267, 271,
NOVATIAN (*Epist.*)		35	173			289, 290
(= Cypr., *Epist.*)		36	174		4	54
XXX 1	448	37	174		8	47, 48n
2	448	14–19	211	IV		289
3	448	18 24	352	V 5		173
XXXVI 1	448	V 5	240n	VI		265
				VII		265
ONOMASTICA (*Vatic.*)		TERTULLIAN (*Ad uxorem*)			1	265
14 56	42	II 2	312		2	282
		VI 2	84	VIII		286
ORIGEN (*Contra Celsum*)				IX		265, 269,
III 59	39	TERTULLIAN (*Adv. Herm.*)				270, 281
		II	200		1	265, 269
ORIGEN (*Frag. in Ex.*)		IV	355		21–22	304
XII PG 285D–288A	310	1	371		22	304
		VI 4	354		25	304
ORIGEN (*Hom. I. Cor.*)		VII 2	354		26	279n, 441
II 8	143	3	371		30	441
		4	357, 371	X		265, 269,
ORIGEN (*Hom. Josh.*)		XII 1	219			270, 271
II 1	80	4	219		5	301
III 5	310	XV	215		6	301
		XIX 1	366, 367		7	302
TATIAN (*Diatess.*)		5	367		7–8	301
III 10	87	14	368		8	302
		XX 1	368		10	303
TATIAN (*Or./Discourse*)		2	368		12	275
12	374	XXV 1	354		13	275
13	374	3	353		14	266
16, 1	410	XXVIII 2	369		18	266
		XXIX 1	369	XI		269
TERTULLIAN (*Ad mart.*)		XXX	346		9	140, 277
III 1–2	449	1	370	XII		289
		XXXI	370		12	278
TERTULLIAN (*Ad nationes*)		XXXII	370	XIII		265, 271,
I 12 12	348n	2–3	373			281, 286,
16	450	XXXIII	370			289, 290
16 12	458n	XXXIV	370		1	266
II 1 6	209	XXXV	370		9	315
8	211	2	348		10	141
2 5–6	209	XXXVI	217, 370		11	266, 277,
5	212	XXXIX 1	219			298, 299
2	212	XLI	217		12	314
3	212	XLV 6	354		13–14	141
3–6	213				14	266
8–14	213	TERTULLIAN (*Adv. Jud.*)			20–21	301
13–15	213	I	114		24	271
15–17	213	1	273		26	54
7	212	4	267	XIV		270
10	212	II	105, 107n		3	304

6		270, 285
7–10		270

TERTULLIAN (Adv. Marc.)

I	4	187
	13 3	240n
	23 6	358
II	2 6	247n
	4 4	34, 306
	5 1	350
	5	382
	8 2	375
	9 2–3	373
	10 3	172
	4	130, 172
	4–5	352
	25 1	169
	3	53, 169
	4	169
	35 7	86n
III		290, 297
	4 15	374
	5 4	297, 307
	6 7	158
	7 6	285
	9 6	384
	13 1	281
	18 2	301
	3	301, 302
	5	302
	19 1	280
	20 6	351
	21 1	280
	2	48
	3	48
	23 21	183
	24 2	144
	3	144
	3–4	144
	5	145
	8–9	114
	25 2	41
IV		264
	1	351
	5	68n
	5 1	183n
	2	184, 350
	3	350
	6 3	353
	11 1	302
	8	311
	11	222
	15 1–7	70n
	16 11	358

	17	68n
	17–18	70
	21 3	47
	23 2	54
	25 11	54
	26 4	373
	29 1	346
	5	358
	7	146
	29–31	146
	30 2	146
	31 6	54
	7	146
	32 1	147
	35 10	302
	40	330
	6	302, 318
	41	323
	42 6	54
	48 5	54
	49 6	351
V	1 5	176
	2 3	353
	4 3	47
	6 6	150
	7 3	303
	8 4	441
	8	441
	10	70
	10	298n
	7	376
	12	76
	11 8	303
	12	158
	15 7	348
	8	216, 348
	17 6	441
	18 8–14	307

TERTULLIAN (Adv. Prax.)

II	4	347
III	1	157
	4	150
	5	351
V	1	157, 190
VII	7	216
	8	348
VIII	4	348
	7	359
IX	3	360
XII	2	142
XIII		284
	4	331
XIV	1–4	332

XV	10		158
XVI			330
		6	334
XXVII	1		56, 158
		6	220
		8	220, 221
		10	347
XXXI	1		157

TERTULLIAN (Adv. Valent.)

II	3	21n
III		187
	1	306
XI	4	191

TERTULLIAN (Apol.)

X	6	352
XII	5	348n
XVII	1	190
	2	192
	4	213
	4–6	193
	6	194
XVII–XXI		430
XVIII	7	175
XIX	1	174
	6	175
	10	174
XXI	13	359
XXII	1	409
	2	409
	3	164, 166
	4	411, 421
	5	411
	6	411
	7	411
	8	411
	9	411
	10	411
	11–12	411
XXIII	1	411
	8–10	411
XXIV	3	244n
XXVII	2	419
XXIX	1	420
	4	420
XXX	1	420
XXXV	12	163
XXXIX	1	431
	2	353
	4	433
XLVII	13	308n
XLVIII	1	206, 229

	2	230		*12*	225	VI	*3*	384
	3	229, 230	XXV	*2*	225		*9*	384
	4	230	XXVI		224	VIII	*5–7*	160
	8	207	XXVII		226		*11–12*	384
LXIX	*10*	183n	XXX	*1*	226	IX	*2*	384n
				2	226	X	*1*	386

TERTULLIAN (*De anima*)

I	*1*	350,372,	XXXII	*1–9*	227	XI		216
		378		*1–10*	230		*1*	386, 387
II	*2*	372		*3*	227		*4*	348
	3	161, 163		*4*	220	XII	*2*	387
III		187		*6*	228		*6*	387
	2	441	XXXVII	*1*	143	XIII		346
	4	372	XXXVIII	*1*	107n,		*1*	386
IV		379			226, 351		*5*	160
	1	355, 379	XL	*1*	349	XIV		150
V	*5*	441	XLI	*10*	49		*2*	150, 388
V-VII		379	XLIII	*3*	441		*3*	149, 150
VI	*3*	216		*5*	441		*4*	149
	6	217		*10*	308		*5*	151, 389
VIII		379	XLVIII	*1*	441	XV	*1*	385
IX		216	L	*3*	323		*3*	385
	1	379		*4*	47		*9*	150
	2	379	LIII	*3*	441	XVI	*1*	385
	5	224, 379		*6*	143		*2*	385
X	*1*	379	LVIII	*2*	392	XVII	*3*	389, 390
XI		379		*8*	144		*4*	298
	3	376					*5*	307
	4	307	TERTULLIAN (*De bapt.*)			*5–6*	299
XII	*1*	379	III	*2*	373n	XVIII	*7*	390
	5	379		*3*	143	XXI	*6*	359
	17	372		*14–27*	143	XXIII	*2–6*	176
XIII	*3*	380	IV	*1*	313			
XIV		409	V	*1*	312,373n	TERTULLIAN	
	1	379		*5*	143	(*De corona milit.*)	
	4	231		*6*	143	XI	*1*	418
XV	*1*	379		*7*	377		*1–4*	449
XVI	*2*	380	VI	*1*	143		*4*	418
XVIII		216, 380	VIII	*2*	315, 336	XV	*7*	394n
	4	81		*3–5*	313			
XX		380	IX	*1*	313	TERTULLIAN	
	1	215, 351		*2*	313	(*De cultu fem.*)	
XXI	*1*	381		*3*	313	I		163
	2	307, 376,	XVI	*6*	314		*2 1*	162, 164
		377	XX	*2*	143	II		163
					157		*1 1*	164
	4	219					*10 2*	163
	6	219, 225,	TERTULLIAN			*3*	164
		380, 381	(*De carne Christi*)	III	*1–3*	162
	7	218, 381	III	*4–5*	220		*3*	162
XXII	*2*	355,372,		*5*	220			
		379, 380		*6*	220,334,	TERTULLIAN	
XXIII	*1*	226			335	(*De exhort. cast.*)	
	5	224	V		216	I	*3*	377
XXIV	*2*	373		*7*	351, 390		*4*	84, 357

II	3	107	TERTULLIAN (De orat.)			XXIX	2–4	183
V	3–4	308	XI		171	XXX	1	223
VI	1	312		1	155	XXXII	2	349
				2	155	XXXIII	5	178
TERTULLIAN (De fuga)			XV	1	153			
II		325	XVI	1	152	**TERTULLIAN (De pud.)**		
	1	420		2	153	V	9	458n,
IV	1	353	XVIII	6	155			460n
XI	1	357	XXII	5	162	VI	16	300
			XXIX	1	321	VII	1	154
TERTULLIAN (De idol.)				4	170	VIII	10–12	147
IV	1–3	165				IX		81
	2	165	**TERTULLIAN**				2	148
	3	165	**(De paenit.)**				8	353
IX	1	166	III	5	376n		21	82
	11	163	IX	1	147		22	148
X	1–2	415	XII	6	147	X	8	357
	2–4	415		9	168		10	441
	6	415					12	153
XI	2	415	**TERTULLIAN (De pallio)**			XIV	8	441
	9	415	II	2	200	XVIII	14	441
XII	1	415		3	175	XX	2	441
XIII	1	415		6	226		10	450n
XV		323				XXI	5	441
	4–5	416	**TERTULLIAN (De pat.)**				5–8	434
	6	165	V	5	422		16–17	440
	10	321	XIII	8	176	XCVIII		441
XVI	2	416	XIV	5	324			
	5	416	XV	3	154	**TERTULLIAN (De res.)**		
XVII	1	416				VII	3	398
	3	417	**TERTULLIAN**			VIII		397
XVIII		414	**(De praescrip.)**				3	399
	3	417	VII	7	187	IX		398
	7–8	417	VIII	1	177, 184	X	3	161
XIX	1	418	IX	4	185	XI		397
	2	418, 449	X	4	82n	XIII	2–4	115
				6	185	XIV		397
TERTULLIAN (De jejun.)			XIII	1–6	186	XV	3	398
III	2	107, 377	XIV	1–5	186	XVII	1	399
VII	7–8	321	XIX	1	181		2	399
IX		323	XX	2	181		6–8	399
	5	321		7	181	XIX	2–3	399
X	4	321	XXI	6	182, 349		7	400
	7	449		7	348n	XX	3	400
XVII	9	441	XXII	2	177	XXIII	1	400
XXXII		307		3	177	XXIV	8	353
			XXIII	2	178	XXV	2	144
TERTULLIAN				5	178	XXVI	1	144
(De monog.)			XXIV	6	178		1–14	400
III	7	90n	XXV	1	178		9	145
IV	2	349	XXVI	9–10	182	XLV	15	401
V	5	349	XXVII	1	182		16	401
	7	308	XXVIII	2	182	XLVI	13	401
VI	4	304		3	183	XLIX	11	402

L	4	402		6–7	412	VIII		109, 323
LI	1	384		10	412		6	441, 445n
	4	402		12	413		7	321
LIII	16	403	XI	2	415	VIII–IX		37, 38
LV	8–12	221		9	415	X	6–7	142
LXI	1	170	XII	1	413, 415	XI	4	148
LXII	2	346		5–6	413			
	11	144, 316	XIII	1	415	THEODOTUS (Valentinian)		
	14	170	XV	2	154, 413	See under Clement of		
XXIX–				4–5	416	Alexandria, *Exc. ex Theod.*		
XXXIII		400		8	413			
XXXI	1	25	XVI	2	416	THEOPHILUS OF ANTIOCH		
XXXII	1	166		5	416	(*Ad Autol.*)		
XXXIII	2	401	XVII	1	416	II	4	369
	9–10	399		3	417		15	106, 128
	10	401	XVIII	3	417	III	28	121
XL	3	401		7–8	417			
	4–5	401	XXIV	2	413, 414	VICTORINUS		
XLII	3	221	XXVI	4	413	(*Comment. Apoc.*)		
LXV	6	140				I	6	124
	9	140	TERTULLIAN			III		133
LXIX	1–21	160	(*De test. animae*)			XI	3	22n, 124
			I	1–2	210	XII	6	124
TERTULLIAN			II		193	XIII	3	123, 124
(*De spectac.*)				4	209	XIX	1	125
II	12	412	III	2	409	XX	2	124
IV	1–2	414				XXI	1	124
VII	2	412	TERTULLIAN					
	3	412	(*De virg. vel.*)			VICTORINUS		
VIII	1	415	I	6	223	(*De fab. mundi*)		
	2–3	412	VII	1–4	162	3		130
	9	412	XI	2	107	4		130
IX	1–2	412, 415				6		123, 130
X	2–4	415	TERTULLIAN (*Scorp.*)			7		131
	6	415	VI	7	357	30		132

MISCELLANEOUS WRITINGS

ALBINUS (*Didask.*)			**8**		238	APULEIUS (*Met.*)		
XV	4	237	**19**		239	VIII	27	410
XXV		225	**19–21**		239			
			21		239	ASCLEPIUS		
APULEIUS (*Apol.*)			**24**		241	**26**		256
90		408	**25**		241	**31**		192
			29		237	**36**		204
APULEIUS (*De Deo Socr.*)			**33**		237			
6		407, 410				AULUS GELLIUS		
9		407				(*Noct. attic.*)		
			APULEIUS (*De Plat.*)			III	10 11	256
			I	5	371			
APULEIUS (*De mundo*)						CICERO (*De nat. deorum*)		
1		237				II	5 13–15	213
2–3		233	APULEIUS (*Flor.*)				15	189
4		234, 236	**10**		235n			

7	238, 240	
11	241	
22	242	
28 71	196	
35	237	
37 95	201	
39	233, 234, 235	
98	201, 202	
100	202	
45 116	202	
46 118	205, 206	
47	204	
21	202	
48	204	
50 127	202	
52 130	204	
53 138	202	
56 140	203, 247	
III	*11*	239, 240
IV	*14* 37	206
XV	*41*	208
XXXVII	*103*	195

CICERO (*Fin.*)
III	*6* 20	192

CICERO (*Leg.*)
II	*11* 26	197, 241

CICERO (*Tusc.*)
I	*25*	197
	28 68	200, 201
	70	200

HIPPOCRATES (*Vet. med.*)
7	249

LUCRETIUS
(*De nat. rerum*)
II	*1104ff*	256
V	*407–410*	205

OVID (*Metam.*)
I	*201–208*	247

PLATO (*Leg.*)
715c	244

PLATO (*Phaedo*)
60c	224

PLATO (*Phaedrus*)
246e	244n

PLATO (*Symp.*)
195e–196a	408
202d	407
e	408

PLATO (*Tim.*)
28c	191
d	407
31c–32a	237
40d–e	407
41a	205
51a	369
69c	224
90a–b	247

PLUTARCH (*De
  animae procr. in Tim.*)
7	371

SALLUST (*Jugurtha*)
II	*3*	255

SENECA (*Benef.*)
VII	*1* 7	190, 252

SENECA (*Cons.*)
VII	*1–2*	226

SENECA (*De ira*)
II	*22* 1	252

SENECA (*Dial.*)
XI	*10*	255

SENECA (*Epist.*)
XXI	*13*	255
XXXVI	*11*	207
XLI	*1*	197
	2	196
	5	197
XLVII	*10*	252
LXXXIII	*1*	197
XC	*37*	247
	42	190
	50	196
	110	248
XCV	*47*	197

SENECA (*Quaest. nat.*)
II	*4*	233, 241n
	1	236
IV	*1* 2	201
V	*15* 3	248
VII	*30* 3	189

TACITUS (*Hist.*)
V	*5*	29

VIRGIL (*Aen.*)
VI	*730*	443n
IX	*105*	208

GENERAL INDEX

Aaron, 38

Abel, 37, 42, 114, 300, 321, 325, 327, 424

Abercius, inscription of, 71

Abraham, 19, 36, 107, 126, 265, 332

Abraham's bosom, 142, 392, 393

Acts of Paul, 84, 91, 96, 155, 156, 157

Acts of the Apostles, 15, 177

Acts of the Scillitan Martyrs, 7

Acts of Thomas, 83n

Adam, 36, 41-42, 43-45, 53, 79–80, 90, 101, 104, 107, 109, 112, 123, 126, 127, 129, 131, 151, 160, 168-173, 246, 265, 298, 299, 307, 325, 349, 374, 376-377, 381, 397, 421-422

Adamantius, 45

Ad Demetrianum (Cyprian), 252, 253, 258

Ad Donatum (Cyprian), 253, 450

Ad Fortunatum (Cyprian), 37, 288, 289, 294, 431, 440, 452

Ad martyres (Tertullian), 431, 448-449

Ad nationes (Tertullian), 209, 211, 214, 358, 410, 429

Ad Novatianum (Ps.-Cyprian), 82, 167

Ad Quirinum (Cyprian), see under *Testimonia*

Adultery, 153-154

Adversus Apelleiacos (Tertullian), 384

Adversus haereses (Irenaeus), 104, 465, 474

Adversus Hermogenem (Tertullian), 159, 343, 358, 361, 366, 369

Adversus Hermogenem (Theophilus), 369

Adversus Judaeos (Ps.-Cyprian), xiv, 17, 18, 19, 30, 31–39, 40, 43, 107, 108, 272, 273, 290n

Adversus Judaeos (Tertullian), 46, 47, 263-273, 291, 293, 297, 430, 465

Adversus Marcionem (Tertullian), 47, 144, 159, 263, 264, 293, 297, 343-344, 465

Adversus Praxean (Tertullian), 149, 157, 291, 293, 337, 344, 361

Adversus Valentinianos (Tertullian), 271, 377, 465

Aelius Aristides, 410

Aesculapius, 410

Ahab, 38

Albinus, xv, 223, 224, 225, 226, 228, 369, 475

Alexander (Valentinian), 385, 389, 403

Alexandria, school of, xv, 261

Altercatio Simonis Judaei et Theophili Christiani, 274, 287

Ammonius Saccas, 223, 230

Ananias, 321-323, 327, 445

Angels, 61, 73-74, 82, 102-104, 117, 142-144, 149-151, 187, 216, 220, 242, 243, 331, 352, 356, 367, 373, 384, 388-389, and change, 220, creation of, 73, 130, 172, existence of, 409, fall of, 162, 409, 422, fallen, 161, 163-166, 405-411, prayer of, 170-171

Animation, 225

Antichrist, 116-119, 294, 424-425, 427

Antioch, school of, xv, 261

Antisemitism, 33, 101, 267, 272-273, 289-290, 291, 293

Antonianus (Bishop), 457

Apelles, 179, 383–384, 403

Apocalypse of Adam, 172-173

Apocalypse of Baruch, 118

Apocalypse of John, 11, 13, 14, 22, 23, 53, 59, 116, 119, 123, 144, 427

Apocalypse of Moses, 168, 170

Apocalypse of Paul, 177

Apocalypse of Peter, 11, 15, 118, 142

Apocrypha, quoted as Scripture, 154–157

Apocryphon of Ezekiel, 19n, 176

Apocryphon of John, 177

Apollo, 412

Apologeticum (Tertullian), 189, 211, 414, 417, 429, 465

Apology (Justin), 210, 465

Apostles, 128

Apostolicity, 182–186

Apostolic Tradition (Hippolytus), 94, 95, 415

Apuleius, xv, 223, 228, 233n, 237, 244, 405, 406, 407-408, 410-411

Arianism, 363

Ariston of Pella, 158

Aristotle, 190, 239, 241, 244, 345, 372

Ark, 309, 313

Arts, 412-413

Ascension of Isaiah, 60, 62, 103

Astrology, 163, 166

Athanasius, 363

Athenagoras, 104, 172, 375, 406, 422

Augury, condemnation of, 9

Augustine, 44n, 45, 100, 132, 198, 211, 223, 252, 383, 428, 461, 466

Authority in the Church, 182–183; see also Bishops

Azarias, 321–323, 327, 445

Bacchus, 412

Baptism, 47, 68, 72, 84, 97, 143, 290, 312–315, 322, 427, 438, 453, 461, 463

Basilides, 90

Bible, Latin translations of, 5–8

Bishops, 184, 349–350, 433–436, 439–440, 445, 446–447, 454, 456–457,

459–461
Blood, 75–77, 159, 160
Body, 215–218, 401,
402–404; see also under
Resurrection
Book of Adam, 167–173, 176
Book of Degrees, 159
Book of Jubilees, 168
Book of the Weeks, 162

Caecilius, 198–200, 315
Caesar, 190, 194
Cain, 72, 114, 168
Calcidius, 233
Callistus, 101
Callixtus, 23
Capella graeca (Catacombs of
Priscilla), 301, 313, 314
Cardea, 416
Carmen Apologeticum (Com-
modian), 104, 119,
273–288
Carpocrates, 391
Cassian (encratite), 84n, 86,
87, 90, 91, 92
Catacombs, 312, 313, 314,
see also Capella graeca
Celerinus, 451
Celsus, 39, 139, 207
Census (in Tertullian), xvi,
222, 344, 348–352, 353,
363
Cerinthus, 120, 213
Change, 218–223
Christianity, 59, 210,
429–440
Chrysippus, xv, 240, 379
Church, 19-22, 257–258,
341, 429–464; apostolic
origin of, 349–350; as an
army, 448–453; as a
woman with white hair,
62; as mother, 20n; birth
of, 49–51; compared with
dove, 21–22; concord in
(Cyprian), 453–464; con-
frontation of with the
Empire, xv, 93, 405, 450;
decadence of, 257–258;
institutions of, 472–474;
official language of, 3;
persecuted by the Empire
419–428; replaced Israel,
297; types of, 298,
306–312, 318; unity of

183, 462–464; vigour of
(Cyprian), 440–448
Cicero, xv, 189, 191, 196,
198, 201, 204, 214, 231,
234–244, 324
Circumcision, 267–268, 290
Cleanthes, 189, 379
I Clement, xiii, 9–10, 12, 40,
95, 190, 435, 465
II Clement, 10
Clement of Alexandria, 21,
36, 39, 73, 83–92, 144, 176,
179, 185, 188, 223, 324,
369, 371, 416
Clement of Rome, 3, 23, 349
Clementine Homilies, 76,
115, 175; see also
Ps.–Clementines
Codex Bezae, 7
Columella, 78n
Commentary on Daniel (Hip-
polytus), 312
Commentary on John (Origen),
368
Commentary on Mark (attrib.
Jerome), 44n
Commentary on Matthew
(Origen), 145
Commentary on the Apocalypse
(Victorinus), 123, 132
Commodian xv, 17, 19, 23,
99–125, 141, 145, 152,
159, 167, 173, 205, 222,
263, 272, 273–288, 289,
293, 384, 389, 477
Continence, 356–357, 444
Coquetry, 164
Corinthians, 14n
I Corinthians, 316
Cornelius (Pope), 424, 433,
438, 443, 447, 453, 457,
463
Cosmetics, 163–164
Covenant, break between
old and new, 33; series of
in ancient times, 36–37;
the new, 32, 35
Creation, 73–74, 366–371,
403
Cremation, 418
Crowns, 29, 431
Crypt of Lucina (Catacombs
of Calixtus), 322
Cyprian xv, 5, 7, 12, 26, 31,
40, 51, 55, 63–67, 69n, 84,

91–92, 93, 96, 99, 100,
137, 140, 141, 167, 183,
194–195, 204, 251–258,
261, 263, 274–288,
289–295, 298, 303,
304–306, 308–319,
321–328, 335, 336, 341,
393, 394, 406, 408,
420–428, 429–464, 465,
472, 473, 477

Daemon of Socrates
(Apuleius), 223, 407
Damascus Document, 38
Daniel, 321–323, 326, 327
Daniel, 321
David, 300, 305, 325, 327,
329, 351
De aleatoribus, 11, 14–15, 58,
93–98, 155–156
De anima (Tertullian),
48–49, 160, 230–231, 344,
350, 361, 371–372, 378,
380, 386, 399, 466
De anima et resurrectione
(Gregory of Nyssa),
227–231
Death, acceptance of, 437
De baptismo (Tertullian), 143,
312, 373n
De bono patientiae (Cyprian),
294, 325, 327
De carne Christi (Tertullian),
146, 298, 344, 383, 389
De censu animae (Tertullian),
350, 371–372, 380
De centesima, sexagesima et
tricesima, xiv, 9, 35n, 40,
59, 63–92, 96–97, 103,
112, 130, 145, 146, 148,
149, 150, 151, 152, 155,
159, 194, 288, 367, 389
De cibis judaicis (Novatian),
245, 249
Decius, 423, 424, 438, 440,
450, 454
De corona militum (Ter-
tullian), 29, 418
De cultu feminarum (Ter-
tullian), 63
De Dominica oratione
(Cyprian), see under De
oratione
De duabus viis, 8–9
De extasi, (Tertullian), 307

De fabrica mundi (Victorinus), 123, 130–133

De habitu virginum (Cyprian), 63, 65, 66, 91, 92, 294, 436–437

De idololatria (Tertullian), 165, 414, 419

De infantibus qui praemature abripiunter (Gregory of Nyssa), 396n

De lapsis (Cyprian), 326

De laude martyrii (Ps.–Cyprian), 11, 142, 255

Demetrian, 252, 444

Demon, see under Devil

Demonology, 405–411

Demonstration of the Apostolic Preaching (Irenaeus), 104, 158, 293, 474

De montibus Sina et Sion, xiv, 12n, 17, 33n, 34, 39–57, 105, 114, 122, 126, 127, 128, 145, 149, 159, 168, 271, 287, 288

De mortalitate (Cyprian), 431

De mortibus persecutorum (Lactantius), 442

De mortuis (Gregory of Nyssa), 229

De mundo (Apuleius), 233n, 234, 235–238, 239, 242, 243, 244, 250

De natura deorum (Cicero), 215, 237, 244, 245, 250

De opere et eleemosynis (Cyprian), 294

De Opificio (Gregory of Nyssa), 233, 240, 246

De oratione (Cyprian), 294, 311, 431, 436, 455

De. oratione (Tertullian), 455

De Pascha (anon.), 310

De Pascha computus, xv, 44n, 99, 126–129, 133, 145, 367

De patientia (Tertullian), 324

De praescriptione (Tertullian), 177–188, 343, 404

De pudicitia (Tertullian), 147, 149

De rebus divinis (Varro), 211

De resurrectione (attrib. Athenagoras), 396

De resurrectione (Ps.–Justin), 397, 403

De resurrectione (Tertullian), 146, 167, 297, 344, 361, 382–383, 395

De spectaculis (Novatian), 235, 236, 237, 240

De spectaculis (Tertullian), 412

De spe fidelium (Tertullian), 144

De testimonio animae (Tertullian), 195, 211, 343, 387, 392

De Trinitate (Novatian), 233, 240, 329, 330

De unitate (Cyprian), 311, 426, 454, 455, 458

Devil (demons, Satan), 40, 52, 72, 97, 107, 111–112, 125, 132, 166, 172, 325, 352, 405, 406–428, 432, 435, 443, 458

De zelo et livore (Cyprian), 72, 300n

Dialogue of Jason and Papiscus (Ariston), 158

Dialogue with Trypho (Justin), 47, 264, 267, 269, 270–272, 286, 465

Diatesseron (Tatian), 7, 8, 35, 39, 78, 92

Didache, 8–9, 69, 83, 95, 155, 156, 157

Didascalia, 95, 155, 156

Didaskalikos (Albinus), 225

Dio Chrysostom, 243

Dionysius the Stoic, 211

Dioscuri, the, 410, 412

Docetism, 351

Docta ignorantia, 192

Dove, as type of the Church, 306–307, 309; as type of the Holy Spirit, 307, 313

Easter homily (anon.), 310

Ebion, 151, 388

Ebionism, 38, 146, 151

Ekpurōsis (conflagration), 204–208, 256

Elect, number of, 25

Elijah, 35, 36, 38, 116, 124, 300n, 306, 327, 394

Elisha, 314

Elkanah, 311

Elkesai, 36

Empedocles, 206, 227, 228,

372

Encratism, 66, 77, 82, 83–92, 156, 159, 385

Enoch, 42, 162, 394

I Enoch, 62, 161, 162–167, 168, 174, 176, 186, 405, 406, 422

II Enoch, 25n, 43–44, 73, 103–104

Ephraem, 84

Ephraim, 114, 315, 336, 338

Epicureanism, 198, 200, 203, 256, 372, 380

Epicurus, 205, 379

Epistle of Barnabas, 8, 10, 12, 17, 34, 40, 41, 43, 51, 52, 53, 65, 70, 126, 141, 266, 267, 294

Epistle of Clement, see *I Clement*

Epistle of John (apocryphal), 41, 154, 156

Epistle of the Apostles, 81, 177

Epistles, (Cyprian), 323, 424, 431

Epistles (Seneca), 244, 250

Epistles to the Athenians, 14n

Epistle to the Laodiceans, 14n

Eros, 407, 408

Esau, 46n, 114

Eschatology, 23–24, 45, 204–208

II (4) Esdras, 17

V Esdras, xiv, 17–31, 33, 61, 107, 118, 124, 141, 152, 156, 273, 307

Essenism, 76, 95, 118n

Eteocles, 190, 194

Eucharist, 97, 153, 312, 314, 315–318, 461–464

Eve, 49, 90, 132, 298, 299, 300, 307–308, 309, 325, 374

Evil, 352, 366, 371

Expositio quattuor Evangeliorum (anon.), 44n

Fabian, 433

Fall of man, 107, 111–112

Fasting, 74–75, 327–328, 431

Feast of Tabernacles, 28–29

Feast of the Lord, 26–27

Felicissimus, 435, 447

Fire, 205–208, 211; see also *Ekpurōsis*

Firmilian, 311
Fish, as symbol of Christ, 71
Flood, as a type of baptism, 313
Flora, 415
Forculus, 416
Freedom, 213, 246, 380, 381
Free will, 219

Gabriel, 151, 388
Gaius, 13, 23
Gaudentius, 127n
Gelasian Decree, 168
Genesis, 244, 367
Glory, 27, 103
Gnosis, 176–177, 184, 187, 188, 343, 389
Gnosticism, 81, 139, 145, 179, 182–188, 192, 223, 224, 303, 343, 357n, 362, 365, 366n, 374, 390, 393, 394, 395, 396, 399–400, 428
God, 101–103, 107, 109–110, 111, 169, 200, 216, 240–244, 347, 355–356, 357–358, 395; and change, 218–223; distinct from the world, 212–213; existence of, 213, 429; invisible, 331–332, 337, 408; is one, 362; Minucius on, 190–198; theophanies, 103, 329–338; unity of, 210; without origin, 355; will of, 436–437
Golden rule, 9, 69, 70, 155
Gospel(s), 14, 130, 446; first preached in Greek, 3; law of, 222, 246, 430–431; symbolised in the four seasons, 128
Gospel of Peter, 60
Gospel of Philip, 106
Gospel of Thomas, 71, 77, 79, 85, 96
Gradus (in Tertullian), 356–360
Gregory of Nyssa, 127n, 207, 219, 227–231, 234, 235, 250, 396

Hagar, 46n, 312, 332, 333, 338
Hananiah, 38

Hannah, 311
Heaven, 25–28, 169, 392–395; see also Paradise
Hebion, see Ebion
Hebrews, 317
Heraclides, 159
Heraclitus, 379
Heresy, 427–428
Hermes Trismegistos, 174, 192, 408
Hermogenes, xiii, 159, 346, 350, 354, 366–383, 403
Hesiod, 256, 407
Hieracles, 230
Hidden people, the, 118
Hilary, 42
Hippocrates, 240, 248
Hippolytus, 13, 45n, 101, 111, 305, 306, 310, 319, 322, 391, 415, 465
History, 257
Holy Spirit, 35, 55–57, 65, 72, 96–97, 154–155, 182, 184, 307, 359, 360, 376–378, 381–382, 402–403, 437–440, 445
Homer, 407
Homily on the Narrative of David and Goliath (Hippolytus), 305
Homily on the Passion (Melito), 19, 31, 35, 37, 38, 265, 266–267
Hostanes, 406, 408
House of Rahab, 310
House of the Passover, 310

Ialdabaoth, 74
Iamblichus, 230
Idolatry, 95–96, 165, 405–411, 424, 427, 429, 432
Instructions (Commodian), 119, 273
Irenaeus, xiii, xvi, 14, 21, 23, 26, 49, 80, 81, 101, 104, 109, 112, 114, 120, 122, 123, 124, 125, 131, 140, 145, 162, 168, 172, 182, 184, 246, 271, 273, 281, 292, 298, 299, 300, 301, 303, 312, 314, 318, 330, 332, 337, 338, 344, 349–350, 362, 365, 377–378, 381–382, 385,

391, 393, 394, 404, 422, 466, 474
Isaac, 19, 126, 265, 266, 300, 301, 302, 3-4, 311, 325, 332
Isaiah, 33, 37, 38, 108, 131, 265, 279, 300n, 324, 329
Ishmael, 338

Jacob, 19, 46n, 114, 300, 301, 302, 315, 325, 327, 334–336
Janus, 416
Jealousy, 72, 300n, 422
Jeremiah, 37, 38, 108, 124
Jerome, 7, 42, 157
Jerusalem, 46, 53
Jesse, 359
Jesus Christ, 56–57, 60–61, 79, 109–110, 126–127, 160, 265, 273, 286, 292–293, 315–317, 346–347, 351, 417, 437–438, 462; as angel, 149–152, 291, 333, 335, 388–389; as the Lord Sabaoth, 73–74; blood of, 76; death of, 45, 122; descended from Jesse, 359; descent into hell, 80, 112; distinct from the Father, 330–331; flesh of, 383–390; inaugurates new period, 297; in Tertullian's rule of faith, 185–186; model for Christians, 436; numerical symbols of, 127–129, 131–132; of great stature, 29, 60; rejected by the synagogue, 20; represented by figure 1, 127; resurrection, 329; revelation of God, 430; second coming, 292; symbolised by fish, 71; transfiguration, 36, 221; types of, 298–306, 317; typified by Melchizedek, 317; virgin conception and birth of, 7, 151, 291, 293, 383, 389–390; water and blood from side of, 49–52
Jewellery, 163

Job, 324–326, 327
Job, 236, 321, 324–326
John, 13, 14, 127, 198, 314, 316
I John, 427
John Damascene, 475
John the Baptist, 108
John the Evangelist, 13, 14, 184, 349
Joseph, 114, 265, 266, 300, 302, 311, 321, 325, 327
Josephus, 175
Joshua, 303
Judah, 302, 318
Judaism, 17, 261, 273
Judas, 38
Jude, 162
Julius Africanus, 121
Jupiter, 410
Justin (Gnostic), 28
Justin Martyr, xiii, xvi, 14, 23, 47, 49, 51, 101, 103, 109, 120, 124, 162, 209, 210, 214, 222, 264, 266, 267–268, 269–271, 273, 277, 281, 289, 291, 292, 297, 298, 301–306, 313, 314, 318, 330, 331, 336–337, 344, 369, 393, 395, 396, 411, 419, 420, 450, 465

Kingdom, 25–26

Laberius, 206, 229
Lactantius, 124, 406, 408
Lapsed, the (lapsi), 323, 425–426, 437–438, 440, 444, 446, 450–452, 454, 456, 472
Law, 105–106, 113, 221–222, 242, 244, 246, 264–265, 290, 297, 304, 430
Leah, 114, 311–312
Letters to Lucilius, 215
Letter to Rheginos, 395, 396, 399, 400
Levi, 302
Life of Adam and Eve, 161, 167–168
Limentius, 416
Logos, theology of, 14, 334
Lucian, 206
Lucifer, see under Devil
Lucretius, 205

Macarius, 77
Malachi, 19
Man, 104–105, 159–161, 203–208, 247–248, 349, 361, 402–403, 437–438; creation of, 34, 104; see also Fall, Soul
Manasseh, 38, 114, 315, 336, 338
Manna, 315–316
Marcellus of Ancyra, 363
Marcion, xiii, 86, 146, 147, 159, 352, 358, 383, 392, 393
Marcionites, 7, 179, 183, 222, 343, 395
Martyrdom, 22, 47, 48, 59, 75–76, 79, 80, 81, 82, 84, 289, 322, 357, 440, 449
Mary, 132, 299, 300, 307, 351, 359
Matthew, 22, 33
Maximus of Tyre, 406, 410
Maximus the Confessor, 475
Meat, 248–249
Melchizedek, 317
Melito, xiii, 14, 266, 267n, 272, 278, 292, 298, 303, 306, 318, 362, 404
Menander, 47
Metempsychosis, 206, 219–220, 225, 226–229
Methodius of Olympus, 104, 396
Methuselah, 162
Michael, 151, 388
Military service, 418
Millenarianism, 23, 100, 114–125, 128, 144–145
Minerva, 415
Minucius Felix, xv, 59, 65, 137, 167, 175, 189–208, 210, 214, 215, 406–411, 419, 428, 429, 466, 475, 477
Misael, 321–323, 327, 445
Modalism, 337
Monarchianism, 13–14, 57, 100, 111, 158–159, 366
Monogamy, 357
Monotheism, 111, 157, 190, 429
Montanism, 23, 144, 145, 158, 307, 361–362
Moses, 35, 36, 37, 42, 151,

175, 265, 300, 302, 303, 325, 329, 369, 430
Moses (Bishop), 435
Muratorian Canon, 7, 10n, 11, 13–15, 59, 72, 94, 142, 152, 288
Muses, the, 412

Nero redivivus, 116, 117, 119, 123
Neo-Platonism xvi, 223
Nicaea, Council of, 366
Noah, 36, 162, 173, 300, 302, 313, 316, 321, 322, 326
Noetus, 362
Novatian, xv, 7, 137, 149, 190, 198, 202, 214, 215, 218, 233–250, 263, 329–338, 403, 424, 426, 427, 428, 429, 433, 437–440, 444, 447–448, 454, 456–457, 463, 464, 475
Numenius, 223
Numerical symbolism, 81–83, 123, 126–129, 145

Octavius (Minucius), xv, 189–208, 406, 429
Oikonomia, 365
On Hannah and Elkanah (Hippolytus), 312
Onomastica, 42
Origen, 36, 37, 39, 42, 72n, 146, 159, 188, 192, 275, 281, 310–311, 344, 368, 384, 388, 392, 394, 396
Ovid, 204

Paganism, 195, 200, 211, 214, 261, 406, 410, 442, 450
Palms, 29, 62
Panetius, 205
Papias, 14, 80, 120, 125, 145, 176
Parables, exegesis of, 77–82, 145–148
Paradise, 27–28, 60–61, 119, 123, 142, 169, 171, 299, 306, 308, 394, 432; see also Feast of the Lord, Heaven, Rest
Parousia, 22–23, 45, 101, 257, 293
Paschal Homily (Ps.–Hip-

polytus), 157
Passio Perpetuae, xiv, 18, 22, 30–31, 59–62, 142, 152, 154, 394
Patience, 215, 324–326, 431, 437
Paul, 3, 15, 69, 89, 155, 178, 297, 313, 400
Pauline Epistles, 14, 394
Peninnah, 311
Perez, 114
Peri archōn (Origen), 344
Peri kósmou (Ps.–Aristotle), 190, 233n, 244
Perpetua, 59, 60, 477
Persecution, 116, 423, 440, 453
Persecution of the just, 37; see also under Church
Persona, 364–365
Peter, 15, 178, 349, 459
I Peter, 23–24, 313
Phaedrus (Plato), 243, 244
Philo, 42, 168, 175, 192, 195, 334, 369, 375
Philosophers, philosophy, 161, 163, 187, 189, 205, 206, 209–214, 353, 378, 382, 407
Phoenix, 115
Pius I, 15
Plato, xv, 174, 175, 205, 206, 216, 223–231, 369, 372, 379, 388, 407, 409
Platonism, xvi, 190, 198, 207, 223–231, 241, 344, 366, 370, 374, 380, 386, 405, 475
Pliny, 10n, 230, 231
Plotinus, 218, 223
Plutarch, 405, 407
Polycarp, 349
Polynices, 190, 194
Pompey, 190, 194
Porphyry, 223, 228
Posidonius, 190, 197, 201, 205, 206, 211, 231, 234, 237, 247, 248, 250, 256
Praescriptio, 180–183
Prayer, 170–171, 327, 431, 454–456, 476
Praxeas, xiii, 56, 57, 101, 157–158, 361–363, 366
Preaching of Peter, 74
Primordial waters, as a type

of baptism, 312–313
Prophets, persecution of, 37–38, 107
Ps.–Aristotle, 190
Ps.–Barnabas, 64, 222, 272, 292, 298
Ps.–Clementines, 38, 299; see also Clementine Homilies
Ps.–Cyprian, see Ad Novatianum, Adversus Judaeos, De laude martyrii
Ps.–Hippolytus, 60
Ps.–Justin, 396
Pythagoras, 206, 226, 372

Qumran, 38, 76, 143, 162
Quod idola dii non sint (Cyprian), 65, 194, 294, 408, 429, 440

Rachel, 114, 311–312
Raphael, 327–328
Rebecca, 114
Redemption, 111–113
Regula fidei, see Rule of faith
Remus, 190, 194
Repentance of Adam, 168
Rest, 26, 392
Resurrection, 23, 115–116, 124, 160, 170, 206–208, 346, 390–391, 395–404; of the body, 23, 24, 166, 215, 390, 392; of the just, 24, 119
Rhodon, 384
Rock of Horeb, 314
Rock of the temple, 45
Romans, 88
Romulus, 190, 194
Rule of faith, 474; in Cyprian, 292; in Tertullian, 185–186, 188, 343

Sabbath, 268, 290
Sabellius, 338
Sacraments, 461, 472, 476; typology of, 312–319; see also Baptism, Eucharist
Sacrifices, 195, 196, 268, 290
Sallust, 255
Samuel, 311
Samuel, 319
Sarah, 46n, 312

Satan, see under Devil
Saturn, 174, 175, 410, 415
Saturus, 59, 60, 61
Scaevola, 211
Scorpiace (Tertullian), 38, 148, 149, 431
Seal of the just, 30
Seneca, xv, 189, 195, 198, 204, 207, 214, 215, 231, 238, 247, 251, 324, 380, 431
Sennacherib, 42n
Septimius Severus, 449
Septuagint, 6, 272, 392
Serapis, 410
Seven witnesses, 36
Shepherd of Hermas, xiv, 3, 10–11, 13, 15, 18, 23, 30–31, 40, 52, 53, 57, 59, 65, 73–74, 94, 95, 96, 98, 105, 112, 139, 150, 151, 152–154, 156, 157, 388, 389, 413, 423, 465
Sibyl, the, 173, 174, 175
Sibylline Oracles, 25n, 71, 104, 117, 152, 161, 173; see also following entry
Sibylline Oracles III, 173–176
Simeon, 302
Simonians, 81
Simon Magus, 147
Sinai, 42, 45, 51
Socrates, 407, 409
Sodom and Gomorrah, 331
Song of Songs, 307, 309–310, 311, 319
Soranus, xv, 217, 379
Soul, 25n, 206, 215, 218, 219–220, 224–231, 346, 348, 350–351, 354–355, 371–383, 385–388, 392, 401–404
Spiritual Homilies (attrib. Macarius), 77
Statues, Christian polemic against, 195, 196
Status (in Tertullian), 352–356
Stephen (Pope), 437, 461
Stephen (protomartyr), 324
Stoicism, 190–208, 209–231, 233–250, 251, 252, 256,

324, 346, 372, 379, 386, 388, 403, 428, 431, 436, 438, 444, 447–448, 454, 456, 470, 475
Stone, as a type of Christ, 304–305
Subordinationism, 338
Substantia (in Tertullian), 345–348, 351, 353, 356, 363, 365
Susannah, 311, 312
Symposium (Plato), 407
Synagogue, replaced by the Church, 113–114

Targums, 140, 156
Tatian, 87, 92, 112, 159, 374
Teaching of Plato (Apuleius), 223, 228
Te Deum, 61
Temple, 35, 45, 48, 54, 126
Tertullian, passim. For major entries, see Contents
Testament of Adam, 168, 171
Testament of Job, 176
Testament of Levi, 60
Testaments of the XII Patriarchs, 176, 285
Testimonia (Cyprian), 5, 12, 91, 268, 271, 273–288, 289–295, 311
The Animation of the Embryo (Porphyry), 225
Theodotus, 374, 375
Theology, negative, 192
Theophilus of Antioch, 121, 173, 344, 366, 375
Thessalonians, 14n
Thomas, 85
Thrason, Catacomb of, 71n

Timothy, 178, 179
I Timothy, 14, 94
II Timothy, 14, 94
Titus, 14, 94
Tobias, 71n, 328
Tobit, 327–328
Tobit, 321
Tradition, 140, 153, 182–186, 297, 404, 434
Traducianism, 226, 349
Trajan, 10n
Transmigration of souls, see Metempsychosis
Tree of life, 27, 28, 106, 112–113, 277
Tree of the knowledge of good and evil, 90, 104–106, 113, 245, 299–300, 430
Trinity, 109, 128, 157, 338, 347, 351–352, 355, 359, 361–366, 367
Two commandments, 69, 70
Two ways, 67, 95, 106
Typology, 297–319

Valentinians, 81, 179, 183, 374, 381, 383, 404
Valentinus, xiii, 179, 219, 369
Valerian, 440
Varro, 211–214, 226, 231, 352
Venus, 412
Vetus Latina, 140, 141, 393
Victor, 93
Victorinus of Pettau, 74, 79, 123–125, 130–133, 145, 263, 371
Virgil, 407
Virginal conception, see un-

der Jesus Christ
Virginity, 64–66, 356, 437, 444
Vitae Prophetarum, 108
Vulgate, 7, 13

War of the Sons of Light and the Sons of Darkness, 117, 448
Waters of Marah, 313
White garments, 30
Will, 246; see also Free will
Wine, 300, 302, 315, 316–318, 461
Wisdom, 318, 365, 367–368
Wisdom, 288
Word, 13, 101, 103, 109, 110, 111, 151, 160, 216, 220–221, 250, 363, 367; adaptation of to men, 337; as the seventh day, 73; mission of, 292, pre-existence of, 109, 291, 292
Work, 247
World, 198–203, 361, 432; age of 251–258; see also Creation

Xenocrates, 405

Yeser ha̅–ra̅, 78
Yetserim, 76

Zechariah, 37, 38, 108, 118, 300n, 327, 389
Zeno, 212, 242, 379
Zephyrinus, 101
Zerah, 114
Zeus, chariot of, 243–244
Zion, 42, 46–48, 51, 53